The Making of ....

The Making of the Modern Self

Identity and Culture in Eighteenth-Century England

DROR WAHRMAN

Yale University Press
New Haven and London

לאבא ולאמא זכרונה לברכה

For information about this and other Yale University Press publications, please contact:
U.S. Office: sales.press@yale.edu yalebooks.com
Europe Office: sales@yaleup.co.uk www.yalebooks.co.uk

Set in Ehrhardt by SNP Best-set Typesetter Ltd, Hong Kong
Printed in the United States of America

Library of Congress Cataloging-in-Publication Data

Wahrman, Dror.
   The making of the modern self: identity and culture in eighteenth-century England / Dror Wahrman.
      p. cm.
   Includes bibliographical references and index.
   ISBN 0-300-10251-8 (alk. paper)
   1. Great Britain—Civilization—18th century.   2. Identity (Psychology)—Great Britain—History
—18th century.   3. Self (Philosophy)—Great Britain—History—18th century.   I. Title.
   DA485.W34 2004
   126'.0941'09033—dc22

                                                                                2004001544

A catalogue record for this book is available from the British Library

ISBN 0-300-12139-3 (pbk)

10 9 8 7 6 5

Published with assistance from the Annie Burr Lewis Fund.

Contents

List of Illustrations

Acknowledgments

In the spectacular desert of Southern Sinai there is a mountain called Jebel Madsus, meaning (more or less) the secreted or concealed mountain. It got its name from the experience of climbing it: every time you think you have reached the top, a new vista opens up that shows you an even higher summit still to be ascended. I no longer remember the name of the *dalil* (guide) who led my way up Jebel Madsus. But I do remember with much pleasure the many friends and colleagues who have guided the way up my own mountain, and who helped me see, every time I thought I had attained the summit, that I still had a long way to go. Many who have generously shared their on-going work, or who enlightened me on specific points, are thanked in the relevant sections of the book. Others have read various segments and incarnations of what follows – some, half a mountain ago, when this was still going to become a book about gender – and made innumerable valuable comments: Donna Andrew, David Armitage, Eitan Bar-Yosef, David Bell, John Bodnar, Ian Burney, Christopher Clark, Norma Clarke, Linda Colley, Seth Denbo, Vince DiGirolamo, Rebecca Earle, John Efron, Elizabeth Elbourne, Jim Epstein, Dena Goodman, Lige Gould, Mike Grossberg, Phil Harling, Colin Jones, Sue Juster, Tom Laqueur, Peter Mandler, Mary Catherine Moran, Sonya Rose, Naama Sheffi, Danny Unger, Jeff Veidlinger, Shula Volkov, and Kathleen Wilson.

Over the last few years I have been fortunate to be part of the vibrant community of eighteenth-century scholars at Indiana University (eighteenth century, for the purposes of our group, being interpreted rather ecumenically): Fritz Breithaupt, Michel Chaouli, Konstantin Dierks, Jonathan Elmer, Mary Favret, Connie Furey, Oscar Kenshur, Sarah Knott, Deidre Lynch, Richard Nash, and Jonathan Sheehan. They have left their imprint on this book through their criticism, suggestions and ongoing conversations, and in many cases through their own work.

The final version of this book was read closely (often more than once!) by three great friends and collaborators in all matters *dix-huitièmes*, who deserve at the very least to be mentioned again: David Bell, Sarah Knott, and Jonathan Sheehan. Their patience with me was matched only by the acuity of their readings. Patience was also the much appreciated virtue of everyone at the London office of Yale University Press – Robert Baldock, Candida Brazil, Ewan Thompson, and Kevin Brown – and of my indexer, Marie Deer. The final stages in this book's incubation took place while I was on an ACLS Frederick Burkhardt Residential Fellowship at the Newberry Library, and benefitted much from the help and comments of the Newberry community and staff.

This book will put up a good fight for its argument, perhaps overdoing it on occasion: this is the main debt it owes my late mentor Lawrence Stone, for whom arguments – forceful, uncompromising, unapologetic – were the lifeline of intellectual progress. Some of the earlier chapters he subjected to his unparalleled critical rigor; the later ones suffered from his not being there to peer over my shoulder in person, but only in spirit. Looking over my shoulder I can also see the kind guidance of two other giants of historical writing whom I have had the good fortune to count among my teachers. The late Edward Thompson, whose startling admission one day in his Wick Episcopi study, that the analytical category of class had reached its sell-by date, was a key stepping stone in moving from my previous book to this one, even if it took me a while to realize its full impact; and Natalie Zemon Davis, whose experiences in writing about an early modern impostor opened my eyes to the possibility that imposture and identity play were indeed the stuff that history is made of.

The last paragraph in the present genre is conventionally reserved for one's family, an inevitability which, like all predictable generic prerequisites, dulls the desired effect. This is a shame, since my debts on this score are truly enormous – to Noa, Shani and Maya, without whom none of this would have been worthwhile, and to my father and my late mother, without whom none of this would have been possible in the first place.

Preface

Before the Self: The Ancien Régime of Identity and the Revolution

Mem[orandum]: Carefully to omit defining of Person,
or making much mention of it
(George Berkeley, c. 1708)

You cannot call up any wilder vision than a city in which
men ask themselves if they have any selves
(G. K. Chesterton, 1908)

It's not the assertion of identity that's important;
it's the assertion of non-identity
(Michel Foucault, 1978)[1]

"Before the self" is a phrase meant not to tease but to be historically precise. In this book "the self" stands for a very particular understanding of personal identity, one that presupposes an essential core of selfhood characterized by psychological depth, or interiority, which is the bedrock of unique, expressive individual identity. That this self has a history is an assertion that we no longer find all that surprising. The first to have recognized that different cultures, or cultures at different historical moments, have had different understandings of identity and self were probably the anthropologists. From Marcel Mauss to Clifford Geertz they have repeatedly told us (in Mauss's words of 1938) that "far from existing as the primordial innate idea, clearly engraved since Adam in the innermost depths of our being", the modern Western sense of a self or a person (thus Geertz half a century later) "as a bounded, unique, more or less integrated motivational and cognitive universe, a dynamic center of awareness, emotion, judgment, and action, organized into a distinctive whole and set contrastively against other such wholes" is in truth "a rather peculiar idea within the context of the world's cultures".[2]

But the anthropological insight (with its subsequent echoes in neighboring disciplines, such as philosophy and literary criticism) – that the supposed universality of the individual subject with a well-defined, stable, unique, centered self is in truth a charged, far from natural, recent Western creation – puts the ball squarely back in the historian's court. For if this creation is not universal and trans-historical, then what were the specific historical circumstances that can account for its emergence, development, and ultimate naturalization as a supposed universal? This book proposes an answer to this question. It seeks to do so while avoiding the pitfall of admitting historical change and yet still taking the interior self as a self-evident category, and perhaps even an essential feature of human nature, that stands outside history: a strategy that simply replaces the self as an ahistorical universal given with a superficially historicized self as a latent bud waiting patiently for the sun rays of modernity to wake it to life. Instead, what follows offers a specific historical narrative – unfolding in England in the long eighteenth century, but with an eye to the West more broadly – of how and when the modern notion of identity came to be synonymous with precisely such a self. It thus also points to an earlier historical configuration in which this was not at all the dominant understanding of personal identity: a configuration and an understanding of identity, that is, "before the self".

If "self" in this book is thus well defined and historically specific, "identity" is used more loosely. This is deliberate. Identity, as has often been noted, encompasses within it – in its etymology as well as in its common application for the variety of possible responses to the question "who am I?" – a productive tension between two contradictory impulses: identity as the unique individuality of a person (as in "identity card"), or identity as a common denominator that places an individual within a group (as in "identity politics").[3] In the former sense, sometimes akin to self, identity is the essence of difference: it is what guarantees my quintessential specificity in relation to others. In the latter sense, identity is the obverse, or erasure, of difference: it is what allows me to ignore particular differences as I recognize myself in a collective grouping. (I will sometimes refer to this meaning of identity as "identicality".) Rather than constrain identity to mean only one or the other, what follows suggests that the balance between these two meanings has itself been subject to historical change, and can thus help us in the task of identifying and distinguishing two radically different configurations of understandings of identity in the eighteenth century.

This book approaches this task from two different directions. I begin the inquiry not with "identity" *tout court*, but with specific *categories* of identity: gender, race, class, and the distinction between humans and animals. The earlier chapters establish certain patterns – persistent, far-reaching, and to me highly intriguing patterns – that had characterized the understandings of these key categories of identity (but not others like nation or religion) in a wide variety of cultural sites and forms during most of the eighteenth century, overriding the important differences between these categories. These patterns will furthermore be seen to contrast sharply with those prevalent at a later stage toward the end of the century. Subsequently I will turn to other cultural sites that allow us a more direct glimpse into eighteenth-century understandings of personal identity itself: here the broadest contours of these shared patterns will become discernible, in sharp contrast again with a very different situation toward the end of the century. It will be important to keep in mind that this is in fact a significant convergence, not a logical inevitability: a priori, there is no reason to expect the historical development of understandings of personal identity to mirror that of categories of identity such as gender or race. The fact that in our particular historical moment they *did* mirror each other, and moved in tandem, will thus prove important in assessing the full meaning of these repeated patterns. By the end of our tour up and down the eighteenth-century cultural terrain, therefore, we will come to recognize a consistent and wide-ranging set of assumptions that defined the meaning, significance, and limits of identity up to the last two decades of the century. I will call this distinctive eighteenth-century configuration, many aspects of which may strike the reader as strange and counter-intuitive, the *ancien régime of identity*.

Like any other historically specific phenomenon, the *ancien régime* of identity had a beginning and an end. It will be seen that some aspects of this *ancien régime* emerged in the late seventeenth and early eighteenth centuries, while others were carried over from earlier. But the focus of this book is less on those beginnings than on the end: the sea change in the last two decades of the eighteenth century in which this distinctive configuration lost its cultural ground and was rapidly superseded by another. The new, alternative identity regime was defined by a fundamental emphasis on self, and we are thus more likely to find it familiar. Indeed, it underlay many new departures of this later period that are often taken as heralding the arrival of the modern. We also often associate these new departures with *revolution*: this was, after all, the "Age of Revolutions", a label that has weathered remarkably well the recent waves of revisionist attacks on its twin planks of sudden economic and political ruptures.[4] This book reaffirms the vision of the late eighteenth century as a period of radical discontinuity, albeit of a rather different nature: hence, with apologies to Tocqueville, the "*ancien régime* of identity and the revolution" in the title of my preface. Characterizing this shift as a revolution – a "cultural revolution" – is meant to highlight the surprising rapidity of the transformation from one identity regime to another, the far-reaching range of its effects, and the magnitude of the change it brought about – that is to say, how very dissimilar the new regime of identity was to the *ancien régime* that had preceded it. So dissimilar, indeed, that we will repeatedly encounter turn-of-the-century observers who looked back at the eighteenth century with expressions of distance, incomprehension, and disbelief.

"Revolution", like "making", also conjures up the notion of historical *process*. This is the final goal of this book, crucial of course to a historical inquiry: to chart the sharp and distinctive transformation that led from one identity regime to the other, and to explain how and why it happened. In fact, what needs explaining is twofold, for it is first necessary to account for the emergence of the eighteenth-century *ancien régime* of identity itself, with its peculiar characteristics that distinguished it from what had come before. Only then can we return to the question of its subsequent demise, seeking an explanation that can account both for the extraordinary abruptness of this late-eighteenth-century cultural revolution and for its extraordinary reach.

But do we not already have a magisterial answer to the questions posed here, one so immense in scope as to leave, seemingly, little room for another? I am thinking of course of Charles Taylor's *Sources of the Self*. Taylor's call to historicize the changing meanings of identity and self is as persuasive as it is uncompromising. For instance:

> So we have come to think that we "have" selves as we have heads. But the very idea that we have or are "a self", that human agency is essentially defined as "the self", is a linguistic reflection of our modern understanding and the radical reflexivity it involves. Being deeply embedded in this understanding, we cannot but reach for this language; but it was not always so.

Practicing what he preaches, therefore, in a dazzling feat of intellectual history, Taylor has lined up most of the important thinkers in the Western tradition and many lesser ones to chart a narrative for the emergence at a specific time and place – or rather, through a punctuated series of historical moments, culminating in the late eighteenth century – of notions of self characterized by inwardness and uniqueness that undergird what he boldly calls "the modern identity".[5] Problem solved?

Not quite. Taylor himself – by disciplinary affiliation a philosopher and political scientist rather than a historian – has indicated as much, in repeatedly flagging the limits of his own inquiry. Whereas the grist for Taylor's mill is the writings of philosophers and other contemplative authors, this is not where prevailing ideas about identity and self primarily reside. "The kinds of ideas I'm interested in here", Taylor writes, "for the most part exist in our lives through being embedded in practices"; cultural practices of infinite variety, permeating "all levels of human social life: family, village, national politics, rituals of religious communities, and so on". For most people, participation in these cultural practices, even as they reinscribe prevalent notions of identity or self, is unencumbered by self-aware reflection or formulation, but rather remains at a level of "some unstructured intuitions". Subsequently, for some thinkers, the more explicit ideas "arise from attempts to formulate and bring to some conscious expression the underlying rationale of the patterns"; the patterns, that is, in these ubiquitous cultural practices. But the crucial thing to realize – here Taylor is at his most remarkably frank – is that "as articulations, ideas are in an important sense secondary to or based on [these] patterns". The process of change in understandings of identity and self "takes place over the whole culture", far beyond the pronouncements of philosophers. The reason that he succumbed to "the temptation to give the priority to the philosophical formulation", Taylor admits, was "the fact that it *is* a formulation"; this in contrast to "the movement through the culture [that] is something diffuse and ambiguous, hard to pick out and define".[6]

It is precisely this diffuse and ambiguous movement across a whole culture of understandings of identity and self that is the subject of the present inquiry. This book, therefore, only rarely marshals forth the self-aware, articulate reflections of contemporaries on the topics of identity, categories of identity, or self. Rather, it pushes and probes as wide and diverse an array of cultural materials as it can – some predictable, others perhaps more surprising – with the hope of picking up the unselfconscious traces, the unintended marks, the signs of those "unstructured intuitions" that underlay people's fundamental assumptions about who they were and who they could be. The goal is not simply to expand the choice of subject matter, and thus add some new materials to the more explicit philosophical articulations. For these philosophical articulations are "secondary" in the important sense that it was the underlying set of assumptions about identity and self, those "unstructured intuitions" permeating a whole culture, that constituted the enabling and shaping precondition for the very articulation of such ideas. If Taylor's inquiry is "historical philosophy", that which I propose here, digging for the underlying assumptions that enable – and limit – people's actions and thoughts, can perhaps be called "historical epistemology".[7]

From this distinction, indeed, follows a methodological consideration that goes to the very heart of the questions this book wishes to answer. In contrast with the intellectual historian for whom individual enunciations that are especially articulate and explicit are the most valuable, in what follows a single enunciation or act does not and cannot by itself carry much weight. Rather, a key question that I will pose with regard to any enunciation or practice is the extent of its *resonance*. I am thinking of resonance as a gauge of conditions of communication and transmission, one that distinguishes (along a continuous spectrum) enunciations or practices that have little echo – those that "fall flat" –

from those that are picked up to be reproduced or mirrored or objected to or bounced around again and again and that thus continue to reverberate against a background buzz of similar enunciations or practices. A single act or pronouncement is like the plucking of the string of a violin: it is only the prior presence and depth of the adjacent soundbox that turns a barely perceptible flickering movement into a resonant sound, and a sequence of such movements into music. Consequently, moreover, the following analysis pays only limited respect to the integrity of particular texts or behaviors and to the overall intentions of their particular authors or perpetrators. Rather, though mindful of individual intent and particular context, it freely weaves together fragments from many texts and many lives in an effort to reconstruct as far as possible this underlying cultural soundbox, at the price of leaving out the full exposition of where and how these fragments fit into the larger wholes of their individual originators. So that even when this inquiry returns to the philosophers, say, as it occasionally will, their role in our *mise-en-scène* will turn out to be quite different than for the intellectual historian.

The other price paid for the laborious effort of reconstructing the underlying cultural soundbox is the imposition of certain temporal and spatial limits on the investigation. Thus, while the long eighteenth century was indeed a crucial period in ushering in recognizably modern notions of "self", the focus on this time frame leaves out both earlier developments and the subsequent twists and turns that carry the story into the nineteenth and twentieth centuries. The "modern" in my title should therefore be understood as a direction and a process but not as an endpoint. Second, this book focuses on one country, England (occasionally Britain), arguably the first country in the West to have undergone the particular transformation that will preoccupy us in the following pages. The fact that England did not experience the discontinuity of a political revolution during the "Age of Revolutions", moreover, makes a discontinuity in cultural terms both more revealing and easier to trace in its own terms. Indeed, for the most part what follows is limited further, owing to the nature of the evidence, to the literate and sometimes semi-literate circles of metropolitan and metropolitan-oriented England. It should be remembered, however, that by the eighteenth century these circles were in fact quite expansive, comprising a large segment of the urban population and a fast-growing proportion of the English population as a whole. At the same time, in considering the larger historical significance of this story we will also cast comparative glances at America and France, in order to speculate about the relationship between the particularities of the English case and the broader Western narrative of the historical changes in understandings of identity and self.

Overall, then, this book can be seen as retelling one of the oldest stories in the Western canon, that of the rise of modern individualism. It retells this story, however, in a way that may appear unfamiliar and strange. So strange, perhaps, as to risk the incredulity of some readers, especially those steeped in post-Romantic assumptions about selfhood. "How can one write a book about 'The Making of the Modern Self'", they might ask, "that is not in the main a history of the ways that expressions of interiority, or of deep emotions, changed over time?" While I do not at all want to suggest that a history of emotional experience, say, cannot be a valuable enterprise, I do want to insist that equating interiority or deep emotion with self at the outset of the inquiry, as a universal human experience rather than as a historically specific understanding of this experience, presupposes what needs to be demonstrated. And it is a presupposition that flies in the face of historical difference: as the following foray into eighteenth-century culture will remind us, the past *is* a foreign country.

Foreign, but perhaps not altogether alien. For, paradoxically, the earlier part of the story, "before the self", is at the same time likely to strike the reader not only as strangely remote but also as uncannily close. Many contemporary intellectual-political movements, from feminism through post-colonialism to multiculturalism, have emblazoned their banners with the imperative of destabilizing and denaturalizing modern Western notions of identity and self, emphasizing instead the liberating post-modern potential in recognizing their limits, their gaps, and their contingencies. It may thus prove somewhat disorienting to discover, as we become better acquainted with the *ancien régime* of identity, that some of those charged political goals that our contemporaries have set for a better future had been (*mutatis mutandis*) taken for granted by our predecessors two and a half centuries ago.

It is for this reason that I have lined up the three particular epigraphs that open this preface (which, however, given what I have said about single quotations, should be read as no more than illustrative mnemonic devices). The most self-assured is that by G. K. Chesterton, who professed in the early twentieth century an inability to imagine anyone even imagining – let alone inhabiting – a time or a place before the self. Chesterton's confidence seems out of synch with both George Berkeley's early-eighteenth-century diffidence and Michel Foucault's late-twentieth-century contrariness. Conversely, one can more readily imagine the post-modern Foucault, asserting the value of non–identity, engaged in a dialogue with the pre-modern Berkeley, whose skepticism about the meaning of identity and person will cross our path again: an imaginary conversation that would have gone way over Chesterton's head. Indeed, some readers may see this whole book as a continuation of Foucault's imaginary dialogue with Berkeley and his contemporaries, given the echoes in it of Foucault's insistence on the need to escape from a universalized unitary fixed self and on a fundamental rupture in the Western episteme in the late eighteenth century. (Others may respond, though, that the kind of questions and analytical moves that drive this book along call for the stripping of any Foucauldian badge to which its author might have wished to lay claim.) Be that as it may, I suspect the picture of the pre-modern eighteenth century that will emerge in this book may owe its appeal, in part, to a whiff of the post-modern, long *avant la lettre*. Indeed, I have become increasingly convinced that the explosion of interest in the eighteenth century in the last couple of decades, especially among British historians who have no revolution to explain and who had long neglected this "forgotten century", is not unrelated to the frisson caused by the realization that through studying the eighteenth century we can establish a conversation – a conversation marked by alternating bouts of suspicion and familiarity, alienation and intimacy – between the historical bookends of modernity.

PART I

Snapshot: On Queen Bees and Being Queens

Shortly after the Glorious Revolution, one Joseph Warder, a physician from Croydon, published a tract that went through no fewer than nine editions in the next half-century; a tract that sang the praises of a particular matriarchal society headed by a "glorious" queen. This warlike queen, "Terrible to her Enemies", was so powerful that "the Grand Seignior with all his janizaries about him . . . is not half so absolute", nor commands such "Loyal Awe" from his subjects. When the second edition came out in 1713, Warder could not but dedicate it to his own female monarch, Queen Anne: "I here present Your Majesty with a true State of these *Amazons*, or rather, a State of the true *Amazons*; and tho' there be Male as well as Female amongst them, 'tis not for nothing, nor by chance, that He who is Wisdom itself, should thus place the Government of their famous Monarchy in a Queen." In many ways, Warder contended, this monarchy led by the "*Amazonian* Dame" was the perfect polity.

This perfect polity was of course the beehive. Long a source of fascination, investigation, and speculation, the beehive was famously seen by early-modern people as a parable – indeed, a divine allegory – on human society. Key to the understanding of the beehive, always heavily anthropomorphized, was its perceived gender relations: it was during the seventeenth century that bees had come to be recognized as a society whose warring and governance were wholly female. Discussions of bees can therefore serve us too as a parable, an allegorical window into bigger questions regarding eighteenth-century under-standings of gender categories and identities.

Warder's apiary manual had the evocative title *The True Amazons; or, The Monarchy of Bees.*[1] The appreciative image it put forth was pretty much the common one from the late seventeenth through most of the eighteenth century. Writers on bees regularly made the analogy between the valorous, magnani-mous, and intrepid bees – in contrast to the feeble drones – and the warlike

Amazons. (At least two other early-modern apiarian texts carried the title
"The Feminine/Female Monarchy".) In particular, the queen at their helm
was praised as a "strong and vigorous" ruler, commanding the absolute and
unswerving loyalty of the community: what a famous mid-eighteenth-century
poetic tribute to the bees referred to as "the martial Dame" heading "the
Female State".[2]

But then things changed. By the closing decades of the eighteenth century,
the common language of bee-texts was veering away from images of female
governance and Amazonian warfare.[3] The image of the queen bee in particular
was now completely different: she was "the mother of her people", who "is to
be considered in no other light than as a layer of eggs". Some texts even went
so far as to declare the queen "the only person [in the hive] of her sex", and
the laborers as creatures "of no sex". The drones were the subjects of more
creative reimagining, whether as effeminate degenerates (who thus deserve
their unmanly fate), as "lazy gentry" (thus shifting the germane distinction
from a gender to a class axis), as self-sacrificing altruists who hide their true
manliness for the good of the community, or even as the (unappreciated)
epitome of caring fatherhood. And to come back to the queen, far from being
a fierce ruling Amazon, late-eighteenth-century bee authors now proclaimed
her to be of an "extremely pacific" nature, "boast[ing] no military pride", and
(without a sting) "unfit by nature for th'embattled fray". Rather, distinguished
by her "modesty", she was surrounded by "the body-guard, a brave, a faithful
band, [who] Round the QUEEN-MOTHER close embodied stand": a naturally
demure female with an entourage – or so the reader was led to suppose – of
valiant protective males. Crucially, it was her position as QUEEN-MOTHER – in
this text's screaming typography – that was "the only title by which she lays
claim to royalty". It was also the sole explanation for the so-called loyalty of
the bees to their queen, which in truth was nothing more than "an attachment
to the mother, somewhat similar to the attachment of young birds to the female
that brings them up". Rather than the political attachment of subjects to ruler,
it was the instinctive bonds between mother and offspring that now turned out
to be the glue that held the beehive together.[4]

It consequently seemed only logical to the writer who penned this last quotation in 1792, the well-known surgeon and naturalist John Hunter, to try to
do away with the royal image altogether. He failed: ultimately, Hunter found
it impossible to disregard the common usage by which "the breeder, is [com-
monly] called the queen". But then he hastened to add with unusual if unwitting candor: "and I shall [therefore] keep to the name, although I do not allow
her voluntary influence or power".[5] How far have we moved from those
Amazonian bees of the previous hundred years, always in control of the fate of
their matriarchal polity. Whereas the earlier writers had drawn attention to –

and were fascinated by – the gender reversals suggested by relations in the beehive, the later ones, in Hunter's revealing formulation, could not "allow" an image of powerful female governance over a community embodying apparently reversed gender roles, and thus went through some remarkable mental contortions to make the bees conform to rigid gender boundaries and expectations.

*

Eighteenth-century depictions of the beehive, then, to which many more could be added, seem to fall into a clear pattern. First, throughout most of the eighteenth century, up to about 1780 – a period that I will sometimes refer to (adapting a familiar scholarly usage) as "the short eighteenth century" – we see an interest in, and appreciation for, the "Amazonian" bees. Then, toward the end of the century, we see an increasing difficulty in allowing for a gender-reversed picture of female governance, and consequently a recourse – sometimes unselfconsciously, sometimes even comically – to a variety of strategies to circumvent or suppress those aspects of bee society that had previously proven of such interest.[6]

So far so good: the dedicated, if small, community of bee historians will be delighted. But what is the larger historical significance of such an observation? I would like to suggest that this pattern in bee-texts was neither a coincidence nor a phenomenon peculiar to apiologists and natural historians. Rather, it offers us a valuable thread end that we can follow in order to begin to untangle and unravel a much wider transformation. Imagine part I of this book, therefore, as drawing a series of increasingly expanding circles around the bee, circles that will illuminate how this localized observation fits into broader and broader contexts that endow it, in turn, with further meaning. The most immediate circle is that of the cultural materials that went directly into the anthropomorphizing depictions of the queen bee: the Amazon and the queen mother. From there we will raise our eyes to the next level, that of the more general understandings of gender categories in the eighteenth century manifested in a wide variety of cultural forms and materials, of which the Amazon and the mother will turn out to have been but particular examples. Next we will expand our perspective to a still broader circle of categories of identity, of which gender itself will now prove to be but one particular example: other categories that we will consider include race, class, and the boundary between humans and animals.

The first part of this book, then, makes its arguments in two registers. On the one hand, each chapter makes its own distinctive contribution to the history of a different identity category: the first two chapters are a contribution to the history of gender in the transition from the pre-modern to the modern, the third chapter is an analogous (but far from identical) intervention in the history of race, and the coda adds a consideration of the history of the distinctions between humans and animals as well as a corrective to my claims in an earlier book about the history of class. Taken separately, and understood internally within the long-term evolution of each category of identity, these chapters tell rather different stories, highlighting the particularities of each category in its own specific historical path. But ultimately it is the second register of the argument that will prove more important for this inquiry as a whole: the lateral, simultaneous look at all these stories together, placed side by side. Such a perspective will suddenly bring to center stage their common features at one particular moment in time. It will thus highlight the extraordinary depth and breadth of the unifying historical pattern shared across this whole terrain. This realization, in turn, is the necessary backdrop for the more direct discussion of identity and self in part II.

I

Varieties of Gender in Eighteenth-Century England

If bees are good to think with, as early-modern people certainly believed, let us inquire further into the cultural currents that intersected in the driving of the Amazon queen out of the beehive by the late eighteenth century and in the emergence of the queen mother as her most likely replacement. This chapter therefore begins by tracing the evolution of both sides in this balance – the image of the Amazon on the one hand, and that of the mother on the other. Both, I want to suggest, went through parallel shifts during the same period: shifts from understandings capacious enough to allow for individual deviation from dominant gender norms to more inflexible understandings that rendered such deviations very costly. It was as a consequence of this double shift that "Amazon" became an unacceptable characterization for a female – whether bee or human – just as maternity was about to become an inescapable one for her very essence.

First, then, the Amazon. In looking at the cultural position of the Amazon, scholars have often asserted – or rather assumed – that her image, involving a more or less radical renunciation of prevailing gender norms, has always pre-sented, by definition, a threatening challenge to patriarchy. Therefore, this line of reasoning continues, Amazons became an inevitable target of repression and vilification throughout the history of Western society – what one writer summed up as "the war against the Amazons".[1] But this can readily be shown not to have been the case: in fact, Amazons were not necessarily perceived as threatening, and they were as likely to have a good reputation as they were a bad one, depending on historical circumstances.

Thus, throughout the short eighteenth century, the lot of human Amazons, like that of Amazonian bees, was overall quite a good óne.[2] This for instance was how Ephraim Chambers began the relevant entry in his famous *Cyclopædia* of 1728: "Amazon, in Antiquity, a Term signifying a bold, courageous Woman: capable of daring, hardy Atchievements. See VIRAGO, HEROINE, &c." Thus, *tout court*: a heroic bundle of extraordinary qualities. These qualities of the Amazons – their "greatest Valour and Heroism" (1758) – were often commented upon: "Have we not read of *Amazons* of Old," versed another mid-century writer, "How great in *War*, how resolute and bold?" Yet another not only complimented "Amazonian Ladies", but insisted they were the best that "Dame Nature design'd". In Oliver Goldsmith's *Vicar of Wakefield*, Olivia was to be "drawn as an Amazon, sitting upon a bank of flowers . . . and a whip in her hand" as part of an idyllic, flattering family portrait. Contemporary art critics would have approved: Goldsmith perhaps got the idea from Joseph Spence's observation in his recently published learned treatise on the imagery of classical mythology, that the ancients had done well to represent Virtue as a manly, armed Amazon, in order to highlight her "firmness and resolution". Spence in turn may have got the idea from the Earl of Shaftesbury, who earlier in the century had suggested that the firmness and manliness of Virtue – "a martial Dame" – could be well conveyed by clothing her like an Amazon.[3]

Moreover, throughout most of the eighteenth century one can readily find representations of actual Amazon queens – be they avowedly mythical or supposedly historical – as noble, honorable, and heroic.[4] Nor were these only the Amazon queens of antiquity: Joseph Warder, after all, considered it genuinely flattering to dedicate his account of the "glorious" Amazonian queen bee and her entourage to his own queen, Anne. Warder's effort resonated with other contemporary attempts to portray the queen as a martial Amazon, from Anne's coronation medal that showed her as the warrior goddess Pallas actively engaged in warfare, to the "Amazons, with Bows and Arrows" that greeted her ceremonial entry into Bath in 1702 (fig. 1). (These attempts, it is also true, did not go very far, but this was because of their incongruity with Anne's personal inclinations, rather than because the Amazonian image itself was unacceptable.)[5] Indeed, nobody understood better the positive implications of Warder's Amazonian tribute than an adversary in the debate on bees, one Robert Maxwell: Maxwell, who was convinced that the head of the beehive was in fact male, accused Warder of deliberately misrepresenting it as an Amazonian female only in order to be able to sway the queen with a "fine Compliment".[6]

So the Amazon, literal or figurative, was doing rather well until the last two decades of the eighteenth century, and was routinely seen as an evocation of ancient glory, more a compliment than a complaint. This is not to say, of course, that there were no pejorative invocations of the Amazons during this period. But such negative characterizations sat side by side with more positive ones, allowing for a wide range of possible evaluations of the Amazon in which the former did not impart the dominant tone.

1. Queen Anne's coronation medal, 1702

But then the fortunes of the Amazons changed rapidly and dramatically. One would be hard pressed to find many writers in the 1780s and 1790s employing the epithet "Amazonian" in anything but a pejorative sense. When the *Historical Magazine* carried in 1792 a putative eyewitness report of a matrilineal and matriarchal society in Lesbos, the closest to "an Amazonian commonwealth" that had ever been found, it turned out that these "lordly ladies" were distinguished "by a haughty, disdainful, and supercilious air", their dress was "singular and disadvantageous", and their usurpation of male prerogatives had led to the disintegration of the natural social fabric even to the point of having these "unnatural daughters" turn on their own parents. And when a turn-of-the-century critic wished to denounce Gothic literature for its unwholesome unnaturalness, the characteristic that he chose – rather surprisingly – to single out as that in which "every law of nature, and every feature of the human character are violated and distorted", was the Gothic's encouragement of "amazonian spirit". Elsewhere it became commonplace to invoke, in the context of the critique of modern times, the Amazon's "*folly*, as a reward for her manhood" (1787), or "the unpleasing airs of an Amazon, or a virago" (1789) – words that now carried very different connotations from those, say, in Chambers's *Cyclopædia* of 1728. "I am no Amazon," declared the milkwoman poetess Ann Yearsley in 1796. As such Yearsley endowed her portrait as a bare-breasted figure of liberty with a sorrowfully imploring feminine expression, as a clear repudiation of the Amazonianism that "profanes [the] heart by nature made". She had moved quite a distance away from her predecessor of half a century, the washerwoman poetess Mary Collier, who, when she had published *her* poems, proudly imagined herself at the head of "an Army of Amazons".[7]

By the 1790s, this change – which had already begun in the 1780s – became much easier to dress in a more explicit political garb. But the renunciation of the Amazon was true not only of anti-revolutionary conservatives, who predictably vied with each other in denouncing Mary Wollstonecraft and her ilk as "the Amazonian band". It was also true of radicals like William Godwin, whose vindication of Wollstonecraft – his erstwhile wife – sought to play down and explain away the "somewhat amazonian temper, which characterizes some parts of [her] book", a temper that he too found to be distasteful, and to emphasize instead her "essential character", as "a woman, lovely in her person, and in the best and most engaging sense, feminine in her manners". Far from being an Amazon – Amazonian behavior, Godwin wrote a few years later, was "absurd, indelicate, and unbecoming" – Wollstonecraft as he now reconstructed her turned out to have been a living reaffirmation, in a proper juxtaposition to her husband, of the basic gender distinctions between men and women.[8] Or take Godwin's friend, the painter James Barry, who also tried to defend Wollstonecraft's reputation, offering her together with her *Vindication of the Rights of Woman* as an example of "why the ancients . . . have chosen Minerva a female". But Barry proved unable to stick by this "feminist" stance for very long: by the next page we find his Minerva advocating "the superior sentiment and graces of feminine softness" as the sole base of women's social position. Barry's turn-of-the-century Minerva, domesticated and properly feminine, was but a faint shadow of that Amazonian Minerva who had been celebrated by his eighteenth-century forerunners in art criticism, Shaftesbury and Spence, for her "sternness that has much more of masculine than female in it".[9]

In a less freighted context, consider the successive editions of the *Encyclopaedia Britannica*. The first and second editions, of 1771 and 1778, included entries on Amazons that were neutral if not appreciative in tone. But in the third edition, of 1788, these were replaced with an avowedly critical essay that presented the Amazons as terrible, barbaric, and politically dangerous. Or take the correspondence of Horace Walpole, as good an indication as any of tremors in the tectonic plates of eighteenth-century culture, given the extraordinary scale and longevity of his letter-writing career. From the mid-1780s, and more insistently in the years following the French Revolution, we find Walpole using the term "Amazonian" frequently to denounce those virago supporters of political radicalism, both in France and at home. But twenty years earlier Walpole had actually written to a lady friend – a "heroine" in his words – in appreciation, not condemnation, of her "real Amazonian principles". In the intervening years, in Walpole's letters as well as in the other cultural registers we have seen, the overtones of "Amazon" shifted from an expression of admiration for female heroism to a denunciation of female transgression. This sudden shift, moreover, did not go unnoticed by at least one (female) contemporary, who observed in 1793 that "Amazonian virtue" had recently gone out of fashion.[10] Small wonder, therefore, that with it the Amazonian queen bee went out of fashion too.

*

The Amazonian queen bee, we recall, was replaced by the mother queen. However natural this substitution might seem, given the structural relations of the hive, it too can be analogously situated within a late-eighteenth-century cultural context.

To begin to see this, we can turn to the novelist and educator Maria Edgeworth. In 1801 Edgeworth published the highly didactic novel *Belinda* – she herself called it a "moral tale" – which set forth her vision for the dawning century. *Belinda* participated in the virulent anti-Amazonian campaign of these years: the novel's bad guy (I use this phrase advisedly) is an Amazonian "*man-woman*", a woman with "bold masculine arms" whose favorite pastimes include hunting, electioneering, sword-fighting, and above all donning male clothes. With a characteristic disregard for subtlety, this person is named Mrs. Harriot Freke ("Who am I? only a Freke!" she cries on one occasion, when mistaken for "a smart-looking young man"). Freke is the agent of corruption for Lady Delacour, Belinda's London patron, who after the death of two children renounces her maternal role for the third. It is this disavowal of motherhood that underlies Delacour's association with Freke, and its consequences are disastrous. Cajoled by Freke, Delacour agrees to a cross-dressed pistol duel with a female enemy – a scheme that backfires, literally, inflicting on her a "hideous" wound in one breast. The bad mother thus turns – as Lady Delacour herself does not fail to appreciate – into a literal one-breasted Amazon, a transformation that threatens to consume her body, her peace of mind, her independence, and ultimately her life. In a particularly poignant scene, Lady Delacour's surviving child attempts to hug her: but when "she pressed close to her mother's bosom", "Lady Delacour screamed, and pushed her daughter away", thus graphically linking her Amazonian wound and her renunciation of maternal duty.[11]

The point to note about this exchange is its physicality: feminine maternal identity in *Belinda* is innate, physical, and impossible to shed at will. The renunciation of motherhood thus necessarily entails a physical corollary on Lady Delacour's very body, the mutilated breast, just as the resolution of the novel must involve the simultaneous restoration of Lady Delacour to the role of mother and the almost miraculous cure of her breast wound.[12] Indeed, the antithesis (over-)drawn in *Belinda* between unredeemable monstrous Amazonianism and idealized natural motherhood – recall again the transformation of the queen bee – can readily be found elsewhere at this juncture. Thus, when Ann Yearsley asserted in 1795 that she was "no Amazon", she too resorted to the same double breasted imagery: pitting the blissful image of a baby at his mother's breast against that of a woman whose refusal to suckle her baby ominously results in breast disease ("Too proud to nurse, maternal fevers came –/ Her burthen'd bosom caught th'invited flame"). In fact, even a cursory search can establish the diseased breast as a recurrent trope in a variety of turn-of-the-century contexts, making it the quintessential physical embodiment of unfeminine and unmaternal behavior.[13]

More broadly, the closing years of the eighteenth century were strewn with assertions of the natural, biological-physical basis of maternity: assertions, for example, of women's natural "destiny of bearing and nursing children", which for one writer of 1787 meant that "the order of nature would be totally reversed" if a woman opted for "the cold, *forbidding* pride of a studious virginity". "The principal destination of all women is to be mothers" (1790). "Maternal feeling" is a law of "all-powerful Nature" that transcends the differences between people in all corners of the globe (1799). Another text, of 1803, by the renowned doctor William Buchan, not only insisted obsessively on the "naturalness" of motherhood, but actually posited the maternal role as *the* key to feminine identity that determines the whole of women's physical and spiritual essence. "[No] virtue [can] take deep root in the breast of the female that is callous to the feelings of a mother" – a woman who thus renders herself an "unfeeling monster" by her "unnatural conduct". This, of course, was essentially the same insistence on maternity *qua* femininity that had appeared in Edgeworth's *Belinda* two years earlier – all the way to the warning about the physical injury to a woman's body that would inevitably result from her neglect of maternal breast-feeding.[14]

It is important to clarify what I am *not* saying here. It would be wrong to suggest that the emphasis on motherhood was a novelty of the last two decades of the eighteenth century. Quite the contrary: the widely researched scholarly consensus is that "a distinctive and historically nuanced fascination with the maternal" already characterized England – and indeed the West – by the mid-century at the latest. The same was also the case for the increasing preoccupation with the maternal breast; most famously, perhaps, for Rousseau and Linnaeus, or in Dr. William Cadogan's influential *Essay upon Nursing and the Management of Children* (1748).[15] But then – to go back to our original inquiry, triggered by the queen bee – the mother and the Amazon are not straightforward equivalents: the mother, after all, was the normative figure, whereas the Amazon, even when tolerated or appreciated, was always the counter-normative one. It is therefore the *non-mother* that is the more precise counterpart of the Amazon: and the question is, when did the woman who chose *not* to mother become a fundamentally unacceptable and disturbing figure? It is here, I want to suggest, that we see again clear marks of a late-eighteenth-century turning point; a turning point that in this case produced the final twist in the long-term advent of new understandings of maternity that we may wish to call "modern". Dr. Buchan, one of the most influential figures in propagating these understandings, recognized very well this change in his own writing. In the forty years that had passed between his first advice manual for mothers and that of 1803 discussed above, Buchan admitted, his emphasis had shifted from the health of the child to the natural duties of the mother, which led him to disallow *any* mother any deviation from the prescribed models that he had formerly set up only in general terms.[16]

The suggestion, then, is that the distinctive shift peculiar to the late eighteenth century was one from maternity as a general ideal, broadly prescriptive but allowing for individual deviations, to maternity as inextricably intertwined with the essence of femininity for each and every woman. In the latter understanding, what was ruled out was the possibility of *choice*: a woman choosing not to exercise these essential maternal instincts, rather than being forced into such a situation through circumstances beyond her control, was now most likely to be branded "unnatural".[17] Earlier, however, one could readily find plenty of acknowledgements of women's ability – even right – to choose to remain single, and not to mother, without this choice necessarily reflecting damagingly on them. Thus, in contrast to the prescriptive texts of the turn of the century that asserted in unison that motherhood and even marriage were "of natural instinct", mid-century contributions to the same conventional genre had been surprisingly undogmatic on this point. "She, who lives to be an old maid, against her will, is unfortunate," one popular conduct book told its readers in 1740. "But where this state results from a free choice . . . then it may properly be called a life of angels." No less. "I know nothing that renders a woman more despicable, than her thinking it essential to happiness to be married," John Gregory echoed in his even more popular conduct book of 1774: "besides the gross indelicacy of the sentiment, it is a false one, as thousands of women have experienced."[18]

In a different textual register, Sarah Scott's utopian novel *Millenium* [sic] *Hall* (1762) depicted a community of chaste, nonsexual women whose lives presented an alternative to marriage and biological motherhood; an alternative, crucially, which they followed by choice, not as a consequence of unfortunate circumstances. To be sure, the women of Millenium Hall "consider[ed]

matrimony as absolutely necessary to the good of society". But they saw it as
"a general duty", from which individual women could "be excused by . . . sub-
stitut[ing] . . . others". The novel is consequently strewn with instances of
motherhood (and occasionally fatherhood) being relegated, displaced, assumed,
or renounced, with little consideration for the "natural" ties of biological
parentage. It is especially telling that when Scott does introduce a mother
characterized by unfeminine "boldness" combined with a lack of maternal
feeling, she turns out to be not a prototype of Lady Delacour, with her
deficiency of innate maternal instinct, but rather her precise opposite: in
Millenium Hall the unnatural Amazonian mother is in fact a *stepmother*, and
it is her unwillingness to *assume* the maternal role – to let her acquired duty
overcome her lack of natural attachment – that turns her into the narrative's
villainess.[19]

Again, we should certainly not paint too rosy a picture: the point is not
simply that good times were replaced by bad times. Throughout the eighteenth
century the lot of "old maids" was often a harsh and abusive one. The non-
mother, like the Amazon, was a counter-normative figure, and as such was often
subject to criticism or worse. But up to the late eighteenth century this criticism sat side by side with the ability – on the part of both men and women –
to imagine these alternatives to the prevalent norms as viable, tolerable,
unthreatening, at times even appreciable. It is this ability that subsequently
seems to have disappeared. Such counter-normative figures were now driven
underground or forced to come out into the open as explicit, charged, politi-
cized challenges to the whole gender order.[20]

Moreover, as we shall see further in chapter 2, even vituperation has room
for different configurations of possibility. To give but one example now, consider the contrast between two texts of 1713 and 1785. In 1713, *A Satyr upon
Old Maids*, one of the most vicious attacks of its kind in the eighteenth century,
concluded its barrage of abuse with the surprising exculpation of those women
"who continue *Maids* to *Old Age*, through Choice", who "deserve all the
Encomiums [that] can be merited by the *Best* of their *Sex*". By contrast, when
the poet William Hayley penned a well-wishing *defense* of single women in 1785,
his self-proclaimed posture as a "Friend to the Sisterhood" extended – as he
hastened to explain – only to those women who remained unmarried "not as
the effect of choice, arising from a cold and irrational aversion to the [married]
state in general", but rather because of unfortunate circumstances beyond their
control. By choice, Hayley insisted, every acceptable woman would marry, and
she who would not must be "utterly devoid of tenderness". So, whereas the
1713 satirist had excluded from his blanket antipathy those women whom he
respected for not fulfilling their roles as wife and mother through their own
choice, the 1785 essayist excluded from his blanket empathy those very same

women, who lost his respect by making precisely that choice. (Hayley dedicated his work to the unmarried Elizabeth Carter, and was reportedly bewildered and wounded when she failed to appreciate the gesture.)[21]

*

Two parallel and complementary trends in late-eighteenth-century culture, then, intersect in our story of the beehive. On the one hand, there was a reversal of fortunes in the reputation of Amazons and in the connotations of all things Amazonian, which after decades of relative tolerance and often positive appreciation suddenly came to be seen as irredeemably negative, signifying a disturbing affront to nature. On the other, there was a simultaneous shift in the eighteenth-century focus on maternity, which essentialized maternity as an innate precondition of femininity, the renunciation of which became – again – an unredeemable affront to nature. In light of these developments, it is not surprising that, after many decades of absolute rule over the beehive, the Amazon queen bee was unceremoniously driven out and replaced by her more properly gender-conformist counterpart, the bounteous queen mother.

Nor was she the only Amazon queen to suffer such a fate. A very different queen comes to mind here, one who was cast in the Amazonian role – rather unflatteringly – by none other than William Shakespeare. She was Margaret of Anjou, the "warlike Queen" of the feeble Henry VI, whose martial spirit and feisty exhortations egged the king on when he was ready to concede his son's right to the throne. A glance at several eighteenth-century incarnations of Queen Margaret in the third part of Shakespeare's *Henry VI* will prove a telling complement to our foray into the representations of the queen bee.

In 1724, Theophilus Cibber – son of the better-known Colley Cibber – restaged *Henry VI* in an "altered" form. Cibber's revisions are suggestive. Not only did he introduce Margaret's Amazonian behavior earlier and more prominently than in Shakespeare's *mise-en-scène*, he also "cleansed" it of the negative connotations it had had in the original text – for instance, by replacing a hostile comment on Margaret as "an Amazonian trull" with an appreciative one (though uttered by Margaret's enemies) on "the bold Amazon Queen". Overall, Amazonian behavior is not condemned in Cibber's *Henry VI*. As the queen herself says, in another addition peculiar to this eighteenth-century adaptation, such behavior on her part was not unnatural (this word she reserved for the king's willingness to disinherit his son), but rather a justifiable "disguise [of] fair nature" in order to attain a higher goal.[22]

But when Margaret returned to the stage in another adaptation of *Henry VI* in 1795, this one by Richard Valpy, the theatrically inclined head of Reading School, the effect was completely reversed. Gone was the feisty Amazonian

behavior, gone (almost) was the intrepid female warrior charging to battle, gone
was the woman who disguised nature in order to encourage the men to fight to
the bitter end. In part Valpy achieved this transformation simply by reducing
considerably Margaret's active role in the play: she no longer spoke of going
into battle, and the last remaining reference to "her more than manly spirit"
was only hearsay. (The word "Amazon" itself was nowhere to be found.)
Instead, on the couple of occasions when Margaret did appear on stage to do
what the story demands of her, namely to encourage her weaker husband, she
did so briefly and in a proper wifely fashion.[23] More centrally, though, her now
muffled Amazonian tendencies were overshadowed by another heroic role – that
of the mother: first protective and then aching mother of the prince who is dis-
inherited and ultimately killed. The climax of Margaret's maternal role, from
Shakespeare onward, comes in her parting words over the body of her dead
son. But whereas formerly this maternal pain had stood side by side with
Margaret's no less powerful Amazonian actions, and without apparent contradiction, in Valpy's 1795 staging Margaret's maternal speech completely eclipsed
any other aspect of her performance.[24] In short, in this late-eighteenth-century
production – which announced at the outset its intent to tell the story in a way
"neither offensive to delicacy, nor repugnant to the principles of modern taste"
– we are back where we started: Margaret the Amazon queen, just like the
queen bee, was also now recast exclusively as a queen mother.[25]

Queen Margaret's refashioning, however, was harder to achieve for those
more closely accountable to the historical record. This might explain why an
1804 biographical portrait of Margaret of Anjou, in trying to account for her
mixture of Amazon and mother, rather lost its bearings. With confusing inconsistency it characterized Margaret either as a woman "tainted with ferocity",
or as an unfortunate woman "unsexed" through situations beyond her control;
but at the same time, miraculously, also as a woman exhibiting feminine devo-
tion to "a husband and son she had so faithfully served". What a distance we
have moved from the 1766 example of the same biographical genre, which had
been able to find no higher praise for Margaret than that "nature had endowed
her with all the virtues of the men without their defects" – a mixture that
in the eyes of that mid-eighteenth-century biographer had been the most
generous gift nature could bestow upon her. Its 1804 counterpart, by contrast,
made an effort to turn Margaret's Amazonian battles, in the final count, into
little more than her own – albeit peculiar – way of fulfilling the role that this
text wanted her above all else to fulfill: as good wife and mother.[26]

Let us go one step further. When a 1766 account of the manly Queen
Margaret flatteringly detailed how she "commanded her army herself", "rode
thro' all the battalions", "drew up her troops in order of battle, and encouraged them with a speech", it was conjuring up unmistakable echoes of another
queen at her warlike Amazonian best: Queen Elizabeth, in her famous horse-

back speech at Tilbury before the defeat of the Spanish Armada ("I know I have the body but of a weak and feeble woman; but I have the heart and stomach of a king"). In fact, Elizabeth's eighteenth-century reputation went through a transformation much like Margaret's. Throughout most of the century we find considerable appreciation for Elizabeth's heroic manliness ("Tho' a woman, she hid all that was womanish about her," Viscount Bolingbroke wrote approvingly in 1749). By association this approval carried over to the "manly genius of Eliza's days", often set as a glittering foil to the enervated present; not least that hardy manliness of *women*, who in those days had been admirably "rough as their lords".[27] It was this side of Queen Elizabeth that late-eighteenth-century accounts, by contrast, tried to hide as much as possible, either by rewriting the scene at Tilbury so as to erase its gender-unsettling aspects, or by emphasizing Elizabeth's femininity as against the manliness of her support staff ("Wise were her Counsellors, her Warriors brave./ But she was *woman* still, and passion's slave" [1790]). Thus, take Mary Hays's *Female Biography* of 1803. In Hays's hands Elizabeth's speech at Tilbury became an apologetic declaration of "her intentions, *though a woman*, to lead them herself against the enemy": the heart of a king was nowhere to be found. This declaration, moreover, naturally brought forth the manly protective instincts of those around her, resolved to perish in "the defence of their heroic queen". Indeed, sympathetic and admiring as this portrait was, penned by an erstwhile "Wollstonecraftian", it even came close to pronouncing the virgin and childless queen as unnatural ("as a *woman*, [she was] cut off . . . from the sympathies of nature").[28]

But unlike the perhaps irredeemable Elizabeth, Queen Margaret did have a redeeming maternal side, which allowed her to be pushed all the way to the other extreme of what now became an axis of incommensurate opposites – that of the Amazon versus the mother. How far Margaret *could* be pushed became apparent when an early-nineteenth-century female author, Margaret Holford, devoted almost five hundred pages of poetry to retelling the queen's misfortunes. Emphatically, and against centuries of historical precedent, this retelling was not a warring saga: Holford's Margaret only ever heard the sounds of battle from a distance. Instead it was a voyage of discovery of the "maternal softness" that suddenly "stole/ With force resistless, o'er her soul", chasing away her more Amazonian tendencies:

> In Margaret's fierce and stormy breast
> A thousand warring passions strove,
> Yet now, unbid, a stranger-guest
> Dispers'd and silenc'd all the rest –
> Thy voice, Maternal Love!

Against the backdrop of this therapeutic apotheosis of maternal love (bringing to mind the radical reformation of Lady Delacour), we can return in conclusion to the symbolic meaning of dedications. Whereas Joseph Warder had prefaced his early-eighteenth-century *True Amazons* with a perhaps over-determined dedication to his queen, one suspects even more of an overdeter-mined inevitability in the dedication of Margaret Holford, who presented her anti-Amazonian *Margaret of Anjou* – how else? – to "my dear Mother".[29]

Percy's Prologue

It is easy to see the common threads that run through the shifts in the fortunes of Amazons and in the understandings of maternity in the late eighteenth century. In both cases, prevailing gender norms were redefined as essential and natural, thus pulling the cultural rug from under behavior or images that seemed to offer alternatives to these dominant norms, enabling individuals to dodge them. But to what extent can these observations be generalized, as indications of a broader cultural pattern? And how broad *is* "broader"? The remainder of this chapter will attempt to answer the first question, by tracing parallel transformations in eighteenth-century understandings of gender that reach beyond bees, Amazons, and mothers. The next chapter will address more directly the question of how broad is broad, and how a cultural historian can go about demonstrating such breadth – breadth in terms of genres, of cultural forms, and of social locations – in order to make a plausible case for a far-reaching pattern of historical change, one that may even be described as a "cultural revolution".

So first, to see how indicative is the pattern we have identified, we need another thread end, another path into the meanings and possibilities associated with gender in the eighteenth century. The guide I have chosen to lead the way might seem a surprising one, given that she is the contemporary figure associated perhaps more than any other with iron-clad unambiguous gender distinctions. This "Victorian" *par excellence* and *avant la lettre* is the educator and publicist Hannah More, that prim paragon and prophetess of a properly gender-divided view of the world in which "men and women occupied separate spheres by nature as well as custom and propriety", and for whom (as Leonore Davidoff and Catherine Hall authoritatively assert) "the emphasis [wa]s on sexual *difference*".[30] It is not for nothing that Richard Polwhele, in his rant against the "unsex'd females" led by the "Amazonian" Wollstonecraft, found the latter's "diametrically opposite" ideal in Hannah More. In 1799, for instance, More went on public record (as she was to do many times thereafter) in a vehement protestation against the models for womanhood set by "self-complacent heroines" or "Amazons" who adopted "masculine manners": namely, "the bold and independent beauty, the intrepid female, the hoyden, the huntress, and the archer; the swinging arms, the confident address, the regimental, and the four-in-hand".[31] In the anti-Amazonian climate of these years, More was certainly not one to remain microphone-shy – which is what makes her earlier public persona so interesting. Consider More's image as it was evoked in association with her tragedy *Percy*, performed more than twenty times in the first two months following its debut in Covent Garden in December 1777, and whose first published edition in 1778 sold 4,000 copies in a fortnight. The unusual fact that this tragedy was written by a woman prompted the doyen of eighteenth-century English theater, David Garrick, to embellish it with a prologue dedicated to singing the praises of crossing gender boundaries. *Percy*'s prologue addressed itself to the women in the audience with the following words:

> I'll prove, ye fair, that let us have our swing,
> We can, as well as men, do any thing; . . .
> Mount the high horse we can, and make long speeches;
> Nay, and with dignity, some wear the breeches;
> And why not wear 'em? – We shall have your votes,
> While some of t' other sex wear petticoats.
> Did not a *Lady Knight*, late *Chevalier*,
> A brave, smart soldier to your eyes appear?
> Hey! presto! pass! his *sword* becomes a *fan*,
> A comely *woman* rising from the *man*.
> The French their Amazonian maid invite –
> She goes – alike well skill'd to talk or write,
> Dance, ride, negociate, scold, coqet [sic], or fight.[32]

Garrick's prologue to *Percy* was nothing less than an ode to gender transgression, the light tone of which should not obscure its genuine intention to celebrate Hannah More's feat. The contrast with the later More is startling: the images of female "masculine" prowess evoked by Garrick's prologue were precisely the same that were to incur More's wrath at the turn of the century. Indeed, she came back to the same list rather obsessively: "An Amazon", she stormed a few years later, with her predilection for "the cap, the whip, the masculine attire . . . the intrepid look, the independent air"; "a huntress – a politician, and a farrier . . . [who] excel[ed] in driving four-in-hand, and in canvassing at an election"; a woman like that was so "disgusting" that any man "would not for the world that she should be his wife or daughter". And yet in 1778 Garrick, a close personal friend of More's who had taken an active role in the production of her play, could associate her with these same images, indeed with the very success of such a gender-crossing, and get away with it without making it seem particularly loaded, discomforting, or threatening. Quite the contrary: the Hannah More of the late 1770s had thought that Garrick's verses were "excellent", and noted with much satisfaction on *Percy*'s opening night that "the prologue and epilogue were received with bursts of applause". As the applause indicated, moreover, these verses did not jar with More's public image at the time: enthusiastic spectators found proof in *Percy*, just as Garrick had suggested, that "the fair had won the cause".[33]

To be sure, this striking reversal of More's public image can readily be explained – and rightly so, no doubt – in terms of her own biography, which conventionally hinges on her well-known Evangelical conversion of the 1780s. But there might be more to it than that. For it is surely significant that the supposedly personal transformation undergone by More was paralleled by uncannily similar shifts in the fortunes of the various indicators of gender-crossing that had been associated with her name in Garrick's prologue to *Percy*. What was true for the Amazon was just as true for the others: the woman wearing the breeches, the female chevalier, the female orator and politician, and indeed the very use of theatrical prologues and epilogues to highlight the instability of gender boundaries, all experienced – as we shall see – a similar "conversion" or transformation at the very same moment. More's personal metamorphosis, in other words, should be understood within a broader cultural pattern, precisely of the kind we are after.

Following in the footsteps of the queen bee, the Amazon, and the non-mother, then, what the following pages demonstrate with regard to the elements that were found together in *Percy*'s prologue is likewise two-fold. First, it will be suggested that these various evocations of the possibilities for crossing gender boundaries were all stock tropes and themes reworked time and again in multiple cultural sites throughout the preceding decades, repeatedly intersecting and cross-referencing each other. On one level, of course, it remains true that the ode to gender transgression in *Percy*'s prologue was a celebration of the *extraordinary*; a fact emphasized by form as well as by content, since it was spoken by a woman rather than a man, itself an infraction of conventional theatrical practice. But I want to suggest that, on another level, this construction of the extraordinary would not have struck the audiences of the 1770s as bizarre, but rather as a comfortably familiar recycling of themes and forms they had encountered many times before. We can therefore use *Percy*'s prologue as a path into the web of allusions and references that together produced the meaning of gender in the eighteenth century: a dense web of mutually reinforcing symbolic reminders of the limits of gender categories, within which Garrick's prologue was snugly situated and from which it derived its meaning and resonance. Here we will find the first part of the broader pattern within which to fit the Amazon, the woman who chose not to mother, or the regal queen bee. The decades leading up to *Percy* were characterized by a resigned

– if not humoring, or even appreciative – willingness on the part of many (albeit never all), at least within metropolitan literate and semi-literate society, to accept that gender categories could ultimately prove inadequate; and therefore that individuals or actions were not necessarily always defined or fixed by the boundaries that these categories delineated.

Then, in each and every case, we will see the shift – the same late-eighteenth-century shift that produced the transformation in the representation of the beehive. Within a remarkably short period of ten or fifteen years after the first performance of *Percy*, the various components of this eighteenth-century cultural environment either vanished, lost their resonance, or reversed their meaning. Reactions characterized by tolerance or begrudging acceptance – let alone humor – were superseded by ones of anxiety and disbelief. Suddenly, the dense web of interlocking eighteenth-century practices and forms that had capitalized in one way or another on the relative elasticity of former perceptions of gender became socially unacceptable and culturally unintelligible. It is this cultural shift that provides the broader context for the transformation undergone by the queen bee, or for the "conversion" undergone by Hannah More between the prologue to *Percy* and her own later enunciations. I have previously called this transformation "gender panic", and will continue sometimes to use this phrase below, although it will prove to be of limited use once we proceed in subsequent chapters to situate this transformation within an even broader context that will transcend the history of the category of gender.

*

That Garrick used the label "Amazonian" in his tribute to More should come as no surprise. We have already seen the positive connotations of this term in the decades leading to the 1770s. In *Percy*'s prologue the image of the Amazon is associated with the related figure of the female knight: the woman who could ride, wear soldier's clothes, handle a sword, and fight. Let us start then with the eighteenth-century fortunes of the female knight.

To a greater extent even than the Amazon, the female knight or warrior in the short eighteenth century was more in danger of becoming a cultural cliché than of raising puzzled eyebrows. Her ability to put on male garb, successfully pass as a man, and excel in the mostly manly pursuit of all, war, was formulaically celebrated in hundreds of street ballads with titles like "The Female Warrior", "The Maiden Sailor", "The Soldier Maid", or "She Dressed herself Like a Duke". Her actual performance in manly military exercises, "in a style that would have done credit to any corps of regulars" (in the words of one raving critic), was a regular audience-drawing feature of eighteenth-century theater. Her confidence in fulfilling these masculine roles as well as any man ("No Warlike Weapons are to me unknown/ I'll Exercise with any one in

Town") was commonly reaffirmed. Her appearance was happily imitated, becoming a familiar feature of actual female dress: most clearly, perhaps, in modish riding habits, donned by fashionable women for an increasing variety of circumstances, that were known for their distinctly masculine cuts (they made women appear "most officer-like").[34]

Moreover, eighteenth-century Britons heard often enough about heroines whose reputed exploits carried the trope of the female knight – complete with her breeches, her dueling sword, and her military prowess – from the literary, dramatic, or aesthetic realms into real life. Such was the case of Mrs. Christian Davies, whose successful double act as "a brave Soldier, [and] a tender Mother" (recall the contemporary portrayals of Margaret of Anjou) was put forth at mid-century as a model for the fair sex, "highly worthy their imitation". Such was the case of the beautiful Jenny Cameron who famously became a female officer under the Jacobite Young Pretender, because "so glorious a Cause had raised in her Breast every manly Thought, and quite extinguished the Woman".[35] Most prominently, such was the case of the celebrated Hannah Snell, the best-known female soldier of the eighteenth century. Snell's popular biography, *The Female Soldier* (1750), exuded self-conscious pride on the part of its subject. Already as a child, it recounted, Snell "used often to declare to her Companions, that she would be a Soldier if she lived", and indeed she led her own gang, "stiled young *Amazon Snell*'s Company", which was "admired all over the Town". When she "boldly" joined the army, her deception was entirely successful: "Hannah in Briggs [breeches] behav'd so well,/ That none her softer Sex could tell." Moreover, her anonymous biographer assured readers that "no doubt she had a Right to do so" in pursuing her objectives, and that in fact, aside from family ties, "there are no Bounds to be set . . . in the female Mind".[36] Extraordinary as Snell's life had been, the book's moral insisted on the more general proposition that there were no uncrossable boundaries set by gender difference; precisely the proposition that animated Garrick's invocation of the female knight in his tribute to Hannah More in 1777–8.

Now the point is surely not whether such stories were true or false. Rather, what is of interest is their successful circulation and their remarkably unanxious reception. These supposed real-life accounts resonated with familiar themes and conventions in the narratives of female warriors that cropped up in eighteenth-century culture in so many different places; in turn, they were obviously also shaped by these conventions. It is therefore precisely in the way that such stories were told and retold that we can best see the signs of impending change.

Around the end of the eighteenth century, the most prominent female soldier was Mary Anne Talbot, who had allegedly spent several years in the navy under a male identity in the 1790s. From the very title of Talbot's 1804 memoirs it was clear that the telling of her life story was to be modeled to a considerable extent after that of Hannah Snell. And yet this self-conscious imitation could not mask the deep differences between the two. Instead of Snell's mid-century unbounded self-confidence and pride, Talbot's turn-of-the-century memoirs evinced throughout a sense of apologetic uneasiness. She hastened to assure her readers that "this mode of life" as a female soldier "was by no means congenial to my feelings". Moreover, she explained, she had been forced into this role by a man who had seduced her: "I was to become the object of more degradation; . . . for, conceiving me properly subjugated to his purpose . . . he produced a complete suit of male attire; and for the first time made me acquainted with the unmanly design he had formed" – namely, boarding a ship with her disguised as a man. Talbot's masculine disguise, it turned out, was a "degrading" consequence of compulsion, and *unmanly* compulsion at that: unwelcome, unexpected, and completely beyond her control. (The fact that Talbot persisted in such a garb for many years, however, long after her seducer had died, might suggest to us that these assertions actually had more to do with the presumed expectations of her audience than with her own inner convictions.)[37] In short, even as Talbot tried stepping into Snell's shoes – boots, rather – her conspicuous discomfort indicated a great distance between them, and perhaps between their respective cultural worlds.

Indeed, the (figurative) battlefields of the late eighteenth century were strewn with the debris of the conventional trope of the female knight, as embarrassed heroines repeatedly stumbled in their efforts to re-enact the feats of their foremothers and successfully pass for heroic men. Thus, a "female chevalier" in an obscure novel of 1799, who tried to follow in the footsteps of countless predecessors in disguising herself as a man while pursuing a lover, discovered to her chagrin that it had become harder to assume a different sex. When she tried, observers pointed out that this person could "hardly be deemed of any sex at all" and that s/he had "a very effeminate voice". From its title onward the novel presented this attempt at crossing gender boundaries as an "indiscretion", and as one that could not succeed, leading inevitably to "grotesque" results. The heroine herself, moreover, hastened to concur: "I felt excessively aukward [sic] in boots – I assure you." A comparison of two frontispieces to subsequent editions of a play involving a female duellist says it all: the feisty self-assurance of the successfully cross-dressed 1725 heroine as against the inactive femininity of her 1792 incarnation, standing sheepishly beneath a comically ill-fitting masculine hat (figs. 2–3). Another pair of portraits (figs. 4 and 5) again bears silent witness to the same transformation. When Middleton and Dekker's 1611 play *The Roaring Girle* immortalized the highwaywoman Mary Frith (a.k.a. Moll Cutpurse), who had notoriously committed her deeds cross-dressed as a highway*man*, the title-page of the published text showed her with a sword, a

2. Frontispiece to Charles
Johnson, *The Country Lasses;
or, The Custom of the Manor*,
London, 1725. The masculine
appearance of the assertive
female duellist, arm akimbo,
is underscored by the visual
parallels between her costume
and that of her rival

pipe, and masculine facial features: like Snell a century later, Moll was indistinguishable from a real man. Then, when in the late eighteenth century
the play was republished, its historically aware editor left the original text
untouched, but did take one liberty: he allowed himself to replace the original
portrait with another that endowed Moll with a distinctly feminine countenance. Moll Cutpurse, too, was retouched to become, it seems, more acceptable
in a changing climate.[38]

Another heroine (this one in an early-nineteenth-century ballad), who "sung
like a linnet, and appeared like a dove", could conceal her innate femininity
only up to a point: "She drest like a sailor as near as could be." *As near as could
be*: a woman could don man's clothes, but she no longer had the potential for
truly passing as a man. If she were the heroine of a female warrior ballad,
however, as was the case for this almost manly sailor, she had no choice but to
keep on trying, forced into her formulaic masquerade by the rigid conventions
of the genre she inhabited: and the inevitable consequences soon became all
too apparent, as the very logic of the genre unraveled under these conflicting
pressures. Thus, for another such female warrior in a ballad of 1791 it turned

THE COUNTRY LASSES.

M.ʳˢ MARTYR as AURA.
*I think this is the seventh duel I have
engaged in for her and Flora__ or the eighth.*

London. Printed for J. Bell British Library Strand Jan.ʸ 2₃ 1792.

3. *Bell's British Theatre*, London, 1797, frontispiece (1792) to reprint of Charles Johnson, *The Country Lasses*. Counteracting the boastful line beneath the image, the cross-armed female duellist is given a passive, feminine look, accentuated by the angle of her head and hat, and the tight-fitting costume

out that while she could still dress in manly clothes, "the fifes were screech-owls to her ears" – a sign of feminine delicacy that would have left her role models from previous decades roaring with hearty laughter. Or take the telling case of one female warrior ballad that had appeared in several variations throughout the century. Its final version, of about 1800, compromised the essence of the genre through one small, almost imperceptible change of words. Whereas in earlier versions, when wounded in battle, the man pursued by the heroine had been brought to the care of "the Surgeon's *Mate*" who turned out to be his cross-dressed love, in the last version he discovers his love at the same moment in the guise of "the Surgeon's serv[ing] *maid*". Maid, not mate: what a sea change was signaled by these few altered letters on a broadsheet.[39]

I want to pause here over one more account of a female soldier, an unusual one in that it details a true-life encounter that was not intended for public circulation and thus, presumably, was less consciously crafted with audience expectations in mind. Moreover, this was an encounter that by fortuitous coincidence happened to take place precisely at the time I want to propose here as that of abrupt change, and that registered the pressures of this change with

4. Thomas Middleton and Thomas Dekker, *The Roaring Girle*, 1611, title-page

unusual clarity. In the early 1780s the future novelist Amelia Opie, then a young teenager, met a real-life female sailor, a meeting that made enough of an impression on her to merit a lengthy entry in her memoirs written many years later. But Opie's story was coming apart at the seams. The cross-dressed sailor was said to have played her role successfully for years without ever letting her true identity slip. But Opie also wanted her reader to believe that in the course of a single evening a friend of hers, playing host to the female sailor whom he had never seen before, immediately sensed "something in the young man's manner which he did not like", and – aided by hints from other family members, who likewise could not really be fooled – exposed the charade, and set upon "a reformation in her". Subsequently, when Opie came to meet this person, she too, like her reforming friend, strongly disapproved of the female sailor's masquerade, which she thought to be "utterly offensive" and the consequence of "a deranged mind". And yet her "consternation" and repulsion were mixed with undisguisable fascination (fueled, as Opie recalled, by the reputation of Hannah Snell), even admiration for this woman with "her large, dark, and really beautiful, though fierce eyes". Beautiful yet fierce, attractive yet repulsive, ready to be reformed yet of deranged mind, romantically successful yet inevitably unsuccessful: through an unmistakable veil of uneasiness and consternation

THE ROARING GIRLE:

O R,

MOLL CUT-PURSE.

As it hath lately beene Aɛted on the Fortune-ſtage by
the Prince his Players.

Written by T. Middleton and T. Dekkar.

My caſe is alter'd, I muſt worke for my living.

Printed at London for Thomas Archer, and are to be fold at his
Shop in Popes head-pallace, neere the Royall
Exchange, 1611.

VOL. VI.   A

5.   The altered portrait of Moll Cut-
purse on the reprinted title-page of *The
Roaring Girle* in 1780: note again the
angling of the head and hat – together
with the substitution of a very different
type of pipe, and shapelier legs – in the
recasting of the image as more feminine
than that of 1611

about the female warrior we can still sense the remnants of the grip that this
figure had formerly held over eighteenth-century imaginations.[40]

Late-eighteenth-century heroines, then, simply could not pull it off. The
more female warriors of this period tried to mask their femininity, the more
irrepressibly it re-emerged. (In one further account, not only did the female
warrior arouse suspicion by "her figure or her reserved manners", like Opie's
sailor, but her futile efforts to repress her femininity by lacing her chest too
tightly raised the specter of breast cancer – poignantly reminiscent of Edgeworth's Lady Delacour.)[41] These female knights or warriors were all now
proving that gender boundaries were indeed impassable, that gender identities
could not be shed at will, and that gender categories were absolute. No matter
how closely a woman imitates a man, went a typical turn-of-the-century assertion, we are

always in the knowledge that the object before us is *a woman assuming the
character of a man*; . . . we may safely pronounce, there is no woman, nor ever
was a woman, who can fully supply this character. There is such a *reverse* in
all the habits and modes of the two sexes . . . that it is next to an impossibility for the one to resemble the other so as totally escape detection.[42]

This was light years away from the confidence exhibited throughout most of the eighteenth century in the possible success of precisely such gender crossings, success that had provided repeated testimony to the limits of gender identities, and that had been met by many contemporaries – like Garrick in his prologue to *Percy* – with appreciation, not disapprobation.

From the vantage point of the new and powerful conviction of the turn of the century, by contrast, vestiges of those earlier plots and possibilities were now dismissed out of hand, amid barely concealed laughter, as "improbable", "ridiculous", "disgusting", and "unnatural". And if they could not be dismissed – for instance, if they happened to have been immortalized in Shakespeare's plays – then they had to be rewritten. The great many young people introduced to the Bard through the early-nineteenth-century mediation of Charles and Mary Lamb, for instance, found there heroines whose experiences would have greatly surprised those familiar with Shakespeare's originals. Thus as Ganymede in *As You Like It*, the Lambs assured their readers, Rosalind could assume only "feigned manliness and forced courage", which failed her soon enough. Viola in *Twelfth Night*, as she "put on the most manly air she could assume" (note the resemblance to the ballad heroine who dressed as a man "as near as could be"), had only her forlorn situation in a foreign land to "plead her excuse" for that "strange fancy in a young lady to put on male attire, and pass for a boy". And *Cymbeline*'s Imogen discovered the hard way that "it is not merely putting on a man's apparel that will enable a young lady, tenderly brought up, to bear the fatigue of wandering about lonely forests like a man". (Contrast the Lambs' treatment of Imogen with that of an earlier, 1759 version of *Cymbeline*. In this mid-eighteenth-century version, not only had Imogen's part been stretched to have her spend more time on stage – as well as deliver a proud epilogue – in man's attire, but the plot had also been recast to make Imogen's cross-dressing her own choice and initiative, rather than Pisanio's as Shakespeare had had it.)[43]

Once again, we appear to have entered a new cultural world. Looking back at the eighteenth-century public that had crowded the theater in one instance to behold "two women pass through [a] whole play, without exciting the least suspicion of their sex, for two men", Elizabeth Inchbald told her early-nineteenth-century readers that they were "as far removed" from such "wonders" of "Old England as the metropolis of Madrid". After all, Inchbald asserted confidently – if not very consistently – on another occasion, "neither history, nor tradition, gives any cause to suppose, that the English ladies were accustomed to attire themselves in man's apparel"; and what is more, "reason assures us, that they could seldom, if ever, have concealed their sex by such stratagem". Such things could not happen, and even if they could they did not, and even if they did they had occurred long before the world as the readers knew it had taken shape. How far removed this new world was from that in which Garrick could have complimented Hannah More by imagining her as a female warrior was also made clear by More herself, who declared in 1799: "I am not sounding an alarm to female warriors, or exciting female politicians: I hardly know which of the two is the more *disgusting and unnatural character*."[44]

Small wonder, then, that even the adventures of that most famous of all female warriors, Hannah Snell, had to be refashioned and repackaged to suit these new sensibilities. Not only did an 1801 reprint of her life story replace her former in-your-face masculine portrait – how else? – with a more feminine one (figs. 6–7). More creatively, a biographer who retold Snell's life in 1803 chose to omit any mention of her childhood propensities for "masculine" behavior, and to assert knowingly – with a striking disregard for Snell's own self-assured tone – that in fact her masquerade, forced upon her by necessity, had involved "acting such parts as in secret gave her *the utmost disgust*" (that word again!). Another biographer, of 1806, went even further: he completely transformed the story of Snell's life by casting it as profoundly immoral, by doubting her actual ability to pass as a male soldier ("to mention only one seeming inconsistency, how is it possible that she could have been twice flogged without a discovery of her sex?"), and by capping it with a new ending. Contrary to what had been "pretended" in all former accounts, this writer claimed "upon good authority" that, following Snell's (inevitable) exposure as a woman, "an Irish officer took her under his protection, and that by this gentleman she had two sons". Even Hannah Snell, by this point, had to be remade into a properly maternal and domestic woman, duly protected by her manly husband.[45]

*

Garrick's prologue to *Percy*, in fact, did more than associate Hannah More with the Amazon and the female warrior as generic tropes that signaled the limits of gender categories in eighteenth-century culture. As any contemporary would have immediately recognized, Garrick's "French Amazonian maid" and "Lady Knight, late Chevalier" were also specific allusions to a real contemporary flesh-and-blood female chevalier. This was the famous Chevalier D'Eon, a person whose peculiarities chime uncannily well with the rhythm of our story.[46] The French aristocratic Chevalier D'Eon, captain of the dragoons and veteran of the Seven Years' War, arrived in London on a diplomatic mission in 1762 and stayed for fifteen years. During the 1760s and 1770s the "CHEVALIER, *alias* Mademoiselle D'Eon made no small figure in the world, as a man-lady of the *doubtful gender*!" Indeed, D'Eon became quite a celebrity, owing his/her fame in large part to the increasing mystery about his/her real sex – a mystery that s/he was reputed (probably wrongly) to have fueled by the way s/he dressed, but that s/he certainly did little to resolve (fig. 8). The English public of the 1770s got a lot of mileage out of this enigma: whether through a wave of betting

6.   Hannah Snell in the frontispiece to her life
story, 1750

on D'Eon's unsettled sex (bets that were large enough to end up in court), through repeated topical references in London's theaters (where any number of characters that year were at "risk of being mistaken for another Female Chevalier"), or as a general topic of light conversation:

> Sir, or Madam, chuse you whether,
> Since Report has made you either;
> Bulls and Bears can't find you out;
> But with me there is no doubt;
> Whate'er Nature may design,
> A Petit Maitre's Feminine.[47]

The last couplet in this bit of doggerel, penned by an Eton teacher as a model epigram, suggestively overruled nature's design as the ultimate determinant of D'Eon's identity. Instead, contemporaries allowed for D'Eon's sex and gender, as we now understand these terms, to go their separate ways: "[D'Eon] is really, verily and truly, as to Sex, a WOMAN, as to Courage, Spirit, and Enterprize, to all intents and purposes a MAN."[48] What better or more vivid demonstration could there be of the limits of gender categorization, those limits that were brought to Garrick's mind by More's success?[49]

7.   Hannah Snell in the frontispiece to the reprint of her life story, 1801 (central figure on the right)

D'Eon left England in 1777, and returned in late 1785, to remain there till his death in 1810. During this second stay in England, however, D'Eon's public image evolved rather differently. Whereas during the earlier London sojourn the public seemed to draw excitement from his/her gender ambiguity, now the same public appeared to accept its definitive resolution with few raised eyebrows; and moreover to maintain this confidence in D'Eon's now stabilized feminine identity despite sometimes extravagant behavior, especially in highly publicized public dueling matches that might have led some to think otherwise.[50] To be sure, this change accorded with D'Eon's own self-presentation solely as a woman, to which she had become increasingly committed since the mid-1770s, and which was moreover demanded of her by the French king. But just as Hannah More's personal transformation gains further meaning from its wider context, so D'Eon's transformation needs to be seen not only in terms of his/her own personal motivations – a lively topic of speculation for biographers and scholars – but also in conjunction with the concurrent transformation in the attitude of the public of the late 1780s and the 1790s, which made it willing and perhaps even relieved to accept this resolution, and to collude with D'Eon's self-presentation only as a female, rather than to continue to

MADEMOISELLE de BEAUMONT, or the
CHEVALIER D'EON.
Female Minister Plenipo. Capt. of Dragoons &c.&c.

8. "Mademoiselle de Beaumont, or the
Chevalier D'Eon", *London Magazine*,
Sept. 1777

highlight and play with the mystery of his/her true sex. Surely this was owing
not simply to a collective lapse of memory – many in the 1790s must have
remembered D'Eon's former fame – but rather also to an active process of collective denial.

Only such a process, for instance, could have allowed Mary Wollstonecraft
to include "Madame D'Eon" matter-of-factly among her highly selective list
of exemplary women through the ages who proved that with proper education
women could achieve "courage and resolution" (and moreover without Wollstonecraft's critics, keen as they were on exposing the gender-defective nature
of the author and her work, capitalizing on this potentially damaging incongruity).[51] Only such a process could have induced biographers during these
years to play down the gender-destabilizing aspects of D'Eon's story, if not (as
one had boldly done) by implausibly ignoring them completely, then by rele-
gating them to minor instances, preferably beyond her control and if possible
in pre-pubescent childhood ("her parents obliged her"). Whether D'Eon was
reported now to have been forced to dress as a boy by her parents, or by her
king, or by unavoidable circumstances, what these turn-of-the-century biographical accounts all had in common was that they ruled out the possibility

that D'Eon did what she did out of free choice. Once again we see the signs of cultural change: that former and freer understanding of gender identity, which had allowed a 1778 satire on D'Eon to highlight his/her unfettered agency – recounting how s/he "duly reason[ed] pro and con" before "boldly put[ting] the breeches on/ And sall[ying] forth a man" – became, by the closing years of the century, overwhelmingly unacceptable.[52]

Once the autopsy following D'Eon's death in 1810 had revealed that anatomically he appeared to be a man – not to mention the reputed public auctioning of his testicles – such circumventions of the issue became more difficult to sustain. A detailed account of D'Eon's life published shortly after his death, therefore, completely reversed the story. It now turned out that D'Eon's masquerade had been no more than another deception in a life of "intrigue", a calculated swindle "with a view to profit" (through the bets on his sex). D'Eon's dressing as a woman, a practice that he supposedly had to continue to prevent his exposure, therefore had nothing to do with sexual identity, with gender boundaries, or with this or that psychological predilection; nor had there been any signs of it in his childhood. Even more revealingly, this retelling of D'Eon's story was at pains to assure its readers that the chevalier, in truth, did not pass as a woman particularly well. Not only did his ingrained masculine behavior – notably, his attentions to the ladies – betray his true identity, but his physical masculine characteristics were irrepressible as well: "her chin [wa]s furnished with some hair, which she employ[ed] herself with nipping". Of the striking fact that D'Eon continued in this mode of self-presentation for more than thirty years with remarkable success, this account said nothing.[53]

However different these turn-of-the-century accounts were, they all ended up doing the same thing: like a long string of other reminders of gender ambiguity, D'Eon's unique capacity to embody such ambiguity – a capacity that had resonated widely in the 1770s – was now as much as possible effaced from the record. One 1785 commentator, indeed, took matters to the other extreme: "it is hoped", this writer opined, that D'Eon's clear-cut feminine identity upon his return to England "will operate so forcibly as to induce such ladies who have usurped a right of wearing breeches, to leave them off".[54] Quite. And who could signal the change better than Hannah More herself? In 1789, coming finally face to face in 1789 with D'Eon, that erstwhile illustrious model for female emulation that had been offered to the late 1770s audiences of *Percy* in appreciation of More's own achievement, More could only find her military pretensions "ridiculous" and her behavior "a great curiosity". "But *one* D'Eon is enough," More now concluded, "and *one slice of her quite sufficient*".[55]

Having traveled considerable distance in the company of bees and queens, Amazons and female knights, Hannah More and the Chevalier D'Eon, we have arrived at what seems to be a suggestive pattern of change – what I have called "gender panic": a pattern of change that decisively reversed, over a relatively short period of time, a variety of interconnected cultural forms through which eighteenth-century Britons signaled their recognition of the potential limitations of gender categories. It is now time to evaluate the meaning, significance, and scope of this transformation. But first, a couple of correctives are in order: one with regard to the understanding of the early birth pangs of modern feminism, the other with regard to the place of men in this cultural shift.

Today, gender subversion, or any exposure of gender as a limited construction, carries strong political overtones, central as it is to a modern feminist agenda. For some scholars, this has been true throughout Western history, since – in their view – any demonstration of the limitations of gender categories always undermines the patriarchal power structure predicated upon them. But this universalizing perspective glosses over major differences between different historical circumstances. Thus, the assumptions of some modern scholars notwithstanding, we should not see the eighteenth-century acceptance or even celebration of Amazons, or single women, or women who pass successfully for men, as *prima facie* evidence of fault lines in – or proto-feminist challenges to – the prevailing system of patriarchy; pre-modern fault lines or challenges that then supposedly disappeared as patriarchy got stronger. While these *were* indications of a readiness in the short eighteenth century to contemplate the limits of gender boundaries, they did not in and of themselves imply weaker patriarchal authority or greater symmetry of power. On the contrary, it was presumably because all these possibilities were *not* immediately perceived as politically charged that they could be widely entertained and tolerated without becoming particularly threatening. But the late-eighteenth-century "gender panic" changed all that: it raised the stakes in denying and denouncing those gender-transgressive images, and thus turned every attempt to reproduce them into a charged political challenge.

Recall now the well-known feminist writers of the 1790s, spearheaded by Mary Wollstonecraft, together with the vehement reactions they elicited. Why the vehemence? After all, similar things had been said before. To be sure, these writings drew a lot of fire because of the new political climate in the wake of the French Revolution, characterized as it was by bolder and more threatening political visions and by acutely radicalized sensibilities. Yet the tenor of the responses to these feminist interventions seems to have exceeded the actual threat they posed, since in truth, unlike the situation in France where female political participation was momentarily imaginable, in Britain a feminist agenda manifestly had no real potential to affect political outcomes. But perhaps the developments sketched in these pages can illuminate the energy and urgency infused into this debate from a different angle. The late eighteenth century was the moment when the gender-transgressive woman was losing her ground culturally, and was thus forced to come into her own politically. The reaction to Wollstonecraft resulted not only from sudden anxieties about what she had to say, but also from the very fact that she and like-minded women continued to say it: an act that flouted those gender boundaries that had recently and abruptly hardened.[56] The edge of late-eighteenth-century feminism, which some might suppose to have been a *cause* of the changes in understandings of gender during these decades, should perhaps be seen more appropriately as their *consequence*.

That this was the case is suggested by the eighteenth-century fortunes of the female orator and politician: she who makes long speeches and covets the vote, the "Wollstonecraftian" *avant la lettre*. In *Percy*'s prologue the female orator/politician joined the Amazon, the female knight, and the Chevalier D'Eon as yet another marker of the limits of gender categories: no more, no less. And her fate during this period replicated that of other gender-crossing figures: no more, no less. Thus, the decades leading up to *Percy* were strewn with numerous light-hearted assertions of women's rights to "politicks debate", to "a female Magna Charta", not to be "exclude[d] . . . from the legislature", and so on. For the most part, they did not signal either aspirations for or anxieties about actual female political empowerment. This remained true even when the female orator spilled over from cultural trope into social practice, right around the time of *Percy*'s success, in a wave of female debating societies with names like the Female Parliament or Female Congress, in which the rights of women to debate every political issue were publicly and earnestly asserted. For even the female debating societies were a social phenomenon that lacked a real political edge, as their absence from the annals of feminism attests. Rather, the various appearances of the female politician throughout the short eighteenth century were yet another marker of the potential porousness of the boundaries of gender. They too demonstrated the ability of a heroine – as a fictional female politician explained in 1732 – to "throw off all the Softness of [her] Sex" in taking on a manly pursuit: an act for which this particular exemplar, in line with so many other assertive eighteenth-century heroines, earned praise rather than criticism.[57]

Subsequently, as was the case with other gender-transgressive figures, the relatively good standing of the female politician was sharply reversed in the late eighteenth century. This reversal was apparent, among others, in the 1780s (pre-revolutionary) decline of the female debating societies. It was also apparent in the abuse suddenly heaped on the Duchess of Devonshire during the notorious elections of 1784, when in truth she did little more than follow in the electioneering footsteps of many eighteenth-century female precedents.[58] Another telling illustration of the change, also pre-1789, can be found in one of the most popular entertainments of the second half of the eighteenth century, George Alexander Stevens's *Lecture on Heads*. Like any good stand-up comedy, this routine – which wittily satirized social types with the aid of papier-mâché busts and wig blocks as props – changed with time to accommodate the current tastes, humors, and concerns of its audiences. And sure enough, one of the most conspicuous changes introduced between the original published version of 1764 and the revised one of the mid-1780s was an intensified preoccupation with the dangers of gender-bending. Nowhere was this more viciously evident than in the case of the female politician, "President of the Lady's Debating Society", mocked for marshaling "the examples of many heroines, from the days of Boadicea, who headed her own armies, down to Hannah Snell, who served in the ranks" in support of her ludicrous ideas about women in government and the army. The exceptionally long tirade ended with a familiar assertion of the impossibility of passing. "Surely no woman of sense would suppose we meant to offend her", the comedian insisted with less than his usual dose of humor, "if we said she was the most improper person in the world to be made a Captain of Horse, or a Member of Parliament."[59]

This gender-panicked comedian, by the way, was no longer George Stevens, but rather the actor Charles Lee Lewes, who had purchased Stevens's equipment and had a friend update the text. In other comic productions of the late 1780s, Lewes displayed the same anxiety and disbelief about "grotesque" and "unnatural" gender transgressions that were a leitmotif of his *Lecture* routine. But this did not mean that in earlier years Lewes himself – recall the "conversion" of Hannah More – had not thought differently, or even appeared himself in gender-crossing roles. In fact, it was Charles Lee Lewes to whom it had fallen in 1777–8 to bend the gender conventions of the theater and come on stage instead of the customary actress in order to recite Garrick's epilogue (not prologue) to More's *Percy*.[60]

*

Percy's epilogue as recited by Lewes provides a convenient segue into the second corrective I want to offer here. Pointing out the limitations of gender categories has so far been exclusively a female affair: but what about *men*? On the one hand, it makes perfect sense in an asymmetrical patriarchal power structure to find women pushing the gender envelope more often than men. Still, albeit less frequently, we can find eighteenth-century men in most equivalent situations to those we have seen for women. In several female debating societies, for instance, where the prohibition on male attendance reversed the common masculine prerogative, we come across stories of men passing as women in order to get in. Occasionally we even encounter a man following in the footsteps of the female warrior – as in the 1775 story of one such hero who dressed as a woman in pursuit of his lover, and who passed so well as to fool even his lover herself.[61] And when we are able to trace change over time with these rarer male figures, they appear to tell the same story as the female ones: be it a 1771 novel about a young man "brought up and educated, without discovery, as a female", which an early-nineteenth-century critic dismissed as "improbable", the situations "unnatural", and the characters "such [as] not to be found in real life"; or the note that a contemporary hand added to an ephemeral *Apology for Bachelors!!* in 1808, insisting not only that it was "a *modern* Unique" – the pun on "eunuch" reinforcing the sense of unnatural strangeness – but also that the author must have been sitting on this pamphlet for some thirty years, since its contents suited the "foolery" of 1780 more than the present "modern" times; or an oft-repeated classical tale about a man cross-dressing as a woman in order to enter an all-female gathering, which in the hands of a late-eighteenth-century commentator became a tale of bungling farce as it proved utterly impossible for the man to disguise his gender iden- tity; or an apology for their inevitable failure offered by early-nineteenth- century sailors acting a play with women's parts, since such parts, they explained, flew in the face of their uncontrollable heroic masculine nature; or a 1790 "scientific" discussion of men with apparent feminine manners that, controverting much earlier eighteenth-century wisdom, dismissed them as "*monsters*" with an essential "*female stock*"; or a scene in Edgeworth's *Belinda*, which in complement to the novel's critique of female gender-crossing also had the talented Clarence Hervey – "a man who might be any thing" – discover that "any thing" did *not* include a woman, as his attempt to pass for one was instantly defeated by his irrepressible masculine behavior.[62] By now these all seem very familiar.

Furthermore, we can also find eighteenth-century cultural forms that man- ifested the same ability to imagine and even appreciate porous gender categories specifically in the case of men. I want to close here briefly with one such case (another will turn up in chapter 2), an alternative model for masculine behavior that was much in vogue in the second half of the eighteenth century: the man of feeling.

Here we can take our cue from the epilogue to *Percy* as it was recited by Charles Lee Lewes. *Percy*'s epilogue recommended to modern men, who unlike their "Gothic ancestors" could no longer excel in warfare ("we wear no armour now – but on our shoes"), to cultivate their manly sensibility. Garrick's epilogue to *Percy* was thus a direct counterpart to his prologue: having used the prologue (unconventionally delivered by a woman) to speak appreciatively of women's counter-normative manly behavior, the epilogue (unconventionally delivered by a man) recommended the flip side – a counter-normative mode of male behavior that was recognized to be distinctly feminine.

Eighteenth-century manly sensibility, writes Janet Todd, which was at the height of its cultural purchase in the years leading up to *Percy*, "stressed those qualities considered feminine in the sexual psychology of the time: intuitive sympathy, susceptibility, emotionalism and passivity". Its most exquisite expression was in the shedding of tears, an act that was perceived to be at odds with dominant masculine norms: "tears . . . are no signs of an *unmanly*, but, contrarily, of a humane nature"; "I burst into a flood of tears – but I am as weak as a woman"; and so on. "Though a man, and a man of business," went a fan letter to Hannah More that likewise drew attention to its flouting of conventional manliness, "I too can shed tears and feel the luxury of shedding them; your *Percy* has cleared scores between us in that respect." More can hardly have been surprised at this correspondent's manly tears ("one tear is worth a thousand hands," she had noted after *Percy*'s second performance, "and I had the satisfaction to see even the men shed them in abundance"). But she must have been particularly gratified by them, for the eyes that shed them belonged to the grand master of lachrymose effusions, who probably did more than any other to propagate this alternative masculine ideal: the Scotsman Henry Mackenzie, author of the novel *The Man of Feeling*.[63]

The Man of Feeling, whose first edition sold out within a couple of months of its publication in 1771, was in a sense the manual for how to be a man of sensibility. Its hero, Harley, eschews manly power, manly pursuits (such as commerce and money-making), and manly sexuality (he never approaches the woman he loves), and assumes instead the womanly qualities of exquisite emotions and intense susceptibility: the novel's narrative is little more than a record of Harley's encounters with misery in multiple forms and the effusive tears he sheds each and every time. That Harley represented an alternative ideal of masculinity was driven home in a scene in which he converts a military officer to feeling: the soldier "laid his left hand on his heart, the sword dropped from his right, [and he] burst into tears". The tears gaining over the sword, that traditional symbol of manly honor: the whole thrust of the book in a nutshell. The spectacular success of *The Man of Feeling* – it was "one of the great blockbusters of sentiment" (Todd again) – was due to its resonance with an important streak in contemporary culture, running from Pope's androgynous manly ideal ("Heav'n, when it strives to polish all it can/ Its last best work, but forms a softer Man"), through Richardson's *Sir Charles Grandison* (a "male virgin") and Sterne's *Sentimental Journey*, to the repeated theme of real-life male tears as in Mackenzie's letter to More.[64] The flip side of the female warrior – she who picked up, as it were, the sword that the susceptible soldier had dropped – the gender-flexing man of feeling was also valued as a possible model for emulation, like the "brave *rough soldier*" who was celebrated by Garrick, in another dramatic epilogue contemporaneous with *Percy*, for appearing when "down his cheeks run trickling nature's tide".[65]

But then the man of feeling – both the novel and the type – performed a striking vanishing act. To be sure, this disappearance was part of the well-known decline in the cultural purchase of sensibility: a shift often illustrated with the laughter that Lady Louisa Stuart encountered in the early nineteenth century when she tried to re-create her youthful memory of collective cathartic weeping in response to a group reading of *The Man of Feeling*. But I want to point to the confluence of this development with the gender-change story we have been following. The embodiment of *this* change was perhaps less the disappointment of Lady Louisa than the uneasiness of her close friend Sir Walter Scott. Writing a tribute to Mackenzie, the "Northern Addison", in 1822, Scott felt the need to offer an apologetic assurance of Harley's manliness. A couple of brief moments of "spirited" and "animated" conduct on the part of Harley in *The Man of Feeling*, he explained, were "skilfully thrown in, to satisfy the reader that his softness and gentleness of temper were not allied to effeminacy; and that he dared, on suitable occasions, to do all that might become a man". Contrary to all appearances, Scott insisted, Harley was not a "feminine" man, a claim that for Scott was key to salvaging his manly credentials. This apologia would have baffled Mackenzie's former comrade-in-tears Hannah More, who had asserted with confidence during his heyday that "his *Man of Feeling*, is a man indeed".[66] So here we have the closure of the eighteenth-century potential for imaginable gender play all over again, but now for men. Previously, Harley could have proudly embodied an alternative type of masculinity, one that More found commendable precisely for that behavior that seemed to defy gender boundaries. Now, for Scott, this behavior had to be explained away in order to make Harley comprehensible, let alone commendable.

Indeed, even before the culture of sensibility went out of fashion, it had already lost its gender-bending edge. By the 1790s, as Claudia Johnson has pointed out, sentimental traits that had previously been considered feminine were redefined as masculine, thus disarming sensibility of its potential to disrupt gender categories. As long as they remembered that "softness of manners must not be mistaken for true sensibility", Hugh Blair told the audience of his enormously popular late-eighteenth-century sermons, they need not doubt that "manliness and sensibility are so far from being incompatible". Wollstonecraft, on the other hand, was militantly anti-sentimentalist precisely because she did see these two qualities as incompatible.[67] Nowhere was this gender-conforming realignment of sensibility more evident than in the hasty retreat of the moist-eyed man of feeling. Public displays of men's tears – real or fictional – became more problematic and less common. Where they did linger on, they were typically reduced to a single tear, rolling down a "manly cheek" and emanating from a "manly heart", and accompanied by defensive hand-waving. This, for example, was the thrust of Thomas Day's *The History of Sandford and Merton*, the 1780s response to the 1770s *Man of Feeling* in shaping ideal men of sensibility. Obsessed with the advantages of hardy manliness over effeminate delicacy, this didactic novel repetitively taught its juvenile readers that even a solitary tear compromised the "appearance of manly fortitude". So when Day's hero completed his own conversion to proper man-liness, he "turned his face aside, and shed a tear of real virtue and gratitude, which he instantly wiped away as unworthy of the composure and fortitude of his new character". This cry-shy epigone – who in sharp contrast to the van-ishing man of feeling was to become one of the most popular bequests of the eighteenth century to the nineteenth – was indeed a "new character" when seen from the perspective of the world formerly inhabited by Mackenzie, Garrick, and the early Hannah More.[68] Whereas in that older world "it [could] be ques-tioned whether those are properly men, who never weep upon any occasion", as one mid-century text had it, in the new one the gushing man of feeling was more likely to be seen as fit for the madhouse.[69]

Making Gender in the Eighteenth Century

Let us take stock of this whirlwind tour through some aspects of eighteenth-century culture. The parallel transformations in the representation of the queen bee and in the public image of Hannah More led us into a variety of cul-tural sites where a shared pattern appeared to be discernible. Throughout the first three-quarters of the eighteenth century these various sites displayed understandings of gender categories that had a remarkable capacity to acknowl-edge their limits. Although expectations of "femininity" and "masculinity" were generally well defined, contemporaries did not perceive them as neces-sarily pinning down each and every individual, and could readily be found to react to an apparent subversion of these expectations – be it by an Amazon, a non-mothering woman, a female warrior, a man of feeling, a female politician, or by the exotic Chevalier D'Eon – with resignation, tolerance, or sometimes even appreciation. (This, to repeat once more, is not to say that such counter-normative acts and figures did not also elicit much moralizing criticism. But not only was the condemnatory tone not necessarily the dominant one, it will also be seen in chapter 2 that even moralizing pontifications bore the signs of the times.) Moreover, the various reminders of these limitations of gender cat-egories reinforced each other, forming together that soundbox in which any contemporary plucking of the violin strings of gender determinacy would have resonated. We can call this eighteenth-century cultural environment gender's *ancien régime*.

But then, in the closing two decades of the century, this relative porousness, which allowed eighteenth-century categories of gender to be imagined as occa-sionally mutable, potentially unfixed, and even as a matter of choice, disap-peared with remarkable speed. In a sharp, uneasy reversal, made possible at times only through mental contortions, long-standing forms and practices that had formerly capitalized on (and sometimes wallowed in) the acknowledged limitations of gender boundaries now became socially unacceptable and culturally unintelligible. Thus, these decades witnessed the transformation of the Amazon from a figure of heroism to an object of derision; the delegitimation as unnatural of the woman who chose not to mother; the refocusing of the regal queen bee – and other, human queens – as queen mothers; the cultural disappearing act of the female warrior and the man of feeling; the evaporation of any sense of humor toward female politicians; the rewriting of stories of boundary-crossing figures like the Chevalier D'Eon and Hannah Snell so as to minimize their potential to disrupt gender categories; and the sudden conviction that one sex passing for another was patently impossible, indeed inconceivable.

Before we begin to interpret these observations, recall again their limits. Overwhelmingly, the voices heard in these pages originated in England's literate circles. And yet the social range of "literate" in the eighteenth century was considerable: my sources range from high-brow philosophical, literary, artistic, and encyclopedic treatises, through middle-brow novels, romances, magazines, and pamphlets, to materials that delve as far down the social scale as printed sources can ever lead us, into the semi-literate audiences of cheap broadsides, chapbooks, and street balladry. And I have not yet mentioned the theater (which will return in force in the next chapter), a cultural form that probably did more than any other during this period to cross social divides and mingle social classes. To the extent, therefore, that the evidence used in this book spans the whole gamut of eighteenth-century print culture, it can plausibly be seen to represent quite a broad segment of society. At the same time, however, it *is* slanted by the predominance of the metropolis. Although we have heard some soundings from the provinces, the extension of the argument outside metropolitan circles must await a more systematic analysis of provincial culture, one that will distinguish London-influenced strands from local ones. Having said this, however, I have encountered little evidence to suggest that developments in the provinces were not roughly in synch with those in the metropolis: a tentative observation reinforced by occasional sources that do cross the metropolitan–provincial divide, like the array of bee-texts that opened this inquiry, written primarily by provincial bee experts across the nation.

Within such limits, then, what remains now is to understand the full meaning of these observations. The patterns that attracted our attention in this chapter can be situated in two separate stories: one along a vertical (or, as the jargon would have it, diachronic) temporal axis, the other along a lateral (or synchronic) axis. The next few pages will first place these developments within a long-term narrative of the history of gender and sex: here I posit both the eighteenth-century gender play and the late-eighteenth-century gender panic as pivotal stages in the shift from early-modern to modern notions of gender.

The second story, which will preoccupy us in subsequent chapters, is that in which key characteristics of the late-eighteenth-century gender shift will be seen to have been not peculiar to gender alone, but common to other identity categories at precisely the same historical juncture. The cumulative result, therefore, will be a picture of a broader historical development that was not fundamentally about gender at all.

*

So now for the history of notions of gender in the long eighteenth century. Unlike the sweeping, confident narratives that originated in women's history and that are concerned primarily with social arrangements and structures of power (e.g. "the creation of patriarchy", "the separation of spheres"), we do not yet have a comparable narrative for the understandings of gender, the very understandings that underlay these arrangements and structures. Recent scholars groping in this direction, led by history-conscious literary critics, have tended to be more tentative, painting their picture with pointillist dabs rather than with wide brushstrokes.[70] But we can perhaps go further.

The obvious starting point is Thomas Laqueur's pioneering *Making Sex*. I am interested here in one particular aspect of Laqueur's argument: the shift that he identifies sometime between the early-modern period and the eighteenth century in the status of sex (that is, the way people perceive sexed bodies) in relation to gender (that is, their understandings of the scaffolding of putative masculine and feminine traits erected around these sexed bodies) in the determination of sexual identities. "Sex before the seventeenth century", Laqueur writes, "was still a sociological and not an ontological category." It was "the epiphenomenon, while *gender*, what we would take to be a cultural category, was primary or 'real'", a key plank in the divine order of things. But sometime around the late seventeenth century, as gender lost its divine moorings, sex gradually replaced it as the primary category, deriving its sway not from the certitudes of godly providence but from those of scientific biological knowledge.[71]

Laqueur, interested in "the making not of gender, but of sex", focuses from this point onward on perceptions of sexual bodies, but does not dwell on the consequences of this shift for contemporary understandings of gender. But these consequences, arguably, were no less important, and we might hypothesize them as follows. As a result of the anchoring of sex in nature, socially constructed gender was operationally separated from biologically grounded sex. Whereas, previously, sex and gender had been (in the words of Michael McKeon) "bound up in a circle of meanings from which escape to a supposed biological substratum [was] impossible", now the firm grounding of sex in nature made possible the conceptualization of masculinity and femininity as social and cultural attributes, distinct from male and female bodies.[72] Thus, this late-seventeenth-century development, perhaps counter-intuitively, rather than *fixing* gender (as is the underlying assumption of Laqueur's narrative, for instance), in fact left it as the looser category. While eighteenth-century sex had already acquired the putative uncompromising rigidity of biology, eighteenth-century gender was still allowed some of the fluidity and versatility of culture. The consequent autonomy of gender from the dictates of sex, it can then be suggested, created *a space for play*, that is, a space for imaginable dissonances of gender over (supposedly) stable sexual bodies.

Such a sex–gender configuration can therefore account for what is likely to strike the modern observer as the most remarkable feature of this *ancien régime* of gender: the willingness to accept the possible freedom of an occasional biological "woman" or "man" to sidestep the cultural expectations of "femininity" and "masculinity". Contemporaries repeatedly asserted this key point in no uncertain terms. "Man", one mid-eighteenth-century text maintained, could in fact be "all Woman, except some Distinction of Sex in *Bodies*"; "I have known a beau", seconded another, "with everything of a woman but the sex"; a particular woman, insisted a third, had "nothing of the Woman about her, but the mere nominal Distinction of Sex"; another – thus a fourth – had "nothing feminine about her but the sex"; yet a different woman, echoed a fifth, "had no more of her sex than her body"; a sixth – a woman – said of her sister that "she has then, perhaps, a soul of the *other* Sex in a body of *ours*"; and finally another, with a more picturesque flourish, described how one particular man was "all Woman, except the masculine Peg which is hung on by Nature". What these voices – and they were just the front row of a large chorus – made explicit is what was implicit in the various markers of gender play that pepper the foregoing pages: occasionally, at least, eighteenth-century Britons could imagine – without being overly disturbed – a person's gender roaming away from his or her sex, or even a person donning and doffing gender identity at will. "I am metamorphosed into this Dress", to quote one more mid-century heroine in male garb, *"because it pleases my fancy."*[73]

But then, as we already know, things changed. Before our concluding move forward, however, let us pause for a moment to cast a brief glance backward. The sex–gender configuration described here was not simply "pre-modern", a timeless prelude to some modern transformations: rather, it was a configuration specific to the eighteenth century that had as clear a beginning as it was to have an end. Indeed, it is possible to use the same indexes of change-over-time we have been following to trace the late-seventeenth- and early-eighteenth-century shifts that had set this particular sex–gender configuration in place, although doing so here would take us too far afield.[74] An investigation of this beginning point would pay attention, for instance, to the seventeenth-century fascination with transformations of bodily sex rather than of gender: a fascination that preceded the eighteenth-century gender play and was largely eclipsed by it. This is why hermaphrodites, the embodiment of the indeterminacy of sexual bodies (rather than gender), were so much more in vogue in the seventeenth century than in the eighteenth, when they were mostly dismissed as fictions or turned into metaphors. In lieu of a detailed inquiry into this shift, it can be illustrated quickly by returning to that model epigram penned by the witty Eton teacher at the expense of the Chevalier D'Eon (see above, p. 30). The rhymes he used to impress his students, it turns out, were in fact silently lifted from a much older poem of 1640. But whereas the Eton master adapted these rhymes to express the indeterminacy of D'Eon's gender over "Whate'er Nature may design" in terms of bodily sex, the original poem by John Cleveland – appropriately titled "Upon a Hermaphrodite" – had been a celebration of indeterminacy of *sex*, not gender, as designed by nature itself: "Sir, or Madame, chuse you whether,/ Nature twists you both together."[75] The contrast encapsulates the difference between the seventeenth and the eighteenth centuries nicely.

But to go back to – and conclude – our story, as it takes its final twist in the closing decades of the eighteenth century: the "gender panic" that we have witnessed many times over, it can now be suggested, was the sweeping closure of the eighteenth-century space for imaginable gender play, that imaginative space for which *Percy*'s prologue had been such an eloquent if unwitting swan song. In its stead emerged new, recognizably "modern" notions of gender; notions reconceptualized so as to reinforce, in the words of Judith Butler, "the belief in a mimetic relation of gender to sex whereby gender [necessarily] mirrors sex".[76] Gender, the behavioral and cultural attributes of masculinity and femininity, collapsed into sex, that is, into the physicality inscribed on the body of every individual. There was thus no longer any conceivable individual escape from the dictates of the sexual body through a play with gender. This, in turn, increased the stakes in dismissing any potential evidence to the contrary as ominously unnatural or well-nigh impossible. So we can see why, in such a different psychic environment, all those former tropes and practices that had relied on the recognition of the limitations of gender boundaries – that is to say, on the recognition of the potential autonomy of gender from the dictates of sex – were now destined to make their exit from the late-eighteenth-century cultural stage. The scene was set for the inflexible, overdetermined understanding of gender categories that was to remain in place for many decades to follow.

2

Gender Identities and the Limits of Cultural History

The previous chapter has led this inquiry head-on into what is perhaps the most problematic methodological quagmire of cultural history. It can be described as the difficulty of the "weak collage":[1] the historian, identifying a seemingly similar phenomenon in several disparate cultural spheres at the same historical moment, declares it to be a pattern of historical significance. This pattern is therefore reified as a "thing" that has an existence independent of these spheres, and then extrapolated beyond them to a larger swathe of culture, perhaps even to culture as a whole – a "zeitgeist" event touching on everything and everyone that comes within its temporal reach.

Now, on the one hand, this difficulty is hard to avoid altogether, unless we are also willing to give up the investigation of habits and structures of thought and feeling that are rarely observable directly, but are nevertheless an essential underpinning of the way people experience their world. On the other hand, the problems involved in such a procedure, as the critics often point out, are considerable. First, the historian needs to make a plausible case that the different phenomena observed in their disparate cultural spheres are in fact manifestations of the same underlying pattern: the pattern that can then be elevated to the status of a "thing", even if not observed directly, and carried over into other domains. Here, a certain level of repetition can be most helpful. While the observed phenomenon might be explainable in completely unrelated terms in one sphere, and perhaps in two or three, its reappearance across several cultural locations that *are* disparate and different from each other makes it increasingly plausible that the common denominator of these disparate observations is indeed the proposed pattern. We can call this "repetition in the first degree" (to distinguish it from what follows): while still always a collage, the more effective the repetition, the less the collage is a "weak" one. Thus, chapter 1 pointed to a remarkably consistent pattern of change in understandings of gender that crossed several different eighteenth-century cultural forms (within broad social limits); a pattern which it then seemed reasonable to extract as a meaningful historical phenomenon in its own right. (Subsequent chapters will extend this exercise further, moving beyond gender to establish the repetition of a meaningful pattern across multiple categories and understandings of identity.)

Second are the hazards of inductive reasoning, that is, of extrapolation from the particular examples, once we are persuaded that they do share a common pattern, to a broader general statement. While such reasoning may be common practice for some literary critics with their sometimes different disciplinary procedures, for historians it immediately brings up the old chestnuts of typicality and representativeness. This is where social historians used to raise – and with good reason – the banner of quantification. But as cultural historians know all too well, meanings and significations cannot for the most part be quantified, since quantification requires the equivalent weighting of whatever is being counted. This does not mean that some form of enumeration is not possible – as we shall see in the pages below. But even such attempts at enumeration are usually within one cultural form rather than cutting across multiple domains, which in the end is the crucial requirement for a more generalized argument. The goal of the present chapter, therefore, is to experiment with another strategy, by striving to push the hypothesized pattern to its limits: that is, to seek its repeated occurrence across as many cultural, generic, and social boundaries as possible, moving from more likely to increasingly less likely social and cultural locations for its occurrence. Such a strategy may also then discover the *limits* of the pattern under observation, those social or generic or other boundaries beyond which it does not extend and which, if discovered, sharpen our understanding of the origins and meaning of this pattern. We can call this strategy "repetition in the second degree": unlike repetition in the first degree, where common sense can suggest when sufficient evidence has been adduced to make a plausible argument about a meaningful shared historical pattern, for repetition in the second degree the goal is not *sufficient* evidence – that is impossible – but only increasing persuasiveness across wider and wider, though still limited, cultural spans.

Furthermore, even once a reasonably persuasive case for a broadly repeated cultural pattern has been established, another key question remains: that of the dynamics of transmission that can explain *how* this particular cultural pattern was diffused across the disparate spheres in which it is observable – and all the more so when this is supposed to have happened, as is the case here, over a relatively short period of time. It is a common peril of "zeitgeist" arguments, with their almost mystical overtones, to mistake simultaneity for explanation: as if the moment in time has in and of itself some inherent characteristic, as well as the power – the driving power of "the spirit of the age" – to shape all things sharing the same temporal bracket to meet this characteristic. I am not sure that historians have developed good models to think about this question: some of its ramifications for the current inquiry will be addressed in part II.

The present chapter has two objectives, crucial respectively to both of these methodological concerns. First, it is concerned with establishing more rigorously the gender-play-to-gender-panic pattern as a meaningful, wide-ranging eighteenth-century development. Striving to approach what I have called repetition in the second degree, what follows singles out four cultural domains that push the argument and its limits in variously revealing ways. The analysis moves from theater and fashion, domains where play with identity categories was likely, to domains at the opposite end of the spectrum that were much less likely to register awareness of the limitations of gender categories: the milieu of learned classical translators and the conventionalized genre of moralizing jeremiads. Since my basic narrative of change over time hinges on a sharp shift in the understanding of gender categories from playfulness to rigidity, each of these examples turns out to be an instructive limiting test case. The discussion of varying cultural susceptibilities also raises the possibility of time lags between different cultural domains, which is important in unpacking an arguably wide-ranging cultural transformation. In addition, the following test cases provide the opportunity to consider specific methodological questions, such as the importance of evidence from opposite sides of the putative divides between discourse and practice, or between description and prescription, in which historians tend to put much stock; and to experiment with specific methodologies for gauging cultural change, especially quantification and micro-textual comparative analysis.

The first objective of this chapter, then, is to add depth and breadth to the pattern uncovered in the previous pages, while experimenting with the methodological limits of cultural history. To this extent, the reader who is more keen to see how the plot thickens, rather than the evidence, may choose to hurry ahead to chapter 3, where the next steps in the larger argument are taken. But the present chapter also supports a second conclusion that is important for this larger argument. It is a conclusion not about gender itself, but about establishing (not yet explaining) the peculiar dynamics of cultural transmission, diffusion, and transformation that took place in the closing decades of the eighteenth century. Such dynamics, involving a rapid, swift, far-reaching rupture that spread like wildfire through the thickets of contemporary culture, are a rather unusual historical occurrence. The following chapters will gradually stake a claim for the late eighteenth century in England as the scene of such an occurrence. But while the full transformation was broader and bigger than merely that in the understandings of gender, a close study of its unfolding in the well-bounded case of gender identity, for which the richness and variety of the evidence are exceptional, can help establish the contours of this sharp and comprehensive late-eighteenth-century rupture: a rupture that may even merit the epithet of "cultural revolution".

Gender Roles

At the heart of the distinction between the *ancien régime* of gender and the new sex–gender regime that replaced it was whether gender identity was understood to be *assumable* – so it could be learned, imitated, performed, donned and doffed at will – or whether it was understood as innate, essential, and predetermined by sex. Nowhere were such questions more explicitly explored than on the dramatic stage. The theater was the arena most likely to foreground experimentation and fluidity, where identities were self-consciously constructed and reconstructed, and liberties could be expected to be taken and stretched to their permissible limits. By the same token, it was presumably also the arena least likely to display unease when faced with the limits of identity categories. In opposite ways, then, the theater presents a limit case for both gender play and gender panic.

And, sure enough, eighteenth-century theater capitalized in a big way on contemporary willingness to contemplate the limits of gender categories. We have already seen examples of this in *Percy*'s prologue and similar productions. But I want to focus now not on dramatic writing, but on an actual theatrical practice that assumed considerable importance in the late-seventeenth and eighteenth centuries: "breeches parts". In these, women were cast in male roles – and occasionally (though not under the same label) men in female roles – throughout a play; not as a requirement of the narrative, as was the case for some Shakespearean heroines we have met, but as a casting choice neither required by the plot nor explicitly revealed during the action. Such gender-crossings on stage were a famous selling point for eighteenth-century audiences, and a boost to many an actress's career.[2] Such, for example, was the case of the celebrated Peg Woffington: her mid-century reputation can thus serve as a good illustration of what the practice of breeches parts could achieve.

When Woffington walked on stage – as she did often in the 1740s and 1750s – in the character of a man, especially in her favorite role of the rake Sir Harry Wildair in George Farquhar's *The Constant Couple*, her success was widely and enthusiastically acknowledged. "In the well-bred rake of quality, who lightly tripped across the stage," one critic raved upon her Wildair debut in London in 1740, "*there was no trace of the woman*. The audience beheld only a young man of faultless figure, distinguished by an ease of manner, polish of address, and nonchalance that at once surprised and fascinated them." Others singled out for praise her ability to maintain an ambiguous sexual identity:

That excellent Peg
Who showed such a leg
When lately she dressed in men's clothes –
A creature uncommon
Who's both man and woman
And the chief of the belles and the beaux!

Spectators and critics dwelt on this theme: "Her charms resistless conquer all,/ *Both sexes* vanquished lie"; and again, "it was a most nice point to decide between the gentlemen and the ladies, whether she was the finest woman, or the prettiest fellow". One admirer even blamed his passionate love for Woffington – without any self-conscious awkwardness – on her ability to pass so well for a male that she swept women as well as men off their feet. Her cross-dressed heroes were seen as exhortations to patriotic virtue, or as models for emulation for women with "manly hearts". Most revealingly, fans of Woffington's breeches parts resorted to *nature* to drive home their point: one addressed her as the "true judge of Nature", another marveled at "lavish nature, who her gave/ This *double power* to please" (both sexes), and a third commented on how "she has more than most players of either sex, given a loose to nature" in expressing her "great sensibility".[3] Far from being an embarrassment to nature or somehow outside it, Woffington's ability to step into a man's boots was seen – with tongue only partly in cheek – as a triumph of nature itself. (By another coincidence, Woffington's main lover at the height of her fame was none other than David Garrick, many years before he was to express his appreciation for another gender-crossing woman in the shape of Hannah More.)

But when we come to the pronouncements of dramatic critics and writers at the turn of the century, we easily recognize the familiar change in attitudes as they now stumbled over each other in their rush to denounce cross-dressing on stage. Among them we find the Yorkshire theater manager Tate Wilkinson who exclaimed with horror at an actress's choice of a breeches part "for her *own amusement*" – her assertion of free will truly got his goat – that it was "so determinately wrong, [that it] is to me inconceivable!" Or actor Charles Dibdin, whose stage history of 1800 found Woffington's Wildair an affront to "female delicacy" and a serious blemish on her otherwise extraordinary record. Or critic William Cooke, who perversely insisted that Garrick himself had declared Woffington's claim to fame as "a great attempt for *a woman*, but still it was *not* Sir Harry Wildair". Or our acquaintance Charles Lee Lewes, who dismissed breeches parts as "strange" and inevitably doomed to failure, depicting an actress in a male role as having "a voice only fit for the monster in the Tempest". Or Elizabeth Inchbald, who asserted that the earlier eighteenth-century presentation of Wildair by female actresses "must be considered as a disgrace to the memory of the men of fashion". Or James Boaden, who was soon to insist with impatient disbelief that "dress [an actress] how you will, the spectator [always] sees that it is a woman".[4]

And again: when an extravagant 1781 George Colman production of *The Beggar's Opera* with *all* parts sex-reversed resurfaced in early-nineteenth-century memoirs, it was repeatedly recalled – the actual success of the staging notwithstanding – with disgust. Colman's sex-reversed *Beggar's Opera* was "as truly laughable as it was strange"; it left one "scandalized at the public indecency"; and it was a "nauseous entertainment" into which "theatrical despotism" must have coerced the performers, since "it is difficult to suppose that they were all volunteers". In any case, this last writer concluded, it "may be doubted . . . whether the existing state of society would tolerate" a production of this sort. The fact that this last expression of critical incredulity came from the pen of none other than George Colman Junior, Colman's own son and successor, made it all the more poignant.[5] As these comments suggest, moreover, the hindsight chorus of disapproval extended to men's acting as well as to women's. Thus, for one critic, when male operatic singers – a familiar counterpart to females in breeches parts – renounced "the manly part of singing for the less natural . . . *falsetto*", this unfortunate choice left them "bewildered", "injured [their] reputation and rendered those gifts of nature contemptible". Another tried to salvage the reputation of an earlier actor who in 1780 had performed a female role: not only was he surely "embarrassed" by this role, but it must have been forced upon him only because there was no actress available to take the part. And as for the well-known Renaissance boys who had played Shakespeare's ladies, they were now declared by Charles Lamb (flying once again in the face of the Bard and his contemporaries) to have been able only "with awkward art/ And shrill sharp pipe [to] burlesque the woman's part". When early-modern audiences encountered men acting female roles, the antiquarian James Peller Malcolm concluded on a familiar note, they were simply "disgusted".[6]

What these commentators on theatrical cross-dressing registered most of all, as they marshaled one by one their belief in the unbridgeable difference between the sexes, was their own unbridgeable difference from their forebears. They could only view this formerly popular practice through a glass darkened by pooh-poohing incredulity (how *could* they fall for it?) and sniggering incomprehension (how could they *enjoy* it?). Here, in sum, is another instance of an eighteenth-century cultural form that appears to have derived its resonance from the *ancien régime* of gender, but then lost its cultural intelligibility as understandings of gender changed.

Predictable, then? Not quite. This particular shift is in fact more surprising than it first appears: for if cultural domains differ in their susceptibility to identity play, and if theater is where we expect experimentation to be at its most adventurous, then one can also reasonably expect it to be more *resistant* to the rigidifying moves that arguably limited the space for such identity play in the late eighteenth century. So, is there any indication of resistance to this pattern of change in the theatrical sphere?

One might begin by pointing out that the assertions crammed into the previous litany of voices critical of gender-crossing on stage were all made somewhat *later* than those we have seen in other cultural domains, closer in this case to the turn of the century and beyond. This short time lag is perhaps an indication of stronger residual resistance to the contraction of gender play that we have seen elsewhere. But even a dozen pronouncements, however central the figures that uttered them, are not sufficient to make this observation conclusive. Fortunately, however, we can examine it another way with a more sensitive and more precise gauge of cultural change, through the stage performances themselves. We have a detailed record of the shows performed on the London (and some provincial) stages every night throughout the century, which allows us to examine the actual day-to-day choices made by managers and performers. The results of such an exercise for the key decades in our story are revealing.[7]

Take for instance Woffington's old vehicle, Sir Harry Wildair in the ever-popular *The Constant Couple*. In London in the 1770s and 1780s, six different actresses tried to step into Woffington's boots in this role (fig. 9): most notably Dorothy Jordan, who made *The Constant Couple* more successful than it had ever been since the days of Woffington. In the two and a half years between May 1788 and October 1790, Wildair appeared on the London stage twenty-eight times, acted either by Mrs. Jordan or by two other actresses, but never by a male actor. The subsequent reversal was striking: the following equivalent period saw the play staged only once – and then with a *man* playing Wildair, not a woman. During the whole subsequent decade this formerly popular breeches part was attempted only three more times.

The indications of change are even more marked with the character of Patrick in John O'Keeffe's *The Poor Soldier*, easily the most popular breeches part on the London stage in the period after its inception in Covent Garden Theatre in 1783. Between November 1783 and March 1789 the play enjoyed ninety-eight performances in Covent Garden, always with a woman playing Patrick (during this period, in another theater, it was attempted on a single occasion with a male actor). In the following eleven years, by contrast, from September 1789 to May 1800, the play was performed fifty-five times in Covent Garden with *male* Patricks, but only twice with women. During this period other London theaters tried to launch *The Poor Soldier* six times with various female leads, but their hopes of capitalizing on Patrick's erstwhile popularity

CONSTANT COUPLE.

Dodd del.   *Goldar sculp.*

M.ᴿˢ *BARRY as* SIR HARRY WILDAIR.

Sdeath, I'm afraid I've mistaken the House

Publish'd May 19.1777 by J. Lowndes & partners.   Act II. Sc. 2.

9.   Ann Barry in breeches as Sir Harry
Wildair in *The Constant Couple*, 1777

as a breeches part came to naught. One can hardly imagine a more stark reversal.

The stage history of other plays tells a remarkably similar story, not least that of Colman's all-sexes-reversed *Beggar's Opera*, which, after starting with a bang for a couple of seasons in the early 1780s, rapidly declined, experiencing a few sporadic and half-hearted revival attempts before finally exiting with a whimper in 1792.[8] The conclusion, therefore, seems to be two-fold. First, we do see the final triumph of the broader cultural pattern, as this popular eighteenth-century gender-crossing practice went out of fashion so sharply at the end of the century. But second, this unusually finely calibrated gauge of change also seems to show an unmistakable lag – of about a decade – between the stage and the other domains we have looked at. Whereas indications of change in other cultural arenas had begun in the early 1780s, breeches parts continued strongly until the early 1790s. It is tempting to see this lag as a sign of a more protracted resistance among theatrical performers and managers to the imminent closure of space for gender play: a resistance that would accord with our expectations of the importance of identity play to the theater.

Nowhere was this resistance more defiant than in the career of Dorothy Jordan, who was manifestly loath to give up those roles in breeches that had been so important in establishing her reputation. The late-eighteenth-century critics sounded the tocsin, their enthusiasm for Jordan in breeches noticeably cooling. Thus, one unfavorable reviewer dismissed a breeches part of hers in 1788 as "offensive and disgusting", while a year later a better-disposed colleague gave her a backhanded compliment for appearing "chaste and natural . . . *in spite of* the disadvantage of appearing in a male dress". Audiences were becoming less appreciative as well: in 1789 Jordan's Wildair met "not with the violent applause she was then accustomed to", from a provincial audience reportedly less able to stomach this character "when represented by a female". Playwrights were no more cooperative. When one did produce for Jordan an afterpiece entitled *The Female Duellist*, seemingly in the manner of eighteenth-century precedents, she discovered this cross-dressed role to have been one that conspicuously involved only *talking* about duels but never fighting one, and that unraveled inexorably within the logic of the piece when "the woman was so strong within her, that she couldn't resist impeaching herself". Another writer had Jordan end such a performance with an apologetic epilogue that exhorted women not to emulate her.[9]

But the ultimate blow came in a prologue to a 1797 play in which Mrs. Jordan again tried a breeches part, albeit (as was now typical) that of a teenage boy:

> To prevent disappointment, but not to forestall,
> To one little hint your attention we call:
> For this 'tis but right we should tell of his plan –
> You must fancy a female is really a man;
> Not merely conceal'd in the manly array,
> But a man, *bona-fide*, throughout the whole play;
> This we own, as it else might your feelings perplex,
> Since she charms you so much in her own proper sex.[10]

What this striking prologue did, unnecessarily from an earlier eighteenth-century perspective, was carefully to prepare the audience for the breeches part that was to follow. One cannot easily imagine a better indication of how alien this practice – and with it Mrs. Jordan's casting preferences – had become than the fact that such an explicit and apologetic forewarning, explanation, and request for suspension of disbelief were now deemed necessary.

And as Mrs. Jordan was being forced to adapt to a different cultural environment – with or without a short time lag – what was happening to the

reputation of the famous Peg Woffington? It is testimony to the force of the
new winds blowing at the turn of the century that the answer to this question
is so predictable. As with Hannah Snell, or the Chevalier D'Eon, a whole array
of commentators stood ready to reinterpret and repackage the long-dead
Woffington in order to render her acceptable, indeed comprehensible, to the
early-nineteenth-century readers of the popular genre of theatrical memoirs-
cum-criticism. Thus, it was a consideration of Woffington's life that led
William Cooke to insist (as we have seen in the previous chapter) on the absolute
impossibility for a woman to act the role of a man "so as totally [to] escape
detection". Never mind that the goal of those former theatrical events had never
been a total avoidance of detection – a preposterous proposition in view of the
publicity surrounding such performances – but rather the pleasure that
eighteenth-century audiences had been able to draw from the indeterminacy
predicated on what one scholar has called their "knowing forgetfulness". But
Cooke now had a different interpretation, and he was willing to tamper with
his evidence to prove it. He thus told his readers that Woffington had started
her career at the age of ten when one Madame Violante, directing a children's
production of *The Beggar's Opera*, "fixed upon [Woffington] as her *Macheath*".
Although in truth, as Cooke was well aware, little Peg had played not Macheath
but Polly in this children's production, this story served his exculpatory
purpose well: "had not the character of Macheath been assigned her, it is more
than probable, she would have gone on in the usual line of acting, without ever
being celebrated as the best male rake of her day". Woffington's career in
breeches was thus the consequence of "an early and accidental decision", one
that took place at a pre-pubescent age and that was "more than probabl[y]" out
of her control. Moreover, much of Cooke's information was drawn from the
earlier theatrical memoir published by Thomas Davies in 1780. According to
Davies, Woffington had played the rakish Wildair "with so much ease, elegance,
and propriety of deportment, that *no male actor has since equalled her in that
part*". But when Cooke reproduced this passage (failing to mention its source),
he admitted only her "ease, elegance, and deportment [no longer "*propriety* of
deportment"], which seemed almost *out of the reach of female accomplishments*".
A telling alteration: Woffington could no longer compete in representing a man
with *male* actors, as had been suggested by Davies, but rather only with performers of her own sex.[11]

But Cooke was still a model of accuracy in comparison with another
acquaintance of ours, Charles Lee Lewes, and the liberties that *he* took with
Woffington's biography. Fantastic as it might seem, throughout his retelling
of Woffington's life Lewes managed to keep silent about those breeches parts
that had been her most singular claim to fame. Instead, in his version of the
youthful beginnings of her career, he asserted that "her young bosom panted

for the wide extending hoop, the long rich train, laced shoes, and brocaded suits, instead of the long drawers, short jackets, and flat pumps, she was used to wear". Fantastic indeed: what Peg Woffington had really been after all along, it now turned out, was nothing more than innocently to accentuate her *femininity*. And finally, pride of place among Woffington's remodelers must go to James Boaden. It was simply the case, Boaden insisted, that Woffington herself "was not aware" of the real meaning of her breeches parts performances. He therefore addressed her directly in order to set her straight: "No, Mrs. Woffington", while you believed you were successful in your disguise, "it was the *travesty*, seen throughout, that really constituted the charm of your performance, and rendered it not only gay, but innocent."[12] Conveniently for Boaden, Woffington and her eighteenth-century admirers were not there to respond.

*

Theatrical breeches parts, then, demonstrated stronger resistance to the limiting consequences of the transformation to the new sex–gender regime than other cultural forms we have examined. I have attributed this lag to the performative nature of the theater. But we can also look at it somewhat differently, emphasizing cultural *dynamic* as well as cultural form. For it stands to reason that the preferences of individuals long set in their professional ways – performers like Dorothy Jordan, or theater managers – will shift more slowly, and more reactively, than the preferences of audiences and critics who are more susceptible to short-term fashions and trends. That this was indeed the case is suggested by the following analysis of a particular theatrical genre that was unusually sensitive to changes in cultural climate, that of dramatic prologues and epilogues. At the same time this exercise will provide a complement to the analysis of change in the theater that is more quantitatively significant and serially systemic; a crude yet revealing experiment in cultural-historical enumeration.

The genre of prologues and epilogues is exceptionally suitable for such an exercise. A customary feature of English dramatic performances from the late seventeenth to the early nineteenth centuries, prologues and epilogues were free-standing pieces spoken by leading actors/actresses, commonly (as in the case of *Percy*) bearing little relationship to the plays themselves, often contributed by someone other than the playwright, and circulating independently in print. In order to understand why prologues and epilogues became (in the words of Gillian Russell) such prominent "vehicles for the distinctive self-consciousness that characterized the Georgian theatre", we need to consider historical changes in the meaning of theatrical representation. During the heyday of this genre key distinctions fundamental to modern understandings of theater – distinctions between on-stage and off-stage, between dramatic character and actor/actress's persona, between "fiction" and "life" – were more easily blurred. The relationship of these eighteenth-century understandings of theatrical performance to contemporary notions of identity will demand our attention in chapter 5; here I only want to suggest that it was the function of prologues and epilogues as reminders of this possible blurring that may account for much of their cultural energy during this period (and perhaps also for their subsequent petering out). Prologues and epilogues effected such a blurring when they offered a meta-commentary on the goings-on on-stage intertwined with a commentary on current events outside the theater; when they directly addressed the public, in what Janet Todd has described as a kind of "winking at the audience, excluding the playwright from an audience–actor compact"; and when they were recited by actors/actresses still in character but also appearing under their real names and reputations.[13] Prologues and epilogues were therefore especially apt vehicles for reflections on the possibilities latent in the making, unmaking, and remaking of identities: we now understand better why Garrick chose this particular genre for his paean to the crossing of gender boundaries in Hannah More's *Percy*. Moreover, importantly for our purpose here, the fact that prologues and epilogues routinely situated performances within the specific temporal context of the world outside the theater made them closely attuned to the concerns and interests of the audience at any given moment. And because of their light and humorous tone, they were given considerable leeway to deliver their cultural commentary more freely and boldly. All this rendered dramatic prologues and epilogues a sensitive gauge of cultural moods. And given the further, obvious advantage that they have survived in large numbers, peppering profusely every decade of the century, they lend themselves to an analysis of these cultural moods that is both quantitative and serial.

To be sure, "quantitative" here should be taken with more than a grain of salt. As with any other attempt to count meaningful utterances, the difficulties in categorizing and enumerating commentaries on the elasticity or inflexibility of gender boundaries, often made obliquely or ironically, are considerable. But as it turns out, a tentative analysis of the prologues and epilogues of over nine hundred eighteenth-century plays has produced a pattern so sharp as to appear to override the obvious limitations of the exercise.[14] The procedure was simple. First, I singled out those prologues/epilogues that offered any kind of commentary on questions of gender boundaries and identities. Such "gender-interested" prologues/epilogues constituted between a fifth and a quarter of the total – a significant portion in its own right, and one that in fact increased to almost a third of all productions in the period between 1770 and 1800, when, according to my argument, these questions could be expected to become the subject of mounting attention. Second, I attempted to identify those productions that appeared to gesture toward the limitations and elasticity of gender categories (like *Percy*'s prologue and epilogue), those that appeared on the other hand to insist on their fixed and rigid nature, and those that made no clear gesture one way or the other.[15]

The results of this crude exercise are striking. Consistently, decade by decade from 1711 to 1780, those prologues/epilogues that appeared to gesture toward the limitations or the elasticity of gender categories numbered no less than a third, and mostly more than half, of all gender-interested productions. At the same time, the prologues/epilogues during these decades that seemed insistent on the fixity of these categories were at most about 8 per cent of the total, and often none at all. (It is interesting to note, however, that the hundred-odd productions between 1701 and 1710 did *not* fall into the clear pattern of the subsequent decades: an indication, perhaps, of a chronological *starting point* for this gender pattern?) But in the last two decades of the eighteenth century we see a radical change. During this period (beginning, as a more refined count at five-year intervals has demonstrated, already during the first half of the 1780s), prologues/epilogues allowing for any elasticity or porousness of gender boundaries all but vanished, appearing as a mere 0 to 3 per cent of the total. Instead, they were replaced with prologues/epilogues that conspicuously insisted on the essential, rigid nature of gender categories: their share of the whole rose sharply to between a third and three-quarters of all gender-interested productions.[16]

Since we have not encountered yet these latter, "gender-panicked" productions, a few examples may be helpful in order to give a flavor of their decisively new tone, now saturated *ad nauseam* with the most formulaic advocacy of rigidly demarcated gender boundaries: "Ye, who in marriage, wealth and grandeur seek,/ Think what a blessing is a wife that's meek"; "And tho' the sphere be small in which we [women] move,/ Great is the recompence when you approve"; "Beyond our sphere we Women should not roam:/ Enough for us, I think, to – rule at home"; "May manners masculine no more deface/ The charms that constitute each female grace"; "Say those manly ladies what they will,/ Our surest maxim is – be women still"; "Ladies! . . . Shun contradiction – worst of all disasters –/ You *should* be mistresses – but *not* be masters!"[17] How different were those late-eighteenth-century exhortations from the repetitive assertions of various heroines in earlier decades (to add a few more examples to *Percy*'s prologue and others we have seen): "I'll huff, to prove my Title to the Breeches/ . . . I'll draw and bid Defiance to the Vicious"; "Custom cries, why do these Men wear Breeches?/ . . . Who knows but soon, to make the Wonder less,/ Custom may win [the women] to take on their Dress?" "I must own, the Breeches please me most/ Tho' in the Wearing, my weak sex is lost"; "to-night's example teaches,/ . . . That things go best when – women wear the breeches"; "farewel to *petticoats*, and *stitching*,/ And welcome dear, dear *breeches*, more bewitching!/ . . . If e'er I grow a *man*, 'tis now, or never."[18] Even if such pronouncements had often been recited with tongue at least partially in cheek, this was evidently a direction in which late-eighteenth-century tongues, even in jest, were now loath to go.

But to come back from the argument-by-example to a more systemic enumeration: the results of this exercise can also be put differently to highlight the dramatic shift that had taken place by the late eighteenth century. Of the almost six hundred plays contributing to the final count of prologues and epilogues between 1711 and 1780, the number of possible *exceptions* to the pattern suggested here – that is, prologues or epilogues that appeared to be invested in the fixity of gender boundaries or that manifested anxiety about their porousness – was at most *six*.[19] By the same token, of the over two hundred productions of the last two decades of the century, the number of counter-examples to the reversed sensibilities of this period – that is, instances in which categories of gender were put in question – was no more than *four*. Together, then, there were at most ten exceptions to the prevalent pattern in more than eight hundred plays between 1710 and 1800, of which no fewer than 180 prologues/epilogues touched on the issue of gender boundaries.

In sum, therefore, even though this exercise is indeed rather crude, and even once we allow for as much margin of error as is necessary to take account of subjective readings and possible misinterpretations, these results still lend strong quasi-quantitative support to the picture of a sharp and distinct cultural shift between the 1770s and the 1780s. Moreover, because of the particular cultural responsiveness of this genre, the shift manifested in the prologues and epilogues was more in synch with the broader patterns of change outside the theater than with the slower-to-change ones among the professionals within it.

Changing Habits

Inevitably, given the nature of the evidence, my inquiry is weighted toward discursive practices, that is to say, toward practices manifested in the uses of words. Now I do not want to push the distinction often alleged between discursive and social practices very far: some historians' skepticism notwithstanding, discursive practices are obviously as much a social practice as any other. And yet they are all the same particular kind of social practice, and surely not the only one through which meaning is produced. It is thus useful to test the limits of the argument against some other kinds of social practices that are not primarily discursive (although this does not make them wholly non-discursive; the distinction, we need to remember, is a heuristic one). Such has been the case in our foray into eighteenth-century theater, which moved from theatrical texts to theatrical practice in the shape of those performers who came or did not come onto the stage cross-dressed. Here I want to examine briefly another realm of social practice, one that involved active choices on the part of a larger number of people as they literally fashioned their self-presentation: that of dress. We will see that the fashions of the closing decades of the century accentuated gender differences, with a distinct emphasis on masculinity for men and on ultra-femininity for women; whereas those of the earlier decades, by contrast, for women as well as men, had noticeably eroded or subverted clearly demarcated gender distinctions.

"On meeting a company on horseback now-a-days," observed "Portia" in 1760, "one shall hardly be able to distinguish, at first sight, whether it is composed of ladies or gentlemen." What "Portia" had in fact seen was a group of women riders. Her comment was prompted by the then-popular female riding habits which had (to an eighteenth-century eye) distinctly masculine cuts, all the way to left-over-right buttoning and stiffened sword pleats at the waist. "They should be called Amazons," she concluded. This was another cultural cliché of this period: throughout the short eighteenth century, fashionable women in such "half-coat, half-petticoat" habits, which they increasingly donned also as walking costume, when traveling, or even when posing for portraits (fig. 10), were characterized as "Hermaphroditical" (1713), "half-Men, half-Women" (1745), "Amazonians" who "wear the breeches literally as well as metaphorically" (1774), "*habillé en homme*" (1777) and "most officer-like" (1781).[20] The woman wearing the breeches, the female officer, the female rider, and of course the Amazon: these riding habits carried on their coat-tails the same familiar range of cultural markers for the subversion of gender boundaries. And with them came the all-but-ubiquitous comments in the manner of "Portia" on the resulting gender confusion, often through the generic tableau of the encounter with a rider of indistinguishable sex. Nor was this reputed effect limited only to riding habits. Other items of female dress appeared to contemporaries to have the same effect: be they "fierce-cock'd Hats" (thus Fielding's *The Champion*), periwigs, cravats, high collars, low-heeled shoes, boots, or greatcoat-dresses that echoed masculine styles in their long tight sleeves, caped collars, and double-breasted fastening or false waistcoat front (fig. 11).[21] And while these gender-stretching fashions had many critics, reactions were on the whole more jocular than anxious, more tolerant than repressive. In the words of the most knowledgeable student of these fashions, Aileen Ribeiro, "instead of heavy moral denunciations of their sin and folly, they were laughed out of countenance" – though not, of course, by the many women who had chosen to wear them.[22]

The contemporary sense that the distance between men's and women's dress

10. Sir Joshua Reynolds, "Lady Worsley", late 1770s. The jacket of Lady Worsley's red riding habit, adapted from the uniform of her husband's regiment, follows a man's coat in the gold epaulettes, the front edges and the cuffs that are turned back, and the white silk waistcoat and lace cravat underneath

was shrinking manifested itself in remarks about male fashions as well: such as the men in petticoats who made a passing appearance in *Percy*'s prologue, or those who "have curl'd their Hair, and spread their Skirts in Imitation of Hoop-petticoats" (Fielding), or those whose coats – "like our Mantuas" – led one Sarah Osborne to declare in 1722: "I believe the gentlemen will ware petty-cotes very soon." Eighteenth-century social commentary boasted a long line of extravagantly dressed gender-ambiguous male figures: from the fops who "quit our Sex – to dress for another", to the Italians whose gender-blurred reputation was captured in Samuel Richardson's memorable three-way division of the character list in *Sir Charles Grandison* into "Men", "Women", and "Italians". (Imagine a theater featuring three doors at the back marked "Men", "Women" and "Italians".)[23] In the 1770s, the stock character that came to embody gender-indeterminate male fashions was the "Macaroni", an exaggerated type drawing on the contemporary penchant for oversize wigs, brightly colored tight-fitting coats, and impractical accessories. The Macaroni "of the double Gender" was

11. "The Sporting Lady", 1776. The appearance of the lady with the fowling piece and the partridges on her shoulder echoes masculine dress in her long boots, her cocked hat with plumes, her wig with parallel curls at the ears, and her coat that mirrors that of her man-servant

an easy target for jokes ("A macaroni being told that not one of his fraternity could keep a secret: Yes, cried he, but we can; for no one yet knows whether we are *male* or *female*"), plays (like *The Macaroni*, about one specimen who made "such large advances to the feminine gender, that in a little time 'twill be difficult to tell to which sex [s/he] belonged"), doggerels ("But *Macaronis* are a sex/ Which do philosophers perplex"), or satirical prints (such as "The Macaroni Duelists" (fig. 12), mocking their inability to hold a sword, aim a pistol, or fight a duel). This image of the Macaroni, with his "aversion to a sword out of its scabbard", brings to mind the sword-dropping gender-flexing man of feeling. As contemporaries of the same decade, each representing a counter-normative model for manhood, the Macaroni, who was reputed "to be moved at nothing – to feel nothing", was often set up as a foil for his worthier alter ego. And yet, however different from each other, the Macaroni and the man of feeling inhabited the same cultural universe.[24]

Now, to be sure, these comments on male dress had a rather different edge

THE MACARONI·DUELISTS.

12.   "The Macaroni Duelists", 1772

to them than those on women's fashions – their critique more in earnest, their
satire more biting. And given the asymmetrical gender power structure in
eighteenth-century society, this is not very surprising. But still a few important
points need to be made. First, the Macaroni was a caricature, but one that drew
on recognizable social behavior. So although 1770s England was hardly flooded
with *bona fide* Macaronies, any more than it was suddenly submerged by the
gushing tears of men of feeling, the resonance of these cultural types depended
on a widespread familiarity with the various components of their exaggerated
portrait: they represented the excess rather than the antithesis of acceptable, if
counter-hegemonic, modes of behavior. Second, as Susan Staves and Philip
Carter have pointed out, despite the seemingly inevitable censure, fops in the
eighteenth century were in fact in better repute than before or after, encountering often affectionate criticism rather than contempt – especially when they
were taken to embody unusual levels of refinement and sensibility.[25] Third, and
perhaps most incomprehensibly for modern observers, even when Macaronies
and other fops did meet with severe criticism, it was not directed at their
subversion of gender categories as often as we might expect. It is true that the

bugbear of these critiques was *effeminacy*, that key plank in the eighteenth-century assault on luxury. But the eighteenth-century critique of effeminacy in and of itself did not necessarily imply a concern with the blurring of gender boundaries. Rather, effeminacy became shorthand for numerous deleterious effects of luxury – such as corruption, degeneracy, enervation, supineness, and self-indulgence – which were not necessarily conceived as gender-specific. Significantly, therefore, effeminacy in this eighteenth-century sense was used to characterize *women* as well as men, both "male and female fops". As Fielding wrote once, the "*Effeminacy* of the present Times" characterized "Coquettes about Town of *both Sexes*". It was commonplace, as we have seen, to juxtapose this modern effeminacy with the manly hardiness of both sexes during the time of Queen Elizabeth.[26]

So while satirical and often critical, the interest in the Macaroni, and in the fop more generally, should not be read backward as a *prima facie* indication that the stretching of gender categories that such figures embodied was considered in and of itself beyond the cultural pale. Rather, like characters in comedies of manners, they represented an exaggerated take on familiar contemporary predilections, even if always the predilections of a minority. That this was indeed the case becomes more apparent when we make our usual move to the closing decades of the eighteenth century. Here we find again a sharp turning point at which the Macaroni too – just like the man of feeling – abruptly disappeared, both in social practice and as a cultural type.

In terms of what men actually wore, the late eighteenth century witnessed the supplanting of the foppish peacock-like dress that some men had sported through the 1770s by somber attire with a limited palette, often reminiscent of military uniforms. "Male dress changed," observed one contemporary, "the colours . . . are more grave. Deep blue, dark browns, mixtures, and black, are worn by the sedate and gay, the young and the old." Linda Colley has persuasively placed this transformation within the refashioning of the image of the British ruling class from a parasitic leisured class to a patriotic service elite. But dressing up *en militaire* was also a public affirmation of men's most distinct masculine role. Indeed, one may wonder how far a sudden interest in the display of unambiguous masculinity contributed to the unprecedented scale of patriotic mobilization during the 1790s, which for most male citizens meant a relatively safe but publicly decorous participation in quasi-military local formations. Some skeptics, at least, were quick to dismiss the raging "military mania" as not "contributing in the least to that military defence", but only to a "*military style of [self-]importance*" and overstated manliness: "Each man, (a sight at which his Lady swoons,)/ [wears] Belt, sabre, helmet, spurs, and pantaloons!" In contrast, when the *Gentleman's Magazine* had identified in an earlier decade a "Rage . . . for the Military Dress" (1781), it had attributed it

a Jessamy

13.   "A Jessamy", 1790

not to men but rather to "the ladies".[27] By the 1790s military mania was exclusively a male affair.

Furthermore, at the same time that the gender-stretching Macaroni style
went out of fashion, the Macaroni *type* was making a hasty retreat as well. So
much so, in fact, that an early 1790s dictionary of "Cant Language" chose
"Maccaroni" (sic, idiosyncratically spelled, which of course speaks volumes) as
an example of such words that, "falling into disuse, or being superseded by new
ones, vanish without leaving a trace behind". *The Collector*, a compilation of
antiquarian anecdotes of 1798, likewise included "the true origin of that once
popular folly, Macaronyism," among those "curiosities" long since gone.[28] The
Macaroni had lost his cultural currency and had thus become a proper subject
for antiquarian interest. Indeed, if the horror with which turn-of-the-century
admirers of Garrick washed their hands of his successful mid-century playing
of fops is anything to go by, the Macaroni's fate was shared by the fop more
broadly. Thus, one declared Garrick's fop "so disgusting that . . . the public

Ladies Dress, as it soon will be.

14. "Ladies Dress, as it soon will be", 1796. One of the many satirical prints poking fun at the 1790s trend in female fashion toward increased transparency and exposure of the female body form

very properly revolted at it" – which of course they had not. Another, while conceding the fop's former topicality, asserted at the same time that such a character sighted "some years since at a village in Surrey" was definitely "the last of the puny race". Which of course it was not: it was hardly true that all narcissistic fops in England were suddenly overtaken by an irresistible urge for public duty. But now, even the fop – or so claimed the text accompanying a 1790 print of "A Jessamy" – "assumes a military air and places a cockade in his hat" (fig. 13). This was a time when "fops, nay, cowards, are in gorgets clad,/ And all the world is military mad".[29]

So much for the transformation in the appearance of men.[30] As for women, the decades at the turn of the eighteenth century notoriously saw – often with a wincing eye – a conspicuous trend toward dresses that clung to the body, and toward fabrics that were more transparent than before, with the effect (noted by many contemporaries) of accentuating the natural female body form (fig. 14). "The dress of women should differ in every point from that of men," went one fashion statement. "This difference ought even to extend to the choice

15. James Gillray, "The Fashionable Mamma, or The Convenience of Modern Dress", 1796. While demonstrating the tendency of 1790s fashions to wear maternity on their sleeve, the emotionless expression of Gillray's fashionable mamma – contrasted with that of her nursemaid, dressed in an older, now outmoded style – was a jab at what the satirist saw as the hollowness of this new visual emphasis

of stuffs; for a woman inhabited in cloth is less feminine than if she were clothed in transparent gauze, in light muslin, or in soft and shining silks." A key focus for these new fashions – which included the radical discarding of the stays, now seen as detrimental to motherhood, and the sudden popularity of false bosoms – was the maternal breast.[31] This trend was captured in James Gillray's print of 1796, "The Fashionable Mamma, or, The Convenience of Modern Dress" (fig. 15). The print shows a fashionable lady in evening dress about to go out (a waiting carriage is visible through the window), fully equipped with feathered turban, choker, gloves, and fan. And yet her "modern" dress is cut in such a way as to lend itself spontaneously to the suckling of an eager infant, whom she satisfies en route to the door. This "fashionable mamma" wore her maternal role on her sleeve, as it were; a point that Gillray hammered home by adding a large picture on the wall of a breast-feeding woman, entitled "Maternal Love".[32]

So we are back with the familiar late-eighteenth-century emphasis on

The Pad Warehoufe.

16.   "The Pad Warehouse",
from the *Bon Ton Magazine*,
1793. A satire on the new
fashion, published in a periodical which frequently bor-
dered on the pornographic,
shows women stand in line to
be fitted with pads simulating
various stages of pregnancy

maternity and its embodiment in the maternal breast, here extended to changing modes of female dress. But nothing, perhaps, illustrated more graphically
the new sartorial emphasis on the maternal form than a curious fashion that
appeared in the streets of London in late 1792: a new contraption that women
wore under their dresses, called "the pad", which gave them the distinct semblance of being many months pregnant. In spite of much ridicule (fig. 16),
objections from the fashion-setting royal family, and even an eponymous play
teeming with women being mistakenly assumed to be pregnant, the pad became
a fad, spreading to women of differing conditions, social and marital. "The
fashion of dressing, at present," commented *The Times* in March 1793, "is to
appear *prominent* . . . holding out a wish to be thought in a thriving way, even
without the authority of the *Arches Court* of Canterbury." The pad – thus the
Morning Chronicle – "makes the barren Matron breed" while also allowing
maidens to be in love without "fear[ing] a swelling waist". So what can we make
of the fact that women were now lining up to associate themselves with this

visible sign of maternity, an accessory before the fact? With due caution about the difficulties in the interpretation of fashions, it is at least suggestive to consider the pad as a perhaps extreme indication – even a parody – of the extent to which maternity, albeit fabricated, acquired an increased weight in defining womanhood at this juncture, an essential foundation of feminine identity which could therefore be shared by *all* women.[33]

This discussion of fashion has been moving back and forth between actual clothes (primarily those worn in fashionable metropolitan circles) and the commentaries about them. Since the latter were mostly, by their nature, voiced by critics, I have paid particular attention to their *tone*: jocular or anxious, humoring or foreboding. And just as the Macaroni lost in the closing decades of the century both his cultural resonance and his humorous overtones, so a striking chasm opened up on both counts for female fashions as well. For the change in tone, listen for instance to the late-1780s writer who, in considering the "masculine" female riding habits of previous decades, insisted with a new sense of urgency that they "conceal every thing that is attractive in a woman's person . . . [and] wholly *unsex* her". "We daily *feel* the *unnaturalness* [of such transgressions]. We forget that you are *women* in *such a garb*, and we forget to love." Unnatural, unsexed, and unlovable: by 1789, this was clearly no laughing matter.[34]

Small wonder, therefore, that these riding habits were disappearing fast. They were "almost entirely laid aside except by walking Amazons", the *Lady's Magazine* observed in 1784. Another contemporary text actually allows us a glimpse of the very process of transition, captured mid-motion in freeze-frame. In December 1786 *The Girl in Style* was staged at Covent Garden Theatre: appropriately for a play set in the middle of the American revolutionary war, it was crowded with women in riding habits and variously *en militaire*. But the prologue revealed an uncomfortable consciousness that times had since changed:

> Some years are flown, since first our author's brain
> Teem'd with this farce, – not teem'd, we hope, in vain,
> Since therefore follies which have reign'd of yore,
> Dethron'd by fate, or fashion, reign no more.

The prologue became increasingly apologetic about the play's anachronistic women, who "wore leather stocks, and criticiz'd field pieces"; women who must seem odd, alien, and even frightening to "our Girl" of 1786 as she "attends half dead with fear" while "enfold[ing] her infant daughter in her arms". In between the writing of the play and the addition of the prologue – or so the latter suspected – the audience, confronting such images, even if conjured up only to poke fun at, had lost their sense of humor.[35]

In fact, we can find numerous late-eighteenth-century commentators unable to imagine such female fashions ever to have been part of their own world. When their existence was recalled, these gender-subverting practices were represented as strange and unacceptable (as in the prologue to *The Girl in Style*), or as exotically alien (like the writer who associated them exclusively with the French, without acknowledging their currency among his own English audience only a short time before), or as decisively extinct (so that one critic could change her perorations against such fashions from present tense in 1781 to past tense by 1800). In 1794, a provincial newspaper had this to say about the then-fashionable pad: "When our grandmothers were pregnant they wore jumps to conceal it. Our modern young ladies, who are not pregnant, wear pads to carry the semblance of it." The only thing this newspaper writer got wrong was the time frame. The truth of the matter was that this reversal had taken place not over two generations but over less than two decades; and the very fact that the former practices seemed now so very distant was in itself a telling sign of how complete this cultural transformation had been.[36]

Gender in Translation: How the English Wrote Their Juvenal

The goal of this chapter, we recall, is to push the pattern we are exploring as far and as wide as it will go – not least, to foray into places increasingly less likely to have been susceptible to its influence. The remainder of the chapter, therefore, moves as far as possible away from those cultural sites that could be expected to foreground experimentation, fluidity, and playfulness: sites like theater and fashion, perceptions of on-stage and off-stage cross-dressing, ballads about women passing as men, drama and fiction. Of course we have also visited domains of culture that were less obviously performative or playful, such as encyclopedias and biographical dictionaries (which, if the reader's patience were of no concern, could have supported a full chapter in their own right), or the texts discussing bees, or the moralizing and pontificating tracts that occasionally surfaced in the above pages and that will demand our more sustained attention shortly. Such forms were not as self-consciously on the cultural cutting edge, nor particularly renowned for their sense of humor, and were thus less likely to register the kinds of shifts we are looking for. But at this point I want to set a perhaps higher bar for the argument: for few domains would appear, at least at first glance, to be further apart from cultural experimentation and performance than that to which the next few pages turn, namely the world of classical learning. In particular, I want to look at one of the pet projects of Augustan classical scholars, the English translations of the Roman satirist Juvenal.

I have already laid down this analysis in considerable detail elsewhere, so allow me to summarize it here briefly.[37] The exercise involved a close comparison of a series of sixteen translations of Juvenal's Sixth Satire into English, produced between the mid-seventeenth and the early nineteenth centuries. *Prima facie*, I suggested, Juvenal and his Sixth Satire constitute as unlikely a site for the present investigation as one could hope for. I thus pointed out that the world of classical learning, to judge by its social composition as well as by its self-image as the bulwark of *gravitas* set against the unbearable lightness of the fashionable world, was much more likely to resist contemporary cultural trends than to spearhead them; that in particular it was seen as a social and intellectual bastion of unwavering manliness, and thus could be expected to be least amenable to fluid notions of gender, and if anything most committed to opposing them; that even if in truth these representations did not necessarily apply to the classics as a whole, contemporaries would have probably voted Juvenal as the one classical writer whose satires on the corruption of late-imperial Rome had proven his credentials as an impregnable rock of manly virtue in a sea of luxury and enervation; and that the pinnacle of Juvenal's vaunted manliness was the scathing attack on Roman women in his Sixth Satire, which by virtue of its sweeping misogyny could be expected to exhibit schematic, polarized, and rigid sexual categorizations.

Late-seventeenth- and eighteenth-century translations of Juvenal's Sixth Satire, then, all produced by men who epitomized the more conservative side of the educated establishment (mostly divines, as well as public writers and professionals, and primarily Oxford graduates), appear to be a particularly remote route to investigating the changing fluidity in understandings of sex and gender during this period. But obviously I was setting up the argument in this manner in order to suggest precisely the opposite. Translations, surely, however much they are driven and constrained by the original text in its ancient-historical context, are at the same time products of the translators' own mental environment. In imputing particular meanings to the ancient authors, in interpreting them in certain ways rather than in others, and in the countless choices of words and formulations involved in rendering them into English, translators necessarily loaded their productions with the cultural baggage of their own times. Furthermore, translators may well render their texts especially valuable in the unselfconscious registering of their own cultural contexts, more than authors of other kinds of literary productions, because of their self-conscious attempts to eliminate their own active involvement and let their original authors "speak for themselves". And further still, the special status of *classical* texts renders them once again particularly suitable for such an analysis, since the belief in their universal timelessness is precisely what encourages every generation to retranslate them in its own image.[38] So there are grounds to suppose that such translations, of a text as suffused with issues of sex and gender as Juvenal's Sixth Satire, may actually provide a sensitive if unwitting prism for reflecting contemporary understandings. And it is a prism that serves as a valuable limit case for the present argument, by taking us into the heart of the seemingly culturally impermeable world of classical scholarship.

Equipped with these presuppositions, I undertook a close comparative analysis of selected key passages in Juvenal's Sixth Satire in this series of translations (which conveniently fell into three groups – three in the late seventeenth century, five in the mid-eighteenth century, and eight between 1785 and 1815). The results were striking. By pulling together the various inflections that translators introduced into these passages, inflections that ranged from subtle alterations to daring flip-flops, this fine-grained analysis brought the whole story told in these pages into sharp focus. Far from being coincidental or random, the variations in the translations of the Sixth Satire appeared to register with remarkable consistency the shifts over time in the scope and the limits of translators' conceptual space for imagining possible – and impossible – configurations of sex and gender.

In lieu of the full-blown analysis, which would be rather time-consuming, let me give here one example of how it worked, from the transmutations of a single passage. In a parenthetical comment prompted by the topic of transgressive athletic women, those who engage in gladiatorial exercises, Juvenal makes the following observation:

> *Where's her chast blush, that puts her helmet on,*
> *And her sex off?* that, though she doate upon
> Man's strength, would not be man, *for but compare*
> *Our pleasures, 'las how little is our share?*

This, of course, is *not* what Juvenal had written, but rather what Sir Robert Stapylton suggested in his mid-seventeenth-century translation that Juvenal might have intended to write. Others, inevitably, phrased it differently. Thomas Sheridan, the learned grandfather of Richard Brinsley Sheridan, preferred in 1739 a prose translation:

> What Modesty can that Woman pretend to, that puts on a Helmet, and puts off the Tenderness of her own Sex? But she loves to look manly, and yet would by no Means be a Man; for alas! have not they much the Advantage of us?

And in the opening years of the nineteenth century William Gifford, the maverick Tory writer and future editor of the *Quarterly Review*, had it again somewhat differently:

> What sense of shame is to that woman known,
> Who envies our pursuits, and hates her own?

> Yet, though she madly doat on arms and blood,
> She would not change her sex, not – if she cou'd,
> For there's a thing she loves beyond compare,
> And men, alas! have no advantage there.[39]

Now, at first glance, it might seem that the textual variations in these three examples are very minor. The passages all appear to mean much the same thing. Indeed, the only additional, external information that seems necessary to complete the understanding of these verses has to do not with the process of translation, but rather with classical allusions: clarifying, that is, that the last couplet is a reference to Ovid's *Metamorphoses*, where Tiresias, who had been both a man and a woman, proclaims from a position of ultimate knowledge that women have greater pleasure in sex.

But we can also read the three passages more closely, shifting our attention from their common ground to their divergences, and thus from the Roman author to his English translators. For instance: in the verses offered by Stapylton, the athletic woman "*puts her helmet on,/ And her sex off*". Now on one level this witty use of syntactical parallelism was simply a literary device characteristic of heroic couplets. But at the same time it relied on a certain plausibility in the underlying analogy, that assuming or shedding sexual identity is as unproblematic as putting on that external and changeable marker of identity, clothes. Sheridan used a very similar parallelism. But, for him, the analogue to the female athlete's "put[ting] on a Helmet" was "put[ting] off *the Tenderness* of her own Sex": not quite her sex itself, but rather a behavioral characteristic with which it was associated. Indeed, more than the other two, Sheridan seems to have been concerned with the appearances and attributes of sexual identity ("she loves *to look manly*") – or with what we would distinguish analytically as *gender*. And, finally, in Gifford's formulation the female athlete "envies our pursuits, and hates her own": she does not cast off her sex, she does not even adopt the behavioral traits of the opposite gender. She is characterized merely by her intentions and desires – her envy of masculine ways – with no indication of her ability to assume them or to escape her own femininity. These differences, moreover, are reinforced by formal structure. The earlier texts had offered antithetical parallelisms in which both parts were supplied from *within* the female athlete's femininity, her behavior as against her sex/gender, thus underscoring in form the instability of her femininity suggested in content. Gifford, on the other hand, dodged this possibility by structuring his own parallelism around the fundamental antithesis of male/female ("our pursuits"/"her own").

These variations, representing each of the three chronological groups of

Juvenalian translations, map nicely onto the changes in understandings of sex and gender with which we are already familiar. In the mid-seventeenth-century text, sex is represented as mutable. In the early-eighteenth-century one, the key to the proposed mutability is shifted from sex to gender. And in the turn-of-the-century translation, the possible instabilities of sex *or* gender are muted or denied. This conclusion is further reinforced by the most striking deviation from the original Latin in Gifford's late translation. "She would not change her sex, not – *if she cou'd*": without any prompting for such a statement in Juvenal, Gifford seems impelled to add this parenthetical caveat, a caveat that in fact went a long way toward emptying these lines of their original meaning. Women, he told his early-nineteenth-century readers, no matter how transgressive, simply *cannot* change their sex. This was a very far cry from Stapylton's female athlete, a century and a half earlier, who had been allowed (however ironically) to don and doff her sex as easily as her helmet.[40]

Other permutations of these same lines retell the same story. Dryden's translation of 1692 also depicted the female athletes as capable of assuming manliness – indeed, even of excelling men in it – before ending this same passage thus:

> Yet to be wholly Man she wou'd disclaim;
> To quit her tenfold Pleasure at the Game,
> For frothy Praises, and an Empty Name.

Dryden left little doubt that it was possible for the female athlete to become "wholly Man": it was simply that the prize was not really worth it. Like Sheridan (and Henry Fielding, in yet another rendition of these lines in the 1720s), Dryden also left gender identity in the final call to the female athlete's choice.[41]

But now juxtapose Dryden's lines with those in Edward Owen's translation of 1785, almost a century later:

> Can helmed dames have any sense of shame,
> Who ape the man and their own sex disclaim?

Like Gifford's, Owen's female athletes are only said to "ape" men, which side-steps the question of their success in doing so. And whereas for Dryden it had been "*to be wholly Man*" that the female athletes "wou'd disclaim", for Owen, whose introduction made clear that he was closely familiar with Dryden's text, it was "*their own sex* [that they] disclaim". One can only disclaim what one could first claim: which for Owen's late-eighteenth-century female athletes was not their potential acquired masculinity, as it had been for Dryden's, but rather their "own" femininity. Perhaps even more telling was Owen's manner of handling the next two lines, those that highlight and explain the athletic woman's active choice *not* to become a man. Gifford, we recall, felt compelled to add an explicit confutation of these very lines, at the risk of losing the coherence of the text. Owen did not even bother to struggle with these lines: he simply omitted them. Not that this in itself was a unique occurrence in Owen's translation: all in all, he expunged some two hundred lines from Juvenal's Satires, declaring proudly his intention to cleanse the classical text of its more repugnant "impurities" and "grosser parts". Rather, what *is* significant in the omission of these particular lines is the fact that the seemingly innocuously phrased comment on the athletic woman's choice not to become a man joined the most explicit sexual and scatological language – on a par, that is, with graphic allusions to the female use of dildos or to homosexuals' dilapidated bottoms – in being censored by Owen as "grosser parts" unfit for late-eighteenth-century ears.[42]

Finally, we can get an unusual glimpse of the hoops that turn-of-the-century translators found themselves jumping through in contending with these lines in Francis Hodgson's effort of 1807. Thus went Hodgson's translation:

> Oh! when she puts her threat'ning helmet on,
> Then ev'ry female, modest, charm, is gone;
> Her sex is alter'd, she becomes a man,
> And violates perverted nature's plan –
> But still retains her own, her proper lust,
> For our poor pleasure has not half the gust.[43]

At first glance, these early-nineteenth-century verses seem to undermine my argument: they retain the possibility of a woman altering her sex. But while maintaining that the female athlete becomes a man, what Hodgson was at the same time denying her – no less strongly than Gifford – was the possibility of reversible choice. Gone was that flexible and self-controlled ability to don and doff gender identities which had been her most prominent asset in the earlier versions, and which by now seems to have become her most threatening aspect. In his own rendition, therefore, once the female athlete puts the helmet on, she *cannot* choose (as Juvenal had had it) not to become a man. Instead, Hodgson's alternative was to force gender into a tightly determined relationship with sex. As soon as the female athlete puts her helmet on, that is to say, as soon as her behavior approaches the masculine, her total and essential sexual identity is irrevocably "violate[d] [and] perverted". Unnatural in behavior – in gender – corresponded inexorably to unnatural in sexual essence.

And yet this transgressive female-turned-male, however consistent in her unnaturalness, left Hodgson uneasy. We know this because of a groaning footnote that he appended to the text, offering another, wishful-thinking version of this passage: one that he would have liked to substitute for the verses just quoted, had he been less constrained by a discomfiting original text. "I would recast the passage into something of this kind," he explained:

> Oh! when she puts her threat'ning helmet on,
> Then all the woman is for ever gone –
> All but one passion of her glowing soul,
> Too sweet for change, too mighty for controul.

If Hodgson had his way, then, if he could cast off the shackles of what he took to be his responsibility to his classical author, this would have been his preferred translation: a translation in which the female athlete, while still losing her womanhood, would have discovered that a sex-altered and nature-perverting manhood was no longer a mentionable option. Of course, the very fact that Hodgson felt the need to add such an unusual footnote is in itself forceful testimony to how loaded the possibilities raised in these lines had become by the beginning of the nineteenth century.[44]

*

The popularity of Juvenal in eighteenth-century England has led scholars to assert the importance of his Sixth Satire as an inspiration for images of and attitudes toward women among the classically educated classes in the long eighteenth century.[45] What such assertions obscure is the fact that the English possessed not one Sixth Satire but many different versions thereof. And yet it is precisely the existence of such a rich series of diverging renditions of the very same text that allows us to reverse the question, searching not for the marks of Juvenal's Sixth Satire in contemporary English understandings of women, but rather for the marks of contemporary understandings of women – or, more broadly, of contemporary understandings of sex and gender – in the changing forms of the Sixth Satire itself.

And indeed, although space does not permit to expand this micro-textual history here, its application to other passages in Juvenal has yielded a very similar pattern.[46] Seventeenth- and eighteenth-century translations up to the 1770s were characterized by elastic categories of gender, capacious enough – as we have seen so often before – to accommodate and even draw attention to those chinks in the armor of gender differentiation. Within these translations, furthermore, there was a divergence between the earlier ones of the seventeenth century and the second group of the middle decades of the eighteenth. The former tended to be more preoccupied with the contingencies of *sexual bodies*, arguably an indication of the transition to biologically grounded sex during precisely this period. Particularly revealing are instances in the earlier translations in which this transition proved to be not yet complete, allowing some show-through of lingering traces of the pre-modern willingness to accept the conditional nature of sex and the power of gender to shape sexual bodies; a power expressed, for instance, in surprising images of women growing beards, or urinating like men while standing up. The mid-eighteenth-century translations took for granted the stability of sexual bodies. At the same time they were more explicitly exploratory – and remarkably more relaxed – about indeterminacies of gendered behavior and appearance, not least those effected through the exercise of unfettered free will. Finally, the third group of translations, from 1785 through the early nineteenth century, signaled that sharp departure from their predecessors that we have come to recognize elsewhere. Showing visible signs of the strain, and at times stepping beyond the limits of plausibility warranted by the original text, these later translations registered time and again the increased stakes in the denial of gender instabilities, in the suppression of the possible role of choice or agency in the shaping of gender identity, and in the insistence on the determined correspondence between gender and sex. We have ended up, then, with one more piece of evidence for the late-eighteenth-century redrawing of the boundaries and movements of sex and gender. It is a perhaps unexpected piece of evidence, demonstrating that the cultural pattern we have been following, both in its earlier possibilities and its later constrictions, did in fact extend into the seemingly inaccessible recesses of masculine scholarly endeavor.

Moreover, the sharp break at the turn of the eighteenth century was once again accompanied by retrospective incomprehension of what had come before. It is thus fitting to end this discussion of Juvenalian variations with a footnote that one Charles Badham appended to his own translation of the Sixth Satire in 1814, when he reached the passage about the female athletes:

> The picture which follows is so entirely abhorrent from the habits of modern times, that it cannot now be much relished. . . . One cannot but admire [i.e. marvel] that women should not at all times have well understood their own real strength, that they should ever have had recourse to exploits which men must in every age have detested, that, in fine, they could possibly overlook the undeniable proposition that, to be amiable, a woman must be supposed to need protection.[47]

What this footnote betrayed, most of all, was a puzzled inability to imagine a gender world different from the author's own – that which was self-assuredly "undeniable", self-evidently known to men in every historical age, and (the internal inconsistency notwithstanding) at such enormous distance from the "entirely abhorrent" practices of ancient times. Indeed, viewed through such safe cultural distancing, most of the eighteenth century could not have been seen but as part of these strange, incomprehensible ancient times.

The Conventions of Prescription

If we imagine a continuum of social types according to their likely responsiveness to cultural play, ranging – say – from actors and dramatists at one end to the learned classical scholars at the opposite end, one group would find itself even beyond the extremity of the ivory tower, indeed, almost completely off the scale. These are the moralizers, pontificators, and other spoil-sports: those self-appointed guardians of social mores who set themselves deliberately against any playful trends. In the remainder of this chapter I want to look briefly at this group: in part as yet another limit test case that is *prima facie* even less likely to be subject to the patterns we have been following, in part in order to pre-empt a particular kind of skepticism that the present argument may encounter.

For surely, the skeptics might say, there is not much new in this late-eighteenth-century "gender panic": can we not find in each and every generation moralizers who speak out against gender-subverting practices? Yes, we can. After all, one cannot easily imagine many finger-wagging pontificators – even in the middle decades of the eighteenth century, long before the late-century reaction – getting up on the podium and calling on their audience to cross-dress in the name of the public good. Rather, the enduring conventions of the genre within which they expressed themselves placed rigid limitations on content. Furthermore, the fact that they were typically the most vocal, articulate, and repetitive – not to say obsessive – speakers on such issues makes their opinions very easy to find. In fact, scholars whose work has involved summary forays into these questions have often tended to dig up primarily such pronouncements – conventional pronouncements which can then be readily mobilized to support a skeptical attitude of *plus ça change . . .*

Now, on the one hand, the perils of relying on such prescriptive preachings to gauge cultural trends, when they are constrained by rigid and unchanging generic conventions, are obvious. Thus, it makes a significant difference in terms of meaning, even if not so much in terms of form, if a prescriptive outburst is riding triumphantly on top of a broader wave of cultural concerns, or stands defensively as the last desperate thumb in a dam cracking under the pressures of cultural currents flowing the other way. Recently, indeed, some historians have gone to the other extreme, dismissing prescriptive sources altogether as too far removed from real social practice to be of much relevance to their investigation: in their eyes, the Jeremiahs are always delivering their jeremiads at the gate, and the world goes on unperturbed. Some contemporaries, at least, would have agreed: "There are few things by which a man discovers the weakness of his judgment more" – thus one mid-eighteenth-century essayist – "than by retailing scraps of common-place sentiment on the tried and thread-bare topic, the degeneracy of the times."[48]

But such an attitude is too easy. First, it can readily be shown that many eighteenth-century people did read or listen to such "scraps of common-place sentiment", pondered them, sometimes reproduced them meticulously in their personal commonplace books, and tried to reconcile them in one way or another with their own lives. Second, and more important for our purpose here, the genre of the moralizing jeremiad – together with its less pessimistic flip-side, the moralizing advice book – is itself as much a cultural form as any other: so that, even if ruled by its own peculiar conventions, it still partakes of the context in which it is embedded. Rather than dismiss prescriptive exhortations, therefore, or treat them simply as a kind of background noise to be filtered out, I want to take them as a cultural site capable in and of itself of registering trends of change. The question can thus again be posed: was this particular cultural form also affected by the patterns we have been tracing? The answer requires us to listen more attentively to the nuances of prescriptive moralizing, nuances that can often be lost in the deafening shrillness of their vitriol.

Listen, for instance, to Benjamin Victor, a theatrical prompter, manager, and commentator. Victor may well have been the harshest critic of breeches parts in the middle decades of the eighteenth century. Asking in 1771 whether it was proper for actresses "to perform the Characters of Men", Victor immediately replied to his own rhetorical question: "I will venture in the Name of all sober, discreet, sensible, Spectators . . . to answer, *No!*" – since when you do so, "you *o'er step the Modesty of Nature*". Strong words, to be sure. So was this simply the timeless conventional disapproval of gender confusion that supposedly characterizes all self-appointed guardians of morality? Not quite, or at least not *just* that: for Victor also turned out to be very much in tune with his times, breeches parts and all. This became most clear when Victor came to the topic of Peg Woffington. No less than his contemporaries could Victor help but admire Woffington's "great Success in the Character of *Sir Harry Wildair*", to the point "of deceiving, and warming into Passion, any of her own Sex, if she had been unknown". Crucially, for Victor it was precisely this *success* that posed the moral danger. Here is the ending of his cautionary dictum: in breeches parts "you *o'er step the Modesty of Nature*, and when that is done, whatever may be the Applause within Doors, you will be injured by Remarks and Criticisms without". The very possibility of a successful gender-crossing (hence the applause), a possibility that Victor *affirmed* not denied, created the danger of immoral behavior and damaged reputation. Our early-nineteenth-century gender-panicked acquaintance James Boaden, by contrast, could not have disagreed more strongly. Boaden believed – or rather hoped – that Woffington's gender-crossing was inherently impossible, and that it had been only this a priori certitude, shared by every person in the audience, that had allowed her "to purify the character" of the rakish Wildair in a performance that was therefore "not only gay, but innocent". Both Victor and Boaden preached the same moralizing position with regard to the impropriety of breeches parts, and yet their assumptions about the possibilities and limits of gender categories could hardly have been further apart.[49]

It is remarkable to discover how many eighteenth-century pontifications turn out, upon close reading, to have registered so unmistakably the imprint of the *ancien régime* of gender that undergirded the very practices against which they set themselves. The list runs the risk of becoming repetitive rather quickly. Among others, it includes the well-known prescriptive writer James Fordyce, who warned women against masculine dress because it *did* in fact eliminate effectively "the distinction of form, which the Almighty had established in the creation"; or the invective likewise aimed at masculine women's dress – dress that "neither decency nor elegance can justify" – since it was so successful in adding "such a masculine fierceness to the figure" that "none but Amazons ought to wear it"; or the critic who wanted women with a penchant for such dress to "know how disgusting they appear to every man of sense or delicacy", but who was prodded into this observation – without any sense of dissonance – by the sight of a "gentleman" about whom only someone in the know could provide the "surprising" clarification "*C'est une dame*"; or the female critic who echoed, mobilizing a standard eighteenth-century tableau, "can any thing be more disgustful to a man, than to see the woman he admires in a habit so like his own, that at a distance he does not know, whether it be the captain of the guard, or the treasurer of his heart who is approaching him?"; or, finally, the 1730s epilogue that warned women against the breeches ("No more usurp the Breeches, not my own,/ But the more proper Petticoat put on") – one of the few above-mentioned exceptions to the prevalent pattern within this genre – but that did so only after making it perfectly clear that as long as the actress speaking *was* wearing the breeches, she cut a perfect and undetectable male figure. All these and many others acknowledged the possibility of successful crossings of gender boundaries even as they were denouncing their consequences. In this, they all sounded quite a different note from their counterparts of the turn of the century, speakers like Isabella Howard, the Countess of Carlisle, who in 1789 warned women to "assume no masculine airs" since "real robustness, and superior force, is denied you by nature; its semblance, denied you by the laws of decency". Nature was now the primary objection that made the transgression impossible, which left only its *semblance* to be proscribed by decency.[50]

Alternatively, a close reading of other eighteenth-century moralists' obligatory finger-wagging against the subversion of gender categories suggests that their heart was not really in it – that their more pressing concerns lay elsewhere. Thus, a standard conduct book "for the improvement and entertainment of young female minds" inveighed against "Martial exercise" as "not being at all adapted to the *delicacy* of a young lady", but then immediately coupled this warning with another against "that foolish affectation which too many women practice". What this female writer was really opposed to, it turned out, was *excess*, so that in her eyes female manliness and female hyper-delicacy were "both equally ridiculous and wrong". The same renunciation of both extremes – rather than actual gender transgression – was also the message of the loose rendition given by Fielding to a jibe at female athletes in Juvenal's Sixth Satire:

> And yet, as often as they please,
> Nothing is tenderer than these.
> A Coach! – O Gad! they cannot bear
> Such Jolting! – *John*, go fetch a Chair.
> Yet see, through *Hide-Park* how they ride!
> How masculine! almost astride!
> Their Hats fierce cock'd up with Cockades
> Resembling Dragoons more than Maids.

By setting masculine riding against its flip-side, the exaggerated feminine delicacy that prohibits riding at all, Fielding directed the satire less at gender transgression than at excess. For these women, affected femininity as well as assumed masculinity were a matter of *choice* ("as often as they please"), and one which on *both* counts could be taken too far. By contrast, a 1789 translator of Juvenal saw the same lines (while missing Juvenal's joke) as differentiating clearly between delicate women "doing right" and masculine women "doing wrong", *tout court*.[51]

But the point I want to make, in the end, is not that criticism leveled within the moralizing genre at gender-flexing behavior had been weaker before the late eighteenth century than subsequently – though it *was* the case that the tone of earlier critics was often lighter, exposing such behavior as more ridiculous than dreadful. The point, rather, is that when moralizing invective *was* voiced in the earlier period, it too bore the imprint of its times; either by not taking the crossing of the gender boundary to be at the core of transgressive behavior, or by admitting the possibility of its successful attainment even as it was denounced, or by making this success the very precondition for the moral danger it posed.

Given that these moralizing exhortations were thus simultaneously shaped by the conventions of the genre and by prevailing cultural understandings at odds with these conventions, it is not surprising that on occasion the resulting tensions rose to the surface. Allow me to present one example at some length, drawn from a country clergyman who in 1736 sermonized on the proprieties and improprieties of dress. "*We Christians*", he roared, are forbidden not only to *wear what belongs to*, but to *imitate the Dress of*, and to *endeavour to appear like* the other Sex. . . . why is it a *Shame* for a *Man* to *wear long Hair*? Why? Because, by it he *assumes the Habit of*, and endeavours to *look like, a Woman*. And is it not then *equally shameful*, to *comb*, or to *pin it up*, as they do. How *unmanly* do *they* look, *who do this?* I say, how do they *deface Manhood*, and *ridiculously depart from the Dignity* of the Sex?

No ifs and buts for this mid-eighteenth-century clergyman: his own sense of gender categories and their boundaries was as sharp as could be. Or was it? By the next sentence, in fact, we suddenly find our preacher unable to hold on to this supposed clarity: "And what makes it the more to be wondered at", he continued, is the fact that "not only the *Smooth* and the *Fair* [men] do this, but even the *Rough* and *Hard-favoured*; in the forming of whom, *Nature* seemed to be in no manner of *Doubt*, of *which Sex* to make them." Suddenly the binary structure of the biblical injunction and its moral was compromised, as the country clergyman felt compelled to distinguish between two kinds of men: the manly men whose sex nature left in no doubt, and the smooth and fair men for whom this injunction was perhaps less severe – those whom he later described in the most hackneyed of all eighteenth-century formulations as men who "would puzzle a *pretty good Grammarian* . . . [in being] of the *doubtful Gender*". However much this preacher was genuinely hoping to shore up those battered gender categories, he still remained part of a world that did not see them as wholly and dichotomously fixable.[52]

A few more examples will suffice. Take John Brown's *Estimate of the Manners and Principles of the Times*, probably the most influential jeremiad of the century. Brown's predictable peroration against effeminacy with its "unmanly Delicacies" was immediately juxtaposed with a less predictable show of *appreciation* for Queen Elizabeth's courage and physical endurance on horseback. If the conjunction of these awkwardly conflicting messages can be explained through the peculiar, non-gender-specific eighteenth-century usage of "effeminacy", consider them together with the more obviously self-contradictory case of James Fordyce. Coming to the topic of Queen Elizabeth, Fordyce felt it necessary to point out in a didactic manner that Elizabeth had been "not very amiably feminine". But then he swiftly moved to drown this fault – a fault that in a prescriptive discourse on manliness and effeminacy could be assumed to be of some importance – in a shower of praise for the Renaissance queen as the source of "the spirit of sobriety, manliness [!], and elevation" of her times. Even more awkward was the position of the author of another run-of-the-mill conduct book who actually delivered his moralizing advocacy of properly demarcated gender distinctions while *himself* being literally cross-dressed – a man writing in the guise of a mother. The peculiar eighteenth-century flavor of his situation may have been matched by that of Lady Sarah Pennington, whose contribution to the prescriptive advice on ideal motherhood was undercut (though, to judge by her success, not very seriously so) by the central revelation of the title of her work: namely, that she was a mother-in-absentia whose natural motherhood over "her absent daughters" had been transferred to a proxy. What was common to all these instances was that the supposedly immutable conventions of the moralizer's pen were inflected through, and sometimes compromised by, the peculiarities of the eighteenth-century cultural environment.[53]

I want to end this consideration of moralizers as mirrors of their times with the best illustration I have come across within this genre of what the following chapters will put forth as a key characteristic of the *ancien régime* of identity during the short eighteenth century. This final piece of conventional didacticism was written in 1755 by the recently appointed physician to King George II, Peter Shaw, in his short-lived periodical with the long-winded title *Man. A Paper for Ennobling the Species*. The fourteenth installment ennobled the species by highlighting its complementary gender distinctions: "As nature hath made a great difference in the external appearance of man and woman," it began, "we may reasonably expect to find as remarkable an one in their moral characters." Most of what followed recycled platitudes about the different abilities, virtues, and duties of men and women in their separate spheres of life. But in between Shaw introduced a significant caveat: "We only propose to consider the two sexes, *in general*; without comparing particular men with particular women. Many of the female sex are, both in body and mind, formed much stronger than many of the male: but . . . we find that the females, in general, are, both in their bodies and minds, weaker than the males." "Men" and "women" were to be considered as collective groupings or ideal types, but Shaw made it clear that his view of gender difference, schematic, fixed, and grounded in nature as it was, nevertheless allowed for occasional individuals to deviate from its prescriptions with impunity. Looked at individually, some women were indeed more manly than some men, and the fact that they were not bound by those gender categories that Shaw's essay was at such pains to reinforce was taken as unremarkable, given the limitations of these categories. Shaw even offered an example, one that was sure to resonate with his eighteenth-century audience. The virtues and duties of men, he wrote, were those that demand "magnanimity, courage, labour, and difficulty", and this remained true "though there may have been *Amazons* in the world; yet the military virtues certainly belong to men".[54] We are once again back where we started: with eighteenth-century understandings of gender categories which even at their most prescriptive were capacious enough to have both clearly defined boundaries *and* appreciation for the Amazons who galloped right through them.

3

Climate, Civilization, and Complexion: Varieties of Race

In the aftermath of the Seven Years' War, the Swiss-born professional soldier Colonel Bouquet led a dangerous expedition to the Ohio country against the Delawares, Shawnees, and Seneca Indians who appeared unaware of the fact that the war had officially ended. After a successful military encounter in the Battle of Bushy Run, Bouquet entered into negotiations with the Indians. Benjamin West's engraving of this diplomatic exchange at the fork of the Muskingum river in late 1764, which accompanied the anonymously published account of the expedition (fig. 17), shows the two rival parties, the Indians and the colonists, clearly separated by the flaming fire. The Indians are part-naked, bald or with "savage" hair styles, their physiognomies fiercely savage and their skins markedly dark; features standing in unmistakable contrast to those of the white colonists, with their light skin, their rounded physiognomies, their European clothes, and their kempt hair. West's image was all about the unmistakable visual markings of difference.

The main achievement of these negotiations was the return of men, women, and children who had been held captive by the Indians, often for many years. Their delivery into the colonists' hands was the emotional high point of the expedition, a "most affecting scene" in which the Indians brought forth beloved – albeit adopted – members of their families, often against their will, to be reclaimed by the colonists. It was a scene, claimed the narrative account, "which language indeed can but weakly describe; and to which the Poet or Painter might have repaired to enrich their highest colorings of the variety of human passions". The artist who answered the call was again Benjamin West, in a second engraving accompanying the text (fig. 18). Here, suddenly, the beholder encounters a rather different gloss on Indian–European difference. Instead of the clear separation of Indians and whites as in the first image, in this one Indians and Europeans – men, women, and children – commingle in one dense

17. "The Indians
Giving a Talk to
Colonel Bouquet in a
Conference at a
Council Fire", Oct.
1764, engraving after
Benjamin West by
Charles Grignion

sea of humanity. In this the image did little more than reproduce the mood of
the text which pointed to this moment as proof of the underlying humanity of
the Indians, a humanity that came into view when the proceedings induced
them to "wholly forg[et] their usual savageness". Their savageness, it further
maintained, was proven to be the result of mere "wrong education", and thus
presumably to be eradicable. And indeed, the savageness of the Indians proved
eradicable even from their visual countenances. With the possible exception of
one figure (behind the child on the right), the physiognomies of the Indians in
West's second engraving were humane rather than fierce, and really not all that
different from the European ones. Likewise, skin color lost its differentiating
effect, with the variations between visages that appeared darker or brighter –
on both sides – being the apparent consequence of lighting in the composition
rather than of group identity. West, however, did not intend wholly to erase the
difference between Indians and Europeans: this is marked plainly enough in

18. "The Indians
Delivering up the
English Captives to
Colonel Bouquet",
Nov. 1764, engraving
after Benjamin West
by Canot

their respective dress and hair styles. But this is precisely what makes West's image so interesting: what remained as the guiding marks of distinction were dress and fashion, those external and mutable attributes, but not the traits of complexion and physiognomy that some might consider as more reliable, perhaps even immutable, markers of difference. Precisely as the text had suggested, the distinction between Indians and Europeans proved to be contingent, circumstantial, and alterable; doubly so, in fact, if one keeps in mind the striking difference between this representation of the Indians and the earlier one depicting the diplomatic negotiations between (male) enemies.[1]

Up to a point, one could account for these observations with reference to the fact that these two images represented rather different alignments of Europeans and Indians – the one of antipathy, the other of empathy. But this obscures important insights that West's efforts to represent "the variety of human passions" can offer us about contemporary understandings of the variety – and variability – of human forms. What does it mean for West to have located human diversity in the external and contingent, rather than in the supposedly immutable physical body? What does it mean for him to have implied that the particulars of the physical body – complexion, physiognomy – were eradicable? For an eighteenth-century beholder, this possibility could well have conjured up a familiar theme in early-modern discussions of Europeans in captivity: namely, their gradual metamorphosis as they became increasingly indistinguishable from their adoptive captors. Thus a seventeenth-century Englishman who had lived for three years among the Indians in Virginia was reputed to have become "so like an *Indian*, in Habit and Complexion, that [the witness] knew him not but by his Tongue". (The skin of a "Virginean" Indian living in England, by the same token, was said to have become "so farre from a Moores or East or West Indians" as to look perfectly English.) A twelve-year-old boy from Maine, after a two-year captivity, "ever after appeared more like an Indian than a white man". A mid-eighteenth-century captive described his family's surprise "to see me so much like an Indian". And another in the first half of the eighteenth century, one John Tarbell, reappeared among his relatives after many years in captivity not only "in his Indian dress" but also "with his Indian complexion". The text accompanying West's engraving also invoked this familiar scenario, telling of "sisters and brothers unexpectedly meeting together after long separation, scarce able to speak the same language, or, for some time, to be sure that they were children of the same parents!" As one contemporary summarized it, it was common knowledge that white captives in such circumstances acquired "a great resemblance to the savages, not only in their manners, but in their colour and the expression of the countenance".[2]

Whites who become indistinguishable from Indians, "savages" and Europeans differentiated through dress but not necessarily through their bodies, "racial passing", understandings of complexion and skin color predicated on climate, or culture, or civilization: these are the kinds of conceivable configurations reflecting eighteenth-century notions of race that are the focus of what follows, as we move from the *ancien régime* of gender to the *ancien régime* of race. "Race" is used here strictly as a descriptive term, since, as will become immediately clear, the very meaning of race is what was at stake: throughout most of the eighteenth century – and before – "race" was understood in ways very different from its modern meaning. At the same time we will see affinities between these earlier understandings of race and those of gender that will alert us to possible shared characteristics of the *ancien régime* of identity: both categories were perceived to be potentially malleable, unfixed, unreliable, changeable through circumstances or even through self-conscious choice. Moreover, I will suggest that, like gender, race underwent a transformation beginning in the closing decades of the eighteenth century, replacing malleability and fluidity with increasing emphasis on innate and essential nature. This is not to say, however, that these categories and their developments – or the ones to be added later (the boundary between human and animal, and the category of class) – were simply parallel or somehow the same. We will see important differences in the respective evolution of their internal developments over time. Yet in key ways their eighteenth-century histories display significant homologies that allow us, I believe, to speak of meta-patterns pertaining to them all.

At the same time, the differences between the categories of gender and race also place limits on our ability to repeat for race the comprehensive exercise we have undertaken for gender. Importantly, in metropolitan culture race was an object of peripheral vision rather than of central focus. As Laura Brown – pioneering the study of both these eighteenth-century categories in relation to each other – has put it, gender was "a category of difference constituted primarily within the geographical purview of the dominant culture", and thus integral to the warp and weft of the cultural fabric. But for Britons not living in imperial peripheries, by contrast, "the understanding of race in this period, despite the increasing visibility of non-European racial groups in England, remain[ed] mainly extrinsic, geographically foreign, a category of difference defined as an external object".[3] Race therefore impinged upon metropolitan culture less frequently. And when it did, it was less often as the unintended subtext of cultural forms not concerned primarily with race – those that can therefore reveal underlying and semi-unselfconscious habits of thought, as we have seen in the case of gender – but rather more in explicit statements directed specifically at the subject.

Moreover, the picture for the category of race will prove to be messier than that for gender, and this because of the very different place that the late eighteenth century occupied in their respective internal evolutions. For sex/gender, as we have seen, the late eighteenth century marked the final stage in a long process of transformation from pre-modern to modern understandings – a transformation that had begun at least a full century earlier. For race, I will suggest, this period represented more the beginning of a gradual dislodging from its pre-modern moorings, likewise a long process of realignment that was to be fully visible only decades later, in the mid-nineteenth-century certitudes of scientific racism. As a consequence the late-eighteenth-century picture for race is one less of sweeping, unified clarity, and more one of transitional multiplicity and confusion. But the contours of change, I believe, are unmistakable.

*

The natural place to begin a survey of eighteenth-century (and more broadly early-modern) understandings of race is climate. In the colonization of India,

Mark Harrison writes, a key question was the possibility of acclimatization: could the Europeans adapt to life in the tropics? According to Harrison, there was a clear shift in colonial medical discourse in the responses that were offered to this question. Prior to 1800 he sees guarded optimism about the prospects of such acclimatization. Toward the end of the eighteenth century, however, this optimism began to fade, a shift that Harrison links to changes in ideas about race as well as to the consolidation of colonial rule.[4]

As Harrison points out, the earlier optimism was a consequence of the prevalent belief that human diversity can be explained through the external effects of the natural environment ("climate" here was taken to include soil, topography, etc.). "It seems agreeable to Reason and Experience", John Arbuthnot affirmed in 1733, "that the Air operates sensibly in forming the Constitutions of Mankind, the Specialities of Features, Complexion, Temper, and consequently the Manners of Mankind, which are found to vary much in different Countries and Climates." So much so that, "in perusing the Accounts of the Temper and Genius of the Inhabitants of different Countries" – such as the Gauls and the French – "we discover in them a great Uniformity, even tho' the Race [i.e. stock] has been changed." A similar effect could be predicted even for Laplanders if they were transplanted to Paris. "Let us then be contented", Oliver Goldsmith echoed in 1760, "in accounting for the variety of the human species, to attribute it to the diversity of climate alone. . . . It is climate alone which tinctures the negroes skin." These were common refrains among eighteenth-century European literati. Among their most notable popularizers were two French aristocrats – Charles de Secondat, Baron de Montesquieu, who counted John Arbuthnot among his sources, and Georges Louis Leclerc, Comte de Buffon, who in turn was a major influence on Oliver Goldsmith.[5]

The sway of climatic theory in the eighteenth century is familiar, and need not detain us long. Its significance for our inquiry is readily evident: climatic understanding of human diversity was intertwined with an acceptance of the mutability of those physical traits that were later to become the hallmarks of race. If climate was the cause of human variance, went this pre-modern logic, then a change of climate should alter these traits of difference. Nothing, therefore, could prove – or disprove – the climatic viewpoint more effectively than the consideration of people who moved from one part of the world to another. And sure enough, as Harrison notes, up to the 1770s (a chronological signpost to keep in mind) reputable medical men maintained that Europeans settling in the tropics would become blacker over generations. According to contemporary medical wisdom, this was but one manifestation of a broader physical adaptation, whereby (in the words of the naval surgeon James Lind in 1768) "the constitution of Europeans becomes seasoned to the East and West Indian climates". So much so, in fact, that some even believed that their constitutions had become

"Indianized" to such a degree that they could no longer go back home. "I am so afraid of you returning to me looking black," one woman wrote anxiously to her husband in India. In fictional writing this notion of "seasoning" produced the trope of the traveler long gone to some tropical region or other, who then returns only to have become unrecognizable to former loved ones; a transformation induced, as one literary character put it, by "the alteration the climate had wrought in me". More scientific texts tended to point to the alteration that climate had produced on migrating groups, like the Spaniards and Portuguese who had settled on the coast of Africa and who were reputed to have "become almost as black as the Negroes". While many writers went to great lengths to explain why the reverse alteration did not readily occur, others occasionally claimed that it did, as in the case of the writer who asserted in 1776 that "blacks in France, turn tawny . . . because the sun is not strong enough".[6]

But no group seemed to provide better proof of the ultimate effects of climate on race than the Jews. "The jews", went one typical example, "who had fled into the southern provinces of Asia and Africa had been all more or less metamorphosed, according to the greater or less degrees of heat in the climate; but that those particularly, who had settled in Abyssinia, were not to be distinguished, either by their physiognomy or colour, from the natives themselves." "No example can carry with it greater force on this subject than that of the Jews," echoed another;

> descending from one stock, prohibited by their most sacred institutions from intermarrying with other nations, and yet dispersed, according to the divine predictions, into every country on the globe, this one people is marked with the colours of all. Fair in Britain and Germany, brown in France and in Turkey, swarthy in Portugal and in Spain, olive in Syria and in Chaldea, tawny or copper-coloured in Arabia and in Egypt.

The Jews, another put it simply, "visibly partake of the Nature of those nations among which they live". Only such a presupposition of the unbounded mutability of the Jews could account for the frontispiece of the late-seventeenth-century eyewitness account of Lancelot Addison – an Anglican clergyman and father of the better-known Joseph Addison – of the Jews in Barbary (fig. 19). The person in the image, supposedly representing a North African Jew, was indistinguishable in attire, accessories, and dark skin color from a Moor (or really an American Indian?).[7] The striking incongruity of this image, in our eyes, highlights the distance we have traveled since those earlier understandings of physiognomy and color as mutable, contingent, and ultimately unreliable markers of identity.

A corrective similar to that introduced earlier with regard to gender is again in order. Just as fluid notions of gender did not necessarily imply weaker

19.   A Jew, a Moor, or an American
Indian? Frontispiece to [Lancelot
Addison,] *The Present State of the
Jews: (More Particularly Relating to
Those in Barbary)*, London, 1675

patriarchal hierarchy, so there was no necessary correlation – our modern sensibilities notwithstanding – between the eighteenth-century emphasis on the
mutability of "race" and a critique of racialist hierarchies of subjugation and
domination. Thus outspoken environmentalists could at the same time be
downright racialists. Oliver Goldsmith's conclusion that environmental factors
produced "all the variations in the human figure, as far as they differ from our
own" did not stop him from continuing in the next sentence: "they are actual
marks of degeneracy of the human form; and we may consider the European
figure and colour as standards to which to refer all other varieties, and with
which to compare them." Sir Richard Blackmore, at the beginning of the
century, was even more blunt. Writing a full-blown poem designed "to express
how far the Disparity of the intellectual Faculties Dispositions and Passions of
Men is owing to the different Situation of their native Countries in respect of
the Sun", he drew from this climatic perspective a clear sense of hierarchy and
superiority:

In vain you hope illustrious Youth will shine
Beneath th'AEquator, or th'Ecliptic Line;
Where Sun-burnt Nations of a swarthy Skin
Are sully'd o'er with blacker Clouds within.
Their Spirits suffer by too hot a Ray,
And their dry Brain grows dark with too much Day.

Pre-modern England – a nation, after all, deeply invested in Atlantic slavery –
was hardly innocent of strongly held beliefs in the superiority of some groups
of humans over others; beliefs of which perhaps the best-known enunciation
was David Hume's notorious footnote about the inferiority of blacks ("I am apt
to suspect the negroes . . . to be naturally inferior to the whites. There scarcely
ever was a civilized nation of that complexion").[8] But of course, the very supposition that what we would today call racism necessarily requires innate and
stable ideas of race postdates – and is predicated upon – the emergence of such
ideas as widely resonant; a development that in the middle of the eighteenth
century was as yet an insignificant blob on the horizon.

Insignificant blob, to be sure, does not mean non-existent. Once again we
arrive at the distinction between intellectual and cultural history: the issue here
is not the *origins* of certain notions of race, or their first recorded appearances
on the historical stage, but rather the significance of the parts they were allot-
ted to play on that stage. Thus, I certainly do not want to suggest that climatic
theory was the only available way of conceptualizing human diversity and variations in human complexion in the eighteenth century. On the contrary, the
point is that contemporaries evinced a wider range of possibilities in racial
thinking than their modern successors. One can find, for instance, the occasional essentializing view of innate racial identity: some – both enraged contemporaries and disappointed scholars – have taken Hume's footnote to be such
a statement. But at this stage in the evolution of race, when the opposition of
its mutable and essential understandings was not necessarily diametric, it was
not always self-evident what such views actually meant. Thus it was not necessarily an a priori belief in ontological racial difference that was revealed in
Hume's footnote: rather, says Emmanuel Eze, it was doubts about Negroes' susceptibility to *civilization* that led Hume to essentializing assumptions about
their epistemological deficiencies.[9] More to the point, throughout the short
eighteenth century – up to the pending turn of the wheel, to be discussed
shortly – the essentializing racialists were minority voices that did not sound
the dominant cultural note.

At the other extreme, we can also find the occasional story falling from
the eighteenth-century presses implying that complexion was even more
contingent, indeed unpredictably capricious – rather, that is, than predictably

correlated with the environment. Such was the effect of reports of white children born to black parents (the phenomenon of albinism was not well understood), or of white mothers giving birth to black or "checkered" babies, or of same-birth twins of different skin colors, or of a remote tribe of milk-white Indians. One account recycled in both the scientific and the popular press told "of the Remarkable Alteration of Colour in a Negro Woman" who had gradually metamorphosed into a woman as white as "a fair European".[10] But in the end, the views of the diversity of human complexion either as capricious and immaterial or as innate and all-encompassing both failed to offer during this period a resonant alternative to climatic theory (which in itself was making an eighteenth-century comeback, after a certain dip in its fortunes in the seventeenth century).[11] At the same time, however, there *was* another way of understanding human diversity that held considerable sway during the short eighteenth century, and that, although often discussed and held together with climatic theory, was in fact distinct: the attribution of diversity to human-made differences – differences, that is, in culture.

The most detailed investigation of this viewpoint to date has been undertaken by literary critic Roxann Wheeler in her *The Complexion of Race*. Throughout the first three-quarters of the eighteenth century, Wheeler argues, cultural markers of difference "were *more explicitly* important . . . than physical attributes such as skin color, shape of the nose, or texture of the hair. Embodied in dress, manners, and language, the concepts of Christianity, civility, and rank were not simply abstract categories of difference; they constituted visible distinctions that are difficult for us to recover." While acknowledging the importance of climatic theory, Wheeler suggests that cultural differentiation assumed particular importance during this period. In part, she attributes this to the influence of the "four-stage theory" of human development emanating from Scotland, which placed all societies on a universal scale of evolutionary stages along the line from savagery to civilization.[12] Surely this makes sense – the Scottish stadial theory was one that privileged civilization, or culture, as a marker of difference, and that had mutability ingrained in its very presuppositions. But at the same time note also the parallels between this observation and those we have made regarding the centrality of culture to understandings of *gender* in the short eighteenth century: parallels that indicate a broader underlying pattern within which the culturalism of the four-stage theory should be understood.

Wheeler's most interesting evidence comes from the fictional sub-genre of "intermarriage novels": that is, novels involving marriage across "racial" lines. Unlike the social opprobrium heaped upon interracial sex in the nineteenth and twentieth centuries, Wheeler finds a rather different world in these eighteenth-century stories, one in which interracial relationships could be looked straight in the eye – indeed, often with a sanguine gaze. Sanguine, primarily, because of their transformative potential: while complexion was not necessarily an important factor in this eighteenth-century genre, culture and, above all, religion were. Consequently it repeatedly allowed for the effective erasure, through religious-cum-cultural education and conversion, of the gulf that had separated the protagonists at the beginning. One tale of 1736, for example, recounted the successful journey of a Muslim woman – via a stint in masculine disguise (the gender-playful conventions of the female-warrior narratives turn up in these race-playful stories with remarkable frequency) – to Christian culture. In another story of 1744, the daughter of a mixed-race (English–Indian) marriage departs India by disguising herself – again – as a black male slave; a successful gender-and-race crossing that she then reverses by washing her skin and donning European clothes, before she completes her religio-cultural transformation. And yet another, of 1767, is even more remarkable: in this novel the protagonist appears as a Christian Englishman, but is in fact a Muslim, who passes so well that he wins the love of his French amour and the consent of her parents for their marriage. The complex resolution involves the cross-dressing of the protagonist as a woman together with a Muslim woman who disguises herself as a black male servant: by the end of such a contrived plot, few markers of identity retain their integrity – and confidence is restored only via the transformative effects of religious conversion.[13]

In previous centuries, as many scholars have pointed out, "the rhetoric of human difference was almost always framed in religious terms" (Alden Vaughan, summing up decades of interest in this subject). Unsurprisingly, one can readily find religion still playing such a role during the period we are interested in here. Thus, a late-seventeenth-century planter revealingly rejected the idea of Christianizing slaves: "*What, those black Dogs be made Christians? What, shall they be like us?*" Upon conversion, that is, blacks would become "like us": the main crux of difference would have been removed. The same logic underlay the early-eighteenth-century travelogue to Gambia referring to black translators who "Here, thro' Custom (being Christians) . . . account themselves White Men".[14] Significantly, another religious interpretation of human difference that had been prevalent earlier but that was less conducive to a mutable view of race – the attribution of blackness to the biblical curse of Ham – declined in importance in the eighteenth century. Moreover, by this period the mutability of race no longer necessarily depended on religious conversion. Rather, religion was now often blended with – or overshadowed by – markers of cultural difference such as custom, education, and level of civilization.[15]

An interesting case in point is the furore that was provoked in 1753 by the "Jew Bill", a somewhat misleading label for a rather limited alteration proposed in the requirements for the naturalization of foreign Jews as British subjects. The debate over the Bill spawned hundreds of public interventions – pamphlets, parliamentary speeches, short pieces in the press, *jeux d'esprit*, and the like. As Thomas Perry has observed in his detailed study of this episode, and as my own readings have confirmed, opposition to the Jew Bill was predicated primarily on restrictionist economic views, on fears for English landownership and the Church, and on xenophobia compounded by anti-Semitism – but was only rarely, even in this last instance, expressed in what can be conceived of as racial terms. James Shapiro, in his excellent discussion of early-modern representations of Jews in England, has since called for more attention to be paid to those racial elements in the debate, unusual as they might have been.[16] Indeed, these are very telling, and well worth a short pause.

One of the most extreme and unusual examples of racialized language was the parliamentary speech of the Duke of Bedford, which Shapiro quotes at some length. Suppose we wanted to naturalize blacks, said the Duke. That would be ridiculous, since they cannot be assimilated, unless we also stipulate that they convert to Christianity and intermarry with whites. Under such circumstances, the Duke continued to weave his hypothetical scenario, "their progeny would in time unite and coalesce with the rest of the people. It might a little alter the complexion of the people of these islands; but they would all be the same people." But – thus the triumphant conclusion – this could never be achieved with the Jews: "for their latest posterity whilst they continue Jews, will continue to be, and will consider themselves as a people quite distinct and separate from the ancient people of this island." For Bedford, Shapiro concludes, Jewishness was an essence even more ineradicable than blackness: a just observation, but one that does not really take into account the fact that for this mid-eighteenth-century speaker, however ironically, the difference signaled by blackness was not really all that ineradicable. (That this was not a completely frivolous scenario is indicated by the contemporary who a few years later put forth precisely the same combination of conversion and intermarriage as a means to be seriously considered for "uniting the [North American] Indians into one people with ourselves".) Moreover, Shapiro does not acknowledge the key caveat posited by Bedford, namely that this ineradicable essence remained so only "*whilst they continue Jews*". Conversion, in other words, had the Jews been willing, would have assimilated them as effectively as blanching the blacks: even at this racialized extreme, religion remained the key to racial difference.[17]

Others in the opposition had it somewhat differently. Whereas Bedford worried about the unconverted Jews remaining an alien and separate element in the midst of British society, some contemporaries were anxious not that the Jews would remain alien and separate, but precisely the opposite – that they would blend in among Britons to the point of non-recognition. Thus, the scare tactics of one anti-Jew Bill compilation included this couplet, supposedly sung by the triumphant Jews:

> We shall grow *truer Englishmen*
> The more we live among ye.

Another opponent of the Bill similarly rhymed:

> Such actions as these most apparently shews,
> That if the Jews are made English, the English are Jews.

The danger was that a mere change in the law would allow naturalized Jews to become indistinct from the English: a prospect echoing those eighteenth-century descriptions of the Jews blending in indistinguishably with every nation among which they live. (One is reminded of the flip side of the coin by Addison's admission in *The Spectator* of the ease with which he would "sometimes pass for a *Jew* in the Assembly of Stock-Jobbers at *Jonathan*'s".) That these markers of difference would ultimately prove unreliable and eradicable was a worrisome possibility, moreover, precisely because it was *not* produced by religious conversion but simply by cultural passing. So much so, indeed, that an *apologist* for the Bill thought it best to deny this possibility by insisting that the Jews, wherever they found themselves across the globe, "were never so blended and incorporated with the Subjects of their Conquerors, as to lose their own separate Existence" – and this through their deliberate choice to remain "separated and distinguished from the rest of Mankind". What was to guarantee the integrity of English identity, then, was not some ineradicable natural barrier to assimilation – other peoples in similar situations, the author admitted, had been "absolutely absorbed" – but rather the Jews' deliberate cultural choice.[18] Ultimately, whether the Jews were a threat or not, the debate made clear how malleable were its underlying categories of difference.

Nothing perhaps demonstrates better the regime of racial identity within which the Jew Bill debates were taking place than the anti-Bill pamphlet that Shapiro actually cites as the best example of racial prejudice. Harping on the old idea that Jews were literally black – seemingly, that is, the most racialized thinking possible – the heavy-handed pamphleteer advised those English readers who wanted to enjoy the new Jewish privileges on ways to make themselves look like Jews. "In order to bring the Skin to a lively Complexion, like that of a new Negro from the Coast of Guinea", went his instructions, take "the Peeling" of "Walnuts" and "carefully rub the Flesh Night and Morning for three Weeks together. Afterwards rub yourselves with a Flesh-Brush," and "it will . . . fix such an indelible Hew that will not come off in six Weeks with all the Water and Soap you can use to it, and this in order to make you compleat Olive Beauties." This was indeed eighteenth-century racial prejudice at its most blatant. Yet it also demonstrates the limits of racial thinking at this juncture. Far from insisting on racial features as essential and innate, the very presentation of difference, sarcastic as it was, was filtered through the contemporary understanding of the physical characteristics of race as mutable, or even as manufacturable, donned or doffed at will (the writer also recommended the fabrication of Jewish looks through "artificial Beards" and "false Hair").[19] Here, the pamphleteer was tapping into a contemporary theme that went far beyond the physical characteristics of the Jews.

*

Consider, for instance, next to the Jews, the early-modern encounters with North American Indians. To the extent that climate was supposed to account for variations in complexion, the Indians presented a difficulty, given the variety of (often cold) climatic conditions in which they lived. Contemporaries were quick to explain: the Indians "use many methods to darken their skins by art, painting them with red oker, and anointing them with the fat of bears". Their "dusky Complexion" is such "because they daub themselves with Bear's Grease and other unctious Substances". "Were it not for the practice of going naked in summer and besmearing themselves with bears grease, etc., they would continue white." "Their skin [is] as white as ours when they are born", but the practice of rubbing babies with bear's oil and exposing them to the sun "gives a red colour to their skin . . . that no time can efface".[20] The Indians, it turned out, manufactured their "swarthy", "olive", or "red" complexions. As for the question "why?", some writers speculated on the functional advantages of painting the skin (it "fills the Pores" – thus one early-eighteenth-century writer – "and enables them better to endure the Extremity of the Weather"). Others, tellingly, explained this practice as a consequence of deliberate aesthetic choice: "the copper colour of the Americans is regarded among them as a criterion of beauty; and it seems to be the object of art, by painting the face with vermilion, to maintain, in all its perfection, the predominant complexion of the Indian race." And again: "they delight in every thing, which they imagine may promote and increase [red color]: accordingly, they paint their faces with vermilion, as the best and most beautiful ingredient." The latter writer, in one of the most detailed discussions of the subject, assured his readers in 1775 that "the Indian colour is not natural", but "is merely accidental, or artificial". It was produced by their "extraordinary anointings and paintings" in which they employed "a certain red root, which, by a peculiar property, is able alone, in a few years time, to produce the Indian colour in those who are white born, and who have even advanced to maturity". That and more: "the colour being once thoroughly established, nature would, as it were, forget herself, not to beget her own likeness", so that "a different colour may be conveyed to the foetus by the parents". The triumph of culture over nature was complete. As Joyce Chaplin has observed, this characterized the colonial understanding of the making of Indian bodies more broadly – an understanding that attributed the peculiarities of these bodies more to the effects of Indian customs, and especially child-rearing practices, than to either climatic or racially inherent factors.[21]

The American Indians, one might object, have always constituted a peculiar case. Alden Vaughan – taking his cue from Thomas Jefferson – has traced a long-standing tendency to play down the differences in complexion between Indians and Europeans, which stood in contrast to how the latter had viewed Africans. This contrast, however, may have been more circumstantial than inevitable. Thus, a close look at European representations of Africans suggests that, while comments on their skin color were certainly more pronounced, they were not necessarily anchored in immutable and innate nature, as is implied in Vaughan's juxtaposition. Kathleen Brown has advocated a revision of our customary ways of thinking about blackness in the early-modern period (derived, above all, from the monumental opus of Winthrop Jordan). Such a revision should give more weight to the role of culture in contemporary notions of difference: in early-modern discussions of Africans, she asserts, "it is sometimes difficult to tell where cultural difference ends and physical difference begins".[22] For our purposes here, a good example that illustrates the underlying contingency in understandings of racial difference is that of the contemporary accounts of the Khoikhoi – the "Hottentots" – of South Africa.

Listen, for instance, to John Hunter, an army physician (not to be confused with his namesake the eminent surgeon) who lectured on "the varieties of man" in 1775. Against new notions of distinct human races that started to circulate during this decade (as we shall shortly see), Hunter emphasized the mutability of human characteristics. While allowing that climate was undoubtedly important in producing differences between humans, as well as pure chance ("if you take such differences as evidence of distinct species," he therefore queried, "would not different species be produced in almost every single family?"), Hunter gave a key role to culture. "There is nothing in which men differ so much as in their customs," he wrote, and therefore different nations, "although they are exposed to the same external causes, still remain different" since they live "in very different ways". To illustrate this, Hunter referred his listeners to the example of Africa, and to the most visible of all human differences, namely black skin: "And this seems to be confirmed by the use of washes, with which the blacks besmear themselves, so as to make themselves blacker." Through deliberate manipulation (transferable – mysteriously, as Hunter admitted – to offspring), "their bodies are rendered blacker, or, as they think, more beautiful".[23] Like the North American Indians, Africans too were supposedly

manufacturing their skin color, at least in part, to suit their aesthetic preferences. An earlier writer, John Harris (who was to become Secretary to the Royal
Society), had elaborated at some length on the possible origins of such aesthetic
preferences in the warmer parts of the world. Their first inhabitants, he suggested, often became swarthy by virtue of the climate, especially those "who
were bold and active Men at Hunting, Fishing, or Feats of War"; as such, they
"would come by degrees to value themselves on the Colour their Bodies had
gain'd by such brave and heroic Exploits". Surely, therefore, "when this *adust
Hew* was once grown honourable, would not every one affect it, and even use
Arts and *Pigments* to procure it?" Harris even had an explanation for the "mysterious" transmission of this acquired taste from one generation to another:
namely, through the effects of the mother's imagination on the foetus.[24] Once
again, culture triumphed over nature.

In making these assertions, Hunter – like Harris – was relying on a familiar
theme in contemporary reports from Africa, especially with regard to the
"greasing" practices of the relatively fair-skinned Hottentots, who had always
held a special place in the proto-anthropological imagination. It is "not that [the
Hottentots] are naturally so black, but they make themselves so by daubing
themselves with Soot and stinking Grease" (1718). In fact, "their Children,
when they are young, are sometimes inclining to be White; and were it not for
their nasty way of greazing them" they would remain that way (1707). "The
Hottentots . . . [have] a Custom, observ'd from their Infancy, of besmearing
their Bodies . . . with Butter of Sheep's Fat, mix'd with Soot that gathers about
their Boiling Pots, in order to make 'em look black, being naturally, as I have
said already, of a Nut- or Olive-Colour. Of this Custom . . . they are so devoutly
observant, that they will not omit it on any Account in the World" (1738).
"They continue constantly to rub themselves with oil or grease, and by degrees
become almost a jet black" (1777).[25] Just as Hunter suggested, the credence
given to such accounts throughout most of the eighteenth century is a testimony to the flexibility and culturalism of contemporary views of racial difference, just as their subsequent disappearance – to which we shall shortly turn
our attention – is a testimony to the beginnings of a profound shift.

But first, recall how we got here. By now, in light of these representations of
North American Indians and South African Hottentots, the ironic how-to
manual for blackening Englishmen into Jews begins to seem less outlandish
(even if no less racialist) than it might have appeared at first glance. Presumably this notion likewise did not seem outlandish when it resurfaced in those
eighteenth-century accounts of captives of the Indians who had become indistinguishable from their captors. At the beginning of this chapter we encountered one John Tarbell, who had reappeared among his relatives after many
years in captivity "in his Indian dress and with his Indian complexion": in fact,

the same report also told its readers how Tarbell actively contributed to this complexion "by means of grease and paints [so that] but little difference could be discerned". The same active assistance being given to nature was also reported in the case of "a Pennsylvanian, a white man by birth", who, within four years of being taken captive by the Shawnee Indians, "by the inclemency of the sun, and his endeavours of improving the red colour, was tarnished with as deep an Indian hue, as any of the camp".[26]

In truth, given the regular recurrence of such comments, we may begin to wonder how often contemporaries, upon first encounters with peoples whose complexion appeared different and unfamiliar, instinctively tried to explain away these differences – all the more so when climatic reasoning proved inadequate – as artificial and man-made. Thus, the Gypsies, say, were asserted by a mid-century writer to be Germans whose Egyptian-looking "subfusk complexions were probably acquired by greasy unguents and suliginous mixtures dried in by the sun". Judging by the most comprehensive cluster of new encounters with completely unfamiliar peoples in the eighteenth century, those that occurred during the exploration of the South Pacific in the 1760s and especially the 1770s, this instinctive reaction appears to have been far from uncommon. Take, for instance, John Hawkesworth, the first person to describe Captain Cook's voyages in print, on the New Zealanders: "The skins of these people, however, are not only dyed, but painted, for as I have before observed, they smear their bodies with red oker." Or take Captain Cook himself, on the Marquesas Islands: "The men are punctured, or curiously *tattooed*, from head to foot. . . . These punctuations make them look dark; but the women, who are but little punctuated, youths, and young children who are not at all, are as fair as some Europeans." Or Captain Cook again, in North America, on the inhabitants of Nootka Sound: "Their colour we could never positively determine, as their bodies were incrusted with paint and dirt; though, in particular cases, when these were well rubbed off, the whiteness of the skin appeared almost to equal that of Europeans. . . . Their children, whose skins had never been stained with paint, also equalled ours in whiteness." Or Cook yet again, on the inhabitants of the island of Tanna: "They make themselves blacker than they really are, by painting their faces with a pigment of the colour of black lead."[27] The pattern, seemingly extending across the globe, is at the very least suggestive. In the case of the last observation, moreover, William Hodges's accompanying illustration (engraved by William Woollett) drove the point home: in "View in the Island of Tanna" (fig. 20), the men appear strikingly darker than the women, who by contrast are almost white. The reader, presumably, was expected to understand this difference, as Cook had observed elsewhere, as a result of the women not being painted like the men, and thus displaying the natural, untampered-with complexion of the inhabitants.

20. "View in the Island of Tanna", 1776, engraving after William Hodges by William Woollett, in James Cook, *A Voyage towards the South Pole*, London, 1777

This image from Tanna merits a short digression, in light of the discussion in the previous chapters. For what Hodges's image lacked in terms of *racial* distinctions – that is, in terms of setting a clear complexion regime to separate the European travelers (and readers) from the local inhabitants – it appeared to make up in *gender* distinctions, using skin color to maintain a clear distinction between local men and women. This emphasis on gender clarity is especially revealing when considered against an episode that Cook recounted from the visit to Tanna. Cook noted certain advances that the locals had made toward one of his men, which suggested that they "were addicted to an unnatural passion". But it then transpired that the islanders "considered him as a female; till, by some means, they discovered their mistake, on which they cried out . . . It's a man! It's a man!" Cook explained: "As the carrying of bundles, &c. is the office of the women in this country, it had occurred to me . . . that the natives might mistake him, and some others, for women." Here, as often during these voyages, the encounter with other peoples reminded the European travelers of the unreliable limits of the category of gender. We should keep in mind that, although it is heuristically sensible to separate our discussions of gender and race in the *ancien régime* of identity, in truth the two were often closely intertwined (as we have seen, for instance, in the inseparable gender-cum-racial masquerading that pervades Wheeler's intermarriage novels).[28] In the case of Tanna, the inability to hold fast to distinctions of gender during the encounter with the islanders was particularly menacing and clearly preyed on the Europeans' minds; which may explain the choice in the accompanying image to focus more heavily on a reaffirmation of clear gender distinctions – those that the adjoining text admitted to have been conditional and unclear – at the expense of racial ones.

But to return to my present storyline, concerned as it is with the understandings of human diversity – or race – in the first three-quarters of the eighteenth century. Jews and Indians, Hottentots and Pacific Islanders: as John Hunter clearly saw, they all bore the marks – often literally – of the contemporary acknowledgement of the contingency, unreliability, and even culturally mediated malleability of racial distinctions. Whereas climatic and environmental views, as well as those focusing on religion, had been around long before the eighteenth century, secular human agency – in the forms of education, custom, and civilization – appears to have been a more peculiarly eighteenth-century addition to the mix. This, after all, was the purpose of Hume's mid-century essay "Of National Characters", however awkwardly vitiated by the footnote on the Negroes: that is, to assert the primacy of "moral" causes – those involving human agency – over the "physical" causes of air and climate in the shaping of differences between people. Shortly thereafter, in 1765, the *Monthly Review* used the American example to make precisely this argument. Despite climatic variation in North America, it quoted a book by the Frenchman Father Gerdil, "the uncivilized Indians differed no ways one from the others", from which observation Gerdil – and the *Monthly* reviewer – concluded that "it is, therefore, very evident, that the want of a civil education has an equal influence on entire nations which inhabit very different climates, and that in the same climate education has the power of civilizing those who enjoy the advantages of it, though the nation they spring from, should be totally barbarous." Civilization trumps climate. The attribution of human variety to environmental causes, Peter Shaw had likewise written, "is absurdly pretending to the inferior properties of brutes, and vegetables, which manifestly derive peculiar excellencies from climate". But humans were not vegetables: even the greatest differences observable between them, Shaw insisted, like those between the Europeans and the Laplanders or the Hottentots, were the consequence of differences not in climate but in education. "Though the complexion and stature of men may differ in different countries, yet . . . the great difference of the species, *entirely depends upon education and custom.*" The point could hardly have been made more clearly and succinctly.[29]

*

In our earlier reconstruction of the malleability of gender identity in the short eighteenth century, one important theme was the repeated stories of success- ful *passing*: that is, of persons of one sex (mostly but not always women) readily picking up the habits – in both senses of the word – of the other sex and thereby becoming indistinguishable from them. Sure enough, the same theme can be found for racial identity as well, as in the cases of the European captives who became indistinguishable from their Indian captors or the exploits of the Muslim Moor whose lover could not see through his Europeanizing disguise. Similarly, we read that the 1770s adventures of the "Indian interpreter and trader" John Long included frequent episodes of his disguising himself as an Indian, "presuming on my appearing exactly like a savage". By this, to be sure, Long did not mean similarity in complexion or physical appearance – those are never mentioned in his memoirs – but rather in his dress and his knowledge of Indian language, dances, and customs: as a consequence of which, he insisted, "no one could distinguish me from the Indians". Racial passing was a two-way street: if Europeans were "to converse unknowingly with *Mahometans* in a *Christian* Dress", a mid-century traveler asserted, "they would look upon them to be just such Creatures as themselves" – entirely indistinguishable, in fact, as implied by the word "unknowingly".[30]

Or take the most famous North American captivity narrative of this period, that of Mary Rowlandson. On one occasion, the reader learns, Rowlandson's hopes of rescue were raised by an encounter with a group of riders whom she took to be Englishmen, "for they were dressed in English apparel, with hats, white neckcloths, and sashes about their waists, and ribbons upon their shoul- ders". Upon approaching closer, however, Rowlandson discovered to her great dismay that the riders were in fact Indians, indistinguishable initially from Europeans because of their dress. Now set this encounter side by side with those in which groups of seemingly male riders were in fact revealed to be equestrian "Amazons": the parallel – in narrative structure as well as in sub- stance – is uncanny, suggesting perhaps a common cultural vein from which both drew their meaning. Like the successfully passing Amazonian female riders, Rowlandson's successfully passing Anglo-looking Indians were a readily recognizable tableau signaling the unreliability of identity categories, which were subject to easy manipulation through the use of cultural accouterments. The ending of Rowlandson's recollection of this episode was no less revealing: when the riders came near, she continued, it suddenly dawned on her that "there was a vast difference between the lovely faces of Christians and the foul looks of those heathens". Rowlandson's sudden revelation of a "vast difference" between lovely and foul looks was grounded in religion; harking back, that is, to earlier certainties – certainties that her own confusion during the encounter exposed as little more than wishful thinking.[31]

Ultimately, then, it was culture – be it religion, dress, education, or level of civilization – that such a perspective privileged above all other markers of difference. This perspective, as we have seen, was well served by the four-stage theory of human progress. "In the habits of his mind or his body, in his manners or apprehensions", the Scottish philosopher Adam Ferguson wrote, nothing distinguishes the ancient German or Briton "from an American, who, like him, with his bow and his dart, is left to traverse the forest". In the end, the diversity – or similarity – of man is molded above all by man himself. It is therefore apt to conclude this discussion with an image that captured this understanding of difference especially vividly: Herman Moll's representation of the four continents, in the shape of four men, in the cartouche at the corner of his "A New and Correct Map of the Whole World" of 1719 (fig. 21).[32] In this image, produced by one of the most important cartographers of the period, what tells the continent-men apart is their dress and their accessories: the Asian's and the European's full-body apparel (which includes armor in the case of the latter) as against the minimal dress of the barefoot Indian and African; the technology and craftsmanship of the Asian's and the European's weapons (swords for both, and a very conspicuously placed gun differentiating the European from all the rest) as against the simpler wooden bows and arrows of the Indian and the African; and the Asian's and the European's banners

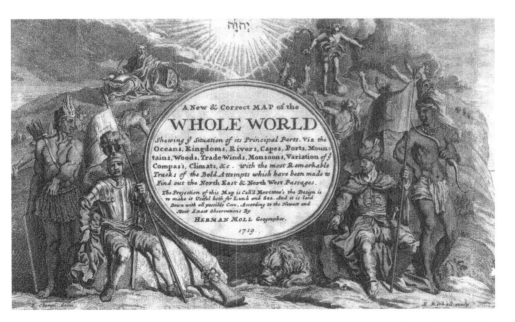

21.   The four continents personified, detail of Herman Moll, "A New and Correct Map of the Whole World", 1719

representing monotheistic religion, for which there is no parallel for the Indian and the African. In short, the key to distinguishing these continental representatives from one another was their level of civilization, manifested in dress, in technology and material culture, and in religion. Conspicuously for the modern observer, the features that did *not* play much of a role in delineating the distinctions between these global types were skin color, physiognomy, and physical appearance. On the contrary, the image employed composition and detail to highlight the affinity between the civilized Asian and European, and to an even greater degree that between the uncivilized African and Indian: uncannily prefiguring Ferguson's suggestion that as long as these two traversed the forest with their bows and darts, there was very little to set them apart.

We are right back where we started. For Herman Moll's cartouche also prefigured Benjamin West's representation of the exchange of prisoners during Colonel Bouquet's expedition to Ohio – the image with which I opened this sketch of the eighteenth-century understandings of race. Both images played down those differences in physical appearance that were later to become the underpinning of racial categories. Both underscored instead the more contingent and malleable elements of cultural difference, which can be donned or doffed through social custom or even through individual choice. Both drew their meaning from understandings of human diversity that did not depend to a great degree on fixed, innate characteristics (the word "innate" itself, in the text of Bouquet's expedition, turned out to mean a trait conditional on a particular stage of civilization).[33] In short, both images were part of what we can call, in analogy to our earlier observations about gender, the *ancien régime* of race: an *ancien régime* that extended back into the early-modern period, and that was about to begin losing significant ground before the eighteenth century was over.

"Imagining Specific Differences among Men"

We can begin to get a sense of the impending change by taking a second look at the "Hottentots". Recall what had been the standard eighteenth-century understanding of the Khoikhoi practice of greasing: as the *Encyclopaedia Britannica* put it in its second edition of 1778, the function of greasing was to "take care to make their children as black as possible . . . much blacker than they really are". But the entry for "Hottentots" in the third edition of the *Britannica* in the 1790s had it rather differently: it now turned the "obscur[ing]" of the Hottentot skin color through greasing into an unintended effect of their penchant for "filth and nastiness". So much for a deliberate attempt to manufacture skin color through aesthetic preference. Once again, this alteration between the editions of the *Britannica* signaled a broader shift: sometime toward the end of the century reports of the Khoikhoi actively assuming black-ness appear to have ceased, and greasing was now interpreted solely in func-tional terms – as enhancing skin protection, or swift movement, or whatever – or simply as a desultory side-effect of their way of life. So whereas one writer earlier in the century had maintained that the Hottentots greased themselves "in order to make 'em look black" (1738), when the *Monthly Review* revisited the same writer in 1776 with the intention of correcting his "false represen-tations", the retrospective reviewer insisted that Hottentots greased themselves in order "to make them[selves] shine". Thus *tout court*: the fabrication of black-ness, here as in virtually all late-eighteenth- and early-nineteenth-century accounts I have seen, no longer appeared as a possibility.[34]

Occasionally we are given a hint of the broader implications of this late-eighteenth-century shift in the representations of Hottentots. One 1780s writer, who attributed greasing to the need for protection "from the influence of the air", also added: "with their skins dressed up with grease and soot", the Hot-tentots "may in a manner reckon themselves fully dressed". No longer seen as involved in the manufacturing of permanent skin color, this writer equated greasing with that ephemeral cultural layering on top of one's body that is *dress*. Another contemporary observer likened the aesthetic preferences manifested in the Hottentot use of grease to those driving a European woman's applica-tion of rouge: "from the same principle of vanity", the Hottentot woman believed that "this sooty coloring added to her charms". Nothing could trans-form greasing better into an ephemeral, superficial accessory after the (bodily) fact. Others, instead of dwelling on the apparently no-longer-imaginable role of greasing in destabilizing distinctions of complexion, chose to emphasize (correctly, as it turns out) its opposite role in *maintaining* distinctions of social position. "The rich", one stated, "display their luxury in a greater quantity of grease"; this was "their distinctive mark of quality and wealth". Another ended a long list of possible uses of this practice among a variety of "savage nations" – ranging from climatic protection through moisture control to insect repel-lence – with the assertion that greasing "served also to distinguish the various ranks and orders of people, in the same manner as difference of dress and insignia of office do amongst us". Rather than blurring the marks of distinc-tion between people, greasing suddenly turned out to bolster them up.[35]

Taken together, these turn-of-the-century observations may indicate a move toward a new understanding of race in southern Africa. Or listen to John Barrow, a future founder of the Royal Geographical Society. In a famous early-nineteenth-century passage, Barrow said of one African group that unusually impressed him that "had not Nature bestowed upon [the Kaffer] the dark-coloring principle that anatomists have discovered to be owing to a certain gelatinous fluid lying between the epidermis and the cuticle, he might have ranked among the first of Europeans". This passage is often cited – plausibly, no doubt – as evidence of *pre*-racialist views of blacks in the era before scientific racism. At the same time, however, it was one clearly removed from the eighteenth-century understandings of African bodies. Instead of the oily substances that had been presumed to grease African skins into blackness, Barrow highlighted the gelatinous fluid *underneath* the skin which guaranteed its natural, essential black color. Elsewhere Barrow referred to greased faces "as if they wore a mask", which was his way of underscoring again the artifice of façade over substance. Most explicitly, he mocked those earlier writers who had believed that racial appearance could be manufactured through "the effect of art": a notion, Barrow assured his readers, that was "without the least foundation in truth".[36]

The same shift in direction can be discerned also in representations of other groups who have earlier afforded us some suggestive glimpses into eighteenth-century understandings of racial mutability. In the case of the North American Indians, Alden Vaughan has pointed out that perceptions of their racial identity gradually changed, moving from climatic explanation of skin color, through an emphasis on artificial skin painting, to viewing Indian skin color as innate: the latter, racializing view, according to Vaughan, became predominant during the closing decades of the eighteenth century. As emblematic of this transition we can take the *pas de deux* of two contemporary writers on North America. The first, one Peter Williamson, published in 1758 an obscure "Summary Detail of the Education, Manners, and Religion of the Indians" which talked about their skin color in terms with which we are already familiar: "The Indians are born tolerably white; but they take a great deal of pains to darken their Complexion, by anointing themselves with Grease and lying in the Sun." The second, John Filson, published in 1784 a well-known description of Kentucky in which he liberally helped himself to Williamson's prose: "The Indians are not born white; and take a great deal of pains to darken their complexion, by anointing themselves with grease, and lying in the Sun." As often in such cases, it is the close word-for-word reliance of one text on the other that makes the few alterations that the imitating author nevertheless chose to introduce all the more significant. It is thus surely telling that while Filson reproduced with precision – albeit without acknowledgement – Williamson's account of skin-darkening, he reversed the beginning of the sentence ("The Indians are *not* born white") so as to eliminate the potential for blurred as well as alterable racial distinctions offered by the original formulation. Moreover, on a second look we see that Filson also replaced the word "but" with "and": if the former was a contrastive preposition implying a *reversal* or *change* in skin color, Filson's subsequent alteration implied a mere *addition* to it.[37]

That doubts regarding "whether the Indians are indebted to nature, art, or the temperature of the climate for the colour of their skin" were in the air at this juncture is also evident in Jonathan Carver's famous *Travels through the Interior Parts of North-America* (1778). Like Filson, Carver acknowledged that all these possibilities had been aired by others, while in the same breath denying that Indian skin color could be anything but "the tincture they received originally from the hands of their Creator". Back in England, the *Monthly Review* was quick to pick up on this new tune, pointing out that in Carver's account, unlike previous writers, the Indians "seem to be a race as totally distinct from the rest of mankind, as the negroes are from the whites". The Tory Irishman Isaac Weld, traveling in America in the 1790s, also reiterated the earlier suggestions that the complexion of the Indians was a consequence of "the burning rays of the sun", or even of "their anointing themselves so frequently with unctuous substances". However, he retorted, even if we admit "that they think a dark complexion very becoming", and even if they do strive to enhance it, "yet it appears evident to me" – and thus, surely, to the sensible reader – "that the greater part of them are indebted for their different hues to nature alone". And even if it were true that Indian children were "white on their first coming into the world", this still did not mean that their final complexion was owing to the diligence of their mothers in "bedaub[ing] them with grease, herbs &c.". Rather, it was through the course of nature alone that their skin subsequently darkened: "just as in the vegetable world the tender blade, on first peeping above ground, turns from white to a pale greenish colour, and afterwards to a deeper green."[38]

Like vegetables, like Indians: neither had much say in their natural physical appearance. Accordingly, toward the end of the eighteenth century and beyond, British accounts of Indians actively manufacturing their skin color – simultaneously with equivalent reports about the Hottentots – are harder to come by. This is not to say that references to Indians painting their skins – especially with vermilion, which had often been singled out by former writers as the key to their altered skin color – disappeared altogether. But when latter-day writers reported that "the males in going to war paint their faces of different colours . . . [and] the females paint a small portion of each cheek of vermillion", or that "a material article in their toilettes is vermilion, which they contrast with their native blue, white and brown earths", or that they "la[y] on fresh paint every day . . . and always study a change of fashion. Vermilion is their favourite colour", in all such cases, a different context gave the same words a rather different meaning. No longer allowed to shape permanent racial appearance, vermilion – precisely as we have seen for the late-eighteenth-century reinterpretations of Hottentot greasing practices – was now transplanted to the fluid realm of artifice and fashion. The deputy postmaster general for British North America, George Heriot, took this reinterpretation even further, with a twist that I find revealing. "These decorations of the body", he explained in 1805, offer the "savage" who knows no alphabet "characteristic figures which personally distinguish him", and thus "become *distinguishing marks of the individual* ". (Body paint served as "a mark of distinction" among Polynesians, an early 1790s traveler to the South Sea similarly observed.) Body painting, formerly seen as instrumental in establishing the collective racial identity of the Indians, became in Heriot's eyes a mainstay of personal identity, that which helped maintain the distinctions between the individual and everyone else.[39]

What about the flip side of the mutable Indians, the white captives who had been reputed to metamorphose into a spitting image of their captors? One 1790 novel, at least, did indeed hark back to this familiar narrative. In this particular retelling of the story, however, its well-worn characteristics no longer appeared satisfactory. Not only did the metamorphosed captive, despite his supposed alteration, remain immediately recognizable for who he "really" was. Even more significantly, the novel revised the explanation for this metamorphosis: rather than embodying a climatic-cum-cultural transformation of skin-and-clothes, as the generic story had demanded, it turned out to have been mere subterfuge, a deliberate disguise.[40] Substitute now gender for race, and note once more how similar these signs of transformation in the presentation of the Indianized captive were to those in the late-eighteenth-century generic female warrior plot, or in the successive retellings of the life story of the Chevalier D'Eon, or in Amelia Opie's account of her encounter with a real-life female soldier. In the same way, one is struck here by the distance between the captivity stories at the beginning of this chapter, or the eighteenth-century stories of racial passing (like that reported by Mary Rowlandson), and this one of 1790, which was evidently coming apart at the seams.

But no weather vane, perhaps, showed more suggestively which way the late-eighteenth-century wind was blowing than invocations of the Jews. Or rather, whether the Jews were or were not a weather vane was now precisely the question. Whereas Jewish variability across the globe had earlier been the seemingly irrefutable argument for climate as the decisive factor in human diversity, by the late eighteenth century doubts were beginning to creep in. "Under all the various governments and climates where their lot is cast", observed James Dunbar in 1780, "the relation of consanguinity" of the Jews "marks their character": while admitting some geographical variance, Dunbar still insisted that "certain marks of uniformity are accordingly discernible among them in every period". Charles White, fifteen years later, cited the oft-repeated clincher of the climatic argument that "nothing is more true than that the English Jew is white, the Portuguese swarthy, the Armenian olive, the Arabian copper, and the African black" – but only strongly to disagree. (Isaac Weld's similar skepticism

while looking back at former views about the American Indians comes to mind.)
First, White said, one needs to take into account the effects of intermarriage:
"the Jews have gained proselytes in every part of the world where they have
resided, and they are at liberty to marry those proselytes" – and it was this that
explained their similarity to their hosting nations. At the same time he also
insisted that "the truth is, that the Jews are generally swarthy in every climate":
that is to say, they were not all that similar to their hosting nations after all.
White was not one to let internal consistency stand in the way of his knockout
arguments against the mutability of Jewish racial identity.[41]

Even more telling was a response to White that expressed disagreement with
him and a wish to reinstate the importance of climate. "The most striking
example we have of the influence of climate is to be found among that persecuted race of people the Jews," began Thomas Winterbottom in a passage that
apparently promised to return to older eighteenth-century understandings of
Jewish appearances: "Dispersed over the chief parts of the civilized globe, but
prevented by religious motives from mixing with the rest of mankind, they still
retain their characteristic features, though they have assumed the complexion
of every country they inhabit." Trying to revive the insistence on the correlation between complexion and environment, Winterbottom found himself
asserting now in the same breath that in all environments the Jews retained their
characteristic, essential features. Within a couple of decades, newcomers to this
question were to find White's position so self-evident as to preclude the need
to acknowledge any alternative interpretation. Thus, one advocate of "hereditary descent" marshaled forth the Jews as "the most striking instance of a
marked distinction of race that is to be met with", since "in every climate . . .
[and] amidst every variety of physical and moral circumstances, the Jews preserve, in their external appearance, incontestible evidence of the race to which
they belong". "In various circumstances, at home and abroad" – thus another
– "every Jew presents the same complexion, or Israelitish face, [which consti-
tutes] the index of their pedigree all over the earth." "The Jews exhibit one of
the most striking instances of national formation, unaltered by the most various
changes," echoed yet another; "they have been scattered, for ages, over the face
of the whole earth; but . . . their colour and their characteristic features are still
the same under every diversity of climate and situation." "However dispersed
among the nations of the earth" – this quasi-identical pronunciation was from
1788 – the Jews "continue peculiar and distinct." It was as if the invocations
of the example of the Jews as proving precisely the opposite had never been
aired.[42]

*

What, then, was the broader framework bringing together these apparent shifts in the representations of Hottentots, American Indians, and Jews? Henry Home, Lord Kames, was one writer in the 1770s who saw the bigger picture very clearly. "In the suburbs of Cochin," Kames wrote, "a town in Malabar, there is a colony of industrious Jews of the same complexion they have in Europe"; from which he concluded that "there are many instances of races of people preserving their original color in climates very different from their own; and not a single instance of the contrary as far as I can learn". Likewise, the fact that "Americans without exception are of a copper colour, tho' in that vast continent there is every variety of climate", again refuted any climatic view. In short, it was inconceivable that skin color – communicable as it evidently was from parents to newborn infants – was determined by the sun. "I should be as soon induced to believe", Kames sneered, "that the negro colour is owing to an ancient custom in Africa of dying the skin black." Enter our third group of reference. "The Hottentots", Kames continued seamlessly, "are continually at work, and have been for ages, to darken their complexion; but that operation has no effect on their children." Here then, within the space of a couple of pages, were all the new "revisionist" assertions about Jewish, Indian, and Hottentot identities, countering their older understandings as mutable – whether through climatic or human intervention, a distinction that mattered little to Kames.[43]

This is not to say that Kames did not take climate seriously. Quite the contrary, he took climatic differences so seriously that he did not believe humans could traverse them. The only way to account for the wide differences between human beings in different climatic conditions, Kames insisted, differences that rendered them so well suited to such disparate environments, and at the same time also to acknowledge the close uniformity within each human sub-group, was to recognize that "there are different races of men fitted by nature for different climates". Kames therefore offered a *polygenetic* account of the origins of man: an account, that is, that assumed multiple origins of several distinct human species. The upshot was that Kames transformed climate, which had been so closely intertwined with the mutability integral to the *ancien régime* of race, into the basis for a new, essentializing view of innate racial identity.[44]

To be sure, Kames's polygenetic position remained a minority opinion throughout this period, and his writing is mostly notable for the spirited retorts it managed to attract. But just as Kames's doubts regarding the earlier representations of Jews, Indians, and Hottentots reflected broader shifts in the understandings of all three groups, so his more general emphasis on the innateness of racial identity resonated with a wider cultural trend, which brought to the fore a mounting skepticism about the role of either climate or culture in the making of race.

Climatic theory, for one, was increasingly on the defensive. Kames's fellow Scot John Millar, for instance, revised the introduction to his celebrated *Origin of the Distinction of Ranks* between the 1771 and 1779 editions to voice his discontent with the prevailing climatic wisdom. The weight of the evidence, Millar finally admitted, amply demonstrated that "national character depends very little upon the immediate operation of climate". Jeremy Bentham's *Introduction to the Principles of Morals and Legislation* (1789) followed a Montesquieuian paragraph on the influence of climate on individual propensities and character with a limiting caveat. "The national race or lineage a man issues from", he explained, is a circumstance that operates "independently of that of climate", so that "a man of negro race, born in France or England, is a very different being, in many respects, from a man of French or English race" – a difference fixed "at the hour of his birth". Birth trumps climate. (Recall, by contrast, those commentators who had been skeptical of the climatic understanding prevalent at mid-century, but for whom climate was trumped by civilization.) When Richard Payne Knight waxed poetic on *The Progress of Civil Society* in 1796, sketching in a familiar Scottish-influenced manner its economic stages as well as the influence of "climate and soil", he too circumscribed the latter, insisting on the anterior existence in the north and the south of "two distinct races of men; the one the farthest removed from, and the other nearest approaching to, the Negro". More emphatic was Isaac D'Israeli's sniggering dismissal of climatic notions (also in 1796) – notions, he asserted in nervous succession, that were "fanciful", "curious absurdities", "prejudice", and "follies". Climatic theory "had been confuted", D'Israeli declared with a confidence betrayed by his palpable agitation, even if at times it "is still believed, for there are some [for] whom no confutation can confute". To suppose that "climate could produce" the variety of "human beings . . . of *so* totally different formations, complexions, and intellectual abilities", the biblical exegete Edward King echoed in 1800, was "contrary to all known experience".[45]

Mark Harrison, in his careful investigation of the changes in the role attributed to climate during this period, points out that climatic theory did not simply disappear in response to such growing unease. Rather, from the late eighteenth century onward it was transformed into what Harrison calls "weak transmutationism": that is to say, a view that still admitted the effects of climate, but that drew them out over a great many generations, thus turning climatic theory in effect into a "genetic" one. Climate became a remote rather than an immediate influence on human development: unlike sheep, one early-nineteenth-century writer explained, who upon transportation to tropical climes changed their wool in the matter of "a few generations", Europeans could not simply adapt and acquire the "sable tint of the inter-tropical natives" – not, in any case, before a great many generations had passed. Or as Johann

Forster observed in 1778, even while defending the monogenetic position ascribing diversity to climate: if blacks transported into colder climes do not intermarry, "the change, if any, is imperceptible in their offspring for many generations". The crucial consequence of this shift in timescale was that the effects of climate were removed from the realm of the individual: racial identity was immutably stamped on each and every person, even if long-term Lamarckian evolution allowed for a future alteration in some distant progeny. While less eccentric than Lord Kames's polygeneticism, weak transmutationism was ultimately another way of essentializing the effects of climate, reversing its earlier association with contingency and mutability. The shift from acclimatization to weak transmutationism, moreover, left its mark on the actual practices of Britons in India. By the turn of the century, Elizabeth Collingham has observed, their efforts at adaptation to Indian climate were reduced to a change of *dress*: they no longer hoped for a transformation of their out-of-place body, but merely for its better protection from the alien environment.[46]

Like Harrison, Roxann Wheeler also points to the last quarter of the century as the turning point in her own account of the eighteenth-century racial imagination – the moment when stories of racial transformation and blurring seem to have lost cultural ground. Within the higher intellectual domain, the contours of this shift have been recently studied in detail by Silvia Sebastiani. Combing encyclopedias and magazines, scholarly tracts and learned periodicals, Sebastiani demonstrates that – especially for Scottish philosophers and naturalists – mutable understandings of human diversity began to retreat from the 1770s, a trend that remained true not only for climatic views of diversity but also for cultural ones, that is to say those based on evaluating different levels of civilization. The *Encyclopaedia Britannica*, as Sebastiani observes, was a case in point, having become noticeably more racialist in each successive edition from the 1770s to the 1790s: most markedly, perhaps, in the "Negroe" entry in the third edition of 1797, the first encyclopedia entry entirely devoted to the discussion of a "race". The *Britannica*, incidentally, was a champion of the monogenetic position, which insisted – *pace* Kames and his followers – that the whole of humankind originated with one human pair. In the debate between polygeneticists and monogeneticists, the emphasis on the essential nature of race was certainly not confined to one side.[47]

This new emphasis, moreover, increased the discomfort with those occasional erratic phenomena like albino blacks that seemed to challenge contemporary notions of racial difference. Whereas such individuals had previously been noted as de facto demonstrations of the limits of racial categorization, late-eighteenth-century reports of equivalent occurrences were no longer allowed as easily to expose these limits. A 1797 report on a "White African", for instance, insisted that "though whiter than any Europeans, [he] still retains the thick lips, fleecy hair, and every appearance (except colour) of the Negro". Another, a decade later, assured its readers that a certain "Spotted Negro"– "so singular a work of nature" – with his clothes on, could "scarcely be distinguished from any other black". Despite their singular complexion, itself a freak of nature, even these rare individuals were still unmistakably racially categorizable.[48]

*

The emerging picture requires a certain revision of the common wisdom regarding the development of modern notions of race. Until recently, scholarship on the history of European racial thinking focused primarily on the nineteenth century, especially on its middle decades, with their blatant forms of scientific racism. (This is in contrast to the historians of race in slave-owning North America, in whose narratives the late eighteenth century – think of Jefferson's *Notes on the State of Virginia* – plays a more obviously prominent, and different, role.) When these scholars briefly cast their eyes on the eighteenth century, they typically looked for precursors of the nineteenth-century developments, a "pre-history" with little distinctiveness or importance of its own, consisting primarily of a few precocious writers – like Lord Kames, or Charles White – who appeared to prefigure what was to come several decades later. What I want to suggest, following the leads of Harrison, Wheeler, and Sebastiani among others, is that these late-eighteenth-century writers were not simply Victorians *avant la lettre*, writers ahead of their times. Rather they were very much a part of their times, indicators of the more extensive epistemological shift that is of interest to us here.[49]

Nonetheless, occasionally some authors, by virtue of the unusual cogency of their vision, removed themselves from the mainstream of their broader cultural milieu to its more eccentric outposts. No one fits this description better than the West Indian planter and administrator Edward Long, whose notorious *History of Jamaica* of 1774 is sometimes presented as the point of origin for modern British racism. Now to be sure, Long fully deserves his bad reputation for his unrelenting emphasis on essential racial difference, leading to a wholesale disparagement of blacks as barbarous, stupid, bestial, and, most memorably, akin to apes. And yet, while Long's vision was extraordinary in its elaborate detail, it drew on the same conceptual shifts evident elsewhere at the same time. Thus, like others at this juncture, Long dismissed climatic theories of human diversity out of hand, citing the seemingly self-evident non-mutability of blacks in North America or Europeans in the West Indies over many generations. Like others, Long also added a reflection on the (non-) effects of culture: "It is astonishing, that, although [the Negroes] have been acquainted with Europeans, and their manufactures, for so many hundred years, they have, in all this series of time, manifested so little taste for arts, or a genius either inventive or imitative." If Long's eighteenth-century predecessors had seen civilization (side by side with climate) as key to human difference, and thus also to the possibility of its erasure, his own conclusion was precisely the opposite: racial differences were ingrained so deeply that no amount of cultural contact or influence could remove them. "When we reflect on the nature of these men", he therefore asserted triumphantly, "and their dissimilarity to the rest of mankind, must we not conclude, that they are a different species of the same genus?"[50]

Even the annals of the most blatant racial prejudice, moreover, bear the marks of a late-eighteenth-century change of emphasis. Thus Long, with his polygenetic essentialism, cut a rather different figure than, say, the provost-marshal of Georgia William Knox had done in the 1760s. As befitted one of the leading racists of the previous decades, Knox too professed strong convictions about the inferiority of blacks. He frankly admitted, however, that his views remained unaffected by the fact that he had no idea whether the difference between whites and blacks was preordained by God or simply the result of developmental circumstances. But when Long's fellow West Indian planter Samuel Estwick revised in 1773 a tract on the question of blacks in England, he asserted – unlike Knox and very much like Long – that blacks occupied a space in creation "the bounds of which they are not capable of passing; differing from other men, not in *kind*, but in *species*". These were assertions of absolute, uncrossable difference.[51]

For Long and Estwick, the insistence on essential racial difference served to reinforce the case for slavery, in response to the recent wave of abolitionist agitation. But the coupling of the mounting racialism with pro-slavery views was not inevitable. Consider the Manchester physician and comparative anatomist Charles White. In many ways White resembled Long, and the two are often paired. Even more explicitly than Long, White acknowledged the prevalent eighteenth-century explanations of human difference through climate or culture, only in order to join the turn-of-the-century chorus of non-believers. Previously, he recalled, "the primitive cause of difference in the colour of man . . . has usually been attributed chiefly to climate . . . But, this being found insufficient, some have added to it the state of society" – that is, the state of civilization. But these views were all inadequate: nothing could be clearer than the imperviousness of people's skin color to transportation across the globe, as was demonstrated so effectively by the example of the Jews. Indeed, White concluded, we should accept that "various differences exist in the human race" that are fundamental; and thus we must "suppose that different species were originally created with those distinctive marks which they still retain". Echoing

Long, then, White offered to overrule climate and culture with a polygenetic narrative, likewise affirming the essential, immutable nature of race. The only difference was that White, perhaps surprisingly, declared himself at the outset to be an abolitionist, not a defender of slavery. Essentialism had no clear political color.[52]

It is beyond my scope here to unravel the intertwining of the campaign for the abolition of slavery with the increasing essentializing of race and of identity. Suffice it for our purpose to raise the possibility that such intertwining characterized *both* sides in this heated debate. The *Encyclopaedia Britannica*, to remind us, retained its consistent opposition to slavery throughout its various editions, regardless of their increasing racialization. "It is true", James Ramsay admitted in one of the better known anti-slavery tracts of the 1780s, that "there are marks . . . as if set by the hand of nature to distinguish them [blacks] from the whites: their noses are flat, their chins prominent, their hair woolly, their skin black": but none of these essential natural differences involved an inferiority of intellect or abilities, as the defenders of their continuing enslavement suggested. Others, by contrast, argued their opposition to slavery on the basis of the shared humanity of blacks and whites: but in elaborating on the immutable, ineradicable essence that constitutes this humanity, they too were speaking the language of the new regime of identity as it was emerging at this juncture. "Some have persuaded themselves", wrote one abolitionist of this variety, "that the negroes are a stupid race, and that their natural insensibility, together with the uncivilized state of society in which they have lived, prevents them from having the nice feelings of the civilized nations of Europe." This opinion, however, was "very erroneous", in that it disregarded the fact that "the affections of the mind are natural, not acquired" – here was the key to the new essentialism – and thus common to all humankind.[53]

For another twist consider the words of the Scottish economist James Anderson. To begin with, this is how he chose to open his own tract against slavery: "The difference observable between man and man is much greater than that which is perceived among the individuals of any other class of animals." Like others in the abolitionist political camp, Anderson made his way from this assertion of fundamental human difference not to an apologia for human subjugation but to a sharp attack upon it. But another arrow in Anderson's abolitionist quiver is more revealing. The advocates of slavery, he wrote, ignored the fact that "there was a time when these very African negroes, as far exceeded the rest of the world in intellectual endowments, as the inhabitants of the most civilized parts of Europe now exceed the much degraded Africans of Guinea". Moses learned everything he knew from the Egyptians; and "there are good reasons for believing, that the sages who taught Pythagoras wisdom, and the learned instructors of Moses, were of the same race of woolly headed negroes

that we now affect so much to contemn". What this move – which we can call
the "Black Athena" argument (foreshadowing Martin Bernal's well-known
late-twentieth-century line) – did, of course, was not to deny race, but rather
to insist on its stability and importance, and yet to make culture central to its
hereditary transmission. Just as we have seen, then, how turn-of-the-century
writings on climate replaced the mutability that had been associated with it with
a more permanent essence, so the "Black Athena" argument replaced the mutability that culture had introduced into eighteenth-century understandings of
race with a view of culture as itself essentialized and hereditary. Thus, however
far removed from Anderson's congratulatory view of the origins of blacks,
when Edward Long had written that "the Negroes seem to conform nearest in
character to the Ægyptians, in whose government . . . there reigned a multi-
tude of abuses, and essential defects", he was offering his readers – in reverse
– precisely the same racialized view of culture.[54]

Nor was this the only logic by which culture was transformed in the late
eighteenth century from a driving force of human mutability to an aspect of
racialized permanence. Thus, in a similar vein to (but more prominently than
in) the "Black Athena" genealogies of Egyptians and blacks, it was precisely
during this period that the notion of Aryanism – introduced by Sir William
Jones in the 1780s – offered an analogous racial-genealogical picture of East
Indian civilization. Humanity consisted of "races of men", Jones lectured in
1792, "that essentially differ in language, religion, manners, and other known
characteristics". This was essential difference anchored in inherited language
and culture (and that prompted at least one reviewer to bring up skin color as
a seemingly major obstacle to the theory). Less famously, Gothicism, as Colin
Kidd has pointed out, was also undergoing a parallel transformation, from an
emphasis on the common stock shared by the British and other Europeans to
an emphasis on "differences [that] are radical; and such that no climate or
chance could produce" (1787). While many had invaded this island, another
writer explained in 1799, "the effects of the Anglo-Saxon settlement have prevailed beyond every other. Our language, our government, and our laws, display
our Cimbric ancestors in every part . . . though more than thirteen centuries
have rolled over." Talk about the inherited fixity of cultural difference. Less
famous still was the Scottish schoolmaster who in 1792 took on the whole progressive historical thinking associated with the leading intellectual lights of his
country to argue that there was no evidence whatsoever for savages making
progress toward civilization, unless they were "impelled by some external circumstance". On the contrary, the schoolmaster asserted, both reason and experience suggest that some peoples were savages in "their original character" and
thus had "a natural and rooted aversion to a civilized state", whereas others
"have been originally civilized" and had never experienced "absolute sav-

agism". Civilization was no longer a transformative force: for this critic, savagery *and* civilization have become natural, original, essential conditions.[55]

Even those who continued to believe in the ultimately transformative powers of civilization could now be seen to develop their own version of "weak transmutationism" (to borrow again Mark Harrison's term for contemporary climatic theory): that is to say, a vision of culture that did allow for its transformative effects, but only over such a long span of time as to make it, insofar as the individual was concerned, completely stable and permanent. Thus James Cowles Prichard, a key figure in early-nineteenth-century anthropology, suggested in 1813 that civilization itself was the cause – not consequence – of racial difference. In an idiosyncratic realignment of the "Black Athena" logic, Prichard suggested that both Egyptians and Indians had originally been black, but became lighter-skinned in a long-term Lamarckian evolution driven by civilization. To be sure, Prichard's was a short-lived, quirky move, from which even he was eventually going to distance himself (though not before Samuel Taylor Coleridge, for one, had experimented with its pessimistic mirror-image, attributing the degenerate state of blacks to a gradual process in which the absence of civilization was diffused so deeply among them as to take control of "the formative principle itself" and become hereditary to the whole race). But it is the underlying impetus to essentialize and racialize the effects of culture that is significant, repeated as it was in all these different forms.[56]

*

Historical change, once again, is surely not all that straightforward. It was to take many more years before rigid, essentialized, racialized, congenital understandings of human difference – those that scholars associate with the mid-Victorians – were to drive their pre-modern flexible, mutable counterparts to the cultural margins, and even then the triumph would not be complete.[57] The closing decades of the eighteenth century witnessed the beginnings of this historical change: beginnings that were often messy, tentative, halting, replete with dead ends, and in which the new jostled and overlapped with the old. In other words, I am not suggesting that we have suddenly been transported into a world of modern racial categories, but rather that we are looking at the onset of a transitional phase pointing in that direction. One telling indication of the transitional nature of this period is the shifts we have seen occurring in the received climatic and cultural ways of thinking *from within*, shifts that pushed them away from their established tendency to highlight malleability to an often incongruous emphasis on racialized essence. The mental contortions involved in attempts to render culture an essential fixed basis for human difference, like the weak transmutationism that did the same for climate, belonged to this transitional phase, in which new pressures were causing the older ways of thinking – even before they were superseded – to strain and eventually come apart at the seams. Often, moreover, the transitional nature of this historical moment – the same pressures, the same contradictory impulses, and the same bursting at the seams – was also evident even within single utterances of contemporaries, as they were trying to confront questions of human diversity with the aid of two mutually incompatible conceptual frameworks, one increasingly discredited, the other not yet quite in place. This veritable plague of contradictions may ultimately constitute the most persuasive evidence for a late-eighteenth-century transition in racial understandings.

Take for instance William Robertson's famous *History of America*. Published in 1777 by "one of the most Montesquieuian of Scottish historians" (the words are Nicholas Phillipson's), it offered what was in many ways the culmination of the eighteenth-century view of American native peoples, filtering the effects of environment and civilization through the Scottish four-stage theory of history. "The disposition and manners of men", Robertson wrote, "are formed by their situation, and arise from the state of society in which they live. The moment that begins to vary, the character of a people must change." However one understood people's "situation" – Robertson went back and forth between "climate and soil" (responsible, *inter alia*, for the "striking variety in the human species" represented by blacks) and "political and moral causes" – this was a mutable, pre-racialist view of human difference. But then, suddenly, when Robertson got to the Eskimos his tune changed. "They are manifestly a separate species of men," he observed, distinct from all other American peoples; and

> there is such a striking similitude in the form of their bodies, and the qualities of their minds, that, notwithstanding the diversities occasioned by the influence of climate, or unequal progress of improvement, we must pronounce them to be descended from one source. There may be a variety in the shades, but we can every where trace the same original colour.

The Eskimos, it turned out, stood outside the variations of the human form that Robertson could imagine to result from environmental and cultural influences, those influences to which he had elsewhere attributed all of human difference. In contemplating this apparent singularity, therefore, Robertson let slip a different understanding of race, one in which fixed, inherited characteristics overrode the secondary effects of climate and culture.[58]

A similar thing happened to fellow Scottish historian William Alexander a couple of years later. Alexander too was convinced that, to the extent that men appear different from each other, "their dissimilarity [is] the effect of art, and of the habits and customs which have arisen from it". Such contingent cultural effects were so powerful that "in many cases [they] obliterate even the laws of nature". But this assertion of culture overriding nature flew in the face of another that Alexander made elsewhere in the very same book: "The human genus has, with no small degree of probability, been divided by naturalists into several distinct species, each marked with corporal differences, which could hardly arise from custom or from climate, and with intellectual powers scarcely less indicative of this division than the marks of their bodies." Like Robertson, Alexander suddenly let through a statement that flatly contradicted his cultur-alist position, admitting with little apparent discomfort that custom and climate were "with no small degree of probability" secondary to innate racial traits.[59]

What I want to stress here is not that such internal contradictions were pos-sible, but rather that during the 1770s and the 1780s they were so very common as to constitute a meaningful historical pattern. Thus, among anti-slavery voices, we have heard James Ramsay put forth in 1784 a rigid picture of racial difference, predicated on "marks" evidently "set by the hand of nature" that "distinguish [blacks] from the whites" – the color of their skin, the texture of their hair, the shapes of their nose and face. This racialist outlook dominated most of Ramsay's tract ("The several families or supposed races have various marks, connecting them with each other, and distinguishing them from the rest"). But then environmentalism began to sneak back in, catching the atten-tive reader unprepared. The older understanding resurfaced at first tentatively – "we know that climate, diet, and the various modes of life have great power over the feature, form, and stature of man" – and then triumphantly. "Negroe children are born white," Ramsay suddenly asserted, and their black skin is simply the consequence of "weather and sun", just like freckles. "A freckle may be defined a partial black skin; a black skin an universal freckle." Ramsay was aware of the fact that his sun-induced "universal freckle" did not sit too well with his statements several pages previously about the original and fixed marks of distinction between races. Whether racial difference was "fixed by the Author of nature" or "caused by climate", he therefore shrugged disingenuously, "is matter of innocent disputation". Hardly. Two years later the influential abolitionist Thomas Clarkson, holding fast to a mutable under-standing of race, borrowed Ramsay's "universal freckle" for his own assertion that differences of color were the consequence of an "*incidental co-operation of causes*", especially climate, but with a bit of culture thrown in. He further main-tained, therefore, that "when the *black* inhabitants of *Africa* are transplanted to *colder*, or the *white* inhabitants of *Europe* to *hotter* climates, their children, *born there*, are of a *different colour from themselves*". The keen reader, however, would have found it well-nigh impossible to square this observation about single-generation transmutations with an apologetic note that Clarkson had inserted a few pages earlier: "We do not mean to insinuate that the same people have their *corpus mucosus* sensibly vary, as often as they go into another latitude, but that the fact is true only of different people, who have been long established in different latitudes." Whether it was an essentialist like Ramsay who could not let go of climatism, or a mutationist like Clarkson who could not ward off the skepticism leading to a more essentialist (weak-transmutationist) view of climate, the result was the same – an unresolvable conceptual muddle.[60]

The examples pile up fast: the physician William Falconer, whose work "on the influence of climate" (1781) did hold on to the general importance of this influence (albeit with the inexplicable exception of the climate-impervious Jews), but only at the considerable price of limiting climatic influence to such traits as temper, disposition, and manners while avoiding any discussion what-soever of the relationship between climate and complexion or skin color; or Captain Cook's natural historian Johann Reinhold Forster, whose adherence to standard eighteenth-century cultural-cum-climatic explanations for "the vari-eties of the human species" (1778) jarred with his natural-historical impulse to essentialize and fixate human types, and flew in the face of his (sheepish) admis-sion that blacks in cold climates "preserve their original complexion . . . change, if any, is imperceptible in their offspring for many generations"; or the East India Company official William Marsden, whose denials of the reputed effects of climate in his *History of Sumatra* (1783) left him so admittedly baffled as to offer on the one hand an idiosyncratic "conjecture" for "the general disparity of complexions" based on humoral imbalances while acknowledging on the other that it was "an hypothesis [that] would not stand the test of experiment"; or the philosopher William Godwin, who a decade later also denied categori-cally the effects of climate on "the characters of nations", only flatly to con-tradict this assertion with an admission on the next page that heat and cold "in their extreme" may be responsible for the character of the Negroes or the Lap-landers; or the Scottish poet James Macpherson (of Ossianic fame), who within a few pages of his *Introduction to the History of Great Britain* had asserted both that the stature and "whiteness of skin" of the ancient Britons could be attributed to climate and that "the Spaniard, exposed to the burning suns of Gallicia, was as fair and florid as the German of the northern Europe". Main-taining further that "no climate, no change of food can raise the Laplander to the height of the German", Macpherson concluded that "among mankind, as in other animals, there seem to be a variety of species". (Note in passing how for Macpherson the Laplander was the clinching argument *against* climatic effect, precisely the opposite of the Laplander's significance for Godwin.) That these difficulties were very much on Macpherson's mind is evident from the additional text he chose to insert into the "Preliminary Observations" of his revised edition of 1773, which reinforced a polygenetic view of distinct races of people endowed with differing susceptibilities for the effects of civilization.

The insistence of these statements made their absence in the previous edition, published a mere year earlier, all the more conspicuous.[61]

So these writers – who include many of the best-known and the most often-quoted British commentators on the question of race during this period – found themselves time and again entangled uncomfortably in a web of incompatible suppositions about racial difference, an inconsistent melange of older and newer ways of thinking. I have saved for last the best example I have come across – of a contemporary whose own writing not only bears the clear marks of this moment of transition, but also displays an extraordinary awareness of the fact that this transition was unfolding around him even as it was taking place. This writer was James Dunbar, professor of moral philosophy at Aberdeen, in his relatively little-known *Essays on the History of Mankind in Rude and Cultivated Ages*, published in 1780. Prodded into writing, in part, by Britain's attempt to assert its superiority over its former American colonies, Dunbar put forth a scathing critique of Europe's wholly misplaced sense of superiority over other nations. "Europe", Dunbar wrote, "affects to move in another orbit from the rest of the species. She is even offended with the idea of a common descent" with "other races"; "and, *by imagining specific differences among men*, precludes or abrogates their common claims". This, then, was a response to what Dunbar – prefiguring my argument here – identified as a rising tendency on the part of his contemporaries to imagine essential differences between people. In so doing, he insisted, they were obliterating the fact that such differences were not the indelible stamp of nature but merely the contingent products of human history. Distinctions between men were "at first few and inconsiderable", but subsequently they "have grown immense in the revolutions of time; and the natural history of the species is scarce able to solve the appearances in civil life". The influence of climate had also been exaggerated; in truth, it is "mechanical and local causes, which, in some respects, so visibly predominate, [that] the imagination invests with a dominion that reaches the very essence of our frame". The attempt to fix human difference – and human individuality – in "the very essence of our frame" was a misplaced fantasy of the imagination: in truth, difference was the result of contingent and random causes.[62]

So far so good: Dunbar appeared to be mounting a comprehensive rearguard defense of what I have described as the *ancien régime* of racial identity, and this while acknowledging that this regime was coming under a growing offensive from new, essentializing – and in his opinion blatantly mistaken – ways of thinking. (I have therefore borrowed the title for this section from his acute critical analysis.) But then, unexpectedly, cracks began to appear in Dunbar's own ability to withstand this assault, cracks that rapidly turned into chasms. The first inkling of this came when Dunbar suddenly sounded a cautionary note not to confuse "the local circumstances we have mentioned" – those contingent causes of limited significance – "with that more mysterious influence which, reaching the principles of our nature, is supposed to produce original and constitutional differences in the human species". Original and constitutional differences: here was a notion that the readers of the earlier pages could not have seen coming. Nor were they better prepared for the final essay in the work, entitled "Of the Hereditary Genius of Nations", which asserted that "hereditary characteristics are interwoven into the genius and essence of the mind"; so much so that "the progeny of savages or barbarians may be distinguishable, both in outward and inward form, from the progeny of a cultivated people". The Jews were the one example Dunbar offered as proof for the triumph of permanent and unifying racial essence over varieties of environment, and he was hoping that "the spirit of Britons" that united the warring parties in the unfortunate American war would prove to be another. It was left to the readers to figure out how any of this could be compatible with what had come before. Dunbar, for his part, seemed unable to do so. Thus, in one place he admitted that "between hereditary, innate, and acquired propensities, it is hard to draw the line of distinction". In several others he acknowledged this hereditary principle to be "mysterious" and unknowable – "the mode of this economy we pretend not to unfold". He then tried to unfold it anyway, tackling head-on the seeming inconsistencies with his earlier statements through a half-formed Lamarckian theory of long-term multi-generational acquisition of hereditary traits, what we have called before "weak transmutationism". It is hard to imagine a writer leaving more signs of his agonizing sense that the argument had spun out of control. The fact that Dunbar the philosopher produced what was at the same time one of the most insightful statements of his generation and one of its most incoherently self-contradictory ones speaks volumes about the transitional nature of the moment in which it was written, a transitional nature of which Dunbar the observer was very much aware.[63]

Coda: Neither Here Nor There – Omai's Lost Identity

British cross-racial interactions in the eighteenth century were much more likely to take place at the outposts of empire across the globe than in the mother country. Consequently, the range of sources that I have drawn upon for this thumbnail picture of the development of race has necessarily been less expansive than the wide range of cultural forms brought to bear on the investigation of gender, and more focused on texts specifically concerned with issues of human difference than on indirect evidence of underlying habits of thought. It is at the outposts of empire, on the other hand, that historians are more likely to discover the consequences of the shift proposed here in actual social practice. Indeed, some have already indicated as much, providing evidence for the suggestion – recently put forth by Eliga Gould – that the British empire in the closing decades of the eighteenth century witnessed a sharpening insistence on the absolute difference between the metropolis and the colonies. Thus Philip Morgan, in a recent synthesis, has reminded us that in the late eighteenth century "the frequency of concubinage and marriages involving British men and Indian and Eurasian women dropped dramatically" in places as far apart as Rupert's Land and India. C. A. Bayly has likewise pointed to the reversal of policy in British India in 1791 that suddenly excluded persons of mixed race from political and military office; a reversal that coincided with the first instances of official consideration of the Eurasians in India as a specific and identifiable racial category. Although the link between the story I have told in this chapter about the shift in metropolitan understandings of racial categories and these developments, involving a wide range of regions and factors, is at present mainly one of temporal coincidence, it is nonetheless a suggestive one. Bayly, indeed, connects the shift in policy in India to what he sees as an increased circulation among British officials in the last two decades of the eighteenth century of notions of "native depravity" common to all Indians: a formulation reminiscent of my argument here.[64]

But I would like to leave the final word on the topic of race to an unusual case of cross-racial interaction that did take place in the metropolis. By fortuitous coincidence, it was precisely the moment of transition of concern to us here that witnessed the fortunes and misfortunes of the most famous dark-skinned visitor to eighteenth-century England, Omai – the Polynesian who was brought to London on Captain Cook's consort ship in his second South Sea voyage and remained there for two years (1774–6). Taken by many to be the epitome of "natural man", or at least as close to it as fashionable London was likely to come, Omai became a public test case for the limits of difference just at the moment when the very understanding of these limits was up for grabs. There was nothing, it seemed, that fashionable London wanted more than to turn Omai into one of them: between their efforts to improve his English, teach him to read and write, Christianize him, instruct him in shooting and riding (a task left to our old acquaintance the Chevalier D'Eon), Europeanize his features (this was the effect of Reynolds's famous portrait of Omai in classical style (fig. 22), which turned him – as Bernard Smith has put it – into "a self-confident civilized patrician"), cajole him into dancing and playing chess, present him in European dress, perfect his table manners, and generally socialize him so as to make him acceptable company for the great and the good (as high up as the King himself), Omai was subjected to an extraordinary concerted effort at cultural conversion. Some observers – European observers: we do not really know what Omai made of all this – tried to insist on the success of this onslaught. They claimed not only that Omai "seemed as easy in our

22. Sir Joshua Reynolds's
portrait of Omai in classical
style, shown at the Royal
Academy in 1776; here copied
in an engraving by Johann
Jacobé, 1780

habit, as if he had been born in Pall-Mall", but even that "his Complexion
much resembles that of an European". But others highlighted rather than
denied difference. What struck Fanny Burney on meeting Omai, for instance,
despite his European dress, was that he was much darker than she had expected.
He was even "browner than most of his countrymen", judged another surprised
contemporary. Even Reynolds, who deviated from his usual practice in making
two preliminary studies of Omai's head before moving to the final portrait,
revealed in those not the Europeanized visage he was going to end up with but
rather a Polynesian with distinctive racial features (fig. 23). The questionable
outcome of this conversion effort was proclaimed in a fictional soliloquy, put
into the mouth of Omai himself:

> Oft' have I gaz'd, and wish'd with ardour too,
> To paint my skin, and only look like you:
> Oft' have I tried, but ev'ry art was vain,
> No colours hid my dark Numidian stain.[65]

23. Sir Joshua
Reynolds, "Omai of
the Friendly Isles"
(1774?), preliminary
study in pencil
displaying features
more distinctively
Polynesian than those
that ended up in
Reynolds's final
portrait

Omai's racial identity – never mind that this versifier could not tell Numidian from Polynesian – proved physical rather than cultural, and ultimately ineradicable.

Culture, however, still had an important role to play in Omai's story. The plan was to take him back to his Polynesian home on Captain Cook's third voyage. But, as the Europeans who accompanied him recounted, the habits that Omai had picked up during his sojourn in England – habits that he was now apparently unable to shed – had made him unsuitable for his original people, even unrecognizable to them as one of their own. These supposed effects of Omai's cultural education were captured most eloquently in Daniel Dodd's fanciful image, "Omai's Public Entry on his First Landing at Otaheite", showing Omai "dressed cap-a-pee [sic] in a suit of armour . . . mounted and caparisoned with his sword and pike, like St. George going to kill the dragon, whom he exactly represented" (fig. 24). Although Omai did indeed bring back a suit of armor, it is doubtful that this composition represented a true scene. Rather, it

24. "Omai's Public
Entry on his First
Landing at Otaheite",
engraving after Daniel
Dodd by Royce, 1781
(Omai is accompanied
in this image by
Captain Cook)

represented how the English travelers understood what was going on: namely,
that while his acculturation in England was not enough to make a dark-skinned
Polynesian into an Englishman, it was enough to transform him into a non-
Polynesian, leaving him suspended betwixt and between as an absurd and
pathetic shadow of an archaic, quasi-mythical English past. In between two
incompatible configurations of racial identity Omai's own identity was lost.
Small wonder that one Englishman described him on his voyage back home as
"acting the part of a merry Andrew, parading about in ludicrous Masks & different dresses". It was as if nothing was left for Omai but to fill the vacuum of
his lost identity with a perpetual masquerade.[66]

Wide-Angle Lens: Gender, Race, Class, and Other Animals

The last quarter of the eighteenth century, then, witnessed the first stages of a shift in the understandings of race, as Britons – to summon once more James Dunbar's perceptive diagnosis – suddenly moved toward new ways of "imagining specific differences among men". Before this transitional moment, race had been basically mutable: changeable either through the effects of climate and the environment, or, in a more specifically eighteenth-century twist, through human interventions in the form of social customs or even individual choice. From the 1770s onward, by contrast, race was gradually and haltingly reconceptualized as an essential and immutable category, stamped on the individual; a transformation resulting in increasing strains in the older climatic or cultural understandings, now ever more on the defensive.

Consider now the emerging picture of the *ancien régime* of race and subsequent transformation alongside that of the *ancien régime* of gender. At times, to be sure – recall Wheeler's interracial marriage narratives, or Hodges's "View in the Island of Tanna" – the intertwining of race and gender was close to the surface, revealing a mutually interlocking relationship. After all, the book in which William Alexander zigzagged between culturalist and essentialist understandings of racial difference was not ostensibly about race, but rather, as its title proclaimed, about "The History of Women". And when Charles White penned his polygenetic *Account of the Regular Gradation in Man*, his essentializing song of praise for the racial superiority of Europeans suddenly shifted focus to locate racial difference in a key marker of natural femininity: where, he asked rhetorically as the very last thought in his lecture, "where, except on the bosom of the European woman two such plump and snowy white hemispheres, tipt with vermillion?" White's gushing effusion transports us right back to the loaded gender-essentializing imagery of the opening sections of this book. Conversely, recall Maria Edgeworth's *Belinda*, the novel that gave the turn-of-the-century preoccupation with the maternal breast as feminine essence such a powerful, embodied expression in the disease and cure of Lady Delacour. The second half of the novel introduced a potential romance between Belinda and a Jamaican creole: this device allowed Edgeworth to match the earlier insistence on the proper boundaries of femininity with an equally insistent cautionary tale – that moreover became more emphatic between the novel's successive editions – about the dangers of miscegenation and racial boundary collapse. The parallel that the novel posited between these two category-threatening situations was unmistakable.[1] Earlier in the eighteenth century, by contrast, one can repeatedly – and predictably – find instances of gender boundary-crossing and successful gender passing that had been intertwined with analogous racial boundary-crossings. In addition to the instances that have crossed our path before, think for instance of Gay's *Polly*, in which Polly's disguise as a "manly" female warrior is mirrored in Macheath's disguise as an unrecognizable black; or of Defoe's *Roxana*, in which the eponymous heroine blends Amazonian and European–Turkish transgressions.[2]

But even when gender and race were not interlocked in such transparent ways, the parallels between their respective late-eighteenth-century transformations are too obvious to miss: the shift from mutability to essence, from imaginable fluidity to fixity, from the potential for individual deviation from general identity categories to an individual identity stamped indelibly on each and every person. Indeed, the close affinity between the fortunes of these two identity categories across such a short period, even as their long-term internal evolutions were not at all parallel to or in synch with each other, is a revealing indication that the historical phenomenon we are observing is at bottom not really about gender or race, but rather took place on an anterior, fundamental, common level. (The attentive reader may also have noted some indications in the previous chapters of a short time lag – of no more than a few years – between the early signs of the late-eighteenth-century transformations in the understandings of gender and of race: while wary of placing too much weight on such a fine distinction, I will return to its possible meaning in chapter 6.)

At the same time, however, there were also significant *differences* between the developments of these two categories: differences that are no less revealing about the underlying logic shaping these developments. To see this point, suppose we resort – as a kind of schematic thought experiment – to an analogy. What is to race as gender is to sex? A plausible answer is *civilization*: civilization, that is, in its eighteenth-century sense – a socio-cultural degree of progress and refinement that characterizes groups of people and differentiates them from others – which is (like gender) the cultural counterpart to physical difference. Up to the late eighteenth century, civilization, from religion to custom, was more often the primary category of difference, at times even the determinative one, whereas race was more likely to prove epiphenomenal, even derivative. What comes to mind of course is the analogous configuration of sex and gender that Thomas Laqueur has posited for an earlier period, before the late seventeenth century, when gender – deriving its sway from divine providence – had been the primary category in relation to sex. If so, then the late-eighteenth-century shift in understandings of race was analogous to that which had characterized the understanding of sex a full century earlier: just as sex had emerged from the late seventeenth century as a scientifically anchored category that took primacy over gender, so did race emerge from the late eighteenth century – buttressed by the developing science of natural history – as the biological-physical substratum on which questions of cultural diversity were evaluated.[3]

But here the analogy suddenly falls apart. In the long-term development of sex and gender, as we have seen, the grounding of sex in biology was followed by an increased *looseness* of the category of gender, which for most of the eighteenth century was still allowed some of the fluidity of culture, before being reconfigured toward the end of the century in a tight one-to-one correspondence with sex. The logical question is therefore this: if the late-eighteenth-century configuration of race/civilization was similar to that of sex/gender in the late seventeenth century, why wasn't the outcome similar as well? Why did civilization not experience a similar disengagement from race as gender had done in relation to sex, with the ensuing dissonance that can be described as looseness or playfulness, instead of increasingly rigidifying throughout the first half of the nineteenth century? The differences between the outcomes of these situations, we can speculate further, cannot be accounted for through the respective internal evolution of these categories over time, which we have taken to be roughly analogous and which thus could have been expected to produce a similar period of conceptual play. Rather, the fact that this did not happen can lead us to surmise that the primary historical factor was a *synchronic* one that affected both categories at the same time but was external to, and presumably more fundamental than, their internal developments. We are inching closer to a need for an anterior notion of "identity regime": that is to say, an underlying, historically specific configuration of epistemological preconditions for the understanding of identity and self on which notions of race and gender – as particular instances of identity categories – depended. It will remain for the second part of this book to sketch the contours of the very different identity regimes that prevailed respectively in the short eighteenth century and in its closing decades, and that provide the common thread for our observations on gender and on race. But first, I would like briefly to point to the same common thread in the simultaneous developments of other identity categories that have not yet crossed our radar screen.

Humans and Animals: Closer and Closer Apart

The cameo appearance of Edward Long in the previous chapter might have left readers familiar with his reputation somewhat puzzled. For I have not yet given Long leave to speak the lines that fixed his reputation as the "pivotal" pro-genitor of modern British racism: the lines that posited the pseudo-scientific association of blacks with apes. Long deduced the close affinity between the supposedly lowest of the human races, the Negroes, and the apes – an affinity that clinched in his eyes the natural hierarchy of races – from the vaunted notion of the great chain of being: the existence of "a regular order and gra-dation, from inanimate to animated matter; and certain links, which connect the several genera one with another; and, under these genera, we find another gradation of species". This chain of fine gradations linked monkeys to apes and apes to humans. "That the oran-outang and some races of black men are very nearly allied", Long asserted, "is, I think, more than probable." Indeed, he pressed his point further: "it is credible that they have the most intimate connexion and consanguinity" – an insinuation made explicit in his report-ing of rumors of sexual intercourse between apes and Negroes (especially Hottentots). In order to secure the distinctiveness of the racial boundary separating Europeans from blacks, then, Long was happy to undermine another boundary – that between humans and animals.[4]

Some twenty years later, Charles White – Long's fellow founding father in the pantheon of modern British racism – returned to the same question in his own polygenetic ruminations. Like Long, White paid homage at the beginning of his treatise to the "gradual and imperceptible steps" of nature's great chain of being, in which "it is often difficult, and sometimes impossible, to draw lines of distinction" between different classes of plants and animals. Like Long, White asserted that "the African . . . seems to approach nearer to the brute cre-ation than any other of the human species". And like Long, White reported the rumors of interbreeding between apes and blacks. "This last circumstance is not, however, certain": suddenly White, who seemed to agree with Long so often on so much, signaled that he was about to change tack. In White's eyes it was inconceivable for the dignity of man to accept "that several species of simiæ [simians] are [also] but varieties of the species Man". God forbid (liter-ally). Unlike monogenesis, therefore, which made such crossings imaginable by allowing for such wide variance *within* a single human species, the polygenetic alternative to which White subscribed "so far from degrading, tends much more to dignify the human race than the opposite one". It was only the poly-genetic scheme that in White's view guaranteed the absolute integrity of the boundary between humans and animals: precisely the opposite consequence for this boundary than that entailed by Long's earlier efforts.[5]

It should be obvious where this is leading. Each of these two racial theorists, I want to suggest, however similar their opinions, represented a different way of thinking about the boundary between humans and apes, and more broadly between humans and animals. The former was broadly characteristic of the short eighteenth century, in both high-brow and popular circles. The latter gave voice to a distinct development of the closing decades of the eighteenth and the early nineteenth centuries. Once again, therefore, in the context of a different (it not unrelated) identity boundary, we can glimpse a pattern that dovetails with our story so far.

To begin with humans and apes. As Arthur Lovejoy noted in his classic study many decades ago, it was during the eighteenth century that the notion of the great chain of being reached the peak of its cultural diffusion and acceptance. This metaphorical scheme of creation was understood to imply, in the words of Joseph Addison, that "the little Transitions and Deviations from one Species to another, are almost insensible". "The wonderful Gradation in the Scale of Beings", went John Hildrop's mid-century recycling of this familiar common-place, renders "all Parts of the Creation . . . so closely linked together, that it is not easy to discover the Bounds between them." "Thus is this wonderful chain extended from the lowest to the highest order of terrestrial beings" – this was Soame Jenyns – "by links so nicely fitted, that the beginning and end of each is invisible to the most inquisitive eye." To be sure, the consequence of this gradualist view of the universe for the status of humans within it was not a foregone conclusion: recall Charles White. Indeed, up to the late seventeenth century the divine sanction of the uniqueness of man, made in God's image, had been sufficient to prevent too much speculation in this direction. But as Lovejoy again pointed out, during the eighteenth century the great chain of being did come to have the conspicuous effect of shrinking the distance between man and those beings immediately below him. Here is Hildrop again: "the Partition betwixt the lowest Degree of Human, and the highest Degree of Brute-Understanding, is so very slender, that it is hardly perceptible." And Jenyns, more poetically: "The superiority of Man to that of other terrestrial animals is, as inconsiderable . . . as the difference of climate between the north and south end of the paper I now write upon." And for a final word, Viscount Bolingbroke: "Man is connected by his nature, and therefore, by the design of the Author of all Nature, with the whole tribe of animals, and so closely with some of them, that . . . the difference of species, appears, in many instances, small, and would probably appear still less, if we had the means of knowing their motives."[6]

When Bolingbroke and his contemporaries conjured up a mental image of "the whole tribe of animals" following close on man's heels, those that led the pack were of course the simians, whom Carl Linnaeus was to join with humans

25. A humanoid orang-utan, from
Captain Daniel Beeckman, *A Voyage to
and from the Island of Borneo*, London,
1718. Beeckman reported acquiring one
specimen that "slept lying along in a
humane Posture with one Hand under
his Head"

in the primate order of mammals; and especially the orang-utan, which was
only then beginning to be known to Europeans and was often confused with
the chimpanzee (fig. 25). A run-of-the-mill paean to the great chain of being,
in which "the Limits and Boundaries of . . . Species seem left unsettled by
Nature", continued thus: "The Ape or Monkey that bears the greatest Similitude to Man, is the next Order of Animals below him. Nor is the Disagreement between the basest Individuals of our species and the Ape or Monkey so
great. . . . The most perfect of this Order of Beings, the *Orang-Outang . . .* has
the Honour of bearing the greatest Resemblance to human Nature." When in
mid-century it was said of the antiquary Martin Folkes, President of the Royal
Society, that he could find "no difference between us and animals", this was
coupled with the report that he therefore "professe[d] himself a godfather to
all monkeys". "I could never look long upon a Monkey", the playwright
William Congreve famously wrote in a letter of 1695, "without very Mortifying Reflections, thô I never heard of any thing to the Contrary, why that Crea-

ture is not Originally of a Distinct *Species*." (I do not know whether William Kent's 1736 Congreve Monument in Stowe, in the shape of a pyramid topped by a monkey looking into a mirror, was inspired by this letter.) Around the same time Edward Tyson dissected an "orang-outang" – really a chimpanzee – with the intention of laying to rest the speculations about its humanity while also exploring its affinity with human anatomy. But as Susan Wiseman has pointed out, Tyson's *Orang-Outang, Sive Homo Sylvestris: Or, the Anatomy of a Pygmie Compared with That of a Monkey* (1699) had precisely the opposite effect, raising the specter of the transformational relationship between human and ape. All that was required to metamorphose one into the other, it seemed (at least to some), was for the ape to be taught to speak.[7]

True to eighteenth-century form – recall the interest in the cultural shaping of gender and race – contemporaries were intrigued by the possibility (famously entertained, among others, by Rousseau) of such a transformation across the human/animal boundary; that is, of turning ape into human through cultural tutelage. Or the reverse: when the *Gentleman's Magazine* concluded that Peter the wild boy, a feral child brought to England from the forests of Hanover, "seemed to be more of the Ouran Outang species than of the human", the implication was that a human bereft of the effects of civilization would degenerate across that labile species line over to its simian side. The same implication was also lurking in James Houstoun's 1722 account of the "barbarous" people of Sierra Leone: "As for their Customs, they exactly resemble their Fellow Creatures and Natives, the Monkeys." Peter Shaw's *Man. A Paper for Ennobling the Species* spelled out what others merely implied. We know of instances of humans born and bred "among wild beasts of the forest", Shaw wrote: "the creatures so educated, spoke no language, ran upon all fours, hunted their prey, and had the cries, actions and gestures, of their foster parents." However, this was not a cause for concern: "as, in the general order of things, brutes stand so near us, it is no great condescension in us to compare them with ourselves. Do not education, knowledge and virtue, constitute the essential difference betwixt man and brute?" The "essential difference" between human and ape turned out to be the mutable and reversible one conferred by civilization; and this, in Shaw's eyes, was indeed grounds "for ennobling the species".[8]

Such a perspective helps contextualize the considerable contemporary investment in the several well-known eighteenth-century feral children captured while roving the woods in different parts of Europe. Commonly seen as indeterminate figures suspended midway between human and animal – consider the three-fold representation of Peter the "Wild Youth" as gentleman with necktie and waistcoat in between his earlier incarnations as animal cub and tree-climbing anthropoid (fig. 26) – feral children were the ideal test case for perfectibility through education. (This fanciful image notwithstanding, these

26.   Before and after: Peter the wild boy between animal and human, from the title-page of *An Enquiry How the Wild Youth*, London, 1726

experiments were typically not crowned with success.) Alternatively, these cul-turalist presuppositions also begged to be tested on sharp-witted apes. One such civilized ape was the orang-utan reported by Buffon to have adopted distinc-tive human behaviors: "But these apparent indications of human sagacity", the *Monthly Review* explained, "are to be considered chiefly as the effect of edu-cation." London got its own example of an ape instructed in what was sup-posed to pass for human behavior in the form of "Madame Chimpanzee", who in 1738–9 became the talk of the town – with the town's tongue only partly in cheek – as a well-dressed, well-behaved, perhaps human creature (fig. 27). Walking upright, sitting to her food, sipping a cup of tea, and lastly "laying in State [as] the African Lady Mademoiselle *Chimpanzee*", this prodigy was exhib-ited to hoards of gawkers of all classes, who were encouraged to conclude – in the words of the president of the Royal Society, Sir Hans Sloane – that she/it was "the nearest to the Human Species of any Creature".[9]

It was but a short distance from admiration for the quasi-humanity of "Madame Chimpanzee" to proposing the cross-breeding of apes and humans in laboratory conditions, though if the rumored experiment was actually attempted, the results were not reported. (The *Monthly Review*, for one, abhorred the very thought that "the striking resemblance which this animal bears to man" might drive a philosophically inclined European to "take a hideous and hairy female *Orang Outang* to his arms, on a mere *possibility* that she might be a woman, and might produce a breed capable of continuing itself".) But then – to return to the more pernicious consequences of this way of thinking – it was not the Europeans who were likely to be seen as sexual partners for the apes. Africans, Lady Mary Wortley Montagu was convinced, "differ so little from their own country people, the Baboons, tis hard to fancy them a distinct race, and I could not help thinking there had been some ancient

27. Madame Chimpanzee holding a tea cup, B. Gravelot after Gerard Scotin, 1738. The text accompanying the plate, dedicated to Sir Hans Sloane, began thus: "This Creature was brought over by Capt Henry Flower in the Ship Speaker from Angola on the Coast of Guinea in August 1738. It is of the Female kind & is two foot four Inches high, walks erect, drinks tea, eats her food & sleeps in a humane way."

alliances between them". Jonathan Swift memorably capitalized on the titillation of such imaginary unions in the scene in which the bathing Gulliver is attacked by a lustful half-human, half-animal female Yahoo with unmistakable intentions.[10] The echoes of this common early-modern refrain were still clearly audible in Edward Long's pronouncements in 1774: while Long partook of a new way of talking about race, there was little novelty in his understanding of the boundary between humans and animals.

By 1795, however, Charles White, while reproducing Long's ideas about race, was speaking from a new and more uneasy perspective on the human/animal boundary. If Tyson's dissection of the chimpanzee had marked the eighteenth-century opening up of potential cracks in the boundary between humans and apes, then their subsequent reclosure was arguably marked by Peter Camper's triumphant announcement in the *Philosophical Transactions of the Royal Society* for 1779 that he had proven beyond any doubt "the absolute impossibility there is for the Orang and other monkies to speak". That this was indeed a sign of a

broader cultural volte-face is evident in the way that the *Monthly Review* chose
to open its report of Camper's discovery, as one that can help explode the
"popular opinion among the honest tars, that monkies could speak if they
would". The suggestion that apes could be taught to speak, or that they were
"of the same species with mankind", a suggestion that had not too long ago
been entertained by sundry scholars and educated lay people, was now dismissed as a vulgar belief befitting only unenlightened sailors.[11] It was a "long
exploded opinion" – thus the sneering Johann Forster in 1778 – that therefore
merited no serious attention. Subsequent denials of the potential proximity of
humans to apes came fast and furious. Upon examining an orang-utan, a contributor to the *Gentleman's Magazine* reassured its readers, he had found that
its appearance "resembled the human countenance much less than I expected".
"His claims to humanity are founded on his being able to walk upright occasionally," wrote another, but in fact, "although the *ourang* can occasionally act
the *biped*, yet he is much better qualified to walk on his fore-feet, and to climb
trees" – not to mention his inability to speak and a variety of other incontro-
vertible arguments against his potential humanity. The gap between apes and
men is immense, the *Britannica* insisted, pouring ridicule on those who "have
endeavoured to level man to the rank of quadrupeds" or, equally absurdly, "to
elevate certain of the brute creation to the same class with their reputed
lords".[12]

   If ridicule was the goal, nobody presented an easier target than the eccentric
James Burnett, Lord Monboddo. A more interesting thinker than critics were
often willing to admit, Monboddo has gone down in posterity as the ultimate
eighteenth-century believer in the orang-utan sharing the same species with
man, to the point of marshaling forth not only stories of human–ape copulation but even of men with tails. The larger argument of Monboddo's *The
Origins and Progress of Language* of 1774 was that speech is not a natural essential human trait, but rather an acquired one: "it will be . . . impossible", he
therefore observed, "for a man who is accustomed to divide things according
to specific marks, not individual differences, to draw the line betwixt the Orang
Outang and the dumb persons among us." For contemporaries who pigeon-
holed Monboddo as the man who had "gone further in brutifying human nature
than any other author, ancient or modern" (thus James Beattie), he became a
convenient peg on which to hang the dismissal of such self-evidently ludicrous
claims. The tone is captured well in a letter of Hannah More's in 1782: "rather
than sacrifice his favourite opinion, that men were born with tails, [Monboddo]
would be contented to wear one himself." Dr. Johnson was moved by
Monboddo's reputed opinions to snigger that "other people have strange
notions, but they conceal them". A satirical pseudo-travel account that marked
Monboddo as its target on its title-page, which bore the motto, "An Ape, and

28. Bringing to light the Monboddian man-animal, from [John Elliott?], *The Travels of Hildebrand Bowman*, London, 1778

Savage (cavil all you can), Differ not more, than Man compared with Man", capped several well-pointed barbs with an image of the "traveler" bringing to light a Monboddian man-animal in the pure state of nature (fig. 28).[13]

The easy sarcasm notwithstanding, it is worth noting that Monboddo was in fact more in tune with his contemporaries' awakening concerns than either they or many subsequent scholars have been willing to concede. Far from dissolving the boundary between humans and animals, Monboddo – true to his system – found it necessary to include the orang-utans in his definition of man in order to *preserve* the clarity of the human/animal distinction. Monboddo was convinced that the difference between orang-utans and men was marginal and "easily to be accounted for from the change which culture and civilization makes upon all animals". It was secondary to the difference between humans and (real) animals, which was natural and essential, "for *nature* is permanent and unchangeable, like its *author*". However bizarre the outcome, Monboddo did declare his commitment to "the Distinction betwixt Man and Brute, [which

is] the Foundation of the Philosophy of Man", and believed that his system
effectively "defended the *humanity* of Man" rather than the reverse. It may be
more fruitful, therefore, to understand Monboddo as yet another contemporary in the expanding gallery of those whom we have seen struggling to reconcile older notions with new pressures during this transitional period.[14]

Once again, the marks of these contradictory pressures can be traced in dissonances that the reader may find by this point rather familiar. Take Oliver
Goldsmith's *History of the Earth*, published the same year as Monboddo's work.
"In some of the ape kind the resemblance [to man] is so striking", Goldsmith
asserted in his characteristic Buffonesque vein, "that anatomists are puzzled to
find in what part of the human body man's superiority consists; and scarce any
but the metaphysician can draw the line that ultimately divides them." The
metaphysician, that is, and Goldsmith himself, at least by the time he wrote a
further couple of volumes of his natural history. Returning again to the
human–ape relationship, Goldsmith now found their undeniable resemblance
to be an "aukward" one, and hastened to add: "From this description of the
Ouran Outang, we perceive *at what a distance* the first animal of the brute
creation is placed from the very lowest of the human species." While it was
still true that "the gradations of Nature *in the other parts of nature* are minute
and insensible", Goldsmith now found it imperative to insist on one exception:
"but in the ascent from brutes to man, the line is strongly drawn, well marked,
and unpassable." No more need for the metaphysician. These uncompromising assertions, moreover, not only flatly contradicted what Goldsmith had
written in the earlier volume, they also jarred with the image that appeared on
that very page (fig. 29). The illustration depicted an orang-utan with accentuated human features, a tradition of representation – recall fig. 25, p. 132 – that
dramatized the affinity between apes and humans, going back to Tyson's
anthropoid chimpanzee. Here was one transitional dissonance on top of
another.[15]

Or listen to William Smellie, the compiler of the first edition of the *Encyclopaedia Britannica* and a distinguished naturalist, whose 1790 magnum opus
remained steadfast in holding to eighteenth-century views, not least with regard
to the finely graded chain of being. (Like Goldsmith, Smellie was deeply influenced by Buffon, whom he had translated into English.) But Smellie too now
found this position increasingly uncomfortable. "In descending the scale of ani-
mation" below humans, he sighed, "the next step, *it is humiliating to remark*, is
very short. Man, in his lowest condition, is evidently linked, both in the form
of his body and the capacity of his mind, to the large and small orang-outangs."
Next come apes and monkeys, who "terminate this partial chain of imitative
animals, which have *such a detestable resemblance* to the human frame and
manners". Great chain of being it still was, but it was no longer the crowning
glory of nature as much as a "humiliating" and "detestable" embarrassment.

The Ouran-Outang.

29.   The orang-utan in Oliver Goldsmith, *History of the Earth*, London, 1774: erect, expressive, and holding a stick partly stripped and shaped like a cane. The possible humanity of the orang-utan is also suggested by the dwellings in the background, bounded by and conforming to the triangular space delineated by the ape's workmanlike stick

Or a "mortifying" one, in the words of William Dickson in 1789. Or "very humiliating" and "odious", as the divine Humphry Primatt admitted in 1776 even as he quoted what he took to be a statement diminishing the distance between human and animal directly from scripture.[16] (One is reminded of those female soldiers who toward the end of the century suddenly became embarrassed and uncomfortable in following the well-trodden paths of their forebears.)

Or take James Dunbar, well remembered for his agonizing vacillation between incompatible understandings of race at precisely this moment. Dunbar was no more certain about the question of humans and animals. On the one hand he maintained that "the boundary is scarce discernible which divides the rational from the animal world", and even granted "some foundation" to accounts of human–animal procreation. But on the other hand he also insisted – all this within the space of two pages – that he was "far from affirming that ever there was no distinction" between humans and animals, since there was always "some decisive mark of superiority in every condition of men". By the time Dunbar added yet another qualification to the qualification – "but the line which measures that superiority is of very variable extent" – the reader was left wondering whether it was human superiority over animals that was very variable, or merely Dunbar's opinion about it.

To be sure, we can find the occasional early-nineteenth-century writer who still capitalized on the affinity between humans and orang-utans. But it is instructive that two such cases that stand out – one an earnest vegetarian manifesto, the other a satirical novel about an orang-utan ("Sir Oran Haut-ton") who becomes a Member of Parliament – have both been described by scholars as out of touch with their times, harking back to bygone eighteenth-century sensibilities. When contemporary readers dismissed the former as "eccentric", "absurd", and "nonsense" – and this *not* on account of its animal-defense position per se, as will become evident shortly – they were demonstrating the same perplexed incomprehension that confronted vestiges of the *ancien régime* of identity whenever they re-emerged long after their sell-by date. It is also telling that when another feral child, Victor of Aveyron, was discovered in 1799, he was no longer interpreted as an exemplar of nature, let alone a missing link between humans and animals, but rather, as Julia Douthwaite has noted, as a medicalized pathological case of human degeneration.[17]

Finally, lest this section fall on the side of the quaintly exotic, we should remind ourselves that the question of the human–ape distinction had pressing political consequences in the late eighteenth century, being closely implicated in the growing campaign against slavery. Abolitionists insisting on the humanity of blacks were quick to mobilize current concerns about the boundary between human and animal by pointing out that the pro-slavery position imperiled the integrity of this boundary. Responding directly to Edward Long, an anonymous magazine contributor put the case very strongly. If blacks could have procreative sex with orang-utans, then "the harmony of the animal system must have been ruined". In truth, however, what prevented "the whole order of animals" from thus imploding "in the utmost confusion" was the "insurmountable barrier" that in fact did exist – *pace* Long – between humans and animals. Another opponent of slavery called it "a chasm": no matter that this supposed chasm was incompatible with the principle of the great chain of being to which this same writer appeared to subscribe. By the impermeability of the barrier between human and animal, wrote another, "every possibility of confusion is prevented, and the world is forbidden to be over-run by a race of monsters". Were it not so, queried a like-minded fictional character, how would we know "where . . . does the man end, and the monkey begin? . . . we shall find ourselves, more degraded than even by the whimsical system of Lord Monboddo".[18] (The fact that Monboddo supported slavery might have had something to do with the universal misreading of his declared intentions.)

*

The transformation in the contemporary disposition toward the boundary between humans and animals was not limited to the human–ape interface on the great chain of being. In a more generalized sense, the distinction between humans and *all* animals was now insisted upon in ways that it had not been in the earlier decades of the eighteenth century. It is not only that this shift was evident in a proliferation – in various contexts – of pronouncements like those of the abolitionists in the previous paragraph, asserting that man was "distinguished from the whole tribe of animals by a boundary which cannot be passed"; and even more so in their sometimes defensive tone that appeared to protest too much (*"how slender so ever it may sometimes appear"*, thus a writer of 1809, "the barrier which separates men from brutes is fixed and immutable").[19] More significantly, key aspects of the ways Britons were approaching the animal world also shifted at the same time, reflecting new ways of thinking and new concerns.

Take the concern for animal welfare. The argument for animal rights can be undertaken from two opposite premises: one of similitude – humans ought not to maltreat animals because they are really not that different from them; and the other from difference – humans ought not to maltreat animals precisely because they have the rational and moral faculties that animals lack. As Keith Tester's authoritative account points out, it was precisely during the late eighteenth century – from the 1770s onward – that the former perspective, predicated on the affinity between humans and other living things, was rapidly superseded by the latter, predicated instead on the privileged status of humanity and the confidence in unbridgeable distance. Here is a mid-eighteenth-century advocate of animal welfare: "Brute Animals are something more than mere Machines, [and] have an intelligent Principle residing within them"; from which the reader must conclude "that he ought to treat them as Beings, very different from Machines". And another: "there is, perhaps, no Passion belonging to human Nature, which may not be found in some Brute Creature in a considerable Degree", and they "have more Reason than they can shew"; consequently "we are obliged . . . to be their Guardians and Benefactors". But compare this retort from the end of the century: "What difference can it make to an oyster whether it be swallowed alive or dead?" – this, to remind us, from another advocate of the *same* moral position! "I answer", this writer continued, "that if only the feelings of the man be concerned [in preventing cruelty], it is enough for my purpose", since this purpose was the safeguarding of the distinctive humanity of man. "When we compare Man and Brute, we find both Excellence and Superiority to center in Man," went another late-eighteenth-century statement; "the distance between us is infinite" – a presupposition from which the speaker proceeded to launch one of the most passionate appeals against cruelty to animals during this period. And then there was Jeremy Bentham's famous plea in 1789: "the question [to be asked about animals] is not, Can they *reason*? nor, Can they *talk*? but, Can they *suffer*?" It too, of course, was based on the argument from human–animal difference. Indeed, this was the mode of argument that dominated all subsequent discussions of parliamentary bills against cruelty to animals, of which there were no fewer than eleven between 1800 and 1835.[20]

The new way of thinking was also evident in the status of veterinary medicine. Was it a coincidence that the short period in which veterinary medicine was institutionalized as distinct from human medicine, with its own schools and training, occurred right in the middle of the transformation we have been following here? Medical historian Roy Porter, for one, thinks not. In his view, the opening of the first veterinary college in London in 1791, with the intention of excluding doctors specializing in humans and establishing the professional independence of veterinary medicine as a distinct pursuit, was indeed a symptom of a conspicuous distancing of animals from humans at the threshold of the modern world.[21] Another such symptom – to shift domains once more – can be found in literary critic Adela Pinch's study of turn-of-the-century Romantic anthropomorphism, which she sees as a peculiarly modern way of thinking. Unlike pre-modern anthropomorphism, which had been an expression of human–animal proximity, its modern form as it emerged during this period was – again – predicated on the distance between humans and animals, a distance that allowed for their metaphorical association.[22]

Following Pinch's cue, it is possible to conceptualize the late-eighteenth- and early-nineteenth-century transformation in the understanding of animals in relation to humans as a shift from synecdoche to metaphor. One contemporary, at least, explicitly embodied this shift in the changing forms of his own thinking. This was John Gregory, in his *Comparative View of the State and Faculties of Man with Those of the Animal World*. The first edition of 1765 repeated the common wisdom about the great chain of being, whose gradations are so close together "that one Species often runs into another so imperceptibly, that it is difficult to say where the one begins and the other ends"; not least, as the title of the work suggested, where animals end and humans begin. By the revised edition of 1777 (reprinted 1785), however, Gregory was in unmistakable discomfort about this suggestion, to the point of wishing that he had given the work a different title altogether. His use of "animal", he now explained in a newly added preface, was primarily a metaphorical way of talking about "man in his savage state" – when "he often displays the instinctive courage of a Tyger or the cunning of a Fox" – rather than an approximation of humans to real animals.[23] To remain within Gregory's chosen metaphorical terrain, here was a contemporary who was caught like the proverbial deer in the headlights of the fast-moving onset of cultural change.

*

In a pioneering inquiry some twenty years ago, Keith Thomas already outlined the contours of this transformation of the human/animal boundary. "In the eighteenth century", he observed, "popular and learned notions about animals combined to weaken the orthodox doctrine of man's uniqueness", resulting in the humbling thought that "there was no firm line between man and beast". But then "human pride . . . was salvaged, at least for Europeans, by the emergence in the late eighteenth century of doctrines which would nowadays be called racialist" – or essentialist; doctrines that in previous decades "had been notably absent".[24] Thomas linked this shift specifically to the development of racial thinking, and rightly so. But we should also be able to see now that the full context of these shifts was in fact a broader one. The pattern, after all, is that of a set of identity categories that had allowed to imagine individuals falling between their cracks, thus exposing the limits of these categories; which was then superseded by an absolute categorization that left little room for crossovers or blurriness. This is precisely the pattern we have seen at this moment for both gender and race, despite their inherent differences. Likewise, the chronology of this evolution is also familiar. The earlier, relatively fluid understandings of the boundary between human and animal appear to have emerged – recall the case of gender – sometime around the late seventeenth century, with the decline of the divinely sanctioned certitudes of man's uniqueness, and to have flourished throughout the short eighteenth century. During this period one could thus imagine in very similar terms a man – in this case perhaps an autistic man – who "except with respect to his figure . . . differed very little from the brute creation" (1748), side by side with a man who could be "all Woman, except some Distinction of Sex in *Bodies*" (1750).[25] Late-eighteenth- and early-nineteenth-century retrospective observers, by contrast, no longer found these earlier gestures toward fluidity comprehensible.

Nor, for that matter, do we. It may be the fact that the human/animal boundary has not been subjected in recent years to the same effective pounding as the categories of gender or race that makes it harder for us to put ourselves in the shoes of eighteenth-century Britons who, say, paid good money to see a Swiss centaur in all his part-man, part-horse glory, or a "man-Tyger" from Angola that "comes the nearest human Nature of any Animal in the World", or a boy covered with fish scales from his neck downward, or an unspecified creature that was "Humane upwards, but Bruit downwards, wonderful to behold". (These were not simply ignorant crowds – in 1699 an account of a man-pig was presented to the Royal Society by none other than Edward Tyson himself.) Nor

would we feel comfortable in the shoes of those contemporaries who believed
that such creatures could plausibly be the offspring of the interbreeding of man
and animal, or indeed that sexual unions between humans and animals could
have any offspring at all. (When in 1716 an American cow "brought forth a calf,
which had so much of a human visage as to make the attentive spectators apprehensive that the poor animal has been impregnated by a beastly negro", this
account was again forwarded to the Royal Society of London, this time by
Cotton Mather.) Still less comfortable would we find the shoes of those who
upon discovering evidence of attempts at such unions took animal as well as
human to be, in some sense, morally culpable, and thus hung them *both* for bestiality. The "*ancien* human/animal *régime*", as it were, produced, if not some
strange bedfellows, then certainly some strange outcomes.[26]

But none, perhaps, was more outlandish – to our eyes, that is – than the event
with which I would like to end the discussion of the human/animal boundary,
an event that "engross'd all Conversation for six Months" in 1726. It was then
that one Mary Toft, an illiterate woman from Surrey, claimed to have given
birth to rabbits – seventeen all told, on average about two a week between
October and December – before her hoax was publicly exposed. The most significant aspect of this story was less the hoax itself than the remarkable fact
that a great many sensible people, including some trained in medicine, were
willing to entertain the possibility that Toft's claims could be true, or at least
to reserve judgement. The story, attested one contemporary, "was generally
believed by sober Persons"; that is (thus another), by "so many Persons of distinguished Sense and Figure". "The whole philosophical World is divided into
two partys," reported Lord Hervey; "& between the downright affirmation on
the one hand for the reality of the fact, & the philosophical proofs of the impossibility of it on the other, no body knows which they are to believe."[27] Many
eighteenth-century Britons, then, immediately saw the hoax for what it was.
But for many others, *prima facie*, the presuppositions underlying this occurrence were not all that outlandish. If, as one more writer who commented on
the human–animal distinction put it, "all the Difference must be only in the
Degrees of *Plus* and *Minus*, and if we judge of this from Matters of Fact, probably there is no Difference at all" – if so, then human rabbit-births were not
out of the question.[28]

But by the early nineteenth century there was no longer any space left for
such a possibility. By this point Toft's story, still circulating in popular memory,
was universally laughed out of the room as "preposterous", "the grossest imposture ever practised on human credulity", "the most obvious fraud that ever was
attempted", and one for which the blame was laid entirely on "this most impu-
dent, profligate, and indecent of imposters" rather than on her public. As Lisa
Cody has pointed out, by the end of the eighteenth century there was nobody

left – let alone any medical authority – who could entertain any doubts whatsoever regarding this episode, or understand how anyone might have possibly taken it seriously before.[29] The incredulous finger-wagging at eighteenth-century people, placing them beyond the pale of comprehension, reminds us once again how effective the shift we are pursuing here had actually been.

The Distinction of Class

Let us summon one more time the Scottish writer James Dunbar. As we recall, Dunbar's efforts to come to terms with new understandings of human diversity led him to conclude his 1780 *Essays on the History of Mankind* with an essentializing plea for "the Hereditary Genius of Nations" that was conspicuously inconsistent with some of his earlier pronouncements. In this sudden and uneasy pitch for "original and constitutional differences in the human species" Dunbar was concerned primarily with the permanence and significance of racial characteristics. But when he speculated in a Lamarckian vein about the origins of "hereditary characteristics [that] are interwoven into the genius and essence of the mind", he introduced an analogy to another category of difference between people: social position. Beginning with the familiar Scottish observation that "different degrees of refinement and civility characterise the various orders of citizens", Dunbar took his argument in a direction that might have surprised his compatriot predecessors: "and the dignity or meanness annexed to the sphere in which they move, is, by no violent transition of imagination, transferred to their immediate, and even to remote descendants, and regarded as appendages of posterity." Transmission to posterity: in effect, this was an extension of the "hereditary genius of nations" to a hereditary "distinction of ranks" (Dunbar's phrase). "Thus families are formed," Dunbar reasoned further, "where men become destined, *from birth alone*, to occupy, in civil society, more or less exalted stations."[30] Like race, in other words, social position – or "class" (which I am using, again, heuristically, with all the prerequisite caveats) – was also innate and congenital.

Now, on the one hand, this move was really not very surprising at this juncture. Class distinctions were often drawn into late-eighteenth-century essentializing discussions of other identity categories. This was the case, for instance, for the turn-of-the-century bee-text that converted the potential gender-destabilizing consequences of the role of the drones into an affirmation of class distinctions. (Where the drones are "differently formed by nature from . . . the majority of the tribe" is in that "they are exempt from all labour", "lazy gentry" whose "life so soft and delicate is [necessarily] of short continuance".) Such was the case for those late-eighteenth-century travelers whom we have seen reinterpreting the greasing practice of the Hottentots not as undermining distinctions of complexion but as reaffirming distinctions between social ranks. (The purpose of greasing was "to distinguish the various ranks and orders of people, in the same manner as difference of dress and insignia of office do amongst us".) Such was also the case for the entry "Negroe" in the third edition of the *Encyclopaedia Britannica*, which shored up the distinction between races with an analogy to "the immense difference" separating European nobles and peasants. ("If they had been separately found in different countries, they would have been ranged by some philosophers under different species.") Such was the case yet again for the animal-rights advocate Humphry Primatt, who equated cruelty to animals with other instances of misuse of natural distinctions ordained by God, like race or class ("for it is no more a man's choice to be poor, than it is to be a fool, or a dwarf, or black, or tawney").[31]

At the same time, however, we should proceed with caution. For it was not simply the case that at some point in the late eighteenth century class categories were suddenly given a resolute shove along the axis from porous and malleable to absolute and inviolable, in a manner similar to those of gender or race. In a way, what took place was precisely the opposite: just think of the decade following the French Revolution, when the possibility that social distinctions *could* be leveled fueled the most turbulent political polarization since the seventeenth-century civil war. In other words, the very question of whether class position was fixed became an explosive and divisive political issue rather than a tacitly accepted precondition for debate.

And yet, despite these differences between class and the other categories we have been following, I do want to make a case for a structural similarity on another level. I will make this case in a rather different manner from that employed elsewhere in this book: not only because the ubiquity of the language of social distinction during this period, especially in its many acres of political prose, would require a whole book of its own just to lay down an adequate slice of the evidence; but also because in a way I have already written this book (though I was not completely aware of doing so at the time). Instead, I will revisit my own work – especially what I now see as the most revealing gap in it – in order to attempt a more comprehensive argument about the language of class in relation to broader developments in notions of identity and self during this period.

In *Imagining the Middle Class* I was concerned with charting and explaining the emergence of a newly resonant map of social categories, centered on the image of the rising middle class, which began to proliferate from the closing years of the eighteenth century. I argued that the introduction of the notion of "middle class" as key to understanding British society was not a straightforward and inevitable reflection of changes in social structure, but rather a contingent result of changing political configurations between the late eighteenth century and the 1830s that had made this vision of society especially resonant. In particular, I accounted for the heightened investment in the notion of "middle class" in the 1790s through the specific characteristics of the political configuration created by the wars with republican France: namely, the need to posit a social corollary to a political map of radicalized extremes and a moderate pro-peace middle (what this means will become more clear in a moment). Since the argument was not about genealogy of formulation but rather about prevalent patterns in political rhetoric, I scoured many hundreds of political sources and heaped up mounds of contemporary enunciations in order to demonstrate these patterns as convincingly as I could.

As I was writing the book, I remained aware of the fact that the political configuration during the wars of the 1790s bore some resemblance to that during the war in America twenty years earlier. The logic of the argument therefore made it reasonable to surmise that a close look at the political language of this earlier war would have yielded a proto-peak of "middle-class" language of a nature similar to its uses in the 1790s; and indeed I added a footnote to this effect.[32] But in fact, I have since undertaken a wide survey of the political materials generated by the American war (for reasons that will become evident in chapter 6), which has yielded very little support for this assumption. Rather the contrary: in hundreds of American war tracts, pamphlets, and speeches, there was precious little "middle-class" language to be found. So little, indeed, that the few exceptions that did surface (about half of which, as it turned out, I had crammed into that hapless footnote) only remind one how resounding this silence really was, especially in comparison to the loaded explosion of this language in the 1790s. It seems safe to say that "middle-class" language, overall, did *not* play a significant role during the debate on the American war. Now, within the politically driven logic of my book, this absence is puzzling. It takes the question away from politics and back to the evolution of class language: can we identify changing preconditions in the understandings of class that made it amenable to such political uses in the 1790s but not in the 1770s? The answer, arguably, brings us straight back into the thick of the present inquiry.

We can begin to see this by resorting one more time to the analogical thought experiment that opened this chapter. To the question: what is to race as gender is to sex? I answered, civilization, and proceeded (with caution) to show certain similarities in their respective relationships, and especially in the putative transformations of these relationships in the late eighteenth century. Suppose we ask now, in a similar vein: what is to *class* as gender is to sex, or civilization is to race? At the risk of pushing the analogy to its limits, and possibly even beyond, there does seem to me to be one answer that makes sense: namely, *the political.* Just as gender was the behavioral-cultural scaffolding erected around perhaps-naturalized sex, allowing for change over time in contemporary understandings of their relative precedence and of the extent to which their relationship was a determined one; and just as civilization was the behavioral-cultural counterpart to physical difference – to "race" – allowing likewise for change over time in contemporary understandings of their relative precedence and the extent of their determinative relationship; so we can see the political as the behavioral counterpart to social position – to "class" – and ask about the change over time in the ways contemporaries understood the correlation between them.

The contours of the analogy may hopefully now begin to emerge. Like the modern assumption of a close correlation between gender and sex, modern politico-historical interpretation – as it developed in the nineteenth century (think Marx) – is similarly predicated on an assumption of a relatively tight link between class and political behavior. Just as individuals cannot escape their sexual bodies to adopt dissonant gender identities without severe complications, so they cannot readily escape their class position to adopt dissonant political ones. In their modern guises, gender mirrors sex, and political behavior mirrors class. Not that there have not been plenty of refutations of this determined relationship, just as has been true, again, for the sex–gender one; but a modern class-society perspective involves a constant investment in explaining away those fissures in what is otherwise a very neat scheme. (Indeed, it is surprising how many of us historians still reach for the comfort of this scheme in interpreting the behavior of past individuals: the familiar tell-me-your-father's-occupation-and-I-will-tell-you-who-you-are fallacy.) But how did this confidence come about? When did political alignments come to be conceptualized as mirroring those of social positions? I would like to propose that it may well have been precisely in the late eighteenth century that social position, the analogue to sex or race, suddenly came to be seen as determining political behavior, the analogue to gender or civilization, to a much greater degree than before; and that from this perspective the eighteenth-century pattern of change in the understanding of class does appear suggestively parallel to what we have seen for gender and race. This proposed shift, moreover, will then allow us to account for those seemingly puzzling differences in the uses of social categories between the American and the French revolutionary wars.

In order to draw the contrast between the infusion of social language into political rhetoric in the closing decade of the century and the prevalent patterns of earlier decades, let me recall briefly some aspects of the 1790s scene as I have sketched it out in *Imagining the Middle Class*. (Since politics now emerges as an additional cultural domain providing grist for our mill, the next few pages involve more political narrative than heretofore.) The key to the political configuration of this decade was its stark polarization. "We live in times of violence and extremes," Charles James Fox declared soon after the war with republican France had broken out. "The nation is reduced to the desperate necessity of chusing one of two extremes," echoed another pamphleteer; and "no mild medium will be allowed". And yet a "mild medium" did want to be heard. In between these two extremes, standing on an increasingly shaky footing, remained the self-proclaimed "middle party": the respectable opposition that distanced itself both from government war policy and from radical agendas, and that was rooting for an end to the war. It was the need of these "moderates" – another label they often used – to justify their claim for a legitimate if unfashionable *political* middle position, I argued, that led them to a concerted emphasis on the legitimacy and virtues of the *social* middle. What they represented, wrote one of their ranks, was "the respectable intervention of the middle ranks of men . . . and active advocates of moderate reform": that is to say, a natural correspondence between the social and political medium. Enter the "middle class": this, in fact, was how this social category was introduced into British political rhetoric in a sustained and resonant way for the first time.[33]

Meanwhile, those greater numbers at the extremes of the political map, radicals and conservatives alike, did their utmost – however unselfconsciously – to ignore this language, if not actively to reject it. Instead, both radicals and conservatives held to a dual social scheme that corresponded neatly to a bipolar vision of the political map. "There never was, or will be, in civilized society, but two grand interests, that of the RICH and that of the POOR," declared James Mackintosh in his defense of Jacobinism; "the differences of interest among the several classes of the rich will be ever too slender to preclude their conspiracy against mankind." "It is in the order of God's Providence that the poor should derive their support from the rich," concurred a preacher from the other corner of the political arena; "the poor can no more live without the rich, than the rich without the poor." A clearly dichotomized social map was the natural counterpart to the Manichean view of the political map that both radicals and conservatives shared. Consequently, as I have shown in some detail, in their exchanges with the moderate opposition they were literally talking past each other, employing different and indeed incompatible schemes of social categorization.[34]

But the most significant observation from our current perspective is what all these different political camps had *in common*. What they shared, regardless of their politics and of their preferred social scheme, was the prior expectation of a correlation between a political configuration and a social one. We can see this correspondence even in the finer detail. Thus, while radicals and conservatives did indeed agree on their basic dual social categories, the former's sense of socio-political alienation led to a polarized social scheme separated by an unbridgeable abyss, while the latter's belief in the possibility of harmonious cross-class coexistence corresponded to a social vision of fine gradations at

small intervals linking the basic two poles of the social map. In short, throughout the heated political debate of the 1790s we can see that one's political map
determined one's social map; which reflected the fact that contemporaries
seemed to take for granted precisely the reverse – that one's social position
determined one's political position.

In fact, however, this had not always been – not even in recent times – a necessary or predominant way of thinking. On the contrary, one of the persistent
enigmas of eighteenth-century socio-political history is precisely the *absence* of
such a correlation. We can appreciate this difference through two especially illuminating political moments, both in the decades immediately preceding the
1790s. First, consider the agitation focused on John Wilkes in the 1760s, which
is often presented as the first episode in the emergence of modern British radicalism. As John Brewer has persuasively shown, however unlikely a figurehead
was the rakish and opportunistic Wilkes, the Wilkite movement drew crucial
energy and numbers from the middling sections of society. The latter found it
a perfect vehicle for their own particular concerns, notably independence, especially from upper-class patrons. And yet the Wilkites failed to develop a viable
"middle-class" language, or a clear political identity as middling sorts. Rather,
the language they used was one that distinguished members of a political
community by their *political* positions and practices rather than by their social
positions, and that manifested seemingly paradoxical continuities with landed
country ideology. Indeed, so consistently was the political behavior and language of the Wilkites silent on the question of their social position that Brewer
had to resort to ingenious anthropological and circumstantial methods – like
the interpretation of the elaborate numerology that pervaded Wilkite symbol-
ism as the symptom of a "bourgeois mentality" of the counting house – in order
to demonstrate how bourgeois, or middle class, this movement really was.[35]
This, then, was a case of an eighteenth-century social middle that did not
manifest an urge to configure politics and political language so as to correspond
to its middle social position.

The second moment of eighteenth-century detachment of the social and
political map I have already mentioned: the American war. Here was the flip
side of the same coin: a political configuration, only a few years after the Wilkite
agitation, that could have easily lent itself to a conceptualization of a political,
and hence social, "middleness". And yet, even as the moderate mobilization
during this crisis involved significant numbers of partisans from socially
middling strata, it nonetheless – in marked contrast to the 1790s – did not
manifest an urge to shore up its position by highlighting this correspondence
between the social and the political maps.

Both of these historical moments draw our attention to a more general
eighteenth-century conundrum, that of the spectral middling sorts: that is to

say, the absence of a clear, distinctive political counterpart to the conspicuous presence of a vibrant social middle in Georgian society. Notwithstanding the presuppositions that underlay all hues of opinion in the closing decade of the century, then, it would appear that Britons had previously been quite willing to accept that social identity did *not* necessarily correspond to political identity and behavior. This suggestion was captured insightfully in Edward Thompson's model for eighteenth-century politics as a "field of force" between patrician and plebeian poles. Thompson's dual model of power relationships manifestly did not correspond to social structure, for which historians have repeatedly taken him to task, especially over the missing "middling sorts". But in fact it is this critique, based on latter-day historians' presuppositions about how social position and political behavior *should* mirror each other, that seems further away from eighteenth-century ways of thinking. (It should also be noted that Thompson saw this model as not applicable to the closing decades of the century, when indeed these eighteenth-century ways of thinking waned.)[36]

Moreover, while the inherent malleability of the category of middle class makes it an especially convenient litmus test for changing understandings of social categories, we can see indications of a similar shift in other categories as well. Take the case of "aristocracy". Throughout most of the eighteenth century, as Paul Langford has reminded us, the term "aristocracy" had more of a political than a social connotation. Deriving its meaning from classical discourses on politics, it referred to a system of government more than to a well-defined body of people. To the extent that it did refer to a body of people, moreover, it was to the "ins" of the political system, as opposed to the "outs", who were "the people" themselves. Such categories allowed therefore for much individual slippage: a title holder heading the opposition, for instance, would have by this fact become a man of the people, overshadowing his membership in an "aristocracy". It was only from the American revolutionary crisis onward, Langford points out, that the meaning of "aristocracy" shifted to denote primarily a social group rather than a political system. This essentializing shift in the understanding of aristocracy as a social category was reinforced in the late-eighteenth-century radical attacks on the "unnatural unfitness" of the aristocracy (the words are Tom Paine's) and on aristocratic vice as inherent if not congenital. Attacks, not on the few aristocrats who happened to be prominent in politics, but on the aristocracy as a class, can again be dated with some precision – thus Langford once more – to the 1770s and 1780s; like that by Thomas Day, who in 1780 declared in unabashedly essentializing language that "from ancient Rome to modern Venice" there had never been an aristocracy "that was not the universal tyrant and inquisitor of the species". The same effect was of course reinforced further by those on the other side who rushed to counteract such attacks with fiery vindications of "the natural aristocracy of the country" – thus one typical early-nineteenth-century follower in Edmund Burke's footsteps – whose "distinctive marks . . . are sufficiently apparent" and who "is more distinguished by the gifts of nature than of fortune". (Compare this turn-of-the-century statement about the middle class: "Amid the vast variety of conduct and character with which the History of Mankind is marked, there is still conspicuous a sameness of manner and sentiment among those that constitute the middle class of society.")[37]

This essentializing redrawing of the social map took yet another form. When the radical Thomas Cooper denounced the oppression of "the People, the lower Classes of Society" by "an aristocracy of property, more or less extended", he was signaling a shift of emphasis in social categories widely observable in the decades around the turn of the century: the metamorphosis of "aristocracy" (or government) versus "people" to "rich" versus "poor". "The English government", expostulated another radical, "is formed by the rich and great, and to them it is favourable, but it has been said to be highly injurious to the poor." We have already come across James Mackintosh's similar affirmation of only "two grand interests" in politics, "that of the RICH and that of the POOR". None of these statements (and I document many more in my earlier book) are very surprising. But I want to draw attention to the significant shift they represented. This shift did not go unnoticed by contemporaries: "I thought it infinitely better to go on", one wrote unhappily in 1795, "with the old dispute of Whig and Tory, than teach men to refer all their causes of complaint to the distinctions of society, and to see only two classes in the state, and those the rich, and the poor." The center of gravity of social categories was shifting to fixed and essentialized social groupings ("independently of all political institutions," wrote Smellie the naturalist in 1790, "nature herself has formed the human species into castes and ranks"). It therefore became more plausible to map onto them political ones, as 1790s Britons – in contradistinction to their forebears – were wont to do.[38]

In *Imagining the Middle Class* I attributed this transformation in the political uses of social language to the logic of politics itself, especially the effects of the French Revolution and the war with republican France in politicizing social class and infusing new social content into the political struggle. But while it is clear that the developments unleashed by the French Revolution did have an important role in crystallizing this shift, it now seems to me that my internalist focus on politics rendered the bigger picture – that which exceeded the political narrative – invisible. The changes in the political uses of class language, I now want to suggest, relied on an anterior, underlying transformation in the very meaning assigned to categories of social identity: a transformation that led people to believe that these categories could indeed have such essential, determinative significance and, consequently, political power. If indeed such an anterior transformation had not yet taken place by the American war, but was in place by the French revolutionary wars, then the ostensibly baffling observation with which I began, about the very different uses of class language in these two politically similar contexts, is immediately explained.

It is therefore highly suggestive, as we are about to turn to the underlying common picture that is the focus of the second part of this book, to note the affinity of the late-eighteenth-century shift in the understanding of social categories with the analogous and nearly-contemporaneous developments in the understandings of other identity categories, developments that were not implicated as directly in the post-revolutionary crisis and indeed preceded it. *Mutatis mutandis*, what we have seen for gender, for race, and for the human/animal boundary also happened to class. (Again, there were obviously crossovers from one category to another: it was precisely during this period, for instance, that we see the beginnings of the racialization of the working class as the domestic equivalent of "darkest Africa".[39]) Class too was reconfigured in the late eighteenth century in more holistic, totalizing, essentialized categories, categories that became more difficult for the individual to circumvent. Expectations of gender, as we have seen, now forced it into a tight one-to-one correspondence with sex. Likewise, expectations regarding political behavior now pushed it into a tight one-to-one correspondence with class – a correspondence that had been far from self-evident earlier in the eighteenth century. And just as we have seen this period of rapid change usher the categories of gender or race into their more recognizable modern guises, so we can locate in this transformation of social categories the seeds of the notions of class cohesion and class difference that underlie our vision of modern industrial society.

PART II

Bird's-Eye View: The Eighteenth-Century Masquerade

Imagine one of those attractive photograph albums that unfold the radical transformation of a modern city by taking the reader on a tour of the townscape through pairs of "then" and "now" shots of key sites taken from exactly the same angles. The first part of this book has performed just such an argumentative function, offering a series of before-and-after contrasts of key sites in the eighteenth-century English cultural landscape. The city album shows the transformation of one neighborhood after another by juxtaposing photographs of changes in a variety of specific locales. I have likewise tried to show the transformation of one category of identity after another by looking at each one as it changed in a variety of specific cultural locations.

In the end, however, the beholder of the photograph album cannot understand the overall pattern of change without a map of the city, demonstrating (presumably with the aid of an accompanying historical essay) the links and connections between localized changes -- this park or that street corner -- that join them into a coherent story of the historical transformation of the urban terrain as a unified whole. It is time now for this book to do the same -- to proceed from specific categories of identity to the broader cultural terrain of which they were part: the long-promised move to the identity regimes that unite our multiple snapshots of "before" and "after" into coherent wholes. Only then can we approach the objective of the mode of inquiry that I have described as "historical epistemology". Mary Poovey, like me borrowing this term from Lorraine Daston, has called on scholars to do precisely this: "we must supplement the identity categories" -- Poovey was talking about race, class, and gender -- "with categories that illuminate not the positionality or identity of [specific] groups or individuals but the assumptions and conventions that constitute the epistemological field that underwrites the salience [and meaning, I would add] acquired by identity categories at various times."[1] The awkwardness of this sentence reflects the complexity of the proposed inquiry, in going beyond – or beneath – categories of identity to the presuppositions about the meaning and constitution of identity that underpin them.

The best historical city albums (I grew up in Jerusalem with a library over-flowing with them) have one other invaluable device to introduce the reader instantaneously to the cumulative effect of their numerous pairs of contrasting snapshots: the aerial photograph. By way of introduction to part II of this book, the next few pages offer an equivalent of the aerial view: one more instance of before-and-after juxtaposition that illuminates not this or that specific category of identity, but rather some aspects of the whole conceptual terrain to which they belong and in which they intersect. The particular element of eighteenth-century culture that had the power to offer such a bird's-eye perspective on everything I have tried to say about contemporary under-standings of identity, and how they changed over time, is that quintessential Georgian institution, the masquerade.

*

It is hard to overestimate – though easy to forget – the cultural significance of the masquerade in eighteenth-century England. Although masques and similar events had of course been known earlier, the masquerade as a large-scale, commercial, non-exclusive public entertainment emerged in London from the 1720s onward, and quickly attained – as Terry Castle has richly documented – a cultural prominence not easily rivaled by other features of eighteenth-century life. The masquerade's triumphant bursting into the center of public life had in fact been prefigured on a smaller scale by a new trend noticeable already in the late seventeenth century in the self-presentation of some fashionable women, who began to wear masks to disguise themselves while out walking in public spaces. Now, the institutionalized masquerades drew large crowds – "Count" Heidegger's "Midnight Masquerades" of the 1720s and 1730s were attended by seven or eight hundred people a week; attendances for mid-century events were estimated in the thousands – and were regularly incorporated into large-scale public celebrations such as jubilees or royal visits, or imitated in numerous private settings. Those who did not participate in them were still apprized of the goings-on by regular detailed press reports: those popular "his-tories of masquerades" that had Horace Walpole lamenting that they occupied "people's thoughts full as much" as key national events.[2] Greater numbers still were confronted with this institution through its ubiquitous invocation in novels, stories, poems, plays, pamphlets, squibs, engravings, not to mention the relentless barrage of shrill moralizing criticism. Overall, eighteenth-century Britons – above all in London, but elsewhere too – were entranced by the masquerade, partly horrified, partly fascinated, and perhaps most often breath-lessly attracted to an unwholesome mixture of both. Indeed, it is remarkable how many contemporaries singled out the masquerade as the epitome of all contemporary moral and social ills, a resonant metaphor for "such masquerad-ing times" as the "dissolut[e]" present.[3]

The essence of the masquerade, of course, was identity play: arriving in costume and masks that made the participants unrecognizable. In the process, the boundaries of every category of identity were explicitly and frequently played with. There were masqueraders dressed as animals: "some, in the shape of Monkeys and Baboons, others, of Bears, Asses, Cormorants, and Owls". Others turned such gatherings to "a Congress of the principal Persons of all the World, [appearing] as Turks, Italians, Indians, Polanders, Spaniards, Vene-tians, &c." – not to mention the popular "blackamores", American Indians, and Polynesian islanders.[4] Of course, the specific context of the masquerade kept such borrowings of alternate identities, for the most part, safely within the boundaries of ludic make-believe. Nonetheless, the potential for less contain-able exposure of the limits of identity categories was never far from the surface. Indeed, I wish to suggest that it was precisely this potential, resulting from dis-tinctive characteristics of eighteenth-century culture, that endowed the mas-querade at this time with a potency – whether to be embraced or condemned – unrivaled in any other historical period.

One could catch a glimpse of this potential, for instance, when two Moroc-can ambassadors in 1726, "Black of Complection", "were introduced to His Majesty King *George* at *St. James's*"; upon which "the Gentry and Quality Flock't around them, *taking them for Masqueraders*". In such a moment of virtual passing – that is, African blacks believed to be masquerading Englishmen passing for blacks – the distinction between real-life encounters with racial dif-ference and masquerade performances of racial difference was fine indeed. This distinction grew even finer in the constant preoccupation of masquerade-goers and masquerade-watchers with the seemingly unavoidable threat it posed to social categorization. When a 1727 account gave the following poetic descrip-tion of a masquerade: "Valets adorn'd with coronets appear", "Sailors of quality with judges mix, – / And chimney-sweepers drive their coach-and-six", one assumes the references were to masquerade costume. But comments about the "confused mixture of different ranks and conditions" at such events, or that "a masquerade, levels all distinctions", or that "the *Peer* and the *Apprentice*, the *Punk* and the *Duchess*, are . . . upon an equal Foot", were obviously expressing anxiety about the undermining of actual social distinctions. Eighteenth-century depictions of the genteel masquerading as peasants and laborers were nervously entwined with reputed instances of peasants and laborers – not to mention pros-titutes – passing as members of the gentility and gate-crashing the festivities.[5]

Finally, masquerades famously undermined distinctions of gender, confounding again playful disguise with the potentialities of actual cross-gender passing. In a run-of-the-mill masquerade at Mrs. Cornelys's renowned establishment in the fall of 1777, for instance, "many assumed the appearance of the opposite sex; men in female habits, and ladies in mens hats and dominos". "Sophia and I were at the Masquerade in Mens Dominos," reported Judith Milbanke to her aunt a few months later; "we made two smart Beaux but I think I wore my Rapier with the better grace & proved the prettiest Fellow of the two." A "Queen of the Amazons", a "romping Hoyden", a "kind of Hermaphroditical Mixture; half Man, half Woman; [with] Coat, Wig, Hat, and Feather", female hussars, pirates and bishops, and other varieties of "belles, clad en-homme"; together with a man "dressed like an old woman", another "in a lady's riding dress", and yet others "transmogrified into Milk-Maids" – all these regular features of eighteenth-century masquerades conjured up those various markers of the limits of gender categories that populate the first two chapters of this book, and through them the possibilities of successful gender passing and gender confusion that they signaled elsewhere in eighteenth-century culture. The resulting observations sound by now very familiar: two sisters and their brother, went one report in 1772, "made a charming group; dressed alike, in a fancy dancing female dress . . . they might, (notwithstanding his sex) have passed for the three graces". On the same occasion "a great many of the ladies of rank and beauty chose to adopt the male dress in domino"; one of them, who "assumed a male character", was "so like a smart, pretty young fellow, that she might have been taken for one, had not (fortunately for them) some gentlemen there had pleasing proof to the contrary, that put her sex out of all doubt". But in the erotically charged milieu of the masquerade – which Castle evokes so well – there could be immediate and unsettling consequences of the fact that "it was not easy to discern the difference of sexes". "It is not certain", warned James Burgh, "that many of the figures [in a masquerade], which passed for females, were not in reality of the other sex in disguise, as it is not certain, that many of the virtuous-seeming ladies at our masquerades, are not rampant wh—s in disguise." The blurring of "the Distinction of Sexes" in masquerades (thus another admonishing voice earlier in the century) could lead even to same-sex dalliances: a titillating possibility that John Cleland, for one, did not let slip through his fingers.[6]

But while bringing to mind the earlier chapters of this book, these invocations of the unreliability of gender identities in the masquerade point us in a more general direction. For the masquerade was not really about gender, any more than it was about any other category of identity. Rather, it was a scene of bacchanalian experimentation with the protean mutability of identity on a more basic level and in all its possible manifestations. "I found Nature turned top-side-turvy," a bemused visitor to a masquerade reported, continuing in breathless succession: "Women changed into Men, and Men into Women, Children in Leading-strings seven-Foot high, Courtiers transformed into Clowns, Ladies of the Night into Saints, People of the first Quality into Beasts or Birds, Gods or Goddesses; I fancied I had all *Ovid's Metamorphoses* before me". Another resorted to verse in order to convey the same phantasmagoric effect:

> So many various changes to impart,
> Would tire an Ovid's or a Proteus' art,
> Where, lost in one promiscuous whim, we see
> Sex, age, condition, quality, degree. –
> Where the facetious crowd themselves lay down,
> And take up ev'ry person but their own;
> Fools, dukes, rakes, cardinals, fops, Indian queens,
> Belles in tiewigs and lords in Harlequins,
>   . . .
> Where sexes blend in one confus'd intrigue,
> Where the girls ravish and the men grow big.

And so he went on and on, unfolding the masquerade's untrammeled collective play with identity metamorphoses.[7]

The masquerade, then, was not simply about people dressing up: it was, at least for some, about a transformation of a different sort, in which "people were so disguised, that without being in the secret, none could distinguish them". In this momentary liberation from the shackles of identity, a contributor to the *Lady's Magazine* explained, "every one divests himself of his borrowed feathers, and following his natural propensity, assumes the character which suits him best". It takes a moment to notice that the masquerade identity is the one that this writer presented as "natural", and the off-masquerade identity as the one that was "borrowed" (I shall return to this suggestive formulation shortly). Masquerade-goers "may possibly forget their own selves in such strange dresses" – thus a mid-century writer – so much so that a masked lady can expect "never once to reflect, who she is" until the event is over. Or even beyond: the transformative nature of such events, to give one final example, was nicely captured in the masquerade scene in Defoe's *Roxana* (1724), which has the heroine exclaim: "I not only did not know any-body else, but indeed, *was very far from knowing myself*." Ironically, however, and tellingly, this identity loss at the masquerade also leads to the reinvention of the heroine, who is assigned during this very scene the name "Roxana" to match her costume as a Turkish princess; "upon which foolish Accident I had the Name of *Roxana* presently fix'd upon me . . . as effectually as if I had been Christen'd *Roxana*". This moment of rebirth is as good as any to demonstrate the potential for identity metamorphosis that was perceived to inhere in the eighteenth-century masquerade; a point driven home even further in the novel when Roxana then proceeds, albeit briefly, to talk about herself – in her new incarnation – in the third person.[8]

*

But then, suddenly and decisively, the eighteenth-century masquerade lost its cultural force. An early indication of what was about to happen came in the middle of the American revolutionary war: "From the thinness of the company at Monday night's Masked Ball," reported one observer in 1779, "it is pretty clear, that these kinds of exotic amusements are so much on their decline, as to promise a total and speedy extinction." How prophetic. Unlike the aftermath of the earlier Seven Years' War ("Though masquerades have been laid aside during the course of a severe and expensive war," the *Lady's Magazine* had then assured its readers, "we are not to consider them as banished for ever"), the 1780s and 1790s witnessed the breathtaking free fall of the masquerade from the lofty heights of its former significance. Modern-day scholars have pointed to this precipitous reversal, somewhat ruefully, as "surely among the most baffling facts about the English masquerade" (thus Terry Castle): its "deinstitutionalisation" and relegation "to the periphery of collective life were so rapid as to suggest *a kind of cultural amnesia*". That the masquerade became moribund so abruptly was plain for all to see. The main venues of former masquerading revelries now fell into decrepitude and disrepair: Carlisle House, the scene of Mrs. Cornelys's renowned masked assemblies, was closed down and auctioned off, house and furniture together, in 1785; the Pantheon, host to the largest masquerades London had ever seen, became (according to Francis Place) "deserted and obsolete", and finally burnt down in 1792 never to be rebuilt; Vauxhall and Ranelagh fell into disuse and subsequently changed their function. Mrs. Cornelys herself, the *grande dame* of masquerading, had to resort to moonlighting in other pursuits before dying in Fleet Prison in utter destitution in 1797. Writers of novels, at the same time, no longer insisted on the formerly *de rigueur* masquerade tableau. Even the barrage of anti-masquerading criticism abated, as if moralizers and their audiences were losing interest.[9]

To be sure, the masquerade did not completely vanish overnight. We can find occasional masquerades continuing into the 1790s and even into the early nineteenth century. But they were a pale imitation of what had preceded them, little more than dusted-off vestiges of a bygone practice – a practice that an early-nineteenth-century chronicler of past London life dismissed as "silly". When one Colonel Armstrong turned up at a Regency masquerade dressed after the fashion of an "old, stiff, maiden-lady of high rank in the reign of Queen Anne. . . . Curiously patched and painted", he himself – in his representation of decayed grandeur, harking back to the days of Queen Anne – was the embodiment of the anachronism that characterized the (considerably fewer) nineteenth-century masquerades. Francis Place, a keen chronicler of changes in manners during his lifetime, reminisced in the early nineteenth century that "the Masquerade at the Pantheon" in the 1770s had been "an amusement far different" from what now passed for a masquerade. Formerly, Place explained, masquerading had been undertaken "with the spirit and vigour which may vainly be sought in a modern masquerade".[10]

Like Place, Elizabeth Inchbald – writing in 1806 – was also acutely aware of the shift that had taken place during "the period of the last twenty-six years, which has produced in the world more wonderful changes in fashions, manners, opinions, and characters, than many a century had done before". What prompted Inchbald to make this observation was her republication of a 1780 play by Hannah Cowley that had included, among "other long-exploded fashions" (Inchbald's words), a masquerade scene; a scene, she noted, that "gives a certain sensation to the reader, which seems to place the work *on the honourable list of ancient drama*". This is a revealing pattern that we have witnessed before: like so many other eighteenth-century cultural practices involving identity play, the masquerade too was now glimpsed through an opaque film of unfamiliarity, a phenomenon already so distant as to be instinctively associated with the ancients. The fact that these final, authoritative words were those of Elizabeth Inchbald, moreover, who had herself romped in men's clothes in a masquerade in 1781 and reputedly passed so well as to have elicited numerous advances from other women, makes this subsequent admission of unbridgeable distance all the more meaningful.[11]

*

So how has the sudden reversal in the fortunes of the masquerade been explained? The authoritative account is Terry Castle's *Masquerade and Civilization*, on which I have drawn throughout the previous several pages. Nothing haunts Castle more than "the mystery of the masquerade's cultural death": she repeatedly returns to this "historical enigma", attacking it with every possible explanatory scheme in the armory of historians of the modern West. Urbanization, industrialization, commercialization, the emergence of capitalism, fragmentation of traditional communities, the rise of the bourgeoisie, the decline of magic (à la Keith Thomas): the rapid and somewhat exasperated succession of these provisional explanatory schemes is in itself testimony to their inadequacy to the task, inadequacy that immediately stands out when one considers the time frames and the timescales of the proposed explanations in relation to the abrupt late-eighteenth-century phenomenon they are supposed to account for. In the end, within Castle's framework, the demise of the masquerade remains, as she admits, "an interesting and perhaps insoluble historical puzzle".[12]

Now, insofar as the history of masquerades is concerned, it should be obvious that I am about to propose the broader story of this book – and in particular the late-eighteenth-century cultural shift that I have been at pains to document – as the context that sheds light on what otherwise does appear to be an insoluble historical enigma. (The reader will also surely not fail to notice the interpretive sleight-of-hand in this move, which rather than *explain* the enigma of the masquerade's demise simply replaces it with another, more comprehensive in scope and hardly less mysterious. Indeed, I have not offered yet any explanations for the patterns we have been observing: but when I arrive at explanatory propositions, as I shall shortly, it will be seen that this more comprehensive context is key to their formulation.) At times the connection between these developments surfaces explicitly. Inchbald herself, in other writings – notably her 1791 novel *A Simple Story* – coupled the shift in the meaning of the masquerade with a particular concern for its potential for compromising gender boundaries, a concern in step with the increasing unease we explored earlier.[13] Likewise, when a woman's attempt in an early-nineteenth-century play to don male clothes for a masquerade is curtailed by a friend who exclaims, "your sex is too obvious", there is surely little point in trying to distinguish whether this was a denial of a woman's possible success in passing for a man – that is, a manifestation of our so-called gender panic – or another nail in the coffin of the eighteenth-century masquerade.[14]

But more important for my purposes here is the light that the history of the masquerade can shed in return on our broader story. For this, however, we need to add to Castle's "mystery of the masquerade's cultural death" the prior mystery of the masquerade's cultural *birth*: how do we account for the masquerade's extraordinary cultural resonance in the previous decades, a resonance without parallel before or since? Castle does not really raise this question, opting to analyze the purchase of the masquerade, with its concomitant understandings of dress and of self, in universalizing and ahistorical terms. Instead, prompted by the striking parallel between the rise and fall of the eighteenth-century masquerade and this inquiry's broader narrative of change over time, I would like to highlight the uncanny suitability of the masquerade to the historically specific understanding of self (with its implications for the understanding of dress) that characterized what I have called the *ancien régime* of identity, and which I now want to explore more directly. The masquerade was a sanctioned, ritualized, to a degree even conventionalized, collective exploration of the possibilities inherent in the *ancien régime* of identity. It thus dovetails with – and pithily epitomizes – the many other ways in which we have seen eighteenth-century Britons touch upon, and admit, the limits of identity categories. This is why I have compared the masquerade to an aerial photograph capable of presenting the whole terrain at once: in drawing together these various elements of the story, the masquerade points to the underlying assumptions about identity and self that unify all that we have seen so far into one fundamental eighteenth-century pattern. It is to this underlying pattern that we now turn. Once we have a better sense of the foundations of the *ancien régime* of identity, moreover, the demise of the masquerade, as soon as a new identity regime had superseded the old one, will appear not only comprehensible but predictable and even inevitable.

4

The Ancien Régime *of Identity*

"The World's All Face"

In the middle of the eighteenth century one A. Betson, an idiosyncratic writer with a scholarly bent, published a treatise on masquerades, setting the scene with a seemingly innocuous definition: "Masquerades, or Masqueraders, are *Persons in Disguise*, representing or acting other Personages, than what they are commonly known to be." Now read this definition again, paying particular attention to how its ending betrays an archaic way of thinking. We might say, "masqueraders are acting personages different than what they *are*", but we are less likely to say that they act personages different than what they *are commonly known to be*. It is not much of a stretch to hear in this formulation an admission that real life was itself not unlike a masquerade: both, it seems, involved assumed identities. The difference appears more one of degree than of kind: whereas in real life one is known to be a particular character most of the time, in a masquerade one sports a character only for an evening.

Betson, accordingly, made it clear that masquerades, contrary to what some may think, had very little to do with that other familiar arena of role-taking and dressing up, the theater. "Plays were originally a Kind of Mimicks of Masqueraders, representing the Actions of others in different Views." Theater was artifice, mimicking the actions of *others*: masquerades, by contrast, were simply expressions of alternative truths of the masqueraders themselves, allowing people "almost [to] change their Nature with their Habit". Furthermore, Betson claimed, perhaps most radically, that the imperative to do so was an essential aspect of human nature: the declared purpose of his learned treatise was to establish masquerades as a natural and universal phenomenon, one "as old as the Worlds second Infancy . . . [and] common to most Nations". More than a person's identity, it was masquerading itself that came closest to characterizing the essence of humankind.[1]

I am not aware of anyone else in eighteenth-century England repeating Betson's historical, or rather ahistorical, line about the primordial and universal origins of the masquerade. But in other important ways, pertaining both to the institution of the masquerade and to its underlying assumptions about identity, Betson was certainly at one with conventional wisdom. Thus, contemporaries would not have been particularly surprised by Betson's suggestion that the masquerade had some fundamental affinity with real life. Quite the contrary: the observation that the masquerade offered a singularly apt lens through which to view and understand broader aspects of "The Times" was put forth by so many eighteenth-century Britons so often that we would be foolhardy not to heed whatever insight they took to be behind it. Witness this (modest) string of examples: "the World being a Masquerade, where borrow'd Vizors so disguised e'ry one, that none knew ev'n his own acquaintance" (Charles Gildon, 1692). "What is human Life, but a Masquerade" (John Trenchard, 1720). "[The present is] such masquerading times/ . . . 'Tis not a world, but Chaos of mankind" (Edward Young, 1728). Society is "a vast Masquerade, where the greatest Part appear disguised" (Henry Fielding, 1743). "The globe is all masquerade" (street ballad, 1750). "The rich and the powerful live in a perpetual masquerade, in which all about them wear borrowed characters" (Samuel Johnson, 1750). "This metropolis is a vast masquerade" (Tobias Smollett, 1753). "Every Place is Masquerade now: There's no knowing a Man by his Face; he always wears two" (a self-consciously cross-dressed dramatic heroine, 1755). "The world's a masquerade! the masquers, you, you, you" (Oliver Goldsmith, 1769, addressing a theater audience). "Society [is] . . . a meer chaos, in which all distinction of rank is lost . . . 'tis one universal masquerade, all disguised in the same habits and manners" (Hannah Cowley, 1781).[2]

On one level, to be sure, such pronouncements were simply recycling that vaunted image in Western social criticism, the *theatrum mundi*, or the world as a stage. And yet, counter to Betson's ahistorical perspective, these speakers were giving this theme, often self-consciously, its own time-specific particularity. "Poets and philosophers, both ancient and modern, have compared this world to a theatre, and considered human life as the grand drama thereof," declared an essayist in the *St. James's Magazine* in 1774; "but as mankind in general seem to act the impostor, I think we may with equal propriety compare human life to our modern masquerade." The timeliness of the invocation of the masquerade as a metonym for society writ large was especially evident in a letter from Elizabeth Montagu to Hannah More in the early 1780s: "it is the ton of the times to confound all distinctions of age, sex, and rank; no one ever thinks of sustaining a certain character, unless it is one they have assumed at a masquerade." We shall return to Montagu's evocative formulation later. For now, it is sufficient to note the resonance of this repeated refrain, as a clue to eighteenth-century presuppositions – presuppositions about disguise and human nature, identity and fluidity – that gave specific meaning to the claim that "the world's all face".[3]

As we unfold these presuppositions that made up the *ancien régime* of identity, the reader will recognize affinities with the patterns identified in part I of this book for the history of specific categories of identity in the short eighteenth century. It bears repeating that, a priori, there was nothing inevitable about such affinities: the fact that in this particular historical configuration they did occur – a synergy that the masquerade embodied so well – points to a powerful shared epistemological framework that underpinned these patterns. In our pursuit of these common underpinnings, two important characteristics of the *ancien régime* of identity stand out. The first is malleability: the sense that one's "personal identity" (a clunky term, but, as we shall see, a contemporary one with a reputable provenance), at least in principle or under certain circumstances, could be imagined as unfixed and potentially changeable – sometimes perceived as double, other times as sheddable, replaceable, or moldable. The second and closely related point is somewhat harder to formulate in its own terms, because we conceive it initially as an absence. This is the absence signaled in the phrase "before the self": indicating a time that lacked a sense of a stable inner core of selfhood like that which will emerge at the turn of the eighteenth century. This "pre-self", as it were, had not been contained or well represented by the spatial model of surface versus depth, which was later to become the main modern visual aid for understanding selfhood. "The world's all face", it will turn out, was more than a metaphor. Instead, we can visualize this eighteenth-century configuration as a set of positions within which one identified oneself – a set of coordinates, or a matrix. One's position in this matrix, which could be prescribed or adopted (thus allowing for both subordination and agency), was relational. Alternatively, we can think of this eighteenth-century configuration as a "socially turned self", to borrow Sarah Knott's felicitous phrase, indicating that its primary leanings were outward rather than inward.[4] Within a post-Romantic terminology, or within the definition of "self" that I insisted on at the beginning of this book, a "socially turned self" is a contradiction in terms. But this contradiction – which also allowed categories of personal identity (as we shall see) to be primarily *collective* rather than individual – actually captures rather effectively this elusive characteristic of the *ancien régime* of identity.

Proteus Unbound: Personal Identity in the Short Eighteenth Century

"Why, then I'd be any thing – and all! – Grave, gay, capricious – the soul of whim, the spirit of variety." Thus exclaims a woman in love in Hannah

Cowley's *The Belle's Stratagem* of 1781 as to the lengths to which she would go for her husband. But how far *was* she willing to go in becoming "the spirit of variety"? She would, as we see, change her temperament. She would "feast with him in an Esquimaux hut, or a Persian pavilion". She would go as far as to "change [her] country". Finally, and more startlingly, she declares her willingness to change even "my sex" (for her lover, no less!). This woman's confident willingness to transform herself extended from behavior and disposition through national identity all the way to gender identity and identity *tout court*; a fact underscored by the playwright's decision to set her profession in the midst of a masquerade scene, thus parading before the play's audience, with all the visual lushness of fancy costuming, the many possibilities of personal metamorphosis. The fact that this masquerade scene, in turn, followed close on the heels of an earlier pronouncement of society – of everyone on and off stage – as "one universal masquerade", guaranteed, in typically unsubtle eighteenth-century fashion, that the audience would not miss the point.[5]

Lord Monboddo surely would not have missed it. A few years earlier he had had the opportunity to proclaim his unshakable belief in the fundamental mutability of man. The occasion was his publication in English of the story of a French feral child, Mademoiselle le Blanc, who, allegedly, began her life as a white girl, was abducted to be sold into slavery and therefore painted black in order "to make her pass for a negroe" (note again the ease of racial passing here taken for granted), before being shipwrecked in France and thus found as the "savage girl" who was now in the process of becoming civilized. Monboddo was quick to dismiss the skeptics. The facts of this story, he affirmed, could only be doubted by such people who against

> all testimony, ancient or modern . . . are resolved to believe that man, the most various of all animals, in the many different states through which he passes, continues still the very same animal, endued with the same powers of mind and body, living in the same manner, and governed by the same notions and opinions; a proposition which appears to me incredible in itself, though it were not contradicted by the whole history of mankind.

Both history and common sense – not to mention the adventures of Mademoiselle le Blanc – proved the protean nature of humankind. James Boswell was another who was glad to make the same announcement. "I have discovered", he exclaimed with excitement several years earlier, "that we may be in some degree whatever character we choose."[6]

To be sure, people in every generation can be found to make such pronouncements. But in the short eighteenth century they may well have *meant* them in a different and more literal way. The female soldier who succeeded in her masquerade for years undetected; the European captive who became indistinguishable from his or her Indian captors; the heroine who lost her own sense of herself at a masquerade; Mademoiselle le Blanc who was painted to pass for black; and likewise a great many of the characters who have paraded before you in the previous chapters with borrowed, assumed, and replaceable identities, together with their public or their audiences who were willing to give credence to their stories; all of them signaled a sense of malleability of identity that is far from our own when *we* say – to borrow a refrain from a 1970s musical – "we could have been anything that we wanted to be". It is for this reason that we have taken the roundabout, hopefully scenic route through eighteenth-century culture in order to see all these characters in their various identity-flexing moments. After all, it was much rarer for contemporaries to formulate and record their understandings of identity in an explicit, self-conscious fashion.

At the same time, certain contexts – typically rather high-brow ones – did occasionally encourage a more direct reflection on the malleability of identity. One such context was, not surprisingly, that of the theorizing of the theater. Where Betson drew a stark distinction between the "real" identity transmutations at the masquerade and the artificial identity charades at the theater, others made precisely the opposite claim for the stage, stressing how *un*artificial, or natural, Georgian acting really was, at least when it was done properly. In the process, their understandings of the potentialities and the limits of identity play came through unusually loud and clear.

In an early contribution to the English theory of acting, the playwright Aaron Hill began with the "first dramatic principle" that "must be always upper-most": "To act a passion well, the actor never must attempt its imitation." Rather, he must move his mind so that he actually *feels* that passion itself, as "when 'tis undesigned, and natural": only in experiencing real feeling can the actor make the audience experience it too. The subsequent step was perhaps more surprising. In order for the actor to "strongly impress the illusion of his performance upon us", repeated John Hill (no relation) in another key work of acting theory adapted in part from French sources, "he must first impress it as strongly upon himself"; and – here comes that next step – as a condition for "his utmost success, it is necessary that he imagine himself to be, *nay that he for the first time really is*, the person he represents". "The player of true spirit" – John Hill again – "is no longer himself, when he assumes his character . . . he lives, not acts the scene." Not step, one might say, but leap: a leap from imaginative representation to actual embodiment. "An *Actor*", Charles Gildon flatly insisted in the first English contribution to this genre earlier in the century, "must transform himself into every Person he represents." A model actor – thus another critic – was a "delightful Proteus, so wholly transforming himself into his part, and putting off himself with his clothes, as he never (not so much as in the tiring-house) assum'd himself again until the play was done." This metamorphosis should hold even away from the view of any audience, in the privacy of the "tiring-house". The same wisdom was echoed in a 1743 essay in the *Gentleman's Magazine*: a good actor is "so much of the *Person* he represents, that he puts the *Playhouse* out of our Heads, and *is* actually to *us* and to *himself*, what *another Actor* would only *seem to be*". Note the essayist's underscoring of "is". Unlike the verisimilitude of bad actors – those examples of "unnatural acting" (thus another authority) who "perform in *disguised* characters" – a good actor *is* whomever he represents.[7]

This good actor, in mid-eighteenth-century England, was no mere academic ideal type, but rather had a well-known identity and an established name: David Garrick. Or rather, this idealized actor had made an established name for himself by conspicuously placing the knowability of his identity in question. Garrick's claim to fame was precisely his ability to lose himself in his roles. Garrick "obtains your Applause", Samuel Foote explained, "by persuading you that *he is the real Man*"; in comparison to him, lesser actors simply appear "ridiculous". Henry Fielding famously capitalized on – and paid tribute to – his friend Garrick's reputation in *Tom Jones*. Upon being taken for the first time to a play, the "unimproved" Partridge – part barber, part schoolmaster – ranked Garrick's performance as Hamlet below that of the strutting, mouthing performer who personated the King, since it did not seem to him like acting at all. This protean reputation, moreover, extended to his life off stage, as in the anecdote about how Garrick, upon encountering a carriage driver who refused to set off with only him and a friend as passengers, re-entered the carriage four times in different characters, thus "succeed[ing] in convincing the man that he had six fares". The ultimate act of passing by the man whose identity was infinitely variable: in the parting words of his friend Oliver Goldsmith, "Here lies David Garrick, describe me who can. . . ."[8]

Now consider Garrick's reputation within the context of the broader questions that are the focus of this book. For, as Shearer West reminds us, the widespread belief that Garrick succeeded so well in actually becoming the characters he was supposed to represent on stage was not just a statement about Garrick's singular acting talent, but also, and perhaps primarily, a reflection of the assumptions and expectations of his audiences, who were confident in his ability – and the general possibility – to do so. Nor were these expectations simply the result of a desire for faithful realism on stage: on the contrary, Garrick's characters, like others before the late-eighteenth-century turn to "authenticity", were often played against the backdrop of incongruous, ahistorical, and unrealistic settings. Rather, these assumptions and expectations of Georgian theatrical audiences offer a revealing glimpse into contemporaries' willingness to imagine personal identity, albeit in unusual circumstances, as

fluid and mutable. For, as Paul Friedland has persuasively argued, in contrast
to our familiar understanding of the theater that supposes its successful effect
to result from the belief (or rather the suspension of disbelief) of the spectator, the onus in the *ancien-régime* theater was placed on *the actor*. It was the
actor who was expected to believe in his own actual metamorphosis in order to
achieve the ideal dramatic effect. Acting was taken to involve a difficult process
in which – to quote one authority of 1759 – the actor "make[s] a temporary
renunciation of himself" and "forget[s] if possible, his own identity". Edmund
Burke, recounting a personal experience of trying to imitate a passion that
resulted in his mind actually "turn[ing] to that passion", likewise admitted that
his own attempts paled in comparison with those of the ultimate mimic, the
man "able to enter into the dispositions and thoughts of people, as effectually
as if he had been changed into the very men". As Garrick himself once wrote, the
superior actor "will always . . . be transported beyond himself". "If you cannot
lend yourself to these metamorphoses," cautioned another, "do not venture
upon the stage."[9] These metamorphoses, involving the suspension of one's
identity, were certainly admitted to be difficult; but the significant point is that
they were considered *possible*.

So what *were* eighteenth-century audiences thinking? Or actors, for that
matter? Did they all simply believe in complete transformation of the identity
of performers on stage? This was the difficulty that Dr. Johnson captured so
well when he observed, "if Garrick really believed himself to be that monster,
Richard the Third, he deserved to be hanged every time he performed it."
Think again of *Tom Jones*'s Partridge, mistaking Garrick's acting for real-life
behavior. After all, Fielding was winking at the reader at Partridge's expense:
a collusion that presupposed that both reader and author knew something about
the theater that the barber-schoolmaster did not. At the beginning of the
century, the playwright George Farquhar wrestled precisely with this question.
In watching Alexander the Great on stage, he wrote,

> we must suppose that we see the very *Alexander*. . . . Yet the whole Audience
> at the same time knows that this is Mr. *Betterton*, who is strutting upon the
> Stage. . . . And that the same Person shou'd be Mr. *Betterton*, and *Alexander*
> the Great, at the same time, is somewhat like an Impossibility, in my Mind.
> Yet you must grant this Impossibility in spight of your Teeth, if you han't
> Power to raise the old Heroe from the Grave to act his own Part.

A person, Farquhar seemed to suggest hesitantly, could embody two identities
at the same time, however difficult this was to comprehend. Occasionally we
can find a critic driven by this difficulty to the language of mystery and the
preternatural – like John Hill, who at one point likened the actor to "the priest-
ess of the Delphic God, who as soon as she ascended the sacred tripod, became

possessed, and uttered with a voice and mien, not her own, the sacred oracles". But I want to call attention to the suggestive possibility raised by Farquhar that drew less on notions of magic – more typically a feature of earlier, seventeenth-century acting theory – than on a potential inherent in contemporary under-standings of personal identity: its possible doubleness.[10]

Nobody, to my knowledge, drew these connections more explicitly than Dr. Johnson's close associate James Boswell. In 1770, Boswell published a series of essays in the *London Magazine*, as a plea to Garrick to write his "Theatrical Testament"; and presumably, if Garrick did not oblige (he did not), to become a substitute for it. In a way, these essays can stand as a testament to the entire *ancien régime* of acting, shortly before it was about to turn obsolete (as will be recounted in chapter 7). Boswell began by "tak[ing] for granted" the conven-tional eighteenth-century wisdom "that a good player is indeed in a certain sense the character that he represents, during the time of his performance": Insisting repeatedly that the fact that the player "*is* what we behold" is a "mysterious dif-ficulty", Boswell then felt obliged – not least, because of the question of moral responsibility raised by Johnson as well – to qualify his argument: "I beg leave to remind my readers", he fidgeted, "that I qualified my proposition by saying that a player is the character he represents only *in a certain degree*; and there-fore there is a distinction between his being what I have said and his being the character he represents in the full sense of the expression." Admitting he was "at a loss" to explain, he tried anyway: "If I may be allowed to conjecture what is the nature of that mysterious power by which a player really is the character which he represents, my notion is, that he must have a kind of double feeling. He must assume in strong degree the character which he represents, while he at the same time retains the consciousness of his own character." Like Farquhar, Boswell was seeing double: in order to account for the difficulty of one person sporting two identities at the same time he pointed to identity's lack of inher-ent unity, invoking, as we shall see later, philosophical authorities to support his point.[11] Be two or not be two, that was the question; and when posed by Garrick's Hamlet, Partridge, for one, did not know the answer.

So the misconception that Johnson mocked, and that Partridge was mocked for, was the failure to understand the complexity of the identity duplication involved in the "mysterious" process of the actor's metamorphosis. At the same time, what both Johnson and Fielding presented as the simpler understanding, the default of the uninitiated with less discernment than themselves, is telling: namely, that actors' identities are truly shed as they assume those of their char-acters. Not identity-splitting, then, but identity substitution. But ultimately, what is important for us is that both the vulgar and the educated views allowed – however differently – for the possible mutability of identities, thus revealing cultural presuppositions about the meaning and nature of identity that they held in common. It is this shared cultural ground, moreover, that may help explain how Boswell, after professing the mysterious and difficult nature of the transformation undergone by an actor like Garrick, could suddenly turn around to claim that in truth "the double feeling" that he had identified in the actor was "experienced by many men in the common intercourse of life", and even that without it "society would not be half so safe and agreeable as we find it". Suddenly everyone turned out to be Garrick. "Like players", Boswell concluded, we all "are to a certain degree a different character from our own": or, as many would have put it, and did put it, the whole world was a masquerade.[12]

We shall see shortly that the possible doubleness or splitting of personal identity surfaced in multiple eighteenth-century contexts, and was a defining feature of the *ancien régime* of identity. But for the time being let me call on just one contemporary witness to give a foretaste of the broader conceptual environment within which these discussions of acting were taking place. Explaining his notion of "sympathy" (which will demand our detailed attention later), Adam Smith gave the following description of how it works:

> when I condole with you for the loss of your only son, in order to enter into your grief I do not consider what I, a person of such a character and profession, should suffer, if I had a son, and if that son was unfortunately to die: but I consider what I should suffer *if I was really you*, and I not only change circumstance with you, but *I change persons and characters*.[13]

The affinity between Smith's meaning in this passage, which itself was closely related to his understanding of theatricality, and the thoughts of the eighteenth-century dramatic theorists about the metamorphosis of the actor, is unmistakable.

For the modern reader, the most remarkable aspect of such statements is that their speakers appeared to be suggesting, indeed often insisting, that they were to be taken literally rather than metaphorically. As we increasingly realize this, familiar themes will re-emerge in a rather new light. Take for instance a statue of Shakespeare that Garrick had commissioned from Louis-François Roubiliac for his Hampton villa, a statue recently rescued from obscurity when its copy was chosen to grace the entrance to the new British Library in London. Garrick, famously, had offered himself as the model for Roubiliac's Shakespeare, a fact that left its indubitable marks on the statue's pose, appearance, and expressive gesture (fig. 30). To what extent then was this statue meant to be seen not simply as Garrick *posing* as Shakespeare, but more literally – and certainly well in tune with other contemporary pronouncements – as Garrick *being* Shakespeare, his actual living embodiment?[14]

Or consider again our encounters with Boswell. In 1762, as we recall, Boswell reported his excited discovery "that we may be in some degree whatever char-

30.   Garrick as Shake-speare: terra-cotta model (1757) for Louis-François Roubiliac's statue of Shakespeare at David Garrick's Hampton villa, posed for by Garrick himself. The final marble statue was somewhat less expressive and theatrical than this earlier model

acter we choose". Now, almost a decade later and in a completely different context, his words were almost identical: the actor "is the character he represents only *in a certain degree*"; and again – like the actor, we too "are to a certain degree a different character from our own". Boswell's detailed dissection of the latter statements may thus further our appreciation of the literalness with which the earlier exclamation could be uttered by himself and understood by his contemporaries. Likewise, we should keep in mind this conceptual environment in reflecting back on some of the formulations in earlier chapters that conjured up the possibility of identity play. In particular, given the present discussion of the eighteenth-century theater, we would do well to consider how Garrick's reputation as the epitome of protean identity added weight and immediacy to the meaning that contemporaries were likely to find in his own confident attribution of protean mutability to *others* – like Hannah More or the Chevalier D'Eon in the prologue to *Percy*.

While bringing to mind episodes from previous chapters, let us also remember that we have encountered the contemporary notion of identity-splitting on stage once before; and that together with many turn-of-the-century critics we have already been puzzled by the difficulty of comprehending what eighteenth-century audiences were actually experiencing or thinking. Recall Peg Woffington, the actress who brought the house down whenever she came on stage in male clothes – which she did as often as she could. Recall further the formulations that enthusiastic admirers invoked to characterize her success. Audiences reputedly could not decide "whether she was the finest woman, or the prettiest fellow"; under her double charms, "*both sexes* vanquished lie"; she was "A creature uncommon/ Who's both man and woman"; it was "nature, who her gave/ This *double power* to please".[15] Woffington's claim to fame, like that of other actresses in breeches parts, was precisely her ability to achieve a doubleness on stage: to be both man and woman at the same time. If one looks at gender as one specific aspect of identity, this reputation appears very much like that of Garrick (Woffington's erstwhile lover), albeit encompassing a more limited repertoire. Eighteenth-century audiences insisted that they were experiencing the performances of actresses in breeches parts as a playful splitting of identity, a splitting literal rather than metaphorical: we may now have arrived at a deeper understanding of what they actually meant. More generally, we may now be able to put a more fundamental gloss on the meaning and experience of *passing* in the eighteenth century: opening up the possibility that a female soldier, say, or the Chevalier D'Eon, or a dressed-up masquerader, together with their audiences, actually believed that they *were* the roles they were assuming, even as they retained consciousness of their original identity.

*

A word of caution: our language is becoming slippery. When Garrick's contemporaries suggested that actors, or masqueraders, or whoever, *were* the roles they were assuming, they did not necessarily imply the same meaning that this phrase is likely to conjure up in our own minds. For the modern ear, who a person "really *is*" invokes the person's true essential self – which is precisely the presupposition that I wish to historicize and problematize rather than let in again through the back door. When eighteenth-century Britons like John Hill and James Boswell used this phrase, as we saw both do, what it connoted for them was indeed, as they insisted, a literal transformation, but it was one predicated on a looser and more mutable sense of what a person's identity was to begin with. What made such views about the doubling, splitting, or transmigrating of identities possible, and to some even plausible, was a nonessential notion of identity that was not anchored in a deeply seated self; which is what rendered it so different from what was to follow.[16]

Nothing, perhaps, illustrates this difference more visibly than where so many eighteenth-century people did locate the semblance of an anchor of personal identity: *clothes*. We have crossed paths with this contemporary notion many times in the previous pages, when the putting on or taking off of clothes constituted the gist of a successful change of identity. Thus, recall Juvenal's female athlete who, in the hands of pre-1780 translators, put her gender identity on or off with her helmet. Or more generally, the significance of the breeches not only in signaling but also in effecting the crossing of the gender boundary. "What is there in the *breeches*", exclaimed one dramatic heroine, "but the *wearing!*" "I must own," declared another, "the Breeches please me most/ Tho' in the Wearing, my weak sex is lost." The very wearing of the breeches constituted the transformation of gender identity; and this was the case, as a 1774 speaker accurately put it, "literally as well as metaphorically". The full meaning of such statements informed the reception of stories like that of a supposed real-life heroine whom nobody recognized when dressed in the clothes of a male sailor, and when she reverted again to women's clothes, the man was once more unrecognizable in the woman: a double identity shift that led an observer in the know to exclaim, "*what an Alteration can Dress make?*" What an alteration indeed. On another occasion, a boy dressed up as a girl for a school play was entrusted with a clear answer:

> What comes from dressing like a Girl, a Lad?
> With my new Garb, I must confess the Change;
> No more I think o'er Hedge & Ditch to range;
> No: I grew nice, as I ungrew a boy,
> And am a Lady – Delicate, – & Coy.
> Stand off Companions; I'm no more ye same.

The humor with which the boy's companions presumably received this confession should not obscure the logic of transformation, the relations of cause and effect, that made it work. It was the same logic that underlay the praise – no joke here, nor mere figure of speech – for the actor who had "wholly transform[ed] himself" on stage by "putting off himself with his clothes".[17] It was the same logic too that underlay, in reverse, the conviction that the unmistakable difference embodied by the Moroccan ambassadors who turned up in London in 1726 must have been the consequence of their donning masquerade costumes. And it was the same logic that allowed Benjamin West to portray Indians and Europeans with equal conviction as very much alike and as very different in the two images accompanying Colonel Bouquet's expedition to the Ohio country.

Of course, the role of dress in the constitution and performance of identity was anything but a peculiarity of the eighteenth century. What *was* more specific to the *ancien régime* of identity was the possible literalness with which dress was taken to *make* identity, rather than merely to signify its anterior existence. As Ann Rosalind Jones and Peter Stallybrass have brilliantly argued, this understanding of dress – thoroughly different from our own – had deep roots in premodern Europe. Its origins were in external authority: the constitution of a person's identity – as a monarch, or a freeman of a guild, or a household servant – through the investiture of clothes. Consequently, dress was taken literally to "transnature" the wearer, a phrase taken from a late-sixteenth-century moralizing tract but still meaningful in Betson's mid-eighteenth-century vision of masqueraders "almost chang[ing] their Nature with their Habit". Again, to match Stephen Greenblatt's Renaissance vignette of the skin-clothed brutish Newfoundland savages that were transformed by English apparel to become supposedly indistinguishable from Englishmen, we can recall eighteenth-century variations on the same theme: be it John Long, say, whose dress made him indistinguishable from the Indians, or, conversely, the Indians mistaken by Mary Rowlandson for Englishmen because of their European clothes.[18]

By the eighteenth century, to be sure, the role of external authorities in conferring identity-constituting dress was long gone (outside some specific professional settings), replaced by the drives of the commercialized market. Clothes were now seen as the products of commodified fashion, and therefore as capricious and meaningless, even as they retained their former power to constitute identity. It will be seen later how this particular conjuncture, in which clothes were still taken to have constitutive power but the authorities that had previously shaped and controlled them did not, contributed to the peculiar tenor of contemporary anxieties about the consequences of fashion. But for now let us note the implications that this conception of the function of clothing had for eighteenth-century understandings of identity. For if clothing was in one sense the anchor of identity, in another it was of course precisely the opposite of an anchor, indicating instead – as in the myriad examples peppering the pages above – the mutable and non-essential nature of what can be assumed or shed at will. It was not yet self-evident that the way to establish a person's identity was by "seeing through clothes". This telling phrase is the title of an influential late-twentieth-century study of dress in Western art, whose wonderful insights are constrained precisely by the presupposition of the universality of the relationship between "inner" self and "outer" costume. Eighteenth-century identities, by contrast, could readily be established by *not* seeing through clothes.

A wonderful indication of this, difficult to document but very revealing all the same, is the theatrical casting of *twins*. What did theatrical managers do when they wanted to signal not difference but rather the opposite, sameness? From the little we know about contemporary casting choices for identical twin roles in plays like *The Comedy of Errors*, it seems clear that actors were not cast for such roles because of their physical resemblance. Instead, and here is the key, the twinness of actors – whatever two actors were available for the parts – was achieved through identical costuming: twins were people who dressed alike. Moreover, the fact that Restoration and eighteenth-century audiences accepted this sartorial generation of identity – here, also in the sense of identicality – without raising too many eyebrows can be inferred from the contrast with the clearly audible resistance with which the practice was to be dismissed, as we shall see, by their turn-of-the-century successors.[19]

Finally, recall what led us to the topic of clothes – the suggestion that the *ancien régime* of identity lacked that key characteristic of the modern under-standing of self, its depth. As Jones and Stallybrass point out, the assumed power of clothes to shape identity – to permeate the wearer – cannot be accom-modated within the determinative surface/outside versus depth/inside scheme that shapes modern thinking about essential constant self versus artificial ephemeral fashion.[20] We tend to think of "the self" as inwardly turned. For the eighteenth century, by contrast, a more helpful image may be of a self (but is it still a "self"?) that was outwardly or socially turned.

The Characterization and Orientation of *Ancien-Régime* Selfhood

In the middle of the eighteenth century, the members of the Society of Dilet-tanti, a highly exclusive London gentlemen's club "for which the nominal qual-ification [was] having been in Italy" – thus Horace Walpole – "and the real one, being drunk", decided to have their portraits painted. The importance of the project was recorded in the minute books of the society: financial penalties were to be imposed on members who did not participate in this venture. To execute the portraits the society chose one of its own members, an insider: the well-respected artist George Knapton, later to be appointed Keeper of the King's Pictures. Knapton accordingly delivered twenty-three such portraits between 1741 and 1749, and they remain the property of the Society of Dilettanti to this day.[21]

Two things strike the modern beholder of these portraits (figs. 31a–c). The first is what they do *not* do – namely, distinguish the sitters by their individual traits. Portraits are often interpreted as revealing the interior self, through the painter's ability to represent psychological depth in the sitter's face. But the portraits of the Society of Dilettanti do anything but that: rather, they stand out for their uniformity – of size, of format, of pose, and even (take a close look at the examples reproduced here) of the subjects' facial features, so spare in distinguishing marks. The second remarkable feature of these portraits is how Knapton, who was personally acquainted with the sitters, *did* introduce individualizing distinctions between them – namely, through their dress and

accessories. Jones and Stallybrass have pointed out the emphasis on clothing in seventeenth-century portraiture, to which facial features were more the background: they thus quote an (approving) account of mid-seventeenth-century portrait artists who had "in readiness a dozen or more Cards ready prepared, and ground laid of severall Complexions", so that for every sitter they could "choose a Card" – that is, a face – "as neare the complexion of the party as they could". Knapton's portraits followed this seventeenth-century practice in introducing clothing to constitute identity, where we might have expected a glimpse of the putative depths of selfhood. "The *common and usual Dress* of a Person is a great addition to *Likeness*," a mid-eighteenth-century authority on portraiture asserted with a similar logic; "for no sooner is the Dress altered, but the Look does the same."[22]

But there is still more to this particular set of portraits, which has to do with the specific garments in which Knapton clothed his sitters. In many cases the members of the society were presented in *masquerade costumes*. Most explicitly, among the examples reproduced here, note the portrait of Samuel Savage (above right), who has a masquerade domino flung over his shoulder – a lady's domino to boot, suggesting his costume involved gender-bending – and a mask in front of him. Here then was a more peculiarly eighteenth-century twist (and one that could be readily found in other eighteenth-century paintings):[23] rather than the habitual clothes of a sitter, signifying profession, status, gender, and so on, individual identity in some of the portraits of the Society of Dilettanti was constituted through the assumed characters of the masquerade.

31.   George Knapton's 1740s por-
traits of the Society of Dilettanti:
Thomas Brand, Samuel Savage, and
Baron Hobergh

The agency offered by masquerade characters, the role of clothing in con-
stituting identity, the generic representation of a group of individuals, the
absence of commitment to the depths of selfhood: Knapton's portraits of the
Society of Dilettanti are in themselves a full set of keys for unlocking the different aspects of the *ancien régime* of identity. Of all these, the most surprising, perhaps, remains the last: that is, the suggestion that I have raised in several
different ways that Knapton's contemporaries were not very much invested in
notions of inner depths of selfhood. How can that be, you may well ask: did
eighteenth-century England not famously witness the emergence of the cultural form uniquely suitable to the exploration of interiority and psychological
depth, the novel?

Indeed it did. At least, that was the basic thrust of the narrative set up half
a century ago by Ian Watt in his influential *The Rise of the Novel*, and which
has been restated by countless followers since. According to this view, the superior roundness of character in the novels of Jane Austen and subsequent
nineteenth-century writers was simply the natural progression from the more
tentative and incomplete attempts to achieve the same psychological depth in
the earlier novels of the eighteenth century. The most notable signpost on this
road was supposedly Samuel Richardson, "whose fifteen-year-old Pamela" –
thus the more recent words of Carolyn Steedman – "is all selfhood, all inside,
and whose depth as a point of reference for female interiority has been
immense". The intrinsic potential for mirroring inner subjectivity – and the
imperative to do so – were inherent in the novel genre, we have been told, from
its eighteenth-century beginnings.[24]

Recently, however, this "rise of the novel" orthodoxy has been debunked
with a loud thump by literary critic and closet cultural historian Deidre Lynch,
who in the process has done more than anyone to liberate the eighteenth
century from its retrospectively imposed interiority complex. We need to
see eighteenth-century novels, Lynch insists, and especially their portrayal of
character, "within systems for categorization and valuation that seem alien
to us". As she demonstrates persuasively, characterization in the first three-
quarters of the eighteenth century – not only in novels, but also in art and
theater – was primarily generic, exhibiting *types* rather than individuals: so
much so that over-particularization of a character was actually frowned upon
by eighteenth-century critics.[25] This was a period, after all, in which narratives
that had *objects* as protagonists – a veritable eighteenth-century mini-genre –
were read as avidly as *Pamela*. With titles like *Adventures of a Bank-Note*, such
tales were "more intent on imagining society than imagining the self" and
cannot really be said to have had "characters". Nor was the interchangeability
of the protagonist confined only to the history of a banknote: Lynch points to
a surprising number of contemporary narratives whose main characters were
deficient in distinguishing features and were consequently mistaken for people
they were not. Furthermore, even the letter form of a novel like *Pamela*, a form
that latter-day critics have often read as offering intimate glimpses into individual psychology, was in fact, as Carol Kay has argued, not an unmediated
window into personal inner depths but rather a *social* performance whose
addressees stood for "representative social authorities". In short, the function
of character in eighteenth-century literature and arts – what Lynch calls the
"*pragmatics* of character" – was primarily not about depth but about "legibil-
ity and replicability". It therefore stood in sharp contrast – not continuity –
with the expanded inner lives of fictional characters in the late eighteenth and
nineteenth centuries.[26]

The affinity and debt of my argument to that put forth by Lynch is obvious.
In particular I want to follow up on her demonstration of the generic or typological nature of eighteenth-century characterization, in which "the individual
specimen of character is meant to refer to an overarching standard of impersonal uniformity". This was true, as Lynch shows, of works of fiction, func-
tioning as "characterological compendia of human nature". It was true of "the
business of a poet", at least as defined by Imlac in Samuel Johnson's *Rasselas*,
namely "to examine, not the individual, but the species; to remark general properties and large appearances". It was true of what the eighteenth century understood by physiognomy, which was in fact – as we shall see in more detail in
chapter 7 – about the commonality of types rather than the distinctions of individuals. (Were it not for the playfulness of nature, John Ray wrote in 1691, "I
see not but the Faces of some Men might be as like, as Eggs laid by the same

Hen": that is to say, essentially men's faces, within groups, are the same.) It was often true of eighteenth-century portraiture, which despite the apparent imperative to reproduce exact likenesses ended up producing large groups of seemingly indistinguishable portraits – think again of the Society of Dilettanti, or of the scores of portraits of apparently identical bewigged Georgian gentlemen in standard "Kit-Cat" format – a phenomenon that art historian Marcia Pointon has described as an "intractable historical problem".[27] It was true of eighteenth-century fashion, which had the distinct effect of blotting out individual character: be it through impersonal accessories like the wig or hair powder (under "the Mode", wrote a 1736 observer, "one Man's Hair is as like that of another as two Drops of Water"), or even more through the treatment of the face, painted by both sexes to conceal natural skin coloring or blemishes. Finally, it was true – to go back to our touchstone of contemporary notions of identity – of the eighteenth-century masquerade, in which people put on not individualized disguise but what one contemporary described as "Charact'ric dress". Famously, the master of masquerading ceremonies "Count" Heidegger refused entry to anyone not dressed in a recognized costume type. The seeming exception, which wasn't really one at all, was the costume of a classical figure, like Hercules or Pallas Athena, in which the individual *was* the type: think, likewise, of the ubiquitous eighteenth-century penchant for public pseudonyms – in publishing pamphlets, in writing letters to the press, even in private correspondence – that were clearly recognizable classical or otherwise generic types, achieving again that same impersonal uniformity.[28]

These peculiar eighteenth-century meanings of characterization as generic and unparticularized had been clearly laid down early in the century by a work of "characterology" with the title *The English Theophrastus* (Theophrastus being the classical author of a work on thirty hypothetical characters, each typifying a single fault). The work opened with a declaration of intent: "*The Subject Matter of the following Sheets is the* Grand-Lesson, *deliver'd by the* Delphian Oracle, Know thy self." But "know thy self" in this work of the early 1700s did not at all signify what the modern reader might expect. Far from soul-searching or introspection of any kind, the book contained a heavy dose of generalized aphorisms and maxims ("*Caprice*, in *Women*, is generally an attendant of *Beauty*", and the like). "Know thy self", it turned out, meant knowing the generic type to which you belong and abstracting yourself, as it were, into a collective category: its imperative was outward, not inward.[29]

Eighteenth-century Britons were frequently explicit in asserting the primacy of collective categories or groupings over the individuals who constituted them. The physician John Arbuthnot seemed at first to go the other way when he acknowledged that human faces are of such infinite variety that "since the Creation of the World, perhaps there were never two that . . . perfectly resembled one another". But he then quickly proceeded to what he saw as a more meaningful observation: faces that "are characteris'd" – that is to say, that have legible meaning – are "not only individual, but gentilitious and national; *European, Asiatick, Chinese, African, Grecian* Faces". Arbuthnot, we may recall, was a great believer in the transformative effects of climate on human appearance – "Transplantation changeth [man's] Stature and outward Shape" – which presumably turned the reading of the individual face into a futile task. Likewise, James Macpherson and John Millar (separately, but in almost identical words) found "the character and genius of a nation" to be stable and meaningful. "But the case is very different with respect to individuals, among whom there is often a great diversity, proceeding from no fixed causes that are capable of being ascertained." In contrast to the intelligible identity of a large grouping, the distinction of every individual was "random", arbitrary, and ultimately meaningless. One is reminded here of the categorizing logic of the naturalist Buffon, who similarly contrasted the "capricious variation" of individuals – among humankind, as well as animals – with the "remarkable stability" of the "general prototype" of the species. Species were *"les seuls êtres de la Nature*, as ancient and as permanent as Nature herself", Buffon delivered his definitive verdict, while "an individual, of whatever species, is nothing in the universe".[30]

Now consider the implications of this generic or typological way of thinking, in which the individual, even if not quite "nothing in the universe", was subsumed under the more salient collective categorizations. Indeed, it can help account for a striking aspect of the *ancien régime* of identity: the relative ease with which, as we have seen, eighteenth-century men and women were willing so often to acknowledge, humor, and sometimes even celebrate the cases of individuals who appeared to defy prevailing categories and boundaries of identity. But if eighteenth-century identity categories were primarily collective, pinpointing groups ("women", "aristocracy", "Indians", "species") rather than individuals, then their conceptual integrity was not unduly shaken by the occasional individual who slipped through their net.

In fact, we have heard the physician-cum-essayist Peter Shaw prefigure precisely this observation. It was in the middle of a paean to gender distinctions, one confident in their reliability rather than anxious about their subversions, that Shaw interjected his revealing caveat. His words bear repeating: "We only propose to consider the two sexes, in general," he insisted, "without comparing particular men with particular women. Many of the female sex are, both in body and mind, formed much stronger than many of the male: but . . . we find that the females, in general, are, both in their bodies and minds, weaker than the males." The salient categories – here, "men" and "women" – were collective, conceptualized "in general" (a phrase that Shaw repeated twice). This allowed "particular" individuals the potential freedom to fall between the cracks, without having the whole conceptual edifice of contemporary understandings of identity come tumbling down after them. A couple of years earlier William Hogarth had made precisely the same point in commenting on the differences in facial proportions between men and women. "Women," Hogarth observed, "when they are dressed in mens-cloaths, look so young and boyish: but" – he hastened to add – "as nature doth not always stick close to these particulars, we may be mistaken both in sexes and ages." Nature allowed some individuals to deviate from its general, collective norm. In such a framework identity signified "identicality" (to invoke again the clumsy terms of the preface) rather than uniqueness: it implied looking outward, toward what one shared with others, rather than inward, at one's quintessence. If you begin splitting categories too often, John Hunter warned apropos his ridiculing of the polygenetic notion of distinct human races, "would not different species be produced in almost every single family? Could it not be said of the same man at different times that he in like way was of a different species from himself?" If anything, it was the over-particularizing gaze, insistent on narrower and narrower distinctions culminating in the uniqueness of every individual, that had the potential to bring down the ceiling on the *ancien régime* of identity.[31]

*

Let us take one more cue from the novel. In the standard retelling of the emergence of the eighteenth-century novel as the birth ground of inner selfhood, novels supposedly contributed to the development of interiority not only in their fictional characterizations but also in their readers. "Reading a novel (in the eighteenth century and not before)" – in the recent words of one historian – "a reader identified with an ordinary person unknown to him or her personally but with whom the reader empathized thanks to the narrative form itself. The novel disseminated a new psychology . . . [it] made the point that all selves are fundamentally similar because of their inner psychic processes; reading the novel drew the reader into those psychic processes."[32] But this assertion is problematic not only in attributing inner psychologies to eighteenth-century novel characters. It also makes significant assumptions about how contemporary readers "identified" or "empathized" with what they were reading; assumptions that can benefit from further scrutiny.

The fundamental eighteenth-century framework for thinking about empathy or identification with others – be they fictional or real-life others – was that of *sympathy*, a key term within the broader language of sensibility. It was the language of sensibility, more than any other, that provided the novel-reading classes in the middle decades of the century with practical guidance about "well-being", in a peculiarly integrated sense that joined together the physical, emotional, and moral aspects of one's life. To be sure, it is often suggested that together with the "voyage into the self" offered by novels – this particular formulation is Roy Porter's – "the key late Enlightenment concept which validated the inner self was sensibility". But did it really? The basis of sensibility, as the word implied, was the senses. Drawing on prevalent medical understandings of the nerves together with the cognitive ideas of associationism, which explained how primary sensations were compounded into feelings, the notion of sensibility allowed for – and extolled – acute feeling derived from external circumstances. Sensibility, in its eighteenth-century sense, did not originate in the heart: it originated in the surrounding environment, and only subsequently left its marks on the heart. This observation is important: for, as Sarah Knott has forcefully argued, to the extent that one could talk about a "sensible self" (which does stretch my own terminology considerably), it was an externally constituted self, drawing its being and nourishment from the outside rather than from one's inner depths.[33]

We should further keep in mind that the notion that one is molded by external stimuli and impressions was not confined to the understanding of sensibility. That it was the *raison d'être* of associationism, formulated most importantly by David Hartley, has already been mentioned. More broadly, it was the most famous tenet that the eighteenth century inherited from the influential educational ideas of John Locke. We are born with no innate ideas, Locke had asserted in his *Some Thoughts Concerning Education*, which went through a staggering twenty-five editions during the century; so that an infant's mind is like "white paper, or wax, to be moulded and fashioned" by the surrounding environment. This image – of the *tabula rasa* – was endlessly recycled in the mushrooming pedagogical literature of subsequent decades, enthralled as it was by the shaping power thus conferred upon education and educators. We have encountered its traces before, in those mid-century writers who confidently asserted that even the most pronounced human differences, like those between Europeans and Hottentots, depended entirely upon education. We even encountered some who were willing to extend this logic to animals: as Joseph Priestley pointed out in his restatement of Hartley's theories, in a framework that emphasized the impressions of the senses and the absence of innate ideas, even the difference between humans and brutes was one of degree, not of kind. The *tabula rasa* will concern us again later, when we ask how this notion fared at the turn of the century. At this point I only want to note the familiarity of the assumption of humans as malleable beings shaped by external forces: an assumption within which the contemporary notion of sensibility made a lot of sense.[34]

Closely associated with sensibility was the notion of sympathy – the feeling extending to fellow men or women and the fundament of sociability. Through the close alliance of sensibility and sympathy, to return to Knott's argument, "this 'sensible self' was socially-turned and socially-useful": that is to say, again turned outward, not inward, not only in its origins but also in its constitutive leanings. David Hume, for one, had no doubts about this constitutive social bent of the "sensible self". "Whatever other passions we may be actuated by; pride, ambition, avarice, curiosity, revenge or lust," he insisted, "the soul or animating principle of them all is sympathy." Consequently, "we can form no wish, which has not a reference to society". Moreover, the very working of sympathy, as it was understood in the eighteenth century, militated against a notion of a deep, well-bounded self. As Hume influentially explained it, sympathy was the process whereby an idea that we conceive of an emotion in others, through external signs in their countenance or behavior, is "converted into an impression, and acquires such a degree of force and vivacity, as to become the very passion itself, and produce an equal emotion [in us], as any original affection". The operation of sympathy – Edmund Burke described it as "a sort of substitution, by which we are put into the place of another man" – was possible, to return to Hume, only because "nature has preserv'd a great resemblance among all human creatures". It was "a very remarkable resemblance" that "must very much contribute to make us enter into the sentiments of others; and embrace them with facility and pleasure". Sympathy in this sense was based on what people shared, not on what distinguished them from each other. As Hume explained further, "we must be assisted by the relations of resemblance and contiguity, in order to feel the sympathy in its full perfection". So the very notion of sympathy blurred the boundaries between "sensible selves", and emphasized again the generic – the similar and the contiguous – over the particular.[35]

Indeed, for David Hartley at mid-century this was the ultimate meaning of human coexistence. Hartley's dense psychological theory involved a full cycle of selfhood from initial vacancy, devoid (à la Locke) of innate ideas or character, through shaping by physical responses to external impressions and by social conditioning, to an ultimate final state of the "perfect annihilation" of "self" (itself understood as just a locus of contradictory impulses). This final state was the supreme triumph of sympathy: the moment in which socially turned identification with others overwhelms every other self-oriented inclination, and thus eradicates particularity – or the boundaries between those "sensible selves" – in favor of a unity of them all under God.[36]

Once again, then, we find ourselves in a conceptual environment in which there was considerable fuzziness about personal identity. Sensibility and sympathy partook of a world where "self" was externally constituted and socially turned rather than inward-looking, and where we cannot readily locate "the concept of a bounded, stable ego", as literary critic Catherine Gallagher has noted. Gallagher in fact discusses sympathy in the context of people reading novels: if this is what eighteenth-century readers meant by relating to another person's experience, she suggests, then fictional characters were those with whom they must have found it easiest to identify – or sympathize. (Listen to Samuel Johnson's description of reader identification with novel characters, which could have been taken straight out of Hume, and indeed would also not have been out of place next to contemporary acting theories: such identification, Johnson wrote, "is produced by an act of the imagination, that realises the event however fictitious . . . by placing us, for a time, in the condition of him whose fortune we contemplate; so that we feel, while the deception lasts, whatever motions would be excited by the same good or evil happening to ourselves".)[37] So, given the understanding of identification through sympathy, and the implications of contemporary notions of sympathy for the meaning of personal identity, surely we cannot simply announce the birth of interiority as brought into the world by the twin eighteenth-century handmaidens of sensibility and the novel.

I want to pause briefly to consider the other well-known discussion of sympathy from this period, that in Adam Smith's *Theory of Moral Sentiments*. I have already invoked a passage from Smith on the doubling of identity for its affinity with contemporary acting theory: a passage in which Smith suggested that my sympathetic identification with your grief takes place only when "I change person and characters" as "if I [were] really you". Smith said this again, indeed on the very first page of his hefty treatise. "By the imagination", he explained, we place ourselves in another person's situation, "we enter as it were into his body, and become in some measure the same person with him", thus reproducing his sensations in ourselves. (This is in contrast to the senses, which on their own, without the imagination, "never did, and never can, carry us beyond our own person".) This is why sympathy, for Smith, could not be "a selfish principle": since "this imaginary change is not supposed to happen to me in my own person and character, but in that of the person with whom I sympathize".[38] In fact, as David Marshall has pointed out, although Smith's notion of sympathy involved "a loss of self, a transfer and metamorphosis", he did not simply mean a total identification whereby we exchange persons and characters with those we identify with. Thus, we can feel sympathy for a madman, while he himself is perfectly content, or even for the dead who can feel nothing at all. Rather, precisely like Boswell's difficulties in making sense of the transformation of the actor without falling into Partridge's misconceptions, Smith wanted to hold to a *doubleness* of personal identity that allows us both to remain ourselves and to experience a transference of identity at the same time, even if this sounds – as Smith himself admitted – "perhaps . . . impossible".[39]

Doubleness was equally key to the other pillar of Smith's moral theory, the concept of the impartial spectator. Smith's impartial spectator was a mental construct, an imaginary "inmate of the breast" that passes judgment on our conduct and thus helps us behave in ways that we would feel are worthy of approbation. A conscience, we might say. But listen to Smith's own language: "When I endeavour to examine my own conduct, when I endeavour to pass sentence upon it . . . it is evident that, in all such cases, I *divide myself, as it were, into two persons*; and that I, the examiner and judge, represent a different character from that other I, the person whose conduct is examined into and judged of." Smith was in fact following a path along which the Earl of Shaftesbury had already traveled half a century earlier. "That celebrated *Delphick* Inscription, RECOGNIZE YOUR-SELF," Shaftesbury had written in his essay on soliloquy, "was as much as to say, *Divide your-self*, or *Be* TWO"; it is through soliloquy that a person "becomes two distinct *Persons*. He is Pupil and Preceptor. He teaches, and he learns." Lest the reader took this transformation lightly, Smith added: "But that the judge should, in every respect, be the same with the person judged of, is as impossible, as that the cause should, in every respect, be the same with the effect."[40] We are right back where we started – recall again Boswell's or Farquhar's thoughts on acting – that is, with an insistence, joined with an awareness of the ensuing difficulties, on the possibilities of literal doubleness, splitting, and transference of identity. Now again, to be sure, these passages do allow for a more literal or a more figurative reading (and by the final revision of his text in the 1790s, as we shall see, Smith would nudge them noticeably toward the latter). But given the potential for polymorphous identity play – and interplay, and double play, and counter-play – that was never far from the surface of the *ancien régime* of identity, a literal reading of these passages would have leapt off the page much more readily for Smith's mid-eighteenth-century readers than for us.[41] All the more so, indeed, for the well-informed readers of Shaftesbury, Hume, Hartley, and Smith, for reasons that must now demand our attention.

The Philosophical Debate on "Personal Identity"

In the last few paragraphs we have started to listen in to the most self-consciously high-intellectual conversations taking place in eighteenth-century Britain. Readers familiar with eighteenth-century philosophy may have wondered why it has taken us so long to get here, and in particular why no reference has been made in the preceding pages to one debate during this period that confronted the questions of the unity and stability of identity head-on: the debate on personal identity begun by John Locke and carried on by many subsequent philosophical and theological luminaries. The reason for this omission bears repeating. The goal of this book has not been to reconstruct a historical

string of ideas, an inquiry in which the most self-conscious and articulate discussions of identity would have been at a premium. Rather, what it has been
striving to reconstruct – to return to the image of the violin – is the cultural
soundbox that produced the resonance and echo of the plucking of this string;
and for this purpose it has placed its emphasis on patterns within a cultural
environment, patterns that accrue meaning by virtue of their diffusion through
(typically) far less articulate – but far more widespread – soundings. The philosophical debate that I am about to discuss now should therefore be seen as yet
another manifestation of the possibilities opened up by the *ancien régime* of
identity, but not necessarily as the most important one or the driving force
behind the others. Indeed, by placing this debate within the much broader
ensemble of eighteenth-century voices hinting at the imaginable possibilities
for thinking about identity, I want to circumvent the (largely unanswerable)
question of assessing relative importance. To play further with my musical
metaphors, there is little value in arguing whether the woodwinds are more
important than the strings: it is only their combined and mutually reinforcing
effects, joined with all the other instruments of the orchestra, that create the
harmony of the symphony.

And indeed, in turning our attention now to this particular episode in the
history of philosophy, it is remarkable how its definitive study, written from a
completely internalist perspective of the philosophical tradition and without
any concern for (or apparent awareness of) external cultural links, has ended
up with a narrative that parallels very closely the one offered here for this
broader cultural context. "In the eighteenth century in Britain," Raymond
Martin and John Barresi open their excellent account, "there was a revolution
in personal identity theory." They explain:

> the self as immaterial soul was replaced with the self as mind. This replace-
> ment involved movement away from substance accounts of personal identity,
> according to which the self is a simple persisting thing, toward relational
> accounts of personal identity, according to which the self consists essentially
> of physical and/or psychological relations among different temporal stages
> of an organism or person.

This "revolution" remained a heatedly debated topic throughout the eighteenth
century, before petering out at the beginning of the nineteenth. The endpoint
will interest us later, when we look at the patterns of change at the end of the
ancien régime of identity. But here, first, allow me to give a quick account of
what this very specific philosophical revolution was all about. In retelling this
story, I am concerned less with the details of the positions offered by this or
that contributor to the debate than with the range of possibilities that they
found imaginable, let alone discussable.[42]

To begin, then, with Locke, the unchallenged father of modern identity theory. Writing in 1694 against the Cartesian dictum that thinking itself guarantees the existence of a substantial self, as well as against the early-modern belief in the immaterial and immortal substantiality of the soul, he asked the question: in what inheres the persistence of "personal identity"? Locke meant "identity" in the sense of "identicality" rather than uniqueness: in this case, identicality over time – what guarantees that I will be the same person tomorrow that I am today. In response he made two fundamental points, one negative, one positive. First, the persistence of a person cannot depend on any material substance of which a person is composed, since all such material is replaced over time. Second, what guarantees a person's identity (i.e. temporal identicality) is consciousness: having the same consciousness tomorrow is what will make me the same person I am today. In Locke's words: "as far as this consciousness can be extended backwards to any past Action or Thought, so far reaches the Identity of that *Person*; it is the same *self* now it was then." But having identity be determined by consciousness had its pitfalls. "But that which seems to make the difficulty is this, that this consciousness, [is] being interrupted always by forgetfulness", not to mention by sound sleep; and consequently, "doubts are raised whether we are the same thinking thing; *i.e.* the same substance or no." Personal identity turned out to be insubstantial, indeed mutable. Moreover, it could even, theoretically, be split. "Could we suppose", Locke speculated, "two distinct incommunicable consciousnesses acting the same Body, the one constantly by Day, the other by Night"; in which case, "the *Day* and the *Night-man* [would] be two as distinct Persons, as *Socrates* and *Plato*". And if "the same individual Man should be two Persons", perhaps it was also possible that one consciousness would inhabit two distinct bodies, thus having one person – one identity – double up.[43] In short, as Locke spins out the consequences of his reflections on personal identity, we find insubstantiality, mutability, and doubleness: precisely those fluid aspects of the *ancien régime* of identity with which we are by now familiar, all wrapped up together in a neat theoretical package.

"The nature of *personal identity*", David Hume wrote some half a century after Locke, "has become so great a question in philosophy, especially of late years in *England*." And so it had. Locke had provided the script for this debate; his disciples and his detractors acted it out; and England's educated elite was the part-bemused, part-anxious audience. Thus the Earl of Shaftesbury, Locke's personal pupil, returned repeatedly – if not always with the profundity of his master – to the point that if identity depended only on memory, since "Memory may be false", there was nothing left for him but to "take my Being *upon Trust*". "'Tis good fortune", therefore, "if a Man be *one and the same* only for a day or two. A Year makes more Revolutions than can be number'd." Not that this was a cause for concern: "If, whilst I am, I am but as I should be," Shaftesbury wrote in his journal, "what do I care more? and thus let me lose self every hour, and be twenty successive selfs, or new selfs, 'tis all one to me." (Or was it? One wonders, in reading Shaftesbury's rather desperate private portrayals of himself as "hav[ing] lost My Self" or as populated by two contrasting and incommensurable personalities, whether he had not in fact taken Locke's Day-man and Night-man example quite personally.) George Berkeley in the 1730s concurred, proposing again that the same man might be several persons, if there is a break in consciousness between them (and recall his revealing note to himself, given the heterodox nature of such thoughts: "Mem: Carefully to omit defining of Person, or making much mention of it"). "The *identity* of [a] person", Edmund Law (soon to become the bishop of Carlisle) repeated in 1769, "consist[s] in nothing more, than his becoming sensible at different times of what he had thought or done before." And there were others. But of course, the best-known formulation of this line of thought after Locke was that of Hume himself. In fact, Hume contributed little to the philosophical debate on personal identity (which he took to be a mere game of words), focusing more on the psychological origins and uses of one's mistaken belief in the substance of self. But it was his categorical declarations, that we "are nothing but a bundle or collection of different perceptions", and that "the identity, which we ascribe to the mind of man, is only a fictitious one", that summed up best for his well-read contemporaries – as well as for subsequent scholars – the radical possibilities opened up in this conversation among philosophers.[44]

Others, of course, were apprehensive about those radical possibilities, and did their utmost to quash them. For them, the Lockean argument was patently absurd. "You make *individual Personality* to be a mere *external imaginary Denomination*, and nothing in reality," complained the eminent scholar Samuel Clarke to Locke's friend Anthony Collins in a six-part debate in the early 1700s: surely everyone could see how preposterous this was? "If Consciousness be the ground of Personal Identity" – thus the Dissenting minister Henry Grove (1720) – "and where the same consciousness is wanting there no longer remains ye same Person, a man may and may not be one and ye same Person at the same time." Absurd. Identity, Grove's friend Isaac Watts echoed (1733), "must not stand upon such a shifting and changeable Principle, as may allow either one Man to be two Persons, or two Men to be one Person, or any one Man or Person to become another, or to be really any thing but himself". The suggestion "that Personality is not a permanent, but a transient thing", the divine Joseph Butler agreed, has "been carried to a strange Length". Those who say that "since our present Self is not, in Reality, the same with the Self of Yesterday, but another like Self or Person coming in its Room, and mistaken for it", and thus is the same self only "in a fictitious Sense", were speaking nonsense which required little further attention. "The bare unfolding [of] this Notion", Butler triumphantly concluded, "seems the best Confutation of it." But Butler knew all too well that this notion, however many times it was denounced as "nothing but absurdity and contradiction" (Abraham Tucker, 1763), continued to attract attention. In fact, despite such dismissive attempts to make the problem go away, the stakes in the debate remained high. What was at issue was not only the metaphysical questions of survival, immortality, and resurrection – hardly trivial in their own right – but also the all-important practical question of moral responsibility. If the substantive continuity and unity of personal identity were not guaranteed, asked the self-appointed defenders of personal identity, how can anyone be held responsible for acts committed in the past? (Dr. Johnson, we recall, raised the same concern, however jocularly, regarding the possible consequences of doubleness in contemporary acting theory.) As James Beattie put it in 1770, "to a man who doubts the individuality or identity of his own mind, virtue, truth, religion, good and evil, hope and fear, are absolutely nothing." Naturally, the other side made considerable efforts to show how their reasoning did *not* undermine the basis for a sustainable theory of morality.[45]

Ultimately, for my purposes here, it matters little what were the specific contributions of every participant in this debate (a story that in any case has been told before), or who appeared to have the upper hand (which in fact no side really did). What matters to this inquiry, first and foremost, is that this debate actually *happened*: that is, that such configurations of identity were within the realm of the conceivable in the eighteenth century, and furthermore that this was a singular development in the history of philosophy, unparalleled until the second half of the twentieth century.

It also matters to us that this debate had an audience, and that this audience received it, again, as within the boundaries of the imaginable. Several of the contributions to the debate went into multiple editions; the nub of their claims also circulated in periodical publications like *The Spectator* or the *Monthly Review*, and in popular reference works like Ephraim Chambers's *Cyclopædia* of 1728, whose entry for "Identity" was in effect cribbed from Locke. This debate may also have left its mark in the oft-quoted identity-puzzle exchange in Laurence Sterne's *Tristram Shandy*: "my good friend, quoth I – as sure as I am I – and you are you – And who are you? said he. – Don't puzzle me, said I." It certainly left its mark in the opening pages of Charles Johnstone's popular *Chrysal: Or, the Adventures of a Guinea* (1760), in which a coin launches its musings about the world with a long, footnoted disquisition on the fluidity of self-as-consciousness, manifested in the self's grammatical – and gender – doubleness.[46] Likewise, Boswell was quite aware of the philosophical debate on personal identity when he penned his essays on acting theory. He therefore made sure to draw the line between his own thoughts on people's "double feeling" and their potential to be "transmuted into various characters", and "what Mr. David Hume very seriously says of man in general, that 'they are nothing but a bundle of perceptions'", a formulation that Boswell obviously found more extreme than his own purpose required.[47]

Finally, I cannot fail to mention one more place where the debate on personal identity left its stamp, provoking in the process what was perhaps the most ingenious treatment of the difficulties posed by the eighteenth-century willingness to contemplate the fluidity of identity: the "memoirs" of Martinus Scriblerus. In this satirical production of the Scriblerus Club – which included among its members John Arbuthnot, Jonathan Swift, John Gay, and Alexander Pope – the "hero" has the misfortune to fall in love with one half of a pair of Siamese twins conjoined in their sexual organ. (The twins, incidentally, are described as complete opposites: in this they joined a whole sequence of fictive disharmonious or disparate twins that appear to have been an eighteenth-century innovation, contrasting with earlier portrayals of twins as indistinguishable in appearance and character.[48] Was this another manifestation, or projection, of the eighteenth-century interest in the splitting and mutating of identity?) The challenge to Scriblerus from the lover of the other twin, involving charges of rape and incest, leads to a learned argument in court, whether "the individual wife of the Plaintiff, is not one, but two Persons". This "disputation" allows the locus and essence of individuality to be debated at length before they are declared to inhere in the organ of generation. This elaborate and fantastic episode drove *ad absurdum* the ramifications of the debate on personal identity – a debate that the satirists invoked explicitly as the "great noise about this Individuality" – in connection with the potential divisibility of the self.[49]

But, the inherent interest of such examples aside, the broader argument I want to make with regard to the eighteenth-century debate on personal identity ultimately remains one about congruity and resonance rather than influence. We can be fairly certain that the consumers of female warrior ballads, or the travelers who left accounts of the Hottentots, or the provincial writers on bees, or most frequenters of masquerades, or the authors and readers of stories about captives who turned Indian, or the actresses who appeared on the Georgian stage in breeches parts and their enthusiastic audiences, or those contemporaries who fell for Mary Toft's rabbit breeding, or the many other eighteenth-century people who populate these pages, were not for the most part within earshot of the circumscribed philosophical conversation on personal identity, and were rarely molded by it – whether consciously or unconsciously, directly or indirectly – in their participation in this cultural milieu. But at the same time it also seems undeniable that all of them shared a common epistemological environment with the philosophers: it is this environment, with its clear and distinctive characteristics, that I have called the *ancien régime* of identity. The philosophical debate on personal identity, in the end, was but one symptom – albeit one distinguished by a unique level of reflexivity – of this particular historical configuration, one thread in the thick mesh of cultural indicators signaling the *ancien régime* of identity that I have been weaving throughout this book.

Rather than looking for the marks of the philosophical debate on personal identity in this broader cultural context, therefore, we can turn the question around and look for the marks of the broader cultural context in the contributions to the debate on personal identity. Thus we can note, for example, that when Shaftesbury wanted to explain the mutability of personal identity that allows a person to become "*another Creature*", the analogy with which he chose to introduce this notion was to a friend who through sickness or through travels to "the remotest parts of the East, and hottest Countrys of the South, return[ed] to us so alter'd in his whole outward Figure, that till we had for a time convers'd with him, we cou'd not know him again to be the same Person".[50] How familiar. Not, of course, that this climatic understanding of human diversity was exactly the same kind of metamorphosis as the one Shaftesbury was about to propose: but it was one that he obviously felt would resonate well with his readers, and was thus an effective analogy to draw upon as a pedagogical aid.

Or we can note that in the whimsical arguments put forth by Martin Scriblerus's legal counsel regarding the perhaps divided identity of the Siamese twins, his insistence that individuality resides in the sexual organ is based on the observation that "when we behold this one member, we distinguish the Sex, and pronounce it a *Man*, or a *Woman*". He therefore proclaims "the Sameness and Individuality of each sex" as equivalent to the sameness and individuality of identity. But the supposed clarity of the sameness and individuality of each sex, as we by now know well, was hardly taken for granted in the eighteenth century. The Scriblerians knew it too: they made this very clear in two separate invocations of hermaphroditism inserted completely gratuitously into the Siamese twins episode – one highlighting the analogy between the conjoined twins and a hermaphrodite, the other a matter-of-fact discussion of the legal standing of hermaphroditical marriage immediately preceding the legal arguments of Scriblerus's counsel. What the satirists were actually doing, of course, was to recall to their readers' attention familiar understandings of the *limits* of gender identity in order to undermine further the clarity of identity that this facetious "argument" was supposed to shore up. (It is worth noting that the predominant contributor to the Scriblerians' *jeu d'esprit* was probably John Arbuthnot, whose belief in the malleability of human complexion we have already encountered; and, more to the point, who also penned an analogous satire on the confusion of the sexes that was supposedly going to result from "the *Metamorphostical* Conjunction" of the planets, a satire that in a similar manner drove *ad absurdum* the possibilities inherent in unreliable gender boundaries.)[51]

In these examples, then, the interlocutors on personal identity were drawing on familiar understandings of identity categories – whether of gender or race – in order to help get their points across. But I find even more suggestive the occasional moments when contributors to the philosophical debate not only drew on this broader context of the *ancien régime* of identity, but actually, because of their level of articulate self-awareness, gave its key features – as I have been trying to reconstruct them – unusually forceful expression.

Take the *Monthly Review*. In 1763, it published a skeptical critique of Abraham Tucker's attempt to defend the "unchangeable individuality" of personal identity, countering that he was "not *quite so great a* master in the *noble science of SELF-defence*" (Tucker's book title begged this quip). "Suppose", the *Review* conjectured, "that a man or woman should be so much altered in their size, make, features, voice and sentiment as not to be known again by others." (Again, the reviewer's beginning point presupposed that the possibility of a person's transformation to the point of indistinguishability – of complete passing – could be taken for granted.) Suppose further that their memory was impaired as well, so that "their external form and interior constitution are so altered, that they are not known to be the same persons, either by themselves or others". In this case it was only the memories of other people that could maintain this changed person's former identity: had this transformation taken place on a desert island, the review triumphantly rested its case, there would be nothing to preserve it at all. But it is the general conclusion that the reviewer drew from these considerations that I find most interesting: "it appears pretty evident that personal identity consists not in the sameness of any particular Being, independent of other Beings; but in the sameness of the relations which such Being bears to all others."[52] This is as close a contemporary formulation of the argument proposed here regarding the relational making of *ancien-régime* identity, determined outwardly by a matrix of social relations, as one could hope to find.

Or take a letter from an unnamed friend that Edmund Law appended to his own 1769 defense of Locke, a letter that again made some very clear points in its dismissal of "personality" – or personal identity – as "an absurd expression". "The word person", it stated, should be taken as "standing for a certain guise, character, quality, i.e. being in fact a mixed mode, or relation, and not a substance". The words "relation" and "mixed mode" echoed the relational, outwardly turned social matrix of the *Monthly Review*. But in this case it is the significance of "guise" and "character" to which I want to draw attention. "When person is considered as a character, and not a substance," this letter explained further, "it amounts to no more than saying, a man puts on a mask – continues to wear it for some time – puts off one mask and takes another."[53] Identity – here equated with character – can be put on or taken off like a mask: a mask that is not only easily replaceable but that also does not hide a "true" substance underneath. Recall now the importance of masks and masquerading, and of the wearing of character, to the arguments made in the above pages: again, it would be hard to sum up the *ancien régime* of identity more succinctly or forcefully.

For my last example I want to return to Locke. In particular, to his distinction between person (or self) and man. "I know", Locke wrote, "that, in the ordinary way of speaking, the same Person, and the same Man, stand for one and the same thing." But Locke wanted to be more precise. "Man" he took to mean a certain biological kind to which all individual humans unproblematically belonged. Person was something different: "*Person*, as I take it, is the name for this *self*. . . . It is a Forensick Term, appropriating Actions and their Merit; and so belongs only to intelligent Agents capable of a Law, and Happiness and Misery." Person was the sum of the attributes of the man's consciousness, which necessarily included thought, moral responsibility, and emotion. The thrust of Locke's argument, in short, was that personhood, or selfhood, can in certain cases roam away from the man, move to another man, or be superseded by another self within the same man. (Edmund Law was later to repeat the same distinction and separation, though his definition of "person" singled out moral responsibility as its sole essential attribute.)[54] Surely this sounds familiar? One can hardly fail to notice the close parallel between the relationship of person to man as Locke conceived it and the relationship of gender to sex as I have laid it down earlier in this book. Gender, we said, the behavioral-cultural scaffolding erected around biologically grounded sex, was conceptually allowed during this period to roam away occasionally from the sexual body. This was the basis of the "*ancien régime* of gender" that prevailed until the late eighteenth century. Likewise we noted the analogous configurations of civilization and race, or the political and class, for which eighteenth-century people could envision similar dissonances that were later to become much harder to imagine. We can say, then, that person in Locke was to man as gender was to sex, or civilization to race, or the political to class; and thus that in its different permutations, this conceptual doubling, and especially the dissonances that it allowed one to imagine as possible, appear to have been a persistent thread that ran through the *ancien régime* of identity. Locke's formulation, therefore, situated him, and the debate on personal identity that followed from it, snugly within the broader logic of this *ancien régime*.

5

Religion, Commerce, and Empire: Enabling Contexts of Identity's Ancien Régime

We are coming close to the end of our tour of the short eighteenth century. Within the itinerary constraints resulting from the limitations of the vehicles that have been carrying us from one viewpoint to the next, and none more disabling than our very restricted access to the countryside, we have surveyed the eighteenth-century cultural terrain from a great many angles, and have come up with a remarkably consistent set of observations. I have given the patterns that emerged from these observations – patterns insistent, widespread, and distinctive enough to be considered as defining properties of this terrain – the label "the *ancien régime* of identity". In a phrase, this was a regime of identity characterized by the relatively commonplace capacity of many to contemplate – without necessarily facing some inescapable existential crisis (and often the reverse) – that identity, or specific categories of identity, could prove to be mutable, malleable, unreliable, divisible, replaceable, transferable, manipulable, escapable, or otherwise fuzzy around the edges. Conversely, it was a regime of identity *not* characterized by an axiomatic presupposition of a deep inner core of selfhood.

Obviously, this last characterization-through-absence points to where we must go next: namely, the sudden demise of this historical configuration that provides the dramatic telos for my story. But before going there, or rather as a first step toward getting there, I want to situate better the *ancien régime* of identity in its own century: that is, to flag those enabling conditions and circumstances of the eighteenth century that made this particular identity regime not only possible, and plausible, but also widely resonant. This chapter, then, can be seen to provide a "socio-cultural context" – an anchoring of the *ancien régime* of identity in specific social and cultural developments of this period.

This is also where I begin the task of explanation. The explanatory significance of the social and cultural developments I am about to discuss is double-sided. On the one hand, they will make the *ancien régime* of identity as it emerged during this period more understandable and perhaps less surprising. On the other hand, they will also reveal sources of unease during this period that took the very same characteristics of the *ancien régime* of identity to be signs of a potentially dangerous new departure. These signs of unease were like a background noise that eighteenth-century Britons seemed mostly to get accustomed to and contain with little effort. But without the constant corrosive action of this gradually swelling undercurrent of unease we cannot understand the force of the flood that was to occur when the dam of Georgian confidence finally cracked (an occurrence that we will witness in the next chapter). I am therefore also laying down here a crucial block for the explanation of the late-eighteenth-century ending of this *ancien régime*.

In moving to identify the long-term social developments underlying this story, the following propositions will not come as a big surprise. On the contrary, I want to anchor the distinctiveness of the *ancien régime* of identity in what historians have come to see as the most fundamental features of eighteenth-century British society. It has become commonplace – following Linda Colley's inimitable historical synthesis – to identify three such essential features, the primary colors of eighteenth-century society from which all its hues and shades were mixed: Protestantism – or, more broadly, religion; commerce; and empire.[1] Mixing all three on our palette, albeit in different quantities, will allow us to paint on a broad canvas the grounds on which the *ancien régime* of identity could flourish, but at the same time also to note in the edges of the composition the lurking shadows of its subsequent disappearance.

*

I begin with religion not because it was somehow more important than other anchors of this peculiar eighteenth-century configuration, but because chronologically and logically it came first. The reader, moreover, should readily recognize the place of religion in our story, as signs of it have been scattered throughout the previous chapters.

Recall for instance the case of "race", or of human diversity. In the eighteenth century religion continued to be crucial to the understanding of human difference. But we saw it blend with culture and education as aspects of human agency, which then became the basis for the human organization of categories of difference. This edged out an alternative understanding of difference, based on divine agency: thus we noted that invocations of the Curse of Ham, a notion that imposed *God*'s supposed categories of organization on humans, appeared to decline sharply during this period. Likewise, the divine ordering of gender as the primary category in relation to sex receded in the late seventeenth century.

This development, in turn, was a key precondition for the subsequent emergence of eighteenth-century gender play, a play superimposed upon sexual bodies whose supposed stability was now grounded in the putative certainty not of providential decree but of natural science. And again, it was the retreat of the divine sanction of the a priori uniqueness of man that allowed the long-standing great chain of being its peculiarly eighteenth-century effect of shrinking the distance between humans and brutes, often to a vanishing point.

Similarly, in the evolution of the understanding of conscience, as Edward Andrew has shown, it was the retreat of the judgemental clarity of God's watchful eye, which had previously turned the workings of Protestant conscience to solipsistic introspection, that now led eighteenth-century moral theorists to develop new understandings of a moral sense that was socially turned and reliant on the judgement of others (and that could then be applied to one's own conduct).[2] And once more: it was against the early-modern religious self located in the immaterial soul that the novel Lockean speculations on an empirical, insubstantial self located in consciousness were set. The sundry eighteenth-century variations on the theme of the mutable self were no longer ruled out by the axiomatic immateriality and immortality of the soul, just as eighteenth-century writers on acting theory no longer found it convincing to invoke magic and the supernatural – as their predecessors had commonly done – in order to explain the transformation of the actor, and just as the enthusiastic educationalists of the period were no longer prevented by notions of innate and transmittable depravity from imagining the infant as a *tabula rasa*. Indeed, the prehistory of this famous metaphor registered the change: while the phrase "*tabula rasa*" had in fact been employed before Locke, earlier uses had not focused on the child's susceptibility to the formative influences of its earthly environment shaped by humans, but rather on its being a receptacle for the word of God.[3] Another intriguing manifestation of the same historical shift has been noted by Phyllis Mack in the changing interpretations of dreams. Looking in particular at the Quaker and Methodist experience of dreams, Mack sees a clear difference between seventeenth-century accounts which invariably focused on the question of the dream's origins – did it originate with God or the devil? – and those from the eighteenth century. While still interpreting dreams as deep spiritual experiences, eighteenth-century religious dreamers were concerned less with their origins (a concern that was to return in a different form toward the nineteenth century) but rather with their effects in signaling the capacity for malleability and even transformation of one's own personal identity. The adult alternative, one might say, to the *tabula rasa*.[4]

The pattern is easy to see. In each instance God's active and authoritative ordering of the world was superseded by man's own, more tentative and open-ended, which prompted the reconstitution of the relevant notions and cate-

gories of identity. Such a narrative is not unfamiliar: historians have incorporated this insight into various accounts of change during this period – be it to
explain changes in attitudes toward financial vicissitudes, say, wrested from the
hands of providence and reinterpreted as the consequences of human actions,
or to chart the decline in the interpretation of pain as a sign of divine displeasure. French philosopher Marcel Gauchet has put forth a more generalized
account of this transformation. In his view, the shift in the relationship between
God and man that took place toward the end of the seventeenth century in the
Christian West was nothing short of "the deepest fracture ever in history". It
was this period, Gauchet writes, that witnessed the decisive break in a long-
term process of separation between the human and the divine: the break – he
calls it "the disenchantment of the world" – that spelled God's final retreat as
an alien "Other" from daily involvement in the terrestrial world. The outcome
was not necessarily secularization or the triumph of reason, as Max Weber
meant when he had originally talked of "disenchantment". Rather, the consequence was that eighteenth-century people – secularists and religious apologists alike – were left to their own devices to make sense of their world in their
own terms: what Gauchet has elsewhere described as "the unlinking of the
celestial order and the terrestrial order". By around 1700 in the Christian West,
he asserts, "the complete organization of the human-social sphere by religion"
was over.[5]

Keith Baker and David Bell have been quick to point out the historical ramifications of Gauchet's insight. Looking at the example of France, they have
shown how this new conceptual vacuum led to the emergence precisely during
this period of new foundational concepts of social organization: society, nation,
patrie, civilization, public. Social relations had to be redefined, boundaries had
to be redrawn, categories had to be reinvented. Simultaneously, and no less fundamentally, the receding of divine determination and order led – in Gauchet's
words again – to a "restructuring [of] difference, separation, and human conflict" through human rather than divine imperatives. Without compelling godly
sanction, categories of identity and difference had to be anchored elsewhere:
and as the previous paragraphs remind us, we have seen in our own inquiry
ample examples of this process. Furthermore, and crucially for our purpose,
since the terms for understanding and organizing the newly conceptualized terrestrial order were now human rather than divine, they were no longer absolute
or preordained. Rather, "the disenchantment of the world" created a situation
whereby the bases for this terrestrial order could prove to be flexible, changeable, even ameliorable.[6]

It was thus, in sum, that a new space of potential possibilities opened up
around the beginning of the eighteenth century: one in which boundaries of
identity called for new demarcation, while the identity categories underpinning

them could be imagined, or experimented with, as flexible and malleable. This was the enabling precondition that the religious realm contributed to the particular configuration of eighteenth-century understandings that I wish to reconstruct. Without the retreat of God and the decline in the immediacy of the divine order of things, the space for play that was such an important defining aspect of the *ancien régime* of identity could not have come into being.

*

The contribution of religion to the conditions of possibility for the *ancien régime* of identity was one of absence or lack rather than one of presence: a retreat that opened up a new conceptual space where new imaginings could potentially take hold. The effects of the second fundamental aspect of eighteenth-century English society that I want to flag now, by contrast, were more active and direct: this was the unprecedented development of commercial society in its urban settings.

These effects were also much more evident to contemporaries. Throughout the eighteenth century it was a commonplace (especially among critics of commerce, to be sure) that in the modernizing, commercializing urban centers, and above all in the metropolis, the comfort of knowing who people were by how they looked and dressed had been replaced by the play of unreliable appearances. How reassuring is the traditional countryside, observed one social commentator, "where each person, his family, and connections are known to every body", and where assigning people an identity "is the easiest thing in nature". But how different – and unfortunate – is the situation "in the great metropolis of the British empire", where "characters are so blended and intermixed, that it is a difficulty for the nicest speculator to distinguish the persuasions and principles of each individual so as to form a just estimate" of who people really are.[7]

Or take the shrill – if unsurprising – jeremiad against the effects of luxury spouted by one Erasmus Jones in 1735. The metropolis, he warned, had been overtaken by novelty, both in its endless stream of commercial entertainments – "the *Mall, Play-houses,* and *Masquerades*" – and in its variety of consumer goods, especially items of apparel: "the Shopkeepers wear a different Garb now, and are seen with their long Wigs and Swords, Velvet Breeches and Hunting Caps, rather than with their own Hair, Bands, and Aprons, as was formerly the Figure they made." The lamentable consequence was what Erasmus Jones described as a radical change in self-representation:

> People where they are not known, are generally honoured according to their Clothes and other Accoutrements they have about them. . . . It is this which

encourages every body . . . to wear Clothes above his Rank; especially, in large and populous Cities, where obscure Men may hourly meet with fifty Strangers to one Acquaintance, and consequently have the Pleasure of being esteemed by a vast Majority, not as what they are, but what they appear to be.

The anonymity of the large city, together with the abundance of shopping opportunities it offered, allowed people to don and doff identities with impunity – in Jones's predictable words, to "appear in *Masque*, and act a Part to make Sport". Enters once again the inescapable masquerade. Indeed, when Tobias Smollett declared at mid-century, as we have already heard him do, that "this metropolis is a vast masquerade", it was precisely this characteristic of the modern city that he had in mind: "this metropolis is a vast masquerade, in which a man of stratagem may wear a thousand different disguises, without danger of detection."[8]

Erasmus Jones's words, then, were common knowledge. In fact, they were not even his own. Perhaps the most telling aspect of Jones's formulation was its unacknowledged provenance: as it turns out, he had lifted it *in toto* from Bernard Mandeville's *Fable of the Bees*.[9] Mandeville's, of course, was the century's most celebrated *defense* – not critique – of luxury. And yet, as Jones penned his diametrically opposite tirade against luxury, he had no difficulty in availing himself of Mandeville's vision of the modern eighteenth-century city. Even if these two social commentators could agree on nothing else, they could still agree on the consequences of luxury for the new possibilities of masquerade-like identity-fashioning.

This agreement extended far and wide among eighteenth-century social observers and commentators. The contemporary city, they all knew, provided the *opportunity* to pass oneself off as something or someone that one was not. The consumer revolution, with its baffling array of goods, provided the *means*, by making all markers of distinction available to anybody for a price. (This was a world "where looks are merchandise", Dr. Johnson wrote in his poem "London"; "now," thus another writer, "alas! every one wears, whatever his *Wealth enables*".)[10] And the pursuit of luxury and social emulation, leading to a general corruption of morality, provided the alleged *motive*.

The latter point, in particular, was a favorite of every moralizing pundit. Long before Thorstein Veblen, aping one's social superiors was presented as a universal imperative – "the characteristick, and almost universal passion of the age" (1761) – that required, it seemed, no further explanation or justification. In a mid-century diagnostic of England's social ills, Henry Fielding pinned the blame on the scramble for emulation that had been unleashed by "the vast Torrent of Luxury which of late Years hath poured itself into this Nation": "Thus while the Nobleman will emulate the Grandeur of a Prince; and the

Gentleman will aspire to the proper State of the Nobleman; the Tradesman steps from behind his Counter into the vacant place of the Gentleman. Nor doth the Confusion end here: It reaches the very Dregs of the People, who [are] aspiring still to a Degree beyond that which belongs to them." "In England the several ranks of men slide into each other almost imperceptibly," echoed another self-appointed social diagnostician: "hence arises a strong emulation in all the several states and conditions to vie with each other. . . . In such a state as this, fashion must have uncontrolled sway." And here is *The Craftsman*'s formulation of this ubiquitous refrain: "In this almost universal Vying with one another," it observed, "the Furniture and Expences of every Tradesman now equal those of the Merchant formerly; those of the Merchant surpass those of the first-rate Gentlemen; [and] those of the Gentlemen the old Peers." The same applied at least as much to women. "By their Extravagance in Dress," another like-minded critic asserted, "the Maid [is] striving to out-do the Mistress, the Tradesman's Wife to out-do the Gentleman's Wife, the Gentleman's emulating the Lady, and the Ladies one another."[11] Everyone had a place in the emulation rondo.

The most revealing enunciation in these clichéd accounts, all of which bore an uncanny resemblance to contemporary warnings about the imminent collapse of the distinctions along the great chain of being, was Fielding's phrase, "the Confusion". There was nothing like an unhealthy dose of competitive emulation, it seemed, to confound social – and, by extension, all – identity categories. The notion that "all ranks and degrees of men seem to be on the point of being confounded" (*London Chronicle*, 1773) was brought closest to home – literally – by the oft-conjured tableau of the mistress who found herself indistinguishable from her maid, or the gentleman from his servant. "The *Domestic*" – thus one example – "will make such an Appearance that if from *behind* he should accidently slide *into* the *Chariot*, the *Mistake* would not be easily *perceived*. It requires a correct *Remembrance* of *Faces*, to distinguish at all Times between my *Lady*, and my Lady's *Woman*." Nobody at that time – thus another – could fail to notice "the exact consanguinity which there appears in the manners of the man of fashion and his gentleman. So nicely do they seem matched, in every respect, that it is impossible to distinguish the master from the man, by any other criterion than their different offices at the table." "The present rage of imitating the manners of high-life hath spread itself so far among the gentlefolk of lower-life", exclaimed one periodical writer in 1763, "that in a few years we shall probably have no common people at all." The rage for social emulation through consumer goods, itself "the offspring of fashion, [which] spreads from the capital into provinces", was apparently threatening to undermine – even annihilate – familiar categories of distinction and identification. When "a whole Nation gives an indiscriminate Loose to their wild passions for *Dress, Furniture and Diversions*", a mid-century satirist wrote in what was neither his funniest nor his most original observation, this was a sure sign of the "forgetting [of] those necessary Distinctions that arise from *Age, Rank*, or *Profession*".[12]

So how many eighteenth-century servants or maids really could be mistaken for their masters or mistresses? Surely not many – perhaps not any. Nor were the English lower classes really in imminent danger of self-annihilation through over-dress. It is not that eighteenth-century processes of commercialization actually brought about the erasure of distinctions, although they sometimes appeared to be contributing to such an effect. Rather, the point is that such observations, repeated so often, provide us with an insight into how contemporaries experienced these social developments: that is, as undermining the integrity and reliability of familiar categories of social distinction – a danger that was further compounded by a rising sense of jitteriness.[13] Now, to be sure, commercial change had been around long before the eighteenth century. But this century saw a radically new breakthrough in its variety, its pace, its level of innovation, the extent of its social reach, and the growing awareness of its consequences among a widening span of English society. In the early 1980s, Neil McKendrick coined the phrase "the consumer revolution of eighteenth-century England", and while some historians today would rather avoid the revolutionary epithet, a growing body of scholarship has largely confirmed this basic picture for most of the century.[14]

It is therefore not a coincidence that it was *fashion* that most often formed the subject of such social commentaries, as the few examples in the previous paragraphs suggest. Most obviously, fashion signified the constant manufacturing and remanufacturing of identity through clothes: the century was strewn with the predictable warnings of outraged pontificators and spoil-sport moralizers that all those markers of identity that had formerly guaranteed the distinctions between people – between men and women (recall the examples in chapter 2), young and old, rich and poor, masters and servants, Englishmen and foreigners – were now on the verge of extinction, swept away by the wanton fashions of a commercial age. As a consequence of present-day fashions, went a typical "Essay on Fashions" in 1736, " 'tis difficult to make a Distinction, [between different people] tho' at never so little Distance".[15] But there was more to changing fashions than simply the possibility of aping one's betters or assuming a different identity. Fashion was characterized by an "infinite variety" (Samuel Johnson) of "objects of mutability" (Bernard Mandeville), "changing like the moon" (John Wesley), or even "pass[ing] from shape to shape with the rapidity of thought": its very essence was transience and jitteriness.[16] Of course, fashion had had this reputation long before the eighteenth century. But there is little doubt that the eighteenth century experienced an extraordinary increase in the prevalence and shrillness of this nervous-cum-fascinated discourse on fashion. Confronted with Georgian social commentaries, a Martian of a gullible nature might well have been led to believe that it was ruffles and chintzes and periwigs that were about to bring civilization as contemporaries knew it to an untimely end. We should understand this obsessive preoccupation with fashion in the context of the broader experience of commercialization, which exposed an increasing number of contemporaries to what was for them an unprecedented phantasmagoria of commodities in a bewildering variety of (relatively) transient forms. In harping endlessly on the effects of fashion as the epitome of the effects of commerce, therefore, eighteenth-century Britons were not only addressing one key mode of identity masquerade that was becoming more widely available: they were also coming as close as they could to concretizing their emerging awareness of the destabilizing effects of change itself.

Moreover, we should consider where most of this change took place: namely, England's fast-growing cities, and above all London, the largest metropolis in Europe. In his classic exploration of the nature of human interactions in eighteenth-century London, Richard Sennett distinguishes between two types of modern migrant-city milieus: that in which the stranger on the street is readily placeable – through language, occupational signs, ethnic type, or neighborhood; and that in which the stranger on the street typically cannot be placed. Early twentieth-century New York is an example of the former; eighteenth-century London is *the* example of the latter. The reasons for this, Sennett suggests, were structural. As a consequence of capitalization of agriculture and of industry, of the development of a wage labor market, of the improvement in possibilities of transportation, and of the growing number of opportunities in London, the metropolis was teeming with recent migrants. As Anthony Wrigley has famously calculated, at least one in six eighteenth-century English people actually lived for a period in London – a much larger proportion than that of Londoners in comparison to the total English population at any given moment. In such an urban scene, the stranger who was alone, came from a significant distance, and was largely unknowable became a disturbingly familiar and important figure. (Sennett presumably does not assume that *all* Londoners were thus unrecognizable: his point, I think, is that the unknowable stranger was a familiar enough figure to draw attention to him/herself as the defining figure of the metropolitan scene. This was in contrast to, say, nineteenth-century London, whose image was that of a city where people were generally decipherable into familiar class and ethnic types, despite the actual presence of many inscrutable strangers.) Similar situations, furthermore, were increasingly replicated in other booming urban centers. In such circumstances old categories of distinction lost their meaning. Instead, people "stepped into clothes whose purpose was to make it possible for other people to act as if they knew who you were", and were encouraged "to create, borrow, or imitate behavior which all agree[d] to treat arbitrarily as 'proper' and 'believable' in their encounters".[17] Or, to put it in terms that Sennett's subjects themselves were more likely to use, these were circumstances that encouraged people to move through social life in a perpetual masquerade.

So far, then, I have suggested that the experience of eighteenth-century commercial society in its urban settings was an important enabling precondition for what I have identified as the playful aspect of the *ancien régime* of identity. It led contemporaries to an increasing awareness of the mutability – indeed transience – of forms, of which fashion was the best embodiment. More specifically, it led them to an awareness – kept constantly in the public eye by every moralizer worth his mettle – of the potential unreliability of those forms involved in the marking and the recognition of identity.

But there was yet another aspect to the effects of commercialization, one that reinforced the other defining characteristic of the *ancien régime* of identity: namely, that it did not rely on a belief in an underlying bedrock of a stable, inner core of identity, an inner "self". To begin seeing this second point, think once more about eighteenth-century fashion, and especially about its peculiarities in contradistinction to previous and later periods. We tend to think of fashion, following its many critics, as the opposite of substance, an immaterial superficiality. But as Jones and Stallybrass have reminded us, this picture is both too simple and not sufficiently historical. Thus, in the sixteenth and seventeenth centuries, when clothing was invested by external authorities, it was anything but superficial: on the contrary, investiture was "the means by which a person was given a form, a shape, a social function, a 'depth'". Only thus can we understand the apparent oxymoron that Shakespeare put in Henry V's mouth: "I will deeply put the fashion on." In the nineteenth century, by contrast, the situation – we will come back to it later – was rather the reverse: clothing was taken to "express" the person – that is, to be an outer sign determined by an inner self. In the intermediate eighteenth century, however, dress was not yet grounded in anterior inner selfhood, but was also no longer seen to acquire "depth" conferred by external authorities. As a sign of this change we can take the resistance to and disdain for livery, so prevalent indeed that such garments lost in the eighteenth century most of their value in the second-hand clothing market. Sumptuary legislation likewise disappeared, together with its driving logic which had made it an important form of social control in earlier centuries.[18] In a more profound sense than we usually assign to these words, fashion in the eighteenth century was about appearances alone – a play of surfaces without real substance, referent, or true value.

But in this respect fashion – and the same point can be made also for the externalities of manners, likewise an all-important eighteenth-century preoccupation – once again epitomized a much broader aspect of the contemporary experience of commercializing society, and one that bears an important if elusive relationship to our story. As Jean-Christophe Agnew has pointed out, a key axis for the ways that commercial society was experienced – whether to be embraced or resisted – was that of transparency versus artifice. As the concreteness of pre-modern commodity exchange in the marketplace gave way to monetarized market relations based on anonymous exchange, commercial activities lost their former transparency and accountability. They became more opaque, more mediated, more dependent on representations. This development was pushed further by new mediums of exchange that were strictly representational, culminating in the worst bugbear of all, paper money. Representation came to stand at the center of market (and other) relations, and with it the nagging doubts about the representational relationship between seeming and being: was there really a gold standard behind paper money? Did a copy presuppose an original? For many it seemed as though representation had run amok, the unreal had become the real (Karl Marx's phrase "all that is solid melts into air" immediately comes to mind). Small wonder that the resulting anxieties, as Agnew demonstrates, became increasingly analogous to those associated with the theater.[19] Or, for that matter, with the masquerade.

Furthermore, the very nature of commodification – the conversion of use value into exchange value – was, as William Sewell has reminded us, "exceptionally transposable. It kn[ew] no natural limits; it c[ould] be applied not only to cloth, tobacco, or cooking pans, but to land, housework, bread, sex, advertising, emotions, or knowledge, each of which c[ould] be converted into any other by means of money." Commercialization rendered all value forms – cultural, moral, personal – measurable in terms of monetary value, which itself was recognized to be shifty and unreliable. The "effects of commerce", one eighteenth-century observer wrote, are the "danger when money becomes [the] sole distinction". Traditional values metamorphosed into detached and manipulable commodities. This metamorphosis, in turn, had profound consequences for notions of identity. John Pocock has described them well: "Once property" – and with it everything else – "was seen to have a symbolic value, expressed in coin or in credit, the foundations of personality themselves appeared imaginary or at best consensual: the individual could exist, even in his own sight, only at the fluctuating value imposed upon him by his fellows."[20] Like money, and like fashion, identity itself was in danger of coming out of the commercializing smelting kiln without real substance, referent, or true value.

To be sure, these statements are sweeping and general. While they reflect developments that had been set in motion at least a century or two earlier, they accelerated and matured in the eighteenth century as never before. But the eighteenth century also witnessed a more time-bound transformation that contributed to the distinctive specificity of this century within the longer history of commercializing society, a specificity especially significant for our purposes here. I am thinking of course of the transition that is commonly referred to as "the financial revolution", signaled by the establishment of the national debt and the Bank of England in the 1690s. Indeed, the one aspect of socio-economic change during the early eighteenth century that can be truly described as spectacular was the bursting into full bloom of a new financial culture based on artificial forms of wealth: banknotes, paper money, bills of exchange, annuity schemes, stocks, bonds, shares, and securities. Without precedent or a reassuringly comprehensible parallel – this was a form of property, critics like Bolingbroke and Swift pointed out, that had previously been unknown and unimaginable – these seemingly immaterial forms of wealth were suddenly thrust into the center of economic activity, generating considerable attention and concern among propertied and literate circles.[21]

The moment that famously turned this new reality into a national *cause célèbre* was the so-called South Sea Bubble, a mania of frenzied speculation in South Sea Company stocks ("The town is quite mad about the South Sea . . . one can hear nothing else talked of") that ended in summer 1720 in financial disaster. But what kind of disaster? Julian Hoppit has recently shown that the financial and economic consequences of the South Sea collapse were in fact considerably less severe than the feverish responses to it have led most historians to believe. Many, to be sure, lost money. What many others lost, however, was their bearings – suddenly all that seemed solid *did* appear to melt into air. The shock led to a feverish bout of collective soul-searching. For the South Sea Bubble was not an isolated event: the decades following the Glorious Revolution had seen an unprecedented flurry of monetary experiments and financial projects – land banks, lotteries, visionary coinage schemes, insurance companies, and numerous joint-stock enterprises. The year preceding the South Sea Bubble alone witnessed the flotation of no fewer than 190 such projects – "monstrous Beasts of uncommon nature. . . . *Men call'd them BUBBLES*." This, as Defoe aptly dubbed it, was "*The Projecting Age*".[22]

These new financial departures reinforced the concerns for the loss of substance and the triumph of the immaterial in this new age. The fact, moreover, that they were often spearheaded by "the Monied Interest", that is, men – often upstarts – who themselves could be seen as lacking substance (i.e. land), did little to help. Various metaphors were invoked to convey the insubstantiality of such early-eighteenth-century "projects" – not only bubbles, but also cobwebs, smoke, clouds, vapors, apparitions, wind, and moonshine. But it was again Defoe who captured the psychic meaning and consequence of this new reality – if it can be called reality – better than anyone. Credit, he wrote in 1710, acts all Substance, yet, is it self Immaterial: it gives Motion, yet it self cannot be said to Exist: it creates *Forms*, yet, has it self *no Form*; it is neither Quantity nor Quality; it has no *Whereness*, or *Whenness, Scite*, or *Habit*. If I should say it is *the essential Shadow of something that is Not*, should I not puzzle the Thing, rather than explain it, and leave you and my self more in the Dark than we were before?

Small wonder that Defoe's contemporaries, sitting in the darkness cast by the essential shadow of something that was not, were willing to contemplate surfaces that had no substance, referent, or underlying inner value.[23]

In subsequent decades, even as the novelty of paper finance wore off, the puzzlement did not. Consider the dismay of the 1770s periodical correspondent "Regulus" at the credulousness of his contemporaries, who continued to "believe the wealth and power of a great nation to be truly and substantially exprest and represented *by scraps of paper*". How could they fail to see that these paper scraps "signify nothing truly, but imposture on the one hand, and credulity on the other"? "I begin to suspect", Regulus continued, "the Thames before my eyes to be no better than a theatrical river made of paper or tinsel; and I have frequently my doubts, from the strong propensity I find to paper, whether I am myself of any better materials." Half a century after the South Sea Bubble, Regulus was no less adamant about the insubstantiality of value in a society so thoroughly commercialized. At the same time it is telling to note his other reference points. Regulus's characterization of this *"paper age"* was inseparable from his revealing references to imposture, to the theater, and even to the immateriality of the speaker himself.[24]

Regulus's contemporaries, in fact, were already familiar with the elision of paper finance and personal imposture. It was precisely this combination that animated the figure that haunted eighteenth-century economic life, triggering the period's most relentless policy of capital punishment: the forger. In a period deficient in specie or banks, the bulk of the credit resources that were the lifeline of economic activity was in the form of a bewildering variety of personal paper notes. Such notes depended on hand-written signatures for their veracity, and on the reputation of their signatories for their credibility. They depended, in other words, on the reliability and substance of particular persons: and the ease with which such signs of personal identity could be forged and thus shown to be *un*reliable and *in*substantial was matched only by the severity of the punishment meted out to the offenders. (It was not a coincidence that forgeries were the capital crime least likely to be pardoned in the eighteenth century.) In short, just as the economy of paper was so easily undermined by the unreliability of the identities it presupposed, so notions of identity were undermined by the flimsiness of an economy of paper. The forger and the

impostor were really two sides of the same coin – or rather of the same counterfeit paper note.[25]

We are back with questions of personal identity. It was but a small step from
the general concern for the absence of underlying substance in the modern,
unprecedented commercial society to the unreliability of identity, now reinforced by its own lack of underlying essential substance. In an age when "very
awkward copies pass for originals", proclaimed one writer in 1772, "it is not
difficult to impose upon the world". Indeed. It is therefore telling that it was
the South Sea Bubble, that ultimate exposure of the airiness inherent in paper
finance, that drove John Trenchard (and not him alone) to exclaim in a vein so
familiar from the previous pages: "What is human Life, but a Masquerade."[26]
Why masquerade again? Because if apparent value no longer represented true
substance, but rather inhered only in paper-thin surfaces, then persons –
identities – were as unreliable as paper property.

*

I have suggested, then, that the multiple and cumulative effects of commerce
were important enabling preconditions for the emergence of the *ancien régime*
of identity. While these aspects of urban commercializing society were not all
new, their combined impact had never before been as pronounced as during the
eighteenth century – a century ushered in by the revolution in public credit and
subsequently the scene for the most developed and widespread consumerism
the West had ever seen. The fluidity of forms, the unreliability of markers of
distinction, the interchangeability and abstraction of all forms of value, the play
of appearances without a necessary underpinning of substance: all of these consequences of commercialization fed directly into – and were again reinforced
by – the playfulness and the insubstantiality that characterized understandings
of identity during this period.

And yet the multiple effects of commercialization cannot all be captured
under the umbrella of "enabling preconditions". If commerce was crucial to the
emergence of the *ancien régime* of identity, it also brought with it the seeds of
this regime's subsequent demise. For with the potential for new imaginings and
the space for new possibilities that are implied in the word "enabling" came also
increasing unease, an unease that accompanied the gradual erosion of confidence
in familiar notions of identity and the increasing preoccupation with the plas-
ticity and deceptiveness of appearances. When Fanny Burney's Evelina was told
that "this is not an age in which we may trust to appearances", it was not only
a perceptive recognition of these aspects of eighteenth-century urban life, but
also a warning to the ingénue coming to London about its imminent dangers.
And when Elizabeth Montagu observed that "it is the ton of the times to

confound all distinctions of age, sex, and rank; no one ever thinks of sustaining a certain character, unless it is one they have assumed at a masquerade" – again, her insightful characterization of the *ancien régime* of identity was inseparable from her disapprobation.[27] Indeed, this unease is distinct in many of the voices we have been listening to, ranging from subtle signs of discomfort to the shrill prognostications of the self-appointed guardians of public morality. Not everyone, of course, shared – or even paid attention to – their gloomy vision of a world about to be drawn to a premature end by the siren call of commerce. Many more – among the propertied classes, that is – were too busy scurrying to capitalize on the fresh possibilities that this new world offered to worry too much about denunciations of luxury, fashion, and modern urban life. But these denunciations were constantly there, like an unremitting background noise muffled by the hubbub of a bustling commercial society. Or, to return to an image at the opening of this chapter, picture a trickle of criticism gradually turning into an undercurrent of unease, the corrosive effects of which were for a long time safely contained behind the walls of Georgian confidence and complacency. But, if new circumstances were suddenly to produce a crack in these walls, this heretofore pent-up undercurrent would threaten to come gushing forth. How this could happen, and did happen, is the story of the next chapter.

*

But first, a word – a quick word – about empire, the third remaining pillar of eighteenth-century society that I wish to flag in thinking about the conditions of possibility for the *ancien régime* of identity.

It is of course a common-sensical truism that encounters with new peoples and unfamiliar societies in the course of exploration, travel, and conquest had the potential to undermine Europeans' confidence in their own sense of identity. For eighteenth-century Britain this was perhaps true above all in the traversing of half the globe to reach the remote South Seas, a repeated and highly publicized experience that could result – in Jonathan Lamb's recent words – in the explorers' sense of personal identity becoming "a doubtful point of reference in any effort to define the exotic or the marvellous". (Interestingly, Lamb suggests that this was also a physical bodily phenomenon: "with scurvy rampant", as it inevitably was on these global circumnavigation vessels, its hallucinatory effects meant that "the eye, and the 'I', [could] no longer be trusted".) In this the voyages to the South Sea stood at the tail end of a long history of contact and discovery going back to the beginnings of European exploration.[28]

But I am more interested here in the outcomes of the more specific experiences of transplantation and colonization. Above all, I am thinking of North

America, the most important and the most populous part of the British global presence in the eighteenth century. It is the thrust of much recent work on colonial North America to emphasize the multiple ways in which the New World experiences of the colonists were chafing away at their confidence in the identity categorizations that they had brought with them from the mother country. In Greg Dening's evocative summary, "early America was a place of thresholds, margins, boundaries. It was a place of ambivalence and unset definition. The search for identity in that place was multivalent and unending."[29]

From Michael Zuckerman's call in the 1980s to take a close look at the "unease in Eden", as British colonists found it difficult "to maintain the boundaries of their increasingly brittle identities", to Karen Kupperman's more recent assertion that, "as colonists and native peoples observed each other, they also thought in novel ways about their own identities", the story historians have told has followed the same logic. It was in the seventeenth- and eighteenth-century colonial context, as the shock effect of early encounters was superseded by sustained interaction and closer long-term familiarity, not to mention frequent interdependence, that the impact of contact on the colonists' notions of identity was the most profound. Richard White has posited a compelling model of this process of mutual transformation. When Europeans and Indians first met, White writes, they "regarded each other as alien, as other, as virtually non-human". But then, "over the next two centuries" – as they became trading partners, allies, and occasionally enemies – "they constructed a common, mutually comprehensible world". In this new "middle ground", in White's influential phrase, the older ways of ordering the world had to change: colonists, like Indians, found that the boundaries of their respective universes "melted at the edges and merged".[30] Even without an obvious new shared middle ground, moreover, the older boundaries could still melt. Such was the case, for instance, in the encounter with the gender practices of the eastern Algonquin peoples. Here was a society with an apparently viable gender system in which – in the words of one Marylander in 1666 – the women were "Butchers, Cooks, and Tillers of the ground", and men thought it "below the honour of a Masculine" to do anything but hunt. Familiarity with the Algonquins thus forced the colonists to confront (or consciously avoid) the possibility that their own gender presuppositions were neither natural nor inevitable.[31]

Another interface of contact in colonial North America was that between the European settlers and the Africans transplanted through the transatlantic slave trade. We have already seen that the relative pliability of the *ancien régime* of race extended also to the edges of the black/white distinction. What remains to be said now is that the experiences of the New World, in which contact between Europeans and Africans was much more pervasive and regular than in the mother country, again compounded the opportunities for pressures on the integrity of identity boundaries, and this despite the vested interest of the institution of slavery in keeping this destabilizing potential in check. In 1765, for instance, in the colony of Georgia, it was decided not only to encourage immigration of free colored people – itself a unique step – but also to grant free mulatto immigrants the right to be naturalized *as white men*, like "any person born of British parents". If this striking move to nullify racial difference by legal decree had no parallel in the North American colonies, it was more in keeping with the confusion surrounding racial differences in their counterparts in the West Indies. In Jamaica, for instance, legal statutes of 1733 regarding mulattos had the effect – in the words of Winthrop Jordan – "of publicly transforming Negroes into white men". Several factors in the Caribbean colonies came together to produce a much more conspicuous potential for the blurring of boundaries: a colored population of both freed and enslaved persons, a smaller proportion of Europeans to blacks as well as of European men to women, and the influence of the Spanish multi-level system of racial classification. The English colonies in the Caribbean were populated not only by negroes, but also by mulattos, samboes, quadroons, and mestizos.[32]

Illustrations of the potential for boundary-blurring in the Caribbean are not hard to find. In the case of eighteenth-century Jamaica, for example, Philip Morgan has pointed out the many opportunities for, and the considerable success of, the passing of mixed-color people – especially women – as whites. Passing in the West Indies, art historian Dian Kriz explains, "depend[ed] on local knowledge of genealogies and social performance, rather than the lightness of one's skin". Kriz makes this observation in her wonderfully suggestive analysis of a series of paintings by the Italian-born artist Agostino Brunias, paintings that the British commissioner of Dominica, St. Vincent, and Tobago had commissioned in order to promote interest in Caribbean emigration among Englishmen back home. What is striking about these scenes of West Indian life is the figure that Brunias chose as their centerpiece, and who was thus presumably supposed to convey most effectively the appeal of the Caribbean colonies to metropolitan viewers: the mulatto woman (fig. 32). Brunias's insistent and deliberate focus on the mulatto woman, Kriz concludes, was a celebration of undecideability. Quite: it was a celebration of the undecideability entailed by the realities of racial mixing that revealed the limits of identity categories. ("I have seen many Mulâtresses", remarked a late-eighteenth-century English captain passing through the West Indies, "as white, if not whiter, than the generality of European women.") It was precisely this undecideability that Brunias foregrounded as a distinctive and recognizable, and appealing, feature of the colonial West Indian experience.[33]

Finally, colonial North America also became the setting for conspicuous figures who in their very persons and lives embodied the limitations of

32. Agostino Brunias, "Market Day, Roseau, Dominica", c.1780. The light-beige-skinned mulatto woman, surrounded by market goers who are variously skin-pigmented, dominates the composition and invites the gaze of everyone, including the viewer

familiar categories of identity on this permanent cross-cultural frontier. In the mid-eighteenth century such figures included William Johnson of Johnson Hall, an Irishman of humble origins who as a successful colonial Indian agent represented himself alternately as an English gentleman and a Mohawk chief, a doubleness carried over to his personal life as the paterfamilias of two families – one European and one Mohawk – and the master of a hybrid colonial house replete with Mohawk artefacts. They also included Mohawk leader "Teoniahigarawe alias Hendrick", Johnson's many-time partner, whose multiplicity of names, like his hybrid Euro-Indian dress and appearance, signaled an inseparable blending of European and Indian life experiences. Then there was Eve Pickard – or was it Eghye Pickerd? – a mulatto woman who lived much of her life as a Mohawk matriarch and was integrated enough within Mohawk society to represent her brethren in several land-fraud court cases, but who was then denounced by her erstwhile adoptive community as one of "the white people" when she herself attempted what they saw as the white crime of land stealing. There was also the Canadian métis Andrew Montour. Son to Oneida leader Currundawanah and the French "Madame Montour" – herself an intriguing but unfathomable mixture of French and Iroquois identities – Montour made a career as interpreter and go-between at numerous intercultural conversations between the Indians, the French, and the English (other than when he preferred to join one side or the other). His multilingual abilities, his undetermined loyalties, his impressive collection of names, and his unclassifiable appearance – complete with hat and waistcoat, earrings, and paint – led one well-informed contemporary to exclaim that Montour was "really *an unintelligible person*". He was right. Repeatedly, such frontier people – individuals with "stretched identities", in the words of Karen Kupperman, "who lived within and between cultures" – proved to be unintelligible and unclassifiable within the understandings of identity that the colonists had inherited from their metropolitan homelands. However desperately the colonists tried to shore up these category boundaries that protected their sense of difference, figures like Johnson, Hendrick, Pickard, and Montour – or Johnson's nephew, Colonel Guy Johnson (fig. 33) – were walking proofs of the inadequacies of these boundaries in the colonial setting.[34]

The conclusion I want to draw from these brisk observations is a double one. First, it stands to reason that as the reports and rumors of colonial experiences found their way back to the mother country – both Johnson and Hendrick, for instance, were well-known figures in England; not to mention Brunias's images that were intended specifically for metropolitan consumption – they too contributed to the conditions of possibility of the *ancien régime* of identity. This effect was not limited to figures from the New World empire: one need only recall the image of the notorious hookah-loving "nabob" returning from India, a reputed hybrid of British and Indian culture whose identity was ceaselessly queried (had the nabob become, as one writer put it, "himself of a blackamoor nature"?).[35] It is in this sense that I have pointed to the empire as one of the enabling preconditions feeding into the long-term undermining of traditional categories of identity, categories that were repeatedly found wanting in accounting for such quintessential colonial experiences.

We should also consider, however, that from a colonial perspective the effects of the same experiences may well have been more anxiety-provoking than from a metropolitan one. Not only were these encounters for the colonists a much closer, more immediate, and often more threatening fact of life. They also came on top of the fundamental disruption of uprooting emigration and transplantation that defined colonial existence, confirming yet again the colonists' immense distance from the world they had left behind. Recall then in closing the image of the undercurrent of unease that was gradually building up beneath the *ancien régime* of identity, its corrosive pressure held in check by the

33.   Benjamin West, "Colonel Guy Johnson and Karonghyontye (Captain David Hill)", 1776. This portrait of William Johnson's nephew and successor as superintendent for Indian affairs of the northern colonies seamlessly blends a European identity with an Indian one, manifested in Johnson's leggings, beaded sash, and moccasins. This blending of identities is notable in the beaded and feathered cap of the Indian Department in Johnson's hand, as well as in the blanket hanging over his other arm, which was likely to be recognized as Indian in design and function but British in manufacture

dam of eighteenth-century confidence. We can safely assume that the "unease in Eden" – to return to Zuckerman's felicitous phrase – added one more tributary to this undercurrent. But more important was its contribution to the unraveling of our story. Given the peculiarities of colonial unease, it should come as no surprise that when the winds of change did begin to blow – the winds that were to unleash the flood that was to bring the *ancien régime* of identity to an end – they began blowing from across the Atlantic ocean.

6

The Ancien Régime *and the Revolution*

In early 1776, two English clergymen had an argument over tea. The first was Richard Price, the pro-American Dissenting minister whose *Observations on the Nature of Civil Liberty* was one of the most influential pamphlets in the run-up to the American Revolution. In arguing the case of the colonists, Price commented on their struggles against the tax on tea; "and at BOSTON", he reminded his readers in passing, "some persons in disguise buried it in the sea." Our second interlocutor was the founder of Methodism, John Wesley, who penned one of the most influential responses to Price. Writing with the angry zeal of a recent convert to the anti-American campaign, Wesley could not let such a quick and neutral reference to what became known as the "Boston Tea Party" go by. This event, he stormed indignantly, was an "eminent instance" of the colonists' pernicious fraudulence.

> The famous Mr. John Hancock, some time since, brought into Boston, a ship-load of smuggled tea. . . . All Europe knows what was done: "Some persons in disguise," Doctor Price tells us, "buried the English tea in the sea." It was not so commonly known, who employed them, or paid them for their labour: To be sure, good Mr. Hancock knew no more of it than the child unborn![1]

How predictable: what one pamphleteering minister accepted as part of a patriotic ideological struggle, his adversary highlighted as a cowardly, self-interested act of fraud. More striking, perhaps, is what this exchange left conspicuously unsaid. As any American child who has ever enacted this originary moment of national mythology in a school play knows, the colonists were disguised as Mohawk Indians: a fact that has since assumed considerable significance in the narrative of American self-fashioning. To cite one recent example, Philip Deloria has described the "powerful imputation of Indian identity" at the Boston Tea Party as "a catalytic moment . . . through which Americans redefined themselves as something other than British Colonists".[2] On our two British commentators, however, this powerfully catalytic significance of the Indian masquerade seems to have been lost. Rather, both chose to convey the meaning of this event by referring simply to its participants being "in disguise", whatever that disguise might have been.

On the part of anti-revolutionary English writers, at least, this apparent omission (which was repeated by others)[3] may well have had something to do with an attempt to conjure up a familiar legal analogue: one possible frame of reference for interpreting the actions of the Bostonians was that of the Black Act, which made the very act of disguise under such circumstances into a capital offense.[4] But perhaps we can take the explanation further, to the particular significance and resonance of notions of *disguise* in the English perspective on the events in America in the mid-1770s. This point will prove to be a key one: the meanings that the notion of disguise came to carry at this particular juncture, I want to suggest, go not only to the heart of contemporaries' experience of what was probably the most traumatic national crisis in their lifetime, but also to the heart of the transformation we are seeking, which brought the *ancien régime* of identity to an end. That disguise was indeed at the core of these accounts of the Boston Tea Party can perhaps be inferred further from what Wesley did with the story when he came back to it a year later, after the Americans had declared independence. "The Bostonians," Wesley now wrote, "under the auspices of Mr. Hancock . . . scorning to do any thing secretly, paraded the town at noon-day, with colours flying, and bravely threw the English tea into the sea. This was the first plain overt act of Rebellion." In this retelling, not only was the disguise of the Bostonians gone, it has been replaced by its opposite – complete transparency, aided by the midday sun (never mind that the actual event had begun at dusk), ensuring that nothing would be done in secrecy. This new perspective proved key to Wesley's second pamphlet: in declaring independence, he stated, the colonists "wholly threw off the mask", and showed their true colors "without any disguise, or reserve".[5] Now that the Americans revealed their true intentions that had formerly been hidden, the Tea Party came to stand metonymically for the whole of the great American fraud. But even as Wesley reversed the narrative of the events in Boston in order to achieve this effect, his repeated recourse to the language of disguise and masquerade only grew stronger and more loaded.

Earlier we saw the central place that disguise and masquerade occupied within eighteenth-century understandings of identity, signaling the limits of identity categories and the playful potential inherent therein. For Price and Wesley in this exchange, however, this language assumed new and rather different overtones. In the following pages we will witness how disguise and masquerade, together with other key elements of the *ancien régime* of identity, were introduced many times over into the language surrounding the unfolding American conflict. But within the freighted peculiarities of this moment of crisis, these elements of identity's *ancien régime* were now invested with distinctly different valences: ominous valences that signaled a profound change. It is this change that we are after.

The previous chapter, we recall, ended with the image of a flood about to be unleashed by transatlantic winds. This image is intended to capture particular dynamics of historical change: those of a swift, radical, far-reaching transformation that brought the *ancien régime* of identity to an abrupt end. The discussion so far has drawn attention to a steady trickle of unease at the edges of this *ancien régime* that remained safely pent up behind the largely impervious dam of Georgian complacency and self-confidence. What now remains to be seen is the sudden collapse of this dam, which sent a powerful current gushing forth rapidly and indiscriminately through the cultural landscape, engulfing everything in its path. In the manner of a hydrological flood, the very abruptness of the disruption gave additional force to a current that under less dramatic circumstances might have in part seeped into the ground and dissipated. William Sewell is one historian who has carefully thought through this type of historical discontinuity, which even if building on pre-existing long-term processes is ultimately initiated and carried forth by specific, sharply defined events – events with "momentous consequences, that in some sense 'changed the course of history'". Such events, Sewell writes, generate high levels of insecurity and emotional intensity, negotiated through "bursts of collective cultural creativity" that often result in consequences far exceeding the event itself.[6] It is precisely such a dynamic that concerns us here: which is why the present chapter, unlike others in this book, is largely focused on the meaning and consequences of a single historical event. This event that in Sewell's words changed the course of history – the slice of history we are interested in, that is – was the American revolutionary war.

That the American revolutionary war played this historical role is far from self-evident and requires several layers of explanation. In brief, the argument I will make focuses on what was for the English the most disturbing and unfamiliar aspect of the American war. In contrast to other wars in recent memory, this one was irreducible to any clearly demarcated map of "us" and "them" based on a stable criterion of difference. Instead, the tension between sameness and difference – resulting, as we shall see, from the lack of clarity about who the Americans were, enemies or brethren – returned inescapably to undermine and destabilize the rhetoric of all sides. In the fraught years before and after the declaration of American independence, English commentators of all political stripes tried to impose virtually every identity category imaginable on the American conflict, in repeated and often desperate attempts to create order out of chaos. But these attempts to identify who was against whom in this national crisis were time and again baffled by the actual complexities of the situation, complexities that exceeded any conceptual tools available for dealing with them.

The consequences of this state of affairs went far beyond the direct political context that triggered them. They led to intense pressures on prevalent understandings of identity, and to an insistent preoccupation – a preoccupation signaled, *inter alia*, by a pervasive recourse to the language of disguise and masquerade – with the constitution of identity: its inherent versus contingent traits, its natural foundations, its boundaries, and its possible permeabilities. These pressures placed the characteristics of the *ancien régime* of identity – and not least, the long-standing prognostications of doom favored by its critics – in a different light. Ultimately, this situation created a sense of urgency about the need to counteract the ever more apparent inadequacies of familiar notions of identity with new, more reliable ways of conceptualizing differences between people. Here then was the transatlantic storm that cracked the dam that unleashed the flood that was to submerge identity's *ancien régime*.

The present chapter, therefore, has a logic, a rhythm, and an array of historical voices rather different from those of the rest of this book. Its goal is to demonstrate the relationship between the contemporary experience of the one event, the American revolutionary war, and the suddenly increasing pressures on the *ancien régime* of identity. Like most aspects of our inquiry, this relationship was rarely made explicit, and thus requires a patient and sometimes circuitous route through the heated political rhetoric of the mid-1770s in order to unearth the ways in which people's understandings of this momentous event were informed by, and inadequately served by, prevalent notions of identity. In Kuhnian terms, this historical moment can be described as the crisis point at which a prevalent paradigm, having long been able to filter out considerable levels of troubling noise as little more than an irritating background hum, suddenly collapsed under the weight of its own limitations, only to be replaced abruptly and comprehensively by another.

The English Problem of Identity in the American Revolution

So why the American war? Historians of late-eighteenth-century Britain (including the author of the present lines) have often glossed over the events of the 1770s in their haste to reach the "real" turning point of their period, supposedly located in the tumultuous 1790s with their dramatic realignment of British politics and social relations in the wake of the French Revolution. Recently we have seen a salutary revival of interest in the American revolutionary war in Britain, proposing that it should be studied on its own terms and not simply as a corridor to the 1790s.[7] My argument here follows in the footsteps of this scholarship: it may even venture one step further, in suggesting that in certain ways the destabilizing effects of the American war had greater historical significance than those that accompanied the events in France a couple of decades later.

For a first hint that this might have been the case, consider a scene that will appear familiar to any connoisseur of "the Age of Revolutions". The rage of Edmund Burke, exasperated by a confrontation that in his view must send the course of history into a catastrophic tailspin, is inflamed – or rather distilled – by the picture of a lone woman overtaken by the advance of the uncivilized hordes inflicting destruction on all that Burke holds dear. Trapped and captured in her domestic surroundings, the woman-victim embodies lofty sentiments that throw the barbarity of her pursuers into sharp relief. Burke envelops the scene with powerful pathos in the self-consciously vain hope that the effects of a striking tableau on his audience might check the course of events.

Only that the tableau I have in mind is not that of the imprisonment of Marie Antoinette by the French revolutionary crowds in October 1789, perhaps the most scholar-beguiling passage in Burke's oeuvre. Rather, it is the virtually unknown one of the woman who reputedly torched a quarter of the city of New York in September 1776 in order to snatch the fruits of victory from the hands of the advancing British army. Now my point in placing these two Burkean flourishes next to each other is not so much to suggest some conscious or sub-conscious genealogical link – in the overdramatized effusions of the man who turned sentimental pathos into a political art form, other such images may well be found – but rather to direct attention to the *differences* between these two analogous pictures, set as they were in their respective revolutionary settings some fifteen years apart.

For in every other respect, Burke's two heroines were as different as night and day. Marie Antoinette was a "great lady" of "exalted rank", embodying feminine beauty that "glitter[ed] like the morning-star", as well as "amiable qualities" and "lofty sentiments", "in a manner suited to her rank and race"; while her pursuers – including, famously, "the furies of hell, in the abused shape of the vilest of women" – were those who threw off "that generous loyalty to rank and sex" that had been abrogated by the French Revolution. The arsonist of 1776 was in almost every way the precise opposite. She was a "miserable woman", a low-life with no name, "with her visage besmeared and smutted over". Most significantly, she, "with her single arm, did that, which an army of a hundred thousand men could not do": arrest the progress of the British. Marie Antoinette embodied conspicuous femininity and nobility; the New York arsonist was a barely recognizable gender-reversed female warrior.[8]

Now, first, we should note that the fact that Burke positioned himself quite differently vis-à-vis the American and the French revolutions cannot in itself account for this contrast, since in both cases the woman in question represented the side that Burke happened to favor. But rather than offering an insight into Burke's thinking, perhaps this contrast can illuminate a difference in the perceived nature of the two revolutionary situations that elicited his rhetoric. Burke's *Reflections on the Revolution in France* underscored the contrast between the English nation – sober, organic, historical, natural – and the French revolutionaries, who were experimental, rationalist, anti-historical, and unnatural. This was a vision predicated on well-defined, mutually constitutive opposites. Burke's portrayal of female heroism in this context, therefore, pitted Marie Antoinette, the embodiment of an orderly world of rank and gender, against her pursuers who were the convenient combination of all its unnatural and disorderly opposites. But in Burke's portrayal of female heroism in the American revolutionary tableau, by contrast, virtue and disorder were inextricably intertwined. Far from pitting one clear-cut world against another, his colonial heroine was herself unable to sustain a clarity of rank (hence her social anonymity), of gender (as attested by her more-than-manly action), and even the integrity of racial appearance (recall her visage "smutted over"). To the extent therefore that she too, like Marie Antoinette, embodied the nature of the conflict in which she found herself embroiled, it was one distinguished by internal tension and disharmony, involving the perhaps unnatural confusion of fundamental identity categories. That this was how contemporaries in fact experienced the American conflict is the thrust of what follows.

So, again, what was so special about the American war? This war, as so many commentators did not tire from pointing out, was perceived to be at bottom *a civil war*: what one pamphleteer (anti-American) dubbed "the second civil war", and another (pro-American) "the American civil war".[9] It is hard to convey – but impossible to miss – the density of such references in the mid- to late 1770s, as writers of all sorts competed with each other in detailing the horrors of such an internecine war. "It is not our natural enemy, it is not French or Spaniards, nor rebel Scots, that we are contending with," exclaimed an anguished American sympathizer; "it is our friends, our brethren, with whom we have this unhappy and unnatural contest." "The present War", a relentless critic of the Americans concurred, "is of all Wars the most unnatural", because it is an "unwarrantable civil War". As the political divergence of these few examples suggests, the many hundreds of similar utterances that one could marshal here came from across the political board.[10]

This situation has been noted often by historians, but its ramifications merit further consideration. Inevitably, a conflict that was seen as a civil war forced people to reflect – often with considerable apprehension – on their understandings of identity. The "evils of civil war" force us away from being "true to ourselves". It is particularly pernicious in that "it confounds those distinctions among men which God and nature have established". It "confound[s] all

the social ties of blood". And so the litany went on and on: internal strife desta-
bilized the most basic distinctions of "us" and "them", good guys and bad guys,
friends and foes. In this war "rag[ing] among *brethren*!", a fictional figure in a
novel subtitled "The Miseries of Civil War" exclaimed with ungrammatical
urgency, "whom are *we* . . . to consider them as enemy, and whom as friend?"[11]
After all, the supposed enemy was, in the eyes of many, literally the Englishmen's "brethren". In relation to the English, the Americans were "of the same
language, the same religion, the same manners and customs, sprung from the
same nation, intermixed by relation and consanguinity". And again: "The
Americans are properly Britons. They have the manners, habits, and ideas of
Britons"; they have in common "the same laws, the same religion, the same
constitution, the same feelings, sentiments and habits". Indeed, summarized
one exasperated observer, either the Americans were English, "or they are
fallen out of the clouds, or started up in America like mushrooms".[12] These
speakers – and countless others – shared the strong and painful sense that the
Americans and the English were fundamentally the same.

And yet, against each assertion of sameness, one can counterpose an assertion of difference. The particular geographic and political circumstances of this
"civil war" allowed many others to deny that it was in fact a civil war at all, and
to dispute every aspect of the supposed common ground between Americans
and Englishmen. Richard Price himself complained that every Englishman had
strong opinions about America, "though perhaps *he does not know what colour
they are of, or what language they talk*". The London physician John Fothergill
echoed this surprising assertion of distance and difference. "I soon perceived
when the confusion begun", he wrote, that all sides in the debate in England
"were almost total strangers to AMERICA, to the Country, and to its Inhabitants:
many, to such a degree, as to be ignorant whence the people sprung; what language they spoke; what religion they professed; nay, of what complexion they
were."[13] Tom Paine's *Common Sense*, the single most influential pamphlet of
the American Revolution, took the point even further. "The phrase *parent* or
mother country" – habitually employed to describe England's relationship to the
colonies – masked the truth: "Europe, and not England, is the parent country
of America", since its population consisted of immigrants "from *every part* of
Europe". According to Paine, the arguments based on common ancestry and
national identity foundered on the simple observation that "not one third of
the inhabitants . . . are of English descent". One royalist pushed this line to a
racialized extreme: unlike the loyalists who displayed "no variety in their
appearance, [being] all of one colour – *white*", those favoring independence
were "of all sizes and of all hues! red-skins, yellow-skins, green-skins, grey-
skins, bay-skins, black-skins, blue-skins!" The revolutionaries, it turned out,
were not simply different, they were the embodiment of difference itself.[14]

Little wonder, then, that Fothergill encapsulated the conflict with the words "when the confusion begun". By the end of such assertions of difference, it turned out that the Americans were strangers to the English in terms of ancestry, religion, complexion, even language. So what common ground *did* remain, to justify the simultaneous representation of the very same conflict, as both Fothergill and Price found themselves doing, as a civil war involving the "sheath[ing] [of] our swords in the bowels of our brethren"?[15] It is crucial for realizing the consequences of this freighted situation that this question did not have, and could not have, a satisfying answer. The tension between assertions of sameness and difference irrepressibly surfaced and resurfaced, self-contradictory and unresolvable, to destabilize every supposedly well-demarcated superimposition of identity categories on the alignments of the American crisis. This, again, was true across the political board: neither side in the conflict had a necessary affinity with one pole or the other of the sameness–difference dyad. Those in favor of American independence could highlight *difference* in order to justify their separation from the mother country, but also *sameness* in order to expose how unnatural the war waged against them was, and how truly English their political demands were.[16] Their opponents, in reverse, could highlight *sameness* in order to expose the ungrateful and unnatural essence of the American rebellion, but also *difference* in order to justify the resort to bellicose actions. Even as a civil war, then, this conflict was not stable; whether it was a "civil war" or "the struggle . . . of a nation against a nation" (both formulations were used by one author, Abbé Raynal, within a page of each other) depended on the answer to a question that resonated throughout the whole confrontation: who were the Americans? Nothing, perhaps, encapsulated the problem more eloquently than the scheme of three distinct headings that the *Lady's Magazine* adopted for printing news during the crisis: "foreign news", "home news", and – evidently impossible to accommodate in either – "America".[17]

The irreconcilable tensions between assertions of sameness and difference, moreover, were undermining the internal coherence and logical consistency of interventions on both sides. Take for instance Matthew Robinson-Morris, the second Baron Rokeby. In a passage that evidently influenced Paine's *Common Sense*, Rokeby too denied that England was "the parent country" to the Americans. "The fact is very different," he wrote. The Americans were "hardly our cousin's [sic] cousins, and no man knows how far we might mount towards Adam or Noah to settle the real relation between us." Given this emphasis on almost primordial distance, then, one may be excused the confusion when a few pages later one reads: "We are one nation with the same language, the same manners, and the same religion." So much for a coherent vision of difference, even within a single text. Another pamphlet of 1774 was no less contradictory.

On the one hand it described "our injured American brethren" as "people, descended from the same stock, governed by the same constitution, laws, religion, and wrapt up in the same common interest"; but, on the other hand, it also claimed that "the inhabitants of America are chiefly made up of emigrants from all Europe", and that they "are a people of a very different complexion from the natives of this island". So which was it? And which was it for the anti-American writer who similarly dismissed "the Provincials" as "a Medley of people composed of English, Scotch, Irish, Germans, Swedes, Dutch, French and Indians . . . opposite in manners, religion, and political opinions", only to end up with a hope for reconciliation, entreating "every American to be a Briton, and every Briton to be an American"? And again, take James Macpherson, whom we have already witnessed in different circumstances tripping over his tongue in making incongruous statements about the essential or environmental constitution of racial difference. How could Macpherson now complain that the Americans, "with a perversion of terms, unknown, in any other times", had misleadingly asserted "that a war against America 'is against our own country' [and that] 'they are still our fellow-subjects, and every blow we strike is against ourselves'"; but then with a straight face also affirm, in precisely the same vein, that this was particularly unthinkable when coming from those "whose hands are daily stained with the blood of their countrymen"?[18]

Among supporters of American independence, these contradictory impulses often took the form of a disjunction between national consanguinity and political divergence. Thus, asserting that Americans were "the posterity of true Britons" did not prevent James Burgh from then switching tack: "What difference is there between the British parliament's taxing America, and the French court's laying England under contribution?" Together with the implied answer (none), Burgh also floated the more surprising suggestion – in light of what he had said before – that, politically, the English were to the Americans as the French were to the English. Edmund Burke likewise tempered his emphasis on the close fraternity between Americans and Englishmen with the insistence that forcing English forms of government on the colonists was as "wild" as assuming "that the natives of Hindustan and those of Virginia could be ordered in the same manner". The war against the Americans was "cruel and unnatural", an "unconnected Whig" told his English readers, because "they are bone of your bone, and flesh of your flesh"; and yet trying to unite the English and the Americans under one system of government was as futile as an "attempt to govern the Turk and the Englishman, the Frenchman and the Indian by the same code".[19] The Americans, then, were to the English – the "flesh of [their] flesh" – like the English to the Turks or to the Hindus. Strictly speaking, such assertions were perhaps not logical contradictions: but neither were they models of categorical clarity.

The point of highlighting these observations is not simply to catch contemporaries in contradictions, as if to uncover a hidden weakness that supposedly invalidated their positions. This would hardly do as a historical methodology, or indeed as an effective analysis of political rhetoric in an actual lived debate.[20] The point is rather to underscore the recurrence throughout the American crisis of such contradictory moves in irreconcilable tension with each other. Moreover, far from it being the case that the conflict neatly lined up one party rooting for Anglo–American sameness against another party rooting for Anglo–American difference, in fact each side was rent by this same fundamental tension from within.

Faced with these unsettling difficulties, therefore, contemporaries employed various strategies to get around them; strategies aimed at the wishful reconfiguration of the conflict along more familiar and tangible lines of difference that might explain why this war was taking place. As we shall presently see, these efforts were doomed to failure, at least during the earlier stages of the war. Despite persistent attempts, Britons found it well-nigh impossible to pull these assertions of sameness and difference apart in order to draw a consistent and reliable map of identity boundaries that could make sense of this empire-shattering conflict. Herein lay the key to its profound effect: it was this intractable muddle that made the American war such a source of unease about the inadequacies of the notion of identity itself.

*

Among the seemingly clear-cut categories of identity and difference that could serve to disentangle this messy situation, few presented themselves more readily than that of religion. Consider the efforts of the veteran high-Tory political hack John Shebbeare. On the one hand, Shebbeare asserted the common identity of Americans and Englishmen, who had a shared "*national* mind, if the expression may be allowed me". On the other hand, Shebbeare explained the "vile and unnatural" rebellion of the colonists by referring to their origins in the dissenting religious sects that had fled England (including "*a religious sect called Witches*"): "in these dissenters . . . rebellion is as innate and natural, as stealing poultry is in a fox, or killing lambs in a wolf". This was a sharp change of tack: instead of essentializing common national identity, Shebbeare was now essentializing religious difference – an old favorite of his – by declaring Dissenting rebelliousness innate and natural like an animal instinct. The consequences could hardly have been more blatant: rebutting Price's appeal on behalf of "our [American] brethren", Shebbeare disdainfully asserted (using words from Swift) that they were "our brethren . . . in no other sense, than nature/ Has made a rat our fellow creature".[21] So much for the most common cliché of affinity with the Americans, "our brethren". So much, indeed, for a vision of shared political and national identity, suddenly metamorphosed into one of innate difference grounded in religion.

Now, from the other corner of the religious arena, listen to the Scottish Presbyterian minister John Erskine in a passionate jeremiad triggered by this "calamitous civil war" against "our own countrymen, connected with us by birth, alliance, or commercial interest, so that we cannot hurt them without injuring ourselves". Continuing in a similar vein until the final two pages of his discourse, Erskine suddenly shifted to an assignation of blame, pinning it – surprisingly – on the pernicious proliferation of popery in England. This "truly alarming" development, leading to the increasing clamor for toleration, was driven by artifice and subterfuge, not least by "many who would pass for good Protestants". And thus Erskine brought in the connection with the American crisis, however tenuous: "the disaffected party on the other side of the water, were particularly active in sending over priests in disguise."[22] It was on this note that the text ended, leaving the reader with the distinct sense that the furtive progress of Catholicism was the real cause of the American crisis. Moreover, not only did Erskine thus shift the line of conflict from the blurred distinctions of an "unnatural" civil war among Britons to the clear and comfortably familiar demarcation between Protestants and Catholics, he also removed the disturbing anxieties of the conflict from the former to the latter. The problem of unknowable or indeterminable identities – that key problematic of the American crisis – was now projected onto the Catholics, whose cunning artifice allowed them to "pass for good Protestants" and send "priests in disguise".

Both Shebbeare and Erskine, then, complicated their emphasis on the natural affinity between the two sides in the American conflict with a shared conviction that religious difference was key – *the* key – to making sense of there being two hostile sides to begin with. Moreover, not only were these assertions in tension with the affirmations of sameness with which they were coupled, they were also in tension with each other: whereas Erskine explained the war with the aid of the line dividing Catholics from Protestants, Shebbeare focused on that dividing the Church of England from Dissenters. Both, indeed, represented familiar positions reproduced by many other speakers. Nor were the possibilities here exhausted: the English-born missionary Charles Inglis, for instance, who was similarly convinced that "the present is a *Religious War*", blamed the crisis – like Erskine – on the progress of popery, but in reverse: in his own recasting of the situation, it was the Americans who were under pernicious Catholic influence, not the English. So whereas some presented the Quebec Act of 1774 (recognizing Roman Catholicism, as well as French civil law, in Quebec) as evidence of the crypto-Catholic sympathies of George III and his ministers, others – like *Hypocrisy Unmasked*, a popular pamphlet reverberating with the language of masquerade – put forth the relationship between the Canadians and the colonists as proof of the Catholic leanings of the *latter*.[23] So again, which was it – which side was in fact the crypto-papists? Or was the war really about differences between Protestants? In the end, no amount of tossing and turning could confer on this contest the crystalline clarity that characterized most eighteenth-century wars, in which unblemished British Protestantism was pitted against the black powers of Catholicism.[24] This particular war was jumbled shades of gray, not black and white.

Now it goes without saying that name-calling is part of every conflict, and thus in and of itself not much of an aid to understanding the dynamics of the American one. Rather, the point of this quick and confusing taste of the uses of religious distinctions in interpretations of the American conflict is to show the difficulties in coming up with a conceptual map that could fix the differences between the warring sides within a stable categorical scheme. The very fact that contemporaries found themselves resorting to virtually every imaginable permutation of religious demarcations in their attempts to make sense of the war – Protestants versus Catholics, Catholics versus Protestants, orthodox versus heterodox Protestants – is in itself eloquent testimony to the basic *lack* of clarity in explaining who was against whom and why. Moreover, whatever scheme one chose, the ineradicable tension between assertions of sameness and difference came back to undermine its coherence. At the same time that religion was claimed to be a wedge separating Americans from Englishmen, it was also seen as a unifying bond – "our Protestant Brethren". In the bottom line, then, religious identity, in any shape or form, did not prove capable of becoming the sword that could cut the Gordian knot holding the two sides in this conflict together.[25]

*

Mixing talk about religion with anxieties about civil war was a potent brew in eighteenth-century England, one that could not fail to conjure up the ghosts of the most potent trauma in English collective memory, the civil war of the seventeenth century. By drawing parallels to that earlier civil war, then, and mapping the present divisions onto former ones, could one perhaps render the American war more comprehensible? This was certainly the implication of the emphasis on the sectarian descent of the colonists, which often led – as it did for Shebbeare – to claims about Dissenters' congenital seditiousness and republicanism: depicting the colonists as "the offspring of [a] turbulent and bloody race", say, or as infected with "an hereditary disaffection to the English constitution". So that to Burke's assertion that "the People of the Colonies are the Descendants of *Englishmen*" and thus one with the English, the Dean of

Gloucester, Josiah Tucker, had this to say: "HERE, Sir, you tell some Truth; you disguise some; and you conceal more than you disguise. OUR first Emigrants to *North-America* were mostly Enthusiasts of a particular Stamp. They were of that Set of *Republicans*" and they have not let go of their republicanism ever since. Contra Burke, their particular variety of English blood proved not their affinity with the mother country but their divergence from it, a divergence going back to, and now re-enacting, the divisions of the English civil war.[26]

But none of this historical role-playing was really very convincing. As we have already seen, pulling the warring sides apart to reveal a Dissenting republican camp of puritan descent facing a royalist Anglican camp was not very plausible. Thus, to give one more example, when loyalist Joseph Galloway tried his hand at it, his attempts to derive the colonists' intransigence and independence from their puritan origins flew in the face of his simultaneous assertion that "the [American] people in general" were simply "duped into rebellion" by a small faction, and could easily be led back into the bosom of the British nation. In the end, therefore, Galloway threw his arms up in the air in exasperated resignation: "To sum up the whole weight of this argument in a few words, Do we not daily see Monarchies at war with Monarchies, Infidels with Infidels, Christians with Christians, Catholics with Catholics, and Dissenters with Dissenters? What stress, then, can be justly laid on an attachment arising from a similarity of government, laws, or religion?" Much as he wanted to abide by the clear divisions of the seventeenth century, Galloway ended up admitting that the American war alignments failed to follow that earlier script. And even if one did accept the significance of the Dissenting voice among the colonists, this still did not necessarily result in a clear scheme of difference. As one commentator had it, writing as the "Voice of God" no less, the presence of Dissenters in North America was so reminiscent of the situation back home that it was in itself grounds for considering the colonists not as different from Englishmen but rather as Englishmen themselves. Once again the supposed categorical map of the seventeenth-century civil war failed to account for the present one.[27]

Moreover, consider again the eighteenth-century retreat of God from active involvement in earthly matters, "the disenchantment of the world" in Marcel Gauchet's phrase. Despite the self-confidence of the writer who styled himself the "Voice of God", God's voice was no longer really expected to be heard in specific human conflicts or dilemmas. Herein, arguably, lay an important difference between the issues of identity raised by the seventeenth-century civil war and those raised by the late-eighteenth-century one. In the earlier period, the very choice of a particular side had been sufficient in and of itself to create a distinct primary identity in relation to God-and-King: it was the conflict itself therefore that produced the separate identities that already embodied the absolute difference that, in turn, explained the divisions of the war. In the American war, by contrast, while many people ardently believed that their choice was consonant with God's will, there was less of a sense that the two warring sides were divinely sanctioned in a way that, *prima facie*, endowed them with a self-explanatory axiomatic identity distinct from that of their adversaries. This is what Gauchet meant when he wrote that the disenchantment of the world led to a "restructuring [of] difference, separation, and human conflict" through human rather than divine imperatives.[28] In the seventeenth-century civil war God had been there to give the rival camps their divine and thus primary stamp. By the late eighteenth century the stamp differentiating adversaries from each other was expected to be primarily a terrestrial one – if it could be identified at all.

*

So if the seventeenth-century civil war was unsuitable as a template for explaining the American one, perhaps the more recent civil strife, involving the Scottish-based Jacobites, could fulfill this role better? Some, to be sure, tried this tack, mapping the American war onto a division redolent of familiar political connotations between Catholic-dominated Scots and the Protestant English. In light of the notoriety of the Scottish Lord Bute's influence over George III earlier in his reign, it was perhaps not too much of a stretch to draw a picture of the war – in the words of one critic – as a "ruinous Scotch contest with the *Anglo Americans*". This was also the line taken by *The Crisis*, a virulent anti-ministerial weekly published throughout most of 1775 and 1776. Britons, it hollered, were "reduced to the miserable Condition of being ruled by an Army of Scotch Janizaries, assisted by *Roman Catholics*", and led by Bute, who "most impudently assumed [the character of] the *Father*", practicing his "Mock-paternal Authority" over the nation. (Note in passing the gratuitous introduction of the theme of subverted and unnatural parenthood, to which we shall return.) What threatened to appear an "unnatural War" was in truth nothing of the kind: as the ministerial henchmen attempt to drive soldiers "to sheath their Swords in the Bowels of their Countrymen", *The Crisis* prognosticated triumphantly, they will inevitably discover that it is "in vain to send English Soldiers", since "none but Scotch will do the Business".[29]

Lower on vitriol but higher on creative flair, another concerned writer made the same point through the device of a futuristic travelogue of a third-generation American who in 1899 returns to visit the old "mother country". Mother, however, is no longer home: by 1899, it turns out, Englishness has migrated to America, leaving the old island in the hands of foreigners, above all the Scots. This understanding dawns on the voyager when he happens across a memorial to the 1745 Jacobite rebellion. He is told that what the Scots had been unable to achieve then by arms they obtained later by other means when they "became regents of this kingdom" (a reference, again, to Bute). It was 1745 that "was called the unnatural rebellion": 1776, by contrast, was a natural rearguard action that salvaged the Englishness sapped by the former, albeit in a new setting across the ocean.[30]

But the clarity that this particular understanding ostensibly conferred on the identity of the two sides in the current conflict proved once more to be a hazy mirage unable to withstand closer scrutiny. Nowhere was this more evident than in the imaginary exploits of the futuristic traveler of the previous paragraph, discoverer of the transatlantic Scottish conspiracy. At some point he actually meets a Scotsman in the street – the real McCoy, as it were – who gleefully announces that the very few English left in England will soon be driven "to the devil, or America . . . no matter which!" But at this point the confident distinction on which the whole narrative depends – namely, that between the real Englishmen driven to America and the Scots and their minions back in England – suddenly receives an unexpected blow: the gleeful Scotsman, it turns out, is tempted into sharing this rosy vision of the cleansing of Albion with the American voyager because he has in fact mistaken him for a fellow Scot! So much, then, for the reliability of these distinctions, whether between American and Englishman or between Englishman and Scotsman. Yet another effort at making sense of the American war was undermined by the slippage and unreliability of the identity categories it employed. (That identity slippage was on the mind of the author of this text is signaled elsewhere as well, when the traveler is judged "by [his] complexion" to have "lately arrived from the East or West Indies, no matter which". Through the familiar device of the environmentally transformed European complexion, the text draws attention to its underlying presuppositions about the mutability of identity.)[31]

Likewise, we can return to the inflammatory anti-Scottish and anti-Catholic rhetoric of *The Crisis*. The war, after all, was run not by Bute, by then long removed from a position of influence, but rather by Lord North. This discomfiting complication led *The Crisis* to characterize North in the following words: "though *Born* a BRITON, and *glorying* in the Name, he should be a SCOTS-MAN; though bred a *Protestant*, he should be a *Catholic*."[32] What began as a distancing gambit ended up allowing the slipperiness of identity through the back door: North's identity, it turned out, was a false and misleading disguise. Scots and Catholics were perhaps to be blamed for the crisis, but in fact you could not always tell them apart from Englishmen and Protestants.[33]

*

As the war between the British and the Americans continued to unfold, another strategy of establishing distance from one's adversaries presented itself through the invocation of the so far silent participants in this drama, namely the North American Indians. We can describe this strategy as mobilizing "racial" identity categories, as long as we recall that the *ancien régime* understandings of race were more likely to be climatic and assumable, or historical and developmental, than innate and congenital. Indeed, it was the understanding of racial difference as potentially mutable that made it easier for both sides to use it to deflect the anxieties attendant upon an unnatural civil war, by associating and even conflating the enemy with the unnatural savagery of the Indians. Such rhetorical moves were triggered by the repeated appeals to the Indians for military support by both the British and the Americans.

On the pro-American side, nobody made the case more sensationally than Edmund Burke, who was infuriated by British efforts to recruit "every Class of savages and Cannibals the most cruel and ferocious". Burke illustrated "their way of making war, which was so horrible", with memorably graphic scenes of Indians torturing, scalping, and cannibalizing their victims. Even better than Shebbeare's invocation of witchcraft, there was nothing like cannibalism to establish ultimate and unbridgeable difference. From here it was but a short step to accusing the British themselves, associating with those *"unnatural and savage"* Indian allies, of "Cruelties (O! Shame to Britain) unknown to the most Savage Nations" (fig. 34).[34] Like Britons, like Indians.

The anti-American side was equally melodramatic. The Americans too were denounced for mobilizing "the wild Indians, those tawny savage beings, who resemble Devils more than men . . . against the King's troops". A reputed incident at Lexington, "a tale so shocking to humanity", when two wounded British soldiers were allegedly "scalped by the savage Provincials", clinched the case: having "throw[n] off the mask", the colonists themselves were turning into savages like their Indian allies – and thus, needless to say, were distinctly different from the British.[35] To be sure, when one Tory claimed that the rebels' rhetoric revealed them as *"Indian chiefs"*, savages whose *"Os frontis"*, according to "the observation of a learned physiognomist", was "uncommonly flat", he was simply scoring rhetorical points. But even if the Americans were not coming to resemble the Indians physically (although a writer for the *London Evening Post*, for one, clearly believed in the possibility of mistaking an Indian for an American colonist), they could readily be depicted as choosing to be like them. After all, their actions betrayed a predilection – in the words of Wesley's friend and disciple John Fletcher – for "the lawless liberty of a *savage*, who lives under no sort of government" instead of "the lawful liberty of a *subject*, who is protected by a civil government". The Americans, quipped another,

34. "The Allies. – Par nobile Fratrum!", London, 3 Feb. 1780. A sharp-edged anti-ministerial print that depicts George III sharing a cannibal feast with an Indian chief, holding a smoking bowl made of a skull, and surrounded by the head and limbs of a dismembered white-skinned infant whose body is being bled by the other two Indian "allies" participating in this anti-colonist feast. In the front a dog vomits

"Prefer their Mohawks, and their Creeks,/ To Romans, Britons, Swiss, or Greeks". In actively opting for "the native unrestrained Freedom of a Savage" over "being Men", the Americans were choosing to shed their European identity and shade into an Indian one. The consequences for colonial identity categories were signaled by the phrases with which this last writer chose to characterize the American rebels: "men disguis'd", "Ambiguous Things", and "men undefin'd, by any Rules".[36]

It was even better to transport the troubling unease about unreliable distinctions between people still further away, to the Indians themselves. Perhaps the most common trope in describing "the merciless Indian Savages" was their "known rule of warfare [which] is an undistinguished destruction of all ages, sexes, and conditions". "Their way of making war is well known. They spare neither age nor sex." The characterization of the Indians as blind to the fundamental distinctions between people was standard fare, even making it into the Declaration of Independence. Even more than scalping or cannibalism, it became *the* formulaic hallmark of barbarity, the opposite pole to civilization;

and as such we can find both sides trying to taint their adversaries with this sign of savagery, as if it had rubbed off on them from their Indian allies.[37] Once again, the inability to maintain clear distinctions, which we have seen haunting this conflict, was being projected as far from one's own domain as possible – in this case, onto the Indians and their allies. In the most explicit projection, the Indians were declared unable to distinguish friend from foe – precisely the formulation that captured so resonantly the problem of this civil war. The Indians, Burke roared, "murder man woman and child – friend and foe in one promiscuous carnage". Their "most barbarous acts of cruelty", echoed another, were "without discrimination of friend or foe". This latter enunciation was provoked by the famous incident of the death of Jane M'Crea, a young Tory woman who was engaged to one of General Burgoyne's lieutenants; on the eve of the wedding, she was shot and scalped by Indians siding with the British, who had mistaken her for a rebel.[38] What better proof could one require for the alleged inability of the Indians to discriminate between people?

The Indians, then, turned out to be unable to tell a white friend from a white foe; the ultimate demonstration of how different the Indians actually were. But by now, what had seemed at first a strategy for distancing the enemy, and thus clarifying the differences between warring adversaries, doubled back to achieve precisely the opposite. When the Earl of Chatham painted a graphic image for the House of Lords of "the massacres of the Indian scalping knife, [and] the cannibal savage torturing, murdering, roasting, and eating – literally, my lords, *eating* the mangled victims of his barbarous battles!"; in wallowing in the shock effect of these images, he was in fact using the unbridgeable distance from the Indians to shore up his anger at a war leveled against people who were *not* substantially different from the English. It is impossible to justify, he exclaimed, "turn[ing] loose these savage hell-hounds against our brethren and countrymen in America, of the same language, laws, liberties, and religion". If these alleged barbarities involved the "indiscriminate murder" of "any white person, whether European or American" (as former Governor of Massachusetts Thomas Pownall put it to the House of Commons), or the inability to tell which side Jane M'Crea was on, was it really because Indians were but indiscriminate savages, or because the present situation did not offer them any stable distinctions between the warring parties to hold onto?[39]

The same niggling question was raised by other invocations of the Indians that focused not on their presumed cruelty but rather on their natural sagacity. Many stories circulated about Indians who reacted to the American war in words similar to those of the Oneida chiefs and warriors: "we cannot intermeddle in this dispute between two brothers, the quarrel seems unnatural. . . . The present situation of you two brothers is new and strange to us."[40]

Invoking the Indian presence, then, rather than somehow helping in sorting out the lines of difference that justified this war, achieved the reverse. Whether it was the image of the ravaging Indians killing the indistinguishable Jane M'Crea, or of the puzzled Indians watching an incomprehensible confrontation, the outcome did little to resolve the difficulties in pinning down categories of identity that might have dispersed the cloud of confusion hanging over the American battlefield.

*

Recall again the contemporary voices in the previous section that invoked the American penchant for the "savage" state of nature. Where, indeed, does the ideology of the American Revolution – to which these comments were obvious gestures – fit into the present argument about categories of identity? Unsurprisingly, the egalitarian ethos permeating the rhetoric of the revolution fed directly – at least for some – into the broader anxieties about the threat to familiar distinctions between people. Imagine, for instance, the possible reactions of the Cambridge audience of Richard Watson, the Whiggish future Bishop of Llandaff, to a sermon in 1776 which he opened with the following words:

> Mankind may be considered as one great aggregate of equal and independent individuals, whom various natural and moral causes have been contributing for above four thousand years to disperse over the surface of the earth. . . . God, as an impartial parent, has put us all upon a level; we are all sprung from the same stock, born into the world under the same natural advantages.

Watson summed up equality as a natural law: "An inferiority of one Species of Beings to another, and an equality of individuals in the same Species, are general Laws of nature, which pervade the whole System." The natural distinction between species was for Watson a backdrop for the denial of the naturalness of any distinctions between humans: and one could readily see such language as a potential threat to the received map of categories with which people made sense of others around them. Even Burke, close as he was to the American revolutionaries, saw the danger: "it is this very rage for equality, which has blown up the Flames of this present cursed War in America. I am, for one, entirely satisfied, that the inequality, which grows out of the *nature of things* by time, custom, succession, accumulation, permutation, and improvement of property, is much nearer that true equality, which is the foundation of equity and just policy." Alarmed by the possible implications of the American position, Burke was asserting here – as he was to do many times subsequently

– that it was the social distinctions themselves, rather than their erasure, that had an essential basis in the *"nature of things"*.[41]

Critics of the Americans, therefore, were quick to point out the subversive implications of their rhetoric for the fundamental distinctions between people. One common trope – feeding also on the well-known truncated social structure of the colonies – was that of the cobbler-turned-prince and vice versa. American pretensions and insubordination, suggested Adam Ferguson, were encouraged when "one man is brought from behind the counter, to be member of a sovereign Congress . . . [and] another from a barber to be a colonel". American republicanism, asserted "Integer", "turns cobblers into kings, and gentlemen into pedlars". "Men of fortune", echoed a third, will upon American independence "place themselves, and their Wives and Children, on a Footing with the meanest Peasants". And what a fourth described as "all ranks and distinctions . . . fall[ing] to the ground", a fifth preferred to put in verse: "See Taylors, Tinkers, Parsons, Pedlars, Crones,/ At morn in muck – at midday blaze on thrones."[42] For some anti-American writers – though not too many – this vision of subversion of social boundaries was also conveniently joined with a clear-cut mapping of the conflict along the lines of social divisions. The generality of the rebels, one Henry Hunter explained dismissively, "have not much property of their own", and indulge in this rebellious act in the hope of appropriating that of their neighbors. "Every man of property" supports the government, affirmed another; while those who oppose it are "those who have neither *property* nor *character* to lose". The revolution was basically easy to make sense of if it could be presented – however implausibly – as a war of the propertyless against the propertied.[43]

Such observations on the dangers of leveling are of course a familiar outcome of the debate on natural equality in the American Revolution. But the present inquiry perhaps allows us to see them from a different angle. Arguably, their resonance needs to be seen, at least on the British side, against the backdrop of the more diffuse and less articulated unease generated by this crisis, unease that both increased the emotional charge of this intellectual-political debate and in turn was fueled by it. At the same time that these were commentaries on the potential subversion of social hierarchy entailed by ideas of natural equality, they were also ways of talking about the danger that colored how Britons experienced this conflict from the start: the danger posed by the unsettling of those categories of identity that had previously been comfortably reliable.

To see this double message, let us take a second look at some of the examples just quoted. "Integer", for instance, did not limit the consequences of American actions only to the subversion of social distinctions: "we may therefore justly expect to have, in a little time, a black assembly, a black council, a black governor, and a black Common Wealth; so that we shall soon be 'black and all black'." Not only social distinctions, but also racial ones were under threat. Likewise, the anonymous writer who predicted that men of fortune in America would end up "on a footing with the meanest Peasants", also foresaw in the same breath that American society would be reduced to "*Whites, Indians and Blacks*, promiscuously cutting each others Throats", thus again linking the commingling of social categories with that of racial ones. And Henry Hunter, who tried to portray the revolution as a well-defined act of the propertyless against the propertied, ended up losing his confidence in this supposedly clear demarcation. Instead he admitted that the only way to restore satisfactory clarity to this war – a war unlike any other in that it failed "to unite all hearts, and to join all hands" – was by physically separating all the supporters of America and persuading them to undertake "voluntary exile". What these examples had in common was that the critique of the social implications of the revolution was inseparable from the by now familiar unease about the broader threat to the integrity of identity itself. It was perhaps the versifying critic who signaled this elision most clearly, when he reinforced his crone-to-throne vision with an ominous warning: the current plot for "the fall of Britain" was conjured up by none other than Satan himself, who alone could contrive "such magic pranks" as were worked by these mutable and unreliable "PROTEAN PATRIOTS".[44]

It would not be difficult to carry on this exercise over many pages. The ideology of the American Revolution could be – and was – associated with the subversion of every basic identity category, thus shading easily into concerns about the protean and inadequate nature of these categories. As John Fletcher put it succinctly, "to attempt to bring about a representation equal *in every respect*, is as absurd as to attempt making all our fellow-subjects of one size, one age, one sex, one country, one revenue, one rank, and one capacity".[45] But we may wonder whether the ideology of the revolution could, in and of itself, do the extensive cultural work necessary to produce these concerns in so many different forms. Rather, we may want to look at this the other way round: to ask, that is, whether it was not the wider problematic of the American crisis, within which these aspects of the revolutionary ideology unfolded, that infused them with an additional powerful charge. The subversion of social distinctions could be used metonymically to talk about the anxiety haunting this war with regard to the indeterminacy of identity and its categories. Indeed, fault lines in *any* category of identity could be used in a similar manner – *vide* Fletcher, or Burke's portrayal of the New York arsonist – as a way of talking about the broader problem with identity posed by the peculiarities of this war: which brings us to one final category that was especially well suited to convey all these elements together – that of gender.

*

In the first instance, gender distinctions were introduced into the American revolutionary debate as further blows – indeed, for some, the *coup de grâce* – to colonial notions of equality and representation. John Fletcher, whose warning against the leveling of all categories of distinction we have just heard, was in fact principally (not to say obsessively) preoccupied with gender. Fletcher chuckled anxiously over the absurd inducement given to women by the American claims to stage an uprising against "the reasonable dominion which all husbands have over their wives" and demand the vote for themselves. This was a position no more sensible than recommending "for all the women who have freeholds in England, to change their sex". Fletcher's sneers echoed the repeated barbs of his mentor, John Wesley ("by what right . . . do you exclude women, any more than men, from chusing thei[r] own governors?"), as well as many other anti-independence writers who warned against the imminent collapse of gender distinctions and matrimonial order.[46] The same blend of delectable horror – to give one more example – was the culminating masterstroke of one pen-wielding lawyer whose response to Price's pro-American stance was reminiscent of Fletcher's concern for the fate of all categories of distinction. The inevitable consequences would echo the fate of ancient Rome, he warned: there, once "the distinction between Patricians and Plebeians was abolished", a confusion of social categories so ruinous ensued that "they sunk at last so low, if history is to be believed, as to chuse a Horse for their Consul". Signs of this very type of confusion were already creeping in "in America, where *men* and *cattle* are offered for *sale* in the same advertisement". Having conjured up the specter of vanishing social boundaries, as well as those between human and animal, the lawyer-turned-pundit went in for the kill: "Are women included in the rank of legislators? . . . Every woman too is her own legislatrix. Good Doctor, reprint this sheet; add, but in *capitals* – 'EVERY WOMAN IS HER OWN LEGISLATRIX.' – These words alone will sell at least nine more editions of your work."[47]

On one level, then, such arguments offered gender subversion as yet another example of the undermining of accepted identity distinctions that was projected onto the Americans: to this extent they had a similar rhetorical effect to pointing out that American ideas would bring votes to blacks or Indians or the poor.[48] But more than this direct, explicit link to the immediate political consequences of undermining gender distinctions, I am interested here in the broader function that gender performed in this debate. Gender provided a convenient language for talking about the bigger issues raised by this crisis, those of the worrying inadequacies of identity categories. Indeed, once we begin looking, instances of gender distinctions introduced in this fashion into the rhetoric surrounding the American revolutionary war prove remarkably thick on the ground.

Take for instance a pamphlet by John Cartwright, produced early in his long career of sensible support for radical causes. Cartwright championed American independence. The claim of king and parliament for supremacy over the colonies, he reasoned, was as unnatural as if they claimed the "power to make white men black men . . . and to transform millions of the human species, into calves and camels". That the government's position was tantamount to denying the boundaries between blacks and whites or between humans and animals was for Cartwright an indication of a bigger problem: the need to recognize that people's identity is determined by "*the inevitable constitution of their original nature*". Driving his point home with more profuse underlining, Cartwright insisted that this was an essential law "*which may in no wise be overturned by any human constitution whatsoever*".[49]

But it was only at the close of his pamphlet that Cartwright's concern for shoring up natural identity categories revealed itself in full force. Suddenly changing tack and tone, Cartwright made an unexpected analogy between the British–American relationship and a courtship involving a manly, protective suitor (Britain) and a demure, tearful, feminine virgin (America). "He shall court her to his embrace with a manly and generous frankness . . . while she, wiping away the last falling tear . . . shall, with angelic loveliness and heart-felt rapture, fly into his protecting arms." Carrying on in this belabored manner for four full pages, until the properly constituted marriage of the lovely couple makes conflict unimaginable, Cartwright took the analogy far – very far – beyond what was required to make a rather simple political point. Rather, the analogy allowed him to wax sentimental, in a seemingly superfluous and interminable digression, on the meaning of gender distinctions and proper gender roles in marriage: "and herein are laid, by the laws of nature, the true foundations for all the superior influence and control that is proper or desirable for the husband; and in which America, as a dutiful and faithful wife, will ever acquiesce with pleasure."[50] At the same time that Cartwright's pamphlet was a sometimes roundabout commentary on the desirable resolution of the current political crisis, it was also an unmistakable commentary on the desirable reconstitution of natural, essential categories of identity as an inseparable prerequisite for this resolution.

Examples of American-war-related interventions that seemed to make similar moves, and whose indirect purpose was signaled by the seemingly gratuitous manner in which they were often grafted onto the argument, are too numerous to reproduce in detail. To give but a flavor of a few, they included a bizarrely disconnected association of the British side in the American conflict with a

"hermaphrodite ass, [who] would not be without its use, if it had but a sex";
an anti-American outburst that conjured up not only Catharine Macaulay's
"Amazonian fire" (she did, after all, intervene in the debate) but also an utterly
gratuitous image of "Woffingtons in breeches" (Peg Woffington, famous for her
masculine breeches parts in the first half of the century, now long dead); a
curious rumor circulating in some quarters that George Washington, the father
of the new American nation, was in truth a woman; and even a mock report of
a "trial" of the sexually ambiguous castrati singers, who had formerly been so
much in vogue, resulting in the recommendation that their expulsion to America
would be "the most effectual way of putting an end to all our intestine broils
and disturbances". Naturally.[51] Perhaps even richer in such allusions was the
flurry of publications at this time – one is tempted to call them a mini-genre –
of allegorical visions and topical flights of fancy: among those, indeed, it may
take some effort to find one that did *not* introduce subverted gender boundaries
into its commentary on current events. Many revolved around the contrast
between unfeminine women ("Begirt, bebooted, and bebuckler'd") and femi-
nized men ("Betrim'd, beribbon'd, and belac'd"); or, similarly, between manly,
unnatural women (revealing a breast "with many a scar") and properly feminine, maternal ones (whose "well-conceal'd . . . bosom plays/ Beneath the
envy'd blond and stays"). Others conjured up allegorical villains characterized
by gender transgression, such as the Tory vision that portrayed the Americans
being led astray by a double-sexed seducer, maid by day and rake by night, later
joined by Lady Discord, herself a disgusting, unfeminine Amazon.[52]

At times such interventions – recall Cartwright's – left little doubt as to the
link that the reader was expected to make between subverted gender boundaries
and the problem of identity in the current crisis. When some wits proposed to
epitomize the present gender disorder in an "inevitable" marriage between Lord
George Germain, Secretary of State for the Colonies and a man with a reputation for cowardice, and the Chevalier D'Eon, the French military veteran whose
reputation as a woman in disguise was reaching its peak at precisely this time,
one of them tellingly explained that the union of an unmanly man and a manly
woman was "very fitting to direct the operation of – an UNNATURAL war".[53]
Another effusion on "the unhappy contest between Great Britain and America"
introduced D'Eon as man/woman, together with fanciful "male and female
politicians" who are "so like you'd scarce know one from t'other", as segues
into its real central concern: that the patriots "have forgot,/ Whether
they're Englishmen or not". Even more fanciful was the supposed vision of an
inhabitant of the New World – himself an evident hybrid of an Ohio Indian and
Omai the Polynesian – which was likewise peopled with an array of ambiguous
figures, including a sometimes-man-sometimes-hermaphrodite (thus doubly
unstable) as well as "an *ancient* JUVENILE" who was indeed "a *thing* amphibious".

This piece too made explicit the connection of these "amphibious" figures to the bigger issue at stake, by blaming the war – the present "civil discord" – on an unnamed protean figure "who various shapes in various parts displays", with "forms too blendid [sic] ever to be known".[54] This was the problem that was flagged through the invocation of figures like D'Eon, the hermaphrodite, or the indistinguishable male/female politicians: the problem of shifting, unreliable identity categories "too blendid ever to be known".

To be sure, concerns for gender roles had turned up in the context of other wars as well: think for instance of the well-known critiques of effeminacy during the Seven Years' War. But in the case of the American conflict these concerns went beyond the predictable positing of war as a test of manliness against womanish opponents. Instead they emerged as a conspicuous and multifaceted subtext that cannot be subsumed under the familiar patterns of wartime machismo. It seems to me that only the problem of identity categories haunting the American revolutionary war can account for the density and the peculiarities of this gender subtext. The very allusions to such images and figures – rapidly following one another, often contextually disconnected and gratuitously introduced – were in and of themselves a gesture, even if sometimes an unacknowledged or unwitting one, to this wider unease.

Moreover, there was an added logic to singling out gender in particular for talking about the inadequacies of identity categories in the American war. The belief that this was indeed an unnatural civil war was frequently expressed through images of an unnatural family affair or domestic strife: historians long ago suggested that the language of disrupted family relations was "the very lingua franca of the [American] revolution". Not that this fact is very surprising. But its consequences are worth noting: for it was but a short step from the anxiety about a malfunctioning family to that about proper gender roles within the family, whether between husband and wife or between parent – especially mother – and child. Was Great Britain a caring or an unnatural – and unfeminine – mother to the colonies? Was King George an unnatural father? This was a question, as Jay Fliegelman has brilliantly shown, that reverberated with considerable consequences throughout the American crisis.[55] One satirical attack on the king gendered him feminine, "Queen Georgiana", in order to describe him as an "unnatural" mother who "threw off the gauze covering of ceremony, renounced her natural feelings", and went to war against her own son. A government supporter, by contrast, stressed, perhaps over-literally, that Britain-as-mother was "more than equal to any of her sex", in contrast to her main detractor, Richard Price, who was a bachelor and therefore "knows but little . . . of the tender feelings of a parent".[56] Such invocations of well-functioning family relationships were inevitably also references to proper gender roles (Cartwright again leaps to mind). Inadequate gender identities fused together the harmful consequences of civil war both in disrupting family relationships and in disrupting identity categories; as a critique of the war they therefore packed a double punch.

Once again I have saved my most elaborate example for last. In 1780 the former clergyman and actor Samuel Jackson Pratt published a sentimental epistolary novel titled *Emma Corbett: Or, the Miseries of Civil War*. It tells the story of a pro-American Englishman, Charles Corbett, whose son is killed during the revolutionary effort, but whose daughter's lover and his own former ward joins the British forces fighting against the Americans. The driving force of the novel from its title onward is this unnatural civil war, "rag[ing] among *brethren*!", in which "a large, and once *loving* family divided against itself": a family dilemma embodied by Emma Corbett, the eponymous heroine who is forced to choose between her father and her lover. Emma's lover is banished by her father for his intention "to go forth *amongst* your countrymen, *against* your countrymen", a choice – here was the key – which "bears in it something shocking to my nature". Nature was shocked: Charles Corbett ceaselessly hammers the point that this was an "open rebellion against the *laws of nature*". "[America], Nature herself lies bleeding on thy shore, and *there* the inhuman mother has plunged the dagger (with her own barbarous hands) into the bowels of her child!" Piling such unrelenting images of familial disruption on top of each other, the novel insists that unnatural acts have dreadful consequences – an inevitability driven home by the gloomy realization that at the end of the belabored plot practically everyone is dead.[57]

Like the many other voices we have heard, Pratt's novel flagged the unease about this unnatural civil war – a war in which there were no guidelines for whom "to consider them as enemy, and whom as friend" – through the gratuitous insertion of markers signaling the subversion of gender identity. The dilemma facing Emma's lover, for instance, is referred to twice as "unmanning", and repeatedly as demanding of him to become "neuter". Emma's own unnatural choices, by the same token, "violated the softness of [her] sex" and rendered her "sufficiently *soldier'd*".[58]

But it was in Emma Corbett's actions resulting from this unnatural family breakdown that the point – and the link to the broader theme of the present inquiry, going back to its very beginning – was driven home most forcefully. Emma decides to follow her lover to America, to which end she boards a ship headed for America *disguised as a man*; from here on she appears to follow in the footsteps of the myriad Amazonian cross-dressed female warriors whose similar actions under analogous circumstances had been celebrated in diverse forms throughout the short eighteenth century. But Emma's experience of the same adventures is very different, reflecting the shift with which we are already familiar. Prefiguring other late-eighteenth-century heroines, Emma finds the donning of male disguise a distressing source of numerous "embarrassments". Her manifest reluctance to enact the script of her female-warrior part results in increasing strains on the conventions of the genre. Although in some passages her masculine disguise is so effective that even her lover and her brother do not recognize her, in others it turns out that she is "all feminine and gentle", that "her man's apparel became no longer a veil", and that she can barely maintain her disguise even among strangers. The whole adventure, as Emma sums it up, is nothing but "a scheme, which is *most terrible to my nature*". These words, echoing almost verbatim her father's revulsion at the unnatural American war, reveal the full meaning of this largely gratuitous twist in the novel. The unnaturalness of the problem of identity in the American war was mirrored and replicated in the unnaturalness of crossing the gender boundary. It was further mirrored even in the waters of the ocean itself, which Emma describes as suddenly and dangerously beset by "tempests which have *deformed its bosom*": forced to witness Emma's unnatural masculine masquerade, even mother earth – or ocean, rather – revealed a diseased breast.[59]

In this particular commentary on the problem of identity in the American war, then, we can see, first, a striking example of the projection of the unease about the boundaries of identity onto boundaries of gender (and also of race – at one point Emma besmears herself with berry juice, creating a stain "deep, strong, and apparently fixed, [which] resembled almost exactly the hue of some of the savages").[60] But we can also recognize in Pratt's novel something further: unmistakable early signs of the new regime of gender – the impossibility and discomfort of gender play, the unnaturalness of gender transgression symbolized in the diseased breast – that was now poised to replace the more playful patterns characteristic of the short eighteenth century. While *Emma Corbett* was unusually explicit, it was far from unique: the same signs of the imminent change in understandings of gender were also evident in previous examples – in Cartwright's insistence on essential categories and on the proper gender distinctions in marriage, in the urge to purge the gender-ambiguous castrati, in the image of the unnatural mother with the scarred breast, or in the disgust that was supposed to be evoked by the image of the Amazonian Lady Discord. In short, we have returned full circle to the transformation with which I opened this book, here connected directly to the specific difficulties of the American war.

The American Revolution and the Denouement of the *Ancien Régime* of Identity

In March 1773 Allan Ramsay, painter to George III, had a severe accident. Shaken by a press report of a fire that had claimed several lives, he climbed onto the roof of his house to show his family the way to safety in case of a similar emergency. But as he was coming down the unfortunate Ramsay missed a step, falling to the ground from a considerable height and permanently disabling his painting arm. But what the court – and the world – lost in terms of a distinguished artistic career, it gained in Ramsay's second career as a court pamphleteer, poised for action just as the American crisis was gaining momentum. At the same time, the argument I have been unfolding here gained its most articulate prefiguration. Let me therefore follow Ramsay's analysis as a convenient device for taking stock of the argument of this chapter thus far, before returning to the broader inquiry that led us into this detailed investigation of a single event in the first place.

Ramsay put forth his reading of current events in 1775, with remarkable self-confidence, as "the single light" that will dispel "the sophistry of the American Pamphleteers". He explained at length why the Americans found such sophistry necessary. "The English Nation has hitherto divided the whole human race into two classes only, viz. Foreigners, who are always supposed to be, at bottom, enemies; and Englishmen, who are always supposed to be, at bottom, friends to England." But this simplicity, "not ill founded in the nature of things", was now a thing of the past: "unfortunately, there has lately started up to view in America a new class of men, who will be found upon examination to belong to neither of those two classes." Their very existence will "give great perplexity" to the people of England "till their true nature, and their true relation to Great Britain is accurately known". By claiming the same descent, language, laws, customs, and religion as Englishmen, Ramsay continued, and by "the practice of calling themselves *Englishmen*, and us *brethren*, they have artfully persuaded the people of England that they are their fellow-citizens, and Englishmen like themselves, to all intents and purposes". This was the familiar argument for sameness of Americans and Englishmen, that sameness belied so blatantly by the present conflict. But Ramsay was a court propagandist, not a disinterested observer: his whole point – which promised to restore the clarity of a "single light" – was that "this [was] altogether a fallacy". The truth was that an American Englishman was hardly different from a "Frenchified Englishman" who chose to live in France and became assimilated there. "Politically speaking", Ramsay asserted, Americans were *not* Englishmen.[61]

The Americans, however, had made every effort to obscure this simple fact, by "avail[ing] themselves of every ambiguity in our language". Ramsay explained:

> They have called themselves our *Fellow Subjects*, knowing, all the while, that they acknowledge themselves to be such, only from a circumstance which belongs to them in common with the people of Hanover. They have talked constantly of their *Mother Country*, and have founded their absurd

pretensions on their British descent; when they know, that there are thousands amongst them who join in those demands upon their *Mother Country* who were born in Westphalia . . . and they have lately talked to us, in the tragic strain, about the horrors of a *civil war*, when they know, that . . . there will no true Englishman fall in it, except he be from amongst those brave men who have lately sailed from England.

Here was the whole problem of the American war neatly summarized: was this a civil war between Englishmen, or was it a war with aliens (many of whom – recall Tom Paine – were not even of British descent) disguising themselves as Englishmen with the aid of linguistic ambiguity and confusing representations? This, Ramsay asserted, was the question that would "ever continue to perplex" Englishmen until the "true nature" of the identities underlying these contradicting claims of sameness and difference was clarified.

We have seen the diverse ways in which this question did indeed perplex Britons of all shades and stripes, as they struggled to make sense of the American war through some reliable lines of differentiation. Eighteenth-century British wars, as Linda Colley has pointed out, had typically been glorious nationally formative experiences that played a key role in shoring up a common identity.[62] But in this perhaps civil war, when national identity was more the problem than the cure, Britons mobilized practically every category of difference imaginable – religion, race, class, gender, even the human/animal distinction – in more or less plausible attempts to stabilize, to explain, to grasp a conflict that so many believed was an unprecedentedly momentous one. But we have also seen how these attempts repeatedly foundered. The American war, to use a fashionable formulation, was a war without a stable "other". As a consequence, the adequacy, and thus usefulness, of prevalent notions of identity were put in doubt. These notions of identity were now in urgent need of reconstruction, with a more solid foundation in what Ramsay called their "true nature". Small wonder therefore that we can find Paine laying in *Common Sense* a bedrock foundation of reliable categories – "Male and female are the distinctions of nature, good and bad the distinctions of heaven" – as a reassuring (and necessary) Archimedean point from which to begin; or that Cartwright insisted so vehemently on "the inevitable constitution" of essential, inalterable identity categories determined by "their original nature"; or that another commentator on the events of these years, who had variously noted their destabilizing effects on distinctions between Indians and whites, men and women, Catholics and Protestants, Americans and Britons, admitted even more forthrightly the need for the institution of newly anchored, essential, invariably dependable categories of identification. "The times", this writer declared,

"render it necessary *that new distinctions should take place*, not as badges of petu-
lance and illwill . . . but such distinctions as must in their very nature discriminate between the lover of the country, and the betrayer of it."[63] Wishful
thinking indeed.

Or was it? While contemporaries were finding it difficult to come up with
such distinctions as could reliably "discriminate between the lover of the
country, and the betrayer of it", as this last writer had hoped, the exhortation
"that new distinctions should take place" can at the same time be seen as a beck-
oning call – however unwitting – for the far-reaching cultural transformation
that we have been tracing throughout this book. This, I want to suggest, is what
happened as a consequence of the singular configuration in which the English
found themselves during the early years of the American revolutionary war.
The troubled preoccupation with the meaning, constitution, and limits of identity during this national crisis, as an essential precondition to its very understanding, was the critical blow that cracked the dam, releasing and stimulating
further the currents of unease about these same issues that had been slowly
building up over decades. Conversely, it is only against the background of the
ancien régime of identity's long-standing undercurrent of potential unease that
we can fully understand the extent of the preoccupation with the limits of identity in the public concern over the American war. Here was the nightmare come
true. The stakes changed almost overnight: the problem of unreliable identities turned from the easy-to-ignore pet peeve of moralizers and doomsayers,
alarmed by the fashionable consequences of commercial society, into a disturbing, inescapable underpinning of the conflict that was threatening to pull
the British nation and empire apart.

The American war, in short, brought to a cataclysmic head trends that had
long been developing gradually and imperceptibly beneath the surface, turning
them from tentative potentialities to overbearing actualities. This observation,
in fact, was already Edmund Burke's. "Many things have been long operating
towards a gradual change in our principles," he declared in April 1777. "But
this American war has done more in a few years than all the other causes could
have effected in a century." The war had many effects. The one of interest to
us here is that it unleashed, arguably, that transformation that was forceful
enough to bring about the demise of the eighteenth-century *ancien régime* of
identity. To vary my imagery, we can see the war – as John Brewer once wrote
in a somewhat different context – as the catalyst that transformed a mildly
aching tooth into a sudden swirl of agonizing inflammation, spreading pain
from head to toe and demanding immediate and radical attention.[64]

*

Let us now revisit some of the cultural sites of earlier chapters that bore the marks of a late-eighteenth-century transformation, to see whether the present argument can illuminate them further.

The first thing to note is that the Atlantic ocean has already played a role – albeit one not yet spelled out – in this inquiry: it played the revealing role of *boundary*. Early on I made the general observation that wherever one can find a limiting demarcation for a cultural pattern, a line beyond which it did not extend, the location and nature of this limiting line provide us with important clues for the understanding of the pattern in question. I also suggested that, within the broad social limits of the literate and semi-literate English urban classes that have provided the bulk of my evidence, such a boundary for the *ancien régime* of identity or for its subsequent transformation could not readily be found. But in fact this was not quite true. One boundary did present itself with notable consistency: the Atlantic. And it presented itself in a specific and telling fashion. Apparently it was not there for the first part of the story: on the contrary, all indications I have seen suggest that the patterns characteristic of the eighteenth-century *ancien régime* of identity were common to both sides of the Anglo-American Atlantic, a transatlantic world in which many of the same eighteenth-century cultural materials circulated. But the opposite was unmistakably the case for the subsequent, late-eighteenth-century transformation. Even a cursory look at late-eighteenth-century America yields ample evidence for a continuing and even heightened potential for identity play on that side of the ocean during the very decades in which a reversal was already well under way on the English side.

One need only mention, say, the American heroine Deborah Sampson, whose claim to fame in the closing years of the century was as an undetected female soldier in the continental revolutionary army. Sampson's life story followed closely in the footsteps of her English predecessors, including Hannah Snell, whose biography was republished in America in 1775: it was a reputation that in England, as we have seen, was by now much harder to credit, let alone celebrate. Or one can summon the post-revolutionary public career of the Rhode Islander Jemima Wilkinson as a cross-dressed and supposedly reborn-as-male preacher. The possibility of Wilkinson's drawing considerable fascination as well as consternation while practicing her ministry up and down the eastern seaboard stands in stark contrast to the inability of the English by this point to imagine such actions at all. (Nowhere was this more evident than in the English biographical compilation of 1803 that cleansed Wilkinson's life story thoroughly – and implausibly – of any hint of gender transgression.) Or one can look at the 1788 frontispiece to the *Columbian Magazine*, a new miscellany for the fashionable American reader, that celebrated "Concord" as a conspicuously and shiftily transgendered figure, portrayed in text and image as

35.   Frontispiece to the
Philadelphia-based
Columbian Magazine,
1788. The classically
dressed central figure
(addressed by the angel)
appears as feminine as
Clio who is kneeling
beside her with match-
ing garb and hair style.
And yet the text
beneath the image iden-
tifies the standing figure
as "Concord, fair
Columbia's son". The
accompanying "Address
to the Public" then
recasts Concord again
as a woman

both male and female (fig. 35). Or one can point to the repeated invocations of
Joan of Arc as a model for emulation in post-revolutionary America, so unlike
the decline in her appeal in England.[65]

Nor was this contrast confined to gender. It does not take much digging
in the American sources to find multiple assertions in the 1780s and 1790s of
the old wisdom regarding human mutability as the explanation for "racial"
diversity: "the physical differences between nations are but inconsiderable"
(Philadelphia, 1797); "the difference is not fixed in nature, but is the mere effect
of climate" (New York, 1793). The best-known exposition of such views in the
early republic was delivered to the American Philosophical Society in 1787 by
Princeton's vice-president (later president), Rev. Samuel Stanhope Smith.
Stanhope Smith demonstrated the mutable effects of climate, of civilization,
and of deliberate manipulation through cultural choice with the whole gamut
of familiar eighteenth-century examples, from the painted Indians through the
greased Hottentots to the climatically inflected Jews. For the ultimate proof of

this environmentalism, however, Stanhope Smith turned to the Americans themselves. Their "change of complexion", which ever since their immigration to the New World had already been melding them into an increasingly homogenized people, "is not easily imagined by an inhabitant of Britain". Although this was not quite what Stanhope Smith meant, it is undoubtedly true that by this point the kind of environmentally induced mutation he had in mind was not easily imagined by an inhabitant of Britain. In this age of "changes and revolutions", another citizen of the young republic summed up the same year, man is the most "variable" being on earth. "He is a creature perpetually falling out with himself, and sustains two or three opposite characters every day he lives."[66] These were statements deeply embedded in the *ancien régime* of identity: a regime that on the other side of the Atlantic ocean was already in full retreat.

To be sure, these American enunciations are a haphazard collection. But the fact that they are so easy to find does indicate that the late-eighteenth-century transformation that brought an end to the English *ancien régime* of identity did not affect the new republic in North America in quite the same way and at quite the same time as it did the mother country. Given this chapter's line of argument, however, it is hardly surprising that the Atlantic ocean would emerge as such a limiting boundary. Rather, this observation reinforces the conclusion that the nature of the moment of Anglo–American divergence – that is, the American war – was implicated in the making of this far-reaching cultural transformation.

The colonists, after all, experienced the American revolutionary war very differently from the English. Rather than a civil war among brethren, the American patriots saw the conflict as a coming of age, a liberation from the yoke of parental tyranny. So while their own revolutionary experience was inevitably also one that unsettled familiar notions of identity, for them this was but one facet of the intoxicating revolutionizing of the social and political order in which they were involved. "In the newly formed United States of America" of the 1770s and 1780s, Carroll Smith-Rosenberg has observed, "identities forged over a lifetime fractured, alternative personae multiplied. . . . The exhilaration born of new possibilities fused with fears of the unknown." The fears of the unknown were naturally considerable – in this, the situation in post-1776 America did differ from the previously less freighted *ancien régime* of identity. But these were fears of the political possibilities suddenly opened up through the empowering realization of the mutability of identity in uncharted terrain, responding to Hector St. John de Crèvecoeur's famous post-revolutionary question, "What then is the American, this new man?" They were a far cry from an imperative, patently implausible in a revolutionary context, to deny that such mutability was possible at all.[67]

It stands to reason, therefore, that for the Americans in the immediate post-revolutionary context mutability gained rather than diminished in significance. It makes sense to find that, in contrast to the English observer who blamed the present civil war on the disgusting gender-unnatural Amazonian "Lady *Discord*", the *Columbian Magazine* offered its American readers precisely the opposite message in celebrating post-war "Concord" as a figure of conspicuously undetermined gender identity (as seen in fig. 35, p. 294). It makes sense that the post-revolutionary emergence of a perhaps disturbing category of free people of color was accompanied by a sudden surge of American interest in accounts of blacks who changed their color (leading the American revolutionary physician Benjamin Rush, after examining such a case in 1792, to diagnose blackness simply as a symptom of skin disease).[68] And it makes sense that when Stanhope Smith marshaled forth his vision of the environmental mutability of human beings in the 1780s, its apotheosis was in the assertion that the American climate was molding all the inhabitants of North America into one new unified nation; just as that other citizen of the early republic proclaimed this age of "changes and revolutions" as precisely the time when man was at his most "variable", "sustain[ing] two or three opposite characters every day". The same events that signaled the retreat of a flexible understanding of identity in England spelled for the Americans the beginnings of an unprecedented period of experimentation – lasting for at least a couple of decades – with the full, albeit daunting, potential of such flexibility.

*

So much for the Anglo-American comparison. Is there also an added perspective to be gained from the proposed role of the American revolutionary war on our earlier observations regarding developments within England itself?

Think back, for instance, to the public preoccupation with the categories of gender before and during the transformative decades of the late eighteenth century. In fact, a closer look at the chronology of these developments during the late 1770s and early 1780s shows not simply a transition to decline, but rather a double movement: first a sharply intensified interest in those markers of gender play that had been stock themes throughout the previous decades, and then an anxious reaction, resulting in an equally sharp repression of those same themes. I have examined the latter phase in much detail in the opening chapters. The former phase – the peak before the decline – was apparent, for instance, in the spate of dramatic pieces spawned by the American war with self-explanatory if repetitive titles, like *The Female Officer* (1778), *The Female Chevalier* (1778), *The Female Captain* (1779) and *The Female Warriors* (1780); not to mention the dozens of female soldiers strutting about in numerous theatrical representations of the military camps of these years (and see fig. 36).[69] Or recall Garrick's prologue to Hannah More's sentimental tragedy *Percy* of 1777–8, which offered such a convenient epitome of the fascination with gender play precisely during those years. What I neglected to point out earlier was the topicality of the play *Percy* itself. Portraying as it did the tragic consequences of war and violence within a family group, and staged in the middle of the American war – More actually interrupted a report to her sister about the final preparations for *Percy*'s opening night to exclaim, "What dreadful news from America! we are a disgraced, undone nation" – *Percy*'s immediate context was unmistakable.[70]

The heightened preoccupation with gender boundaries during these early war years was also expressed in numerous cultural forms and events that had, on the face of it, little or nothing to do with the war: be it the universal fascination with the suspected sexual masquerade of the Chevalier D'Eon, whose story con-

36. Capitalizing on the heightened interest in female soldiers during the American war: "Corporal Cartouch Teaching Miss Camp-Love her Manual Exercise", after John Collet, 1780

veniently broke in 1777–8 just at the right moment to galvanize this general interest; or the conspicuous surge in what I have crudely called "gender-interested"
dramatic prologues and epilogues in the 1770s, just before the radical shift in attitude toward gender elasticity in the 1780s; or the peculiar 1777 publication *The
Goat's Beard*, which was simultaneously obsessed with gender transgression in
a manner reminiscent of *Percy*'s prologue and insistent on the need for "innate
essences [to] remain"; or that oft-noted "rage for military Dress" which the
Gentleman's Magazine attributed in 1781 not to men, but to "the ladies" (see fig.
10, p. 60);[71] or the sudden and short-lived mid-war wave of female debating societies such as the "Female Parliament" and "Female Congress"; or – in what was
perhaps the most baroque manifestation of this interest, as well as its self-
burlesquing swansong – George Colman's eccentric mid-war production of
Gay's *Beggar's Opera* with all characters gender-reversed.

Allowing then for a short time lag between the political debate and its effects
on the broader cultural scene, we can now see both sides of this more refined
chronology of the public discussion of gender boundaries as two sides of the
same coin, linked to the specter of unreliable identities raised by the American
war. The initial mid- to late-1770s intensification of interest in gender categories and their limits should be understood in the context of the repeated
attempts to use gender to articulate the problem with identity categories that
the war had suddenly posed. Subsequently, the intense discomfort with which
such gender play was met from the early 1780s – spelling the beginning of the
end of the *ancien régime* of gender – signaled the anxious reaction to these same
developments.

Beyond gender, the present argument can help illuminate another short time
lag that may well have already caught the reader's attention. A closer look
at the chronology of the shifts described in the first part of this book also
suggests that the early signs of transformation in understandings of race had
perhaps preceded the parallel transformation in understandings of gender by
a few years. Whereas the signs of the reaction against the *ancien régime* of
gender appeared in the early 1780s, those of the strains in the *ancien régime*
of race had been noticeable in some instances already from the mid- to late
1770s. Now, given the elusive nature of these transformations, and the rather
different types of materials I have analyzed for each category, this tentative
second-order refinement of the story needs to be approached with caution. But
should there be some truth in it, this would not be very surprising. If indeed
the pressures on the *ancien régime* of identity began at the periphery of empire,
it stands to reason that the categories of human diversity – "race" – would have
shown the earliest signs of these pressures. It is therefore also suggestive
that the cluster of texts on human diversity that I singled out in chapter 3 as

"transitional", because of their conspicuous intermingling of incompatible perspectives on racial identity, emerged precisely in the midst of the American war.
Almost without exception, these texts, allowing us glimpses of the actual
process of transition to new understandings of racial difference, were all dated
from the mid-1770s to the early 1780s.

Some of these wartime writers on human diversity, indeed, did not fail to
acknowledge the unfolding of the American crisis around them: for instance,
William Robertson's *History of America* of 1777 – one of the earlier examples
of the inconsistent vacillation between environmental and innate understandings of race – that opened with a gesture to the "civil war [of the American
colonies] with Great Britain".[72] But for no one was the importance of this
timing more manifest than for the extraordinarily self-aware James Dunbar. In
his *Essays on the History of Mankind*, Dunbar made it clear that his meditations
on European claims for superiority over other nations – meditations that led
him, as we have seen, to agonizing, self-contradictory reflections on racial difference – were sparked, at least in part, by the misconceived assertion of British
claims over the American colonies. In particular, Dunbar's surprising shift to
unremitting essentialism in his concluding essay, "Of the Hereditary Genius of
Nations", may become more comprehensible when seen against the author's
urge to leave the reader with hope for a resolution of the American crisis. For
if indeed "the spirit which now animates American councils, was the spirit of
Britons in a former age", as Dunbar now insisted, and if furthermore "the
Britons, in the same province, are distinguishable from every other tribe", then
it was not impossible to imagine that the "temporary and precarious union" of
the Americans with foreigners like the French "may dissolve apace", driving
them to "re-unite them, by more *natural and indissoluble ties*, to the British
monarchy".[73] More crisis-driven wishful thinking.

This exercise – tracing the imprint of the American war in the early signs
of the transitions we followed in earlier chapters – can be carried further.[74] Take
the satirical pseudo-travel account of 1778 that already on its title-page
announced its intent to mock Lord Monboddo's disregard for the boundary
between human and animal (see fig. 28, p. 137). Shifting its commentary to the
events in America, it also poked fun at the man who "pretends to stand neuter"
(that word again) in the present conflict. Such inability to differentiate friend
from foe, it stated, was "very extraordinary", so much so "that one would think
they actually forgot the difference betwixt right and wrong". (France, by
contrast, was an unmistakable "natural enemy".) Once again, the combination
of the timing and the linking by association of the critiques of uncertain identity boundaries with uncertain boundaries between the warring parties in
America is suggestive. On rare occasions we can even find contemporary
accounts that are utterly frank about these connections. A good example is the

unusually perceptive anonymous 1777 analysis of the problem of identity in the modern metropolis, where "characters are so blended and intermixed, that it is a difficulty for the nicest speculator to distinguish the persuasions and principles of each individual so as to form a just estimate" of who people really are. What triggered these observations, peppered as they were with concerns about the consequent loss of gender distinctions, social distinctions, and national distinctions? Our 1777 author, unexpectedly, gave a very precise answer: these observations on the limits of identity arose directly from the contemplation of the "deceitful patriotism" of the Englishmen who supported America during this national crisis – America which "in the beginning of the dispute, we were wont to consider . . . as a branch of ourselves".[75]

*

Ultimately, however, the multiplication of such individual examples can go only so far in adding to the plausibility of my argument here, that the identity problematics of the American war and the sudden retreat of the *ancien régime* of identity were essentially, rather than circumstantially, connected. To conclude, therefore, I would like to return to one aspect of the public debate on the American war that can illuminate this connection more generally and directly. I have frequently suggested that the eighteenth-century language that distilled better than any other the conceptual framework of the *ancien régime* of identity was the language of disguise and masquerade, evoking the possibilities, or the dangers, inherent in the contingency and unreliability of identities. It therefore seems appropriate to close this analysis with a look at the role of the language of disguise and masquerade in the American crisis.

For if the language of disrupted family relations was the lingua franca of the revolution, then that of masking and disguise was not far behind. This language has already surfaced many times in our romp through contemporary thoughts on the American crisis: in Erskine's Catholic "priests in disguise", in Dean Tucker's attack on Burke's concealment and disguise (in fact only a small taste of Tucker's obsessive use of such formulations in his wartime writings), in the unnatural motherhood of "Queen Georgiana" revealed as s/he "threw off the gauze covering", in the savage nature of the scalping Americans that was supposedly revealed when they "throw off the mask", or in the characterization of the rebels as "men disguis'd". In fact, these are but a random handful of examples of the ubiquitous recourse to this language throughout the American debate. At times it was invoked literally: as in stories about Americans disguised as Indians in pursuit of their savage war, or of gentlemen disguised as rabble, or of women disguised as men.[76] Few accusations were hurled more frequently at the Americans and their supporters than that they were falsely wearing "the mask of patriotism" – or "the Mask of Friendship" or "the Masque of Religion" – and "put[ting] on every Disguise", and also (forget the inconsistency) that they had but waited for "a convenient opportunity to unmask", and now "have boldly thrown off the mask" to reveal their true intentions (the words were George III's).[77] On the other side, Jay Fliegelman has noted how Americans identified Britain with artifice, dissimulation, and theatricality.[78] The sustained recourse to this language was not at all partisan. Its capacity to synthesize the problem of identity categories and their limits, now a matter of considerable urgency, is nicely illustrated in what may qualify as one of the most convoluted charges ever raised against a politician for changing his mind. "Your lordship", *The Crisis* accused Chatham when it suspected him of reneging on his pro-American support, "has at last thrown off your *American* mask, and not only resumed the *Englishman*, but commenced a *ministerial* man. . . . If your lordship will not now confess yourself an *American* once more, I must tell you that you are unworthy to be called an *Englishman*."[79] The mask here stood at the epicenter of what was so clearly – almost to a comical extent – an unresolvable muddle.

Moreover, just as the preoccupation with gender boundaries transcended the political debate to pass into a wider cultural sphere, so the war years witnessed a conspicuous public obsession with disguise and masquerading in multiple forms. From all corners came urgent warnings against what Henry Hunter decried as the present "criminal" penchant for "Disguise and Dissimulation", a "universal" and unprecedented "contagion". Within the space of just over a month in winter 1775, for example, the readers of the *Morning Post* were thrice warned: against the "very numerous gang of *impostors*, *disguised* under the denomination of patriots", but also against "the villainy of such impostors" on the royalist side, who fortunately don "too thin a disguise to impose upon the most undiscerning"; and, most generally, not "to be deceived by false appearances". "Beware of counterfeits", this latter correspondent summed it all up, "for such are abroad." The plague of the present times, echoed another with a professed penchant for "unmask[ing]", was the ubiquity of "impostors" who threaten "people in every part of the world". The present propensity for false appearances – thus yet another – was "an indelible stain upon the times". Tellingly, a verse "Apology for the Times" in 1778 contrasted the "White" of goodness not, as one might expect, with the straightforward blackness of evil, but rather with the shifting colors of "Camelions [that] take all Colours but the White". It was Proteus, the figure that had often embodied the malleability central to the *ancien régime* of identity, who was now found to be at the core of present ills: "In ev'ry Shape this *Proteus* can appear, / All but the honest, manly, and sincere."[80]

Of course, denouncing the dangers of disguise and masquerading was

JOHN BUNCLE, Junior,

GENTLEMAN.

L O N D O N:

Printed for J. JOHNSON, in St. Paul's Church-Yard;

MDCCLXXVI.

37.   Frontispiece to Thomas Cogan's
novel, *John Buncle, Junior, Gentleman,*
London, 1776

nothing new: the theme of *fronti nulla fides* (trust not to appearances) of the frontispiece of a 1776 novel, showing a mirror revealing the inner truth behind a misleading façade (fig. 37), was a venerable time-worn trope. But there *was* something quite new, and revealing, about the extraordinary intensity of this chorus at this particular moment, an intensity that went well beyond the simple logic of the political circumstances. One way to gauge its pervasiveness, spilling over from the political to the cultural, is by looking at the pages of periodical publications, which bring together many short items on unrelated subjects that are combined into one whole only by virtue of simultaneity. As a random example we can take the 1776 volume of *The Sentimental Magazine*. Within the pages of a single octavo volume, readers found side by side an "Essay on Patriotism" that noted "some thing ominous" in the "duplicity" of pro-American "gentry who strut in the garb of Patriotism" and who are really "wolves in sheep's cloathing"; an account of the new farce *The Impostors*, in which a man "is not the person whose character he assumed"; a critique of "the Moral Tendency of the Beggar's Opera" for staging "characters, where the shades of good and evil are so artfully and insensibly blended, that the nicest eye alone, is capable of ascertaining the bounds of either"; and a social commentary on today's "man of the world" who "is intirely [sic] in masquerade": "Being never himself, he is always strange and uneasy when he is forced to

become so; what he is, does not signify; what he appears, is every thing to him."
As if this were not enough, the magazine also carried a wealth of documents,
anecdotes, and even a portrait relating to the one *cause célèbre* that galvanized
this public theme better than any other: the case of Mrs. Margaret Caroline
Rudd and the Perreau brothers.[81]

The most notable fact about this affair – a complex forgery-cum-masquerade
swindle that involved the endlessly manipulative and protean Mrs. Rudd,
reputed *inter alia* to have practiced her sexual wiles (on the same man!) while
disguised as several different women, and her soon-to-be-executed accomplices
(or dupes), the Perreau twins, eerily indistinguishable in appearance yet complete opposites in character – was how much publicity it generated. The
public's interest in this story, which unfolded in 1775–6 just as the American
crisis was coming to a head, seemed boundless. "I find", one newspaper correspondent wrote in rueful exaggeration, "that the *important* Affair of the two
Perreaus has, at length, driven the American Business out of all Conversation."
Perhaps not quite; and yet, as its recent historians Donna Andrew and Randall
McGowen reasonably point out, the immense energy released by this story
cannot be explained solely on its own terms, but rather requires us to realize
that it "played into deeper sources of unease". While "giv[ing] substance" to "a
growing uneasiness about the unreliability of appearances in social and economic life", Andrew and McGowen conclude, especially within the context of
the dangers of insubstantiality in commercial society (the crime here, after all,
was forgery), the confusing Rudd–Perreau hall-of-mirrors "served to com-
pound the growing crisis of confidence brought on by colonial difficulties". Precisely. Just as the Chevalier D'Eon was such a convenient peg on which to hang
the current interest in gender-blurring, so the Rudd–Perreau case proved to be
equally effective in crystallizing the preoccupation with the unreliability of
identities. It was probably inevitable that someone would be tempted to tie all
these ends together. It would be well for the nation, one pundit ruminated, if
Mrs. Rudd could indeed be like the Chevalier D'Eon: change her sex and
become a man. This ingeniously wrought transformation would give her the
power to "assert the honour and dignity of the Mother-country, by taking
such vigorous measures as will force the stiff-necked rebellious Yankies to
bow submissively to her supreme authority".[82] The epitome of gender ambiguity and the quintessential impostor joining forces to bring about a resolution
to the identity-unsettling rebellion against the mother country: who could ask
for more?

The extraordinary grip of the sensational Rudd–Perreau case on the attention of the public, then, had in all likelihood a great deal to do with its coincidence with the crucial months of the American crisis, a time when, just like
the Perreau twins, England and America appeared so very different in charac-

ter yet vexingly indistinguishable. Moreover, we should also remind ourselves that imposture had not always had such a uniformly bad reputation. The earlier eighteenth century, unsurprisingly, had often given it a much kinder reception. Indeed, one could readily sketch the contours of the *ancien régime* of identity all over again through the public images of its notable gallery of impostors. In addition to causing us to cross paths again with the many cross-dressed and otherwise disguised impostors we have already met, such an exercise would also introduce us to figures such as Bampfylde-Moore Carew, "King of the Beggars", whose habitual masquerading as "all Sorts and Degrees of Persons, and that in all Shapes and Characters", was offered to mid-century readers, in several multiple-edition publications, for their "agreeable Amusement and Instruction"; or George Psalmanazar the counterfeit Formosan, who despite the eventual exposure of his extended attempt at cultural masquerade was declared by Dr. Johnson as "the *best* man he had ever known"; or Charles Price, "otherwise Bolingbroke, otherwise Johnson, otherwise Parks, otherwise Wigmore, otherwise Brank, otherwise Wilmott, otherwise Williams, otherwise Schutz, otherwise Polton, otherwise Taylor, otherwise Powel, &c. &c. &c.", whose "Proteus character", able to change disguises endlessly with complete success, was reportedly developed – how quintessentially eighteenth century – in his father's tailoring shop, "where he had opportunities to shift clothes as he pleased".[83]

Perhaps no episode brought this aspect of the *ancien régime* of identity to light more clearly than the rebellion of 1745, a moment that witnessed a veritable festival of imposture, misrecognition, and disguise; and nowhere was the contrast with the future American war more pronounced. At the center of the earlier political crisis stood the Young Pretender – note his sobriquet – who also famously cross-dressed to escape his pursuers (the Pretender was "making Merry with our Disguises", went one account, "while [he] himself personated by Turns, the various Ranks and Characters of the Highlanders of both sexes"). By his side was Jenny Cameron, "one of the most agreeable Women of the Age", who, acting under the influence of "a pure State of Nature", became a celebrated female officer in his service. Around them one could find a wide array of characters, real and fictional, whose identity was put in doubt at some point during these events. Thus Peter the wild boy, Bampfylde-Moore Carew, Fielding's Tom Jones, and Smollett's Count Fathom were all supposedly mistaken on one occasion or another for the Jacobite Pretender himself – effectively a double imposture or identity-crossing; and in *Tom Jones*, Sophia Western was also mistaken for his cross-dressed female warrior, Jenny Cameron.[84] Few of these moments of doubt, moreover, carried connotations that were especially negative.

During the American war, by contrast, as is evident from the previous

examples and from wherever else I have looked, the overtones of the ubiquitous language of disguise and masquerade were unreservedly negative, associated with words like ominous, criminal, contagion, plague, disease, villainy,
dishonesty, and evil. It is this strong valence of disguise, to give one more
example, that may account for the acute discomfort of John André – Benedict
Arnold's British collaborator who was captured by the Americans, tried, and
ultimately executed – at having been apprehended while in disguise. Although
the disguise was relevant to establishing his guilt, André's efforts at explaining
it away went well beyond what was required for his attempted self-vindication.
On one occasion he insisted that his disguise was unintentional, an unwitting
mistake; on another he provided a detailed account of his actions without mentioning the disguise at all, following it with a sheepish postscript that admitted
to his "hav[ing] omitted mentioning" – did it simply slip his mind? – that "I
changed my dress". Colluding with Arnold was compatible with André's insistent claim to "the honor of an officer and a gentleman"; donning disguise, evidently, was not.[85] So when Elizabeth Montagu in 1782 made that resonant
declaration that "it is the ton of the times to confound all distinctions of age,
sex, and rank", and furthermore that "no one ever thinks of sustaining a certain
character, unless it is one they have assumed at a masquerade", hers was no
mere aphorism about enduring truths of human nature.[86] Rather, it was an
extraordinarily shrewd observation that well captured the particular mood of
the war years, concerned as it was with the supposed current plague of imposture, masquerading, disguise, and otherwise unreliable identities.

What about the masquerade itself, then, as a cultural institution? Surely, if
the masquerade had been the consummate eighteenth-century collective exploration of the possibilities inherent in the *ancien régime* of identity, then it could
not have emerged unscathed from this moment of intense unease about the
perils inherent therein. And indeed it did not. Rather, as we have already seen,
after decades at the center of the cultural stage, the masquerade, replete with
its transformative potential, suddenly went into a precipitous and conspicuous
decline. And the first signs of this decline appeared, yes, right in the middle of
the American war. Another coincidence? The writer who in 1779 embarked on
a quest "to search out the *primary* cause" of the "fatal" descent into civil war
did not think so. On the contrary. At the top of the litany of moral vices that
had transformed the English into "a divided people" plagued by "discord", this
writer placed one particular cause, adding further emphasis through screaming
typesetting: "the INFERNAL MIDNIGHT MASQUERADE". At first glance, this was an
odd choice. But no more odd than that an anti-American critic in 1777 should
have chosen to blame the masquerades, continuing as they did "notwithstanding the American war", for their tendency "to diffuse *a spirit of liberty*, by
reducing all men to an equality . . . the noble peer is confounded with the

ignoble peasant; the order of things is inverted". Enter again the familiar peer-turned-peasant formulation: the subversion of identity distinctions at the masquerade – its "freedoms" which "must endear it to every lover of his country" – was found to be the hothouse of those subversions of social distinctions promulgated by the dangerous American taste for equality.[87] Once again the urgently unnerving aspects of the American war and the suddenly unnerving aspects of the *ancien régime* of identity – here represented through the disguise and identity play at the masquerade – have become inseparable.

Finally, having taken a long and circuitous route, we are ready to get back to the exchange between Wesley and Price that opened the discussion of the American war. Both, the reader will recall, fixed their attention – and that of their audience – on the use of disguise in the Boston Tea Party, without further consideration of what that disguise might have been (namely, Indian costumes). The same emphasis remained paramount in Wesley's subsequent retelling of the story, which did away with the actual disguise but still represented the event through the lens of transparency versus dissimulation. However unself-conscious these selective representations of the Boston events may have been, we can begin now to appreciate the depth of the overtones conjured up by their focus on disguise *qua* disguise. The language of disguise and masquerade, reverberating with the echoes of endless repetitions, signaled the problem of the potential inadequacy and unreliability of identities: a problem that was an endemic, freighted, and inescapable preoccupation of Britons of all political stripes as they strove to make sense of their own experiences during the American crisis.[88] The questions of whether the colonists were brethren or enemies; whether American identity had evolved far enough to make this a foreign rather than a civil war; whether one could put forth *any* reliable category of identity to clarify who was against whom in this conflict and why; whether identity categories could now be trusted at all, and whether the *ancien régime* of identity was not really too perilous an environment to live in; the faint palimpsest of all these questions could be read in the tea leaves that got Price and Wesley into an argument in that fateful spring of 1776.

A Short (Double) Postscript

In February 1779, no fewer than seventy-five British provincial towns held popular demonstrations to celebrate the acquittal of Admiral Augustus Keppel in a court martial for alleged misconduct during a naval engagement with the French fleet. Keppel, a known opponent of the war against the American colonists, had nonetheless agreed to command a fleet against the French once they had joined the hostilities in spring 1778. His trial was widely seen as the result of ministerial intrigue. But how can we account for what one observer proudly described as "the Excesses of popular Joy on the late glorious Occasion of Admiral Keppel's Acquittal", given that at best Keppel could be said to have provided tepid leadership in an inglorious and indecisive naval battle? The nationwide fervor unleashed by this event – a "cathartic" release, in the words of one historian – signaled an important turning point in the American war, shifting attention away from those unsettling difficulties that had bedeviled its earlier years and thus bringing one strand of my story in this chapter to a close.[89]

The pivot of this turning point was the entry of the French (and the Spanish) into the war. Despite the gravity of this development, it released an audible national sigh of relief, as Britons – like Keppel – now rallied to a war against their perennial, natural foes. Here is one poetic example addressed to Britannia in the wake of Keppel's trial:

> Turn from this ill-omen'd war:
> Turn to where the truly brave
> Will not blush thy wrath to bear;
> Swift on th' insulting Gaul, thy native foe.

How wonderful that the unnatural and discomforting "ill-omen'd war" was now eclipsed by a glorious war against a "native foe". A year earlier one commentator had expressed hope for "an attack from our natural foes" that "would yet suspend the differences subsisting at present amongst a people so uncommonly irritated against each other"; now at last Edmund Burke was able to relax in his armchair and write to a friend, apropos the Keppel commotion: "Indeed Miss Pelham you can hardly conceive the unanimity of this place." A wish come true. The immediate effect on Burke's mood was unmistakable, as he abruptly replaced his previously unrelenting references to a "civil war" with constant allusions to the war against France and Spain.[90] From now on the war could make sense, even in defeat. The English problem of identity in the American Revolution was no more.

Nor was it allowed to linger in memory. Historians have often commented on the surprisingly swift and radical excision of the trauma of the American "civil war" from British national consciousness – what David Armitage described as the "imperial amnesia" that was "the result of post-Revolutionary repression". It is only such a national effort at erasure that can explain how Joseph Cawthorne, in 1782, could write with a straight face about the mistake of "an *unnatural internal* war" in America, and turn out to have meant *not* that heavy, disconcerting weight that these very same words had carried with them just a few years back, but rather the simple strategic mistake of choosing to fight "an internal perilous war, in an enemy's country (for so we may call it) against nature" instead of picking a more advantageous battleground.[91] Likewise, it is perhaps only such a concerted national effort at collective forgetting that can explain why, when King George III continued to bemoan the loss of the American colonies throughout the 1780s in terms that were little more than reiterations of the widespread apocalyptic formulations of the 1770s, his refusal to partake of the national amnesia was taken to be a clear sign that the king was, indeed, downright mad.

*

Looking back from the early nineteenth century at the American war, the historian Thomas Somerville reminisced precisely on this transition in the English reactions to the conflict. Whereas his whole generation – he had been in his mid-thirties when the war began – used "to express themselves with a passionate zeal on this subject", they then suddenly "have not only changed their sentiments, but seem to have forgotten them". The amnesia. But it is Somerville's next few words that I find curiously pregnant with historical meaning. He and his peers let go of their passions regarding the American conflict so comprehensively, he explained, "as much *as if they had lost all sense of personal identity*".[92] However unwitting, this formulation is uncannily close to what I would like to suggest did in fact take place.

On the one hand, it is true that the circumstances of the early years of the American conflict, which had generated such a crisis of confidence in categories of identity, disappeared from view as swiftly as they had begun. But the consequences of this crisis in understandings of identity, a crisis long in the making and now brought to a head by the American war, were arguably enduring, long-term ones. On the immediate political level, one can readily trace echoes in subsequent events that were now, predictably, interpreted through the lens of disguise and masquerading. In particular, such an analysis – which goes beyond my intentions here – would be likely to focus on the shocking Gordon Riots of June 1780, which raised again the specter of civil war together with renewed concerns about religious, sexual, and social masquerading. It would then be likely to pay attention to the notorious elections of 1784, the discourse around which raised a storm of allegations of social and sexual boundary transgressions that was not obviously merited by the occasion. And it would not miss out the infamous coalition between Lord North and Charles James Fox that preceded these elections, the alleged duplicity of which was captured most eloquently in James Sayers's print "The Mask", which showed a composite double-identity Janus-like mask accompanied – how else? – by the inevitable epigram *fronti nulla fides* (fig. 38).[93]

But the consequences of this crisis of confidence in prevalent understandings of identity went far beyond politics. As I have suggested by now many times over, this moment spelled for the English the end – or the beginning of

38. James Sayers, "The Mask", May 21, 1783

the remarkably quick end – of the particular set of eighteenth-century pre-suppositions and expectations that I have labeled the *ancien régime* of identity. Even if not quite what Somerville intended, this is one way to understand his recollection that the American war resulted in the loss of "all sense of personal identity": for which, read personal identity in its very specific eighteenth-century sense. In place of the *ancien régime* of identity, the pressures of these events ushered in the swift re-anchoring of notions of personal identity in what may be seen as more "modern", essentializing foundations. A new regime of identity was on the horizon.

7

The Modern Regime of Selfhood

Soundings of a New Order: Twelve Fragments

New regime fragment 1

In May 1783 James Sayers published the print "The Mask", which I offered at the end of the previous chapter as an example of the continuing resonance of the language of disguise and masquerade immediately after the American war (fig. 38). And so it was. But on second glance it becomes clear that what this print called a "mask" was in truth the antithesis of one: it revealed duplicity rather than hid it, and represented an identity transformation or doubling that was grotesque rather than successful. This print was as much about the conspicuous failure of masquerading as about duplicity. (Recall fig. 37, p. 257 which presents the same theme under the same apothegm, *fronti nulla fides*: in 1776, more in line with the logic of this motto, it took a supernatural "mirror of truth" to reveal what hid behind a façade.) Coincidence? Compare a print attacking Charles James Fox and the Duchess of Devonshire in May 1784, "Cheek by Joul or the Mask" (fig. 39). In this identical composition, lest the incompatibility of the attempted fusion of identities fail to strike the viewer powerfully enough, the accompanying text drove the point home: "Two faces here in one you see design'd,/ Each strongly mark'd declares the inward mind." The inward mind (note this phrase) irrepressibly and ineradicably marked the face. Both prints, ultimately, suggested that masquerading and identity-doubling were impossible. *Fronti tota fides.*

New regime fragment 2

In 1780, a couple of years after the French joined in the American war, an anonymous author published a forgettable novel called *Masquerades; or,*

Cheek by Joul   or the MASK

39. "Cheek by Joul or the Mask", possibly by John Boyne, 3 May 1784

Two faces here in one you see defign'd,   One rough & virulent th' other fair & free.
Each ſtrongly mark'd declares the inward mind, with looks that promiſe ſenſibility.
One ſeems ambitious of a daring ſoul,   When ſuch as theſe in harmony unite,
The other ſoft the paſſions to controul.   The contraſt ſurely muſt amaze the fight.

What You Will. Its appearance coincided with the increased interest in masquerading during these years. Its title seemed to reproduce that sense of agency in the fashioning of identities, central to the *ancien régime* of identity, that the masquerade had encapsulated so well. And yet its representation of an actual masquerade, working to fulfill the promise of the title, took the reader in a somewhat different direction. This scene required one character to seek another who would impersonate him at the masquerade. Far from being a matter of simple disguise, however, the person who was singled out as able to succeed in this impersonation was chosen because of a similar body type, and was then equipped with "a domino wrapt close about him, which could I thought conceal the difference in person".[1] Disguise here – a domino was a generic, characterless masquerade cloak – did not make the man, as we have come to expect, but was rather a means for hiding him: there was a difference in persons that the masquerade could not erase, but merely obscure through a closely wrapped domino. In this case, identity – even during a masquerade – was all about "seeing through clothes".

New regime fragment 3

The same year, 1780, saw the publication of a travelogue by an officer of the East India Company, whose experiences while traveling up the Red Sea in Arab garments led him to make the following observation:

> there is a peculiar characteristic in the individuals of every nation, that will distinguish them through the disguise of dress and language. This is exemplified daily amid the neighbouring states of Europe, whose habits and manners are nearly the same, and cannot so much excite wonder in our case [in Arabia], where the whole temperature of our minds and bodies was so contrary to that of the people, whom we endeavored to personate.[2]

Not only did disguise not make the man, it could not really hide him either. Even the distinctions among Europeans – let alone those between Europeans and Arabs, whose minds and bodies were so very different – inevitably prevented effective impersonation.

New regime fragment 4

Shortly after the end of the war, several publications, undoubtedly hoping to recapture the success of the Rudd–Perreaus case as a popular media event, brought to the public's attention the exploits of two other extraordinary forgers-cum-impostors. One has already been mentioned – the chameleon-like Charles Price, with his endless repertory of borrowed identities. What I have not yet said about this case is that when Price's mid-eighteenth-century story of successful serial imposture was told in 1786, its teller could not refrain from indulging in a dose of incredulous skepticism: "incredible as it may appear, his master did not know him", etc. In the other case, the true identity of the impostor in disguise was supposedly exposed, despite himself, "when a bye-stander took notice of his thumb-nail, which he recollected . . . to be of the shape of a parrot's bill".[3] This particular charade, then, was brought to an end through an irrepressible physical trait that penetrated willy-nilly through the most skillful masquerade. (The analogous retelling of the stories of the Chevalier D'Eon or the latter-day female warriors, failing in their masquerades through irrepressible signs of their real identity, immediately comes to mind.) In both cases, therefore, the mid-1780s verdict was that a full identity-alteration through disguise was well-nigh impossible.

New regime fragment 5

In 1787 Quobna Ottobah Cugoano, an African ex-slave now living in London, published a radical attack on "the evil and wicked traffic" in slaves (recommending, unusually, the immediate abolition of the institution of slavery, not merely of the slave trade). For Cugoano the fact that by God's design blacks "cannot alter or change" their skin color – he was certainly no believer in racial mutability – was in itself an argument against turning it into a basis for their subjugation. Cugoano continued:

> It does not alter the nature and quality of a man, whether he wears a black or a white coat, whether he puts it on or strips it off, he is still the same man. And so likewise, when a man comes to die, it makes no difference whether he was black or white, whether he was male or female, whether he was great or small, or whether he was old or young; none of these differences alter the essentiality of the man, any more than [if] he had wore a black or a white coat and thrown it off for ever.[4]

Even as Cugoano was keen on erasing the significance of racial difference, however immutable, he found himself insisting – note his choice of words – on man's "essentiality". Far from dress making the man, its meaningless superficiality was precisely the opposite of the true essentiality of man.

New regime fragment 6

In the mid-1780s, the newly formed *Artist's Repository and Drawing Magazine* offered its readers this advice on the subject of portraiture: "as the intention of a portrait is to preserve to posterity the likeness of a person, it appears to me, to be the effect of a vicious taste, when any one is painted as it were in masquerade." It was almost as if the author of these words penned them while frowning disapprovingly at George Knapton's mid-century portraits of the honourable members of the Society of Dilettanti (fig. 31, pp. 180–1). These earlier portraits, as we recall, had been precisely the opposite: they appeared less interested in preserving the individualized likenesses of sitters, and more in particularizing their dress and accessories, especially if they were those donned at a masquerade. Moreover, given this difference – the mid-century Dilettanti themselves, one supposes, had not found their valued portraits, commissioned from one of their own members, "vicious" – it is suggestive to compare these earlier portraits to those of the Dilettanti painted by another

40. Sir Joshua
Reynolds, group
portrait of
members of the
Society of
Dilettanti, 1777–9

insider, Sir Joshua Reynolds, a generation later, precisely in the middle of the
American war (fig. 40).[5] Rather than representing individual members separately, generically, and indistinctly, as Knapton had done, Reynolds chose to
make a group portrait: the collective composition ensured that the immediately
recognizable differences between the individualized likenesses of the members
could not be overlooked. (Also note in passing the lady's garter clutched by
John Taylor at the back left: what a different message regarding the performance of sexual identity this offered than the lady's masquerade dress on
Samuel Savage's shoulder in his portrait of 1744!)

New regime fragment 7

In 1786 Reynolds, lecturing to the students of the Royal Academy on art's
aspiration to a higher aim than mere imitation, made a telling retrospective
observation.

Our late great actor, Garrick, has been as ignorantly praised by his friend Fielding; who doubtless imagined he had hit upon an ingenious device, by introducing in one of his novels, (otherwise a work of the highest merit,) an ignorant man, mistaking Garrick's representation of a scene in Hamlet, for reality . . . [and] what adds to the falsity of this intended compliment, is, that the best stage-representation appears even more unnatural to the person of such a character, who is supposed never to have seen a play before, than it does to those who have had a habit of allowing for those necessary deviations from nature which the Art requires.

The scene that drew Reynolds's censure of Fielding's lack of discernment – Erasmus Darwin was soon to refer to it as Fielding's "bad judgment" – was of course the scene in *Tom Jones* in which Partridge, upon his first visit to the theater, dismisses Garrick's performance since he believes that Garrick *is* the character he is representing on stage. It was a scene, as we have seen, that was very much in tune with eighteenth-century understandings of acting in general, and with Garrick's reputation in particular. For Reynolds in 1786, however, this scene was puzzling, even irritating: surely acting must have had, on an uninitiated spectator, precisely the opposite effect? How could Fielding, otherwise an author of "the highest merit", have made such an ignorant error? And how could he possibly have imagined it to be an ingenious tribute to a great friend?[6] (The gulf of impatient incomprehension separating Reynolds from Fielding – or Garrick, for that matter – brings to mind those late-eighteenth-century assessments of breeches parts, so popular earlier in the century, that dismissed them now with precisely the same puzzled irritation.)

New regime fragment 8

Also in 1786, a "Lady of Distinction" published a tribute to Sarah Siddons, the actress who in the previous four years had blazed a meteoric career path across the London stage. The Lady's praise was interrupted, however, by her account of one of Siddons's roles, that of Jane Shore in the tragedy by that name, that she found less pleasing: "her representation [was] so near real life, that, under that persuasion, when she appeared tottering under the weight of an apparently emaciated frame, I absolutely thought her the creature perishing through want . . . shocked at the sight, I could not avoid turning away from the suffering object; I was disgusted at the idea." (Note the use of that litmus-paper of change again, "disgust".) What Reynolds could not understand, the Lady of Distinction could not stand. Nor did she have to: Jane Shore notwithstanding, Sarah Siddons, together with her brother, the celebrated actor John Philip Kemble, inaugurated a new style of acting focused on internal character development which they advanced explicitly against that associated with the late Garrick. As an account of Kemble's career put it, this new acting style took for granted the impossibility – and undesirability – of "representing characters literally as they would be in nature, that is in reality, with all the peculiarities of both mind and person". "Playing, after all, is an art"; and thus "the charm lies in seeing a man . . . adapting his mind and features to such a personation; and the more distant we know his real character to be from that he is assuming, the greater is his merit." James Boaden, a friend of Kemble's and a partisan of his style, provided sound reasoning for his disbelief in Garrick-like transformations: "though we are as men all liable to the same influences, they are greatly modified by our personal qualities and individual habits."[7] Every actor – *pace* Garrick – is constrained by his own inescapable individual identity, "his real character".

New regime fragment 9

One more theatrical fragment: in June 1798 Thomas Rees, a professional mimic, was hired by Covent Garden Theatre to play the part of Dromio in *The Comedy of Errors* opposite Joseph Munden. Rees was not a regular actor on this stage: he was brought in specifically for his mimicking abilities, so that he could act his Dromio – as the playbill explained – "in imitations of Mr. Munden's voice, manner &c." This is the earliest recorded attempt to cast the twin characters on the basis of resemblance, after decades of achieving twinness – among whatever actors happened to be available, and often switching partners – through identical costuming. In actuality, Rees failed: critics noted that his imitation did not really resemble Munden at all. But it was this new expectation on the part of audiences and critics that was so telling. Thirteen years later, when Munden tried the Dromio role again against William Blanchard, it was quickly pointed out that he "was considerably shorter than Blanchard and could not be well mistaken for him"; this in contrast to the two Antipholuses of that production, who reportedly "were very well suited". A few years subsequently Leigh Hunt dismissed two other Dromios as "persons no more resembling each other than moisture to drought, or a bowl of cream and a tobacco pipe, or a plum pudding and a pepper-box". The fragments of information we have about the casting of twins suggest that by the early nineteenth century dress could no longer generate identity, and guarantee identicality, as it had done before: no effort of masquerading could now turn plum pudding into a pepper-box. Indeed, for one critic – Sarah Siddons's son Henry – it was folly even to try: "We have never seen two men so exactly conformable in their physical appearances as to be enabled to represent the Dromios of Shakespeare in a way that could mislead our senses or bewilder our imaginations even for a moment." Elizabeth

Inchbald also agreed, but argued that far from attempting to mislead, the Bard had actually counted precisely on the "improbability" of casting two identical twins, since telling them apart was necessary for the success of the play.[8] Given the unmaskable uniqueness of every individual, Siddons and Inchbald were insisting, each person is necessarily a plum pudding to another's pepper-box.

New regime fragment 10

In 1790, shortly before his death, Adam Smith published a new edition of *The Theory of Moral Sentiments*, significantly revising and altering the original text of 1759–61. One particularly long addition elaborated Smith's notion of the impartial spectator. We have seen how Smith's mid-century discussion of the impartial spectator posited a doubleness of identity, and how this account was likely at the time to have been read – and written – more literally than simply figuratively. In the later edition, however, we can see Smith moving – hesitantly but unmistakably – away from the literal and further to the figurative. The highest authority to which men can appeal the public sentence on their conduct, Smith now wrote, was "to the tribunal of their own consciences, to that of the *supposed* impartial and well-informed spectator, to that of the man within the breast". "The jurisdiction of the man within", he continued, "is founded altogether in the desire of praise-worthiness, and in the aversion to blame-worthiness"; but in the next sentence we find Smith sliding seamlessly into talking about "*our natural sense* of praise-worthiness and blame-worthiness". Ours or his? The man within pronouncing judgement, whom Smith's earlier text of 1759–61 had described as "a man in general", who could not possibly "be the same with the person judged of", was in this new passage elided with our "own consciences" and "natural sense". Small wonder that the impartial spectator was now merely "supposed", a qualification that Smith meaningfully repeated twice in this passage. Smith's 1790 revisions pushed the impartial spectator, however subtly, from being an actual, distinct character, involving the splitting of one's identity, toward becoming a metaphorical reference to one's natural internal conscience (which is moreover how critics ever since have preferred to understand him). In a similar manner, when Isaac D'Israeli in 1796 invoked Shaftesbury's earlier notion of the divided self, on which Smith had relied, he left little doubt that such formulations were "only a metaphorical expression".[9]

New regime fragment 11

In 1805 the young William Hazlitt published his first work, a foray into meta-physics that critics for the most part have happily ignored. The *Essay on the Principles of Human Action* was in many ways the culmination of the eighteenth-century debate on personal identity launched by Locke; in other respects, however, it differed substantially from its predecessors. On the one hand, Hazlitt accepted Hume's basic contention that the self was a fictional construct. On the other, he went to great lengths to explain how development from early childhood entrenches personal identity as if it had an essential, natural existence after all. Once a sense of their own personal identity is formed in young children, Hazlitt explained, "the mind makes use of it to strengthen its habitual propensity, by giving to personal motives a reality and absolute truth which they can never have". Here was Hazlitt's main innovation – in his emphasis on developmental psychology, and especially in his account of the development and importance of self-conceptions. Raymond Martin and John Barresi, having recently rescued Hazlitt's work from the oversight of posterity, describe his approach as a "psychogenetic" understanding of self.[10] It can also be described as another instance of what I have called "weak transmutationism": namely, the positing of a notion of identity, or self, that is still taken to be conditioned by external forces but that is now also seen as becoming gradually innate and "genetic". So Hazlitt's work was a turning point in this high-philosophical debate: first, in its decisive moves toward a more essentialized notion of self; but second and even more significantly, in its very airing of such eighteenth-century questions – especially those of the divisibility of identity and consciousness that went back to Locke's Day-man and Night-man. Hazlitt was the last to discuss them for a long time: after him, our expert witnesses attest, nobody else was again to raise these philosophical possibilities until the 1960s. Hazlitt's 1805 work, even as it shifted the ground of the earlier exchange on personal identity, was also the final terminus of this exchange.

New regime fragment 12

Around the late 1780s, the juvenile Mary Anne Galton (later Schimmelpenninck), born in the middle of the American war, had a collection of human profiles which she used to dress up "with every variety of costume". Recalling this playful experience years later, as an adult art critic, she wrote:

> The different effect of these costumes was very apparent. It could not fail to strike the most inattentive eye, that whilst some of them only travestied the individual, so as completely to disguise him, and others produced a burlesque incongruity of appearance; some of them, on the other hand, imparted a new and bold relief to the expression; and, as with the touch of Ithuriel's spear, bid the original character start up to light, in all its native magnitude.[11]

This striking statement can be seen as nothing short of an epitaph to the malleability of identity, a theorized eulogy for the end of "passing". We are back where we began, only more so: not only did disguise not make the man (but could only hide him, sometimes, if not too incongruous), it was in fact the man who made the disguise. A disguise, Schimmelpenninck told her readers a generation after the American war, could only reinforce an "original", "native", ingrained character. Even "the most inattentive" observer – even a playful child – must surely have realized that disguise could not make one pass (unless burlesqued) for something one was not already.[12] What an apt conclusion for our assemblage of post-war fragments of a new order: surely it is hard to imagine any assertion more diametrically opposed to the understandings of disguise that had been such a fundamental feature of the *ancien régime* of identity throughout most of the preceding century.

Identity as Self

Why twelve fragments? Twelve, because a round dozen seems a reasonable compromise in the delicate balancing act between the eagerness of the writer and the resilience of the reader. Fragments, to signal the incompleteness of this compromise – i.e. that the writer *did* have more up his sleeve – and because the reader is by now familiar enough with the eighteenth-century cultural landscape to situate each fragment in its proper place among the interconnected indicators of contemporary notions of identity and self.

Moreover, these twelve fragments, originating for the most part in the decade following the American war, readily fall into place within the broader jigsaw that we have been slowly piecing together. As has been suggested before, this observation in itself – that the transformations of specific categories of identity that we followed in part I coincided with, and paralleled so closely, those that I am about to unfold in the present chapter – will prove to be a significant aspect of this late-eighteenth-century moment, one that explains both its comprehensive outcome and some of its internal contradictions.

The remainder of this chapter will thus do two things. It will sum up the main characteristics of this new identity regime, echoing in its juxtaposition with the earlier eighteenth-century configuration the many "before-and-after" contrasts we have already encountered. At the same time, while one eye will be looking backward to differentiate the late eighteenth century from what had preceded it, the other will be casting a more speculative glance forward, to new departures leading into the nineteenth century. I will ask to what extent these new departures – departures that are often posited as quintessential to the culture and practice of modernity, in domains ranging from pedagogy through literary and artistic theory and practice to science and politics – relied as a necessary precondition on the epistemological transformation from one identity regime to another.

Beginning the final rounding-up of this late-eighteenth-century "cultural revolution" by contrasting it once more with earlier decades, we are again struck by the sharp retreat or reversal of formerly central aspects of the *ancien régime* of identity. It suddenly became much harder for people to imagine identities as mutable, assumable, divisible, or actively malleable – be it through the donning of disguise, the transformative abilities of the actor, or the workings of conscience as the philosopher envisioned them. Nothing illustrated the difficulty in imagining all these better than the rapidly narrowing range of reactions with which contemporaries, as we have seen so often, now greeted such possibilities: impatience, irritation, incomprehension, dismissiveness, incredulity, laughter, and disgust. Instead, in parallel to categories of identity such as gender, race, class, and the human/animal divide, the more fundamental and anterior notion of personal identity also came to be seen in the late eighteenth century as an innate, fixed, determined core: that "essentiality of man" posited by Cugoano, or the "real character" heralded by the account of Kemble's career.

Consider the early-nineteenth-century observations of Thomas Carlyle and Sir Walter Scott on the writing of fiction in previous generations. Carlyle was commenting on Goethe, whose characters, he maintained, had "a verisimilitude, and life that separates them from all other fictions of late ages. All others, in comparison, have more or less the nature of hollow vizards, constructed from without inwards, painted *like*, and deceptively put in motion." And here is Walter Scott, making precisely the same observation about a 1777 novel by Clara Reeve: "The general defect in novels of [Reeve's] period" had been the "total absence of peculiar character"; "every person [was] described [as] one of a genus [rather] than as an original, discriminated, and individual person". Our picture of the *ancien régime* of identity has confirmed that both observations were close to the mark. The key point to note now, of course, is that these early-nineteenth-century critics knew it. By this point they were self-consciously expressing a very different understanding of the novel, one that actively sought characters that were "original" and "individual" and projected out from their "inwards". The Romantic understanding of the novel has arrived, based on a new emphasis on inner psychological depths.[13]

Deidre Lynch, who cites Carlyle and Scott in her account of the origins of this Romantic understanding, dates its first appearance quite precisely to a series of Shakespearean critical interventions running from the middle of the American war to the late 1780s. In this she follows Margreta de Grazia, who has drawn attention to these interventions as having endowed Shakespeare's characters with "inner regions of [the] psyche" for the first time. Simultaneously, de Grazia shows further, Shakespeare himself was also endowed with an autonomous well-defined self expressed in his authentic oeuvre, now claimed to be faithfully reconstituted for the first time in Edmond Malone's edition of 1790. It was the same "inner regions" or depths that were now contrasted with, and sometimes seen as expressed by, the superficial veneer of clothing, masks – Carlyle's "hollow vizards" – and disguise. Unsurprisingly, it was also during the same decades that the epistolary novel, as a form privileging social performance over expressions of interiority (latter-day critics' assumptions to the contrary notwithstanding), went out of fashion.[14] These new departures in the novel and in literary criticism – to which we can add the meaning now assigned to reading as a way for individuals to expand their own interior resources – all revolved around the broader transformation in the understanding of identity that is of interest to us here: identity became personal, interiorized, essential, even innate. It was made synonymous with self.[15]

Together with these interiorizing and essentializing transformations, late-eighteenth-century identity became synonymous with self – that is, self in the specific meaning I assigned it at the beginning of this book – in one other important sense. Both Scott and Carlyle, in critiquing their forebears, made the point that eighteenth-century characters had been "painted *like*", as "one of a genus", rather than as "original" individuals. The mid-eighteenth-century portraits of the Society of Dilettanti again come to mind as exemplifying this type of generic characterization, in contrast to Reynolds's subsequent representation of the Society's members as individuated personalities. Here was the crucial shift from identity as "identicality" – or the collective grouping highlighting whatever a person has in common with others – to identity as that quintessential uniqueness that separates a person from all others. (It seems hardly a coincidence that the OED's earliest recorded use of "personality" in the sense of "that quality or assemblage of qualities which makes a person what he is, as distinct from other persons" dates to 1795.)

Assertions of individual uniqueness now followed fast on the heels of one another. "Our souls," Isaac D'Israeli insisted in 1796, "like our faces, bear the general resemblance of the species, but retain the particular form which is peculiar to the individual." "In the original frame or texture of every man's body" – thus Jeremy Bentham in 1789 – which is a circumstance "coeval to his birth", "there is something which, independently of all subsequently intervening circumstances" guarantees his development "in a manner different from that in which another man would be affected by the same causes". There is "such an infinite variety in nature", a contributor to the *Gentleman's Magazine* wrote in 1786, "that no two things, however in appearance they may seem so, are found, on a strict enquiry, to be exactly alike. Thus two brothers have been seen so alike as hardly to be distinguished, but have often been taken one for another, and yet, when they have appeared together, the differences, the variation, has been very visible." (Forget then what everyone had said about the indistinguishable Perreau brothers only a decade earlier.) Or listen to James Ramsay in 1784: "Now, in the eye of true philosophy, the distinguishing attributes of the individual, an hair more or less of this or that colour, a particular feature predominant, have as certain a distinct cause in nature, as what makes the difference between the fairest European and most jettiest African." Admittedly, the force of this analogy is somewhat attenuated when we recall that Ramsay, writing for the abolitionist cause, could not ultimately decide whether the difference between the fairest European and the jettiest African was "fixed by the Author of nature" or "caused by climate". But when push came to shove, Ramsay too lined up with "true philosophy" in asserting the ultimate uniqueness of the individual as guaranteed by nature. In this insistence Ramsay was joined by the aging actor Charles Macklin, who takes the prize for the most pithy assertion of individual uniqueness: "What is character? The alphabet will tell you. It is that which is distinguished by its own marks from every other thing of its kind."[16] And for the bizarrest practical conclusion derived from this new emphasis, the prize undoubtedly goes to Bentham, who proposed that a new centralized system of personal nomenclature be "so arranged, that, in a whole nation, every individual should have a proper name which should belong to him alone"; and – to top this literal enactment of individual uniqueness with an equally literal enactment of ingrained identity – that this unique name should be tattooed on the wrist of every individual.[17]

Surely, however, such an emphasis on unique individuality was something quite different from the insistence on rigid categories such as race, class, or gender? Yes and no. On the one hand, listen to the turn-of-the-century words of the playwright and dramatic theorist Joanna Baillie when she self-consciously advocated a shift to uniqueness. "Above all," Baillie insisted, "it is to be regretted that those adventitious distinctions amongst men, of age, fortune, rank, profession, and country, are so often brought forward in prefer-ence to *the great original distinctions of nature*." The contingent collective categories must pale in comparison to those original natural distinctions that differentiate one individual from another: distinctions, in Baillie's words, that "give a certain individuality to such an infinite variety of similar beings". What Baillie said about drama, *The Artist's Repository* repeated about art. The magazine insisted that "every person is not exactly alike", and that collective categorizations of people were therefore insufficient to account for "the almost infinite diversity of character, which we remark in the human countenance".[18]

On the other hand, in practice we often find the emphases on individuality and on essentialized identity categories seamlessly braided together. *The Artist's Repository* itself, for one, readily joined its concern for the undisguisable uniqueness of every person with a gratuitous injunction against cross-dressing as "contradict[ing] the course of nature", describing "a woman [who] acts the hero, or becomes a good fellow" as having "*forgotten her very self*". What

278 The Making of the Modern Self

allowed such a text to insist simultaneously on rigid identity categories and on individual uniqueness was that in the new regime of the late eighteenth century, gender, race, and class were not understood primarily as collective categories, but as individual traits stamped on every person. In the *ancien régime* of identity, by contrast, the preference for generic categorization had meant that collective categories that identified groups had primacy over categories that identified individuals. It was for this reason that the mid-eighteenth-century speakers whom we have heard contemplating the undeniable variety of individual differences had dismissed these differences as random, arbitrary, and meaningless.[19] And it was this primacy of the collective categories that had accounted for the relative ease with which the conceptual edifice of this *ancien régime* could absorb the shock of individuals who had slipped between its cracks. But in the new configuration of the late eighteenth century such categories contributed to the generation of unique identity before they generated the identicality of a collective group, and were thus closer to the new understandings of self.

Consequently, just as it became harder to imagine a person's gender roaming away from his or her sex (without severe consequences), or civilization from race, or political behavior from class, so it became harder to imagine – to revert to Locke's formulation – that personhood, or the self, could roam away from the man. Once again the stakes increased in denying, or ignoring, or explaining away any evidence to the contrary. (Or in medicalizing it: was it a coincidence that the first three recorded cases of that specifically Western modern condition that we call multiple or split personality, including a German woman who reportedly "exchanged her personality" and an American man who "seemed to have two distinct minds" – a state, mind you, in which Garrick was reputed to have found himself regularly, and that Adam Smith had attributed to every moral person! – came from the two decades on either side of 1800?)[20] By the turn of the century, in short, identity-as-self, innate and even congenital, was supposedly stamped on each and every individual. In this, the anchoring of self in the person mirrored that of the identity categories we discussed earlier. And yet it remains true that the tension between the uniqueness of each individual thus constituted and the essentializing categories of this new regime – a tension that will surface again in the following pages – was to become an inescapable aspect of modern notions of identity, and one that in the eyes of some bedevils identity politics to this day.

*

I have been putting off offering an important qualification to these arguments that the last statements make impossible to postpone any further. My account in this book revolves around the parallel and simultaneous transformations of several key categories of identity – gender, class, race – and of understandings of identity and self (while always keeping in mind the important caveats about their differences). Given that there is no a priori reason to expect all these developments to occur in tandem, I have suggested that the fact that they did is in itself of considerable significance. But in that case, what about other categories of identity that do *not* fit into this framework? It is easy to see that for some identity categories the story told here is inadequate. This is especially true for two categories that were central, in different ways, to the shake-up of the American war: religion and nation. What can we make of this observation?

First, we should note that one can indeed find some attempts toward the end of the century to essentialize both categories of nation and religion as innate and ingrained in the individual, in a similar vein to what we have already seen. Thus, one could cite Hugh Blair's Herderian claim that "instincts implanted in our nature" extend "the ties of natural affection" from family to nation, "our native land"; or William Wilberforce's urge to stand up to those increasing numbers who chose to see Christianity as a "hereditary religion" fully formed upon a "child's coming out into the world".[21] Yet it is also obvious that such moves did not really carry the day: that ultimately national identity did not come to be seen as being as innate as racial identity, or religious identity as being as much of a burden of birth as class.

Put differently, it is certainly true that within these particular identity categories it remained possible to continue to imagine individuals crossing boundaries. Thus, in the case of religion, boundary-crossing was commensurate with the thrust of Evangelicalism, the important late-eighteenth-century religious movement, in which Wilberforce was a leading light, that gave marked precedence to "vital religion" in a Church Invisible of all true believers over sectarian divisions and denominational differences. Additionally, we can also recall the gradual, apparently seamless, drifting of figures like John Henry Newman, Henry Edward Manning, and Robert Wilberforce from Evangelicalism toward Catholicism. As for nation, perhaps the most conspicuous indication of the limits of this category in pinning down every individual was the band of cosmopolitan "citizens of the world" who were physically or at least mentally prancing around Europe and America during the "Age of Revolutions" in the hope of not missing any. Their deliberate denial of national belonging, in claiming to speak for generic "friends of humanity", was epitomized in the famous welcome extended by the French National Assembly in 1792 to a delegation of eighteen such citizens of the world who now also became honorary Frenchmen. Comprising seven Britons (including Joseph Priestley, Jeremy Bentham, David Williams, and – who else? – Thomas Paine), four Germans, three Americans, an Italian, a Dutchman, a Swiss, and a Pole, they demonstrated triumphantly that in the case of national identity, as Sophie Rosenfeld has recently put it, late-eighteenth-century persons could still retain a "fungible individuality".[22]

So religion and nation did not follow the innatist, essentializing route of other categories toward the turn of the eighteenth century. Yet perhaps their relationship to our story here may nonetheless have been closer than it first appears. Recent scholarship has raised the intriguing possibility of an alternative path through which these categories may have arrived at the threshold of modernity, at the same historical juncture, in a different but not unrelated form.

In the case of religion, Susan Thorne has pointed to the vigorous blossoming of British missionary societies as an important new departure that began, once again, in the 1780s. Why then? Thorne asks. Not because of major innovations in theology, she answers, since evangelical (small "e") revivalism had already been around for at least two generations. (Nor would it do, she insists, to dismiss this development, drawing as it did on considerable metropolitan resources, merely as a reflex reaction to an expansionist imperialist drive.) However, there *was* an important difference between eighteenth-century evangelicalism and turn-of-the-century Evangelicalism, in their respective understandings of sin and salvation: a difference that can help explain the sudden urge of the latter for missionary activity, and one that Thorne formulates in terms closely related to our inquiry here. For Wesley and his mid-century generation, she writes, sin and salvation were "the attributes of individuals; they did not yet mark the boundaries that separated discrete communities from one another". Eighteenth-century Methodists did embark on missionary travels: but their efforts everywhere, far and near, were based on the belief that heathenism and Satan were present within every community, and that the missionary's efforts had to extend "right down to the individual evangelical". Ultimately, "sinners and saved were on the surface indistinguishable". Evangelicals from the 1780s onward, by contrast, had a very different vision, "predicated on the assumption that heathenism resided outside the individual, that it was a characteristic feature of entire communities". Turn-of-the-century missionary efforts – thus Thorne's argument – could therefore be institutionalized to target such communities as a whole, be they indigenous communities across the empire or communities of the poor at home.[23] For our purposes here, meanwhile, the point to note is how the understanding of sin and salvation changed: not in parallel with other categories we have seen, from a collective, group identity to an internalized, individual one, but rather the other way around. Even as this new missionary activity drew on the emerging rigidities of racial or social boundaries in distinguishing the sinner and the saved – this in line with the broader imperative to fix and clarify identity boundaries – its own attribution of religious identity went in precisely the opposite direction to what the previous pages might have led us to expect.

As for nation, it has been a commonplace – albeit not an unchallenged one – in the classic literature on this topic, from Hans Kohn to Benedict Anderson, that the emergence of the peculiar form of modern nationalism, with its modern sense of national identity, occurred in the West in the late eighteenth century. I find especially suggestive the recent affirmation of this basic timeline in the work of David Bell: for him, what differentiated modern nationalism from earlier sentiments of national belonging was a shift from seeing the nation as natural, innate, and a given, to seeing it as an artifice in need of active efforts of construction through political action. "The meaning of 'nation' itself", Bell writes, "was changing, from a fact of nature to a product of political will." Note that Bell's point is not simply that nation is a construction – hardly earth-shattering news – but rather that the emergence of late-eighteenth-century nationalism involved a new active investment of contemporaries in this fact. (The term "nationalism" itself, we may add, was another neologism of the closing decade of the eighteenth century.) Bell has made his case, very persuasively, for revolutionary France. But if his logic holds for changing opinions in Britain as well, which is not unlikely – only in "the Irish revolution of 1782", Burke once wrote, did the Irish patriots "beg[in] also to recollect that they had a country" – then once again we may be observing a category of identity in transformation during the same loaded decades, but in an unexpected direction. Like religion, the trajectory of the hypothesized transformation of nation was also opposite to that of other categories discussed in this book: from individual to collective (all citizens, the revolutionary Abbé Grégoire insisted, had to be "melted into the national mass"), and from innate and natural to knowingly constructed. The goal – thus another revolutionary – was "to endow the nation with its own, unique physiognomy": an active constructionist formulation which in the context of late-eighteenth-century notions of individual identity and individual physiognomy, as we shall shortly see, was a nonsensical oxymoron.[24]

Now I do not know whether these preliminary speculations will survive further scrutiny. But if they do, they may lead us to see the development of nation and religion as the mirror-image of the same late-eighteenth-century transformation that is the subject of this book. It would be intriguing, in other words, to inquire further whether nation and religion also partook in the broader shake-up in the understandings of identity during this period (triggered in our Anglo-specific scenario by the identity difficulties inherent in the American revolutionary war, in which both categories played an important part); and whether their own trajectory toward the threshold of modernity was different, indeed perhaps in some key ways opposite – and thus complementary – to that followed by the categories of gender, race, and class.

Moreover, if these speculations prove not too far off the mark, then we may find ourselves in a position to explain a peculiarity that lies at the heart of modern, and post-modern, understandings of identity and self (and indeed of this book): namely, the different status of different identity categories as attributes of modern selfhood. Why do race, class, and gender (to which we may need to add sexuality) have a different relationship to the making of the modern self from that of nation and religion? Was it the fact that gender, race, and class were those categories that were reconfigured from the late eighteenth century as essentialized and stamped on the individual that turned them into the privileged sites of modern subjectivity? Have we then stumbled upon a historically anchored rationale for the seemingly over determined prominence of the often deified or blasphemed "holy trinity" of race, class, and gender in post-modern efforts to unravel this modern construction of selfhood?

The Age of Innocence: Childhood in the New Regime of Identity

Aficionados of the decades around the turn of the eighteenth century have often drawn attention to another conspicuous new departure during those same years: what Norma Clarke has described as the late-eighteenth-century "cult of childhood". It was of course not the case that childhood had not been important before. Yet it is also not hard to see that a regime of identity insisting on the unique, ingrained, enduring inner self did place more weight on the child's shoulders. It turned the child – even the newborn infant – into the self-contained bud of potential that would subsequently bloom into the full adult. "The Child is father of the Man", as Wordsworth famously put it. Or as Adam Sibbit, an obscure clergyman, expressed it less famously and less succinctly: "We are endowed by our benevolent Creator, with a capability of improvement, with the seeds of talents and of virtues ready to blossom, and to produce delightful fruit, if they are fostered and cherished by a good education."[25]

There was nothing inevitable about this developmental vision. Earlier eighteenth-century wisdom, as we recall, had been rather different. "It is the *Education*, that makes the Man. To speak all in a few words" – words that rightfully belonged as much to Locke as to this early-eighteenth-century disciple – "*Children* are but *Blank Paper*, ready indifferently for any Impression." No child "was better than another", Dr. Johnson echoed decades later, "but by difference of instruction". The purpose of education was not to foster but to create.

A more complex perspective on the *ancien-régime* educational position was offered in 1745 by the Scottish moral philosopher David Fordyce in the form of a dialogue. Fordyce assigned one of his interlocutors the role of rehashing the standard analogy of the newborn child to "a kind of *Tabula rasa*, or like a Piece of blank Paper, that it bears no original Inscriptions". Consequently "we owe all the Characters afterwards drawn upon it, to the Impressions made upon our Senses; to Education, Custom, and the like". This socializing process was bound to work, Fordyce's imaginary speaker continued less predictably, because "we have an innate, and almost insuperable Propensity to Imitation, and imbibe Manners as easily as we do Opinions". The word to note here is "innate", which in proximity to Lockean ideas could be used only with deliberate intent. Fordyce's Lockean voice, counter-intuitively (but with precedents dating back to Aristotle), concluded with an innate human feature, but one that was distinctively socially turned, to go back to our earlier formulation, an innate trait directed outward rather than inward. His imaginary interlocutor, on the other hand, rejected the analogy of the child's mind to blank paper: "I would rather compare it to a Seed, which contains all the Stamina of the future Plant, and all those Principles of Perfection, to which it aspires in its After-growth, and regularly arrives by gradual Stages." But this was not the same developmental understanding that was to become prevalent at the turn of the century: for what this side of the argument took to be innate in a child's mind turned out to be not individualized talents and virtues, but rather universal platonic principles of perfection. Fordyce thus offered the mid-century reader a choice between a *tabula rasa* combined with an innate tendency for socially turned imitativeness on the one hand, and a generic congenital seed of unindividuated platonic principles on the other: either way, a far cry from the individual, differentiated, unique selfhood that was to occupy center stage for his turn-of-the-century successors.[26]

I cannot do justice here to the sophisticated views on childhood and education of Fordyce's contemporaries. Let me only invoke therefore one recent study of views on education of considerable importance in the short eighteenth century: those propounded by the Comte de Buffon between the 1740s and the 1770s. Actually, Buffon did not think much of the role of childhood in shaping adult identity. But, as Adriana Benzaquén has shown, if childhood for Buffon was negligible from the perspective of *individual* identity, it carried enormous significance as a *collective endeavor*: delimiting nothing less than the definition, the history, and the distinctiveness of the human species. "Buffon", she writes, "made childhood indispensable to an understanding of human identity, not in an individual but in a collective sense, and not as the key to adult selfhood but as the source of a binding responsibility for the other"; the source, that is, of "sociability [as] an essential component of human nature". How familiar. We are back in *ancien-régime* territory of collective categories and of identity as socially turned – or "necessarily intersubjective", as Benzaquén prefers to put it.[27]

By contrast, to return to the later period, one could hardly imagine a verdict on education more different from these soundings of the short eighteenth century than that which John Wilson Croker pronounced in the *Quarterly Review* early in the nineteenth. Since it is a fact, he began, that "the varieties of the human mind and temper are innate and indefinite"; since "they admit of no uniform law"; and since "the qualities of the mind and temper are nearly as numerous as the individuals of our species"; consequently, Croker concluded triumphantly, "we hardly can imagine a wilder scheme than the attempt to educate one child by a system of observations made upon another".[28] So much for the hope of creating a better education system, a hope shattered on the rock of unique individuality. Few turn-of-the-century educationalists, for obvious reasons, would have agreed with this rather extreme conclusion. But its underlying premise, that the uniqueness of essential individual identity extended to young children, was certainly in tune with broader tendencies in the new identity regime. And thus, if in the *ancien régime* of identity the figure that had embodied ultimate malleability was a child, the feral child, by the early nineteenth century the understanding of feral children had also changed, as they now came to manifest innate reason, emotions, or virtue.[29]

Nowhere, perhaps, was this new perspective on childhood more evident than in contemporary visual art. As a 1990s exhibition entitled *The New Child* at the University of California, Berkeley delectably reaffirmed, the late eighteenth century witnessed a sharp rise in artistic interest in young children, focusing more emphatically than before on their individuality and character. The leader of the artistic pack, in this as in so many other things, was Sir Joshua Reynolds, who from the 1780s found himself spending increasing amounts of time on such "fancy-pictures" and their young subjects. "He used to romp and play with them", his student and biographer James Northcote recalled, "and talk to them in their own way; and, whilst all this was going on, he actually snatched those exquisite touches of expression which make his portraits of children so captivating." Reynolds's "Master Hare" of 1788 (fig. 41) can stand in as an example. With its composition that placed the child at the front of the picture plane so as to dominate the landscape, with its point of view lowered to a child's perspective rather than presenting the child through adult eyes, with its attention to the details of the boy's uncut locks and frock that is falling off one shoulder, and with its expressive re-creation of the personality of the young sitter, this painting confirmed Lady Grantham's judgement that "Sir Joshua is undoubtedly the best at discovering children's characters". Even very young children – Master Hare was only two years old – had characters to be "discovered". Reynolds's innovation – and there were many similar examples by him as well as by other turn-of-the-century artists – is put into relief by a comparison with a typical earlier, mid-century, depiction of children (fig. 42). Although portrayed in the midst of childish play, these two children are really small

41. Sir Joshua
Reynolds,
"Master Hare",
1788

adults, with adult-like clothing and postures, generic features, flat and distracted expressions. The overall effect is symbolic and emblematic rather than realistic. Such adult-focused purpose, characteristic of representations of children in the short eighteenth century, was sharply distinct from what can be found in the much greater number of child images produced at the turn of the century.[30]

The notion that a child had a character to be discovered raised the question of its origins: a question made uncomfortable by the continuing weight of Locke's attack on the doctrine of innate ideas. Adam Sibbit, having declared the newborn child to contain "the seeds of talents and of virtues ready to blossom", immediately hastened to insist that "we have no innate ideas, as that great philosopher has observed". Recognizing that these two statements could not easily be reconciled, Sibbit tried to explain:

42. Joseph
Francis
Nollekens,
"Children at
Play",
probably the
artist's son
Jacobus and
daughter
Maria
Joanna
Sophia,
1745

> Our mind is, therefore, like a *carte-blanche*, ever ready to receive impressions
> and characters of every kind. . . . But there are, it may be said, some few of
> a happier mould, of a more delicate organization, who antecedently, and
> independent of all instruction, are more disposed to virtue than others; that,
> previous to education, 'they are more feelingly alive to each fine impulse;'
> . . . and that Genius, with all her inspiration, glows in their breasts.

All children are born equal, but some are more equal than others. Or listen to
the master of a Cambridge college who in 1788 qualified his statement that "the
approbation of Good, and the dislike of Evil, will arise from the Original
Constitution of human nature" with the rather unconvincing caveat: "I hope I
shall not be so misunderstood as to be thought to advance the doctrine of Innate
Ideas, or Innate Instincts." And again, the same quandary also tied in knots the
clergyman whose 1802 tract on education opened with the familiar Lockean
image of the newborn infant as "a portion of paper without any impression",

so that "the most simple of our ideas are not innate and unborrowed", but rather are all "what we owe to education". Soon, however, this author too was forced to admit "that certain individuals are endowed by nature with faculties peculiarly adapted to certain pursuits, and that a bias upon the mind often clearly points out the employment, to which those faculties are destined". Indeed, "that nature grants to different men intellectual talents in very different degrees is too obvious to require argument".[31]

Turn-of-the-century views on education, then, were often complex and not necessarily consistent mixtures of "environmental" and "organicist" strands.[32] It was another move, however, that largely circumvented the tensions between these incompatible impulses and allowed contemporaries to have their Lockean cake and eat it too. This is what Charles Taylor has identified as the late-eighteenth-century "return in force of biological models of growth, as against the mechanistic ones of association, in the account of human mental development", and what Clifford Siskin has described as "the Romantic redefinition of the self as a mind that grows". It was a focused emphasis on the developmental journey from the child to the adult or, in Thomas Reid's words of 1785, on "the gradual progress of man, from infancy to maturity". It is here that we find the distinctive contribution of this period to the consideration of childhood in relationship to selfhood. For Carolyn Steedman, indeed, this developmental view was at the very core of the making of the modern "self *within*", leading directly from the 1780s – where she too identifies its beginnings – to Freud. "The interiorised self," Steedman writes, "understood to be the product of a personal history, was most clearly expressed in the idea of 'childhood', and the idea of 'the child'."[33] The investment in one's personal history – recall also Hazlitt's "psychogenetic" understanding of the childhood development of personal identity – made it possible to see the child as the seed of the subsequent adult while at the same time focusing on childhood as a distinct and passing stage. The adult was ingrained in the newborn child *in potentia*, just as the full-grown oak is already present in the acorn.[34]

So if late-eighteenth-century art manifested a growing investment in the distinctive character of the individual child, we can also note the complementary artistic investment in the distinctiveness of childhood itself. Art historian Anne Higonnet has singled out this new trend – she describes it as the English-led invention of the innocence of childhood – as a major cultural shift, "the last major change in ideas about childhood" before our time. The novelty – signaled by another of Reynolds's child portraits, appropriately entitled "The Age of Innocence" (c. 1788) – was the representation of "an innocent child body, a body defined by its difference from adult bodies". As *The Artist's Repository* advised budding portrait artists in 1788: pay attention to "that kind of character which marks their years [that] is so clearly discernible in CHILDREN",

43. Sir Joshua
Reynolds,
"Penelope
Boothby"
(sometimes also
known as "The
Mob Cap"),
1788. Penelope,
daughter of Sir
Brooke Boothby,
was three years
old when this
portrait was
taken; she died
three years later

children who will indeed manifest "indications of genius or stupidity" even at
a very young age, lest they would appear as "men and women, differing only
in stature". Unlike earlier predecessors (recall fig. 42), therefore, turn-of-the-
century children were – in Higonnet's words – "endearingly miniaturized" so
that "they seem to be in masquerade even when wearing adult clothing". Consider Reynolds's "Penelope Boothby" (fig. 43): the young Penelope, wearing an
adult woman's dress, seems to be nestled in an oversized cocoon, her mob cap
in particular striking the viewer as amusingly big and grown-up.[35] Children like
Penelope were no longer made to pass for adults. Such representations simultaneously reinforced children's inherent unique identity together with the transient uniqueness of childhood.

It is therefore hardly surprising to discover that it was during this decade,
the 1780s, that a new and unprecedented form of children's literature came
into being. Led by the father-and-daughter educational duo Richard and
Maria Edgeworth, whose well-known *Practical Education* was an impor-

tant contribution to the developmental model of children's maturation, the new approach was predicated on a sequence of books "geared to progressive developmental stages". "In the last two decades of the eighteenth century," continues Alan Richardson in the best-informed account of this development, "the modern children's library – with its stratification by age-groups . . . was all but fully established."[36] The modern child, in sum, complete with the panoply of artefacts for its understanding and support, was a key new departure of the late eighteenth century, riding on the coat-tails of the new regime of identity.

And there is more. If children were now proclaimed to have an individual identity already as infants, a core of selfhood subject to continual maturational development, why stop at the threshold of parturition? A close look at embryology – that is, at theories of generation from conception to birth – suggests an intriguing extension of this late-eighteenth-century pattern. Prior to this period, as Andrea Henderson has shown, theories of generation had been dominated by preformationist understandings of the fetus. Preformationism took fetal growth to be the mechanistic increase in size of a fully formed complex creature in miniature (like a child in adult clothing?). In the late eighteenth century, by contrast, Henderson finds an abrupt shift to epigenesis: that is, to the theory that the embryo *develops* from conception to birth, as its supraphysical inner impulses shape it into an increasingly complex and uniquely individuated being. The simultaneous turn to a developmental epigenetic perspective on the embryo before birth and to a developmental perspective on the child after birth is at the very least highly suggestive. And the fact that epigenesis as a theory had actually been available already from the late seventeenth century, but did not really catch on until the end of the eighteenth, makes the proposed link to the broader cultural context more suggestive still.[37]

Finally, once a putative enduring self was shored up with a developmental outlook on a personal history unfolding since early childhood, it remained but a short step to the retrospective recounting of this personal history in the form of a connected narrative. Not everyone would agree with Michael Mascuch that modern autobiography – distinct from earlier personal life stories in employing a unified, retrospective, first-person narrative to represent the development of one's unique self-identity – arrived on the cultural scene on one particular day in 1791, with the publication of the arguably unprecedented memoirs of the bookseller James Lackington. And yet other students of the genre have also affirmed the qualitative difference between late-eighteenth-century autobiographies, telling the connected stories of inner selves, and the typical self-narratives of the short eighteenth century. The short eighteenth century, Felicity Nussbaum has argued, had a specific form of self-narrative that did not necessarily "add up to a coherent self", and that was to disappear by the 1790s. Another scholar has characterized the eighteenth-century precursors of autobiography as showcasing the "exemplary self", meaning a presentation of personal identity that was generic and ideal-typical rather than individual and singular. It was thus probably more than a coincidence that the word "auto-biography" itself was also a neologism of the last decade of the eighteenth century, popularized further – until it no longer called attention to itself – in the opening decades of the nineteenth.[38] Joining the many other newly coined terms in the emerging conceptual toolbox of the new regime of identity, "auto-biography" became the name for the self-reflexive genre that put "The Child is father of the Man" into personalized narrative form.

The New Regime of Identity and the Romantics

Summoning up the figure of Wordsworth, as I have now done for the second time, begs the question of the place of the Romantics in this story. After all, many of the developments routinely associated with literary Romanticism are precisely those I have identified for the new regime of identity: the character-ization of self in terms of psychological depth; the emphasis on human differ-ence and individuality; the rekindled interest in innate, intuitive, and instinctive traits or behaviors; the developmental perspective on human growth. Thus, the following lines from Wordsworth's 1805 *Prelude* could have served well as an epigram for the discussion of the new emphasis on interior depths:

> When I began to inquire,
> To watch and question those I met, and held
> Familiar talk with them, the lonely roads
> Were schools to me in which I daily read
> With most delight the passions of mankind,
> There saw into the depths of human souls –
> Souls that appear to have no depth at all
> To vulgar eyes.

The poet's task is to reveal "the depths of human souls" that are invisible to vulgar eyes. Likewise, another image in *The Prelude* – subtitled, after all, "Growth of a Poet's Mind" – could have served to frame the intensified emphasis in the new regime of identity on the experience of childhood and on the innate capacities of the newborn child:

> – blest the babe
> Nursed in his mother's arms, the babe who sleeps
> Upon his mother's breast, who, when his soul

Claims manifest kindred with an earthly soul,
Doth gather passion from his mother's eye.
Such feelings pass into his torpid life
Like an awakening breeze, and hence his mind,
Even in the first trial of its powers,
Is prompt and watchful, eager to combine
In one appearance all the elements
And parts of the same object, else detached
And loth to coalesce.

The infant, the poet suggests, has an active mind that participates from the moment of its birth in the shaping of its sensations: the innatist anti-Lockean position.[39] For the newborn's active mind and inborn powers we could also turn to the poet and essayist Anna Barbauld. "What powers lie folded in thy curious frame," she addressed an embryonic child just before birth; "Launch on the living world, and spring to light!" William Blake was there too, hardly mincing his words: "Innate ideas are in Every Man, Born with him; they are truly Himself." We could go to Blake again for the emphasis on individual uniqueness: "Man varies from Man more than Animal from Animal of Different Species." And for the inner self as essential, enduring, and anterior, to Samuel Taylor Coleridge: "In looking at objects of Nature while I am thinking . . . I seem rather to be seeking, as it were *asking*, a symbolical language for something within me that already and forever exists, than observing anything new." Or, once more, to Wordsworth: "I was often unable to think of external things as having external existence, and I communed with all that I saw as something not apart from, but inherent in, my own immaterial nature."[40]

It is not surprising, therefore, that Charles Taylor places Romanticism at the center of the final turning point in his account of the rise of the modern self in Western thought. Taylor calls this Romantic turning point the "expressivist turn", by which he means the turn to inner depths of selfhood (a phrase, he asserts, rarely encountered before the Romantic period): inner depths that are the locus of the voice of nature, and thus truth, within us. Expressivism in Taylor's terms is thus the knowledge and articulation of this inner voice: one's goal – a quintessential Romantic goal – is to express oneself, and thus to live one's unique inner truth. In thus characterizing Romanticism, to be sure, Taylor chimes with conventional critical wisdom that has identified time and again the Romantic "conceptual shift" – this particular formulation is Clifford Siskin's – as that "by which man reconstituted himself as the modern psychological subject", sporting "a self-made mind, full of newly constructed depths".[41] (For Siskin, indeed, this shift was the very condition for the invention of the discipline of literature as we know it.)

But as I approach the end of this book, it may be useful to recapitulate once more the difference between my own project and Taylor's, a difference that defined my methodological starting point several hundred pages ago. The thrust of the present inquiry is to uncover not intellectual genealogies but rather patterns of broad cultural resonance. From this perspective a well-defined intellectual movement or trend beckons us to ask whether it was part of a more general cultural pattern, of which it may have been a symptom or a particular manifestation, but not necessarily a privileged locus or driving force. So just as I have identified the eighteenth-century philosophical debate on personal identity as one instance among many of the possibilities inherent in the *ancien régime* of identity, so I now want to posit literary Romanticism as one of the many new departures suddenly made possible – and resonant – by the new identity regime that superseded it: no more, no less. Indeed, Charles Taylor himself, well aware of these methodological considerations and wary of making cultural claims that exceed his high-intellectual base, has anticipated this point. He has therefore chosen to reject the "tempting" identification of the late-eighteenth-century shift with Romanticism, in favor of a formulation that recognizes this shift as "a crucial part of the conceptual armoury in which Romanticism arose".[42] Precisely.

Such a perspective may also shed light on an interesting challenge that literary critic Andrea Henderson has posed to this Romanticist consensus. Henderson has attempted to pull the rug from under the hegemony of the "depth model" of identity in Romantic studies by unearthing alternative ways of conceptualizing subjectivity that lurk within Romantic texts – with examples from Byron, Percy Shelley, Mary Shelley, Scott, and even a Wordsworth play.[43] Now suppose we grant Henderson's case, which seems overall plausible: is it all that surprising? If there was indeed a late-eighteenth-century moment of pressing challenge to received notions of identity, surely creative minds so confronted could be expected to explore other alternative conceptualizations? It is not this, it seems to me, that needs explaining. Henderson has given us a map of roads not taken. It thus begs the question: why did these roads turn out to be dead ends? And why, even as dead ends, did they remain largely invisible, so far off the Romantic beaten track that their very existence has been so effectively occluded in the many surveys of this terrain? Arguably, the answer to this question – why certain literary moves resonated widely, while others had little echo – falls outside the rhetorical effects of Romanticism itself, pointing the finger once again at its broader cultural environment.

Alan Richardson recently set himself precisely this task of uncovering the imprint of the broader cultural environment on literary Romanticism, in relation to its understanding of selfhood. He therefore cast a comparative cross-disciplinary look at a non-literary field of knowledge: the scientific understanding of the brain, or neuroscience. In this rather distant and distinct field Richardson has drawn attention to significant new developments that were simultaneous with literary Romanticism and that mirrored its key concerns.[44]

The late eighteenth and early nineteenth centuries, as historians of neuroscience and biological psychology have long recognized, witnessed the emergence of unprecedented claims about the brain and nervous system. Spearheaded by figures like Erasmus Darwin, Charles Bell, and William Lawrence in Britain, together with Franz Joseph Gall and Pierre-Jean-Georges Cabanis on the Continent, these claims (not always consistent with each other) focused on the biological basis of the mind, on its embodiment in the brain, and on the innate and internally active nature of some of its basic faculties. The operations of the mind were essentialized and materialized in the brain: we might say that the mind, for these biological psychologists, now collapsed into the brain – a formulation that is of course meant to bring to mind (or brain) the analogous collapse of gender into sex at the very same time. Richardson shows that these new neuroscientific theories, starting from their own distinct premises and questions, ended up reinforcing many conclusions in common with literary Romanticism: from the emphasis on the innate active mind and on individual uniqueness, through a developmental perspective on maturation since birth, to the assertion of the importance of the unconscious. (The latter was in itself an interesting reincarnation of the notion of a fragmented or split self, radically different from the externalized meaning that the same image had had earlier in the eighteenth century, and one that looked forward, again, to Freud; not least, in the interpretation of dreams, now newly focused on what Erasmus Darwin described as the "internal stimuli" of "internal senses".[45]) Richardson further traces the marks of the new brain science in canonical Romantic texts – from Wordsworth's unusual use of "brain" for "mind" in the 1799 *Prelude* through Coleridge's "Kubla Khan" and Keats's "Ode to Psyche" to Jane Austen's *Persuasion*, in which a knock on the head, in the plot-shaping turning point of Louisa's fall and her subsequent metamorphosis, could easily be read as a loaded intervention in the brain-science debates on the side of the essentialized, embodied mind/brain.

Without wanting to flog a dead horse too often, it bears repeating that the goal of these observations is not to claim priority for one cultural domain over another. We can summon up again the image of the orchestra, whose harmony cannot be attributed to the primacy of the woodwinds over the strings or the other way around. Rather, like the orchestra, the effect is one of *concert*, created when the different instruments, each with its different and distinctive overtones, come together in a mutually reinforcing correspondence of tune and timing. In Richardson's words: "Such specific points of contact and intellectual debts (on both sides) bear witness to a more pervasive set of intersecting

concerns, theories, readings, and key terms common to the scientists and literary artists mutually engaged in rethinking the relations of mind, body, and environment in Romantic-era Britain."[46] Indeed. And yet it should be clear by now
that this pervasive set of intersecting concerns, theories, readings, and key
terms extended far beyond the horizons of scientists and literary writers alike:
its reach extended throughout the cultural configuration that I have called the
new regime of identity, which rapidly took hold in what Richardson now cau-
tiously calls "Romantic-era" rather than "Romantic" Britain.

Masks and Faces

In 1792 appeared the first English translation of Johann Kaspar Lavater's
seminal *Essays on Physiognomy*. The response was astounding. The book was
reprinted, abridged, summarized, pirated, parodied, imitated, and reviewed so
often (between 1792 and 1810 British printers produced more than one edition
or adaptation of Lavater per year) that it is difficult to imagine any literate,
semi-literate, or otherwise culturally conscious person remaining unaware of
its basic, and deceptively simple, claims. The impact of physiognomy was
readily evident not only in directly related fields such as medical practice and
physical anthropology (subsequently branching into phrenology and racial
science), but also in other arenas of cultural production, such as the novel, the
theater, and visual art high and low. All told, the impact of Lavater's *Physiognomy* was extraordinary, even if we do not take too literally the 1801 journalis-
tic assessment that it was now "thought as necessary in every family as even the
Bible itself".[47] Consequently, much more than the rather rarefied discourse of
neuroscience, the sudden frenetic interest in physiognomy – with which it
shared key assumptions about identity and self – is a good indication of how
far-reaching the cultural transformation of "Romantic-era" Britain really was.

   Once again, I am not trying to make a claim about origins. Far from being
something new, physiognomy was a form of knowledge with roots in antiquity
that had thrived in the Renaissance. From the late seventeenth century onward,
however, physiognomy had begun to lose much of its cultural purchase. It
increasingly declined, as Martin Porter has shown, into a form of fortune-
telling, especially in relation to matrimonial or business prospects, and was
often practiced as a more or less bawdy parlor game. For many eighteenth-
century Britons, the only plausible response to physiognomic claims was one
of dismissive scorn: recall James Macpherson's and John Millar's assertions
that the distinctions of individual countenances were random, contingent, and
meaningless – a reasonable position for those who maintained that complexion
and appearance were environmentally, culturally, or self-consciously mutable.
Others in the short eighteenth century nurtured instead their own alternative

hermeneutics of faces: I will quickly mention two. One such alternative was a classically inspired focus on the generic "Principles of Beauty, Relative to the Human Head". As the painter Alexander Cozens, who wrote a book by this title, explained, such an approach to faces called for the *erasure* of physiognomic particularity in order to attain "a beautiful face unmixed with character". This "simple beauty" remained the ideal even if the artist then conceded to allow character to be "superinduced" with a few distinguishing physical characteristics or, equally effective, through accessories like "dresses of the hair". (The most prominent advocate of this perspective was Sir Joshua Reynolds in his earlier Discourses on Art, to which we shall return in a moment.) Another alternative was to focus on pathognomy, the study of expressions, that privileged evanescent gesture over fixed features. In the words of a mid-century authority on "human physiognomy", the only form of physiognomic knowledge with any scientific basis had nothing to do with the "general Shape of the Face, or any of its Parts", but only with "the Actions of the Muscles" as they voluntarily correspond with "the Passions of the Mind". Even when Henry Fielding penned what seemed like a *defense* of physiognomy, which he found at mid-century to be "of so little Use and Credit in the World", it turned out to be all about the interpretation of "Actions of Men [which] are the surest Evidence of their Character". Actions spoke louder, or clearer, than looks: those "Marks which Nature hath imprinted on the Countenance" that in the end proved "liable to some Incertainty".[48]

Let us linger for another moment on the meanings of physiognomy earlier in the eighteenth century. It is easy to see that both these eighteenth-century hermeneutics of faces – the unparticularized generic and the unfixed pathognomic – were drawing on the *ancien régime* of identity. The same was true for the 1763 work on physiognomy that gratuitously paused to describe gypsies who had transformed their complexion by smearing themselves with greasy unctions. It was also true of the 1760 writer whose admission that "there is at least some truth in physiognomy" turned out to have been intended as an admonition to "every young lady to be very careful of her looks" precisely because external appearance can lead others to *wrong* conclusions about one's character. It remained true when Burke revealingly identified the best example he knew of a protean man, one who could transform himself into other identities "as if he had been changed into the[se] very men", as none other than "the celebrated physiognomist Campanella". In these instances, and many others, it cannot fail to strike us that the eighteenth-century understanding of physiognomy was fully compatible with an underlying belief in the mutability of identity. Small wonder, therefore, that the clergyman-satirist John Clubbe, author of the 1763 work *Physiognomy* with the interest in face-altered gypsies, could barely contain his laughter in proposing to replace physiognomy – "a fallacious

44.   "The Weighing House", after William Hogarth, frontispiece to [John Clubbe], *Physiognomy*, London, 1763. The key below the image provides the measure of gravity for every order of men variously suspended in mid-air by the fantastical weighing machine

way of judging" – with a "weighing machine" that would tell people's generic types simply from their weight (fig. 44). The artist who rendered Clubbe's weighing machine in visual form was none other than William Hogarth, whose own writing on reading faces tempered the artistic interest in their potential as an "index of the mind" with the warning that faces could metamorphose, mislead, be subject to contingencies and manipulations, or act as masks. Hogarth hastened to elaborate these caveats, he explained, "least I should be thought to lay too great a stress on outward shew, like a physiognomist". Perish the thought.[49]

How very different was the late-eighteenth-century science of physiognomy, reinvented by Lavater and now riding back triumphantly on the waves of a turning cultural tide. Its premises were now in tune with the new regime of identity, not the old. "Physiognomy" – thus Lavater, in the words of Holcroft's popular translation – "is the science or knowledge of the correspondence between the external and internal man, the visible superficies and the invisible contents". Physiognomy provided "solid and fixed principles by which to settle what the Man really is". Forget Cozens, whom Lavater actually singled out for his alleged unnatural and characterless treatment of classical profiles; and forget the generic measures of Clubbe's fantastical weighing machine. Rather, more like Mary Poppins's magical tape measure, the skilled (even if hard to attain) application of Lavaterian principles was guaranteed to recover for each and every person nothing short of a unique "individual self". For Lavater, the skill of the physiognomist was in the discernment of the depths of individual character. Cozens, by contrast, had wished for a skilled penetrating elite who "will think the charactered beauties imperfect" but "whose nice discernment and taste inclines them to admire the simple beauty" – that characterless, unindividuated beauty which for him was precisely what was hidden in those underlying depths. But to go back to Lavater: "Man is free as the bird in a cage. He has a circle of activity and sensibility whose bounds he cannot pass. As the human body has lines which bound it, every mind has its peculiar sphere in which to range; but that sphere is invariably determined."[50] Deep and consequential, fixed and real, determined and determining: it does not take much of an imaginative leap to see Lavater's bird as the newly fixed inner core of selfhood, and the cage as those impermeable boundaries of identity, now essentially inscribed in the physicality of the body, from which the self can no longer fly away. One could hardly conjure up a more concrete, embodied image of the new regime of identity-as-self.

Lavater's physiognomic theory, furthermore, represented a new departure not only in relation to physiognomy's low point of the eighteenth century: it was also distinctly different from that which had characterized the earlier heyday of physiognomy in the sixteenth and seventeenth centuries. When Renaissance humanists had read faces, Roy Porter has reminded us, they were reading for *types* of universal characters and emotions: the face of fear, or dignity, or nobility, or anger. And they found the signs of these generalized types not in the face as a whole, but atomistically, in this or that particular trait: a mole on a cheek, hairy eyebrows, lobeless ears. Late-eighteenth-century physiognomists, by contrast, read the integrated ensemble of the face, and they did so in the belief – in Lavater's words – that "each man is an individual self, with as little ability to become another self as to become an angel". Consequently, it was crucial for the modern physiognomist to realize that "all faces, all forms, all created beings, differ from one another, not only with respect to their class, their genus, their species, but also, with respect to their individuality".[51] Again, it would be hard to find enunciations summing up the new regime of identity that were more categorical and uncompromising.

Perhaps too uncompromising. For if human appearances came in an infinite variety, corresponding to the infinite diversity of unique selves, how could they be reduced to a manageable system of generalizations reproducible in a work like Lavater's? *The Artist's Repository*, for one, was struck by this problem. It is true, the magazine happily conceded, that "the face is the index of the mind", an oft-repeated cliché of physiognomic wisdom. But although "some great artists" have consequently taken up physiognomy, it was in truth "a science 'puzzled in mazes, and perplexed with errors'", since "the almost infinite diversity of character, which we remark in the human countenance" makes it "impossible to say, determinately, that as such and such features compose the countenance of a certain individual, therefore he is a morose, a glutton, &c."[52] We are back once more with the internal tension inherent in the new regime of identity, which had also struck John Wilson Croker in reviewing contemporary theories of education, between its contradictory emphases on individual uniqueness and essentializing generalizations.

Many contemporaries were likewise aware of this contradictory tension – not least Lavater himself, who warned of the hazards of proposing too formulaic a system – and tried their best to square the circle. Blake, for instance, made a note in his copy of Lavater to distinguish substantial "true character" from insubstantial accidents. "Substance", Blake commented to himself, "gives tincture to the accident, and makes it physiognomic": that is, it is the inner substance, which does yield itself to generalized categorization, that makes a feature that is in itself accidental, and thus of infinite variety, indicative of a person's true character. It hardly needs pointing out that Blake's solution was as much in tune with the presuppositions of the new identity regime as the stricter physiognomic theory on which he was commenting. The same was equally true of another move that tried to get around this difficulty by affirming that physiognomic knowledge was itself part of the innate essence of human identity. It is doubtful, one critic wrote, whether physiognomy can be theorized or taught in the manner of Lavater, since in truth it represents knowledge that "is, at best, a sort of instinct given to man, as instinct is given to the beasts". For Charles Bell too, writing in 1806, the capacity to read faces was inborn and not learned: it was therefore observable in its purest form in infants – who thus found themselves once again at the forefront of turn-of-the-century speculation.[53] But if the reading of faces was inborn in each and every person, then it was compatible with the infinite differences of innate selves, and did not require – or indeed allow for – generalized theorizing.

Another critic of a more fanciful bent hit the nail right on the head. In this critic's scenario set in an imaginary land, a native school of physiognomists brought "the physiognomic art" to "an incredible pitch of perfection". They did so by practicing the art not with Lavaterian drawings but rather with *real live heads*. Here was a solution for the incompatibility of generic generalization and unique individuality: each head in this fantastical picture was taken to represent the physiognomy only of itself.[54] What this critic intuited through this ironic jest was that the only way to bridge the incongruous impulses to individuate and to essentialize was by circumventing altogether the mediation of representation. Lavater himself recommended eliminating the mediation of representation as much as possible through the use of silhouettes: a newly fashionable technique for the replication of heads that could supposedly retain, as John Randolph put it in a letter to his sister Fanny in 1805, "in each face the peculiarity of character it possesses". Nor did one have to stop there. The late 1780s saw the invention of the "physionotrace", a profiling machine that could reputedly replicate an exact face in an immediate and unmediated fashion. Tellingly, the physionotrace was introduced to Britain by the sons of another major personage in the pre-photographic quest for the perfect unmediated replication of human likeness: namely, Madame Tussaud, as she began touring Britain in the post-revolutionary years, making her wax figures while her sons wheeled behind her the newfangled profiling machine.[55]

These various developments can be interpreted, first, by placing them within the shifting history of representation. The *ancien régime* of identity, we recall, had witnessed concerns for the unprecedented preponderance of representation: did a copy presuppose an original? These late-eighteenth-century developments can therefore be seen as one reaction, admittedly extreme, through the insistence on the elimination of representation altogether, so as to annihilate, hopefully, the very distinction between copy and original. But more to our point here, we can also place the well-known vogue for wax figures and wax museums in the late eighteenth and early nineteenth centuries, together with the efforts of the profiling devices and silhouette artists, within the shifting history of identity and selfhood. They were all responses, more or less successful, to the premium that the new regime of identity now placed on embodied, unique, unmediated physiognomy.

*

Physiognomy, as is often recognized, has an intimate relationship with art. I would like therefore to close this consideration of Lavaterian physiognomy, which crystallized several aspects of the new regime of identity (regardless of whether the theory itself was embraced or, as was often the case, rejected), by drawing attention to the affinities of physiognomic logic and presuppositions with late-eighteenth-century developments in the theory and practice of both (so-called) high and low visual art.

No eighteenth-century institution represented high art more authoritatively than the Royal Academy of Arts, and no figure represented this august authority more famously than its first president, Sir Joshua Reynolds, who from its opening in 1769 addressed its members and students in a series of annual "Discourses on Art". Early on in his *ex cathedra* pronouncements Reynolds laid down a general "presiding principle" of art: "perfect form", art's object and purpose, "is produced by leaving out particularities". From this he then derived a clear theory of portraiture. "If a portrait-painter", went his address of 1771, "is desirous to raise and improve his subject, he has no other means than by approaching it to a general idea. He leaves out all the minute breaks and peculiarities in the face . . . if an exact resemblance of an individual be considered as the sole object to be aimed at, the portrait-painter will be apt to lose more than he gains." "Peculiar [individual] marks" – he added a couple of years later – were "defects", which, although useful for making us "cognizable and distinguished from one another", the artist should seek to avoid as much as possible. It is only by eliminating such peculiarities – by achieving, in other words, what Alexander Cozens was to recommend as "a beautiful face unmixed with character" – that the artist can approach a common form, one that is shared by all individuals and that is the grounds for social sympathy between them. Here we have again the theory of the socially turned generic representation of the *ancien régime* of identity, valorizing intersubjective identicality over individual identity.[56]

With this flashback to Reynolds's lectures of the early 1770s in mind, consider now the break represented by what the same distinguished audience was to hear in 1785 from the academy's recently appointed professor of painting, James Barry. John Barrell has provided us with a detailed contrast between Barry and Reynolds, which can be summarized as follows. Barry basically accepted Reynolds's account of characterless ideal beauty, but rejected outright his injunction to the artist never to deviate from this ideal. Following Reynolds's generalized ideal would not only be "tasteless and insipid" as well as "lying and contradictory", but also could not be "advantageous to morality and the interests of mankind". This was because it is only through the particular tasks that individuals perform, tasks physical or intellectual that distinguish one person from another, that man achieves his moral purpose and the highest development of his nature. For Barry, therefore, a man is – and ought to be – what he does; which in turn depends on a combination of inborn individual suitability and education. But even the external influence of education, Barry explained further (prefiguring the early Hazlitt), is then internalized as man's second nature, by which his body is entirely determined and individualized: character may be the result of development and education, but once it is fixed it cannot be changed.[57]

What Barry told his audience, therefore, was that variety was for an artistic work not a flaw but a virtue. His theory sought not to eliminate the range of individual identities but, in Barrell's words, "to categorise and distribute [them] . . . into physiognomic types". Moreover, just as Reynolds's lectures had been in tune with other eighteenth-century voices in the public discussion of art, including those of Hogarth, Cozens, even Gainsborough, as well as Jonathan Richardson earlier in the century,[58] so Barry's physiognomic approach also chimed with others during his own moment at the close of the century. We can mention in this company Archibald Alison (who in 1790 declared the height of beauty to be found in the "expressions" of "peculiar characters or dispositions of the MIND"), Charles Bell ("The noblest aim of painting unquestionably is to reach the mind . . . [and] the emotions of the mind, as indicated by the figure, and in the countenance" [1806]), William Hazlitt ("general character" and "individual peculiarities" are "so far from being incompatible with, that they are not without some difficulty distinguishable from, each other" [1816]), and Henry Fuseli. Fuseli's belief that good characteristic portraiture was physiognomic led him to tamper even with Lavater's work: when Lavater was translated into English, Fuseli took out a generalized portrait of Brutus (after Rubens) that had graced the original German edition and replaced it with his own, still modeling his Brutus on the Rubens head but now endowing it with particularized and expressive features.[59] In sum, if Reynolds had lectured with both legs firmly planted in the *ancien régime* of identity, Barry was in good company in getting his feet wet in the new.

The reader may wonder at this point how Reynolds suddenly came to represent the *ancien régime* of identity, given that earlier in this chapter – in his portrait of the Dilettanti, or his paintings of children – his role was rather that of the bellwether of the new. To explain this, we need to keep in mind that Reynolds's Discourses were an ongoing endeavor, delivered annually (and later biannually) from 1769 through to his retirement in 1790. As Barrell has painstakingly shown, when read as a temporal sequence, the Discourses reveal unmistakable shifts in Reynolds's opinions. Of these, one of the most conspicuous is Reynolds's retreat in the later Discourses from the categorical preference for the general over the particular. Admitting now that individual particularities "have still their foundation, however slender, in the original fabrick of our minds" – note well this last phrase – Reynolds increasingly doubted whether the portrait painter should not really be allowed considerable license in taking them into account. The later Discourses therefore repeatedly wrestled with the implications of this altered position for the practice of art in general and portraiture in particular. Perhaps unsurprisingly, Reynolds saved his most upfront admission of his change of heart to another venue, an unfinished essay on Shakespeare. There he conceded readily that this was a new age that "demand[ed] a new code of laws", one "more agreeable to the nature of man" and attentive to "those accidents" that his earlier theory had dismissed.

By now Reynolds had certainly traveled quite a distance from his earlier pronouncements. Finally, in view of what the previous pages have suggested regarding chronology, consider this: as it turns out, we can pinpoint with some precision the moment of Reynolds's change of heart. According to expert witness John Barrell, it first became apparent that Reynolds was changing his opinion and leaving the *ancien régime* of identity behind in his seventh Discourse, which he delivered to the Royal Academy on 10 December 1776.[60]

*

So much for high art. But the American revolutionary war, art historian Amelia Rauser tells us, also saw the arrival in force of a new visual genre that is commonly categorized as low rather than high: the political caricature. How could it be new, you ask: was Hogarth's century not already replete with political prints? Yes, but they were not the same. Rauser, following the lead of Diana Donald, distinguishes two different representational modes in political prints. For most of the eighteenth century, political prints were conceived overwhelmingly in an emblematic mode: that is to say, using a complex visual language of signs and symbols, inherited and adapted from the popular emblem books of the seventeenth century, which typically involved a multilayered interaction of image and text and a surfeit of symbols crowding the surface of the print in cells of different time and space. Individuals were subordinated to this emblematic composition in ways that rendered their representation stereotypical and impersonal, and thus routinely required textual clarification of their identity.[61]

By contrast, the late eighteenth century – the age of Gillray, Rowlandson, and Cruikshank, among others – saw the heyday of the caricatural mode, a mode that was insistently subjective and individualized. In caricatural political prints the issues at hand were invested in the particularized representation of distinct and distinguishable persons. The stance of the caricatural mode toward such individuals was ironic, promising to strip away unreliable signs in order to reveal the deeper underlying truth. Consequently, this new mode was inherently physiognomic. In a mutually reinforcing relationship with the explosion of interest in physiognomy, the manipulation of individuated personal traits through a physiognomic eye – in contrast to the recycling of familiar symbols that had been typical of the emblematic mode – became the key to the new ironic purpose of the political caricature.

As a typical example, albeit one uncommonly explicit about its source of inspiration, we can take Gillray's caricature of 1798, "DOUBLÛRES of Characters; or Striking Resemblances in Phisiognomy" (fig. 45), which revealed the true character of known political figures (like Charles James Fox, top left) with

45. James Gillray, "DOUBLÛRES of Characters; or Striking Resemblances in Phisiognomy", 1798

the guidance of an aphorism from Lavater – "If you would know Mens Hearts, look in their Faces".[62] Gillray's "doublûre", a doubleness of inner self delimiting outer appearance, or outer appearance revealing inner self, could hardly be further from that vision of unfettered and roaming doubleness of identity – à la Garrick, Boswell, Woffington, Locke, or Smith – that had been commensurate with the presuppositions of the previous generations. Indeed, by this point it seems almost superfluous to spell out how closely the contrast between the late-eighteenth-century physiognomic, particularized, inner-gazing caricatural mode and the earlier generic, impersonal emblematic mode maps onto this book's broader story: both onto the contrast between the *ancien régime* of identity and the new regime that came to replace it, and onto the chronology that singles out the American revolutionary war as the caesura that marked the break.

Of course, this is not to suggest that there had not been physiognomic prints before: Hogarth's famous 1763 caricature of the squinting, cross-eyed, ugly Wilkes leaps to mind as the ultimate counter-example. But rarely has there been an exception that proved the rule more effectively. For, as Rauser insightfully demonstrates, Hogarth's caricature spectacularly backfired: like Balaam's ass, it was intended to vilify Wilkes, but was instead picked up by his supporters (and Wilkes himself) to be recirculated with considerable enthusiasm. As Rauser continues to explain, the print missed its purpose because it used a visual language that was resolutely at odds with contemporary practice and expectations, and thus beyond the interpretive horizon of its audience. Hogarth, stung by a private feud with his erstwhile friend, released his personalized caricature in the middle of the political episode that in fact elicited the last major flourish of eighteenth-century emblematic prints (the ubiquitous and rich symbolic use of a boot for "Bute" was but one memorable example of this emblematic mode). Consequently Hogarth's offensive gambit fell flat, and became available for misappropriation by his rival's supporters. Similarly, we can point to several other instances when eighteenth-century caricatures failed to resonate, notably the witty drawings of Marquess Townshend in the late 1750s for which he was summarily reproved by his contemporaries (a "false start", says Donald).[63] After all, caricature was a recognized art form, having been popularized by seventeenth-century Italian fine artists from Annibale Carracci to Gianlorenzo Bernini: a tradition undoubtedly familiar to eighteenth-century Grand Touring Englishmen. That this mode of representation did not catch on for most of the century, therefore, had to do not with its unavailability but with its lack of resonance. But then, suddenly, the situation changed. If it was rare to see political caricatures before 1780, thereafter they became exceedingly common, quickly becoming the dominant mode. (So much so that when an early-nineteenth-century antiquarian encountered an earlier emblematic political print, he dismissed it as a "curious jumble of Hieroglyphics".)[64] Why the sudden change? Donald, somewhat unconvincingly, tries to explain the continuing resonance of the emblematic over the caricatural mode during the short eighteenth century, and then their abrupt reversal of fortunes, in terms of the exigencies of political rhetoric at these respective moments. Rauser, on the other hand, seeks to locate this shift within a broader cultural explanation: one that would also be able to account for the simultaneous and obviously pertinent rise of physiognomy. An explanation, to be sure, very much consonant with the shift proposed here from the *ancien régime* of identity to the new.

The relationship between the emergence in force of the caricatural-cum-physiognomic mode and the new regime of identity becomes even more apparent when we consider what Rauser rightly emphasizes as the key function of caricature and physiognomy: namely, *to unmask*. One of the main indicators of change in her story is therefore a sudden and conspicuous rise in prints devoted to unmasking: a trend that, as she carefully documents, "surged around 1780" and then "increased rapidly in the early 1780s". This observation is loud with reverberations from our earlier discussion. It takes us back to the outbreak of contemporary preoccupation with masking and disguise that was triggered just then by the American war (a connection clearly registered in Rauser's examples). It takes us back to the unexpected, precipitous decline in the cultural status of the masquerade that began precisely at this moment. Indeed, it takes us straight back to the very first "fragment" that opened this chapter, which featured two of these unmasking prints as signs of the impending change. These two prints, moreover, have allowed us to see that this 1780s preoccupation was not simply about unmasking, but about the wishful assertion of the very impossibility of successful masquerade and disguise. The same assertion was of course also dear to the hearts of the physiognomists – think again of the implication of Gillray's "Doublûres of Characters". It thus seems overdetermined that, when Mary Anne Schimmelpenninck summoned her childhood memories of playing doll dress-up in the 1780s, a pastime that had taught her the inevitable preponderance of ingrained character over disguise and masquerade (recall New regime fragment 12, pp. 273–4), she could not separate them in her mind from the recollection of being left alone as a young girl – how else? – with the heavy tomes of Lavater.[65]

We have thus closed one more circle. If the decline of the masquerade has served us as the lens through which to observe the late-eighteenth-century transformation in understandings of identity and self, we can now add the rise of the physiognomic mode across so many cultural forms as its complementary flip side. Masks were the opposite of faces. Contemporaries, to be sure, knew this. In the 1780 novel *Masquerades; or, What You Will*, which I discussed at the beginning of this chapter as undermining the potential for identity play at a masquerade, contrary to the implication of the novel's title, there is in fact a second masquerade scene. In this case the anonymous author seems at first glance to have allowed for the unrecognizability of individuals at a masked ball: but the novelist's real intent is made clear to the reader in the deliberate framing of this scene, before and after, with carefully placed references to a "physiognomic eye" and to the value of being "a true physiognomist". So much for the masquerade's potential for transforming or disguising identity, undone through the power of physiognomy.[66] Masks or faces: there was nothing like the shift in cultural investment from one to the other to epitomize the ousting of the *ancien régime* of identity by the new.

Coda: Self in the Age of Revolutions

In the preceding pages I have sometimes referred to the late-eighteenth-century transformation in the regime of identity and self as a "cultural revolution". This phrase is intended to draw attention to the pervasiveness of this

transformation's reach, to the abruptness of its unfolding, and to the significance of its consequences.[67] But it also gestures to the familiar picture of this
period as the "Age of Revolutions", and thus begs the question of their relationship – the relationship, that is, between the cultural revolution proposed
here and the emergence of modern democratic politics that is commonly dated
to the same historical moment. Now this is a very big topic to arrive at the end
of an already rather big book, and one that in truth would require a volume of
its own and a whole range of new sources. *Faute de mieux*, I would like to end
this discussion of the new departures riding on the coat-tails of the new regime
of identity with some preliminary observations on its possible relationship with
the birth of modern politics, which might serve to outline some areas for future
research.

The first point to be made is a negative one. It is an all-too-common histor-
iographical move to finger major political events as the prime movers of changes
in other spheres of life, as if this causal relationship were so self-evident as not
to require either logical justification or detailed demonstration. This book, by
contrast, has suggested that the major political revolutions and ideologies of the
Age of Revolutions were *not* the prime motor behind the story it has been
trying to tell. I am not arguing that these revolutions and ideologies had no
impact – that would be foolhardy and wrong. But already on the grounds of
chronology (the transformation charted here was well under way before the
French Revolution and the dramatic political departures of the 1790s)
and scope (it reached far and wide, crossing many social, cultural, and indeed
political lines) it is impossible to defend the singling out of political developments as the cause from which all other layers of change followed. This remains
true even of the American Revolution, which I have invoked less for the impact
of its innovative political ideology than for the broadly diffused effects of the
conflict that accompanied it, and which in any case filled in my scenario the
role of trigger rather than prime mover. Instead I have pushed for a reversed
perspective that asks whether the broad cultural framework was in itself a conditioning factor in political developments; or, in other words, whether there is
something to be gained from treating politics as an arena of culture, rather than
culture as an arena of politics. Specifically I have therefore asked, for instance,
whether we should look less for how American revolutionary ideology produced
the cultural anxieties accompanying the American war than for how these
diffuse anxieties conditioned the reception and effects of American political
ideology. Or whether we should try to see the onset of a new regime of gender
as a precondition for the new political edge of late-eighteenth-century feminism, rather than assume that it was the backlash against the political feminism
of the 1790s that generated a realignment of gender understandings. Or
whether we should see the resort to the language of the "middle class" in the

1790s not simply as a consequence of the political configuration of this decade – as I myself once argued – but rather as a consequence of anterior cultural transformation that had made this particular interaction of politics and social language plausible.

Following a similar line of reasoning, therefore, we can ask more generally in what ways the cultural revolution proposed in this book constituted an enabling precondition for the political revolutions of the Age of Revolutions. (I realize of course that I am posing this question at the end of an inquiry focused on a country that, unlike France and America, did *not* experience a political revolution: I will return to this comparative point shortly.) Consider one of the most significant contributions of this period to modern political language: the notion of inalienable natural rights. To be sure, the idea of natural rights was not a new one: it had an important early-modern provenance. But in framing the question of natural rights in terms of continuity and change, two observations can quickly be made. First, the prevalent understanding of natural rights throughout most of the eighteenth century, derived as it was from early-modern theories of natural law, was not as open-ended claims of individuals, but always in conjunction with matching duties to others. As Knud Haakonssen has shown, natural rights, following the formulation of the influential late-seventeenth-century natural law theorist Samuel Pufendorf, entailed a package deal comprehended in the Latin term *officium*, or office, which encompassed duties and rights together. In terms we have used before, this can be described as a socially turned understanding of natural rights. Its particular intersubjective bent may have depended, in part, on a relative decline in the weight accorded to the direct and active duty to God in the conceptualization of natural rights (recall Gauchet's vision of the disenchantment of the world); but it was distinctly different – this is Haakonssen's point – from the more sharply individualistic meaning assigned to the "rights of man" during the Age of Revolutions.[68] A more extensive discussion, moreover, would consider these developments in political theory next to the familiar picture of political practice in the short eighteenth century, in which the primary derivation of political legitimacy relied on the communal claims of *custom*; and custom, as Nicholas Rogers and Douglas Hay have reminded us, was a collective language that "had many of the resonances that came at the end of the century to be struck by the word 'rights'".[69]

The second observation on continuity and change goes back to the remarkable pre-modern prefiguration of the modern notion of individual, inalienable, natural rights in the hands of certain groups of radicals, especially the Levellers, during the English Revolution of the mid-seventeenth century. But not only were these radicals a very small group – "a minority within a minority", in David Zaret's words – their breakthrough – unprecedented and "distinctively modern" (Zaret again) – fell flat without real historical echo, leaving the modern observer with the familiar sense of this episode as an isolated moment out of synch with its times.[70] It seems plausible therefore to pose the question again in terms of the specificity of the late eighteenth century: why was it this particular juncture that saw natural rights shift from a socially turned to a more individualistic understanding, and why did this political language now resonate so widely – as it had not done before – among supporters and detractors alike? For the first half of the question, the connection to the cultural transformation charted in this book requires no further commentary. But what about the ultimately more important second half: was this cultural transformation a factor in enabling the language of natural rights to become such a wide platform for popular mobilization in modern politics?

Charles Taylor, for one, has anticipated a positive answer. The novelty in modern notions of natural rights, according to Taylor, was not in their moral imperatives, largely shared by their predecessors, "but in the place of the subject" in their conceptualization, relying on an autonomous active individual able to claim these rights. Historians have only lately turned their attention to the implications of this insight. "How did 'rights'", Joan Scott has asked, "come to be understood as something individuals possessed?" We can get even closer to Taylor's meaning by reversing Scott's question: how did "individuals" come to be understood as something – or someones – that can possess rights? This is precisely the shift in focus that has recently been recommended by the doyenne of the cultural history of the Age of Revolutions. "The belief in the self-evidence of the human rights of autonomous individuals", Lynn Hunt insists, "depended not only on alterations in the intellectual climate but also on subtle changes in the perception of bodies and selves." And again: "the credibility of natural rights flows from new conceptions and practices of what it means to be a self as much as from previous intellectual or legal influences."[71] The credibility of natural rights – what I might call here their resonance – depended on new meanings of self.

But which new meanings? Political philosopher Edward Andrew has proposed one specific change in conceptions and practices of selfhood that underlay the emergence of the language of natural rights in the late eighteenth century. Natural rights, he argues, rest on a notion of individual inner conscience: a conviction that was shared by both sides in the late-eighteenth-century debate – as represented most influentially by Thomas Paine and Edmund Burke – and picked up, among others, by the Romantics (Byron's "small voice within"). This notion, Andrew further shows, was itself an innovation, distinctly different from the prevalent eighteenth-century conscience – recall Adam Smith's impartial spectator – that was other-oriented and socially turned. (This eighteenth-century conscience, in turn, had been distinct from its solipsistic but God-driven Protestant predecessor.) So while Andrew does not frame this change explicitly as a question of self, his reasoning can readily be seen to affirm Hunt's line of thinking.[72] It also, obviously, dovetails with my own framework in this book. Indeed, the broader question that I would like to leave the reader with is whether those new conceptions and practices of self-hood that Hunt seeks as the missing link in our understanding of natural rights in the Age of Revolutions were not precisely the outcomes of the transforma-tion that we have been following here. Was the new regime of identity that emerged at this very moment privileging a self that was stable, well-defined, and reliable, and thus capable of possessing inalienable individual natural rights, an enabling epistemological precondition for the bursting of this pivotal concept onto the Western political stage? The making of the modern subject, we may find, relied on the prior making of the modern self.

The reader may reasonably protest that the notion of natural rights was central to the American Revolution of 1776, and thus preceded the shift that in my *mise-en-scène* arrived subsequently. And yet American historians – Michael Zuckert, for example – have repeatedly pointed to a paradoxical dis-crepancy between, on the one hand, the place of the language of natural rights in the Declaration of Independence and in the statements of the nascent states and, on the other, the tendency to ignore, deny, or deprecate natural rights as irrelevant to American actions during the revolution. Yes, the language of natural rights did appear from the 1760s onward – although not too frequently – in American pronouncements during the confrontation with the metro-politan government. But no, this language did not necessarily mean yet what we now take it to mean, but rather drew on the same eighteenth-century socially turned and duty-bound understandings just noted. And when the language of natural rights suddenly seemed to open up new meanings, the revolutionaries, who – in Daniel Rodgers's words – stumbled upon these new potentialities "hesitantly, pushed by circumstances", did not quite know what to do with them. Constitutional historian John Phillip Reid has gone as far as to declare "the irrelevancy of natural rights" to the revolutionary moment. Taking on a powerful retrospective "mythology", he notes that even in the Declaration of Independence natural rights made an impact only on the rhetorical preamble but not on the actual rights claimed, all of which were historical constitutional rights of Englishmen. Still more to the point, even when the Americans did invoke natural rights, they did not have (thus Haakonssen's conclusion) "a clear idea of rights as underived, primary features of the person". This idea, Alfred Young adds, was not really to make a difference to the American political vocabulary until the 1790s.[73] Overall, then, the picture that emerges is of the American revolutionaries being pushed into this new language by the power of events, broaching it in their formal statements in an experimental and sometimes confused way, but before its full implications and mobilizing power had unfolded. The American Revolution certainly made a distinct and crucial contribution to the political career of the language of natural rights, but we can still ask whether it was only in conjunction with the emergence of a new cultural environment that this career could really take off.

*

I would like to conclude these brief observations on the age of political revolutions with a counter trend. As far as I am aware, it is the most significant counter-example – or cluster of counter-examples – for my argument about the late-eighteenth-century demise of the *ancien régime* of identity. However, I want to suggest that the very nature of these exceptions demonstrates once more how different was the cultural environment in which the new political winds were blowing.

This counter trend comes from the radical Jacobin circles of the 1790s. Consider William Godwin's *Enquiry Concerning Political Justice* of 1793, one of the most important – and most profoundly radical – interventions of this period. The basis of Godwin's arguments was a belief in the perfectibility of man. This position perforce required him to combine a developmental perspective on the progress of the mind, seemingly in tune with the new regime of identity, with an *ancien-régime* insistence on the mutable nature of one's identity and character, undetermined by inborn tendencies and wholly shapeable through external influence. "What is born into the world is an unfinished sketch," Godwin asserted, "without character or decisive feature impressed upon it." Who does not know that "in the course of a human life the character of the individual frequently undergoes two or three revolutions of its fundamental stamina?" he asked; "how often does it happen that, if we meet our best loved friend after an absence of twenty years, we look in vain in the man before us" for the person we had once known? Godwin here wheeled out the familiar, if by now dusty, eighteenth-century trope – the traveler unrecognizable after twenty years of absence – in order to drive home his point; namely, that "it is impression that makes the man, and, compared with the empire of impression, the mere differences of animal structure are inexpressibly unimportant and powerless".[74] No mincing of words for Godwin.

So here was an intransigent vestige of the *ancien régime* of identity. But note the difference. What could have been taken for granted earlier in the century, or at least would not have been taken as particularly objectionable, now signaled in Godwin's hands an explicit and loaded radical political program. Indeed, the key point to note is that those who now shared Godwin's rearguard *ancien-régime*-of-identity position – a position that had characterized a broad spectrum earlier in the eighteenth century – were all of his own well-defined political ilk. We can therefore find the echoes of Godwin's position in the so-called "Jacobin novels" of the 1790s, those that were staking the same political territory: like Godwin's own *Caleb Williams* of 1794, which had one character saying, "you did not make yourself; you are just what circumstances irresistibly compelled you to be"; or his friend Mary Hays's *Memoirs of Emma Courtney* of 1796 which declared that "we are all creatures of education".[75] The old had become new: the same familiar eighteenth-century ideas now took on a fresh and unfamiliar meaning as the cultural world around them changed. This was the same reversal that we have seen in the transformation of the *ancien régime* of gender, when the gender-bending woman's loss of her cultural ground in the closing decades of the century was, arguably, a precondition for her emergence as a politically charged figure in the feminist debates of the 1790s. The new edge and the new challenge posed by notions that had been part and parcel of the *ancien régime* of identity were a consequence of the very transformation that had brought this *ancien régime* of identity to an end.

The Panoramic View: Making an Example of the French

The previous section has brought into sharp relief a question that may have been at the back of the reader's mind for some time: what is the relationship between the specifics of the English case and the broader Western history of identity and self that this book purports to retell? Of course this question is important for every stage of the argument, but for none more so than for the linking – however tentative – between the new political departures of the Age of Revolutions and the new regime of identity: a new regime that has been laid down here in detail for the major Western country that, famously, did *not* have a political revolution at all. Are not France and America the more obvious places to look for the new departures of the Age of Revolutions?

My necessarily speculative response is as follows. It seems likely that the array of scholars who have helped set the terms for this inquiry, from Marcel Mauss through Charles Taylor to Michel Foucault, were not too far off the mark in assuming – or intuiting – that the history of identity and self, in its broadest outlines, was not confined by Western national borders. In many fundamental respects the West was one cultural domain with many unifying features. (I take "the West" to include not only western Europe, but also its transatlantic extensions into North and South America.) But the unfolding of the developments laid down in this book – the particular configuration of the *ancien régime* of identity or the new, the triggers of change, the timing and rhythm of transformation, the nature of particular twists – was likely to have taken a specific and different form in each national context, indeed making some cases diverge considerably from the Anglo-centric variation. Establishing these variations is a project far beyond what is feasible in one volume. But rather than simply sidestepping the question, I want quickly to pull together several cues from the work of other scholars to propose a skeletal outline of what such a picture of national variation might look like, and what conclusions we may be able to draw from such a comparative perspective. My example in the next few pages will be the French one, to which I will also add a glance at the American case. While these are the two most natural candidates for a comparative triangulation during the so-called Age of Revolutions, a better-informed writer may be able to extend the discussion also to other places, such as Germany (notable for the most articulated high-academic discourse on the meaning of the self in the late eighteenth century) and Latin America.

As a lead into the French scene we can return to William Godwin's belief in the perfectibility of man, which owed its immediacy and charge to the French Revolution. The notions of "regeneration" and the "new man", after all, stood at the center of the French revolutionary project. No one was a better spokesman for the malleability of identity than Maximilien Robespierre, who in true Lockean fashion proclaimed children to be mere *tabulae rasae* that the revolution could fashion as it pleased. It was also Robespierre who remarked that the revolution had transformed the French, in comparison to other European powers, "as if they had become a different species". When the revolutionaries wanted to advocate a variety of cultural practices as necessary to the forging of this "new man" – be it revolutionary festivals, the new calendar, the new educational code, or the renaming of Paris streets – they did so, as Jan Goldstein has noted, in the eighteenth-century language of associationist psychology, citing the shaping impact of the senses on the imagination of individuals.[1]

While building on such *ancien-régime*-of-identity foundations, however, other aspects of the revolutionary project, as Goldstein also shows, "problematised the nature of the self" in new and radical ways. In particular, she emphasizes the Tocquevillian observation that the revolution swept away the whole corporate order which in pre-revolutionary France had been a major anchor of collective identity – *ancien-régime* identity, a term now returned to its original source – that was prior and anterior to the individual. "Each person", the Parisian glovemakers said as they explained the nature of corporate society, "has an existence only through the corporate body [*corps*] to which he is attached." But with the revolution, the sudden disappearance of corporate bodies raised the danger – thus another contemporary voice – of turning every artisan into "a solitary being, dependent upon himself alone, and free to indulge all the flights of an often disordered imagination".[2] More new than old regime. The same was also true of the revolutionizing of family law, from the new limits on parental authority to the facilitation of divorce, which resulted in the uprooting of individuals from previously solid moorings in multiple family ties and obligations. Overall, it is not surprising that the immediate, unsettling effects of the French Revolution involved conflicting consequences with regard to underlying notions of selfhood.

Demonstrations of these conflicting impulses in the early years of the revolution are not hard to find. Thus, on the one hand, nobody perhaps embodied the revolutionary potential for malleability more personally than the feminist republican Olympe de Gouges, who declared herself "an amphibious animal", "neither man nor woman". De Gouges, to quote Joan Scott, "refused the differentiation of bodies into fixed binary categories, insisting instead on multiplicity, variety, ranges of difference, spectra of colours and functions, confusion of roles – the ultimate undecidability and indeterminacy of the social significance of physical bodies"; a position that she held for race as well as for gender. For de Gouges, who also invented her own name, "there was no pre-existing subject": rather, she "produced a self that had no antecedent to her enactment of it". On the other hand, however, the early 1790s also witnessed powerful reactions like that of Pierre-Gaspard Chaumette, who ranted in a familiar gender-panicked way to the National Convention: "Since when is it permitted to give up one's sex? Since when is it decent to see women abandoning the pious cares of their households, the cribs of their children, to come to public places, to harangues in the galleries, at the bar of the Senate? Is it to men that nature confided domestic cares? Has she given us breasts to feed our children?" De Gouges, after all, ended her revolutionary career on the guillotine – a price she paid, in Chaumette's words, for "this forgetfulness of the virtues of her sex" or, in Scott's words, for the newly pathologized loss of coherent self.[3]

Chaumette's rants, and de Gouges's execution, were part of a sharp rise in the public investment in gender clarity during the Terror (summer 1793–summer 1794), a development that students of the French Revolution have reconstructed over the last twenty years in much detail. It was signaled most clearly by the National Convention's banning of women's political clubs in October 1793, and by its acceptance shortly thereafter of Jacques-Louis David's proposal for a gargantuan statue of a masculine Hercules to replace the feminine Marianne as the symbol of the radical republic. To the extent that this was a reaction – perhaps predictable, for some scholars inevitable – to the threatening space that the revolution had momentarily opened for female political participation, it was one that appears to be readily accounted for within the internal logic and dynamic of the fortunes of gender in the French Revolution.[4]

But for the purposes of the present book I am more intrigued – and here we are getting to the crux of this speculative cross-Channel comparison – by a picture emerging from recent scholarship of a more diffuse and yet seemingly far-reaching transformation that took place somewhat later in the French revolutionary decade. Explorations from several different angles have come together in identifying a moment of cultural realignment during the Thermidorian reaction (the revolutionary phase named after the ninth of "Thermidor" – i.e. 27 July 1794 – when Robespierre and his supporters were arrested and subsequently executed, bringing the Terror to an end) and into the rule of the Directory (lasting through 1799). In terms not unfamiliar to the reader of the foregoing pages, they posit this transformation as one involving notions of self.

William Reddy, for instance, has recently charted a shift in France from eighteenth-century sentimentalism – the reign of externalized emotions, or sensibility (which, as we recall, should not be confounded with interiority) – to nineteenth-century Romanticism, characterized by "psychological introspection". Exemplary of the latter was Victor Cousin, who rejected sensationalism outright in favor of an essentializing view of self-as-substance. Reddy dates this transformation, which also entailed a retrospective forgetting of the previous importance of sentimentalism, quite precisely: it took place "almost immediately after Thermidor" and was virtually complete within two decades. Sean Quinlan argues more explicitly that the post-Terror period in the revolutionary decade was the key turning point in the inauguration of a new understanding of selfhood, one that was inextricably linked to physical experience: personhood came to reflect an underlying biological reality.[5]

Several intellectual projects that were launched in France during the second half of the 1790s can be seen as precursors of such new discourses on identity. One example is provided by the career of the *idéologue* Pierre-Jean-Georges Cabanis, who came to prominence under the Directory in the newly established Institut de France. In addition to his contributions to the new "Romantic" brain science that we encountered in chapter 7, we should note his *L'Influence des sexes sur le caractère des idées et des affections morales* (prepared in 1795–6), a work that launched a "mini-genre" of investigations over the next decade reaffirming in shrill tones the absolute distinctions between the sexes.[6] In the Bicêtre asylum, meanwhile, Cabanis's friend Philippe Pinel was busily developing his innovative psychological views (first published 1796–8) on the psyche as a distinct faculty governing the relation of body and self in a unique individual, and on the cure of the mental patient as a return to one's true self (*"retour sur lui-même"*). In Goldstein's opinion, Pinel's views were a major "proto-Romantic" turning point on the road to the modern medical discourse of the psyche.[7] In 1799 both Cabanis and Pinel, together with many other luminaries, joined the Société des Observateurs de l'Homme, founded by Louis-François Jauffret, which made the whole of the "science of man" its domain, approaching it – as Adriana Benzaquén has pointed out – from a distinctly "Romantic" perspective. The first essay prize announced by the society went to an author who proposed that the child was the answer to the riddle of man: a choice that signaled the persistent pedagogical-developmental belief of the members of the society that, in the words of one of its reports, "the exact history of the progress of a child, in its physical and moral aspects, must be the proper basis for the history of man".[8]

More memorably, the Société des Observateurs de l'Homme played a key role in the reception and investigation of the feral child Victor of Aveyron. Their view of this wild child, Julia Douthwaite has shown, differed from the earlier eighteenth-century cases in that the feral child was no longer seen as an exemplar of nature and of the malleability of man, let alone an indication of the potential porousness of the boundary between human and animal. Instead, the Observateurs de l'Homme now medicalized the feral child – most clearly in a report prepared in 1800 by Philippe Pinel – as a pathological case of mental disorder. Douthwaite too places this change within a broader story of the disillusionment with the vision of regenerated and perfectible man that had befallen the revolutionaries in the aftermath of the Terror.[9]

Others have pointed to specific developments during the post-Thermidor years that are also revealing. Take Jane Caplan's inquiry into the modern emergence of the legal immutability of personal names, a key step toward the formal fixed individuation of one person from another. For Caplan, the "paradigmatic case" is the French law enacted on 23 August 1794 (6 Fructidor, An II). This law, which came into being less than a month after Robespierre's execution, forbade French citizens to bear any names other than those registered at birth, and required the resumption of original names that had been changed during the revolution: no more self-inventing identity play à la Olympe de Gouges. Historians of women have likewise pointed out that while the backlash against female participation in politics had begun already in 1793, it was after the Terror that the consolidation of fixed gender-differentiated spheres and boundaries got into full swing, leading, among other things, to the end of women's political activity and drive for legal and social reform. Suzanne Desan, looking at the changing demarcations of gender in the legal reforms relating to marriage, has concluded that while the reforms of the early years of the revolution created new possibilities as well as new problems for women, "after the Terror . . . revolutionary leaders would redouble their emphasis on the conjugal family and gender complementarity as a source of cohesion and gradually abandon their earlier commitment to liberty within the family". In this, moreover, they were responding to a groundswell of popular petitioning in which "Thermidorian disorder" was repeatedly cast "as the subversion of sexual and gender roles within the family". A particularly instructive demonstration of this change was the peculiar case of Suzanne Lepeletier. In January 1793, following the assassination of her father, the eleven-year-old Lepeletier was enthusiastically adopted by the National Assembly: a move in line with the reforms curtailing paternal authority in families and indicative, as Jennifer Heuer has put it, of a sense "that familial bonds were malleable". But when in 1797 Lepeletier's uncles called upon the French legislature to exercise its "paternal" authority and prevent the adolescent from what they saw as a hasty marriage, they were rebuffed by the legislators' rather different emphasis on stabilized, gender-differentiated family bonds, one in which the transfer of paternity to the nation was no longer imaginable.[10]

Again, then, indications of a "gender panic" are intertwined with a broader transformation of identity and self. Recently, however, Carla Hesse has raised a persuasive challenge to the familiar narrative of the contraction of possibilities for women and their increasing domestic confinement after a brief window of opportunities early in the revolutionary decade. It is true, Hesse says, that "the period of the Thermidorian reaction (1795–1800) [was] a critical moment in the elaboration, and more important, the popularization of biological theories of gender difference" – Cabanis again emerges as an important trendsetter – "as a means of justifying the continued civil and political subordination of women". But, insisting that "science, philosophy, and even law and politics are not mirrors of the social world", she offers female literary production as a measure of the public visibility of women that in fact demonstrates an expansion, not retraction, of their actual opportunities in social practice under the Directory. For our purposes here, however, it is especially revealing to follow Hesse's analysis of the strategies used by these women writers to resist "the new chauvinism of the Thermidorian period". Their basic strategy was "to insist upon the fictive nature of their elective public identities". This move was made possible, in turn, by stressing "the gap between inner feeling and its external representation", a gap "in which the self can be seen to exist independently from, and in a determining relation to, its external representations". Even as these women resisted the Thermidorian essentializing of gender categories, they did so by reaffirming the essential nature of the autonomous, anterior, determining inner self.[11]

A pattern, then, begins to emerge: a pattern of interconnected shifts in post-Thermidorian France with unmistakable affinities to the picture sketched in this book for late-eighteenth-century England. These affinities are especially conspicuous in art historian Ewa Lajer-Burcharth's evocatively titled *Necklines*. The seemingly modest goal of her inquiry is to explain the "decisive rupture" in the art of Jacques-Louis David – the most notable and influential artist of the French Revolution – brought about by his imprisonment after Thermidor, a delicate situation from which he was lucky to emerge with his own neckline unharmed. But rather than read the transformations in David's paintings simply as reflections of the changes in his personal fortunes and status, Lajer-Burcharth casts the widest possible net in order to situate them in "the cultural moment" of Thermidor and the Directory. This moment, in her view, "constitute[d] a key phase in revolutionary culture" because "it [was] precisely then that the relations between body and self emerged *as a problem.* . . . The Directoire inaugurated, then, a distinctively modern way of imagining the relation between subjectivity and embodiment" – or, we might say, a distinctive making of a modern self.[12]

Beginning with David's portraiture, therefore, Lajer-Burcharth detects a shift from exemplary or generic representations in the early 1790s – Robespierre's portrait with "a generic quality of likenesses churned out en masse", say, or the preparatory sketch for the *Tennis Court Oath* in which "the deputies appear as clones" – to more personalized portraits by 1794, manifesting a realism that "offered too much of a specific, contingent self on view". She then discusses a series of broader transformations that took place at precisely the same time: "a wider, shared post-Thermidorian belief in physiognomy", which also engendered a flurry of reprints of physiognomical works; new trends in fashions under the Directory, which heralded "the function of fashion as the expression of individual self", including transparent female clothing that presented "a visible, eloquent cultural contour of the self"; "a broader trend discernible in post-Thermidorian culture" that mapped the new republican self onto "the notion of the physical body"; a new emphasis on the married couple in their natural, clearly gender-differentiated roles; and, finally going back to portraiture, a new investment in "the requirement of resemblance, which made the image of the actual body, with all its peculiarities and imperfections, a higher priority than the notion of the *beau idéal*" – what she calls "the post-Thermidorian surge of likeness". By drawing all these themes together, Lajer-Burcharth transforms David's micro-shift into nothing short of "a psychocultural history of the self emerging at the end of the revolutionary decade".[13]

The parallels between this catalog of cultural transformations in post-Thermidorian France and the transformations that this book has identified in post-American-war England are striking. Furthermore, this similarity extends also to the dynamics of the transitional moment itself, a moment (to quote Lajer-Burcharth once more) "of a collective uncertainty about identity [that was] brought about by the Revolution and specifically by the Terror". In our discussion of the American war, the most conspicuous symptom of that earlier moment of collective uncertainty about identity was the unusually intensive recourse to the language of disguise and masquerade. To be sure, this preoccupation also played a key role, no less intense or meaningful, during the French revolutionary decade. James Johnson has chronicled this revolutionary obsession in detail: while masks and masquerades had been banned already in 1790, "the mask remained a central figure in revolutionary discourse so long after its physical banishment". "As the Terror approached," Johnson continues, "masks multiplied in the revolutionary imagination, and their peril took on the highest urgency, as orators warned the nation of their ubiquity."[14] How familiar.

Now it is undoubtedly true that masks and unmasking assumed a distinctive charge in the French Revolution, as Lynn Hunt has influentially shown, because of the fundamental revolutionary investment in their opposite: absolute (and impossible) transparency. But Johnson takes the explanation for their continuing – and mounting – importance further, into the very nature of the Terror. "Far from being incidental to the worldview of the Terror," he writes, "the figure of unmasking came to occupy a principal role in distinguishing friends from enemies." Johnson continues: "The rhetoric of the mask offers great insight into the Janus-faced Republic of the Terror, which, at each moment its citizens seemed on the brink of unanimity, had a disturbing tendency to generate traitors from within." The figure of unmasking embodied the problem of discerning friend from foe: the problem (here Johnson paraphrases a speech of Saint-Just's on 13 March 1794) that "the battle was no longer between revolutionary and aristocrat, us versus them. It was revolutionary against dangerous lookalike, *us versus us.*" It is hard to imagine getting much closer than this to the English problem of identity in the American revolutionary war. And again, when we encounter the Directory in Lajer-Burcharth's story as a period of heightened, almost caricaturized, gender experimentation, but also of increased anxiety and urgency in the inscription of gender difference leading to a more rigid gender regime, we cannot fail to see the parallel to the double movement we have identified in England during the American war. In both cases, this double movement, of intensified interest followed by intensified discomfort, appears to have been directly linked to the specter of unreliable identities that was so central in ushering in a transformation from one identity regime to another.[15]

These last words remind us how very preliminary the present observations must remain. Suppose I am not too far off the mark in speculating – piggybacking as I have done on the experts in the field – that Thermidor was the crux of a shift that in many ways resembled that which some fifteen years earlier had heralded a new regime of identity in England. But a shift from what? The assumption implicit in the previous pages is that France and England shared a broadly similar *ancien régime* of identity. There is certainly some evidence to support such a claim. Many of the manifestations of the *ancien régime* of identity in England had their parallels in France: as starting points one can take Paul Friedland's work on the French *ancien-régime* understandings of theatrical acting as embodiment, or Julia Douthwaite's on the assumptions of malleability underlying the reception of feral children, or Kathleen Nicholson's on generic representation in eighteenth-century French portraiture, or Daniel Roche's on the confusion of sartorial identity signs as a consequence of eighteenth-century French "urban corruption", or Jan Goldstein's on the radical transition between the philosophies of Condillac and Cousin. Or we can summon Joan Dejean's suggestive reflections on the French cultural crisis of the late seventeenth century, "an essential turning point" in the history of subjectivity that suddenly allowed contemporaries "to fracture identity and to question the very possibility of a neatly defined identity": a turning point that seems readily interpretable as the birth pangs, the beginning point, of a French *ancien régime* of identity.[16]

But while we can speculate about many features common to the *ancien régimes* of identity in France and England,[17] we must remember that there were also considerable differences – just think of the difficulties presented by Rousseau, whose unclassifiable writings alternate between "proto-Romanticism" and radical statements of malleability. It is possible, moreover, that in the French case there were more gradual foreshadowings of the transformation from one identity regime to the other before the revolution (Friedland's theatrical evidence from about 1750 onward, for instance, weighs in favor of such a conclusion). After all, unlike the Kuhnian paradigms that I have invoked before, there was nothing inherent in a shift from one identity regime to another that required it to take place in as abrupt a fashion as it did in the English case. So until we actually have a more detailed comparison of the French history of identity and self to the English one, the familiar caveat "*mutatis mutandis*" may actually hide more than is conventionally implied by its pro-forma scholarly invocation.

The comparative perspective on these two moments of transformation on the two sides of the Channel, however, also leads us to a rather different conclusion, one that focuses on convergence rather than variance. For French historians, it is probably easy to accept a scenario in which the Terror, a traumatic episode following on the heels of several years in which so many traditional frameworks had been swept away, produced a profound shift, and moreover that this shift was likely to involve a more restrictive outlook and an attempt to fix and re-anchor some basics of cultural understanding. Surely they are right; just as they are right to see the sudden explosion of the language of unmasking and disguise during the revolutionary years as inherent in the revolutionary process and especially, again, in the Terror. But if we raise our viewpoint to look at this mid-1790s French transformation not only from within the unfolding of the French revolutionary decade, but also in conjunction with the parallel English transformation of a decade or two earlier, an additional logic begins to emerge. For, if indeed these two turning points were similar in so many ways, sharing significant features across a disparity of time and space, then neither one can be fully explained by the unique nature of its own particular context, be it the French Revolution or the American war.

Not would it do, it seems to me, to conclude that it is simply the combination of revolutionary turmoil and warfare that explains both moments of transformation. In order to see this point, let us cast one final comparative glance at the American case. In the early American republic, we recall, the revolutionary war did *not* lead to similar consequences. On the contrary, we have seen suggestive indications that in America the same events led to a period of intense interest in the possibilities and hazards of identity-flexing. Subsequently, moreover, what one revolutionary moment had opened for the Americans, the next may well have closed down. That is to say, there are signs – Jay Fliegelman and Rosemary Zagarri are among those who have spotted them – that from the mid-1790s, following the echoes of French revolutionary events, a change of direction began to take place in the young American republic, from a preoccupation with malleability to a shrinking of the space in which it could be imagined. (For one such sign, consider how Deborah Sampson, the American heroine who had been celebrated during and immediately after the revolutionary war for her exploits as a successful cross-dressed soldier, was described in the late 1790s – by her most important, and sympathetic, biographer – as committing an unnatural act; and one, furthermore, that was equivalent to another unnatural social act: civil war.)[18] Was it the case, then, that by the early nineteenth century America too had completed its transformation to a new identity regime, but that its own route was quite different from either the French or the English, with its own particular to-and-fro dynamic over two decades of nation-building during the Age of Revolutions?

I would like to leave the reader with this parting thought. If indeed a similar pattern of transformation was shared across these different national and temporal boundaries, then the French revolutionary Terror and the American revolutionary war (twice over, experienced differently as it was on both sides of the Atlantic) may best be seen as triggers – triggers that took different shapes within their own specific historical contexts – for a broader underlying historical process. This process was in its most basic outline common to England, France, and the United States (and perhaps also to other Western national contexts), even if it unfolded differently and at different times in each of them: in all, it spelled a distinctive formative stage in the making of the modern self. In comparing how the *ancien régime* of identity gave way to a new regime in different places, therefore, "*mutatis mutandis*" should not be allowed to hide *too* much.

Notes

Preface: Before the Self

1. George Berkeley, *Philosophical Commentaries* (1707–8), eds. G. H. Thomas and A. A. Luce, New York, 1989, p. 94 (entry 713). Gilbert K. Chesterton, *Orthodoxy* (1908), London, 1957, p. 51. Michel Foucault quoted in D. Macey, *The Lives of Michel Foucault*, London, 1993, p. xv.
2. Marcel Mauss's seminal 1938 lecture "A Category of the Human Mind: The Notion of Person; the Notion of Self" is translated and reproduced in M. Carrithers et al. (eds.), *The Category of the Person: Anthropology, Philosophy, History*, Cambridge, 1985, pp. 1–25 (quoted, p. 20). C. Geertz, "'From the Native's Point of View': On the Nature of Anthropological Understanding", in R. A. Shweder and R. A. LeVine (eds.), *Cultural Theory: Essays on Mind, Self, and Emotion*, Cambridge, 1984, p. 126.
3. For an excellent recent discussion see C. W. Bynum, *Metamorphosis and Identity*, New York, 2001, esp. pp. 163–6. (Bynum adds a third possibility, identity in the sense of the "spatiotemporal continuity" of personal identity: as will be seen in chapter 4, this third meaning is of a rather different nature, and in my view not analytically comparable to – or distinct from – the other two, but rather implicated in both.) Etymologically, as one learns from a quick visit to the Oxford English Dictionary, "identity" is a peculiarly formed combination of the Latin *idem*, expressing the notion of "sameness", together with *unitas*, signifying the notion of "oneness".
4. See C. Jones and D. Wahrman, "Introduction: An Age of Cultural Revolutions?", in C. Jones and D. Wahrman (eds.), *The Age of Cultural Revolutions: Britain and France, 1750–1820*, Berkeley, 2002, pp. 1–16, together with the other contributions to this volume.
5. C. Taylor, *Sources of the Self: The Making of the Modern Identity*, Cambridge, 1989 (quoted, p. 177).
6. Ibid., pp. 204, 285, 307. Indeed, the one chapter in Taylor's book that stands out as uncharacteristically schematic and quick is chapter 17, "The Culture of Modernity", which tries to touch on some of those broader cultural aspects that the book as a whole largely refrains from addressing.

7. I have borrowed this term from L. Daston, "Historical Epistemology", in J. Chandler et al. (eds.), *Questions of Evidence: Proof, Practice, and Persuasion across the Disciplines*, Chicago, 1994, esp. pp. 282–3. Daston defines "historical epistemology" as "the history of the categories that structure our thought, pattern our arguments and proofs, and certify our standards of explanation": though her definition is more narrowly geared to the practice of history of science and scientific thinking, it seems to me readily adaptable to broader use.

Snapshot

1. Joseph Warder, *The True Amazons; or, The Monarchy of Bees. Being a New Discovery and Improvement of Those Wonderful Creatures* (1693, 1713), 3rd edn. with additions, London, 1716, pp. ix, 42–4, 66.
2. [John Thorley,] *The Female Monarchy; or, The Natural History of Bees* (1744), London, 1745, pp. 3–4, 6. Joshua Dinsdale, *The Modern Art of Breeding Bees, a Poem*, London, 1740, pp. 18–19. The use of "Amazons" to denote bees was common enough to make it into contemporary reference works, including the first edition of the *Encyclopaedia Britannica*, London, 1771, or Henry Croker et al., *The Complete Dictionary of Arts and Sciences*, London, 1766.
3. These observations are based on a survey of thirty-six texts about bees between the late seventeenth and the early nineteenth centuries; this encompasses the lion's share of full-text discussions of bees and a considerable proportion of shorter discussions during that period. And note J. Merrick's pioneering "Royal Bees: The Gender Politics of the Beehive in Early Modern Europe", *Studies in Eighteenth-Century Culture* 18 (1988), pp. 7–37.
4. *A Short History of Bees. In Two Parts*, London, 1800, pp. 80–5, 90–1. John Hunter, "Observations on Bees", *Philosophical Transactions, of the Royal Society of London*, 1792, pt. 1, pp. 132, 139 (reproduced in *Historical Magazine* 4 [1792], p. 266). Arthur Murphy, *The Bees. A Poem*, London, 1799, pp. 20–3, 37. Robert Huish, *A Treatise on the Nature, Economy, and Practical Management of Bees*, London, 1815, pp. 17, 40. John Evans, *The Bees: A Poem*, Shrewsbury, 1806, bk. I, pp. 17, 29, 31 (and note how his description of the queen is unable to maintain its stability, slipping [p. 32] into a simile of a *male* warrior, and a "manly" one at that). Robert Sydserff, *Sydserff's Treatise on Bees*, Salisbury, 1792. Cf. also *Historical Magazine* 2 (1790), p. 287, adapted from William Smellie's *The Philosophy of Natural History*, 2 vols., Edinburgh, 1790, i, pp. 344–9; J[acob] Isaac, *The General Apiarian*, Exeter, 1799, pp. 39–41; George Strutt, *The Practical Apiarian; or, A Treatise on the Improved Management of Bees*, Clare, 1825, p. 92; and *The Monarchy of the Bees; A Poem*, London, 1821, which creatively turned the worker bees themselves into benevolent males (in contrast to the idle, aristocratic drones) extending their manly protection to their graceful feminine queen as well as to their tender offspring.
5. Hunter, "Observations on Bees", p. 140. The same concession for inadequate common usage was repeated in almost the same words by John Keys, *The Practical Bee-Master*, London, 1780, pp. 1–4; and James Bonner, *The Bee-Master's Companion, and Assistant*, Berwick, 1789, pp. 23–4.
6. For a more detailed demonstration of this pattern see my "On Queen Bees and Being Queens: A Late-Eighteenth-Century Cultural Revolution?", in C. Jones and D. Wahrman (eds.), *The Age of Cultural Revolutions: Britain and France, 1750–1820*, Berkeley, 2002, pp. 251–80.

Chapter 1

1. A. Wettan Kleinbaum, *The War against the Amazons*, New York, 1983.
2. The following observations are based on a survey of over two hundred texts (of widely varying genres and provenances) between the seventeenth and the early nineteenth centuries that made explicit references to literal or figurative Amazons. See also J. Pearson, *The Prostituted Muse: Images of Women and Women Dramatists 1642–1737*, New York, 1988, pp. 87–92. G. J. Barker-Benfield, *The Culture of Sensibility: Sex and Society in Eighteenth-Century Britain*, Chicago, 1992, pp. 351–9 (the Amazon was the "Augustan code-word for female pride and gender crossing"). G. Kates, *Monsieur d'Eon Is a Woman: A Tale of Political Intrigue and Sexual Masquerade*, New York, 1995, pp. 157–8, 203–4. B. Orr, *Empire on the English Stage 1660–1714*, Cambridge, 2001, chap. 6.
3. Ephraim Chambers, *Cyclopædia, or, An Universal Dictionary of Arts and Sciences*, 2 vols., London, 1728, i, p. 74. James Eyre Weeks, *The Amazon; or, Female Courage Vindicated*, Dublin, 1745, p. 3. *Female Rights Vindicated. . . . By a Lady*, London, 1758, preface (in this case the Amazonian allusion was enlisted in support of a proto-feminist argument; but this was the exception, not the rule). *A Lady's Address to the Ladies, to Maintain their Antient Liberty*, n.p., n.d. [c. 1760s]. *The Vicar of Wakefield* (1766), in the *Collected Works of Oliver Goldsmith*, ed. A. Friedman, 5 vols., Oxford, 1966, iv, p. 83. Rev. [Joseph] Spence, *Polymetis* (1747), 2nd edn., corrected, London, 1755, pp. 59, 140–1. Anthony Ashley Cooper, Earl of Shaftesbury, *Characteristicks of Men, Manners, Opinions, Times*, 4th edn., 3 vols., [London], 1727, iii, pp. 362–3, 386.
4. Examples include: Philip Frowde, *The Fall of Saguntum. A Tragedy*, London, 1727, pp. 14–15. *The Famous History of Hector, Prince of Troy*, London, [c. 1750–70], e.g. p. 22. John Grose, *A Voyage to the East Indies*, London, 1766, p. 234. Even the mildly mocking letter by "Thalestris" (the Amazon queen) in Frances Brooke's *Old Maid* 15 (21 Feb. 1756), pp. 87–8 is critical of contemporary *men*, but is not at all anti-Amazonian.
5. C. Barash, *English Women's Poetry, 1649–1714: Politics, Community, and Linguistic Authority*, Oxford, 1996, chap. 5. R. O. Bucholz, "'Nothing but Ceremony': Queen Anne and the Limitations of Royal Ritual", *Journal of British Studies* 30 (July 1991), pp. 295–6 (I am grateful to Seth Denbo for this reference). T. Bowers, *The Politics of Motherhood: British Writing and Culture, 1680–1760*, Cambridge, 1996, pp. 77–9. R. Weil, *Political Passions: Gender, the Family and Political Argument in England 1680–1714*, Manchester, 2000, chap. 7.
6. Robert Maxwell, *The Practical Bee-Master*, Edinburgh, 1747, pp. 10–11.
7. *Historical Magazine* 4 (1792), pp. 40–2. Edward Green, *Observations on the Drama* (1803), 2nd edn., London, 1814, pp. 51–2. Theophilus Swift, *The Temple of Folly, in Four Cantos*, London, 1787, pp. 50, 69–72. John Bennett, *Letters to a Young Lady*, 2 vols., Warrington, 1789, i, p. 241. Ann Yearsley, *The Rural Lyre; A Volume of Poems*, London, 1796, frontispiece, and pp. 30–1, 113–14 (and see D. Landry, "Figures of the Feminine: An Amazonian Revolution in Feminist Literary History?", in M. Brown [ed.], *The Uses of Literary History*, Durham [N.C.], 1995, pp. 107–28). *Poems, on Several Occasions, by Mary Collier*, Winchester, 1762, p. iv.
8. The phrase "the Amazonian band" was Richard Polwhele's, in his anonymous *The Unsex'd Females: A Poem*, London, 1798, p. 6n. (Cf. also William Duff, *Letters, on*

the Intellectual and Moral Character of Women, Aberdeen, 1807, p. 100n.) William Godwin, *Memoirs of Mary Wollstonecraft*, ed. J. Middleton Murry, London, 1928, pp. 55–6, 130–1. Idem, *Fleetwood, or, The New Man of Feeling* (1805), in *Collected Novels and Memoirs of William Godwin*, 8 vols., vol. v, ed. P. Clemit, London, 1992, p. 55.

9. James Barry, in his *Letter to the Dilettanti Society* (1798), as cited and discussed in J. Barrell, *The Birth of Pandora and the Division of Knowledge*, Basingstoke, 1992, pp. 163–8. Spence, *Polymetis*, p. 59. Cf. also the allegorical representation of Minerva as a benevolent Amazon in J. B., *Henry and Minerva. A Poem*, London, 1729, p. 10.

10. *Encyclopaedia Britannica*, 1st edn., 3 vols., London, 1771, i, p. 131; 2nd edn., 10 vols., Edinburgh, 1778–83, i, pp. 279–80; and 3rd edn., 18 vols., Edinburgh, 1797, i, pp. 518–23 (but the first volume was actually completed in Oct. 1788). Walpole's negative uses of "Amazon" include: Walpole to Lady Ossory, 15 Dec. 1786, in *The Yale Edition of Horace Walpole's Correspondence*, ed. W. S. Lewis, 48 vols., London, 1937–83, xxxiii, London, 1965, p. 548; to Lady Ossory, 24 Feb. 1789, xxxiv, London, 1965, p. 41; to Hannah More, 4 Nov. 1789, xxxi, London, 1961, p. 332; and to Mary Berry, 20 Dec. 1790, xi, New Haven, 1944, pp. 169–70. The earlier, appreciative references are from Walpole's letters to Lady Mary Coke, 30 June 1762, xxxi, p. 25 (where he also characterized her, again with approbation, as a "militant dame"), and c. Nov. 1771, p. 160 (and see also 11 Dec. 1771, p. 164). [Laetitia Matilda Hawkins], *Letters on the Female Mind, its Powers and Pursuits*, London, 1793, p. 117.

11. Maria Edgeworth, *Belinda*, 3 vols., London, 1801, i, pp. 60, 66–7, 87, 93–101, 113–22; ii, pp. 23, 76, 139. *Belinda* is often compared with Fanny Burney's *Evelina* of 1778, to which it bears an unmistakable resemblance, and Mrs. Freke with *Evelina*'s Amazonian Mrs. Selwyn. Nonetheless, it is instructive to note the differences between them. Like those of Mrs. Freke, Mrs. Selwyn's understanding and manners "may be called masculine". But unlike her later counterpart, Mrs. Selwyn is not rendered thoroughly reprehensible by this transgression – indeed, she is "very kind and attentive" – but, at most, rather "awkward". And when her "Amazon"-like, "unnatural" person is ridiculed, this turns out to be the opinion of silly fops, in whose exposure as such by Mrs. Selwyn the reader cannot but collude with delight. It is not a properly gender-differentiated character, but rather one that combines the best of both sexes, which is the ideal put forward by this earlier novel: such is what Evelina wishes for Mrs. Selwyn, or what distinguishes the paragon Lord Orville (with his "manly" countenance combined with "so feminine [a] delicacy"). Frances Burney, *Evelina; or, The History of a Young Lady's Entrance into the World* (1768), eds. E. A. Bloom and L. D. Bloom, Oxford, 1982, pp. 261, 268–9, 281, 361–2.

12. Interestingly, in Edgeworth's first draft, Lady Delacour actually dies of breast cancer – her Amazonian state proves to be so innate as to be incurable. See M. Butler, *Maria Edgeworth: A Literary Biography*, Oxford, 1972, p. 282.

13. Yearsley, "To Mira, on the Care of her Infant" (16 Sept. 1795), in *The Rural Lyre*, pp. 115–16. For examples of unfeminine women who contract breast disease, see Robert Jephson, *Conspiracy, A Tragedy*, Dublin, 1796, epilogue. G. H. Wilson, *The Eccentric Mirror: Reflecting a Faithful and Interesting Delineation of Male and Female Characters*, 3 vols., London, 1806–7, ii, no. 12, p. 21; iii, no. 30, p. 30. By contrast, in the early-modern period it was the maternal breast-feeding itself that was often

associated with breast disfigurement and disease: cf. G. K. Paster, *The Body Embarrassed: Drama and the Disciplines of Shame in Early Modern England*, Ithaca (N.Y.), 1993, pp. 203–4.

14. [John Bennett], *Strictures on Female Education*, London, [1787], pp. 123–4. William Smellie, *The Philosophy of Natural History*, 2 vols., Edinburgh, 1790, ii, p. 442. Richard Brinsley Sheridan, *Pizarro: A Tragedy*, London, 1799, epilogue (written by William Lamb). William Buchan, *Advice to Mothers, on the Subject of their Own Health*, London, 1803, pp. 99, 215–17. Cf., among many similar examples, the essay "On the Differences between the Sexes" in the July 1803 issue of *The Lady's Magazine*, as quoted in B. C. Gelpi, *Shelley's Goddess: Maternity, Language, Subjectivity*, New York, 1992, p. 60.

15. F. A. Nussbaum, *Torrid Zones: Maternity, Sexuality, and Empire in Eighteenth-Century English Narratives*, Baltimore, 1995 (quoted, p. 24). Idem, *The Autobiographical Subject: Gender and Ideology in Eighteenth-Century England*, Baltimore, 1989, pp. 205–12. S. Staves, "Douglas's Mother", *Brandeis Essays in Literature*, ed. J. Hazel Smith, Waltham (Mass.), 1983, pp. 51–67. R. Perry, "Colonizing the Breast: Sexuality and Maternity in Eighteenth-Century England", *Journal of the History of Sexuality* 2 (1991), pp. 204–34.

16. Buchan, *Advice to Mothers*, pp. 1–3 and esp. p. 103. Compare his much less stringent (though no less committed) advocacy of breast-feeding in his *Domestic Medicine*, 2nd edn., London, 1772, pp. 664–5. And note Ludmilla Jordanova's suggestion (in "Interrogating the Concept of Reproduction in the Eighteenth Century", in F. D. Ginsburg and R. Rapp [eds.], *Conceiving the New World Order: The Global Politics of Reproduction*, Berkeley, 1995, pp. 369–86) of a late-eighteenth-century shift in the understanding of reproduction to a "Xerox model of reproduction", resulting in an increasingly essentialized – even racialized – conception of the role of the mother.

17. In this context we should also note the late-eighteenth-century surge in the preoccupation with infanticide, the ultimate unnatural maternal act: cf. J. McDonagh, "Infanticide and the Boundaries of Culture from Hume to Arnold", in S. C. Greenfield and C. Barash (eds.), *Inventing Maternity: Politics, Science and Literature, 1650–1865*, Lexington (Ky.), 1999, pp. 215–37 (and note the chronology of this volume, e.g. "Introduction", pp. 24–5, which generally indicates a late-eighteenth-century shift following a surge in interest throughout the century). F. Breithaupt, "Anonymous Forces of History: The Case of Infanticide in the Sturm und Drang", *New German Critique* 79 (2000), pp. 157–76.

18. George Wright, *The Gentleman's Miscellany* (London, 1795), Exeter (N.H.), 1797, p. 106. Wetenhall Wilkes, *A Letter of Genteel and Moral Advice to a Young Lady* (1740), 8th edn., 1766, reproduced in V. Jones (ed.), *Women in the Eighteenth Century: Constructions of Femininity*, London, 1990, pp. 33–4. John Gregory, *A Father's Legacy to his Daughters*, 2nd edn., London, 1774, pp. 104–5. Cf. also [Dorothy Kilner], *Dialogues and Letters on Morality, Oeconomy, and Politeness*, London, [1780?], p. 154, about a woman who might "happen to marry", and who might "chance to have children" – but then again, who might not.

19. Sarah Scott, *A Description of Millenium* [sic] *Hall* (1762), ed. J. Spencer, New York, 1986 (quoted, pp. 37, 115); and contrast Buchan's utter denial in 1803 of the possibility of transferring motherhood: *Advice to Mothers*, p. 362. Other mid-century women's defenses of the choice not to marry include: [Frances Brooke], *The Old Maid*, 21 (3 April 1756), pp. 123–6. *Poems, on Several Occasions, by Mary Collier*,

p. 41. *Tunbridge Epistles, from Lady Margaret to the Countess of B***, London, 1767, p. 34. Also note John Sharp's coronation sermon for Queen Anne, which described the queen as the mother of her people, but "avoid[ed] biological essentialism: kings could nurse as well as queens, and nursing was not confined to biological parents" (Weil, *Political Passions*, p. 167); and Toni Bowers's account (in *The Politics of Motherhood*) of how the literature propagating the maternal ideal from the early 1700s continually, and often against its grain, reaffirmed the possibilities of alternative maternal configurations in which "biological" motherhood could be supplanted or replaced by other, more nurturing relationships.

20. It is thus perhaps not a coincidence that after four successful editions, between 1762 and 1778, the fortunes of *Millenium Hall* were reversed, and it went out of print from the late eighteenth until the twentieth century. For the turn of the tide against the possibilities opened up in *Millenium Hall*, see *Letters of Momus, from Margate*, London, 1778, p. 28.

21. *A Satyr upon Old Maids*, London, 1713, p. 12. [William Hayley], *A Philosophical, Historical, and Moral Essay on Old Maids. By a Friend to the Sisterhood*, 3 vols., London, 1785, i, pp. 12–14. Cf. S. S. Lanser, "Singular Politics: The Rise of the British Nation and the Production of the Old Maid", in J. M. Bennett and A. M. Froide (eds.), *Singlewomen in the European Past, 1250–1800*, Philadelphia, 1999, pp. 297–323. Amy Froide's forthcoming *Never Married: Singlewomen in Early Modern England* confirms the emergence at the beginning of this period of unmarried women as an acknowledged group offering an alternative model of feminine life, though she puts more emphasis on the increase of derision as a consequence. (I am grateful to her for sharing her work-in-progress with me.)

22. William Shakespeare, *Henry VI, Pt. III*, II. i.123; I. iv.114. Theophilus Cibber, *King Henry VI. A Tragedy. . . . Altered from Shakespear, in the Year 1720*, 2nd edn., London, 1724, pp. 7, 16–17, 55, 57. This vindication of the Amazonian Margaret of Anjou was common elsewhere in the eighteenth century: cf. her characterization in 1723 as "In Feature Woman; but, in Heart, a Man:/ Fair as the Queen of Beauty; Bold, as *Mars*" ([Ambrose] Philips, *Humphrey, Duke of Gloucester. A Tragedy*, London, 1723, p. 5); or David Garrick's epilogue to [Thomas Francklin], *The Earl of Warwick. A Tragedy*, London, 1766, which presented her as a courageous, defiant female warrior; or William Whitehead's rather curious *The Goat's Beard. A Fable*, London, 1777 (see below, n. 27).

23. [Richard Valpy], *The Roses; or, King Henry the Sixth; An Historical Tragedy. . . . Compiled Principally from Shakespeare*, Reading, [1795]; cf. pp. 4, 7. The point is not that these lines were necessarily new – they could be based on Shakespeare's own text (cf. *Henry VI, Pt. III*, II.ii.56–7) – but that their selective use accentuated one meaning while obliterating the rest. Crucially, Valpy omitted a key moment in the earlier retellings of the story in which Margaret proves her resolve by announcing her intention to divorce King Henry for his weakness. In the 1795 script, by contrast, she sticks by her husband as a loyal, supportive wife.

24. For another example of the earlier eighteenth-century commensurability of Amazon and mother see Peter Anthony Motteux, *Thomyris, Queen of Scythia. An Opera*, London, 1707, which centers on a flattering image of an Amazon-cum-mother. Its prologue, moreover, once again makes explicit the analogy between this double-sided heroine and Queen Anne, whose public image joined enthusiastic-but-unsuccessful motherhood with successful-though-unenthusiastic Amazonianism. For Anne as both Amazon and mother see Barash, *English Women's Poetry*.

25. Similarly cf. the emphatically maternal Margaret of Anjou played by Mrs. Siddons in the 1780s: *The Beauties of Mrs. Siddons . . . in Letters from a Lady of Distinction*, London, 1786, pp. 31–3.

26. Matilda Betham, *A Biographical Dictionary of the Celebrated Women of Every Age and Country*, London, 1804, pp. 546–7. *Biographium Fæmineum. The Female Worthies; or, Memoirs of the Most Illustrious Ladies*, 2 vols., London, 1766, ii, p. 89.

27. Ibid., ii, p. 90 (and note Elizabeth's Tilbury speech in i, pp. 187–8). Bolingbroke's *The Idea of a Patriot King* (1749), as cited in Weil, *Political Passions*, p. 171. [George] Lillo, *Marina: A Play*, London, 1738, epilogue. *The Adulteress*, London, 1773, pp. 1–2. Cf. also Richard Blackmore, *Eliza: An Epick Poem*, London, 1705 ("She did a Leader *Amazon* appear,/ Forgetfull of her Sex, and ignorant of Fear"). [John Brown], *An Estimate of the Manners and Principles of the Times*, [vol. i], London, 1757, p. 35. James Fordyce, *Addresses to Young Men*, 2 vols., London, 1777, ii, pp. 142–5 (see further below, p. 81). And see Whitehead's *The Goat's Beard* of 1777, which listed both Margaret and Elizabeth among a series of valiant "Amazons" who had exhibited "the most heroic spirit" (pp. 17–18). See further examples, including Hume's *History of England*, in J. Lynch, *The Age of Elizabeth in the Age of Johnson*, Cambridge, 2003, p. 70.

28. John St. John, *Mary Queen of Scots. A Tragedy*, London, 1790, prologue (written by William Fawkener). Mary Hays, *Female Biography; or, Memoirs of Illustrious and Celebrated Women, of All Ages and Countries*, 6 vols., London, 1803, iv, pp. 210–11, 290 (emphasis added). Hays was labeled "Wollstonecraftian" by Richard Polwhele. Matilda Betham, whom we saw rewriting the biography of Queen Margaret, likewise also carefully paraphrased the Tilbury speech in a similar gender-proper manner (*Biographical Dictionary*, p. 343). See also the critique of Elizabeth's lack of femininity in the prologue to "Taste and Learning", 1790 (Larpent Mss., Huntington Library, no. 877); and Elizabeth Inchbald's association of her "masculine" mind with "almost unheard-of despondency" in Henry Jones, *The Earl of Essex. . . . With Remarks by Mrs. Inchbald*, London, [1807], p. 6. Although it would take us too far afield, it can also be shown that another key historical warrior queen, Boadicea, experienced an eighteenth-century transformation parallel to those of Margaret and Elizabeth.

29. [Margaret] Holford, *Margaret of Anjou: A Poem*, London, 1816, dedication and p. 58.

30. C. Hall, *White, Male and Middle Class: Explorations in Feminism and History*, New York, 1992, p. 9. L. Davidoff and C. Hall, *Family Fortunes: Men and Women of the English Middle Class, 1780–1850*, London, 1987, pp. 169, 171.

31. Hannah More, *Strictures on the Modern System of Female Education* (1799), in *The Works of Hannah More*, 7 vols., New York, 1835, vi, p. 41. Polwhele, *The Unsex'd Females*, p. 35n. Polwhele, who was a long-time acquaintance and admirer of More, in fact lifted More's anti-Amazonian passage almost word for word for one of his own: [Richard Polwhele], *The Family Picture, or Domestic Education*, London, 1808, p. 47 n. DD.

32. [Hannah More], *Percy, a Tragedy*, London, 1778, prologue. On *Percy*'s staging and success see M. A. Hopkins, *Hannah More and her Circle*, New York, 1947, chap. 9. Prologues and epilogues were frequently contributed by writers other than the playwright.

33. [Hannah More], *Cœlebs in Search of a Wife* (1808), quoted from the reprinted 1880

edn., introduced by M. Waldron, Bristol, 1995, pp. 157, 160–1. William Roberts, *Memoirs of the Life and Correspondence of Mrs. Hannah More*, 4 vols., 3rd edn., London, 1835, i, pp. 122–3. William Heard's poem, "Impromptu, On Seeing Miss More's Tragedy of Percy", as quoted in Hopkins, *Hannah More*, p. 81; and cf. [Ralph Schomberg], *Fashion. A Poem*, London, 1778, p. iii. More's success was not the only evidence during these years that "the fair had won the cause": other creative women were regularly praised for their putative manly achievements, notably Angelica Kauffman (cf. *Pursuit after Happiness: A Poem*, London, 1777, pp. 41–2) and Catherine Macaulay (cf. *The Monthly Review* 58 [1778], p. 111).

34. For a discussion of these trends in fashion, see below, chapter 2. *Town and Country Magazine* 10 (1778), p. 544; *Morning Post*, 16 Oct. 1778; both quoted in *The Dramatic Works of Richard Brinsley Sheridan*, 2 vols., ed. C. Price, Oxford, 1973, ii, pp. 713, 739. Epilogue to [Charles] Shadwel[l], *The Humors of the Army* (1713), in P. Danchin (ed.), *The Prologues and Epilogues of the Eighteenth Century*, 8 vols., pt. I, 1701–20, i, Nancy, 1990, p. 525. *Gentleman's Magazine* 51 (Feb. 1781), p. 57. The definitive study of the genre of female warrior ballads is D. Dugaw, *Warrior Women and Popular Balladry, 1650–1850*, Cambridge, 1989. And cf. Henry Brooke, *The Female Officer* (1740), in his *Collection of Pieces*, 4 vols., London, 1778, iv, pp. [i–iii], 260–300.

35. *The Life and Adventures of Mrs. Christian Davies, the British Amazon, Commonly Call'd Mother Ross*, London, 1741. J. Wilson, *The British Heroine; or, An Abridgement of the Life and Adventures of Mrs. Christian Davies*, London, 1742 (quoted, p. ii). *A Brief Account of the Life and Family of Miss Jenny Cameron*, London, [1746?] (quoted, p. 70).

36. *The Female Soldier; or, The Surprising Life and Adventures of Hannah Snell. . . . Who Took upon herself the Name of James Gray*, London, 1750 (quoted, pp. 17, 19, 169). Cf. also the confident Mary Slade (i.e. Mary Lacy), *The History of the Female Shipwright* (1773), as excerpted in S. Starke, *Female Tars: Women Aboard Ship in the Age of Sail*, London, 1996, chap. 4.

37. *The Life and Surprising Adventures of Mary Anne Talbot, in the Name of John Taylor. . . . Related by Herself*, London, [1809]; originally printed in *Kirby's Wonderful and Scientific Museum; or, Magazine of Remarkable Characters*, 6 vols., vol. ii, London, 1804 (quoted, pp. 166, 169). Suzanne Starke has plausibly suggested (in her *Female Tars*, pp. 107–10) that Talbot's story was a fabrication, which of course makes the choice of the way it was presented all the more telling. Cf. the story of another early-eighteenth-century woman who had dressed in man's clothes, as it was recounted in *Kirby's Wonderful and Scientific Museum* (vol. iv, London, 1813, pp. 311–12): her tribulations began "when the chapel fell on her, [and] she received a hurt which prevented her ever afterwards from wearing stays" – the ultimate beyond-one's-control rationale for wearing men's clothes if ever there was one.

38. *Filial Indiscretions; or, The Female Chevalier*, 3 vols., Wakefield, 1799, i, pp. 83–5; ii, pp. 154–5; iii, pp. 24, 105–6, 180. [Robert Dodsley], *A Select Collection of Old Plays*, 12 vols., 2nd edn., London, 1780, vi, p. [1]. The frontispieces to *The Country Lasses* are noted and reproduced in C. D. Williams, "Women Behaving Well: Early Modern Images of Female Courage", in C. Mounsey (ed.), *Presenting Gender: Changing Sex in Early-Modern Culture*, Lewisburg, 2001, pp. 62–65.

39. Dugaw, *Warrior Women and Popular Balladry*, pp. 56–62, 69, 71–2 (emphases added). Cf. the demure behavior of "The Female Captain", prodding the men to

do *their* manly duty, in *Roundelay; or, The New Siren, a Collection of Choice Songs*, a new edn., London, [c. 1790?], p. 14. Also note the early-nineteenth-century anti-quarian who ended a description of a 1725 public contest against a courageous female duellist, a "shameful" event in his view, with the assurance that "the deli-cately attenuated nerves of my female reader must perforce be shocked" by this bizarre bygone practice: James Peller Malcolm, *Anecdotes of the Manners and Customs of London during the Eighteenth Century*, London, 1808, p. 339. By con-trast, early-eighteenth-century observers had received this female duellist and others like her favorably, indeed enthusiastically: see Dugaw, *Warrior Women*, pp. 125–6; and my "Gender in Translation: How the English Wrote their Juvenal, 1644–1815", *Representations* 65 (1999), p. 15.

40. Cecilia Lucy Brightwell, *Memorials of the Life of Amelia Opie*, Norwich, 1854, pp. 18–21 (supposedly from an autobiographical fragment).

41. The story of Frances Scanagatti in Wilson, *Eccentric Mirror*, ii, no. 12, p. 21. Inter-estingly, one 1790s text where the successfully passing female warrior could still be found alive and kicking was a highly pornographic compilation (*Hilaria. The Festive Board*, London, 1798; cf. "The Toy", pp. 94–7), which retained the basic generic formulation of her story but in graphically sexualized form. It is a suggestive possibility that gender-flexing cultural forms like the female warrior perhaps did not completely disappear, but went underground, into the very different cultural waters of illicit homosocial humor. For another example see the *Bon Ton Magazine; or, Microscope of Fashion and Folly* of 1791, which between semi-pornographic material interspersed several references to Amazons and similar figures that had disappeared by this point from mainstream discourse (cf. pp. 15, 137).

42. [William Cooke], *Memoirs of Charles Macklin, Comedian*, London, 1804, p. 126 (emphasis in the original).

43. Charles and Mary Lamb, *Tales from Shakespeare* (1807), London, 1987, pp. 67–8, 122, 234 (Shakespeare's *Cymbeline*, III.vi.1–2, by contrast, has Imogen say "I see a man's life is a tedious one,/ I have tir'd myself" – thus relating her fatigue to a *male's* condition, not a *female's*). William Hawkins, *Cymbeline. A Tragedy, Altered from Shakespeare*, London, 1759, pp. 18–19, epilogue. For two other turn-of-the-century expressions of incredulity at Imogen's masculine role see the editorial remarks in *Cymbeline; A Historical Play. . . . With Remarks by Mrs. Inch-bald*, London, [1808], p. 4; and [A. Eccles], *Cymbeline, A Tragedy. By William Shakespeare. . . . To Which Are Added, Remarks by the Editor*, Dublin, 1793, p. 193n.

44. Colley Cibber, *She Wou'd and She Wou'd Not. . . . With Remarks by Mrs. Inchbald*, London, 1807, pp. [3]–4. George Farquhar, *The Recruiting Officer. . . . With Remarks by Mrs. Inchbald*, London, 1807, p. 4. More, *Strictures on the Modern System of Female Education*, p. 13 (emphasis added): a few sentences later in these opening paragraphs, More also denounced the "warlike Thalestris", queen of the Amazons. The most defiant exception of which I am aware to the late-century shying away from such gender twists was Mary Robinson's 1798 novel *Walsingham; or, The Pupil of Nature*, the plot of which revolved around the late discovery of the main protagonist's identity as a woman in disguise. Critics, however, duly pounced on this device as one that – to quote but one commentator – "cannot, we think, be either instructive or amusing" (*Critical Review* 22 [April 1798], p. 557). Cf. J. Shaffer, "Cross-Dressing and the Nature of Gender in Mary Robinson's *Walsing-ham*", in Mounsey (ed.), *Presenting Gender*, pp. 136–67.

45. *The Female Warrior; or, Surprising Life and Adventures of Hannah Snell*, London, [1801]. *Eccentric Biography; or, Memoirs of Remarkable Female Characters*, London, 1803, p. 316 (emphasis added); and cf. the depiction of La Maupin, p. 245. Wilson, *Eccentric Mirror*, vol. i, 1806, no. 8, p. 25; and note the "paroxysm of phrenzy and despair" that Wilson attributed to Mary Anne Talbot, in vol. iv, 1807, no. 38, p. 4. In contrast to Wilson's account, Snell's 1750 biography had concluded with the affirmation that "she is resolutely bent to be Lord and Master of herself, and never more to entertain the least Thoughts of having a Husband to Rule and Govern her": *The Female Soldier*, p. 178. Note also the wholesale feminization of the life of Jenny Cameron, the Jacobite female officer, in James Caulfield, *Portraits, Memoirs, and Characters, of Remarkable Persons*, 4 vols., London, 1820, iii, pp. 83ff.

46. "French Amazonian maid" also carried the more distant reference to Joan of Arc, another female warrior whose fortunes during this period accord well with the narrative of change offered here (though her case must await fuller unfolding elsewhere). First, her eighteenth-century celebration as an exemplary heroine (which replaced her previous, early-modern representation as a witch): e.g. [Sir Richard Blackmore], *The Lay Monastery*, London, 1714, pp. 73–5. Then, from the 1780s onward, her rewriting (even when relying on the same historical sources) in ways that played down her "masculine" prowess and cross-dressing. Instead, later writers highlighted Joan's femininity – variously focusing on her modesty, her pregnancy, and her sexual amours. See for example *Airs, Duets, and Chorusses, in a New Grand Historical Ballet of Action, Called Joan of Arc*, London, 1798 (and cf. Gillian Russell, *Theatres of War: Performance, Politics and Society, 1793–1815*, Oxford, 1995, pp. 52–3): while the production managed to avoid ever mentioning that Joan of Arc was, indeed, a female warrior, the historical pageant that immediately followed celebrated English women who had excelled as helpmeets in the heroic male endeavors against the French. The message was unmistakable: whereas women still had a patriotic role to play, military heroism had by now been safely marked as the exclusive domain of men. Note also Mary Ann Hanway, *Christabelle, the Maid of Rouen. A Novel, Founded on Facts*, 4 vols., London, 1814: a story of a modern Joan, properly demure and feminine, who only puts on men's clothes as a last resort under "unfortunate" circumstances beyond her control, and takes them off again with an audible sigh of relief just as soon as she can.

47. Walley Chamberlain Oulton, *The History of the Theatres of London*, 2 vols., London, 1796, i, p. 72. T[homas] Morell to J. West, 18 July 1771, "On Monsr D'Eon", British Library, Add. Mss. 34728, West Papers, vol. II, f. 204. Sheridan, *The Camp* (1778), in *The Dramatic Works of Richard Brinsley Sheridan*, ii, p. 744. Note also the allusion to D'Eon in John Philip Kemble's unpublished "The Female Officer" (Larpent Mss., Huntington Library, no. 441), p. 50. The immediate issue that brought the D'Eon enigma into the public eye at this moment was a trial in July 1777, presided over by Chief Justice Mansfield, in which a bettor's claim that D'Eon was in fact a woman remained essentially uncontested.

48. *The Public Ledger*, 16 June 1772; in D'Eon mss., Brotherton Library, Leeds University, second volume of newspaper cuttings, f. 310.

49. D'Eon's moorings in contemporary culture are explored in Gary Kates's authoritative biography, *Monsieur d'Eon Is a Woman*. At times, however, Kates also suggests that such gender play as D'Eon's must have constituted a disruptive crisis, rather than an affirmation of expectations different from our own. Literary critic Marjorie Garber has offered the most extreme argument based on a universalized

and ahistorical notion of "crisis": for Garber, D'Eon is but one example of the "consistent and effective functio[n] of the transvestite in culture" – *any* culture – namely, that of "an index . . . of many different kinds of 'category crisis'", which is therefore *always* accompanied by deep anxiety. If nothing else, it is hoped that the present argument demonstrates the necessity of considering differing historical and cultural contexts, differences that such a sweeping, essentializing generalization ignores at its peril. M. Garber, *Vested Interests: Cross-Dressing and Cultural Anxiety*, New York, 1993, pp. 16, 259–66.

50. Cf. the emphasis on D'Eon's inescapable feminine modesty even in the midst of combat in *The Morning Post, and Daily Advertiser*, 12 April 1787, in D'Eon Mss., second volume of newspaper cuttings, f. 146.

51. Mary Wollstonecraft, *Vindication of the Rights of Woman* (1792), ed. M. Kramnick, Harmondsworth, 1985, p. 172. Cf. also Anne Frances Randall (i.e. Mrs. Robinson), *A Letter to the Women of England, on the Injustice of Mental Subordination*, London, 1799, p. 71n: again, while holding "this extraordinary female" as a model for "talents, enterprize, and resolution", this appreciation too was predicated on the insistent assertion of D'Eon's unambiguous womanhood.

52. L[eman] T[homas] Rede, *Anecdotes and Biography, Including Many Modern Characters* (1799), 2nd edn., London, 1799, p. 107. *Eccentric Biography*, pp. 118ff. [James Perry], *An Epistle from Mademoiselle d'Eon to the Right Honorable L—d M—d . . . on his Determination in Regard to her Sex*, London, 1778, p. 9.

53. *Kirby's Wonderful and Scientific Museum*, vol. iv, 1813, pp. 1, 21–3. For another posthumous strategy for explaining away D'Eon's story, by inventing a sexually defective body to match his gender-defective behavior and thus "render[ing] the doubts that had so long subsisted respecting his sex the less extraordinary", see Alexander Chalmers, *The General Biographical Dictionary*, 32 vols., London (1812–17), xi, 1813, p. 480.

54. *The Morning Herald and Daily Advertiser*, 26 Nov. 1785, quoted in L. Friedli, "'Passing Women' – A Study of Gender Boundaries in the Eighteenth Century", in G. S. Rousseau and R. Porter (eds.), *Sexual Underworlds of the Enlightenment*, Manchester, 1987, p. 245. Cf. Wilson, *The Eccentric Mirror*, vol. iv, 1807, no. 34, p. 1: "The successes of Mademoiselle d'Eon were, however, but temporary, and she is a striking example of the disappointment which sooner or later awaits those who step out of the path which nature designed them to pursue."

55. Hannah More to her sister, May 1789, in Roberts, *Memoirs of the Life and Correspondence of Mrs. Hannah More*, ii, p. 156. For a similar aversion to the model set by D'Eon, coming from a rather different political quarter, see Thomas Amyot to William Pattisson, 18 Feb. 1795, in P. J. Corfield and C. Evans (eds.), *Youth and Revolution in the 1790s: Letters of William Pattisson, Thomas Amyot and Henry Crabb Robinson*, Stroud, 1996, p. 120.

56. At the same time, however, we should also not take the present-day image of Wollstonecraft at face value. Her feminist writings displayed less often a desire to eradicate sexual difference than a concern that lines of sexual differentiation had become *too* permeable; which may put her, in truth, in the same cultural boat with her nemesis Hannah More. Cf. C. L. Johnson, *Equivocal Beings: Politics, Gender, and Sentimentality in the 1790s*, Chicago, 1995, chap. 1.

57. For a more detailed analysis see my "*Percy*'s Prologue: From Gender Play to Gender Panic in Eighteenth-Century England", *Past and Present* 159 (May 1998), section

V. Epilogues to [Susanna] Centlivre, *The Wonder! A Woman Keeps a Secret*, London, 1714; [William] Havard, *King Charles I. A Tragedy*, London, 1779 (recycling a prologue spoken on the king's birthday in 1731, and reprinted in Pierre Danchin [ed.], *The Prologues and Epilogues of the Eighteenth Century*, pt. II, 1721–37, iv, Nancy, 1992, p. 452); and Colman, *The Spleen. The Fate of Corsica; or, The Female Politician. A Comedy. Written by a Lady of Quality*, London, 1732, p. 24. Among many others, cf. Gilbert Stuart, *A View of Society in Europe, in its Progress from Rudeness to Refinement*, Edinburgh, 1778, p. 16; [Frances Sheridan], *The Discovery. A Comedy*, London, 1763, prologue; and Garrick's own epilogue to [John Burgoyne], *The Maid of the Oaks: A New Dramatic Entertainment*, London, 1779, invoking "nature's rights" in support of women's political claims. For female debating societies (predictably compared by one 1780 observer to "the Immortal Amazons of Yore") see "On Hearing the Debates of the FEMALE PARLIAMENT, at the CASINO, May 19, 1780" (handwritten), in Daniel Lysons's "Collectanea" (newspaper cuttings, in the British Library), iii, p. 116v; D. Andrew (ed.), *London Debating Societies, 1776–1799*, London, 1994, p. 89 (from *Morning Post*, 11 April 1780) and *passim*; idem, "Popular Culture and Public Debate: London 1780", *Historical Journal* 39 (1996), and "Women and Debating Societies", unpublished (I am grateful to Donna Andrew for the opportunity to read this essay); M. Thale, "Women in London Debating Societies in 1780", *Gender and History* 7 (1995), pp. 5–24.

58. For the Duchess of Devonshire as part of an eighteenth-century tradition of female electioneering, and the unprecedentedness of the furore she provoked, see E. Chalus, "'That Epidemical Madness': Women and Electoral Politics in the Late Eighteenth Century", in H. Barker and E. Chalus (eds.), *Gender in Eighteenth-Century England*, London, 1997, pp. 151–78; J. S. Lewis, "1784 and All That: Aristocratic Women and Electoral Politics", in A. Vickery (ed.), *Women, Privilege, and Power: British Politics, 1750 to the Present*, Stanford, 2001, pp. 89–122; and I. H. Tague, *Women of Quality: Accepting and Contesting Ideals of Femininity in England, 1690–1760*, Woodbridge, 2002, chap. 7 (and note p. 195 for the appreciative 1733 evaluation of a female politician who "must act the man where talking is necessary").

59. *A Lecture on Heads, Written by George Alexander Stevens, with Additions by Mr. Pilon, as Delivered by Mr. Charles Lee Lewes. . . . A New Genuine Edition Corrected*, London, 1785; quotations from Dublin edn., 1788, pp. 8–9, 22–5. Cf. George Alexander Stevens, *The Celebrated Lecture on Heads*, Dublin, 1765 (originally published in 1764 as *Lecture on Heads*), e.g. p. 15. For another vitriolic tirade against political women, this one post-revolutionary, which invoked a female debating society together with the Amazon and the female warrior only completely to reverse their former connotations and overtones, turning them into menacing indicators of the worst crimes imaginable, see *The Female Revolutionary Plutarch*, 3 vols., London, 1806, i, pp. 254–61.

60. Charles Lee Lewes, *Comic Sketches*, London, 1804, pp. 35–8, 67–70, 132–3 (performed for the first time in the East Indies in 1788); and see below, p. 49.

61. Andrew, *London Debating Societies*, pp. 80, 98; and note the device of men cross-dressing to enter female debating societies in two unpublished 1780 plays, "The Belles Association or Female Orators" and "The Female Orators; Or Ladies Debating Society" (Larpent Mss., Huntington Library, nos. 521, 528). *Lady's Magazine* 6 (March 1775), p. 147.

62. *The Disguise, a Dramatic Novel*, Dublin, 1771, in which the boy's real identity

successfully eludes his friends, his lover, and even his own father; subsequently criticized in Stephen Jones, *Biographia Dramatica*, 3 vols., London, 1812, ii, p. 165 (in the previous edition of 1782 *The Disguise* was mentioned but without the critique). *An Apology for Bachelors!! Marriage and Celibacy Considered*, London, 1808, three-page manuscript dated 1812 in the British Library copy. The classical story of Publius Pulcher Clodius, as retold in William Gifford, *The Satires of Decimus Junius Juvenalis, Translated into English Verse . . . with Notes and Illustrations*, 2nd edn., corrected and enlarged, London, 1806, p. 191n; for more detail see my "Gender in Translation", pp. 22–3. *Naval Chronicle* 21 (1809) (address spoken on board the *Albion* in Feb. 1808), as cited in Russell, *Theatres of War*, p. 147. Smellie, *The Philosophy of Natural History*, ii, p. 443 (cf. Sarah Howard, *Thoughts on Female Education: With Advice to Young Ladies*, London, 1783, p. 80n: "I think there is no composition in nature more disagreeable [than an effeminate man], unless it be a masculine woman; they are equally monsters"). Edgeworth, *Belinda*, i, pp. 165, 258 (and contrast the complete success of a mid-eighteenth-century fictional man passing as a woman in *The Male-Coquette; or, Seventeen Hundred Fifty-Seven*, London, 1757, pp. 41–2).

63. It was after reading *The Man of Feeling* that Hannah More wrote to Mackenzie seeking "some compensation for the tears you have made me shed so frequently and so plentifully": this was the "score" that Mackenzie saw as settled after *Percy* (quoted in H. W. Thompson, *A Scottish Man of Feeling: Some Account of Henry Mackenzie*, Oxford, 1931, p. 170). Mackenzie to More, 12 Oct. 1778, in Roberts, *Memoirs of the Life and Correspondence of Mrs. Hannah More*, i, p. 143. Samuel Richardson, *Clarissa*, 7 vols., London, 1748, vii, p. 4. Laurence Sterne, *A Sentimental Journey through France and Italy* (1768), Harmondsworth, 1967, pp. 44–5. J. Todd, *Sensibility: An Introduction*, London, 1986, p. 110. See also J. Mullan, *Sentiment and Sensibility: The Language of Feeling in the Eighteenth Century*, Oxford, 1988. T. Castle, *The Female Thermometer: Eighteenth-Century Culture and the Invention of the Uncanny*, New York, 1995, pp. 33–5.

64. Henry Mackenzie, *The Man of Feeling* (1771), intro. K. C. Slagle, New York, 1958, pp. 37, 46. Todd, *Sensibility*, pp. 100–1, and on *Sir Charles Grandison*, p. 116. For Pope see J. H. Hagstrum, *Sex and Sensibility: Ideal and Erotic Love from Milton to Mozart*, Chicago, 1980, p. 141 (quoting his *Epistle to a Lady*).

65. Garrick's epilogue to John Home, *Alfred. A Tragedy*, London, 1778. To be sure, like the gender-bending figures we have seen before, the man of feeling also got his fair share of derision. Mrs. Fanny Greville, for one, exclaimed in reaction to Sterne's *Sentimental Journey*: "when a man chooses to walk about the world with a cambrick handkerchief always in his hand, [so] that he may always be ready to weep . . . he only turns me sick." But, as the "animated encomiums" of Elizabeth Burney that had provoked Mrs. Greville's outburst attest, criticism was not necessarily the dominant tone. (Frances Burney D'Arblay, *Memoirs of Doctor Burney* [1832]; quoted in *Sterne: The Critical Heritage*, ed. A. B. Howes, London, 1974, p. 204.)

66. *The Novels of Sterne, Goldsmith, Dr Johnson, Mackenzie, Horace Walpole and Clara Reeve* (Novelist's Library, vol. v), London, 1823, p. lv, "Prefatory Memoir to Mackenzie"; and for Scott's writing of this memoir in autumn 1822, see Thompson, *A Scottish Man of Feeling*, p. 317. Indeed, some modern critics have followed Scott: most recently Barker-Benfield, who weaves the most circuitous arguments to try to prove Harley's real, albeit hidden manhood (*Culture of Sensibility*, pp. 144–7, 218, 250, 262, and, perhaps most casuistically, p. 442 n. 157). Cf. J. K. Sheriff, *The*

Good-Natured Man: The Evolution of a Moral Ideal, 1660–1800, Alabama, 1982, esp. pp. 76, 82. Stuart's letter of 1826 is quoted (*inter alia*) in G. A. Barker, *Henry Mackenzie*, Boston, 1975, pp. 50–1; and for the *Man of Feeling*'s going out of fashion by the 1790s see Mullan, *Sentiment and Sensibility*, p. 123. [Hannah More], *Sacred Dramas . . . to Which Is Added, Sensibility, a Poem*, London, 1782, p. 285.

67. Johnson, *Equivocal Beings*, e.g. pp. 12, 14; and on Wollstonecraft, chap. 1. Hugh Blair, *Sermons*, 5 vols., Edinburgh, 1777–94, iii (1790), pp. 36–7.

68. Godwin, *Fleetwood; or, The New Man of Feeling*, p. 231 (Godwin's "new man of feeling" was a misanthrope, not a lachrymose sentimentalist). Cf. [Elizabeth] Inchbald, *I'll Tell You What. A Comedy*, London, 1786, p. 77. [Thomas Day], *The History of Sandford and Merton*, 3 vols., London, 1783–9, i (1783), p. 161; iii (1789), p. 297.

69. [Peter Shaw], *Man. A Paper for Ennobling the Species*, London, 1755, no. 43, p. 4. Those who discovered in the 1790s that weeping in public had gone out of fashion included Major Cartwright, whose shedding of a tear in reaction to the revolutionary events in France was perceived as eccentric and whimsical (see Todd, *Sensibility*, p. 130); and Charles James Fox, when he burst into tears in the House of Commons in May 1791 in response to a particularly vehement anti-revolutionary performance by Burke, to which the public reaction was one of shocked astonishment.

It may be noted that the examples for the constriction of the imagined space open to *men* to flex gender categories appear to be of slightly later dates than those we have seen for women. The evidence here is not sufficient to be conclusive, but such a lag would be readily understandable in a society in which limitations were placed more easily on women than on men.

70. Particularly interesting examples include: T. Castle, *Masquerade and Civilization: The Carnivalesque in Eighteenth-Century English Culture and Fiction*, Stanford, 1986. Dugaw, *Warrior Women and Popular Balladry*. K. Straub, *Sexual Suspects: Eighteenth-Century Players and Sexual Ideology*, Princeton, 1992. Nussbaum, *Torrid Zones*. J. Campbell, *Natural Masks: Gender and Identity in Fielding's Plays and Novels*, Stanford, 1995. M. McKeon, "Historicizing Patriarchy: The Emergence of Gender Difference in England, 1660–1760", *Eighteenth-Century Studies* 28 (1995), pp. 295–322. See also Kates, *Monsieur d'Eon Is a Woman*.

71. T. Laqueur, *Making Sex: Body and Gender from the Greeks to Freud*, Cambridge (Mass.), 1990 (quoted, p. 8). Although Laqueur interweaves this change with his well-known main story, which has attracted much critical attention, of the shift from a one- to a two-body sexual mode, these two suggested developments are in fact distinct from each other – the former, moreover, logically preceding the latter. For seventeenth-century enunciations of the precedence of gender over sex see, for example, John Fletcher's *Love's Cure* (1621), which has "custom" operating "so cunningly on nature" that the heroine "forgot my sex, and knew not/ Whether my body female were, or male" (quoted in S. Shepherd, *Amazons and Warrior Women: Varieties of Feminism in Seventeenth-Century Drama*, Brighton, 1981, p. 90); or the bee-text that explained that "the common Honey-Bees are the Females, but not by virtue of any copulation or conception, but because they supply the place and Office of the Female" (Moses Rusden, *A Further Discovery of Bees*, London, 1679, p. 42).

72. Laqueur, *Making Sex*, p. 128. McKeon, "Historicizing Patriarchy", p. 301. On the fluidity of Renaissance understandings of sexual identity see also S. Greenblatt,

"Fiction and Friction", in his *Shakespearean Negotiations: The Circulation of Social Energy in Renaissance England*, Berkeley, 1988, pp. 66–93. S. Orgel, *Impersonations: The Performance of Gender in Shakespeare's England*, Cambridge, 1996.

73. *Characterism; or, The Modern Age Display'd; Being an Attempt to Expose the Pretended Virtues of Both Sexes*, London, [1750], p. 166 (emphasis in the original). Henry Fielding, *Love in Several Masques* (1728), in *The Complete Works of Henry Fielding, Esq: Plays and Poems*, 16 vols., ed. W. E. Henley, London, 1903, i, p. 21. *The Female Rebels*, Edinburgh and London, 1747, p. 37. *The Works of Christina Queen of Sweden . . . to Which Is Prefixed an Account of her Life, Character and Writings, by the Translator*, London, 1753, p. xiii (extracted from a contemporary memoir). *Biographium Fæmineum*, i, p. 207. Richardson, *Clarissa*, ii, p. 193. Ned Ward, *Adam and Eve*, London, 1714, p. 210. *The Country Coquet; or, Miss in her Breeches. . . . By a Young Lady*, London, 1755, p. 6 (emphasis added).

74. See for instance below, p. 57. Also my "Gender in Translation".

75. *The Poems of John Cleveland*, ed. B. Morris and E. Withington, Oxford, 1967, p. 10. The eighteenth-century decline of the hermaphrodite is noted, *inter alia*, in E. Donoghue, *Passions between Women: British Lesbian Culture 1688–1801*, London, 1993, chap. 1; Campbell, *Natural Masks*, p. 125; R. Gilbert, "Seeing and Knowing: Science, Pornography and Early Modern Hermaphrodites", in E. Fudge et al. (eds.), *At the Borders of the Human: Beasts, Bodies and Natural Philosophy in the Early Modern Period*, Basingstoke, 1999, pp. 150–70; and idem, *Early Modern Hermaphrodites*, Basingstoke, 2002, esp. pp. 158–60.

76. J. Butler, *Gender Trouble: Feminism and the Subversion of Identity*, New York, 1990, p. 6.

Chapter 2

1. This phrase is not my own. I heard it many years ago used in a somewhat different context, but I have been unable since to locate its origins.

2. See, *inter alia*, P. Rogers, "The Breeches Part", in P.-G. Boucé (ed.), *Sexuality in Eighteenth-Century Britain*, Manchester, 1982, pp. 244–58; J. Pearson, *The Prostituted Muse: Images of Women and Women Dramatists 1642–1737*, New York, 1988, chap. 6; and K. Straub, *Sexual Suspects: Eighteenth-Century Players and Sexual Ideology*, Princeton, 1992.

3. Contemporary comments quoted in J. Dunbar, *Peg Woffington and her World*, London, 1968, pp. 39, 60 (emphasis added), 83 (Sir Charles Hanbury Williams, "To Mrs. Woffington", 1740); and in Robert Hitchcock, *An Historical View of the Irish Stage*, 2 vols., Dublin, 1788, i, pp. 107 ("On Miss Woffington's Playing Sir Harry Wildair", 1739), 219 (verses written by "a gentleman of some eminence in the literary world", 1751). *The Life of Mr. James Quin, Comedian*, London, 1766, pp. 67–8. Charles Macklin, *King Henry the VII; or, The Popish Impostor. A Tragedy*, London, 1746, epilogue (which, to oblige the audience, Woffington delivered in breeches, although in the play she had a female role). [John Hill], *The Actor; or, A Treatise on the Art of Playing*, London, 1755, p. 105. See also E. K. Sheldon, *Thomas Sheridan of Smock Alley*, Princeton, 1967, p. 187; S. Richards, *The Rise of the English Actress*, New York, 1993, p. 28; and B. H. Friedman-Romell, "Breaking the Code: Toward a Reception Theory of Theatrical Cross-Dressing in Eighteenth-Century London", *Theatre Journal* 47 (1995), pp. 459–79. Cross-dressing was also consid-

ered appropriate for respectable private theatricals: for a provincial example that elicited praise, see the Diary of John Marsh, Huntington Library Mss., v, pp. 97–100, entries for Oct. 1776.

4. Tate Wilkinson, *The Wandering Patentee; or, A History of the Yorkshire Theatres*, 4 vols., York, 1795, iii, pp. 14–15 (many years before, however, Wilkinson himself – then a personal friend of Woffington's – had been famous for his own cross-gender mimicry, especially in transforming his voice and face into those of a good-looking actress: see C. B. Hogan, *The London Stage 1776–1800: A Critical Introduction*, Carbondale (Ill.), 1968, pp. lxxxvi–lxxxvii). [Charles] Dibdin, *A Complete History of the Stage*, 5 vols., v, London, [1800], p. 208. [William Cooke], *Memoirs of Charles Macklin*, London, 1804, p. 126 (and note his insistence on the impossibility of a successful breeches part as quoted above, p. 27). Charles Lee Lewes, *Comic Sketches*, London, 1804 (performed since 1788), pp. 132–3. George Farquhar, *The Constant Couple. . . . With Remarks by Mrs. Inchbald*, London, [1807], p. 5. James Boaden, *The Life of Mrs. Jordan*, 2 vols., 2nd edn., London, 1831, i, p. 34.

5. Mary Julia Young, *Memoirs of Mrs. Crouch*, 2 vols., London, 1806, i, pp. 114–17 (and note how the evaluation of this production is all about performers' innate physical characteristics in relation to their cross-sexed roles, taking for granted their inability to *assume* such roles). Prince Hoare, *Memoirs of Granville Sharp, Esq. Composed from his Own Manuscripts*, London, 1820, p. 206. Colman Junior is quoted in W. Macqueen-Pope, *Haymarket: Theatre of Perfection*, London, 1948, pp. 154–5. See also Roger Fiske, *English Theatre Music in the Eighteenth Century*, London, 1973, p. 406. Colman Senior's cross-sexed *Beggar's Opera* – which had a successful run of seventeen performances over five weeks in 1781 (and was preceded by a similar production in the Yorkshire theater) – chimed with an upsurge of interest in gender-crossing practices at that particular moment, the last flourish of the *ancien régime* of gender intertwined with its imminent demise: see below, pp. 251–3.

6. Dibdin, *A Complete History of the Stage*, v, pp. 362–5. Young, *Memoirs of Mrs. Crouch*, p. 93. Charles Lamb's prologue to Samuel Taylor Coleridge, *Remorse: A Tragedy* (1797), in *The Complete Poetical Works of Samuel Taylor Coleridge*, Oxford, 1912, p. 817. James Peller Malcolm, *Anecdotes of the Manners and Customs of London from the Roman Invasion*, 2nd edn., 3 vols., London, 1811, iii, p. 82.

7. The following paragraphs are based on the information in *The London Stage 1660–1800*, 11 vols., Carbondale (Ill.), 1960–8.

8. Other examples include Sheridan's *The Duenna*, staged in Covent Garden with a breeches-part lead thirty-seven times between the 1779–80 and the 1789–90 seasons, before becoming the unchallenged preserve of male actors throughout the 1790s, with a single exception in 1800. Or, for a man in a female role, take John Burgoyne's *The Lord of the Manor*: launched in Drury Lane in 1780 with Richard Suett as a female lead, it had two good seasons with twenty-eight performances, and was then intermittently and briefly revived six times during the next seven seasons, before being abandoned by the management in 1789.

Breeches parts were to make a partial return later in the nineteenth century, though with very different, and arguably safer, meanings. As Sandra Richards (*The Rise of the English Actress*, p. 93) writes: "By Queen Victoria's time breeches roles had become a test of female modesty, used by actresses to point up their essential womanly natures" – a very different goal indeed.

9. *European Magazine* 13 (May 1788), p. 372 (and see S. S. Kenny's introduction to *The Works of George Farquhar*, 2 vols., Oxford, 1988, i, p. 126). *Historical Magazine* 1 (March 1789), p. 214 (emphasis added). Wilkinson, *The Wandering Patentee*, iii, p. 80 (and cf. Boaden, *The Life of Mrs. Jordan*, i, p. 46). *The Female Duellist: An After Piece*, London, 1793, p. 42. Miles Peter Andrews, *Better Late Than Never: A Comedy*, London, 1790, epilogue. Cf. also the criticisms voiced by Fanny Burney (1788), as quoted in C. Tomalin, *Mrs Jordan's Profession*, London, 1994, p. 81; and by Leigh Hunt in his *Critical Essays on the Performers in the London Theatres*, London, 1807, p. 168. And see J. I. Marsden, "Modesty Unshackled: Dorothy Jordan and the Dangers of Cross-Dressing", *Studies in Eighteenth-Century Culture* 22 (1992), pp. 21–35.

10. Frederick Reynolds, *Cheap Living: A Comedy*, 2nd edn., London, 1797, prologue (written by John Taylor). The only relatively successful breeches part of Mrs. Jordan's in the 1790s was Little Pickle, a mischievous schoolboy (and one with an unmanly name to boot) in the farce *The Spoil'd Child*. Compare the example of the celebrated Sarah Siddons, who had been praised in 1775 for having "a very good breeches figure", but later refused the customary breeches in roles that required them as part of the plot, opting for a costume that she deemed more modest but that others saw as "ambiguous". At the same time, by contrast, whenever possible, Siddons accentuated natural maternity on stage (so natural indeed that it "hardly deserve[d] the name of acting"), and even transformed Lady Macbeth from the "unsexed" creature she had used to be into a delicate, hyper-feminine figure. *Morning Chronicle*, 3 May 1785 (and cf. Boaden, *The Life of Mrs. Jordan*, ii, p. 19), and the contemporary quotations reproduced in L. J. Rosenthal, "The Sublime, the Beautiful, 'The Siddons'", in J. Munns and P. Richards (eds.), *The Clothes That Wear Us: Essays on Dressing and Transgressing in Eighteenth-Century Culture*, Newark, 1999, pp. 56–79.

11. [Cooke], *Memoirs of Charles Macklin*, pp. 123–7; and see above, p. 27. Thomas Davies, *Memoirs of the Life of David Garrick*, 2 vols., new edn., London, 1780, i, pp. 306–7 (emphases added). "Knowing forgetfulness" is Friedman-Romell's phrase in "Breaking the Code", p. 471; and cf. Straub, *Sexual Suspects*, p. 127.

12. Charles Lee Lewes, *Memoirs of Charles Lee Lewes*, 4 vols., London, 1805, ii, p. 11. Cf. Matilda Betham, *A Biographical Dictionary of the Celebrated Women of Every Age and Country*, London, 1804, p. 849, which likewise alleged that Woffington's "chief merit consisted in the representation of females in high rank". Boaden, *The Life of Mrs. Jordan*, i, p. 127.

13. Russell, *Theatres of War*, pp. 144–5. J. Todd, *Gender, Art and Death*, New York, 1993, p. 12. Generally see M. E. Knapp, *Prologues and Epilogues of the Eighteenth Century*, New Haven, 1961.

14. In fact, the analysis extended to prologues/epilogues for some 1,200 plays, including (but not limited to) all those contained in H. W. Wells (ed.), *Three Centuries of Drama*, Readex Microprint, New York, 1967; the Chadwyck-Healey Verse-Drama CD-ROM; and P. Danchin (ed.), *The Prologues and Epilogues of the Eighteenth Century*, 8 vols., pt. I, 1701–20, and pt. II, 1721–37, Nancy, 1990–2. Only those published at the time, unambiguously datable and strictly comparable, were included in the final count. Dates of publication were adjusted to dates of first performance where known.

15. Those prologues/epilogues that could not be classified were omitted from the count. Moreover, to keep the potential biases of such a crude procedure in check, each category was enumerated within a range, from a minimum number of seemingly clear-cut cases to a maximum including likely but not iron-clad ones.

16. This wide range reflects the fact that it is more difficult to characterize conclusively an insistence on *lack* of flexibility, thus increasing the number of productions that could be classified with likelihood but not conclusively.

17. [John O'Keeffe], *The Young Quaker, a Comedy*, [Dublin], 1788. Richard Cumberland, *The Jew: A Comedy*, London, 1794, epilogue. [Fisher], *"Thou Shalt Not Steal": The School for Ingratitude: A Comedy*, 2nd edn., London [1798], prologue. Frederick Reynolds, *The Rage: A Comedy*, London, 1795, p. 79. Miles Peter Andrews, *Baron Kinkvervankotsdorsprakingatchdern*, London, 1781, epilogue. Sir James Bland Burges, *Riches; or, The Wife and Brother*, London, 1810, p. 102 (epilogue). See similarly, among many others, epilogues to [Richard Cumberland], *The Carmelite: A Tragedy*, London, 1784; Edward Topham, *The Fool, a Farce*, London, 1786 (concluding monologue); Thomas Holcroft, *The Deserted Daughter: A Comedy*, London, 1795; and [Elizabeth] Inchbald, *Wives as they Were, and Maids as they Are: A Comedy*, London, 1797, p. 96.

18. [Gabriel] Odingsells, *The Capricious Lovers: A Comedy*, London, 1726, epilogue, spoken by an actress "in Boy's Cloaths". *Love in All Shapes*, London, 1739, prologue. [John Durant Breval], *The Strolers*, London, 1727, epilogue (and see also the actress-spoken prologue, encouraging the wearing of the breeches). William Hawkins, *Cymbeline. A Tragedy, Altered from Shakespeare*, London, 1759, epilogue. [David] Mallet, *Eurydice. A Tragedy*, London, 1731, epilogue; cited here from *The Works of the Late Aaron Hill, Esq.*, 4 vols., London, 1753, iii, p. 334. (It may be noted that *Eurydice*, like *Percy*, was a tragedy: such lines crossed dramatic genres, and were not confined to comical or farcical contexts.)

19. Moreover, of these six exceptions, two were in fact productions in a school for young girls that repeated the same apologetic verses about females taking men's roles: unusual examples that made it rather anomalously into the sample by virtue of being published, whereas several other contemporary productions in boys' schools, asserting boys' right to play girls' roles, did not.

20. While most female garments were by this time produced by female mantua-makers, these riding habits continued to be made by male tailors. "Portia" in [Charles Allen], *The Polite Lady; or, A Course of Female Education. In a series of Letters, from a Mother to her Daughter*, London, 1760, p. 103. Prologue to George Colman's unpublished *The Suicide*, quoted in *Gentleman's Magazine* 48 (1778), p. 382. John Gay in *The Guardian* 149 (1713), and a letter of Lady Polwarth, 1777, quoted in A. Buck, *Dress in Eighteenth-Century England*, London, 1979, pp. 52–3. *The Female Spectator*, 1745, quoted in A. Ribeiro, *Dress and Morality*, New York, 1986, p. 181 n. 53. *Town and Country Magazine*, 1774, pp. 245–6, quoted in D. Dugaw, *Warrior Women and Popular Balladry, 1650–1850*, Cambridge, 1989, p. 134. *Gentleman's Magazine* 51 (Feb. 1781), p. 57. For discussion of these "masculine" female fashions, see also A. Ribeiro, *Dress in Eighteenth-Century Europe 1715–1789*, London, 1984, pp. 155–7; idem, *The Art of Dress: Fashion in England and France 1750 to 1820*, New Haven and London, 1995, pp. 67–8; E. Mackie, *Market à la Mode: Fashion, Commodity, and Gender in "The Tatler" and "The Spectator"*, Baltimore, 1997,

pp. 116–18; and C. Blackman, "Walking Amazons: The Development of the Riding Habit in England", *Costume* 35 (2001), pp. 47–58.

21. Eighteenth-century comments on the subversion of gender distinctions by such female fashions (comments that went back as far as Samuel Pepys) include, among many, *The Spectator* 435 (19 July 1712); Samuel Richardson's 1741 letter "Against a Young Lady's Affecting Manly Airs; and also Censuring the Modern Riding-Habits", as cited in Ribeiro, *Dress and Morality*, p. 114; [Henry Fielding and James Ralph], *The Champion: Containing a Series of Papers*, 2 vols., 2nd edn., London, 1743, i, p. 149.

22. Ribeiro, *Dress and Morality*, p. 111 (and cf. Blackman, "Walking Amazons", p. 49). We shall look more closely at moral denunciations below.

23. *The Champion*, i, p. 149. Osborne is quoted in I. H. Tague, *Women of Quality: Accepting and Contesting Ideals of Femininity in England, 1690–1760*, Woodbridge, 2002, p. 150. Lady Jane Grey's 1730 epilogue in benefit for Mrs. Sterling, in Danchin, *The Prologues and Epilogues of the Eighteenth Century*, pt. II, 1721–37, iii, p. 338. On Richardson see J. Mullan, *Sentiment and Sensibility: The Language of Feeling in the Eighteenth Century*, Oxford, 1988, p. 112; and on Italians cf. David Hume, "On Refinement in the Arts" (1752), in *Essays: Moral, Political and Literary*, ed. E. F. Miller, Indianapolis, 1987, p. 275. Cf. also the images of the fop ("half girl, half boy") in the epilogue to David Garrick's adaptation of Thomas Tomkis's *Albumazar*, new edn., London, 1773; Hugh Kelly, *The Romance of an Hour*, London, 1774, epilogue; and the *Town and Country Magazine*, March 1772, p. 242. On fops, as tropes and in social practice, see Susan Staves, "A Few Kind Words for the Fop", *Studies in English Literature* 22 (1982), pp. 413–28; P. Carter, "Men about Town: Representations of Foppery and Masculinity in Early Eighteenth-Century Urban Society", in H. Barker and E. Chalus (eds.), *Gender in Eighteenth-Century England*, London, 1997, pp. 31–57; and idem, *Men and the Emergence of Polite Society, Britain 1660–1800*, Harlow, 2001. Carter (following Staves) offers the important reminder that although individual fops might be associated with homosexuality (notably Pope's "Sporus", the bisexual Lord Hervey), as a *type* the eighteenth-century fop was not. For the opposite assertion, refuted by Carter in some detail, see R. Trumbach, "The Birth of the Queen: Sodomy and the Emergence of Gender Equality in Modern Culture, 1660–1750", in M. B. Duberman et al. (eds.), *Hidden from History: Reclaiming the Gay and Lesbian Past*, New York, 1989, esp. pp. 133–5.

24. *The Sentimental Magazine* 5 (1777), p. 281. *Lord Chesterfield's Witticisms*, London, [1775?], p. 67, in a cluster of jokes about Macaronies. [Robert Hitchcock], *The Macaroni. A Comedy*, York, 1773, p. 47. "The Macaroniad", in *The Vauxhall Affray; or, The Macaronies Defeated*, London, 1773, p. 59. Davies, *Memoirs of the Life of David Garrick*, ii, p. 223. On Macaroni satires "affixed in every print shop" see Ferdinand Twigem (pseud.), *The Macaroni. A Satire*, London, 1773, p. [1]. See also A. Ribeiro, "The Macaronies", *History Today* 28 (1978), pp. 463–8; V. Steele, "The Social and Political Significance of Macaroni Fashion", *Costume* 19 (1985), 94–109; and M. Ogborn, *Spaces of Modernity: London's Geographies, 1680–1780*, New York, 1988, chap. 4.

25. After all, three of the most successful actor-manager-playwrights of the period – Colley Cibber, David Garrick, and Samuel Foote – not only opted repeatedly for playing famous foppish roles on stage, but also wrote eminently successful fop roles

for themselves: see Staves, "A Few Kind Words for the Fop" – an essay to which this paragraph owes a great deal; and Carter as cited in n. 23.

26. Epilogue to *Macbeth* (1778), repr. in Samuel Whyte, *The Theatre: A Didactic Essay*, 2nd edn., Dublin, 1793, p. 68. Fielding in *The Champion*, ii, p. 80 (and cf. *Gentleman's Magazine* 5 [1735], p. 186, on "the Foppery and Effeminacy of the Coxcombs of both Sexes"). Note also the critique of the Macaronies that in the same breath also yearned for the manly gender-blurring "Matrons of Queen Bess" in *The Adulteress*, London, 1773, pp. 1–2; and the defense of women against charges of effeminacy in *The Real Character of the Age. In a Letter to the Rev. Dr. Brown*, London, 1757, pp. 2, 12–13. For more details see my "Gender in Translation: How the English Wrote their Juvenal, 1644–1815", *Representations* 65 (1999), pp. 19–20. And cf. M. Cohen, *Fashioning Masculinity: National Identity and Language in the Eighteenth Century*, London, 1996, pp. 5–6 and *passim*; P. Carter, "An 'Effeminate' or 'Efficient' Nation? Masculinity and Eighteenth-Century Social Documentary", *Textual Practice* 11 (1997), pp. 429–43.

27. James Peller Malcolm, *Anecdotes of the Manners and Customs of London during the Eighteenth Century*, London, 1808, p. 449 (and cf. Adam Sibbit, *A Dissertation, Moral and Political, on the Influence of Luxury and Refinement*, London, 1800, p. 130n). L. Colley, *Britons: Forging the Nation 1707–1837*, New Haven and London, 1992, pp. 184–8. Reynolds, *The Rage*, epilogue. Barbara Blunderbuss (pseud.), "Military Mania", from the *Morning Chronicle*, in *The Spirit of the Public Journals for 1798*, 2 (1799), pp. 217–19. "The Military Taylor", from the *Lady's Monthly Museum*, in *The Spirit of the Public Journals for 1799*, 3, London, 1800, pp. 323–8. *Gentleman's Magazine* 51 (Feb. 1781), p. 57. Once again, what was new at this point was not the emergence of the simpler, more somber attire – this can be seen much earlier – but rather the abrupt disappearance of the more flamboyant alternative. Moreover, uniform-like patriotic dress was not the only possible route of change: *vide* Charles James Fox, who within a decade of the American Revolution transformed himself – with the aid of blue and buff clothing – from an elaborate Macaroni into an unkempt man of the people (see Steele, "The Social and Political Significance of Macaroni Fashion", pp. 104–5).

28. [James Caulfield], *Blackguardiana; or, A Dictionary of Rogues, Bawds, Pimps, Whores*, [London, 1793?], p. ii. *The Collector; or, Elegant Anecdotes, and Other Curiosities of Literature*, London, 1798, p. 182. Cf. also [Richard Cumberland], *The Observer*, iv, 4 vols., 3rd edn., London, 1791, pp. 9–10: "We know there are such words in the language as fop and beau, and some can remember them in daily use." And note Christopher Anstey's *Liberality; or, The Decayed Macaroni*, London, 1788, the title of which speaks for itself; here, the gender-blurring aspects of the Macaroni have all but vanished.

29. Dibdin, *A Complete History of the Stage*, v, p. 140. Arthur Murphy, *The Life of David Garrick, Esq.*, London, 1801, i, pp. 308–9. *The Follies of Man* (1790), quoted in Ribeiro, *Dress and Morality*, p. 114. "The Yeoman", in *The Spirit of the Public Journals for 1798*, 2, p. 50. (A gorget is a piece of armor designed to protect the throat.) Cf. also the prologue to [Lady Sophia (Raymond) Burrell], *Theodora; or, The Spanish Daughter: A Tragedy*, London, 1800; and the regimental dress of the foppish Tom Twitter in Mary Ann Hanway, *Ellinor; or, The World As It Is. A Novel*, 4 vols., London, 1798, iii, pp. 118–19.

30. It should also be noted that when the fop made his last-gasp, short-lived comeback

in the 1810s, in the form of the Regency dandy, he cut an altogether different figure, eliminating frills and colors from his costume, and striving – albeit not always successfully – for an "indubitably masculine" appearance (not least with the aid of tight-fitting pantaloons which showed off the male anatomy to such a degree that the pope found it necessary to condemn them). See E. Moers, *The Dandy: Brummell to Beerbohm*, Lincoln (Nebr.), 1960 (quoted, p. 36); and Ribeiro, *Dress and Morality*, p. 120.

31. "Fashion", in *La Belle Assemblée* (1807); quoted in B. C. Gelpi, *Shelley's Goddess: Maternity, Language, Subjectivity*, New York, 1992, p. 54. A. Hollander, *Fabric of Vision: Dress and Drapery in Painting*, London, 2002, p. 106, also notes for this period a new design for stays that made the breasts more pronounced. For false bosoms, see C. W. Cunnington and P. Cunnington, *The History of Underclothes*, London, 1951, pp. 108–9. For a taste of contemporary humor at the expense of this trend – in a story of a lover whose admiration for "the beautiful snowy bosom of his mistress, which laid artfully half concealed under a transparent veil of gauze", gave way to disappointment when she suddenly fainted and "out tumbled a pair of beautiful wax breasts on the floor!!" – see Mrs. [Ann] Thicknesse, *The School for Fashion*, 2 vols., London, 1800, ii, p. 119. For "scientific" condemnations of stays, see Erasmus Darwin, *A Plan for the Conduct of Female Education, in Boarding Schools*, Derby, 1797, pp. 77–8; and William Moss, *Essay on the Management, Nursing, and Diseases of Children*, London, 1794 (quoted in Gelpi, *Shelley's Goddess*, pp. 45–6).

32. Note also the 1794 tribute to the advantages of "the modern manners of the Town" over the dress of former times, centered on an elaborate pas de deux of gender-differentiated "patriot breast[s]": the manly warriors' "breasts unarm'd and bare,/ Save that the shining gorget dangles there", set against the women's bare breasts, "Each in the zone of Grecian Venus drest,/ Freezes her own, to fire her lover's breast". Henry James Pye, *The Siege of Meaux: A Tragedy*, London, 1794, p. 70 (epilogue).

33. *The Times*, 25 March 1793, quoted in John Ashton, *Old Times: A Picture of Social Life at the End of the Eighteenth Century*, London, 1885, p. 70. *Morning Chronicle*, 30 May 1793. Robert Woodbridge, *The Pad. A Farce*, London, 1793. Cf. also the ridicule heaped on the pad in the epilogue to Frederick Reynolds, *How to Grow Rich: A Comedy*, London, 1793. Cf. L. Werkmeister, *A Newspaper History of England 1792–1793*, Lincoln, 1967, pp. 164–5, 328–30 (citing further contemporary reactions); Gelpi, *Shelley's Goddess*, pp. 59–60; and Cunnington and Cunnington, *The History of Underclothes*, pp. 111 and 91 (noting similar female artificial protuberances as early as 1783).

34. John Bennett, *Letters to a Young Lady*, 2 vols., Warrington, 1789, i, pp. 240–1 (closely echoed in the "Amazonian" encounter gratuitously inserted into Charlotte Lennox, *Euphemia*, 4 vols., London, 1790, ii, pp. 164–5).

35. *Lady's Magazine*, 1784, quoted in Blackman, "Walking Amazons", p. 49. [John Scawen], *The Girl in Style*, 1786 (Larpent Mss., Huntington Library, no. 749), prologue. The play ends with the "strange reformation" of its heroine – an ending far enough from the logic of the plot and of the heroine's character to suggest that it might have been tacked on at the same later stage as the prologue.

36. *Domestic Anecdotes of the French Nation*, London, 1794, pp. 264–5. Ann Thicknesse, *Sketches of the Lives and Writings of the Ladies of France*, 3 vols., London, 1778–81, iii, pp. 50–2, and idem, *The School for Fashion*, ii, p. 101 (and cf. George Crabbe's characterization of these habits as distinctly antiquated in 1807,

as cited in Blackman, "Walking Amazons", p. 55). *Chester Chronicle*, 1794, in Cunnington and Cunnington, *The History of Underclothes*, p. 111.

   The changes described here were part of a broad revolution in dress in the last twenty years of the eighteenth century, after many decades of relatively minor shifts in fashion. This sartorial revolution is sometimes attributed to the effects of the French Revolution; but historians of fashion seem to agree – and in accordance with the evidence here – that in fact the change was already well under way before 1789, with the political events in France simply "act[ing] as a catalyst" (Ribeiro, *The Art of Dress*, p. 83).

37. This section presents the rudiments of my argument in "Gender in Translation: How the English Wrote their Juvenal, 1644–1815".

38. The relatively new sub-discipline of Translation Studies has already pointed to the importance of the social and cultural norms of the receiving ("target") language, and indeed predicted the rich potential of comparing multiple translations of the same text over time. This potential lies, however, more in the domain of historians, who have been slow to pick up on this cue. See further in my "Gender in Translation", pp. 6–7, 35 nn. 19–21.

39. Sir Robert Stapylton, *Juvenal's Sixteen Satyrs*, London, 1647, p. 89. [Thomas Sheridan], *The Satires of Juvenal Translated*, London, 1739, p. 153. William Gifford, *The Satires of Decimus Junius Juvenalis, Translated into English Verse*, 2nd edn., corrected and enlarged, London, 1806, pp. 185–6.

40. Gifford's translation betrayed a heightened anxiety also in its tone: note, for instance, how he gratuitously replaced Stapylton's "she doate upon/ Man's strength" with the palpably more agitated "she madly doat on arms and blood".

41. *The Works of John Dryden. Volume IV: Poems 1693–1696*, eds. A. B. Chambers and W. Frost, Berkeley, 1974, p. 169. Henry Fielding, *Miscellanies*, 3 vols., vol. i, ed. H. K. Miller, Oxford, 1972, pp. 112–13. For the earlier period note also Barten Holyday, *Decimus Junius Juvenalis . . . Translated and Illustrated*, Oxford, 1673 (but written before mid-century), p. 96: as with Stapylton's translation, here too one is struck by the matter-of-fact ease with which she who "once a helmet wears" in so doing "has renounc'd her Sex".

42. Edward Owen, *The Satires of Juvenal, Translated into English Verse*, 2 vols., London, 1785, i, p. 117; and pp. [iii], ix.

43. Francis Hodgson, *The Satires of Juvenal*, London, 1807, p. 103.

44. Ibid., notes, p. 432. Rev. Martin Madan's *A New and Literal Translation of Juvenal*, 2 vols., London, 1789, i, p. 263, created a similar effect to that of Hodgson's wishful verses by deftly altering the earlier, mid-century translation on which his own was heavily based (John Stirling, *The Satires of Juvenal*, London, 1760, p. 83).

45. F. Nussbaum, *The Brink of All We Hate: English Satires on Women 1660–1750*, Lexington, 1984, chap. 5 and *passim*. This is the only other study to compare the eighteenth-century series of English translations of the Sixth Satire. L. Brown, *Ends of Empire: Women and Ideology in Early Eighteenth-Century English Literature*, Ithaca (N.Y.), 1993, pp. 140–1. E. Donoghue, *Passions between Women: British Lesbian Culture 1688–1801*, London, 1993, esp. pp. 212–14.

46. Wahrman, "Gender in Translation". Obviously this methodological experiment need not be restricted to Juvenal: cf. p. 41 n. 79 for hints of similar trends in translations of Ovid's *Metamorphoses*.

47. Charles Badham, *The Satires of Juvenal. Translated into English Verse*, London, 1814, p. 155n.

344 Notes to pages 77–86

48. Adam Fitz-Adam in *The World*, 26 February 1756, quoted in H. Guest, "'These Neuter Somethings': Gender Difference and Commercial Culture in Mid-Eighteenth-Century England", in K. Sharpe and S. N. Zwicker (eds.), *Refiguring Revolutions: Aesthetics and Politics from the English Revolution to the Romantic Revolution*, Berkeley, 1998, p. 173.

49. [Benjamin] Victor, *The History of the Theatres of London and Dublin, from the Year 1730 to the Present Time*, 3 vols., London, 1761–71, iii, 1771, pp. 2–8. Boaden, *The Life of Mrs. Jordan*, i, p. 127.

50. James Fordyce, *Sermons to Young Women*, 2 vols., London, 1765, i, p. 105. *The Weekly Register*, 10 July 1731, quoted in Malcolm, *Anecdotes of the Manners and Customs of London from the Roman Invasion*, p. 436. *The Macaroni, Scavoir Vivre, and Theatrical Magazine* 2 (Jan. 1774), p. 155. Thicknesse, *Sketches of the Lives and Writings of the Ladies of France*, iii, p. 50. Epilogue to *The Trip to the Jubilee*, in Joseph Yarrow, *Choice Collection of Poetry by the Most Ingenious Men of the Age*, 2 vols., York, 1738, ii, pp. 97–8. Isabella Howard, Countess of Carlisle, *Thoughts in the Form of Maxims Addressed to Young Ladies*, London, 1789, p. 38.

51. [Dorothy Kilner], *Dialogues and Letters on Morality, Oeconomy, and Politeness, for the Improvement and Entertainment of Young Female Minds*, London, [1780?], pp. 170–2. Fielding, *Miscellanies*, i, p. 113. Madan, *A New and Literal Translation of Juvenal*, i, p. 264. Similarly, it can be readily shown that, where we find critiques of Amazons prior to the shift of the 1780s, they typically directed their hostility less at their Amazonian crossing of the gender boundary than at their alleged ferociousness, vulgarity, and lewdness.

52. *Of Luxury, More Particularly with Respect to Apparel. . . . By a Country Clergyman*, London, 1736, pp. 11–12.

53. [John Brown], *An Estimate of the Manners and Principles of the Times*, [vol. i], 5th edn., London, 1757, p. 36. James Fordyce, *Addresses to Young Men*, 2 vols., London, 1777, ii, pp. 142–5. [Allen], *The Polite Lady; or, A course of Female Education. In a Series of Letters, from a Mother to her Daughter*. Lady Sarah Pennington, *An Unfortunate Mother's Advice to her Absent Daughters*, London, 1761, as discussed in T. Bowers, *The Politics of Motherhood: British Writing and Culture, 1680–1760*, Cambridge, 1996, pp. 225ff. Note also the literarily cross-dressed domestic manual, [John Hill], *On the Management and Education of Children: A Series of Letters Written to a Neice by the Honorable Juliana-Susannah Seymour*, London, 1754. And recall John Gregory's approval of women's choice not to marry in one of the most popular conduct books of the era (see above, p. 13), which one puzzled scholar has described as "highly unorthodox" (J. Fliegelman, *Prodigals and Pilgrims: The American Revolution against Patriarchal Authority, 1750–1800*, Cambridge, 1982, pp. 44–5).

54. [Peter Shaw], *Man. A Paper for Ennobling the Species*, 14 (2 April 1755), pp. 1–3 (first emphasis added).

Chapter 3

1. [William Smith], *An Historical Account of the Expedition against the Ohio Indians, in the Year MDCCLXIV under the Command of Henry Bouquet*, Philadelphia and London, 1766, pp. 26–9; engravings opposite pp. 14, 28.

2. John Mitchell, "An Essay upon the Causes of the Different Colours of People in Different Climates", *Philosophical Transactions [of the Royal Society]* 474 (1744), in

vol. xliii, London, 1746, p. 149, citing John Smith, *The Generall History of Virginia*, London, 1623. William Crashaw, *A Sermon Preached in London*, London, 1610, cited in K. O. Kupperman, "Presentment of Civility: English Reading of American Self-Presentation in the Early Years of Colonization", *William and Mary Quarterly* 3rd ser., 54 (1997), p. 227 (and note also p. 208). For Tarbull see E. L. Coleman, *New England Captives Carried to Canada between 1677 and 1760*, 2 vols., Portland (Maine), 1925, i, p. 296; ii, p. 11. James Smith, *An Account of . . . his Captivity with the Indians, in the Years 1755, '56, '57, '58, & '59*, Lexington (Ky), 1799, cited in J. H. Merrell, *Into the American Woods: Negotiators on the Pennsylvania Frontier*, New York, 1999, p. 94. [Smith], *Historical Account of the Expedition against the Ohio Indians*, p. 27. And see J. Axtell, *The Invasion Within: The Contest of Cultures in Colonial North America*, Oxford, 1985, p. 308. Also of interest are the indecisive debates around the mysterious case of the servant Elizabeth Canning, who was supposedly kidnapped and held captive by Gypsies for a month in 1753: what was her skin color upon her escape? Did it show signs of having become blacker – even "as black as the chimney stock" – during her captivity? See J. Moore, *The Appearance of Truth: The Story of Elizabeth Canning and Eighteenth-Century Narrative*, Newark, 1994 (quoted, pp. 13–14).

3. L. Brown, *Ends of Empire: Women and Ideology in Early Eighteenth-Century English Literature*, Ithaca (N.Y.), 1993, pp. 136–7.

4. M. Harrison, *Climates and Constitutions: Health, Race, Environment and British Imperialism in India 1600–1850*, Oxford, 1999, and his "'The Tender Frame of Man': Disease, Climate, and Racial Difference in India and the West Indies, 1760–1860", *Bulletin of the History of Medicine* 70 (1996), pp. 68–93.

5. John Arbuthnot, *An Essay Concerning the Effects of Air on Human Bodies*, London, 1733, pp. 146–50. Oliver Goldsmith, "The Effect which Climates Have upon Men, and Other Animals" (*British Magazine*, May 1760), in *Collected Works of Oliver Goldsmith*, 5 vols., ed. A. Friedman, Oxford, 1966, iii, p. 114; and cf. his *An History of the Earth, and Animated Nature*, 8 vols., London, 1774, esp. ii, pp. 211–41. On climatic thinking in the eighteenth century see, *inter alia*, C. J. Glacken, *Traces on the Rhodian Shore: Nature and Culture in Western Thought from Ancient Times to the End of the Eighteenth Century*, Berkeley, 1967, esp. chap. 12; F. A. Nussbaum, *Torrid Zones: Maternity, Sexuality, and Empire in Eighteenth-Century English Narratives*, Baltimore, 1995, pp. 7–10 and *passim*; R. Wheeler, *The Complexion of Race: Categories of Difference in Eighteenth-Century British Culture*, Philadelphia, 2000, pp. 21ff. For the earlier roots of climatic theory see M. T. Hodgen, *Early Anthropology in the Sixteenth and Seventeenth Centuries*, Philadelphia, 1964, pp. 276–90; K. F. Hall, *Things of Darkness: Economies of Race and Gender in Early Modern England*, Ithaca (N.Y.), 1995, pp. 92–107; and the sources in note 11 below.

6. Harrison, *Climates and Constitutions*, pp. 11, 25, 45, 215 and *passim*; James Lind, *An Essay on Diseases Incidental to Europeans in Hot Climates*, London, 1768, cited in Harrison, "'The Tender Frame of Man'", p. 74. Hyacinthe Wellesley to her husband Richard Wellesley, c. 1799, quoted in I. Butler, *The Eldest Brother: The Marquess Wellesley, The Duke of Wellington's Eldest Brother*, London, 1973, p. 200. Sarah Scott, *A Description of Millenium Hall* (1762), ed. J. Spencer, New York, 1986, p. 9 (spoken by a character who had spent twenty years in Jamaica); and see Nussbaum, *Torrid Zones*, p. 150. Goldsmith, *History of the Earth*, ii, pp. 228–9; and cf. Mitchell, "Essay upon the Causes of the Different Colours of People", p. 150.

The Sentimental Magazine 4 (1776), p. 317. Also note the suggestion in Thomas Shaw, *Travels; or, Observations Relating to Several Parts of Barbary and the Levant*, Oxford, 1738, p. 304, that the real meaning of "Moor" should not be "a Person of a dark and swarthy Complexion", since this is an incidental effect of the sun; rather, "it only denotes the Situation of the Country he inhabits". On the notion of "seasoning", and its early-modern medical-theoretical basis, see also J. E. Chaplin, "Natural Philosophy and an Early Racial Idiom in North America: Comparing English and Indian Bodies", *William and Mary Quarterly* 3rd ser., 54 (1997), pp. 229–52.

7. *Monthly Review* 42 (1770), p. 524. Rev. Samuel Stanhope Smith, *An Essay on the Causes and Variety of the Complexion and Figure in the Human Species*, Philadelphia and London, 1789, p. 24. [John Toland], *Reasons for Naturalizing the Jews in Great Britain and Ireland*, London, 1714, p. 19. [Lancelot Addison], *The Present State of the Jews: (More Particularly Relating to Those in Barbary)*, London, 1675, frontispiece. On this image, probably "less Addison's than his illustrator's [or publisher's] idea of a typical Moor", see I. Abrahams, *By-Paths in Hebraic Bookland*, Philadelphia, 1920, p. 154. My attention was drawn to this image by S. Volkov, "Exploring the Other: The Enlightenment Search for the Boundaries of Humanity", in R. S. Wistrich (ed.), *Demonizing the Other: Antisemitism, Racism, and Xenophobia*, Jerusalem, 2000, p. 160. Such views represented a shift from earlier sixteenth- and seventeenth-century ones, which often referred to Jews as black.

8. Goldsmith, *History of the Earth*, ii, p. 239. [Sir Richard Blackmore], *The Nature of Man. A Poem*, London, 1711, pp. ii, 4. David Hume, "Of National Characters", in *Essays Moral, Political, and Literary*, ed. E. F. Miller, Indianapolis, 1987, p. 208 n. 10. And see R. H. Popkin, "The Philosophical Basis of Eighteenth-Century Racism", in H. E. Pagliaro (ed.), *Studies in Eighteenth-Century Culture: Racism in the Eighteenth Century*, Cleveland, 1973, pp. 245–62 – in many ways the first salvo in the modern scholarly study of these questions. P. J. Marshall and G. Williams, *The Great Map of Mankind: Perceptions of New Worlds in the Age of Enlightenment*, Cambridge (Mass.), 1982, chap. 8.

9. E. C. Eze, "Hume, Race, and Human Nature", *Journal of the History of Ideas* 61 (2000), pp. 691–8.

10. James Bate, "An Account of the Remarkable Alteration of Colour in a Negro Woman", *Philosophical Transactions [of the Royal Society]* 51 (1760), pp. 175–8 (quoted, p. 176); this story was reported in *Gentleman's Magazine* 31 (1761), p. 361. Examples of such reports include *Gentleman's Magazine* 13 (1743), p. 542, and 36 (1766), p. 403 (unusually varied list of cases); *The British Magazine; or, Monthly Repository for Gentlemen and Ladies* 7 (1766), pp. 483–5; Goldsmith, *History of the Earth*, ii, pp. 240–1; and for mixed-color twins, the diary of Thomas Thistlewood of Jamaica, 1750, as cited by Philip Morgan, "Interracial Sex in Eighteenth-Century Jamaica: Personal Dynamics and Social Consequences", paper presented at the Huntington Library, October 2000 (I am grateful to Phil Morgan for permission to cite this paper). Note also the fictional account of a "fine white girl" born to a black mother in [Henry Neville], *The Isle of Pines*, London, 1668, p. 12; as well as the report in the *Monthly Review* 65 (1781), p. 543, of a white Negro whose description also insisted that "his breast resembles that of a woman" – one category collapse entailing another. And cf. W. D. Jordan, *White over Black: American Attitudes towards the Negro, 1550–1812*, Chapel Hill, 1968, pp. 244–5, 249–52.

11. On climatic theory in the sixteenth century, and its relative retreat in the seventeenth, see M. Floyd-Wilson, "'Clime, Complexion, and Degree': Racialism in Early Modern England", PhD thesis, University of North Carolina, 1996. M. J. Guasco, "Encounters, Identities, and Human Bondage: The Foundations of Racial Slavery in the Anglo-Atlantic World", PhD thesis, College of William and Mary, 2000, chaps. 4–5. Glacken, *Traces on the Rhodian Shore*, chap. 12.

12. Wheeler, *The Complexion of Race*, pp. 7, 35 and *passim*. See also N. Hudson, "From 'Nation' to 'Race': The Origin of Racial Classification in Eighteenth-Century Thought", *Eighteenth-Century Studies* 29:3 (1996), pp. 247–64.

13. [William Rufus Chetwood], *The Voyages, Travels and Adventures, of William Owen Gwin Vaughan*, London, 1736; *The Lady's Drawing Room*, London, 1744; *Memoirs of the Remarkable Life of Mr. Charles Brachy*, Dublin, 1767; as discussed in R. Wheeler, "The Complexion of Desire: Racial Ideology and Mid-Eighteenth-Century British Novels", *Eighteenth-Century Studies* 32:3 (1999), pp. 309–32. Also cf. Wheeler, *The Complexion of Race*, chap. 3; and below, pp. 214–15, for the spectatorial appeal of the racially indeterminate mulatta in the 1770s.

14. A. T. Vaughan, *Roots of American Racism: Essays on the Colonial Experience*, New York, 1995, p. 164 and *passim*; and cf. C. Kidd, *British Identities before Nationalism: Ethnicity and Nationhood in the Atlantic World, 1600–1800*, Cambridge, 1999, pt. I. Morgan Godwyn, *The Negro's [and] Indians Advocate*, London, 1680, quoted in Vaughan, *Roots of American Racism*, p. 68. Bartholomew Stibbs, *Journal of a Voyage up the Gambia*, London, 1738, quoted in Wheeler, *Complexion of Race*, p. 4. Compare also J.-P. Rubiés, *Travel and Ethnology in the Renaissance: South India through European Eyes, 1250–1625*, Cambridge, 2000, pp. 171–6. B. Orr, *Empire on the English Stage 1660–1714*, Cambridge, 2001, esp. pp. 12–25. Jordan, *White over Black*, pp. 17–24, 94–8. Hall, *Things of Darkness*, p. 114.

15. On the late-sixteenth- and early-seventeenth-century emergence of the Curse of Ham as a perspective on Africans see B. Braude, "The Sons of Noah and the Construction of Ethnic and Geographical Identities in the Medieval and Early-Modern Periods", *William and Mary Quarterly* 3rd ser., 54:1 (1997), esp. p. 138. For a persuasive demonstration of the replacement of religion by culture during the eighteenth century, arrived at from a rather different perspective, see Jonathan Sheehan's *The Enlightenment Bible*, Princeton, 2005 (I am grateful to him for sharing this work-in-progress with me).

16. T. W. Perry, *Public Opinion, Propaganda, and Politics in Eighteenth-Century England: A Study of the Jew Bill of 1753*, Cambridge (Mass.), 1962, pp. 88, 108 and *passim*; and cf. F. Felsenstein, *Anti-Semitic Stereotypes: A Paradigm of Otherness in English Popular Culture, 1660–1830*, Baltimore, 1995, chap. 8. J. Shapiro, *Shakespeare and the Jews*, New York, 1996, chap. 7.

17. Quoted in Shapiro, *Shakespeare and the Jews*, p. 208. William Roberts, *An Account of the First Discovery, and Natural History of Florida*, London, 1763, pp. v–vi. Cf. also the claim of *A Modest Apology for the Citizens and Merchants of London . . . against Naturalizing the Jews*, 2nd edn., London, 1753, pp. 8–9, that one can always "know a *Jew* at first Sight". The author explained that "it is not his dirty Skin" by which one can tell a Jew apart, "neither is it the Make of his Body". Rather, "look at his Eyes" for "a malignant Blackness underneath them": if one could always sniff out a Jew, this author nonetheless had to admit that this identification was *not* to be achieved by the Jew's distinctive physical appearance.

18. "Aaron's Show-Box. A New Ballad", in *The Repository . . . in Opposition to All Jews, Turks, and Infidels* 2 (London, 1753), p. 44. *Gentleman's Magazine*, July 1753, p. 346, cited in Shapiro, *Shakespeare and the Jews*, p. 199. *The Spectator* 1 (1 March 1711), in D. F. Bond (ed.), *The Spectator*, 5 vols., Oxford, 1965, i, p. 4. *An Apology for the Naturalization of the Jews. . . . By a True Believer*, London, 1753, pp. 2–4.

19. J. E., *Some Considerations on the Naturalization of the Jews*, London, 1753, p. iv, quoted in Shapiro, *Shakespeare and the Jews*, p. 197. To appreciate the incongruity of this vision with later understandings of race, cf. another scaremongering piece from 1789, which was to use precisely the same heavy sarcasm to warn of the dangers of black presence in England. In 1789, however, the increased blackness on London streets was no longer the consequence of self-blackening, but of misce-genation ("The dark *brunette*, or rather *noisette*, would soon gain in numbers on the fair, and a wonderful alteration would take place in the complexion of future gen-erations by [inter-racial] marriage"); and the concomitant transformation of hair was no longer the result of the application of "false hair" or "artificial beards", but rather of innate natural tendency: "It would save [the British ladies] the expence of *frizzing their hair*, for their hair would *friz of itself.*" This shift in the signs of racial contamination, from artificial hair over manufactured skin color to hair that frizzes of itself over essential biologically modified skin color, is as good as any summary of my argument. "A Lover of Blacks", *The World* 735 (9 May 1789), p. [2].

20. Goldsmith, *An History of the Earth*, ii, 236. W. Gordon, *Every Young Man's Com-panion*, 4th edn., corrected, London, 1765, p. 202 (and cf. Rev. Richard Turner, *A View of the Earth*, London, 1762, p. 16). Letter from Peter Fountaine, a Huguenot Virginian, to his brother, 1757, quoted in J. H. Johnston, *Race Relations in Virginia and Miscegenation in the South*, 1970, p. 170. *Gentleman's Magazine* 23 (1753), p. 326 (and cf. Robert Beverley, *The History and Present State of Virginia* [London, 1705], ed. L. B. Wright, Chapel Hill, 1947, p. 159; Joseph-François Lafitau, *The Customs of the American Indians* [1724], Toronto, 1974, i, p. 89). See also Jordan, *White over Black*, p. 241; K. M. Brown, *Good Wives, Nasty Wenches and Anxious Patriarchs: Gender, Race, and Power in Colonial Virginia*, Chapel Hill, 1996, p. 63; and A. T. Vaughan, "From White Man to Redskin: Changing Anglo-American Per-ceptions of the American Indian", in his *Roots of American Racism*, pp. 8–9.

21. John Lawson, *The History of Carolina*, London, 1714, p. 171. James Dunbar, *Essays on the History of Mankind in Rude and Cultivated Ages*, London, 1780, p. 368. James Adair, *The History of the American Indians*, London, 1775, pp. 1–3 (this discussion opens the book). J. E. Chaplin, *Subject Matter: Technology, the Body, and Science on the Anglo-American Frontier, 1500–1676*, Cambridge (Mass.), 2001, esp. pp. 256–7, 276 (I am grateful to Joyce Chaplin for the opportunity to see her work before publication). For the earlier period cf. also Vaughan, "From White Man to Redskin", p. 10; and Kupperman, "Presentment of Civility", pp. 207–8, as well as K. O. Kupperman, *Indians and English: Facing Off in Early America*, Ithaca (N.Y.), 2000, pp. 58–9. Finally, as the flip side of these understandings of Indian skin color, consider the essay in *The Edinburgh Magazine* 6 (1752), pp. 232–4, on "the gradual decline of blushing in these kingdoms", a development which the author under-stood as "discontinuing a custom" – that is to say, again, not as a physical-bodily phenomenon, but as another aspect of complexion that was elective and culturally determined.

22. Vaughan, "From White Man to Redskin". K. Brown, "Native Americans and Early Modern Concepts of Race", in M. Daunton and R. Halpern (eds.), *Empire and Others: British Encounters with Indigenous Peoples, 1600–1850*, Philadelphia, 1999, pp. 79–100, critiquing Jordan, *White over Black*.

23. John Hunter, "Inaugural Disputation on the Varieties of Man" (June 1775), in *The Anthropological Treatises of Johann Friedrich Blumenbach*, trans. and ed. T. Bendyshe, London, 1865, pp. 357–94 (quoted, pp. 361, 370–1, 376, 392).

24. John Harris, *Navigantium atque Itinerantium Bibliotheca; or, A Compleat Collection of Voyages and Travels*, London, 1705, p. viii. Cf. also John Harris, *Remarks on Some Late Papers, Relating to the Universal Deluge*, London, 1697, p. 66, cited in Kidd, *British Identities before Nationalism*, p. 46.

25. Captain Daniel Beeckman, *A Voyage to and from the Island of Borneo*, London, 1718, p. 184. William Funnell, *A Voyage round the World*, London, 1707, pp. 289–90. Peter Kolb, *The Present State of the Cape of Good Hope*, 2 vols., trans. Mr. Medley, 2nd edn., London, 1738, i, p. 49. Mrs. [Jemima] Kindersley, *Letters from the Island of Teneriffe, Brazil, the Cape of Good Hope, and the East Indies*, London, 1777, p. 68. Cf. also, *inter alia*, Mitchell, "Essay upon the Causes of the Different Colours of People", p. 138; John Bulwer's earlier assertion in 1650 that the Negroes' complexion had its beginning in the "affectation of painting" (cited in Floyd-Wilson, "'Clime, Complexion, and Degree'", p. 142); Awnsham Churchill, *A Collection of Voyages and Travels*, 6 vols., London, 1732, ii, p. 152 (citing John Nieuhoff, 1655); as well as the account – repeated by Buffon – of a Hottentot baby who, having been brought back to Europe and kept away from "dirt and black paints", "soon became as white as any European" (cited in Wheeler, "The Complexion of Desire", pp. 311–12). See L. E. Merians, "What They Are, Who We Are: Representations of the 'Hottentot' in Eighteenth-Century Britain", *Eighteenth-Century Life* 17 (Nov. 1993), pp. 20–2; idem, *Envisioning the Worst: Representations of "Hottentots" in Early-Modern England*, Newark, 2001, pp. 124–7; and R. Elphick, *Khoikhoi and the Founding of White South Africa*, New Haven, 1975, p. 197.

26. Coleman, *New England Captives*, i, p. 296. Adair, *The History of the American Indians*, pp. 3–4.

27. John Clubbe, *Physiognomy*, London, 1763, p. 6. John Hawkesworth, *An Account of the Voyages . . . for Making Discoveries in the Southern Hemisphere . . . in the Dolphin, the Swallow and the Endeavour*, 3 vols., London, 1773, iii, p. 446. James Cook, *A Voyage towards the South Pole, and Round the World . . . in the Years 1772, 1773, 1774, and 1775*, 2 vols., London, 1777, i, pp. 308–9; ii, p. 80, and plate between pp. 62 and 63. James Cook and James King, *A Voyage to the Pacific Ocean . . . in the Years 1776, 1777, 1778, 1779, and 1780*, 4 vols., London, 1784, ii, p. 303. On the European explorers' puzzlement at the variety of complexions in the South Pacific, unaccountable by climate, see Marshall and Williams, *The Great Map of Mankind*, pp. 261–3.

28. Cook, *A Voyage towards the South Pole*, ii, p. 66; and cf. i, pp. 76–7. Kathleen Wilson has discussed these frequent instances of "gender misrecognition" in the South Sea voyages in *The Island Race: Englishness, Empire and Gender in the Eighteenth Century*, London, 2003, chap. 5. See also Wheeler, *The Complexion of Race*, pp. 19–20.

29. *Monthly Review* 33 (1765), p. 42, reviewing Giacinto Sigismondo Gerdil, *Reflections on Education*, [London], 1765. [Peter Shaw], *Man. A Paper for Ennobling the Species*,

48 (26 Nov. 1755), pp. 1–2 (emphasis added). Cf. Thomas Sheridan, *British Education*, London, 1756, p. 6.

30. J[ohn]. Long, *Voyages and Travels of an Indian Interpreter and Trader*, London, 1791, pp. 20, 35. Laugier de Tassy, *A Compleat History of the Piratical States of Barbary*, London, 1750, p. v, cited in Wheeler, "The Complexion of Desire", p. 318.

31. *Narrative of the Captivity and Restoration of Mrs. Mary Rowlandson* (1682), in A. T. Vaughan and E. W. Clark (eds.), *Puritans among the Indians: Accounts of Captivity and Redemption 1676–1724*, Cambridge (Mass.), 1981, pp. 58–9. Ann Little, in her forthcoming "Abraham in Arms: Gender and Power on the New England Frontier, 1620–1760", draws attention to the persistent preoccupation in European–Indian encounters during this period with clothing and the stripping of clothes, thus centering the construction of difference on the savage–civilized distinction. (I am grateful to Ann Little for allowing me to cite her work-in-progress.)

32. Adam Ferguson, *An Essay on the History of Civil Society* (1767), ed. D. Forbes, Edinburgh, 1966, p. 80. Ferguson's observation was echoed in other Scottish texts: cf. William Robertson, *History of the Reign of the Emperor Charles V*, London, 1769, as cited in O. D. Edwards, "Robertsonian Romanticism and Realism", in S. J. Brown (ed.), *William Robertson and the Expansion of Empire*, Cambridge, 1997, p. 111; and Gilbert Stuart, *A View of Society in Europe, in its Progress from Rudeness to Refinement*, Edinburgh, 1778, p. 156. For an analysis of Moll's image see Wheeler, *Complexion of Race*, p. 36 (and cf. the analogous representation of the four continents on p. 34).

33. [Smith], *An Historical Account of the Expedition against the Ohio Indians*, p. 38.

34. *Encyclopaedia Britannica*, 2nd edn., Edinburgh, 1778, v, pp. 3737–44 (quoted, p. 3739); 3rd edn., Edinburgh, 1797, viii, pp. 683–91. *The Monthly Review* 55 (1776), pp. 544–5, 548, invoking Kolb, *The Present State of the Cape of Good Hope*. Examples of functional explanations of greasing that left no room for the intentional modification of skin color include Lieut. William Paterson, *A Narrative of Four Journeys into the Country of the Hottentots, and Caffraria*, London, 1789, p. 116. François Le Vaillant, *Travels into the Interior Parts of Africa . . . in the Years 1780 [to 1785]*, 2 vols., Perth, 1791, ii, p. 27. Captain Robert Percival, *An Account of the Cape of Good Hope*, London, 1804, p. 86. [C. G. Curtis], *An Account of the Colony of the Cape of Good Hope*, London, 1819, pp. 90, 92. Sir George Mouat Keith, *A Voyage to South America and the Cape of Good Hope*, London, 1819, pp. 60–1. Merians, *Envisioning the Worst*, pp. 27, 203, has noted a concomitant late-eighteenth-century decline in comments on the Khoikhoi skin color as distinctly lighter than that of other Africans: a distinction that had been the trigger for the earlier interpretations of greasing as blackening.

35. Anders Sparrman, *A Voyage to the Cape of Good Hope . . . into the Country of the Hottentots and Caffres, from the Year 1772, to 1776*, 2 vols., London, 1785, i, p. 183. *Gleanings of Africa . . . in a Series of Letters from an English Officer*, London, 1806, pp. 232–3. *The Modern Part of an Universal History*, 44 vols., vol. xii, London, 1781, p. 413. William Falconer, *Remarks on the Influence of Climate, Situation, Nature of Country . . . and Way of Life, on the Disposition and Manners . . . of Mankind*, London, 1781, pp. 312–13. Cf. also Thomas Bankes, *A Modern, Authentic and Complete System of Universal Geography*, London, [c. 1795], p. 320.

36. John Barrow, *Travels into the Interior of Southern Africa*, 2 vols., 2nd edn., London, 1806, i, pp. 158–9, 236, 245 (and on greasing as a functional form of skin protection, i, pp. 106–7). Cf. also his *A Narrative of Travels in the Interior of South Africa . . . in the Years 1797, and 1798*, London, 1802, p. 29. And note the review of Petrus Camper in *Monthly Review* 6 (1791), p. 211, which expressed impatience with Camper's "unnecessary parade of learning" intended to disprove the notion that racial appearance could be "ascribed to arts employed for the purpose", since this claim was common knowledge and common sense. (Quoted in M. C. Meijer, *Race and Aesthetics in the Anthropology of Petrus Camper*, Amsterdam, 1999, p. 154.)

37. Peter Williamson, *Some Considerations on the Present State of Affairs*, York, 1758, p. 55. John Filson, *The Discovery, Settlement, and Present State of Kentucke*, Wilmington (Del.), 1784, pp. 98–9 (London edn., 1793). Vaughan sees signs of the shift beginning in the 1760s: "From White Man to Redskin", pp. 13–14 and *passim*.

38. Jonathan Carver, *Travels through the Interior Parts of North-America, in the Years 1766, 1767, and 1768*, London, 1778, p. 223. *Monthly Review* 60 (1779), p. 286. Isaac Weld, *Travels through the States of North America . . . during the Years 1795, 1796, and 1797*, London, 1799, pp. 375–6. Cf. also George Heriot, *Travels through the Canadas*, London, 1805, p. 121. Silvia Sebastiani has noted a shift to increasingly racially rigid representations of the Indians in the successive editions of the *Britannica*, even as the encyclopedia was becoming more positive in its evaluation: "The Changing Features of the Americans in the Eighteenth-Century *Britannica*", in L. Passerini (ed.), *Across the Atlantic: Cultural Exchanges between Europe and the United States*, Brussels, 2000, pp. 39–57.

39. *Memoirs of Charles Dennis Rusoe d'Eres . . . Who Was with the Scanyawtauragahroote Indians Eleven Years*, Exeter, 1800, p. 99 (and separated from the account of their skin color on p. 97). Sir Alexander Mackenzie, *Voyages from Montreal . . . in the Years 1789 and 1793*, London, 1801, p. xciii. George Henry Loskiel, *The History of the Moravian Mission . . . with a Preliminary Account of the Indians, 1740–1814*, London, 1838, p. 25. Heriot, *Travels through the Canadas*, p. 131 (emphasis added). George Hamilton, *A Voyage around the World . . . in the Years 1790, 1791, and 1792*, Berwick, 1793, p. 78. For the possibility that notions of Indian skin color as mutable persisted longer among observers in the early American republic than among Britons, see below, pp. 249–51.

40. Charlotte Lennox, *Euphemia*, 4 vols., London, 1790, iv, pp. 196–200, 209.

41. Dunbar, *Essays on the History of Mankind*, pp. 426–7. Charles White, *An Account of the Regular Gradation in Man*, London, 1799, p. 104, read to the Literary and Philosophical Society of Manchester in 1795. White's account of the older – and in his eyes wrong – climatic view of the Jews was based on Thomas Clarkson, *An Essay on the Slavery and Commerce of the Human Species, Particularly the African*, London, 1786, p. 207.

42. Thomas Winterbottom, *An Account of the Native Africans in the Neighbourhood of Sierra Leone* (1803), 2 vols., London, 1969, i, p. 187 (for more indecisive dithering regarding the effects of climate, see pp. 182–4). John Bigland, *An Historical Display of the Effects of Physical and Moral Causes on the Character and Circumstances of Nations*, London, 1816; and William Lawrence, "On the Causes of the Varieties of the Human Species", from his *Lectures on Physiology, Zoology, and the Natural History of Man*, London, 1819; both reproduced in H. F. Augstein (ed.), *Race: The Origins of an Idea, 1760–1850*, Bristol, 1996, pp. 72–3, 123. William Rae Wilson,

Travels in the Holy Land, Egypt, etc, originally 1823, as cited from the 4th edn., 1847, in A. Cohen, *An Anglo-Jewish Scrapbook 1600–1840: The Jew through English Eyes*, London, 1943, p. 332 (and note there the even stronger formulation from T. Skinner, *Adventures during a Journey Overland to India*, London, 1836). *The Artist's Repository and Drawing Magazine*, 1 (1788), p. 117. Cf. J. M. Efron, *Defenders of the Race: Jewish Doctors and Race Science in Fin-de-Siècle Europe*, New Haven, 1994, chap. 3. Note also Anne Janowitz's suggestive comments on the late-eighteenth-century racialization of the Gypsies as the counterpart to the Jews in her "'Wild Outcasts of Society': The Transit of the Gypsies in Romantic Period Poetry", in G. Maclean et al., *The Country and the City Revisited: England and the Politics of Culture, 1550–1850*, Cambridge, 1999, pp. 213–30 (together with John Barrell's comment, p. 234, on how different the view of Gypsies had been at mid-century).

43. Henry Home, Lord Kames, *Sketches of the History of Man*, 2nd edn., 4 vols., Edinburgh, 1778, i, pp. 27–30 (it is worth noting that Kames still acknowledged the Hottentot *intent* to manufacture their skin color, while denying its possibility). The argument for innate racial identity based on the whiteness of the "White Jews" of Cochin – as distinct from the "Black Jews", a supposed consequence of intermarriage – was repeated in Claudius Buchanan, *Christian Researches in Asia*, London, 1811; see Efron, *Defenders of the Race*, p. 40.

44. Kames, *Sketches of the History of Man* (quoted, i, p. 23). Again, we are not dealing here with a novel idea without precedent. Polygenetic views had been suggested before – notably by Isaac de la Peyrère in the mid-seventeenth century – though not necessarily with the same racialized overtones. Thus, one of the (precious) few early-eighteenth-century arguments for polygenesis, *Co-Adamitae; or, An Essay to Prove the Two Following Paradoxes*, London, 1732, was responding solely to difficulties in biblical exegesis: counter to late-eighteenth-century expectations, it laid down its arguments in full without mentioning complexion, or present-day human diversity, even once. On the polygenetic debate in its biblical context see Kidd, *British Identities before Nationalism*, chap. 3. For an unusual example, however, that did launch a polygenetic argument from differences in skin color, see John Atkins, *A Voyage to Guinea, Brasil, and the West-Indies*, London, 1735, p. 39.

45. John Millar, *The Origin of the Distinction of Ranks* (3rd edn., 1779), repr. in W. C. Lehmann, *John Millar of Glasgow 1735–1801*, Cambridge, 1960, p. 181; these paragraphs were not included in the first edition of 1771. Jeremy Bentham, *An Introduction to the Principles of Morals and Legislation* (1789), eds. J. H. Burns and H. L. A. Hart, Oxford, 1996, p. 67 (and cf. the dismissal of Montesquieu's climatic theory in Rev. David Williams, *Lectures on Political Principles*, London, 1789, lecture xx). Richard Payne Knight, *The Progress of Civil Society*, London, 1796. Isaac D'Israeli, "On the Influence of Climate on the Human Mind", in his *Miscellanies; or, Literary Recreations*, London, 1796, pp. 288–309 (quoted, pp. 288–91). [Edward King], *A Second Part to the Morsels of Criticism*, London, 1800 (vol. iii of his *Morsels of Criticism*, London, 1800), pp. 117–18 and *passim*. Indeed, King was moved by the evidence of the unbridgeable differences between people to a polygenetic reading of the biblical account of creation: see Kidd, *British Identities before Nationalism*, pp. 56–7.

46. James Johnson, *The Influence of the Atmosphere . . . on the Health and Functions of the Human Frame*, London, 1818, pp. 1–2, cited in Harrison, *Climates and Constitutions*, pp. 103–4; and see there *passim*. Johann Reinhold Forster, *Observations Made*

during a Voyage round the World, London, 1778, p. 275. *Monthly Review* n.s., 20 (1796), p. 64 (review of Blumenbach). E. M. Collingham, *Imperial Bodies: The Physical Experience of the Raj, c. 1800–1947*, Cambridge, 2001, e.g. p. 41.

47. Wheeler, *Complexion of Race*, pp. 37, 248–9, and *passim*. S. Sebastiani, "Race as a Construction of the Other: 'Native Americans' and 'Negroes' in the 18th-Century Editions of the *Encyclopædia Britannica*", in B. Stråth (ed.), *Europe and the Other and Europe as the Other*, Brussels, 2000, pp. 195–228; S. Sebastiani, "Progress, National Characters, and Race in the Scottish Enlightenment"; and her PhD thesis, "Razza, donne, progresso: tensioni ideologiche nel dibattito dell'Illuminismo Scozzese", European University Institute, Florence, 2002. I am extremely grateful to Silvia Sebastiani for generously sharing her ongoing research. A similar narrative also underlies D. Bindman, *Ape to Apollo: Aesthetics and the Idea of Race in the 18th Century*, Ithaca (N.Y.), 2002; and F. A. Nussbaum, *The Limits of the Human: Fictions of Anomaly, Race, and Gender in the Long Eighteenth Century*, Cambridge, 2003.

48. *Gentleman's Magazine* 67 (1797), p. 94. G. H. Wilson, *The Eccentric Mirror: Reflecting a Faithful and Interesting Delineation of Male and Female Characters*, London, 1807, ii, pp. 28–33. And note also Charles White's discomfort with such reports: *An Account of the Regular Gradation in Man*, p. 121.

49. Cf. also P. Fryer, *Staying Power: The History of Black People in Britain*, London, 1984, chap. 7; C. A. Bayly, *Imperial Meridian: The British Empire and the World 1780–1830*, London, 1989, p. 155; idem, "The British and Indigenous Peoples, 1760–1860: Power, Perception and Identity", in Daunton and Halpern, *Empire and Others*, pp. 19–41; and Kidd, *British Identities before Nationalism*.

50. [Edward Long], *The History of Jamaica*, 3 vols., London, 1774, ii, pp. 354–6 (and see pp. 351ff.).

51. [William Knox], *Three Tracts Respecting the Conversion and Instruction of the Free Indians and Negroe Slaves in the Colonies*, [London, 1768], p. 16, closely adapted from [Arthur Lee], *An Essay in Vindication of the Continental Colonies of America*, London, 1764, pp. 37–8. Samuel Estwick, *Considerations on the Negroe Cause*, 2nd edn., London, 1773, pp. 81–2. Estwick in many ways laid the ground for Long's more elaborate tract. In the French West Indies, the comparable new departure of the 1780s was the writings of Moreau de Saint-Méry: cf. J. Dayan, *Haiti, History, and the Gods*, Berkeley, 1995, pp. 230–7.

52. White, *An Account of the Regular Gradation in Man*, pp. 83, 99, 110, 131.

53. James Ramsay, *An Essay on the Treatment and Conversion of African Slaves in the British Sugar Colonies*, Dublin (also London), 1784, pp. 172–3. *Gleanings of Africa*, pp. 135–6. Hannah More was one such writer whose anti-slavery position was imbricated in racialism and notions of essential selfhood: see M. Ferguson, *Subject to Others: British Women Writers and Colonial Slavery, 1670–1834*, New York, 1992, pp. 150–1; and A. Diego, "Signifying Bodies: 'Marvels', 'Negros' and the Production of 'Race' in the Eighteenth Century", PhD thesis, Cornell University, 1999. We shall encounter later further anti-slavery voices that formulated their positions precisely within such a framework of essential selfhood. For a related argument, about the paradoxical origins of south African notions of race in the vocabulary of evangelical missionaries at the beginning of the nineteenth century, see D. Stuart, "'Of Savages and Heroes': Discourses of Race, Nation and Gender in the Evangelical Missions to Southern Africa in the Early Nineteenth Century", PhD thesis, Institute of Commonwealth Studies, University of London, 1994.

54. James Anderson, *Observations on Slavery*, Manchester, 1789, pp. [3], 37; and cf. the opening of Ramsay, *An Essay on the Treatment and Conversion of African Slaves*, pp. [1]–2. [Long], *The History of Jamaica*, ii, p. 355. For another anti-slavery "Black Athena" argument see William Dickson, *Letters on Slavery*, London, 1789, p. 63. Unsurprisingly, the late eighteenth century turns out to be an important turning point in M. Bernal, *Black Athena: The Afroasiatic Roots of Classical Civilization*, New Brunswick, 1987.

55. Sir William Jones, "On the Origin and Families of Nations", delivered 23 Feb. 1792, in Augstein, *Race: The Origins of an Idea*, p. 42. On Sir William Jones and the emergence of Aryanism see T. R. Trautmann, *Aryans and British India*, Berkeley, 1997 (for the critique of the *Monthly Review* of 1797, see pp. 169–70); and T. Ballantyne, *Orientalism and Race: Aryanism in the British Empire*, Basingstoke, 2002, chap. 1. John Pinkerton, *A Dissertation on the Origins and Progress of the Scythians or Goths*, London, 1787 (published with his *An Enquiry into the History of Scotland*, 1789), pp. 33–4. Sh[aron] Turner, *The History of the Anglo-Saxons, from their First Appearance*, London, 1799, p. 2. Kidd, *British Identities before Nationalism*, pp. 97–8 and *passim*. David Doig, *Two Letters on the Savage State*, London, 1792, pp. viii–ix, 151–2 (letter dated 5 Nov. 1776). Also note the eccentric views of the English Huguenot philologist Charles Vallancey, who in several publications – especially *A Vindication of the Ancient History of Ireland*, Dublin, 1786 – attempted to prove the glorious eastern origins of Irish culture and language.

56. James Cowles Prichard, *Researches into the Physical History of Man*, London, 1813. On Prichard see Trautmann, *Aryans and British India*, pp. 170–2; and Ballantyne, *Orientalism and Race*, pp. 39–40. Coleridge to J. H. Green, 25 Jan. 1828, quoted in D. Herzog, *Poisoning the Minds of the Lower Orders*, Princeton, 1998, p. 296. For Coleridge's interestingly unstable views on race see P. J. Kitson, "Coleridge and 'the Ouran Utang Hypothesis': Romantic Theories of Race", in N. Roe (ed.), *Samuel Taylor Coleridge and the Sciences of Life*, Oxford, 2001, pp. 91–116. Cf. also the supposition of an ancient racial connection between Egyptians and East Indians, manifest in "hereditary" cultural affinities, in Henry Light, *Travels in Egypt, Nubia, Holy Land, Mount Lebanon, and Cyprus, in the Year 1814*, London, 1818, p. xiii.

57. For reminders of the relative fuzziness of ideas of race even in the mid-nineteenth century see P. Mandler, "'Race' and 'Nation' in Mid-Victorian Thought", in S. Collini et al., *History, Religion, and Culture: British Intellectual History 1750–1950*, Cambridge, 2000, pp. 224–44; and R. Romani, *National Character and Public Spirit in Britain and France, 1750–1914*, Cambridge, 2002, pp. 214–15.

58. William Robertson, *The History of America* (London, 1777), 3 vols., Vienna, 1787, ii, pp. 29, 45–6, 63–4, 71, also pp. 230–1. N. Phillipson, "Providence and Progress: An Introduction to the Historical Thought of William Robertson", in Brown (ed.), *William Robertson and the Expansion of Empire*, p. 61 (and see pp. 58–9). For a long contemporary commentary on the internal contradictions in Robertson's work, hovering between essentializing and particularized statements about the American Indians, see Bryan Edwards, *The History, Civil and Commercial, of the British Colonies in the West Indies*, 2nd edn., London, 1794, pp. x–xiv.

59. William Alexander, *The History of Women, from the Earliest Antiquity, to the Present Time*, 2 vols., Dublin (also London), 1779, i, p. 74; ii, p. 42.

60. Ramsay, *An Essay on the Treatment and Conversion of African Slaves*, pp. 172–3, 177, 180, 183–5. Clarkson, *An Essay on the Slavery and Commerce of the Human Species*,

pp. 198, 201–10 (including the example of the Jews), 197n. A similar example, uneasily lumping together more malleable and more essential understandings of climatic effects, is Dickson, *Letters on Slavery*, pp. 65–6.

61. Falconer, *Remarks on the Influence of Climate* (on the Jews as similar throughout the globe, see p. 180). Forster, *Observations Made during a Voyage round the World*, pp. 252, 275. William Marsden, *The History of Sumatra* (1783), 2nd edn., London, 1784, pp. 40–1. William Godwin, *Enquiry Concerning Political Justice* (1793), ed. I. Kramnick, Harmondsworth, 1985, pp. 150–1. James Macpherson, *An Introduction to the History of Great Britain and Ireland*, London, 1773, pp. 13–14, 262–7; and cf. the "Preliminary Reflections" in the London 1772 edn., pp. 1ff.

62. Dunbar, *Essays on the History of Mankind*, pp. 154–5 (emphasis added).

63. Ibid., pp. 300, 399, 405, 411, 419–20, 425, 430. For Dunbar on the Jews see above, p. 108.

64. E. H. Gould, *The Persistence of Empire: British Political Culture in the Age of the American Revolution*, Chapel Hill, 2000, pp. 209–11. P. Morgan, "Encounters between British and 'Indigenous' Peoples, c. 1500–c. 1800", in Daunton and Halpern, *Empire and Others*, p. 64 (and cf. H. L. Malchow, "The Half-Breed as Gothic Unnatural", in S. West [ed.], *The Victorians and Race*, Aldershot, 1996, pp. 101–11; Fryer, *Staying Power*, pp. 162–4). Bayly, *Imperial Meridian*, pp. 148–9; and p. 7, for the recurrence of this exclusion across British colonial territories around the globe within the next generation. See also C. J. Hawes, *Poor Relations: The Making of a Eurasian Community in British India 1773–1833*, Richmond (Surrey), 1996, esp. pp. 57, 60; and B. F. Tobin, *Picturing Imperial Power: Colonial Subjects in Eighteenth-Century British Painting*, Durham, 1999, chap. 4. For the introduction of formalized racial distinctions into the law in South Africa in the code of 1809 see E. Elbourne, "The Savage and the Saved: Early Nineteenth-Century Khoi Visitors to London and the Ambiguities of Colonialism". (I am grateful to have had the opportunity to read this work-in-progress.)

65. *Omiah's Farewell; Inscribed to the Ladies of London*, London, 1776, p. 2. See E. H. McCormick, *Omai: Pacific Envoy*, Auckland, 1977: Burney and the other contemporary observations in this paragraph are cited there, pp. 102, 106, 109, 125 (and see also p. 114), and for Reynolds's sketch, pp. 174–5. On Reynolds's final painting see B. Smith, *European Vision and the South Pacific*, 2nd edn., New Haven, 1988, pp. 80–2.

66. Cook and King, *A Voyage to the Pacific Ocean*, ii, p. 8. Dodd's image accompanied [John Rickman], *Journal of Captain Cook's Last Voyage to the Pacific Ocean*, London, 1781, facing p. 136, and quoted, p. 134; reproduced in Smith, *European Vision and the South Pacific*, p. 115. The comment on Omai's masquerade was David Samwell's, cited in McCormick, *Omai*, p. 240. Harriet Guest discusses suggestively this aspect of Omai's return in her "Colourful Tales: Fictions of Cultural Convergence in the South Pacific", paper presented at the Huntington Library, Oct. 2000, in anticipation of her book on Cook's second voyage (I am grateful to her for allowing me to cite this forthcoming work).

Wide-Angle Lens

1. For Alexander see above, pp. 118–19. Charles White, *An Account of the Regular Gradation in Man*, London, 1799, p. 135. K. J. Kirkpatrick, "'Gentlemen Have Horrors

upon This Subject': West Indian Suitors in Maria Edgeworth's *Belinda*",
Eighteenth-Century Fiction 5 (1993), pp. 331–48. S. C. Greenfield, "'Abroad and at
Home': Sexual Ambiguity, Miscegenation, and Colonial Boundaries in Edgeworth's
Belinda", *PMLA* 112:2 (March 1997), pp. 214–28.

2. F. A. Nussbaum, *Torrid Zones: Maternity, Sexuality, and Empire in Eighteenth-
   Century English Narratives*, Baltimore, 1995, pp. 34–5. D. Dugaw, "The Anatomy
   of Heroism: Gender Politics and Empire in Gay's *Polly*", in B. F. Tobin (ed.),
   History, Gender and Eighteenth-Century Literature, Athens (Ga.), 1994, esp. pp.
   40–1, together with her *Deep Play: John Gay and the Invention of Modernity*,
   Newark, 2001, pp. 189–94.

3. Some early-modern scholars have noted an earlier shift in notions of race in the
   second half of the seventeenth century, which may raise intriguing possibilities of
   a broad-scope late-seventeenth-century epistemological turning point. See L. E.
   Merians, *Envisioning the Worst: Representations of "Hottentots" in Early-Modern
   England*, Newark, 2001, p. 25, and the sources cited there.

4. [Edward Long], *The History of Jamaica*, 3 vols., London, 1774, ii, pp. 356–75. For
   this characterization of Long see P. Fryer, *Staying Power: The History of Black
   People in Britain*, London, 1984, p. 165; and see p. 162 for Philip Thicknesse's 1778
   diatribe on "the resemblance of the Orang Outang" to Negroes, obviously influenced by Long.

5. White, *An Account of the Regular Gradation in Man*, pp. 1–2, 10, 34, 42, 133.

6. A. O. Lovejoy, *The Great Chain of Being: A Study of the History of an Idea* (1936),
   New York, 1960, chap. 6; and pp. 185, 196 for Addison and Bolingbroke. John
   Hildrop, *Free Thoughts upon the Brute-Creation. . . . Letter II*, London, 1743, pp.
   63–4, 72–3. Soame Jenyns, *Disquisitions on Several Subjects* (1782), in *Works*, 4 vols.,
   1790, iii; reprinted in *Animal Rights and Souls in the Eighteenth Century*, ed. A.
   Garrett, 6 vols., Bristol, 2000, iv, p. 183. Locke had already written in a similar vein
   (*An Essay Concerning Human Understanding* [1700], ed. P. H. Nidditch, Oxford,
   1975, p. 572): "The well-shaped *Changeling* is a Man, has a rational Soul, though
   it appear not; this is past doubt, say you. Make the Ears a little longer, and more
   pointed . . . and then you begin to boggle: Make the Face yet narrower, flatter, and
   longer, and then you are at a stand: Add still more and more of the likeness of a
   Brute to it, and let the Head be perfectly that of some other Animal, then presently
   'tis a *Monster* . . . [that] hath no rational Soul, and must be destroy'd. Where now
   (I ask) shall be the just measure; which the utmost Bounds of that Shape, that
   carries with it a rational Soul?" Recent discussions include K. Thomas, *Man and
   the Natural World: Changing Attitudes in England 1500–1800*, Harmondsworth,
   1984, pp. 31–3. S. Wiseman, "Monstrous Perfectibility: Ape-Human Transformations in Hobbes, Bulwer, Tyson", in E. Fudge et al. (eds.), *At the Borders of the
   Human: Beasts, Bodies and Natural Philosophy in the Early Modern Period*, Basingstoke, 1999, pp. 215–38. L. Brown, *Fables of Modernity: Literature and Culture
   in the English Eighteenth Century*, Ithaca (N. Y.), 2001, chap. 6. Note also the decline
   in urgency, disgust, and holy horror in the contemplation of bestiality in the
   eighteenth-century British Atlantic in comparison with the seventeenth century, as
   noted in J. M. Murrin, "'Things Fearful to Name': Bestiality in Colonial America",
   Pennsylvania History 65 (1998), pp. 8–43.

7. [Sir Richard Blackmore,] *The Lay Monastery*, London, 1714, pp. 28–30. For Folkes
   see Thomas, *Man and the Natural World*, p. 124 (and see pp. 121–36). Congreve is
   quoted in M. E. Novak, "The Wild Man Comes to Tea", in E. Dudley and M. E.

Novak (eds.), *The Wild Man Within*, Pittsburgh, 1972, p. 190. Compare, *inter alia*, John Grose, *A Voyage to the East Indies*, London, 1766, p. 232. See also W. D. Jordan, *White over Black: American Attitudes towards the Negro, 1550–1812*, Chapel Hill, 1968, pp. 28–32, 218–24, 228–34; L. Schiebinger, *Nature's Body: Gender in the Making of Modern Science*, Boston, 1993, chap. 3; S. Volkov, "Exploring the Other: The Enlightenment Search for the Boundaries of Humanity", in R. S. Wistrich (ed.), *Demonizing the Other: Antisemitism, Racism, and Xenophobia*, Jerusalem, 2000, pp. 148–67; and R. Nash, *Wild Enlightenment: The Borders of Human Identity in the Eighteenth Century*, Charlottesville (Va.), 2003, chap. 1 (I am grateful to Richard Nash for allowing me to see this manuscript before publication). It should be noted that although both the great chain of being – in its eighteenth-century interpretation – and the Linnean system of classification undermined the clear separation of humans from apes, they were in fact fundamentally different and indeed incompatible classificatory systems.

8. *Gentleman's Magazine* 21 (Nov. 1751), p. 522. James Houstoun, *Some New and Accurate Observations . . . of the Coast of Guinea*, London, 1725, pp. 33–4. [Peter Shaw], *Man. A Paper for Ennobling the Species*, 11 (12 March 1755), pp. [1]–2. Cf. also Joseph Priestley, *Hartley's Theory of the Human Mind, on the Principle of the Association of Ideas*, London, 1775, pp. 238–49. Another supporter of such notions on the Continent was La Mettrie, who suggested in *L'Homme machine* (1748) that through hard work and good will an ape (like feral children, also suspended between human and animal) may be transformed into "un Homme parfait, un petit Homme de Ville" (cited in J. Douthwaite, "*Homo ferus*: Between Monster and Model", in A. Curran et al. [eds.], *Faces of Monstrosity in Eighteenth-Century Thought*, special issue of *Eighteenth-Century Life* 21:2 [1997], p. 200 n. 45).

9. *Monthly Review* 34 (1766), p. 530. G. S. Rousseau, "Madame Chimpanzee", in his *Enlightenment Crossings: Pre- and Post-Modern Discourses*, Manchester, 1991, pp. 198–209 (quoted, pp. 201, 203); and for similar instances, see A. J. Barker, *The African Link: British Attitudes to the Negro in the Era of the Atlantic Slave Trade, 1550–1807*, London, 1978, pp. 57–8. J. Douthwaite, *The Wild Girl, Natural Man and the Monster: Dangerous Experiments in the Age of Enlightenment*, Chicago, 2002, chap. 1 (for the triptych image of Peter, pp. 24–6, following Novak, "The Wild Man Comes to Tea", pp. 190–2). M. Newton, *The Child of Nature: The Feral Child and the State of Nature*, PhD thesis, London University, 1996.

10. *Monthly Review* 42 (1770), pp. 530–1. *Letters of the Right Honourable Lady M—y W—y M—e; Written during her Travels*, London, 1763, cited in Nussbaum, *Torrid Zones*, p. 92. On stories of black–ape sex, see Jordan, *White over Black*, pp. 31–2 (but also the corrective in Barker, *The African Link*, pp. 56–7); Nash, *Wild Enlightenment*, chap. 4; and Brown, *Fables of Modernity*, pp. 236–45.

11. Peter Camper, "Account of the Organs of Speech of the Orang Outang", *Philosophical Transactions, of the Royal Society of London* 69 (1779), p. 140 (and see M. C. Meijer, *Race and Aesthetics in the Anthropology of Petrus Camper*, Amsterdam, 1999, chaps. 3, 6). *Monthly Review* 62 (1780), p. 220. The *Monthly Review* 33 (1800) actually faulted White himself for not going far enough in securing the human/animal boundary (in H. F. Augstein [ed.], *Race: The Origins of an Idea, 1760–1850*, Bristol, 1996, p. 55).

12. Johann Reinhold Forster, *Observations Made during a Voyage round the World*, London, 1778, pp. 254–6. *Gentleman's Magazine* 68 (1798), p. 947. *Monthly Review* 80 (1789), p. 685. "Comparative Anatomy", *Encyclopaedia Britannica*, 3rd edn.,

Edinburgh, 1797, v, pp. 249–74; quoted in S. Sebastiani, "Race as a Construction of the Other: 'Native Americans' and 'Negroes' in the 18th Century Editions of the *Encyclopædia Britannica*", in B. Stråth (ed.), *Europe and the Other and Europe as the Other*, Brussels, 2000, p. 217.

Of course, the fascination with the similarity of apes to humans was not to go away. But, as Harriet Ritvo has pointed out, unlike the eighteenth century, where the distinctiveness of the human species had not yet been posited clearly, by the nineteenth century human–ape resemblances no longer led to the blurring of the boundary between them. Rather, if anything, they proved the reverse, namely that humans (thus an 1833 formulation) were "infinitely pre-eminent". H. Ritvo, *The Animal Estate: The English and Other Creatures in the Victorian Age*, Cambridge (Mass.), 1987, pp. 31–4, 39. And cf. John Bird Sumner, *A Treatise on the Records of Creation* (1816), 2 vols., 4th edn., London, 1825, ii, pp. 20–3.

13. James Burnett, Lord Monboddo, *Of the Origins and Progress of Language*, 6 vols., 2nd edn., Edinburgh and London, 1774, i, p. 297. James Beattie quoted in E. L. Cloyd, *James Burnet, Lord Monboddo*, Oxford, 1972, p. 47 (and cf. the dismissal of Monboddo's views as "preposterous and unnatural" in *The Progress of Fashion*, London, 1786, pp. 60–2). William Roberts, *Memoirs of the Life and Correspondence of Mrs. Hannah More*, 4 vols., 3rd edn., London, 1835, i, pp. 252–3. Dr. Johnson cited in R. Wokler, "Apes and Races in the Scottish Enlightenment: Monboddo and Kames on the Nature of Man", in P. Jones (ed.), *Philosophy and Science in the Scottish Enlightenment*, Edinburgh, 1988, p. 145. [John Elliott?], *The Travels of Hildebrand Bowman, Esquire, into Carnovirria, Taupiniera, Olfactaria. . . . Written by Himself*, London, 1778.

14. Monboddo, *Of the Origins and Progress of Language*, i, pp. 348, 367, and see p. 311 (the section on "Orang-Outangs" had been added and expanded after the 1st edn. of 1773). Idem, *Antient Metaphysics*, 6 vols., London and Edinburgh, 1779–99, iii (1784), pp. 335, 359. On Monboddo's investment in the human–animal distinction see also his letter to Sir John Pringle, 16 June 1773, in William Knight, *Lord Monboddo and Some of his Contemporaries*, London, 1900, pp. 84–5. These texts have all been reprinted in *Animal Rights and Souls*, vol. vi.

15. Oliver Goldsmith, *An History of the Earth, and Animated Nature*, 8 vols., London, 1774, ii, pp. 310–11; iv, pp. 187–8, 203–4 (emphases added). On eighteenth-century representations of monkeys that combined realism with progressive anthropomorphism see E. K. Levy and D. E. Levy, "Monkey in the Middle: Pre-Darwinian Evolutionary Thought and Artistic Creation", *Perspectives in Biology and Medicine* 30:1 (1986), pp. 95–106. Meijer, *Race and Aesthetics*, pp. 127–34.

16. William Smellie, *The Philosophy of Natural History*, 2 vols., Edinburgh, 1790, i, p. 523 (emphases added). William Dickson, *Letters on Slavery*, London, 1789, p. 68. Humphry Primatt, *A Dissertation on the Duty of Mercy and Sin of Cruelty to Brute Animals*, London, 1776, pp. 95–6, 108.

17. James Dunbar, *Essays on the History of Mankind in Rude and Cultivated Ages*, London, 1780, pp. 14–16. Joseph Ritson, *An Essay on Abstinence from Animal Food, as a Moral Duty*, London, 1802, as discussed in K. Tester, *Animals and Society: The Humanity of Animal Rights*, London, 1991, pp. 133–7 (and see contemporary quotations there). [Thomas Love Peacock], *Melincourt*, London, 1817, as discussed in Nash, *Wild Enlightenment*, chap. 6. Douthwaite, *The Wild Girl, Natural Man and the Monster*, pp. 58–60.

18. *European Magazine and London Review* 13 (1788), pp. 75–6. Dickson, *Letters on Slavery*, p. 67 (and see pp. 67, 71, 82–4). Thomas Clarkson, *An Essay on the Slavery and Commerce of the Human Species, Particularly the African*, London, 1786, p. 187. Charlotte Smith, *Desmond* (1792), eds. A. Blank and J. Todd, London, 1997, p. 329. Compare, *inter alia*, Richard Hillier, *A Vindication of the Address to the People of Great-Britain*, London, [1792], p. 6; and Jeremy Bentham's assertion of the human/animal boundary in the context of slavery in his *An Introduction to the Principles of Morals and Legislation* (1789), eds. J. H. Burns and H. L. A. Hart, Oxford, 1996, p. 283n.

19. William Lambe, *Additional Reports on the Effects of a Peculiar Regimen*, London, 1815, p. 227, cited in Thomas, *Man and the Natural World*, p. 137. William Bingley, *Memoirs of British Quadrupeds*, London, 1809, p. 2 (emphasis added). Cf., *inter alia*, the shocked insistence on the "permanent distinctions" between humans and animals in *The Artist's Repository and Drawing Magazine*, 1 (1788), pp. 151–4 (also pp. 81–2); Sir Charles Bell, *Essays on the Anatomy of Expression in Painting*, London, 1806, pp. 85–8; and Thomas Pennant in 1793, as cited in H. Ritvo, *The Platypus and the Mermaid and Other Figments of the Classifying Imagination*, Cambridge (Mass.), 1997, p. 52. Ritvo has noted a more general investment from the late eighteenth century in the integrity of species: see her "Barring the Cross: Miscegenation and Purity in Eighteenth- and Nineteenth-Century Britain", in D. Fuss (ed.), *Human, All Too Human*, New York, 1996, pp. 37–57. Also note M. Fissell, "Imagining Vermin in Early Modern England", *History Workshop Journal* 47 (1999), pp. 1–29, for interesting observations on the early-modern views of vermin as human-like competitors, capable of language, communication, and social formation, rather than as the targets of unmitigated disgust that they would become in the nineteenth century.

20. Tester, *Animals and Society*, pp. 88, 96–7 (on Bentham), 111 (on legislation), and *passim*. Richard Dean, *An Essay on the Future Life of Brutes*, 2 vols., 2nd edn., London, 1768, ii, pp. 102–3 (and see also pp. 69–70, 104). David Hartley, *Observations on Man*, London, 1749, pt. I, pp. 414–15. Thomas Young, *An Essay on Humanity to Animals*, London, 1798, p. 191 (and see pp. 6–7). Primatt, *A Dissertation on the Duty of Mercy*, pp. 34–5, 100. Bentham, *Introduction to the Principles of Morals and Legislation*, p. 283n. For a later text that still strongly argued the case from similitude see John Oswald, *The Cry of Nature; or, An Appeal to Mercy and to Justice, on Behalf of the Persecuted Animals*, London, 1791, pp. 52, 54, 84.

21. R. Porter, "Man, Animals and Medicine at the Time of the Founding of the Royal Veterinary College", in A. R. Mitchell (ed.), *History of the Healing Professions: Parallels between Veterinary and Medical History*, London, 1993, pp. 19–30. I. Pattison, *The British Veterinary Profession 1791–1848*, London, 1984, chap. 1. J. Swabe, *Animals, Disease and Human Society: Human–Animal Relations and the Rise of Veterinary Medicine*, London, 1999, chap. 4.

22. A. Pinch, "Romantic Anti-Anthropomorphisms", unpublished paper (I am grateful to Adela Pinch for sharing her work-in-progress with me), following the cue in J. Berger, "Why Look at Animals", in his *About Looking*, New York, 1980, esp. p. 9. For early-modern anthropomorphism and its presupposition of human/animal proximity, see E. Fudge, *Perceiving Animals: Humans and Beasts in Early Modern English Culture*, Basingstoke, 2000. Also consider the sub-genre of biographies of animals directed at children. As Samuel Pickering has pointed out (in *John Locke*

and Children's Books in Eighteenth-Century England, Knoxville [Tenn.], 1981, p. 96), whereas in the earlier part of the eighteenth century this had been a genre that anthropomorphized animals to discuss a wide variety of moral and educational issues, toward the end of the century it became much more limited, centering on the one issue of human cruelty to inferior animals: again, a shift from similarity to difference.

23. [John Gregory], *A Comparative View of the State and Faculties of Man with Those of the Animal World*, London, 1765 (based on lectures of the late 1750s), pp. 8–9; new edn., 1785, pp. iii–v, 117.

24. Thomas, *Man and the Natural World*, p. 135.

25. John Blair's lawyers on Hugh Blair, 1748, cited and discussed in R. Houston and U. Frith, *Autism in History: The Case of Hugh Blair of Borgue*, Oxford, 2000, pp. 64–5 (according to the authors, the tone of the depositions regarding Blair's perhaps non-humanity was "curious rather than appalled"). *Characterism, or, the Modern Age Display'd*, London, [1750], p. 166 (see above, p. 43).

26. For these and other instances see [Richard Bentley], *A True and Faithful Account of the Greatest Wonder Produced by Nature . . . the Surprizing Centaur*, [London], [1751?] (note pp. 14–15 for the intimation that the centaur was the outcome of a sexual union of a farmer and a mare). Barker, *The African Link*, p. 58. D. Todd, *Imagining Monsters: Miscreations of the Self in Eighteenth-Century England*, Chicago, 1995, p. 147. Douthwaite, "*Homo ferus*: Between Monster and Model", p. 179. Murrin, "'Things Fearful to Name'", pp. 10, 29, and *passim*. Brown, *Fables of Modernity*, pp. 229–30. Fudge, *Perceiving Animals*, pp. 121–5. Ritvo, *The Animal Estate*, p. 1, reports a 1679 hanging of a woman with her dog for bestiality. John Locke also accepted the possibility that women could be impregnated by mandrills: *An Essay Concerning Human Understanding*, p. 451.

27. L. Cody, "The Doctor's in Labour; or, A New Whim Wham from Guildford", *Gender and History* 4:2 (1992), pp. 175–96, and Todd, *Imagining Monsters* (contemporary quotations on pp. 2, 39–40).

28. [Guillaume Hyacinthe Bougeant], *A Philosophical Amusement upon the Language of Beasts*, London, 1739, p. 37.

29. Mark Noble, *A Biographical History of England*, 3 vols., London, 1806, iii, p. 477. Owen Manning and William Bray, *The History and Antiquities of the County of Surrey*, 3 vols., vol. i, London, 1804, p. 649. *Memoirs and Anecdotes of Philip Thicknesse*, Dublin, 1790, p. 160. James Caulfield, *Portraits, Memoirs, and Characters, of Remarkable Persons*, 4 vols., London, 1820, ii, p. 197. Cody, "The Doctor's in Labour", pp. 189–90 (and further quotations there).

30. Dunbar, *Essays on the History of Mankind*, pp. 398–9, 405–11 (emphasis added).

31. *A Short History of Bees. In Two Parts*, London, 1800, pp. 90–1 (and cf. *The Monarchy of the Bees; A Poem*, London, 1821, p. 15). William Falconer, *Remarks on the Influence of Climate, Situation, Nature of Country*, London, 1781, pp. 312–13. The *Britannica* is quoted in Sebastiani, "Race as a Construction of the Other", p. 222 and n. 97. Primatt, *A Dissertation on the Duty of Mercy*, pp. 11–12.

32. D. Wahrman, *Imagining the Middle Class: The Political Representation of Class in Britain, c. 1780–1840*, Cambridge, 1995, pp. 67–8 n. 80.

33. Fox to Lord Holland, 28 Dec. 1793, quoted in L. G. Mitchell, *Charles James Fox*, Oxford, 1992, p. 130. *The British Tocsin; or, Proofs of National Ruin*, London, 1795,

pp. 36–7. Christopher Wyvill to John Courtney, 18 June 1794, in C. Wyvill, *Political Papers*, 6 vols., vol. v, York, [1804], p. 207. Thomas Bigge, *Considerations on the State of Parties, and the Means of Effecting a Reconciliation between Them*, 2nd edn., London, [1793 or 1794], pp. 7, 31. This argument is laid down, with numerous further contemporary voices, in my *Imagining the Middle Class*, chap. 2.

34. James Mackintosh, *Vindiciae Gallicae. Defence of the French Revolution and its English Admirers*, 3rd edn., with additions, London, 1791, p. 268. James Scott, *Equality Considered and Recommended, in a Sermon . . . April the 6th, 1794*, London, 1794, p. 11. For the skewed dialogue see my *Imagining the Middle Class*, part I.

35. J. Brewer, "English Radicalism in the Age of George III", in J. G. A. Pocock (ed.), *Three British Revolutions: 1641, 1688, 1776*, Princeton, 1980, pp. 323–67; idem, "Commercialization and Politics", in N. McKendrick, J. Brewer, and J. Plumb, *The Birth of a Consumer Society*, Bloomington, 1982, pp. 197–262; and idem, "The Number 45: A Wilkite Political Symbol", in S. B. Baxter (ed.), *England's Rise to Greatness, 1660–1763*, Berkeley, 1983, pp. 349–80 (quoted, p. 374). K. Wilson, *The Sense of the People: Politics, Culture and Imperialism in England, 1715–1785*, Cambridge, 1995, esp. p. 234.

36. E. P. Thompson, "Patrician Society, Plebeian Culture", *Journal of Social History* 7 (1974), pp. 382–405, with his "Eighteenth-Century English Society: Class Struggle without Class?", *Social History* 3 (1978), 133–65. See also Thompson's reply to his critics in his *Customs in Common*, London, 1991, pp. 87–90. For further discussion of this conundrum, interpreting middling-sort behavior in the eighteenth century as a matter of choice between two polar cultural-political positions rather than as a reflection of social position, see my "National Society, Provincial Culture: An Argument about the Historiography of Eighteenth-Century Britain", *Social History* 17 (1992), pp. 43–72.

37. P. Langford, *Public Life and the Propertied Englishman 1689–1798*, Oxford, 1991, pp. 535, 541; and p. 538 for the quotation from Day. Thomas Paine, *Rights of Man* (1791), ed. E. Foner, Harmondsworth, 1985, p. 83. John Merritt, *A Letter to Wm. Roscoe, Esq . . . on the Subject of Parliamentary Reform*, Liverpool, [1811?], pp. 15, 17. [Sir Charles Aldis,] *A Defence of the Character and Conduct of the Late Mary Wollstonecraft Godwin*, London, 1803, p. [iii]. Cf. S. Conway, *The British Isles and the War of American Independence*, Oxford, 2000, pp. 94–5. D. Andrew, "Adultery à la Mode: Privilege, the Law and Attitudes to Adultery 1770–1809", *History* 82:265 (1997), p. 6 (anticipating her long-awaited definitive work on the attacks on aristocratic vice during this period). For the aristocratic counter-mobilization to fend off this critique see L. Colley, *Britons: Forging the Nation 1707–1837*, New Haven, 1992, chap. 4. For Burke's definition of "natural aristocracy" see his *An Appeal from the New to the Old Whigs* (1791), in Edmund Burke, *Further Reflections on the Revolution in France*, ed. D. E. Ritchie, Indianapolis, 1992, pp. 168–9.

38. Thomas Cooper, *A Reply to Mr. Burke's Invective against Mr. Cooper*, Manchester, 1792, pp. 70, 74. G[eorge] Dyer, *The Complaints of the Poor People of England*, 2nd edn., London, 1793, p. 3. [Sir Robert Adair], *A Whig's Apology for his Consistency*, London, 1795, p. 192. Smellie, *The Philosophy of Natural History*, as cited in Schiebinger, *Nature's Body*, p. 145. See further in my *Imagining the Middle Class*, chap. 3.

39. See S. Thorne, *Congregational Missions and the Making of an Imperial Culture in Nineteenth-Century England*, Stanford, 1999, pp. 1–2, 15, and *passim*.

Bird's-Eye View

1. M. Poovey, *Making a Social Body: British Cultural Formation 1830–1864*, Chicago, 1995, pp. 2–3. L. Daston, "Historical Epistemology", in J. Chandler et al. (eds.), *Questions of Evidence: Proof, Practice, and Persuasion across the Disciplines*, Chicago, 1994, esp. pp. 282–3.

2. Walpole to Horace Mann, 10 March 1755, as quoted in T. Castle, *Masquerade and Civilization: The Carnivalesque in Eighteenth-Century English Culture and Fiction*, Stanford, 1986, p. 3. My account of the masquerades owes much to Castle's authoritative work. See also her *The Female Thermometer: Eighteenth-Century Culture and the Invention of the Uncanny*, New York, 1995, esp. chap. 6. For the late-seventeenth- and early-eighteenth-century practice of wearing masks in public see C. Heyl, "When They Are Veyl'd on Purpose to Be Seene: The Metamorphosis of the Mask in Seventeenth- and Eighteenth-Century London", in J. Entwistle and E. Wilson (eds.), *Bodily Dressing*, Oxford, 2001, pp. 121–42: as Heyl points out, masks had sometimes been worn earlier in the seventeenth century as well, but with a distinctly different utilitarian-functional purpose. On the very different nature of seventeenth-century court masques, in which roles were ordained within a decorous representation of power, see J.-C. Agnew, *Worlds Apart: The Market and the Theater in Anglo-American Thought, 1550–1750*, Cambridge, 1986, p. 146.

3. [Edward Young], *Love of Fame, the Universal Passion. Satire VI. On Women*, London, 1728, p. 145. See further examples below, p. 167.

4. *Weekly Journal*, 15 Feb. 1718, and 8 Feb. 1724, as quoted in Castle, *Masquerade and Civilization*, pp. 25, 67 (and cf. p. 60).

5. *It Cannot Rain But It Pours; or, London Strow'd with Rarities*, London, 1726, pp. 5–6 (emphasis added). Christopher Pitt, "On the Masquerades" (1727), cited in Castle, *Masquerade and Civilization*, p. 83 (and cf. p. 28). [Frances Brooke], *The Old Maid* 9 (10 Jan. 1756), p. 66. *Coxheath-Camp: A Novel. In a Series of Letters. By a Lady*, Dublin (also London), 1779, cited in G. Russell, *The Theatres of War: Performance, Politics, and Society, 1793–1815*, Oxford, 1995, p. 39. *Weekly Journal*, 25 Jan. 1724, cited in Castle, *The Female Thermometer*, p. 86. And cf. *Gentleman's Magazine* 5 (1735), p. 186.

6. *Town and Country Magazine*, May 1772, pp. 236–8. [John Elliott?], *The Travels of Hildebrand Bowman, Esquire, into Carnovirria, Taupiniera, Olfactaria. . . . Written by Himself*, London, 1778, p. 307. [James Burgh], *Political Disquisitions*, 3 vols., London, 1774, iii, p. 110. *The Freethinker* 108 (1719), as cited in E. Donoghue, *Passions between Women: British Lesbian Culture 1688–1801*, London, 1993, p. 90. (Cf. also *Love's Invention; or, The Recreation in Vogue. An Excellent New Ballad upon the Masquerades*, 2nd edn., London, 1718, pp. 8, 11.) John Cleland, *Memoirs of a Woman of Pleasure*, 2 vols., London, 1749, ii, pp. 167–8. And note the calm and even approving reference to playful gender-crossing in masquerades in *The Original of Apparel; or, The Ornaments of Dress*, London, 1732, p. 4.

7. Joseph Addison in *The Guardian* 154 (7 Sept. 1713). Christopher Pitt, "On the Masquerades" (1727), in Castle, *Masquerade and Civilization*, p. 83.

8. *Lady's Magazine* 6 (April 1775), p. 240; 7 (Dec. 1777), pp. 637–8. *The Young Gentleman and Lady Instructed in Such Principles of Politeness*, 2 vols., London, 1747, ii, pp. 137–8, quoted in I. H. Tague, *Women of Quality: Accepting and Contesting Ideals of Femininity in England, 1690–1760*, Woodbridge, 2002, p. 56.

Daniel Defoe, *Roxana: The Fortunate Mistress* (1724), ed. J. Mullan, Oxford, 1996, pp. 176–7, 181 (first emphasis added). And cf. F. A. Nussbaum, *Torrid Zones: Maternity, Sexuality, and Empire in Eighteenth-Century English Narratives*, Baltimore, 1995, p. 36.

9. "Masquerade Intelligence", 17 Feb. 1779, quoted in *Mrs. Cornely's Entertainments at Carlisle House, Soho Square*, [London?], [1840?], p. 16 (and see p. 18 for the closure of Carlisle House). *Lady's Magazine*, April 1760, p. 366, as quoted in A. Ribeiro, *The Dress Worn at Masquerades in England, 1730 to 1790*, New York, 1984, pp. 6, 19. Castle, *Masquerade and Civilization*, pp. 98–9 (emphasis added); also idem, *Female Thermometer*, p. 86. Francis Place, "Manners. Morals. The Drama &c", ii, in Francis Place's Papers, vol. xliv, BL, Add. Mss. 27832, f. 177.

10. James Peller Malcolm, *Anecdotes of the Manners and Customs of London during the Eighteenth Century*, London, 1808, p. 406. Place, "Manners. Morals. The Drama", ff. 176–7. On Colonel Armstrong, as reported in an 1825 memoir, see Castle, *Masquerade and Civilization*, pp. 331–2; and cf. p. 99. Note also the late-eighteenth-century lady who claimed to have "outlived these Diversions", namely the masquerades, while also dismissing as a mere "Pretence" the reported indistinguishability of their masked disguises: *The Deportment of a Married Life: Laid Down in a Series of Letters*, London, 1790, pp. 238, 242. Finally, it is suggestive to note where the memory of the masquerades did continue to linger. In early Victorian London masquerading attire could reportedly be found in London's most famous alley of obscenity and pornography, Holywell Street; but even there, according to G. W. M. Reynolds's *The Mysteries of London* (1844–56), it was a practice "all but gone" (L. Nead, *Victorian Babylon: People, Streets and Images in Nineteenth-Century London*, New Haven and London, 2000, p. 174). For the intriguing possibility that some eighteenth-century practices survived in the underground world of pornography see above, p. 330 n. 41.

11. Mrs. [Hannah] Cowley, *The Belle's Stratagem. . . . With Remarks by Mrs. Inchbald*, London, [1806], p. 5 (emphasis added); and cf. Inchbald's comment in her edition of Arthur Murphy, *All in the Wrong*, London, 1806, p. 4: "A veil should now be substituted in this scene, for that old-fashioned appendage to disguise, a mask." James Boaden, *Memoirs of Mrs. Inchbald*, 2 vols., London, 1833, i, p. 140.

12. Castle, *Masquerade and Civilization*, pp. 98, 327, 330; and for explanations of the masquerade's demise, esp. pp. 100–5.

13. Elizabeth Inchbald, *A Simple Story* (1791), eds. J. M. S. Tompkins and J. Spencer, Oxford, 1991, pp. 151–60: this scene, as Castle points out (*Masquerade and Civilization*, pp. 309–10), is unique in lacking the usual content and meaning of the topical eighteenth-century masquerade tableau, emphasizing instead only its hazardous potential to subvert gender distinctions. And cf. Thomas Vaughan's prologue to [Elizabeth] Inchbald, *Such Things Are*, London, 1788, which also denounced the gender-cum-sexual transgressions of the masquerade.

14. John Galt, "The Masquerade. A Comedy", in *The New British Theatre; A Selection of Original Dramas, Not Yet Acted*, 4 vols., London, 1814, i, p. 246 [i.e. p. 264]. Note also the denunciation of the "disgusting" sexual transformations in a masquerade in an unidentified periodical clipping, dated Feb. 1789, in the Papers of the Chevalier D'Eon, Brotherton Library, Leeds, unnumbered file marked "Important D'Eon Papers".

Chapter 4

1. A. Betson, *Miscellaneous Dissertations Historical, Critical, and Moral, on the Origins and Antiquity of Masquerades, Plays, Poetry, &c.*, London, [1751], pp. iv, 10, 14, 45. Cf. also "Of Masquerades", in [James Ralph], *The Touch-Stone*, London, 1728, esp. pp. 177, 179.

2. Charles Gildon, *The Post-boy Rob'd of his Mail*, London, 1692, prologue, p. 20. John Trenchard and Thomas Gordon, *Cato's Letters* (1720), 2 vols., New York, 1971, i, p. 23. [Edward Young], *Love of Fame, the Universal Passion. Satire VI. On Women*, London, 1728, p. 145. Henry Fielding, "An Essay on the Knowledge of the Characters of Men", in *Miscellanies, by Henry Fielding, Esq* (1743), ed. H. K. Miller, Oxford, 1972, i, p. 155. *Truth on All Sides. A New Masquerade Ballad*, n.p., 1750, p. 8 (and cf. similarly *The World in Disguise; or, Masks All. A New Ballad*, London, [c. 1749]). Samuel Johnson, *The Rambler*, eds. W. J. Bate and A. B. Strauss, 3 vols., New Haven, 1969, ii, p. 33 (75 [4 Dec. 1750]). Tobias George Smollett, *The Adventures of Ferdinand Count Fathom*, 2 vols., London, 1753, i, p. 232. *The Country Coquet; or, Miss in her Breeches. Ballad Opera. . . . By a Young Lady*, London, 1755, p. 11. Charlotte Lennox, *The Sister: A Comedy*, London, 1769, epilogue by Oliver Goldsmith (the two examples of masquerading identity shifts in this epilogue are man-turned-woman and white-turned-black). Mrs. [Hannah] Cowley, *The Belle's Stratagem. A Comedy* (1781), London, 1782, p. 27.

3. *St. James's Magazine*, 1 (Oct. 1774) i, p. 444: "Human Life Compared to a Masquerade". Elizabeth Montagu to Miss H. More, Bath, 1782, in William Roberts, *Memoirs of the Life and Correspondence of Mrs. Hannah More*, 4 vols., 3rd edn., London, 1835, i, p. 269. [Thomas Letchworth], *A Morning's Meditation; or, A Descant on the Times. A Poem*, London, 1765, pp. 186–7.

4. S. Knott, "A Cultural History of Sensibility in the Era of the American Revolution", PhD thesis, Oxford University, 1999. See below, pp. 186–7.

5. Cowley, *The Belle's Stratagem*, pp. 27, 59.

6. *An Account of a Savage Girl, Caught Wild in the Woods of Champagne. Translated from the French*, Edinburgh, 1768, pp. vii, xvi (from the preface written by Lord Monboddo). James Boswell, *Boswell's London Journal, 1762–1763*, ed. F. A. Pottle, New York, 1950, p. 47, entry for 21 Nov. 1762.

7. Aaron Hill, "An Essay on the Art of Acting", in *The Works of the Late Aaron Hill*, 4 vols., London, 1753, iv, p. [355]. [John Hill], *The Actor: A Treatise on the Art of Playing*, London, 1750, p. 106 (emphasis added; this work relied heavily and silently on Rémond de Sainte Albine, *Le Comédien*, Paris, 1747); and 1755 edn., p. 110. Charles Gildon, *The Life of Mr Thomas Betterton*, London, 1710, p. 34 (also p. 40). Richard Flecknoe, "The Acting of Richard Burbage" (1664), in T. Cole and H. K. Chinoy, *Actors on Acting*, New York, 1957, p. 91 (and cf. *Reflections upon Theatrical Expression in Tragedy*, London, 1755, pp. 14–15). "The Character of an Excellent Actor", *Gentleman's Magazine* 13 (1743), p. 254. *Theatrical Biography*, 2 vols., London, 1772, i, pp. 149–50. See S. West, *The Image of the Actor: Verbal and Visual Representation in the Age of Garrick and Kemble*, London, 1991, chap. 3; and J. R. Roach, *The Player's Passion: Studies in the Science of Acting*, Newark, 1985. The following paragraphs owe much to Paul Friedland's insightful work – see below, p. 401 n. 16. I am also grateful to Wendy Aron for her advice on this subject.

8. Samuel Foote, *The Roman and English Comedy Consider'd and Compar'd*, London, 1747, pp. 38–9 (emphasis added). Henry Fielding, *Tom Jones* (1749), eds. J. Bender

and S. Stern, Oxford, 1996, pp. 751–4 (echoing the praise for Betterton's earlier Hamlet in *The Laureat; or, The Right Side of Colley Cibber*, London, 1740, p. 31). Goldsmith quoted in L. Woods, *Garrick Claims the Stage: Acting as Social Emblem in Eighteenth-Century England*, Westport (Conn.), 1984, p. 6. Cf. Dr. Franklin's verse compliment to Garrick's Shakespearean performances: "'Tis not a scene of idle mimicry,/ 'Tis Lear's, Hamlet's, Richard's self we see" (in Thomas Davies, *Memoirs of the Life of David Garrick*, 2 vols., new edn., London, 1780, ii, p. 403). See D. S. Lynch, *The Economy of Character: Novels, Market Culture, and the Business of Inner Meaning*, Chicago, 1998, pp. 71, 83, and *passim*. Scott Gordon has also recently written about this reputation of Garrick's, but his premise that a preoccupation with interiority versus exteriority was a contemporary concern (a premise arrived at by conflating self-interest with self-as-interiority) leads him to deny that writers on acting actually imagined any transformation taking place: S. P. Gordon, *The Power of the Passive Self in English Literature, 1640–1770*, Cambridge, 2002, p. 163 and chap. 5.

9. West, *Image of the Actor*, pp. 67–8. For Friedland see p. 401 n.16. Thomas Wilkes, *A General View of the Stage*, London, 1759, p. 92. Edmund Burke, *A Philosophical Enquiry into the Origins of our Ideas of the Sublime and Beautiful* (2nd edn., 1759), ed. J. T. Boulton, Notre Dame, 1958, p. 133. Letter from Garrick to Madame Clairon, Aug. 1769, in Cole and Chinoy, *Actors on Acting*, p. 137. De Sainte Albine, *Le Comédien*, p. 32.

10. Dr. Johnson quoted in P. Holland, *The Ornament of Action: Text and Performance in Restoration Comedy*, Cambridge, 1979, p. 63. George Farquhar, *Love and Business* (1702), in *The Complete Works of George Farquhar*, 2 vols., ed. C. Stonehill, New York, 1967, ii, p. 341. [Hill], *The Actor*, 1755 edn., p. 110. Similarly cf. Joseph Pittard, *Observations on Mr. Garrick's Acting*, London, 1758, p. 11, and [Robert Lloyd], *The Actor. A Poetical Epistle*, London, 1760, p. 4: "No Actor pleases that is not *possess'd*." On the earlier invocations of magic in seventeenth-century acting theory see Roach, *The Player's Passion*, chap. 1. As an example we can take Samuel Butler, *Characters*, c. 1667–9: "A Player . . . assumes a body like an apparition, and he can turn himself into as many shapes as a witch" (quoted in J.-C. Agnew, *Worlds Apart: The Market and the Theater in Anglo-American Thought, 1550–1750*, Cambridge, 1986, p. 101).

11. *On the Profession of a Player. Three Essays by James Boswell*, n.p., 1929 (orig. in the *London Magazine*, 1770), pp. 12, 14–18, 24.

12. Boswell, *On the Profession of a Player*, p. 19. On Boswell's views on the malleability of identity cf. F. A. Nussbaum, *The Autobiographical Subject: Gender and Ideology in Eighteenth-Century England*, Baltimore, 1989, esp. pp. 106–9.

13. Adam Smith, *The Theory of Moral Sentiments* (1759), eds. D. D. Raphael and A. L. Macfie, Indianapolis, 1984, p. 317 (emphases added). See the discussion below, p. 188. For the relationship between Smith's notion of sympathy and the theater see D. Marshall, "Adam Smith and the Theatricality of Moral Sentiment", *Critical Inquiry* 10 (1984), pp. 592–613; and Agnew, *Worlds Apart*, pp. 182–7.

14. D. Bindman and M. Baker, *Roubiliac and the Eighteenth-Century Monument: Sculpture as Theatre*, New Haven, 1995, pp. 77–9. National Portrait Gallery, *O Sweet Mr. Shakespeare I'll Have his Picture: The Changing Image of Shakespeare's Person, 1600–1800*, London, 1964, pp. 28–9. For Garrick's reputation as the actual embodiment of Shakespeare see J. Brewer, *The Pleasures of the Imagination: English Culture in the Eighteenth Century*, New York, 1997, p. 410. I am grateful to Eunice Martin of the Ashmolean Museum Library, Oxford, for her help on Roubiliac.

15. See above, pp. 48–9.
16. A clarification may be in order. It is certainly not suggested that the language of depth was unfamiliar in the eighteenth century: the depth of the heart or the soul is an ancient metaphor with which contemporaries were well acquainted. But it is a metaphor that can refer to different things – to real intentions, to real feelings, to true moral or religious worth – rather than necessarily always presuppose the inner depths of selfhood.
17. *The Works of the Late Aaron Hill*, iv, p. 28 (orig. 1736). [John Durant Breval], *The Strolers*, London, 1727, epilogue. *Town and Country Magazine* 1774, pp. 245–6, quoted above, p. 59. *The Life of Patty Saunders, Written by Herself*, London, 1752, p. 96 (emphasis added). Richard Steele, prologue to a revival of *Tamerlane* at Newcome's School, Hackney, c. 1722, repr. in P. Danchin (ed.), *The Prologues and Epilogues of the Eighteenth Century*, 8 vols., pt. II, 1721–37, iii, Nancy, 1992, p. 82 (and cf. the later epilogue on p. 212). Note also the turn of phrase chosen by one Benjamin Roberts in a letter to William Johnson, 8 Aug. 1770: "People when they come to this side of the Water [America], *they Alter their Way of thinking with their Clothes*" (cited, with thanks, from Kirk Davis Swinehart, "This Wild Place: Sir William Johnson among the Mohawks, 1715–1783", PhD thesis, Yale University, 2002; emphasis added). And compare above, p. 170.
18. A. R. Jones and P. Stallybrass, *Renaissance Clothing and the Materials of Memory*, Cambridge, 2000, esp. pp. 1–4. The chronicler Robert Fabian as cited in S. Greenblatt, *Marvelous Possessions: The Wonder of the New World*, Chicago, 1991, p. 184 n. 55. See also S. Orgel, *Impersonations: The Performance of Gender in Shakespeare's England*, Cambridge, 1996, e.g. pp. 103–4.
19. For twins on stage see R. J. Slawson, "'Dromio, thou Dromio': The Casting of Twins in Shakespeare's *Comedy of Errors*", *New England Theatre Journal* 2:1 (1991), pp. 59–71; and Orgel, *Impersonations*, p. 104. See further below, pp. 271–2.
20. Jones and Stallybrass, *Renaissance Clothing*. A. Hollander, *Seeing through Clothes* (1975), Berkeley, 1993, e.g. pp. xiv, 420, 444.
21. Walpole to Sir Horace Mann, 14 April 1743, in S. West, "Libertinism and the Ideology of Male Friendship in the Portraits of the Society of Dilettanti", *Eighteenth-Century Life* 16 (May 1992), pp. 76–104 (quoted, p. 76); West's article is the main source of information about this group of portraits. See also M. Pointon, *Hanging the Head: Portraiture and Social Formation in Eighteenth-Century England*, New Haven, 1993, p. 82.
22. Edward Norgate, *Miniatura; or, The Art of Limning*, written between 1648 and 1650, as cited in Jones and Stallybrass, *Renaissance Clothing*, p. 35; and see pp. 11–12, 34–58. Gerald de Lairesse, *The Art of Painting*, London, 1738, in M. Rosenthal, *The Art of Thomas Gainsborough: "A Little Business for the Eye"*, New Haven, 1999, p. 136. The primacy of clothes and accouterments over physical features is noted in K. O. Kupperman, *Indians and English: Facing Off in Early America*, Ithaca (N.Y.), 2000, p. 42, for portraits of early-modern Indians; and for eighteenth-century Anglo-American portraits, in T. H. Breen, "The Meaning of 'Likeness': American Portrait Painting in an Eighteenth-Century Consumer Society", *Word and Image* 6 (1990), pp. 325–50.
23. Anne Hollander has noted the turn to fancy costuming in eighteenth-century portraiture, in contrast to the seventeenth century, in her *Fabric of Vision: Dress and Drapery in Painting*, London, 2002, pp. 86–7, 93.

24. I. Watt, *The Rise of the Novel* (1957), London, 1987. C. Steedman, *Past Tenses: Essays on Writing, Autobiography and History*, London, 1992, p. 164 (but see Steedman's more recent view, as discussed below, p. 287).

25. See for instance Henry Gally, *The Moral Characters of Theophrastus . . . [with] a Critical Essay on Characteristic-Writings*, London, 1725, p. 39: to attain "the very Soul of *Characteristic-Writing*" an author "must not dwell too long upon one Idea". Lynch, *The Economy of Character*, p. 9 and *passim*.

26. Lynch, *The Economy of Character*, pp. 4, 7, 44. C. Kay, *Political Constructions: Defoe, Richardson, and Sterne in Relation to Hobbes, Hume, and Burke*, Ithaca (N.Y.), 1988, p. 140 (and cf. M. A. Favret, *Romantic Correspondence: Women, Politics and the Fiction of Letters*, Cambridge, 1993, p. 10 and chap. 1). Lynch's argument is suggestively foreshadowed in R. Sennett, *The Fall of Public Man*, London, 1986, e.g. pp. 67–72, 108. Cf. also M.-P. Laden, *Self-Imitation in the Eighteenth-Century Novel*, Princeton, 1987, where eighteenth-century novels – not least *Pamela* – are seen as representing divided, doubled, surface-based, and non-centered forms of selfhood. An analogous argument has also been made for eighteenth-century dramatic writing in L. A. Freeman, *Character's Theater: Genre and Identity on the Eighteenth-Century English Stage*, Philadelphia, 2002, and for autobiographical writing (see below, pp. 289–90).

27. Lynch, *The Economy of Character*, pp. 40, 47. Samuel Johnson, *The History of Rasselas, Prince of Abissinia* (1759), ed. D. J. Enright, Harmondsworth, 1976, p. 61 (and cf. Johnson's "Preface to Shakespeare" (1765), in *Johnson on Shakespeare*, in *The Yale Edition of the Works of Samuel Johnson*, 16 vols., vol. 7, ed. A. Sherbo, New Haven, 1968, p. 62). John Ray, *The Wisdom of God Manifested in the Works of the Creation* (1691), 2nd edn., London, 1692, as quoted in Pointon, *Hanging the Head*, pp. 81–2 (and cf. West, *Image of the Actor*, p. 138). For portraiture see also Breen, "The Meaning of 'Likeness'", p. 342; Rosenthal, *The Art of Thomas Gainsborough*, esp. p. 66; C. Gibson-Wood, *Jonathan Richardson: Art Theorist of the English Enlightenment*, New Haven, 2000, pp. 159–60; and S. West, "The Darly Macaroni Prints and the Politics of 'Private Man'", *Eighteenth-Century Life* 25 (2001), p. 174. See further below, p. 300.

28. *Gentleman's Magazine* 6 (1736), p. 378. *The Masquerade. A Poem Inscribed to the King of Denmark*, London, 1768, p. 14. Terry Castle, *Masquerade and Civilization. The Carnivalesque in Eighteenth-Century Culture and Fiction*, Stanford, CA, 1986, p. 75.

29. *The English Theophrastus; or, The Manners of the Age. Being the Modern Characters of the Court, The Town, and the City* (1702), 3rd edn., London, 1708, pp. i, 29.

30. John Arbuthnot, *An Essay Concerning the Effects of Air on Human Bodies*, London, 1733, pp. 146–7. John Millar, *The Origin of the Distinction of Ranks*, 3rd edn., 1779, repr. in W. C. Lehmann, *John Millar of Glasgow 1735–1801*, Cambridge, 1960, p. 177; and cf. James Macpherson, *An Introduction to the History of Great Britain and Ireland*, Dublin, 1771, p. 197. William Bewley's review of Buffon's *The Natural History of the Horse*, originally in *Monthly Review* 27 (1762), repr. in H. F. Augstein (ed.), *Race: The Origins of an Idea, 1760–1850*, Bristol, 1996, pp. 2–3. Buffon as cited in A. O. Lovejoy, *The Great Chain of Being: A Study of the History of an Idea* (1936), New York, 1960, p. 230.

31. [Peter Shaw], *Man. A Paper for Ennobling the Species* 14 (2 April 1755), pp. 1–3 (and cf. John Millar, *Observations Concerning the Distinction of Ranks in Society*, Dublin, 1771, p. 17). William Hogarth, *The Analysis of Beauty* (London, 1753), ed. R.

Paulson, New Haven, 1997, p. 100. John Hunter, "Inaugural Disputation on the Varieties of Man", June 1775, in *The Anthropological Treatises of Johann Friedrich Blumenbach*, trans. and ed. T. Bendyshe, London, 1865, p. 361. Cf. also *Some Doubts Occasioned by the Second Volume of an Estimate on the Manners and Principles of the Times*, London, 1757, pp. 17–18: responding to John Brown's panicked alarm that the confounding of gender distinctions was about to result in a complete national collapse, this writer reassured him that while "there [we]re some obvious instances of this" – the actual observation was undeniable – "they seem to be not so common . . . as *Manly* men and *Tender* women". Once again individuals crossing the lines were deemed unthreatening to the broader collective categories. And note Charles Taylor's recent admonition that pre-modern identities were not attributes of individuals but of collectives, in his "Modernity and Identity", in J. W. Scott and D. Keates (eds.), *Schools of Thought: Twenty-Five Years of Interpretive Social Science*, Princeton, 2001, pp. 140–1.

32. L. Hunt, "The Paradoxical Origins of Human Rights", in J. Wasserstrom et al. (eds.), *Human Rights and Revolutions*, Lanham (Md.), 2000, p. 14.

33. R. Porter, *The Creation of the Modern World: The Untold Story of the English Enlightenment*, New York, 2000, pp. 281, 286. Knott, "A Cultural History of Sensibility in the Era of the American Revolution". I am grateful to Sarah Knott for many illuminating conversations on this subject.

34. John Locke, *Some Thoughts Concerning Education*, London, 1692, section 216, repr. in P. Gay (ed.), *John Locke on Education*, New York, 1964, p. 176. Joseph Priestley, *Hartley's Theory of the Human Mind*, London, 1775, pp. 238–49. For Locke's educational ideas and influence see S. F. Pickering, *John Locke and Children's Books in Eighteenth-Century England*, Knoxville (Tenn.), 1981, esp. chap. 1. G. Brown, *The Consent of the Governed: The Lockean Legacy in Early American Culture*, Cambridge (Mass.), 2001, pp. 59–63 and *passim*. See further below, pp. 282–3.

35. Knott, "A Cultural History of Sensibility", p. 20 (and cf. J. Dwyer, *Virtuous Discourse: Sensibility and Community in Late Eighteenth-Century Scotland*, Edinburgh, 1987, pp. 53–4). David Hume, *A Treatise of Human Nature* (1739–40), eds. D. F. Norton and M. J. Norton, Oxford, 2000, pp. 206–8, 234–5. Burke, *A Philosophical Enquiry into . . . the Sublime and Beautiful*, p. 44. On the implications of the eighteenth-century notion of sympathy for understandings of identity see S. D. Cox, *"The Stranger within Thee": Concepts of the Self in Late-Eighteenth-Century Literature*, Pittsburgh, 1980, pp. 28–9, 40, 47. C. Gallagher, *Nobody's Story: The Vanishing Acts of Women Writers in the Market Place, 1670–1820*, Berkeley, 1994, p. 170. Lynch, *The Economy of Character*, p. 95. Also W. Motooka, *The Age of Reasons: Quixotism, Sentimentalism and Political Economy in Eighteenth-Century Britain*, London, 1998, p. 214, for the suggestion that the theory of sympathy was inimical to the comprehension of substantive differences between people.

36. David Hartley, *Observations on Man*, London, 1749; later given wider circulation through Priestley's more accessible *Hartley's Theory of the Human Mind*. Cf. R. C. Allen, *David Hartley on Human Nature*, Albany (N.Y.), 1999, esp. chaps. 7–9; Cox, *"The Stranger within Thee"*, p. 33.

Historian David Sabean, in an intriguing ongoing project, may have found traces of this eighteenth-century notion of sympathy with the similar and the contiguous in an unexpected twist in European marriage patterns during this period. Sabean notes around the 1740s a sharp transformation from marrying strangers to marrying cousins and relatives. This new "incestuous" pattern, he explains, relied on a sense that "the self was formed in an intimate dialectic with another beloved and where 'same' and 'other' became totally implicated in each other". D. Sabean, "Kinship and Issues of the Self in Europe around 1800", paper presented at the American Historical Association annual meeting, Chicago, Jan. 2003 (I am grateful for the opportunity to cite this work-in-progress).

37. Gallagher, *Nobody's Story*, p. 170. Samuel Johnson in *The Rambler* 60 (13 Oct. 1750); quoted in Patricia M. Spacks, *Imagining a Self. Autobiography and Novel in Eighteenth-Century England*, Cambridge, MA, 1976, p. 5. Cf. also Marshall, "Adam Smith and the Theatricality of Moral Sentiment", p. 595; J. Bender, *Imagining the Penitentiary: Fiction and the Architecture of the Mind in Eighteenth-Century England*, Chicago, 1987, e.g. p. 202; and I. Hunter, "Reading Character", *Southern Review* 16 (Adelaide, 1983), pp. 226–43.

38. Smith, *Theory of Moral Sentiments*, pp. 9, 317. Moreover, when Smith and his contemporaries talked of "self" and "selfishness" as the antithesis of sympathy (as in "all now is drawn into the base and narrow Circle of SELF – And . . . all social Ties are at an End"), "self" referred simply to an *un*socially turned self, the flip side of social interaction, but did not necessarily imply an antecedent interiority. The epitome of this was the narcissist who sits in front of his mirror and "finically spends all his time in adorning and making Love to his sweet self", which of course implied anything *but* interiority. *The Tryal of the Lady Allurea Luxury, before the Lord Chief-Justice Upright*, London, 1757, p. 87. [John Philip Kemble], "The Female Officer", 1778 (Larpent Mss., Huntington Library, no. 441), p. 10.

39. Marshall, "Adam Smith and the Theatricality of Moral Sentiment", pp. 598–601 (quoted, p. 600). Smith, *Theory of Moral Sentiments*, p. 12. R. Martin and J. Barresi, *Naturalization of the Soul: Self and Personal Identity in the Eighteenth Century*, London, 2000, pp. 94–102. K. Haakonssen, *Natural Law and Moral Philosophy: From Grotius to the Scottish Enlightenment*, Cambridge, 1996, p. 131.

40. Smith, *Theory of Moral Sentiments*, pp. 113, 130 (emphasis added). Anthony Ashley Cooper, Earl of Shaftesbury, "Soliloquy; or, Advice to an Author" (1710), in his *Characteristicks of Men, Manners, Opinions, Times*, 3 vols., 4th edn., [London], 1727, i, pp. 158, 170 (and see also pp. 195–6, on the "*Self-Inspection*" that allows us a "double Reflection [that] distinguish[es] our-selves into two different Partys"). Cf. Agnew, *Worlds Apart*, pp. 163–5; and D. Marshall, *The Figure of Theater: Shaftesbury, Defoe, Adam Smith, and George Eliot*, New York, 1986, chaps. 2, 7. Note that once again the Delphian injunction "know thyself" was not interpreted as a search for one's interior core of selfhood. Indeed, as Edward Andrew has cogently shown, Smith's impartial spectator stood at the end of a distinctive eighteenth-century discussion of conscience and morality carried on by Locke, Shaftesbury, Hume, and others. The novelty of their perspective was in shifting the emphasis from the early-modern Protestant conscience, which had involved mainly solipsistic judgements on oneself, to a socially turned moral sense involving spectatorial judgements on others and then the application of the spectator's point of view to one's own conduct. E. G. Andrew, *Conscience and its Critics: Protestant Conscience, Enlightenment Reason, and Modern Subjectivity*, Toronto, 2001, pp. 82, 116, 125, and *passim* (I am grateful to Ed Andrew for the opportunity to read his work before publication).

41. Modern scholars who have not allowed for such a literal reading include Motooka, *The Age of Reasons*, pp. 206–7; Bender, *Imagining the Penitentiary*, pp. 218–28; and the excellent account of the impartial spectator in N. Phillipson, "Adam Smith as

Civic Moralist", in I. Hont and M. Ignatieff (eds.), *Wealth and Virtue: The Shaping of Political Economy in the Scottish Enlightenment*, Cambridge, 1983, pp. 186–7. Smith's contemporaries, on the other hand, readily picked up the image of the splitting of sensible selves: like Charles Johnstone's reference (in *The Reverie; or, A Flight to the Paradise of Fools*, 2 vols., London, 1763, ii, p. 133) to "the tender connexions of nature, which, as it were, multiply a man into many selfs"; or Henry Mackenzie's characterization of Hamlet as a man whose sensibility causes him to feel in himself "a sort of double person" (cited in Cox, *"The Stranger within Thee"*, p. 48).

42. Martin and Barresi, *Naturalization of the Soul*, p. ix. Other useful accounts of this debate are C. Fox, *Locke and the Scriblerians: Identity and Consciousness in Early Eighteenth-Century Britain*, Berkeley, 1988; and Cox, *"The Stranger within Thee"*, chap. 2. Also see D. Todd, *Imagining Monsters: Miscreations of the Self in Eighteenth-Century England*, Chicago, 1995, which indeed wants to link this debate to happenings outside it – specifically, the case of Mary Toft – but by treating these two episodes as straightforward cause and effect (cf. p. 125) misses, in my view, the larger picture. For the French parallel, see J. Goldstein, "Mutations of the Self in Old Regime and Postrevolutionary France", in L. Daston (ed.), *Biographies of Scientific Objects*, Chicago, 2000, pp. 86–116.

43. John Locke, *An Essay Concerning Human Understanding*, ed. P. H. Nidditch, Oxford, 1975, pp. 335–6, 343–4. Most of Locke's thoughts on this subject were added to the text in its second edition of 1694, in bk. II, chap. 27: "Of Identity and Diversity".

44. Hume, *A Treatise of Human Nature*, bk. I, pt. 4, section 6: "Of Personal Identity" (quoted, pp. 165, 169). Shaftesbury, *Characteristicks of Men, Manners, Opinions, Times*, ii, p. 350; iii, pp. 193–4; and cf. i, pp. 279–85. For Shaftesbury's journal see Martin and Barresi, *Naturalization of the Soul*, p. 64, and for his notebooks L. E. Klein, *Shaftesbury and the Culture of Politeness*, Cambridge, 1994, pp. 72–4. George Berkeley, *Alciphron; or, The Minute Philosopher*, London, 1732, as cited in Martin and Barresi, *Naturalization of the Soul*, pp. 65–6; and memo as quoted above, p. xi. [Edmund Law], *A Defence of Mr. Locke's Opinion Concerning Personal Identity*, Cambridge, 1769, pp. 3–4. Other contributors to this side of the debate included Catharine Trotter (Cockburn), Anthony Collins, Vincent Peronnet, Joseph Priestley, and the anonymous author of *An Essay on Personal Identity*, London, 1769.

45. Samuel Clarke, *A Third Defence of an Argument Made Use of in a Letter to Mr. Dodwell*, in *The Works of Samuel Clarke*, 4 vols., London, 1738, iii, p. 844. Henry Grove, "A System of Pneumatology", c. 1720, Huntington Library Mss., in Martin and Barresi, *Naturalization of the Soul*, p. 73. Isaac Watts, *Philosophical Essays on Various Subjects*, London, 1733, p. 306. Joseph Butler, *The Analogy of Religion, Natural and Revealed*, 2nd edn., London, 1736, pp. 444–6. Cuthbert Comment (i.e. Abraham Tucker), *Man in Quest of Himself; or, A Defence of the Individuality of the Human Mind, or Self*, London, 1763, p. 50. James Beattie, *An Essay on the Nature and Immutability of Truth*, Edinburgh, 1770, p. 76.

46. *The Spectator* 578 (9 Aug. 1714), in *The Spectator*, 6 vols., ed. D. F. Bond, Oxford, 1965, iv, p. 575. For the *Monthly Review* see below, p. 196. Laurence Sterne, *Tristram Shandy*, London, 1759–67, quoted in Fox, *Locke and the Scriblerians*, p. 119. [Charles Johnstone], *Chrysal; or, The Adventures of a Guinea* (1760), 2 vols., London,

1768, i, pp. 7–9. In terms of the public reaction to this debate, it is also worth noting that Edmund Law published his radical views on the inessential nature of identity *before* he became the bishop of Carlisle, a fact that evidently did not prevent his future appointment to such a prominent position in the Church of England.

47. Boswell, *On the Profession of a Player*, pp. 22–3 (and see Fox, *Locke and the Scriblerians*, pp. 127–8). We can also see traces of the personal identity debate in John Hunter's warning against moving too far along the road from generic characterization to particularization, as quoted above (p. 185): "Could it not be said of the same man at different times that he in like way was of a different species from himself?"

48. On disharmonious twins in the eighteenth century, and their subsequent replacement by biologized twins in the nineteenth, see H. Schwartz, *The Culture of the Copy; Striking Likenesses, Unreasonable Facsimiles*, New York, 1996, pp. 29–31, 390 n. 25. L. Gedda, *Twins in History and Science*, Springfield (Ill.), 1961, p. 9. Also recall the mid-century account of a pair of twins of different skin colors: see above, p. 92.

49. *Memoirs of the Extraordinary Life, Works, and Discoveries of Martinus Scriblerus* (1740), ed. C. Kerby-Miller, New York, 1988, pp. 140, 156: and see chaps. 7, 12, 14–15. For a detailed analysis see Fox, *Locke and the Scriblerians*. Also note Todd, *Imagining Monsters*, pp. 126–35; and C. D. Williams, "'Another Self in the Case': Gender, Marriage and the Individual in Augustan Literature", in R. Porter (ed.), *Rewriting the Self: Histories from the Renaissance to the Present*, London, 1997, pp. 99–104. A similar effect, though in an allegorical rather than a satirical mode, was achieved in *The Spectator*'s essay inspired by this debate (see above, n. 46), which told a story of a woman who commits adultery with her own husband's body while it is inhabited by another man's transmigrating identity.

50. Shaftesbury, *Characteristicks of Men, Manners, Opinions, Times*, i, p. 283.

51. *Memoirs of Martinus Scriblerus*, pp. 143, 154, 157. Abraham Gunter (i.e. John Arbuthnot), *Annus Mirabilis; or, The Wonderful Effects of the Approaching Conjunction of the Planets Jupiter, Mars, and Saturn*, [London, 1722], p. 1.

52. [Abraham Tucker], *Man in Quest of Himself; or, A Defence of the Individuality of the Human Mind, or Self*, London, 1763. *Monthly Review* 29 (Dec. 1763), pp. 452, 460–2.

53. [Law], *A Defence of Mr. Locke's Opinion Concerning Personal Identity*, pp. 39–41.

54. Locke, *An Essay Concerning Human Understanding*, pp. 340, 346. [Law,] *A Defence of Mr. Locke's Opinion Concerning Personal Identity*, pp. 18–20. And cf. George Berkeley's enigmatic notation to himself: "No identity other than perfect likeness [the last four words added at a later stage] in any individuals besides persons" – which seems to say that no identity over time is preserved in a man, despite continuity of external appearance, unless there is also a continuity of person. George Berkeley, *Philosophical Commentaries*, in *The Works of George Berkeley*, eds. A. A. Luce and T. E. Jessop, 9 vols., London, 1948–57, i, p. 21, entry 192.

Chapter 5

1. L. Colley, *Britons: Forging the Nation 1707–1837*, New Haven, 1992.

2. E. G. Andrew, *Conscience and its Critics: Protestant Conscience, Enlightenment Reason, and Modern Subjectivity*, Toronto, 2001, pp. 82, 116, 125, and *passim*.

3. Examples include John Earle's *Micro-Cosmographie* (1628) and John Bunyan's *A*

Book for Boys and Girls (1686); see A. Richardson, *Literature, Education, and Romanticism: Reading as Social Practice, 1780–1832*, Cambridge, 1994, pp. 12, 128. Although I have focused in this book on documenting the later transition that ended the *ancien régime* of identity, similar procedures can be undertaken to chart more precisely its initial phases. Where I have tried to do this, the evidence appears to suggest that most aspects of the *ancien régime* of identity were in the process of becoming around the opening decade of the eighteenth century, or perhaps shortly before: see above, p. 57, and my "Gender in Translation: How the English Wrote their Juvenal, 1644–1815", *Representations* 65 (1999), pp. 1–41. For a contemporary opinion about this difference between the seventeenth and the eighteenth centuries, see Joseph Strutt, *Glig-Gamena Angel-Deod; or, The Sports and Pastimes of the People of England*, London, 1801, p. xlix.

4. P. Mack, "Agency and the Unconscious: Spiritual Dreams in Eighteenth-Century Britain", unpublished paper (I am grateful to Phyllis Mack for the opportunity to read her work-in-progress). Mack quotes a 1695 dream account, by one Francis Stamper, a Quaker, that bears an uncanny similarity to Locke's thoughts on the splitting of identity published the previous year: "I awoke and behold it was a dream yet such was the deepness of ye sense of the thing upon my outward man that I cold scarcely believe my outward eyes whether I was in the body or not."

5. M. Gauchet, *The Disenchantment of the World: A Political History of Religion*, trans. O. Burge, Princeton, 1998, pp. 162, 164. I have benefitted from the explication of Gauchet's work in D. A. Bell, *The Cult of the Nation in France: Inventing Nationalism, 1680–1800*, Cambridge (Mass.), 2001, chap. 1 (and further Gauchet quotation there, p. 232 n. 35). For the retreat of God from the interpretation of financial misfortunes see M. Hunt, *The Middling Sort: Commerce, Gender and the Family in England 1680–1780*, Berkeley, 1996, pp. 34–7; and from the interpretation of pain, D. B. Morris, *The Culture of Pain*, Berkeley, 1991, esp. pp. 44–5. An important reference point remains the final chapter of K. Thomas, *Religion and the Decline of Magic*, Harmondsworth, 1971.

6. K. Baker, "Enlightenment and the Institution of Society: Notes for a Conceptual History", in W. Melching and W. Velema (eds.), *Main Trends in Cultural History*, Amsterdam, 1992, pp. 95–120. Bell, *The Cult of the Nation*. Gauchet, *The Disenchantment of the World*, p. 162.

7. *Pictures of Men, Manners, and the Times. . . . Written in the Year 1777*, 2 vols., London, 1779, i, pp. 191–2; and cf. pp. 55–60 for a Baudelaire-like account of the bustle and confusion of modern city life.

8. [Erasmus Jones], *Luxury, Pride, and Vanity, the Bane of the British Nation*, London, [1735], pp. 6, 13–14. Tobias George Smollett, *The Adventures of Ferdinand Count Fathom*, 2 vols., London, 1753, i, p. 232. Cf. also *London. A Satire*, Portsmouth, 1751, a critique of metropolitan life dominated by images of masks and masquerading, until the inevitable conclusion, "that the whole world [in London] makes up a masquerade" (p. 10).

9. Bernard Mandeville, *The Fable of the Bees; or, Private Vices, Publick Benefits* (6th edn., London, 1732), ed. F. B. Kaye, 2 vols., Indianapolis, 1988, i, pp. 127–8. Among others, the same observation was also put forth by Montesquieu in *The Spirit of the Laws* (1748): see the useful discussion in E. J. Hundert, "The European Enlightenment and the History of the Self", in R. Porter (ed.), *Rewriting the Self: Histories from the Renaissance to the Present*, London, 1997, pp. 72–83.

10. Samuel Johnson, "London: A Poem in Imitation of the Third Satire of Juvenal" (1738), in *A Collection of Poems*, London, 1763, p. 195. *Of Luxury, More Particularly with Respect to Apparel. . . . By a Country Clergyman*, London, 1736, p. 13.

11. Thomas Cole, *Discourses on Luxury, Infidelity and Enthusiasm*, London, 1761, p. 11. Henry Fielding, *An Enquiry into the Causes of the Late Increase of Robbers* (London, 1759), in *The Wesleyan Edition of the Works of Henry Fielding* (no vol. no.), ed. M. R. Zirker, Middletown (Conn.), 1988, p. 77. Nathaniel Forster, *An Enquiry into the Causes of the Present High Price of Provisions*, London, 1767, p. 41. "The Prevalence of Luxury", *Gentleman's Magazine* 12 (1742), pp. 532–3 (from *The Craftsman* 850 [2 Oct. 1742]). *A Trip through the Town. Containing Observations on the Humours and Manners of the Age*, 4th edn., London, 1735, p. 23.

12. *London Chronicle* 34 (1773), as quoted in N. McKendrick, "The Commercialization of Fashion", in N. McKendrick, J. Brewer, and J. Plumb, *The Birth of a Consumer Society*, Bloomington (Ind.), 1982, p. 95; and see pp. 34–99. Abbé Coyer, *A Supplement to Lord Anson's Voyage round the World. Containing a Discovery and Description of the Island of Frivola*, London, 1752, pp. v, 49. *Pictures of Men, Manners, and the Times*, ii, p. 49. *The British Magazine; or, Monthly Repository for Gentlemen and Ladies* 4 (1763), p. 417. *Gentleman's Magazine* 52 (1782), p. 122. Among many other examples, cf. also [James Miller], *The Mother-in-Law; or, The Doctor the Disease*, London, 1734, epilogue; and *Lady's Magazine*, Feb. 1773, as quoted in B. Lemire, *Fashion's Favourite: The Cotton Trade and the Consumer in Britain, 1660–1800*, Oxford, 1991, p. 190. As Lemire points out, eighteenth-century advances in production of ready-to-wear clothing rendered more varieties of dress more readily available.

13. Not everyone, of course, saw this jitteriness as threatening: take, for instance, the 1732 writer who heaped praise on tailors precisely for their valuable contribution to people's possibilities for social mobility "in our modern emulating Days". *The Original of Apparel; or, The Ornaments of Dress*, London, 1732, pp. 7–8 (and note the approval of masquerading, including gender inversion, on p. 4).

14. N. McKendrick, "The Consumer Revolution of Eighteenth-Century England", in McKendrick et al., *The Birth of a Consumer Society*. Other key contributions to this burgeoning literature include C. Campbell, *The Romantic Ethic and the Spirit of Modern Consumerism*, Oxford, 1987; P. Langford, *A Polite and Commercial People: England 1727–1783*, Oxford, 1989 (e.g. pp. 66–7); J. Brewer and R. Porter (eds.), *Consumption and the World of Goods*, London, 1993 (note especially the contribution by John Styles, which considers explicitly the question of periodization); and J. Brewer, *The Pleasures of the Imagination: English Culture in the Eighteenth Century*, New York, 1997, which provides an especially vivid portrait of a frenetic commercial urban culture in which established boundaries were in danger of collapse.

15. "An Essay on Fashions", *Gentleman's Magazine* 6 (1736), p. 377. Compare [John] Dennis, *An Essay upon Publick Spirit; Being a Satyr in Prose upon the Manners and Luxury of the Times*, London, 1711, p. 10: "our ancestors", in contrast to present days, by "their Habits, and the rest of their Customs and Manners were such, as very fairly distinguish'd their Birth, their Age, their Sex, and their Country". Also see vol. i of O. Sedgewick, *The Universal Masquerade; or, The World Turn'd Inside-Out*, 2 vols., London, 1742, which attributed to contemporary fashion the erasure of racial, social, and gender distinctions.

16. S[amuel] Johnson, *The Temple of Fashion: A Poem in Five Parts*, Shrewsbury,

1781, p. 2. Bernard Mandeville quoted in Brewer, *The Pleasures of the Imagination*, p. 74. [John Wesley], *An Estimate of the Manners of the Present Times*, London, 1782, p. 5. Anonymous commentator cited in McKendrick, "The Commercialization of Fashion", p. 54 – this is the classic account of the eighteenth-century obsession with fashion as a new and all-consuming departure. See also J. Raven, *Judging New Wealth: Popular Publishing and Responses to Commerce in England, 1750–1800*, Oxford, 1992 (esp. for the second half of the century). E. Mackie, *Market à la Mode: Fashion, Commodity, and Gender in "The Tatler" and "The Spectator"*, Baltimore, 1997 (esp. for the earlier part of the century).

17. E. A. Wrigley, "A Simple Model of London's Importance in Changing English Society and Economy, 1650–1750", in his *People, Cities and Wealth: The Transformation of Traditional Society*, Oxford, 1987, pp. 133–56. R. Sennett, *The Fall of Public Man*, London, 1986 (quoted, pp. 49, 67–8). See also Mackie, *Market à la Mode*, pp. 89–90. On the trickle-down effect to provincial cities from the late seventeenth century see P. Borsay, "The English Urban Renaissance: The Development of Provincial Urban Culture, c.1680–c.1760", *Social History* 2 (1977), pp. 581–603, and idem, *The English Urban Renaissance: Culture and Society in the Provincial Town, 1660–1770*, Oxford, 1989, esp. chap. 9. P. J. Corfield, "Walking the City Streets: The Urban Odyssey in Eighteenth-Century England", *Journal of Urban History* 16 (1990), pp. 156–8.

18. A. R. Jones and P. Stallybrass, *Renaissance Clothing and the Materials of Memory*, Cambridge, 2000, pp. 2–3. William Shakespeare, *Henry IV, Part II*, V.ii. Sennett, *The Fall of Public Man*, pp. 72, 147. B. Lemire, *Dress, Culture and Commerce: The English Clothing Trade before the Factory, 1660–1800*, Basingstoke, 1997, p. 7. A. Hunt, *Governance of the Consuming Passions: A History of Sumptuary Law*, Basingstoke, 1996, pp. 29, 374–5.

19. J.-C. Agnew, *Worlds Apart: The Market and the Theater in Anglo-American Thought, 1550–1750*, Cambridge, 1996. See also B. M. Stafford, *Body Criticism: Imagining the Unseen in Enlightenment Art and Medicine*, Cambridge (Mass.), 1991, esp. p. 86. J. Fliegelman, *Declaring Independence: Jefferson, Natural Language, and the Culture of Performance*, Stanford, 1993.

20. W. H. Sewell, "A Theory of Structure: Duality, Agency, and Transformation", *American Journal of Sociology* 98:1 (1992), pp. 25–6. James Pye, *The Progress of Refinement*, London, 1783, quoted in R. Young, *Colonial Desire: Hybridity in Theory, Culture and Race*, London, 1995, p. 34. J. G. A. Pocock, *The Machiavellian Moment: Florentine Political Thought and the Atlantic Republican Tradition*, Princeton, 1975, p. 464. P. Brantlinger, *Fictions of State: Culture and Credit in Britain, 1694–1994*, Ithaca (N.Y.), 1996, pp. 36–7.

21. The classic account is P. G. M. Dickson, *The Financial Revolution in England: A Study in the Development of Public Credit 1688–1756*, London, 1967. See also J. G. A. Pocock, "The Mobility of Property and the Rise of Eighteenth-Century Sociology", in his *Virtue, Commerce, and History*, Cambridge, 1985, esp. pp. 108–12; Brantlinger, *Fictions of State*, chap. 2; S. Sherman, "Credit, Simulation, and the Ideology of Contract in the Early Eighteenth Century", *Eighteenth-Century Life* 19 (1995), pp. 86–102; and idem, *Finance and Fictionality in the Early Eighteenth Century: Accounting for Defoe*, Cambridge, 1996.

22. Daughter of Robert Harley, the Earl of Oxford, in H. M. C., *The Manuscripts of His Grace the Duke of Portland*, vol. v (1899); *The Battle of the Bubbles*, London,

1720; [Daniel Defoe], *An Essay upon Projects*, London, 1697; all quoted in J. Hoppit, *A Land of Liberty? England 1689–1727*, Oxford, 2000, pp. 334–6. J. Hoppit, "The Myths of the South Sea Bubble", *Transactions of the Royal Historical Society* 6th ser., 12 (2002), pp. 141–65 (I am grateful to the author for the opportunity to read this paper before publication).

23. Daniel Defoe, *An Essay upon the Public Credit* (1710), London, 1797, p. 8. Brantlinger, *Fictions of State*, p. 60. See also C. Ingrassia, *Authorship, Commerce, and Gender in Early Eighteenth-Century England: A Culture of Paper Credit*, Cambridge, 1998, pp. 5–6 and *passim*. J. Lamb, *Preserving the Self in the South Seas 1680–1840*, Chicago, 2001, pp. 62–8. L. Brown, *Fables of Modernity: Literature and Culture in the English Eighteenth Century*, Ithaca (N.Y.), 2001, pp. 120, 146–9.

24. *London Magazine*, Sept. 1776, cited in D. Andrew and R. McGowen, *The Perreaus and Mrs. Rudd: Forgery and Betrayal in Eighteenth-Century London*, Berkeley, 2001, p. 269.

25. See Andrew and McGowen, *The Perreaus and Mrs. Rudd*, chap. 6.

26. David Williams, *Letter to David Garrick, Esq., on his Conduct*, London, 1772, pp. 3, 20–1. John Trenchard and Thomas Gordon, *Cato's Letters: Essays on Liberty, Civil and Religious, and Other Important Subjects* (1720), 2 vols., New York, 1971, i, p. 23. For the elision of Exchange Alley with the masquerade see Ingrassia, *Authorship, Commerce, and Gender*, pp. 37–8. Cf. Lamb, *Preserving the Self*, p. 174.

27. Fanny Burney, *Evelina; or, The History of a Young Lady's Entrance into the World* (1768), eds. E. A. Bloom and L. D. Bloom, Oxford, 1982, p. 309. For Elizabeth Montagu see above, p. 167.

28. Lamb, *Preserving the Self*, pp. 128, 165; also p. 281. A useful summary remains M. T. Hodgen, *Early Anthropology in the Sixteenth and Seventeenth Centuries*, Philadelphia, 1964.

29. G. Dening, "Introduction: In Search of a Metaphor", in R. Hoffman et al. (eds.), *Through a Glass Darkly: Reflections on Personal Identity in Early America*, Chapel Hill, 1997, p. 2.

30. M. Zuckerman, "Identity in British America: Unease in Eden", in N. Canny and A. Pagden (eds.), *Colonial Identity in the Atlantic World, 1500–1800*, Princeton, 1987, p. 152. K. O. Kupperman, *Indians and English: Facing Off in Early America*, Ithaca (N.Y.), 2000, p. 4. R. White, *The Middle Ground: Indians, Empires, and Republics in the Great Lakes Region, 1650–1815*, Cambridge, 1991, pp. ix, 50. See also K. A. Lockridge, "Colonial Self-Fashioning: Paradoxes and Pathologies in the Construction of Genteel Identity in Eighteenth-Century America", in Hoffman et al., *Through a Glass Darkly*, esp. p. 337; P. J. Deloria, *Playing Indian*, New Haven, 1998, chap. 1; and A. Games, *Migration and the Origins of the English Atlantic World*, Cambridge (Mass.), 1999, esp. pp. 192–3, 206–14.

31. M. B. Norton, "Communal Definitions of Gendered Identity in Seventeenth-Century English America", in Hoffman et al., *Through a Glass Darkly*, pp. 40–66 (contemporary quotation on p. 50). K. M. Brown, *Good Wives, Nasty Wenches and Anxious Patriarchs: Gender, Race, and Power in Colonial Virginia*, Chapel Hill, 1996, pp. 45, 58, and idem, "'Changed . . . into the Fashion of Man': The Politics of Sexual Difference in a Seventeenth-Century Anglo-American Settlement", in C. Clinton and M. Gillespie (eds.), *The Devil's Lane: Sex and Race in the Early South*, New York, 1997, e.g. p. 51. Kupperman, *Indians and English*, pp. 148–51. For encounters with Indians who similarly did not recognize *social* distinctions, thus

causing much alarm, see R. White, "'Although I Am Dead, I Am Not Entirely Dead, I Have Left a Second of Myself': Constructing Self and Persons on the Middle Ground of Early America", in Hoffman et al., *Through a Glass Darkly*, p. 413.

32. W. D. Jordan, *White over Black: American Attitudes towards the Negro, 1550–1812*, Chapel Hill, 1968, pp. 169, 174–7, 255 (quoted, p. 177).

33. P. Morgan, "Interracial Sex in Eighteenth-Century Jamaica: Personal Dynamics and Social Consequences", paper presented at the Huntington Library, Oct. 2000. K. D. Kriz, "Marketing Mulatresses in the Paintings and Prints of Agostino Brunias", in F. A. Nussbaum (ed.), *The Global Eighteenth Century*, Baltimore, 2003, pp. 206–7. Lieut. Thomas Phipps Howard quoted in J. Dayan, *Haiti, History and the Gods*, Berkeley, 1995, p. 180, and cf. pp. 174–5. Similarly see, for French Saint-Domingue, D. G. Grigsby, *Extremities: Painting Empire in Post-Revolutionary France*, New Haven, 2002, p. 16.

34. T. J. Shannon, "Dressing for Success on the Mohawk Frontier: Hendrick, William Johnson, and the Indian Fashion", *William and Mary Quarterly* 3rd ser., 53:1 (1996), pp. 13–42 (contemporary quotation, p. 26). For Johnson and Pickard (among other examples) see W. B. Hart, "Black 'Go-Betweens' and the Mutability of 'Race,' Status, and Identity on New York's Pre-Revolutionary Frontier", in A. R. L. Cayton and F. J. Teute (eds.), *Contact Points: American Frontiers from the Mohawk Valley to the Mississippi, 1750–1830*, Chapel Hill, 1998, pp. 88–113 (quoted, p. 107). J. H. Merrell, "'The Cast of his Countenance': Reading Andrew Montour", in Hoffman et al., *Through a Glass Darkly*, pp. 13–39 (quotation from the Anglican clergyman Richard Peters, p. 17; emphasis added); and idem, *Into the American Woods: Negotiators on the Pennsylvania Frontier*, New York, 1999, chap. 1. Kupperman, *Indians and English*, p. 211. On Johnson and his household, and especially for a detailed reading of Guy Johnson's portrait on which I have drawn, see B. F. Tobin, *Picturing Imperial Power: Colonial Subjects in Eighteenth-Century British Painting*, Durham, 1999, chap. 3; and K. D. Swinehart, "This Wild Place: Sir William Johnson among the Mohawks, 1715–1783", PhD thesis, Yale University, 2002. Recall also Robert Beverley's prefacing of his *The History and Present State of Virginia*, London, 1705, with the declaration "I am an *Indian*" (ed. L. B. Wright, Chapel Hill, 1947, p. 9).

35. [Sir Henry Bate Dudley], *Airs, Ballads, &c. in The Blackamoor Wash'd White. A New Comic Opera*, London, 1776, p. 13. E. M. Collingham, *Imperial Bodies: The Physical Experience of the Raj, c. 1800–1947*, Cambridge, 2001, chap. 1.

Chapter 6

1. Richard Price, *Observations on the Nature of Civil Liberty*, 3rd edn., London, 1776, p. 64. John Wesley, *Some Observations on Liberty: Occasioned by a Late Tract*, London, 1776, pp. 6–7.

2. P. J. Deloria, *Playing Indian*, New Haven, 1998, pp. 2, 6; and cf., *inter alia*, E. Countryman, *Americans: A Collision of Histories*, New York, 1996, pp. 42–3.

3. Cf. another response to Price which likewise recounted how "a small part of the people had separated from the rest in order to disguise themselves; and, being so disguised, entered all the ships, hoisted out the tea, and cast it into the sea" (*Experience Preferable to Theory. An Answer to Dr. Price's Observations on the Nature*

of Civil Liberty, London, 1776, pp. 64–5). In castigating the Bostonians for "being so disguised", this writer likewise did not deem any further detail necessary. This repeated oversight is even more significant, given that for writers of Wesley's frame of mind the association of the colonists with Indians might have become another potentially effective weapon of denigration. For one more example see *Sagittarius's Letters and Political Speculations. Extracted from the Public Ledger*, Boston, 1775, p. 18.

4. This, for instance, was how the issue was discussed in the House of Commons: *The Parliamentary History of England, from the Earliest Period to the Year 1803*, vol. xvii, 1771–4, London, 1813, cols. 1,185–6. This omission, moreover, was not owing to lack of information – cf. col. 940, where the report of the Boston events appeared complete, Mohawk disguises and all.

5. John Wesley, *A Calm Address to the Inhabitants of England*, London, 1777, pp. 10–13.

6. W. H. Sewell, Jr., "Historical Events as Transformations of Structures: Inventing Revolution at the Bastille", *Theory and Society* 25 (1996), pp. 841–81 (quoted, pp. 842–5).

7. See especially L. Colley, *Britons: Forging the Nation 1707–1837*, New Haven, 1992; J. C. D. Clark, *The Language of Liberty 1660–1832: Political Discourse and Social Dynamics in the Anglo-American World*, Cambridge, 1994; K. Wilson, *The Sense of the People: Politics, Culture and Imperialism in England, 1715–1785*, Cambridge, 1995, chap. 5; E. H. Gould, *The Persistence of Empire: British Political Culture in the Age of the American Revolution*, Chapel Hill, 2000; and S. Conway, *The British Isles and the War of American Independence*, Oxford, 2000. Also note J. Brewer, "English Radicalism in the Age of George III", in J. G. A. Pocock (ed.), *Three British Revolutions: 1641, 1688, 1776*, Princeton, 1980, pp. 323–67.

8. Edmund Burke, "Speech on Cavendish's Motion on America", 6 Nov. 1776; in *The Writings and Speeches of Edmund Burke*, eds. W. M. Elofson and J. A. Woods, 9 vols., Oxford, 1996, iii, p. 254. Idem, *Reflections on the Revolution in France*, ed. C. C. O'Brien, Harmondsworth, 1969, pp. 168–70.

9. *Remarks on Dr. Price's Observations on the Nature of Civil Liberty, &c.*, London, 1776, p. 34. *Civil War; A Poem. Written in the Year 1775*, [n.p.], [1775], p. 3.

10. *London Evening Post* 8,391 (30 Dec. 1775–2 Jan. 1776), p. 4. *Independency the Object of the Congress in America; or, An Appeal to Facts*, London, 1776, pp. 6, 18. See P. Lawson, "Anatomy of a Civil War: New Perspectives on England in the Age of the American Revolution 1767–82", *Parliamentary History* 8 (1989), pp. 142–52; Clark, *The Language of Liberty*, pp. 296–303; and Gould, *The Persistence of Empire*, pp. 184–5.

11. *The Delusive and Dangerous Principles of the Minority. . . . By a Friend to the Public*, London, 1778, pp. iii, v. Samuel Stennett, *National Calamities the Effect of Divine Displeasure. A Sermon. . . . February 21, 1781*, London, [1781], p. 8. *The Complaint; or, Britannia Lamenting the Loss of her Children*, London, [1776?], p. 2. [Samuel Jackson Pratt], *Emma Corbett; or, The Miseries of Civil War*, Dublin, 1780, p. 173. Cf. also [James Macpherson], *A Short History of the Opposition during the Last Session of Parliament*, 3rd edn., London, 1779, p. vi.

12. In this sample, again, some voices were for the American cause and some against it; and for our present purpose it does not really matter which was which. *Observations on American Independency*, n.p., [1779], p. 6. *The True Interest of America Impartially Stated. . . . By an American*, 2nd edn., Philadelphia, 1776, p. 52. [Arthur

Lee], *An Appeal to the Justice and Interests of the People of Great Britain* (1774), 4th edn., London, 1776, p. [3]. *Licentiousness Unmask'd; or, Liberty Explained*, London, [1776], p. 40. These assertions echoed formulations that had been repeated ever since the American crisis had begun to unfold: see Gould, *The Persistence of Empire*, pp. 66, 119, and *passim*.

13. Richard Price, *Observations on the Nature of Civil Liberty*, 8th edn., Edinburgh, 1776, p. 22 (emphasis added); and see an exasperated response to this observation in *Remarks on Dr. Price's Observations on the Nature of Civil Liberty*, p. 16. John Fothergill, *An English Freeholder's Address, to his Countrymen*, London, 1780, p. 2.

14. Thomas Paine, *Common Sense* (1776), in *The Thomas Paine Reader*, eds. Michael Foot and Isaac Kramnick, Harmondsworth, 1987, pp. 81–2. *A Triumph of the Whigs; or, T'Other Congress Convened*, New York, 1775, p. 4. For more examples, on both sides of the political divide, see *The Farmer Refuted; or, A More Impartial and Comprehensive View of the Dispute*, New York, 1775, p. 19 (suggesting that to "endeavour to transmute the people of America into those of Great-Britain" is as erroneous as a syllogism proving that if men and horses are both animals, then "a man is an horse"); *The Honor of the University of Oxford Defended, against the Illiberal Aspersions of E–d B–e Esq*, London, [1781?], p. 27. Cf. S. Conway, "From Fellow-Nationals to Foreigners: British Perceptions of the Americans, circa 1739–1783", *William and Mary Quarterly* 59:1 (2002), pp. 65–100.

15. Price, *Observations on the Nature of Civil Liberty*, p. 39. Cf. Fothergill, *An English Freeholder's Address*, p. 14.

16. As has often been pointed out, American radicals and their sympathizers repeatedly presented the Americans as the "undegenerated descendants of their British ancestors", therefore "desir[ing] a Constitution perfectly English": [Arthur Lee], *A Speech, Intended to Have Been Delivered in the House of Commons*, London, 1775, p. 4; and *Morning Post* 707 (1 Feb. 1774), p. 4. Cf. J. M. Murrin, "A Roof without Walls: The Dilemma of American National Identity", in Richard Beeman et al. (eds.), *Beyond Confederation: Origins of the Constitution and American National Identity*, Chapel Hill, 1987, pp. 333–48. As the revolution progressed, however, American assertions of difference naturally grew stronger than those denying this difference.

17. Abbé [Guillaume] Raynal, *The Revolution in America*, London, 1781, pp. 29–30. *Lady's Magazine*, 1775, etc. Note the revealingly oxymoronic reference of one M.P., without the least sense of irony, to "a civil war with America": *Parliamentary History of England*, xviii, p. 186.

18. [Matthew Robinson-Morris, 2nd Baron Rokeby], *Considerations on the Measures Carrying On with Respect to the British Colonies in North America*, London, 1774, in *English Defenders of American Freedoms 1774–1778: Six Pamphlets Attacking British Policy*, ed. P. H. Smith, Washington, 1972, pp. 64, 81. *America Vindicated from the High Charge of Ingratitude and Rebellion. . . . By a Friend to Both Countries*, Devizes, 1774, pp. 9–10, 22, 24. [John Knox], *The American Crisis, by a Citizen of the World*, London, 1777, pp. 19, 26. [Macpherson], *A Short History of the Opposition during the Last Session of Parliament*, pp. 7–9.

19. [James Burgh], *Political Disquisitions*, London, 1774, 3 vols., ii, pp. 309, 313–14; and cf. pp. 320–1. Edmund Burke, *Letter to the Sheriffs of Bristol*, 3 April 1777, in *The Writings and Speeches of Edmund Burke*, iii, pp. 313, 316–17. *An Unconnected Whig's*

Address to the Public; upon the Present Civil War, London, 1777, pp. 56–8, 63, 76–7. Government apologists could also use the same arguments – acknowledging the variety within the British empire – *against* American independence: cf. E. H. Gould, "American Independence and Britain's Counter-Revolution", *Past and Present* 154 (1997), p. 123.

20. Contemporaries, on the other hand, often drew attention to "such contradictory arguments" in the rhetoric of their adversaries, though they typically preferred to see in them proof of the opposition's cynicism and deception rather than a problem that may have been inherent in the conflict itself. For examples see David Hartley, *An Address to the Committee of the County of York, on the State of Public Affairs*, London, 1781, pp. 28–9 (quoted); Caleb Evans, *A Reply to the Rev. Mr. Fletcher's Vindication of Mr. Wesley's Calm Address to our American Colonies*, Bristol, [1776], p. 26; [Josiah Tucker], *A Series of Answers to Certain Popular Objections, against Separating from the Rebellious Colonies*, Gloucester, 1776, p. 55; and idem, *Tract V. The Respective Pleas and Arguments of the Mother Country, and of the Colonies*, Gloucester, 1775, p. vi.

21. J[ohn] Shebbeare, *An Essay on the Origin, Progress and Establishment of National Society; in which the Principles of . . . Dr. Price's Observations, &. Are . . . Fully Refuted*, London, 1776, pp. 21, 91, 93, 108, 119, 135.

22. John Erskine, *Shall I Go to War with my American Brethren?*, Edinburgh, 1776, pp. [iii], 7, 18–19.

23. [Charles Inglis], *Letters of Papinian: In Which the Conduct, Present State, and Prospects of the American Congress Are Examined*, New York and London, 1779, pp. 71–3, 78. *Hypocrisy Unmasked; or, A Short Inquiry into the Religious Complaints of our American Colonies*, 3rd edn., London, 1776, pp. 5–7, 14–15, 18. Cf. also *A Short Appeal to the People of Great Britain; upon the Unavoidable Necessity of the Present War with our Disaffected Colonies*, 2nd edn., London, 1776. For examples drawing the Catholic–Protestant contrast on the other side see *The Crisis* 47 (9 Dec. 1775), pp. 305, 308–9, and *passim*; and *An Unconnected Whig's Address to the Public*, pp. 67–9. For examples focusing on the Anglican–Dissenting divide cf. John Fletcher, *A Vindication of the Rev. Mr. Wesley's "Calm Address to Our American Colonies"*, 3rd edn., London, 1776, pp. 65–6; *Remarks on Dr. Price's Observations on the Nature of Civil Liberty*, pp. 16, 18, 68–9; *Morning Chronicle* 24 July 1777, repr. in A. Grant, *Our American Brethren: A History of Letters in the British Press during the American Revolution, 1775–1781*, Jefferson (N.C.), 1995, p. 175; and [Joseph Priestley], *Address to Protestant Dissenters of All Denominations*, London, 1774, p. 5 (this example being pro-American).

24. Of course, as Eliga Gould reminds us (*The Persistence of Empire*, p. 7), in truth these earlier eighteenth-century wars were not really all that clear-cut in terms of their religious alignments, with Britain often finding itself joining forces with Catholic allies (like the devoutly Catholic queen Maria Theresa in the War of the Austrian Succession in the 1740s). But these earlier conflicts had been readily *representable* as following unambiguous religious lines, a feat that proved more elusive for the American war.

25. Jonathan Clark (*The Language of Liberty*, p. 305) has claimed the American war as "the last great war of religion in the western world". Perhaps: but what the present argument suggests – and what Clark may have failed to appreciate sufficiently – is that many people had a pressing interest in trying to portray it in just this way.

26. *Morning Post, and Daily Advertiser* 711 (6 Feb. 1775), p. [1]. Myles Cooper, *National Humiliation and Repentance Recommended, and the Causes of the Present Rebellion in America*, Oxford, 1777, p. 13. Josiah Tucker, *A Letter to Edmund Burke, Esq*, 2nd edn., Gloucester, 1775, pp. 10–11. Idem, *Four Tracts, on Political and Commercial Subjects*, 3rd edn., Gloucester, 1776, pp. 222–4. Cf. also the penny geneticist who claimed that such "innate principles", inherited from their forefathers, had rendered the "general character" of the colonists as a nation "so opposite to the noble and generous character of Britons" as to make the war immediately comprehensible: *Considerations on the American War. Addressed to the People of England*, London, 1776, pp. 3–5. Cf. also *Sagittarius's Letters and Political Speculations*, p. 22.

27. [Joseph Galloway], *Historical and Political Reflections on the Rise and Progress of the American Rebellion*, London, 1780, pp. 26–7, 32, 45–6, 58, 92–3. [Idem,] *Cool Thoughts on the Consequences to Great Britain of American Independence*, London, 1780, pp. 46–8, 50. *The Voice of God. Being Serious Thoughts on the Present Alarming Crisis*, London, 1775, p. 13.

28. See above, p. 201.

29. *London Evening Post* 8,406 (3–6 Feb. 1776), p. 4; and cf. 8,391 (30 Dec. 1775–2 Jan. 1776), p. 4. *The Crisis* 4 (11 Feb. 1775), pp. 23–4; 13 (15 April 1775), pp. 87–8; 34 (9 Sept. 1775), pp. 225–7. See also *The Conquerors. A Poem Displaying the Glorious Campaigns of 1775, 1776, 1777, &c. &c.*, London, [1778]. The rise in anti-Scottish sentiments during these years is discussed in Conway, *The British Isles and the War of American Independence*, pp. 178–9.

30. *Anticipation; or, The Voyage of an American to England, in the Year 1899, in a Series of Letters, Humorously Describing the Supposed Situation of this Kingdom at that Period*, London, 1781, pp. 6, 163.

31. Ibid., pp. 31, 99.

32. *The Crisis* 31 (19 Aug. 1775), p. 207.

33. In fact, it was not even clear which side the Scots were supposed to be egging on: whereas these voices blamed the Scots for the bellicose behavior of the mother country, others, loyalists, made seemingly equal sense blaming the Scots – whose kirk in North America zealously safeguarded its independence from the Church of England – for inciting the winds of independence and rebellion. See N. Landsman, "Colonial Transculture and the Divisions of Britain", paper presented at the Huntington Library, Oct. 2000 (I am grateful to Ned Landsman for permission to cite this paper).

34. Edmund Burke, "Speech on the Use of Indians", 6 Feb. 1778 ("universally thought the very best [speech] Mr. Burke had ever delivered"), in *The Writings and Speeches of Edmund Burke*, iii, pp. 356, 361; Burke, "Draft Petition on Use of Indians" [1775; never used], p. 180 (and cf. his "Address to the King" and his "Address to the Colonists", both Jan. 1777, pp. 267, 281–2). *The Crisis* 21 (10 June 1775), p. 135; 49 (23 Dec. 1775), p. 322. Cf. also Thomas Day, *Reflexions upon the Present State of England, and the Independence of America*, London, 1782, p. 25.

35. *London Evening Post* 8,393 (4–6 Jan. 1776), p. 3. *An Address to the People on the Subject of the Contest between Great-Britain and America*, London, 1776, p. 10. [John Lind], *An Answer to the Declaration of the American Congress*, London, 1776, pp. 56, 102.

36. Thomas Bolton, as cited in J. Fliegelman, *Declaring Independence: Jefferson, Natural Language, and the Culture of Performance*, Stanford, 1993, p. 75. *London Evening Post* 8,509 (1–3 Oct. 1776), p. 2 (and for another suggestion that some expected

Americans to appear indistinguishable from Indians, *Narrative of Remarkable Occurrences in the life of John Blatchford*, New London [Conn.], 1788, p. 9). J[ohn] Fletcher, *American Patriotism Farther Confronted with Reason, Scripture, and the Constitution*, Shrewsbury, 1776, p. 62 (and cf. *The Double Delusion. . . . A Joco-Serious Review of our American Embroilment*, London, 1777, pp. 14–15). *The Patriots of North-America: A Sketch*, New York, 1775, pp. 3, 12, 18, 27, 33, 39n (written, the preface asserted, for English as well as American readers). And note Edward Long's defensive assertion that England's Indian alliances did *not* turn them into cannibalistic savages in his *English Humanity No Paradox; or, An Attempt to Prove, that the English Are Not a Nation of Savages*, London, 1778, p. 82.

37. [Lind], *An Answer to the Declaration of the American Congress*, p. 106. *London Evening Post* 8,475 (16 July 1776), p. 4. These two examples, again, came from the opposite sides of the political spectrum. Others include "Extract of a Letter from the Hon. Lieutenant-General Gage to the Earl of Dartmouth" in *Gentleman's Magazine* 45 (Sept. 1775), p. 446; William Allen, *The American Crisis: A Letter . . . on the Present Alarming Disturbances in the Colonies*, London, 1774, p. 13; *The Conquerors. A Poem*, pp. 56, 58; and Burke, "Speech on the Use of Indians", p. 361. Also cf. Gould, *The Persistence of Empire*, pp. 196–7.

38. Burke, draft of the speech on the use of Indians, 6 Feb. 1778, in *The Writings and Speeches of Edmund Burke*, iii, p. 366. *Boston Gazette*, as cited in J. Fliegelman, *Prodigals and Pilgrims: The American Revolution against Patriarchal Authority, 1750–1800*, Cambridge, 1982, p. 138; and see pp. 137–9 for the story of Jane M'Crea.

39. *Genuine Abstracts from Two Speeches of the Late Earl of Chatham*, London, 1779, pp. 55–7 (and cf. p. 39). Pownall's speech, of 6 Feb. 1778, is cited in *A View of the History of Great-Britain, during the Administration of Lord North*, London, 1782, p. 293n.

40. *London Evening Post* 8,463 (15–18 June 1776), p. 4; and cf. 8,244 (26–28 Jan. 1775), p. 4. Other examples include *General Evening Post* 6,587 (12–14 March 1776), p. 3; Raynal, *The Revolution in America*, pp. 128–9.

41. Richard Watson, *The Principles of the Revolution Vindicated: In a Sermon . . . May 29. 1776*, Cambridge, 1776, pp. 1–4. Edmund Burke to John Bourke, [Nov. 1777], in *The Correspondence of Edmund Burke*, 10 vols., ed. G. H. Guttridge, vol. iii, Cambridge, 1961, p. 403.

42. [Adam Ferguson], *Remarks on a Pamphlet Lately Published by Dr. Price, Intitled, Observations on the Nature of Civil Liberty*, London, 1776, p. 42. *Letters to the High and Mighty United States of America. By Integer*, New York and London, [1780], p. 47. *A Letter to Lord North, on his Re-Election into the House of Commons. By a Member of Parliament*, London, 1780, p. 34. *Independency the Object of the Congress in America*, p. 44. *Momus; or, The Fall of Britain. A Poem*, London, 1779, p. 18. Among many similar examples, cf. also *The Patriotic Mirror; or, The Salvation of Great Britain in Embryo*, London, 1781, p. 14; and *The Honor of Parliament and the Justice of the Nation Vindicated*, London, 1776, p. 6.

43. [Henry Hunter], *A National Change in Morals, in Measures, and in Politics Necessary to National Prosperity*, London, 1780, p. 37. Letter to Lord North in *Morning Post, and Daily Advertiser* 708 (2 Feb. 1775), p. 1. Cf. *The Voice of God*, p. 10.

44. *Letters to the High and Mighty United States of America. By Integer*, p. 29. *Independency the Object of the Congress in America*, p. 47. [Hunter], *A National Change in*

Morals, in Measures, and in Politics Necessary to National Prosperity, pp. iv, 21–2, 40. *Momus; or, The Fall of Britain*, p. 18.

45. Fletcher, *American Patriotism Farther Confronted with Reason, Scripture, and the Constitution*, p. 27. Cf. idem, *A Vindication of the Rev. Mr. Wesley's "Calm Address to our American Colonies"*, pp. 61–2.

46. Fletcher, *American Patriotism Farther Confronted with Reason, Scripture, and the Constitution*, pp. 25, 63 (and cf. Fletcher, *A Vindication of the Rev. Mr. Wesley's "Calm Address to our American Colonies"*, pp. 16–17). Wesley, *Some Observations on Liberty*, pp. 12–16. And see the heated argument over which side was preparing the ground "for what, in vulgar phrase, is styled *petticoat government*" between Evans, *A Reply to the Rev. Mr. Fletcher's Vindication of Mr. Wesley's Calm Address*, pp. 74–5, and Fletcher's *American Patriotism Farther Confronted with Reason, Scripture, and the Constitution*, pp. 36–7. Other examples include: *Opposition Mornings: With Betty's Remarks*, London, 1779, pp. 11–12; [David Williams], *The Morality of a Citizen; in a Visitation Sermon*, London, 1776, pp. 9–10; and, on the pro-American side, *The Religious Harmonist; or, A Recipe for the Cure of Schism, the Fatal Source of our American Disputes*, London, [1776], pp. 37–8.

47. The force of the argument was somewhat undermined, however, when this writer also asserted at the same time that "an American [in] England . . . is not a stranger, not an alien, a man of *another* country: he is a man of *this* country"; *Three Letters to Dr. Price, Containing Remarks on his Observations on the Nature of Civil Liberty. . . . By a Member of Lincoln's Inn*, London, 1776, pp. iv, 40, 43–4, 46, 82–3, 106.

48. For a warning that the American ideology will lead to votes for Indians see John Martin, *Familiar Dialogues between Americus and Britannicus*, London, 1776, pp. 57–9; for blacks, *Letters to the High and Mighty United States of America. By Integer*, p. 29; and for the propertyless, Wesley, *Some Observations on Liberty*, p. 16.

49. [John Cartwright], *A Letter to Edmund Burke, Esq; Controverting the Principles of American Government*, London, 1775, pp. 6–9.

50. Ibid., pp. 25–8. The same simile, to the same purpose, was used in *A Letter to Those Ladies Whose Husbands Possess a Seat in Either House of Parliament*, London, 1775, pp. 7–9.

51. *An English Green Box; or, The Green Box of the R–t H–e E–d L–d Churllow*, London, 1779, p. 92 (and note the imputation of social and racial indistinctiveness to Lord Thurlow on pp. 100–1). *Liberty and Patriotism: A Miscellaneous Ode, with Explanatory Notes, and Anecdotes*, London, 1778, pp. 2, 11 (and note the subversion of social boundaries invoked there as well). *Daily Advertiser*, 25 Jan. 1783, in D'Eon Mss., Brotherton Library, Leeds University, second volume of newspaper cuttings. *The Remarkable Trial of the Queen of the Quavers, and her Associates*, London, 1778 (quoted, p. 147); and see J. P. Carson, "Commodification and the Figure of the Castrato in Smollett's *Humphry Clinker*", *The Eighteenth Century* 33 (1992), p. 37. See also the uncontrollable sliding of *A Poetical Address to the Ladies of Bath*, Bath, 1775, from the issue of the present internal strife, its intended target, to the question of proper feminine behavior and gender roles.

52. *XSMWPDRIBVNWLXY; or, The Sauce Pan*, London, 1781 (quoted, pp. 41, 55). *Bedlam, a Ball, and Dr. Price's Observations on the Nature of Civil Liberty. A Poetical Medley*, London, 1776, pp. 9, 13 (this text charged Price with subversion of the social order, as embodied in the unsettling of the boundaries of gender – and also, briefly, rank and race – against the dictates of nature). *The Patriots; or, An Evening Prospect on the Atlantic*, London, 1777. Other examples include: *The Family*

In-Compact, Contrasted with the Family Compact, London, 1778; *An Epistle from a Young Lady to an Ensign in the Guards, upon his Being Ordered to America*, London, 1779; [William Preston], *The Female Congress; or, The Temple of Cotytto: A Mock Heroic Poem*, London, 1779; *The Castle of Infamy. A Poetical Vision. In Two Parts*, London, 1780; and *Heroick Epistle from Hamet the Moor, Slipper-Maker in London, to the Emperor of Morocco*, London, 1780.

53. *The Public Ledger*, 28 Nov. 1775; in D'Eon Mss., second volume of newspaper cuttings, f. 300 (with D'Eon's handwritten translation); and cf. f. 301 for *The Public Ledger*, 29 Nov. 1775. *Matrimonial Overtures, from an Enamour'd Lady, to Lord G–G–rm–ne*, London, 1778. See also the critique of the cowardly Germain as confounding gender and other distinctions in the context of the "flames of civil war", in *An Heroic Epistle to the Right Honourable Lord Viscount Sackville*, London, 1783, pp. 6, 14–15. The other side did not fall far behind: cf. the anti-American suggestion of a love affair between the Chevalier D'Eon and a foppish Benjamin Franklin in *History of a French Louse; or, The Spy of a New Species, in France and England*, "trans. from 4th ed of Paris copy", London, 1779, pp. 19–21.

54. [Joseph Peart], *A Continuation of Hudibras. . . . Written in the Time of the Unhappy Contest between Great Britain and America*, London, 1778, pp. 32, 57–8. *The Se'er; or, The American Prophecy. A Poem. Being the Second Sight of That Celebrated Ohio Man, or Indian Seer, Oomianouskipittiwantipaw*, London, 1779, pp. 26, 29, 31.

55. E. G. Burrows and M. Wallace, "The American Revolution: The Ideology and Psychology of National Liberation", *Perspectives in American History* 6 (1972) (quoted, p. 168). Fliegelman, *Prodigals and Pilgrims*. The common "metaphoric transfer of civil war from an external, political realm to inner conflict over sexual choice and the proper gender roles" is discussed in M. R. Higonnet, "Civil Wars and Sexual Territories", in H. M. Cooper et al. (eds.), *Arms and the Woman: War, Gender, and Literary Representation*, Chapel Hill, 1989 (quoted, p. 87). Cf. the analogous argument about the effects of the intra-Grecian Peloponnesian War in P. duBois, *Centaurs and Amazons: Women and the Pre-History of the Great Chain of Being*, Ann Arbor, 1982.

56. *The Annals of Administration. Containing the Genuine History of Georgiana the Queen-Mother, and Prince Coloninus her Son*, London, 1775, pp. 14, 16, 19. Martin, *Familiar Dialogues between Americus and Britannicus*, pp. 5, 40.

57. [Pratt], *Emma Corbett; or, The Miseries of Civil War*, pp. 4, 85, 173, 196.

58. Ibid., pp. 25, 35, 57, 92, 108, 173, 222.

59. Ibid., pp. 213, 219, 230, 235, 248 (emphases added).

60. Ibid., p. 243.

61. [Allan Ramsay], *Letters on the Present Disturbances in Great Britain and her American Provinces*, London, 1777, pp. 16–24; originally published in the *Public Advertiser* early in 1775.

62. Colley, *Britons*. Colley notes the peculiarities of the American war, but in the end incorporates it within her broader narrative together with other eighteenth-century conflicts, in part by focusing predominantly on the final defeat.

63. Paine, *Common Sense*, p. 72., *A View of the History of Great-Britain, during the Administration of Lord North*, p. 397 (emphasis added). The immediate context that prompted this plea was the alleged disappearance of any meaningful boundary or distinction between Whigs and Tories. For the boundaries between Indians and whites see pp. 334–5; between men and women, p. 336; Catholics and Protestants, p. 304; Americans and Britons, pp. 123, 226, 245, 293. Note also Eliga Gould's

argument for the long-term effects of the American war on British notions of empire, pushing them from an emphasis on empire-wide Anglicized similarity to one on diversity within the empire: *The Persistence of Empire*, pp. 209–11; and idem, "A Virtual Nation: Greater Britain and the Imperial Legacy of the American Revolution", *American Historical Review* 104 (1999), pp. 476–89.

64. Edmund Burke, *Letter to the Sheriffs of Bristol*, 3 April 1777, in *The Writings and Speeches of Edmund Burke*, iii, p. 329. See in the same vein *XSMWPDRIBVN-WLXY; or, The Sauce Pan*, p. 5. Brewer, "English Radicalism in the Age of George III", p. 342.

65. *Eccentric Biography; or, Memoirs of Remarkable Female Characters, Ancient and Modern*, London, 1803, pp. 335–43. S. M. Gustafson, "The Genders of Nationalism: Patriotic Violence, Patriotic Sentiment in the Performances of Deborah Sampson Gannett", in R. Blair St. George (ed.), *Possible Pasts: Becoming Colonial in Early America*, Ithaca (N.Y.), 2000, pp. 380–99. S. Juster, "'Neither Male nor Female': Jemima Wilkinson and the Politics of Gender in Post-Revolutionary America", in Blair St. George (ed.), *Possible Pasts*, pp. 357–79. For the gender ambiguous elements in the *Columbian Magazine* frontispiece see C. Smith-Rosenberg, "Dis-Covering the Subject of the 'Great Constitutional Discussion,' 1786–1789", *Journal of American History* 79 (1992), pp. 870–2. For Joan of Arc as a model of emulation in the early republic see Fliegelman, *Prodigals and Pilgrims*, p. 89; Gustafson, "The Genders of Nationalism", pp. 392–3; as well as *United States Magazine*, March 1799, p. 122 (and for the different situation in England see above, p. 331 n. 46).

66. Benjamin Smith Barton, *New Views of the Origins of the Tribes and Nations of America*, Philadelphia, 1797, p. v. Gilbert Imlay, *A Topographical Description of the Western Territory of North America*, New York, 1793, pp. 179–80 (based on Imlay's 1780s American experiences). Rev. Samuel Stanhope Smith, *An Essay on the Causes and Variety of the Complexion and Figure in the Human Species*, Philadelphia and London, 1789 (quoted, p. 26). *American Museum*, 1787, as cited in Juster, "'Neither Male nor Female'", pp. 368–9. Note also Don Alfonso Decalves [pseud.], *New Travels to the Westward; or, Unknown Parts of America*, Boston, [1788], several editions of which appeared from Vermont to Philadelphia between 1788 and 1797; this foregrounded the eighteenth-century trope of the traveler whose appearance is transformed beyond recognition through the effects of climate and culture. On the continuation of environmental and mutable understandings of race in America in the 1780s and 1790s (before receding in the early nineteenth century) see W. D. Jordan, *White over Black: American Attitudes towards the Negro, 1550–1812*, Chapel Hill, 1968, esp. chap. 14; B. W. Sheehan, *Seeds of Extinction: Jeffersonian Philanthropy and the American Indian*, Chapel Hill, 1973, chap. 1; and J. P. Melish, *Disowning Slavery: Gradual Emancipation and "Race" in New England, 1760–1860*, Ithaca (N.Y.), 1998, esp. chap. 4.

67. C. Smith-Rosenberg, "Political Camp or the Ambiguous Engendering of the American Republic", in I. Blom et al. (eds.), *Gendered Nations: Nationalisms and Gender Order in the Long Nineteenth Century*, Oxford, 2000, p. 274; and cf. her "Dis-Covering the Subject", where she explains the post-revolutionary need of the colonists to adhere to complex, non-binary identity categories in order to differentiate themselves simultaneously from the British colonizers against whom they had just rebelled and from the non-white colonized peoples around and among them. J. Hector St. John de Crèvecoeur, *Letters from an American Farmer* (1782), New

York, 1904, p. 54. On Crèvecoeur's environmentalism, based on natural history theories of transplantation, see Fliegelman, *Prodigals and Pilgrims*, pp. 62–3, 180–2. Also note D. Waldstreicher, *In the Midst of Perpetual Fetes: The Making of American Nationalism, 1776–1820*, Chapel Hill, 1997, e.g. pp. 64, 77–8.

68. C. Kidd, *British Identities before Nationalism: Ethnicity and Nationhood in the Atlantic World, 1600–1800*, Cambridge, 1999, p. 25. J. P. Melish, "Emancipation and the Em-bodiment of 'Race': The Strange Case of the White Negroes and the Algerine Slaves", in J. M. Lindman and M. L. Tarter (eds.), *A Centre of Wonders: The Body in Early America*, Ithaca (N.Y.), 2001, pp. 223–36. Sarah Knott's forthcoming *A Cultural History of Sensibility in Revolutionary America* promises to illuminate further the significance of the *ancien régime* of identity to the shaping of the early republic.

69. The highpoint of Richard Sheridan's *The Camp* (1778), for example, was when "Miss Walpole, in performing the military exercise" while dressed as a male soldier, "met with great applause" (*Town and Country Magazine* 10 [1778], p. 544; *Morning Post*, 16 Oct. 1778; quoted in *The Dramatic Works of Richard Brinsley Sheridan*, ed. C. Price, 2 vols., Oxford, 1973, ii, pp. 713, 739). Interestingly, if by now predictably, Sheridan's early-nineteenth-century biographer, flying in the face of the late-1770s success of *The Camp* (a success not repeated thereafter), saw it as a "disgrace", a "contemptible production", and admitted failing to comprehend why Sheridan had not publicly disavowed its authorship (quoted ibid., pp. 714–15). Other examples of wartime stage productions involving female soldiers include: Robert Ashton, *The Battle of Aughrim; or, The Fall of Monsieur St. Ruth. A Tragedy*, Dublin, 1777; Frederick Pilon, *The Liverpool Prize; a Farce*, London, 1779; [Edward Neville], "Plymouth in an Uproar", 1779 (Larpent Mss., Huntington Library, no. 493); [George Downing], *The Volunteers; or, Taylors, to Arms! A Comedy*, London, 1780; and [John Scawen], "The Girl in Stile", 1786 (but written earlier) (Larpent Mss., no. 749). Also note F[rederick] Pilon, *The Invasion*, London, 1778, p. 9; *The Woman of Fashion. A Poem*, London, 1778, p. 19; *Buthred; a Tragedy*, London, 1779, epilogue; and [Elizabeth Craven], *The Miniature Picture: A Comedy*, London, 1781, epilogue. The resulting expectation to encounter women of "a masculine nature" in military camps was interestingly revealed and queried in a 1777 letter in [Thomas Anburey], *Travels through the Interior Parts of America; in a Series of Letters. By an Officer*, 2 vols., London, 1789, ii, pp. 39–40.

70. William Roberts, *Memoirs of the Life and Correspondence of Mrs. Hannah More*, 4 vols., 3rd edn., London, 1835, i, p. 122. On the political connotations of the tragedy *Percy* see K. Newey, "Women and War on Stage: Revolution and Nation", unpublished paper (I am grateful to Kate Newey for sharing this paper with me).

71. [William Whitehead], *The Goat's Beard. A Fable*, London, 1777, p. 38. *Gentleman's Magazine* 51 (Feb. 1781), p. 57.

72. William Robertson, *The History of America*, 3 vols., Vienna, 1787 (orig. London, 1777), i, p. [iii]. And see above, p. 118.

73. James Dunbar, *Essays on the History of Mankind in Rude and Cultivated Ages*, London, 1780, pp. 269, 430–1.

74. This was not the case, however, for the full-blown signs of the transformation of *class*, whose real moment came somewhat later, in the 1790s. In this case, the important factor was the timing of a major political crisis that drew out the implications of the new ways of thinking.

75. [John Elliott?], *The Travels of Hildebrand Bowman, Esquire, into Carnovirria, Taupiniera, Olfactaria. . . . Written by Himself*, London, 1778, pp. 296, 313. *Pictures of Men, Manners, and the Times. . . . Written in the Year 1777*, 2 vols., London, 1779, i, pp. 139–41, 186–8, 191.

76. For disguises as Indians see *An Answer to the Letter of Edmund Burke, Esq. One of the Representatives of the City of Bristol*, London, 1777, pp. 43–4, 52; and *A View of the History of Great-Britain, during the Administration of Lord North*, pp. 335–6. For disguised gentlemen, *The Patriotic Mirror; or, The Salvation of Great Britain in Embryo*, p. 48; and [Macpherson], *A Short History of the Opposition*, p. 18. For disguise undermining religious distinctions see Theophilus Stephens, John Williams, and Charles Thompson, *The Fall of Britain* 6 (14 Dec. 1776), p. 36; and [Thomas Bradbury Chandler], *The Friendly Address to All Reasonable Americans, on the Subject of Our Political Confusions*, New York, 1774, p. 22.

77. [Joseph Cawthorne], *The False Alarm*, London, 1782, p. 26. Josiah Tucker, *An Humble Address and Earnest Appeal*, Gloucester, 1775, p. 86; [Cartwright], *A Letter to Edmund Burke*, p. 10; *Four Tracts, on Political and Commercial Subjects*, pp. 163, 223; and [Tucker], *A Series of Answers to Certain Popular Objections, against Separating from the Rebellious Colonies*, p. 55. *Experience Preferable to Theory. An Answer to Dr. Price's Observations*, London, 1776, p. 57. *The Correspondence of King George the Third from 1760 to 1783*, ed. J. Fortescue, 6 vols., London, 1928, iii, p. 48 (no. 1,361, memoranda by George III, 1773?); and cf. p. 86 (no. 1,427, George III to Lord North, 25 March 1774). Similar instances, *inter alia*, include: *Americans against Liberty; or, An Essay on the Nature and Principles of True Freedom*, London, 1775, p. 39; *General Evening Post* 6,596 (19 March 1776); [Lind], *An Answer to the Declaration of the American Congress*, p. 56; *An Answer to the Letter of Edmund Burke . . . to the Sheriffs of that City, passim*; and Alexander Gerard, *Liberty the Cloke of Maliciousness, Both in the American Rebellion, and in the Manners of the Times. A Sermon*, Aberdeen, 1778.

78. Fliegelman, *Declaring Independence*, p. 90. Cf. T. Gustafson, *Representative Words: Politics, Literature, and the American Language, 1776–1865*, Cambridge, 1992; G. S. Wood, "Conspiracy and the Paranoid Style: Causality and Deceit in the Eighteenth Century", *William and Mary Quarterly* 3rd ser., 39 (1982), pp. 401–41; and J. H. Richards, *Theater Enough: American Culture and the Metaphor of the World Stage, 1607–1789*, Durham (N.C.), 1991, chaps. 9–11.

79. *The Crisis* 65 (13 April 1776), pp. 414–15.

80. [Hunter], *A National Change in Morals, in Measures, and in Politics Necessary to National Prosperity*, pp. iv, 21–2 (and cf. David Grant, *The Living Manners of the Times, and their Consequences. . . . A Sermon*, Edinburgh, 1779, pp. 5–6). *Morning Post* 713 (8 Feb. 1775), p. [1] (letter from "Candidus"); 739 (10 March 1775), p. [4]; 744 (16 March 1775), p. [4]. *The Hypocrite Unmasked* 1 (1 Nov. 1780), p. 3 (and cf. the declared intent "to draw aside that mask" in *XSMWPDRIBVNWLXY; or, The Sauce Pan*, p. 91). [Macpherson], *A Short History of the Opposition*, p. 18 (and cf. Thomas Hunter, *Reflections Critical and Moral on the Letters of Lord Chesterfield*, London, 1776, pp. 185, 260–1). *An Apology for the Times: A Poem*, London, 1778, p. 54 (and cf. the critique of men adopting the "many Shapes as PROTEUS wore,/ As many wily Arts explore" in [Christopher Anstey], *Speculation; or, A Defence of Mankind: A Poem*, London, 1780, pp. 8–9).

81. *The Sentimental Magazine* 4 (1776), pp. 60, 75–6, 103, 110, 425. For the surge at

this very juncture in the preoccupation with unveiling and disguise, as revealed through interpretations of Shakespeare, see E. A. Dotson, "Shakespeare Illustrated 1770–1820", PhD thesis, New York University, 1973, pp. 297, 301. Note also the burst of political caricatures focused on the theme of unmasking that art historian Amelia Rauser has identified at the middle of the American war, as discussed below, pp. 304–5.

82. D. Andrew and R. McGowen, *The Perreaus and Mrs. Rudd: Forgery and Betrayal in Eighteenth-Century London*, Berkeley, 2001, pp. 2, 277 (and additional formulations in the prologue to a longer version of this book which the authors kindly shared with me in manuscript). *Public Advertiser*, 28 March 1775 (and cf. *Town and Country Magazine*, April 1775, p. 205), and *London Chronicle*, 16–19 Dec. 1775; both cited in Andrew and McGowen, *The Perreaus and Mrs. Rudd*, pp. 83, 132–3. Cf. also [James Perry], *An Epistle from Mademoiselle d'Eon to the Right Honorable L–d M–d*, London, 1778, pp. 21–2.

83. *The Life and Adventures of Bampfylde-Moore Carew*, London, 1745, cited in D. S. Lynch, *The Economy of Character: Novels, Market Culture, and the Business of Inner Meaning*, Chicago, 1998, pp. 83–4. Hester Lynch Piozzi, *Anecdotes of the Late Samuel Johnson*, London, 1786, pp. 173–5, cited in F. J. Foley, *The Great Formosan Impostor*, St. Louis, 1968, p. 62 (and see the situating of Psalmanazar in "a larger eighteenth-century crisis in authenticity" in S. Stewart, "Antipodal Expectations: Notes on the Formosan 'Ethnography' of George Psalmanazar", in G. Stocking (ed.), *Romantic Motives: Essays on Anthropological Sensibility*, Madison [Wis.], 1989, pp. 48, 52). *A Minute and Particular Account of That Arch Impostor, Charles Price*, London, 1786, pp. 7, 11; and *Memoirs of a Social Monster; or, The History of Charles Price*, new edn., London, 1790, title-page.

84. The contemporary account of the Pretender's masquerade is cited in Lynch, *The Economy of Character*, p. 92 (and cf. pp. 90–2). *A Brief Account of the Life and Family of Miss Jenny Cameron*, London, [1746?], pp. 26, 35. For the importance of imposture and masquerade in the events of 1745 see also J. Campbell, *Natural Masques: Gender and Identity in Fielding's Plays and Novels*, Stanford, 1995, chap. 5.

85. André's letter to Washington was published in *Gentleman's Magazine* 50 (1980), pp. 610–16, and in *Proceedings of a Board of General Officers, Held by the Order of . . . Gen. Washington . . . Respecting Major John André*, Philadelphia, 1780, pp. 21–2: I am grateful to Sarah Knott for the André citations.

86. Elizabeth Montagu to Miss H[annah] More, Bath, 1782, in Roberts, *Memoirs of the Life and Correspondence of Mrs. Hannah More*, i, p. 269.

87. *An Address to Both Houses of Parliament . . . in Which the True Cause of our National Distresses Is Pointed Out*, London, [1779], pp. 5–6, 15. "An Essay on Masquerades", *Lady's Magazine* 8 (Dec. 1777), p. 638. Cf. James Burgh's long attack on masquerades ("to put on a mask is to put off shame") in the midst of his political argumentation which was so important for the American cause: in his *Political Disquisitions*, iii, pp. 103ff. And note the association of Germain's supposed cowardice, which we have seen linked to gender play, with a masquerade too, in *Captain Parolles at M–nden: A Rough Sketch for the Royal Academy*, London, 1778, p. 7.

88. It was therefore apt that Wesley himself became the object of an attack that leveled the same accusation against him in turn. Penned by a pseudonymous "Patrick Bull", *A Wolf in Sheep's Clothing; or, An Old Jesuit Unmasked . . . in the Form of the Rev. John Wesley*, London, [1775], linked Wesley's supposed masquerade with his incon-

sistent references to the Americans as "brethren" even as he recommended harsh measures against them, which led to "civil dissension" (p. 11).

89. *The Englishman* 9 (14 April 14 1779), p. 55. Wilson, *The Sense of the People*, p. 258; and see pp. 253–9. N. Rogers, *Crowds, Culture and Politics in Georgian Britain*, Oxford, 1998, pp. 122–51.

90. W[illiam] Mason, *Ode to the Naval Officers of Great Britain. Written, Immediately after the Trial of Admiral Keppel*, London, 1779, p. 8; and cf. *John and Susan; or, The Intermeddler Rewarded: A Tale, Address'd to the French King*, Bath, 1778. James Fordyce, *Addresses to Young Men*, 2 vols., London, 1777, ii, p. 325. Burke to Frances Pelham, 12 Jan. 1779, in *The Correspondence of Edmund Burke*, iv, p. 37 (and cf. *Norfolk Chronicle*, 20 Feb. 1779, as cited in Wilson, *Sense of the People*, p. 257). The importance of this turning point for attitudes to the war has been noted by J. H. Plumb, "British Attitudes to the American Revolution" (1964), in his *In the Light of History*, London, 1972, pp. 70–87.

91. D. Armitage, "Greater Britain: A Useful Category of Historical Analysis", unpublished longer version of the essay that appeared in *American Historical Review* 104 (1999). [Cawthorne,] *The False Alarm*, pp. 12–13, 16.

92. Thomas Somerville, *My Own Life and Times 1741–1814*, Edinburgh, 1861, p. 185 (emphasis added).

93. Gerald Newman notes a sudden new emphasis on sincerity in politics at precisely this time in his *The Rise of English Nationalism: A Cultural History 1740–1830*, New York, 1987, esp. pp. 206–7.

Chapter 7

1. *Masquerades; or, What You Will. By the Author of Eliza Warwick* (London, 1780), 2 vols., Dublin, 1781, ii, p. 62.

2. Eyles Irwin, *A Series of Adventures in the Course of a Voyage up the Red-Sea, on the Coasts of Arabia and Egypt*, London, 1780, p. 157. Compare John Andrews, *An Analysis of the Principal Duties of Social Life*, London, 1783, pp. 109–10: "It is difficult, not to say impracticable, to preserve long an assumed and feigned character"; and when we try on such a character, "like clothes that fit us not, [it] must fit very uneasy."

3. *A Minute and Particular Account of That Arch Impostor, Charles Price*, London, 1786, p. 6. *The Lives of George and Joseph Westons, Two Notorious Highwaymen, Forgers*, Edinburgh, 1783, pp. 10–11, cited in P. Baines, *The House of Forgery in Eighteenth-Century Britain*, Aldershot, 1999, p. 129.

4. Ottobah Cugoano, *Thoughts and Sentiments on the Evil and Wicked Traffic of the Slavery and Commerce of the Human Species*, London, 1787, in his *Thoughts and Sentiments on the Evil of Slavery and Other Writings*, ed. V. Carretta, New York, 1999, pp. 40–1.

5. *The Artist's Repository and Drawing Magazine*, 1 (1788), p. 120. S. West, "Libertinism and the Ideology of Male Friendship in the Portraits of the Society of Dilettanti", *Eighteenth-Century Life* 16 (May 1992), pp. 76–104 (Reynolds made two such group portraits). For Reynolds's views on portraiture see below, pp. 300–2.

6. Sir Joshua Reynolds, *Discourses on Art*, ed. R. R. Wark, New Haven, 1997, pp. 238–9 (Discourse XIII, delivered 11 Dec. 1786). [Erasmus Darwin], *The Botanic Garden. A Poem, in Two Parts* (London, 1789), New York, 1798, p. 42. For this scene from

Tom Jones see above, p. 171. Cf. also the mid-nineteenth-century beholder of Hogarth's portrait of Garrick as Richard III, who similarly could relate neither to Garrick's acting style as represented in it nor to the compliment that Hogarth supposedly meant it to be, as cited in S. West, *The Image of the Actor: Verbal and Visual Representation in the Age of Garrick and Kemble*, London, 1991, p. 2.

7. *The Beauties of Mrs. Siddons; or, A Review of her Performance . . . in Letters from a Lady of Distinction*, London, 1786, pp. 47–9 (and recall Siddons's resistance to gender identity play on stage – cf. above, p. 388 n. 10). *An Authentic Narrative of Mr. Kemble's Retirement from the Stage*, London, 1817, pp. xxiv–v, cited in West, *The Image of the Actor*, p. 69 (and cf. *passim*). James Boaden, *Memoirs of John Philip Kemble*, 2 vols., London, 1825, i, p. 173, cited in E. G. Dotson, "Shakespeare Illustrated 1770–1820", PhD thesis, New York University, 1973, p. 72 (and cf. pp. 69–78).

8. Henry Siddons, *Practical Illustrations of Rhetorical Gesture and Action* (1807), London, 1822, p. 363. William Shakespeare, *The Comedy of Errors. . . . With Remarks by Mrs. Inchbald*, London, [1808], p. 5. For the other contemporary quotations, and more broadly for the transformation in the casting of twins on stage, see R. J. Slawson, "'Dromio, thou Dromio': The Casting of Twins in Shakespeare's *Comedy of Errors*", *New England Theatre Journal* 2:1 (1991), pp. 59–71.

9. Adam Smith, *The Theory of Moral Sentiments*, eds. D. D. Raphael and A. L. Macfie, Indianapolis, 1984, pp. 129–31 (emphases added): Smith's earlier ideas were put forth in the 1st edn. of 1759 and the 2nd edn. of 1761, and then remained unchanged until the 6th edn. of 1790. (Cf. W. Motooka, *The Age of Reasons: Quixotism, Sentimentalism and Political Economy in Eighteenth-Century Britain*, London, 1998, p. 210; and J. Dwyer, *Virtuous Discourse: Sensibility and Community in Late Eighteenth-Century Scotland*, Edinburgh, 1987, pp. 170–2.) Isaac D'Israeli, "Some Observations on Diaries, Self-Biography, and Self-Characters", in his *Miscellanies; or, Literary Recreations*, London, 1796, p. 101, where he explained that a divided self was a metaphor for the scrupulous keeping of a diary of one's good and bad deeds. Note also Dugald Stewart's dismissal of Smith's notion of sympathy, mistakenly based on "really" changing places with its object, in his *Elements of the Philosophy of the Human Mind* (1792–1827), in *Collected Works*, 11 vols., ed. W. Hamilton, Edinburgh, 1854, iv, pp. 129–32.

10. William Hazlitt, *An Essay on the Principles of Human Action* (1805), ed. J. R. Nabholtz, Gainesville (Fl.), 1969, p. 140. R. Martin and J. Barresi, *Naturalization of the Soul: Self and Personal Identity in the Eighteenth Century*, London, 2000, pp. ix–x, 139–51.

11. Mary Anne Schimmelpenninck, *Theory of the Classification of Beauty and Deformity, and their Correspondence with Physiognomic Expression*, London, 1815, p. vi. Cf. Richard Sennett's observations on the transformation of dress into an expression of one's true identity, a "guid[e] to the authentic self of the wearer": R. Sennett, *The Fall of Public Man*, London, 1986, p. 153 (and see also p. 147).

12. The same, according to Henry Siddons, was also true on the stage: "To imitate the inherent qualities of grand and sublime souls", he advised actors in 1807, "must presuppose similar qualities in the imitator"; so that "the imitation of an attitude which is foreign to him" – to the actor, that is – will inevitably become "a veritable caricatura" (Siddons, *Practical Illustrations of Rhetorical Gesture and Action*, pp. 218–19, 222). Was it a coincidence that the 1780s also witnessed a vogue

for having the dramatic parts of noblemen on stage played by actual live noblemen? (Cf. P. Langford, *Public Life and Propertied Englishmen 1689–1798*, Oxford, 1991, p. 554.)

13. D. S. Lynch, *The Economy of Character: Novels, Market Culture, and the Business of Inner Meaning*, Chicago, 1998, pp. 3 (Carlyle), 125 (Scott), and *passim*.

14. M. de Grazia, *Shakespeare Verbatim: The Reproduction of Authenticity and the 1790 Apparatus*, Oxford, 1991 (quoted, pp. 223–4). Lynch's earliest example of the advocacy of round characters – of character appreciation – is Maurice Morgann, *An Essay on the Dramatic Character of Sir John Falstaff* (1777), followed by a series of essays on Shakespearean characters by different authors between 1780 and 1788: *The Economy of Character*, pp. 133–4. For the decline of the epistolary novel, and of the fictional uses of letters to represent interpersonal communications, see M. A. Favret, *Romantic Correspondence: Women, Politics and the Fiction of Letters*, Cambridge, 1993 (I am indebted to my colleague Mary Favret for enlightening me on this subject). See also A. Henderson, *Romantic Identities: Varieties of Subjectivity, 1774–1830*, Cambridge, 1996, p. 7 and chap. 2, for a discussion of late-eighteenth-century Gothic fiction as polarizing identity into essential personal identity and ephemeral social identity, which seems to me to complement the present argument (although Henderson's historical perspective is rather different from my own).

15. Moreover, carrying Lynch's investigation deeper into the nineteenth century may reveal – as Alan Richardson has suggested – a further movement of second-generation Romantic novelists to increasingly explicit inherited and congenital understandings of self, as epitomized in his view by Mary Shelley's words in *The Last Man* (1826): "We are born; we choose neither our parents, nor our station; we are educated by others, or by the world's circumstances, and this cultivation, *mingling with innate disposition*, is the soil in which our desires, passions, and motives grow." (Quoted in A. Richardson, *British Romanticism and the Science of the Mind*, Cambridge, 2001, pp. 96–7: Richardson's emphasis.)

16. *Gentleman's Magazine* 56 (1786), p. 772. D'Israeli, "Some Observations on Diaries, Self-Biography, and Self-Characters", p. 97. Jeremy Bentham, *An Introduction to the Principles of Morals and Legislation* (1789), eds. J. H. Burns and H. L. A. Hart, Oxford, 1996, pp. 61–2. James Ramsay, *An Essay on the Treatment and Conversion of African Slaves in the British Sugar Colonies*, Dublin (also London), 1784, p. 177 (and see above, pp. 115 and 119). Charles Macklin, "The Art and Duty of an Actor", in James Thomas Kirkman, *Memoirs of the Life of Charles Macklin. . . . Principally Compiled from his Own Papers and Memorandums*, London, 1799 (date of composition unknown; Macklin died in 1797), cited in T. Cole and H. K. Chinoy, *Actors on Acting*, New York, 1957, p. 162. The first recorded use in the OED of "characteristic" in the modern sense, referring to the essential distinctive quality of a person, dates to 1793. Thus, when a 1798 publication boasted personalized portraits that it said were "striking likenesses" and at the same time "all of them strongly characteristic", it was employing this word in this distinctly modern individualized sense, rather than in the former eighteenth-century generic one (*British Public Characters*, London, 1798, p. xii, cited in M. Pointon, *Hanging the Head: Portraiture and Social Formation in Eighteenth-Century England*, New Haven, 1993, p. 97).

17. Quoted in J. Caplan, "'This or That Particular Person': Protocols of Identification in Nineteenth-Century Europe", in J. Caplan and J. Torpey (eds.), *Documenting Individual Identity: The Development of State Practices in the Modern World*,

Princeton, 2001, pp. 64–5; and note this essay's main narrative regarding the emergence of protocols for individual identification from the early nineteenth century, which may also be connected with the broader framework suggested here.

18. Joanna Baillie, *A Series of Plays*, London, 1798, "Introductory Discourse", pp. 29, 53 (emphasis added). *The Artist's Repository and Drawing Magazine*, i (1788), i, pp. 104, 107–8, 176–7.

19. See above, pp. 183–4. *The Artist's Repository and Drawing Magazine*, i (1788), pp. 174–5.

20. H. Schwartz, *Century's End: A Cultural History of the Fin de Siècle from the 990s through the 1990s*, New York, 1990, p. 213. I. Hacking, *Rewriting the Soul: Multiple Personality and the Sciences of Memory*, Princeton, 1995, pp. 142, 150–2. Also idem, "Double Consciousness in Britain 1815–1875", *Dissociation* 4 (1991), pp. 134–46. Richardson, *British Romanticism and the Science of the Mind*, p. 22. Finally, note Coleridge's painful pathologizing in 1814 of his experience of the dissociation of his will, "deranged" and "frenzied", from his volition, when under the influence of laudanum addiction: *The Collected Letters of Samuel Taylor Coleridge*, ed. E. L. Griggs, 4 vols., Oxford, 1959, ii, pp. 489–90 (I am grateful to Tilar Mazzeo for this reference).

21. Hugh Blair, "On the Love of our Country", sermon preached 18 April 1793, in his *Sermons*, 5 vols., Edinburgh, 1777–94, v (1794), pp. 127, 131. William Wilberforce, *A Practical View of the Prevailing Religious System of Professed Christians*, 5th edn., London, 1797, p. 6.

22. S. Rosenfeld, "Citizens of Nowhere in Particular: Cosmopolitanism, Writing, and Political Engagement in Eighteenth-Century Europe", *National Identities* 4:1 (2002), pp. 25–43 (quoted, p. 32): and note that Rosenfeld sees such writers as retaining a well-defined, centered identity-as-self even as they claimed to cast off *national* identity. T. J. Schlereth, *The Cosmopolitan Ideal in Enlightenment Thought*, Notre Dame, 1977, pp. 133, 213 n. 22.

23. S. Thorne, *Congregational Missions and the Making of an Imperial Culture in Nineteenth-Century England*, Stanford, 1999, pp. 24–5, 32–4.

24. D. A. Bell, *The Cult of the Nation in France: Inventing Nationalism, 1680–1800*, Cambridge (Mass.), 2001 (quoted, p. 15). Henri Grégoire, 1788, and Marie-Joseph Chénier, 1793, as cited in ibid., pp. 14–15. Cf. also C. Taylor, "Modernity and Identity", in J. W. Scott and D. Keates, *Schools of Thought: Twenty-Five Years of Interpretive Social Science*, Princeton, 2001, esp. pp. 143–6. Edmund Burke, *A Letter . . . to Sir Hercules Langrishe, Bart. M.P. on the Subject of Roman Catholics of Ireland*, 2nd edn., London, 1792 (referring to the Catholic Relief Bill of 1782), in *The Writings and Speeches of Edmund Burke*, vol. ix, ed. R. B. McDowell, Oxford, 1991, pp. 616–17. Starting points for substantiating such a claim, beginning with the essentializing reconfiguration during these decades of Anglo-Saxon and Celtic identities, can be found in K. Trumpener, *Bardic Nationalism: The Romantic Novel and the British Empire*, Princeton, 1997; and C. Kidd, *British Identities before Nationalism: Ethnicity and Nationhood in the Atlantic World, 1600–1800*, Cambridge, 1999.

25. N. Clarke, "'The Cursed Barbauld Crew': Women Writers and Writing for Children in the Late Eighteenth Century", in M. Hilton et al. (eds.), *Opening the Nursery Door: Reading, Writing and Childhood 1600–1900*, London, 1997, p. 101. William Wordsworth, "My Heart Leaps Up When I Behold", 1802, in *The Complete Poetical Works*, London, 1888; www.bartleby.com/145. Adam Sibbit,

A Dissertation, Moral and Political, on the Influence of Luxury and Refinement on Nations, London, 1800, pp. 116–17.

26. *The English Theophrastus; or, The Manners of the Age*, 3rd edn., London, 1708, p. 152. Boswell's *Life of Samuel Johnson*, as cited in R. Porter, *The Creation of the Modern World: The Untold Story of the English Enlightenment*, New York, 2000, p. 279. [David Fordyce], *Dialogues Concerning Education*, London, 1745, pp. 114–17. Cf. also James Burnett, Lord Monboddo, *Of the Origins and Progress of Language* (2nd edn., 1774): "we seem to set out in life without any original stock of our own, or any natural talent besides that faculty of imitation, which nature has bestowed upon us in so high a degree" (in *Animal Rights and Souls in the Eighteenth Century*, 6 vols., ed. A. Garrett, Bristol, 2000, vi, pp. 208–9).

27. A. Benzaquén, "Childhood and Identity in Enlightenment Human Science", paper presented at the Bloomington Eighteenth-Century Workshop "Signs of the Self in the Eighteenth Century", May 2002 (I am grateful for her permission to cite this paper). Benzaquén's ongoing project "Children's Progress: The Science of Childhood before Developmental Psychology" promises to be a valuable in-depth account of this subject.

28. *Quarterly Review* 23 (1820), quoted in A. Richardson, *Literature, Education, and Romanticism: Reading as Social Practice, 1780–1832*, Cambridge, 1994, pp. 61–2.

29. Compare for example Monboddo's understanding of the French feral girl (above, p. 169) with William Dimond, *The Foundling of the Forest*, London, 1809: upon first encounter with the girl, "even in the midst of all this misery, there was/ a something so noble and so gentle in her air" – an encounter that in itself, supposedly, brings the girl to stop being dumb and begin speaking. In Mary Robinson's "Savage of Aveyron" (1800), the feral child cannot speak, but has distinct numerical abilities and displays reason, memory, and emotions: see Richardson, *British Romanticism and the Science of the Mind*, pp. 159–60, 178. As Richardson shows, Mary Shelley's *Frankenstein* (1818) – closely related to the Enlightenment representations of feral children – affirms again that the newborn "creature" enters the world with pre-formed passions, propensities, and instincts.

30. J. C. Steward, *The New Child: British Art and the Origins of Modern Childhood, 1730–1830*, Berkeley, 1995, pp. 24, 91–2, and *passim* (Northcote quoted p. 94; Lady Grantham to her father, 1784, quoted p. 98). Note Master Hare's white muslin frock with a sash, similar to the dress of small girls: the ungendered representation of small children, and thus the linking of gender differentiation with puberty, heightened further the collapsing of gender into bodily sexual features. Also see A. Higonnet, *Pictures of Innocence: The History and Crisis of Ideal Childhood*, London, 1998, chap. 1.

31. Sibbit, *A Dissertation, Moral and Political*, pp. 116–18. P[eter] Peckard, *Justice and Mercy Recommended, Particularly with Reference to the Slave Trade. A Sermon*, Cambridge, 1788, pp. 16–17. Rev. William Barrow, *An Essay on Education*, 2 vols., London, 1802, i, pp. 4, 159–60 (and note the further vacillation on p. 166). Cf. also Bentham, *Introduction to the Principles of Morals and Legislation* (1789), p. 66; the contradictory impulses in Henry Home, Lord Kames, *Loose Hints upon Education, Chiefly Concerning the Culture of the Heart* (1781), 2nd edn., Edinburgh, 1782, pp. [iii], 6, 47; and Andrews, *An Analysis of the Principal Duties of Social Life* (1783), pp. 9 versus 91. Earlier eighteenth-century discussions of genius, such as William Sharp's *Dissertation upon Genius* (London, 1755) or Alexander Gerard's

Essay on Taste (London and Edinburgh, 1759) and *Essay on Genius* (London, 1774), placed more emphasis on environment than on inborn talent: cf. S. D. Cox, *"The Stranger within Thee": Concepts of the Self in Late-Eighteenth-Century Literature*, Pittsburgh, 1980, pp. 40–2. For an exception see Edward Young, *Conjectures on Original Composition*, London, 1759.

32. See Richardson, *Literature, Education, and Romanticism*, pp. 11, 13, 17.

33. C. Taylor, *Sources of the Self: The Making of the Modern Identity*, Cambridge, 1989, p. 375. C. Siskin, *The Historicity of Romantic Discourse*, Oxford, 1988, p. 3; for Siskin, indeed, "development" itself, as the ultimate mode of enhancement of one's inner self, was a historically specific notion that emerged in the late eighteenth century. Thomas Reid, *Essays on the Intellectual Powers of Man*, Edinburgh, 1785, cited in Martin and Barresi, *Naturalization of the Soul*, p. 129. C. Steedman, *Strange Dislocations: Childhood and the Idea of Human Interiority, 1780–1930*, London, 1995, pp. 4–5. In Germany, the same shift was formulated as one from *Erziehung* (education) to *Bildung* (cultivation): as Johann Pestalozzi wrote in 1800, turning from institutional change to the interior life of the child, "I seek to psychologize human education" (quoted in J. Sheehan, *The Enlightenment Bible*, Princeton, 2005, chap. 5).

34. The same developmental perspective also made it possible to circumvent Locke's quandary about the continuity of identity, by insisting on the "primeval seeds of life" that "remai[n] unchanged through all the stages of life": Thomas Morrell, *Notes and Annotations on Locke on Human Understanding*, London, 1794, p. 64, cited in F. A. Nussbaum, *The Autobiographical Subject: Gender and Ideology in Eighteenth-Century England*, Baltimore, 1989, p. 61 (and note also Priestley and Drew there, and Thrale on p. 56).

35. Higonnet, *Pictures of Innocence*, pp. 8, 23, 28. *The Artist's Repository and Drawing Magazine*, 1 (1788), pp. 97–9, 170. See also Clarke, "'The Cursed Barbauld Crew'", esp. pp. 99–100; and Kate Redford's promising *The Art of Domestic Life: Representing the Family in Eighteenth-Century England* (New Haven, forthcoming).

36. Richardson, *Literature, Education, and Romanticism*, pp. 130–1.

37. Henderson, *Romantic Identities*, pp. 6, 31–2, and more generally chap. 1.

38. M. Mascuch, *Origins of the Individualist Self: Autobiography and Self-Identity in England, 1591–1791*, Oxford, 1997, pp. 6–8, 19, 206, and *passim*. Nussbaum, *The Autobiographical Subject*, pp. 1–2, 21–3, 56, and *passim*. R. Banes, "The Exemplary Self: Autobiography in Eighteenth-Century America", *Biography* 5 (1982), pp. 226–39. The emergence around the turn of the century of compilations of "eccentric" lives, which popularized a new use of this word to describe the unique life stories of unusual individuals, may well have been another facet of the same broad pattern: examples include *Eccentric Biography; or, Memoirs of Remarkable Female Characters*, London, 1803; G. H. Wilson, *The Eccentric Mirror: Reflecting a Faithful and Interesting Delineation of Male and Female Characters*, London, 1806–7; and *The Eccentric Magazine; or, Lives and Portraits of Remarkable Characters*, London, 1812.

For a similar lack of concern with self in eighteenth-century American life narratives, including Benjamin Franklin's, see, in addition to Banes, M. Sobel, *Teach Me Dreams: The Search for Self in the Revolutionary Era*, Princeton, 2000, esp. pp. 18–24; S. C. Arch, "Besides Benjamin Franklin: Autobiography in America, 1750–1800", in R. Dekker (ed.), *Egodocuments and History*, Hilversum, 2002, pp. 125–36 (Arch's first American example of an autobiography embodying a recognizable self dates to 1790); and idem, *After Franklin: The Emergence of Auto-biography in Post-Revolutionary America 1780–1830*, Hanover (N.H.), 2001, pp. x–xi and *passim*.

39. *Prelude* 1805, bk. xii, ll. 159–67, and 1799 pt. II, ll. 269–80, in William Wordsworth, *The Prelude 1799, 1805, 1850*, eds. M. H. Abrams and S. Gill, New York, 1979, pp. 20, 446. In reading these lines in the context of selfhood I found especially useful, respectively, Henderson, *Romantic Identities*, pp. 1–2, and Richardson, *British Romanticism and the Science of the Mind*, pp. 66–7.

40. Anna Barbauld, "To a Little Invisible Being Who Is Expected Soon to Become Visible", c. 1795, in *The Works of Anna Laetitia Barbauld*, London, 1825, i, pp. 199–201. Blake on innate ideas is quoted in E. G. Andrew, *Conscience and its Critics: Protestant Conscience, Enlightenment Reason, and Modern Subjectivity*, Toronto, 2001, p. 148; and his annotation to Reynolds is cited in Cox, *"The Stranger within Thee"*, p. 24. Coleridge and Wordsworth are cited in Taylor, *Sources of the Self*, p. 301.

41. Taylor, *Sources of the Self*, pp. 368–70, 374, 548 n. 1; and note Taylor's positioning of Rousseau as a halfway step toward this Romantic turn (p. 362). Siskin, *The Historicity of Romantic Discourse*, pp. 11, 13, and *passim*. Among many others, see also J. J. McGann, *The Romantic Ideology: A Critical Investigation*, Chicago, 1983, pp. 67–8.

42. Taylor, *Sources of the Self*, p. 368.

43. Henderson, *Romantic Identities*. I benefitted from many conversations with Andrea on this topic, long before I knew it had any bearing on my own work.

44. Richardson, *British Romanticism and the Science of the Mind*. Key British contributions to this field included Erasmus Darwin, *Zoonomia; or, The Laws of Organic Life*, 2 vols., London, 1794–6; Alexander Crichton, *An Inquiry into the Nature and Origin of Mental Derangement*, London, 1798; Sir Charles Bell, *Idea of a New Anatomy of the Brain*, London, 1811; and William Lawrence, *Lectures on Physiology, Zoology, and the Natural History of Man*, London, 1822. See also L. Jordanova, *Sexual Visions: Images of Gender in Science and Medicine between the Eighteenth and Twentieth Centuries*, Madison, WI, 1989, pp. 55–8.

45. Quoted in Richardson, *British Romanticism and the Science of the Mind*, p. 45. For the late-eighteenth-century interest in dreams as a threatening phenomenon of inner nature, Freudian *avant la lettre*, see also J. Ford, "Samuel Taylor Coleridge and the Pains of Sleep", *History Workshop Journal* 48 (1999), pp. 169–86; and D. Kaufmann, "Dreams and Self-Consciousness: Mapping the Mind in the Late Eighteenth and Early Nineteenth Centuries", in L. Daston (ed.), *Biographies of Scientific Objects*, Chicago, 2000, pp. 67–85. And contrast the earlier eighteenth-century understandings of dreams as discussed above, p. 200.

46. Richardson, *British Romanticism and the Science of the Mind*, p. 37. Richardson only mentions but does not discuss Mesmerism as another related anticipation of depth psychology at the same juncture.

47. *Gentleman's Magazine*, Feb. 1801, quoted in G. Tytler, *Physiognomy in the European Novel: Faces and Fortunes*, Princeton, 1982, p. 345 n. 1. On the late-eighteenth-century burst of interest in physiognomy, see also J. Graham, "Lavater's Physiognomy in England", *Journal of the History of Ideas* 22 (1961), pp. 561–72; R. Porter, "Making Faces: Physiognomy and Fashion in Eighteenth-Century England", *Études anglaises* 38:3 (1985), pp. 383–96; B. M. Stafford, *Body Criticism: Imagining*

the Unseen in Enlightenment Art and Medicine, Cambridge (Mass.), 1991, pp. 84–103; and G. Richards, *Mental Machinery: The Origins and Consequences of Psychological Ideas, Part 1: 1600–1850*, London, 1992, chap. 6. For the influence of physiognomy on British art, discussed in more detail below, see M. Cowling, *The Artist as Anthropologist: The Representation of Type and Character in Victorian Art*, Cambridge, 1989; and L. Hartley, *Physiognomy and the Meaning of Expression in Nineteenth-Century Culture*, Cambridge, 2001. Its influence on early-nineteenth-century theatrical writing is strikingly evident in Siddons, *Practical Illustrations of Rhetorical Gesture and Action*. For physiognomic medical practice see L. Jordanova, "The Art and Science of Seeing in Medicine: Physiognomy 1780–1820", in W. F. Bynum and R. Porter (eds.), *Medicine and the Five Senses*, Cambridge, 1993, pp. 122–33.

48. M. Porter, "English 'Treatises on Physiognomy'", PhD thesis, Magdalen College, Oxford, 1997. Alexander Cozens, *Principles of Beauty, Relative to the Human Head*, London, 1778, pp. 1–3, 6. James Parsons, *Human Physiognomy Explain'd: In the Crounian Lectures on Muscular Motion. . . . Read before the Royal Society*, London, 1747, pp. 46–7 (and cf. pp. 36–7); and see as an example Samuel Richardson, *The History of Sir Charles Grandison*, 7 vols., 1754, ii, p. 8. Henry Fielding, *Miscellanies*, vol. I, ed. H. K. Miller, Oxford, 1972, pp. 157, 164. R. Houston and U. Frith, *Autism in History: The Case of Hugh Blair of Borgue*, Oxford, 2000, pp. 68–9, interestingly note the conspicuous lack of interest of a mid-eighteenth-century court in the facial features of an alleged "idiot", in contrast to his clothes, which were of considerable interest; an indifference, the authors suggest, that within the assumptions of early-nineteenth-century physiognomists would have been implausible.

49. [Charles Allen] *The Polite Lady; or, A Course of Education*, London, 1760, pp. 218–19. Edmund Burke, *A Philosophical Enquiry into the Origins of our Ideas of the Sublime and Beautiful* (2nd edn., 1759), ed. J. T. Boulton, Notre Dame, 1958, pp. 132–3. [John Clubbe], *Physiognomy*, London, 1763, p. 6. William Hogarth, *The Analysis of Beauty* (London, 1753), ed. R. Paulson, New Haven, 1997, pp. 95–6. And see Lynch, *The Economy of Character*, e.g. p. 12.

50. John Caspar Lavater, *Essays on Physiognomy*, trans. Thomas Holcroft (1789), 13th edn., London, 1867, pp. 11, 91. Idem, *Essays on Physiognomy*, trans. Henry Hunter, 3 vols., London, 1792, i, p. 25; ii, p. 21. Cozens, *Principles of Beauty*, p. 8. For Lavater on Cozens see J. Gage, "Photographic Likeness", in J. Woodall (ed.), *Portraiture: Facing the Subject*, Manchester, 1997, p. 129 n. 13. See also Thomas Cooper's 1790 address to the Manchester Literary and Philosophical Society in which he strove to distance the modern science of physiognomy from its "disgraceful" associations with divination earlier in the eighteenth century, as cited in Jordanova, "The Art and Science of Seeing in Medicine", p. 123.

51. Porter, "Making Faces", p. 395. Lavater, *Essays on Physiognomy*, trans. Hunter, i, p. 27. Idem, *Essays on Physiognomy*, trans. Holcroft, p. 91. See also Richards, *Mental Machinery*, p. 252.

52. *The Artist's Repository and Drawing Magazine*, 1 (1788), pp. 104, 107–8.

53. Blake's annotation on Lavater is quoted and discussed in J. Barrell, *The Political Theory of Painting from Reynolds to Hazlitt*, New Haven, 1986, pp. 247–8. "Physiognomy", *The New Lady's Magazine*, June 1794, p. 278. Charles Bell, *Essays on the Anatomy of Expression in Painting*, London, 1806, p. 85 (and cf. Jordanova, "The Art and Science of Seeing in Medicine", esp. pp. 130–3; and Hartley, *Physiognomy*

and the Meaning of Expression in Nineteenth-Century Culture, chap. 2). For Lavater's reservations about seeing physiognomy as a formulaic system see Cowling, *The Artist as Anthropologist*, pp. 20–1.

54. [William Thomson], *Mammuth; or, Human Nature Displayed on a Grand Scale. . . . By the Man in the Moon*, 2 vols., London, 1789, ii, p. 210.

55. H. Schwartz, *The Culture of the Copy: Striking Likenesses, Unreasonable Facsimiles*, New York, 1996, pp. 92–3, 102–3, and p. 95 for John Randolph. See also S. McKechnie, *British Silhouette Artists and their Work*, London, 1978, pp. 4–5, 23–6; J. Fliegelman, *Declaring Independence: Jefferson, Natural Language, and the Culture of Performance*, Stanford, 1993, pp. 84–7; and Gage, "Photographic Likeness". There was nothing in wax models, however, that made them inherently a medium for such supposedly unmediated likenesses: cf. the earlier eighteenth-century wax artist whose models, even self-portraits, were characterized to the contrary by *generic* representation, in R. Messbarger, "Waxing Poetic: Anna Morandi Manzolini's Anatomical Sculptures", *Configurations* 9 (2001), esp. pp. 93, 96.

56. Reynolds, *Discourses on Art*, pp. 57 (see also p. 59), 61, 72, 102. My discussion of Reynolds and Barry draws on Barrell, *The Political Theory of Painting*. And cf. D. Donald, "'Characters and Caricatures': The Satirical View", in N. Penny (ed.), *Reynolds*, New York, 1986, pp. 357–8, for an analysis of Reynolds's actual practice in his portraits that, in tune with his theory, conformed to ideal types and epitomized social roles and achievements rather than some notion of individual depths. Reynolds's contemporaries regularly contrasted his portraits with those of his peer Thomas Gainsborough, whose reputation was built on his extraordinary ability to reproduce exact likenesses. Yet Gainsborough, even as he expressly disagreed with Reynolds's pronouncements quoted here, also acknowledged the limits of portraiture in terms that were pathognomic but certainly not physiognomic: "Had a picture voice, action, etc. to make itself known," Gainsborough wrote in 1771, "no disguise would be sufficient to conceal a person; but only a face confined to one view and not a muscle to move to say, 'Here I am' falls very hard upon the poor Painter who perhaps is not within a mile of the truth in painting the Face only." Elsewhere Gainsborough also emphasized "the amazing Effect *of dress*" on the success of individual portraits – again, in line with his *ancien-régime* contemporaries. See Gainsborough's early 1770s letters in C. Harrison et al. (eds.), *Art in Theory 1648–1815: An Anthology of Changing Ideas*, Oxford, 2000, pp. 746–7; and M. Rosenthal, *The Art of Thomas Gainsborough: "A Little Business for the Eye"*, New Haven, 1999, pp. 33–4, 59–66, 136 (including the opinion of the contemporary miniature painter Ozias Humphry about the reliance of Gainsborough's portraits on the stability of dress for their stability of likeness).

57. James Barry's lectures on design of 1785 are quoted in Barrell, *The Political Theory of Painting*, pp. 174, 181; and see more generally chap. 2. Barry had begun working out some of these ideas in a preliminary and incomplete fashion in his *Inquiry into the Real and Imaginary Obstructions to the Acquisition of the Arts in England* of 1775.

58. In 1725 Jonathan Richardson had written: "Painters should take a Face, and make an Antique Medal, or Bas-Relief of it, by divesting it of its Modern Guises, raising the Air, and the Features" (quoted in D. Donald, "'Characters and Caricatures'", p. 360). For Gainsborough see above, n. 56. Barrell, *The Political Theory of Painting*, pp. 214–15.

59. Archibald Alison, *Essays on the Nature and Principles of Taste*, 1790, and William Hazlitt's contribution to the fourth and fifth editions of the *Encyclopaedia*

Britannica, "Fine Arts" (1816), are quoted in Barrell, *The Political Theory of Painting*, pp. 178, 327. Bell, *Essays on the Anatomy of Expression in Painting*, p. 7 (and cf. pp. 42–3 for the critique of the classical ideal of generalized beauty). For Fuseli, and his sometimes reluctant acceptance of particularized variety – including the representation of permanent physiognomic deformities – as the most suitable for the present historical age, see Barrell, *The Political Theory of Painting*, chap. 4; and for Fuseli's *Brutus*, Dotson, "Shakespeare Illustrated 1770–1820", pp. 61–2. And cf. J. Woodall, "Introduction: Facing the Subject", in Joanna Woodall (ed.), *Portraiture. Facing the Subject*, Manchester, 1997, esp. pp. 4–5.

60. Reynolds, *Discourses on Art*, Discourse VII, p. 141. Reynolds's essay on Shakespeare is quoted in Barrell, *The Political Theory of Painting*, pp. 160–1; and see pp. 141–62.

61. A. Rauser, "Unmasking the Modern Self in Eighteenth-Century Caricature", paper presented at the Bloomington Eighteenth-Century Workshop "Signs of the Self in the Eighteenth Century", May 2002; and idem, *Caricature Unmasked: Irony, Authenticity, and Individualism in Eighteenth-Century British Prints* (forthcoming). I am grateful to Amelia Rauser for generously sharing her ongoing work and for numerous enlightening exchanges. D. Donald, *The Age of Caricature: Satirical Prints in the Reign of George III*, New Haven, 1996, chap. 2. See also Pointon, *Hanging the Head*, p. 86, for an analogous observation regarding eighteenth-century caricatures of criminals.

62. For Gillray's print see Pointon, *Hanging the Head*, pp. 102–3; and D. Bindman, *Ape to Apollo: Aesthetics and the Idea of Race in the 18th Century*, Ithaca (N.Y.), 2002, pp. 120–1.

63. A. Rauser, "Embodied Liberty: Why Hogarth's Caricature of John Wilkes Backfired", in B. Fort and A. Rosenthal (eds.), *The Other Hogarth: Aesthetics of Difference*, Princeton, 2001, pp. 240–57. For the transformation c. 1780 see also idem, "Death or Liberty: British Political Prints and the Struggle for Symbols in the American Revolution", *Oxford Art Journal* 21:2 (1998), pp. 151–71. Donald, *The Age of Caricature*, pp. 9–15, 47, 50–60.

64. James Peller Malcolm, *An Historical Sketch of the Art of Caricaturing*, London, 1813, p. 98. Malcolm has crossed our path before with similarly uncomprehending assertions that early-modern audiences must have been "disgusted" with cross-dressing on stage, or that eighteenth-century female dueling was a "shameful" bygone practice that "must perforce be shock[ing]" to the modern ears of his early-nineteenth-century readers.

65. Rauser, "Unmasking the Modern Self". Schimmelpenninck, *Theory of the Classification of Beauty and Deformity*, p. vi.

66. *Masquerades; or, What You Will*, i, pp. 135, 143. John Cross, *An Attempt to Establish Physiognomy upon Scientific Principles*, Glasgow, 1817, pp. 6–7, similarly put forth physiognomy as the antidote to the problem of the modern street crowded with unfamiliar individuals (prefiguring Edgar Allan Poe's "Man in the Crowd"), since it could aid "in determining the great movements of the individual among other individuals, all acting their respective parts in the great struggle and bustle of life" (cited in Hartley, *Physiognomy and the Meaning of Expression*, p. 15). And cf. "Physiognomy", *The New Lady's Magazine*, June 1794, p. 279, which recycled for this purpose – unacknowledged – Mandeville's line that in the modern city street "we should be liable to fifty errors in a day".

67. For a preliminary attempt to emphasize this perspective see my "On Queen Bees and Being Queens: A Late-Eighteenth-Century 'Cultural Revolution'?", in C. Jones

and D. Wahrman (eds.), *The Age of Cultural Revolutions: Britain and France, 1750–1820*, Berkeley, 2001, pp. 251–80; and the editors' "Introduction: An Age of Cultural Revolutions?", pp. 1–16.

68. K. Haakonssen, "From Natural Law to the Rights of Man: A European Perspective on American Debates", in M. J. Lacey and K. Haakonssen (eds.), *A Culture of Rights: The Bill of Rights in Philosophy, Politics, and Law – 1791 and 1991*, Cambridge, 1991, pp. 19–61; and similarly idem, *Natural Law and Moral Philosophy: From Grotius to the Scottish Enlightenment*, Cambridge, 1996, chap. 10. As Richard Tuck has argued, this potentially paradoxical duality had been inherent in the theory of natural rights since its late-medieval emergence: *Natural Rights Theories: Their Origin and Development*, Cambridge, 1979. J. Waldron, *"Nonsense upon Stilts": Bentham, Burke, and Marx on the Rights of Man*, London, 1987, pp. 12–14. I am grateful to Barbara Taylor and Mary Catherine Moran for helpful conversations on this subject.

69. D. Hay and N. Rogers, *Eighteenth-Century English Society: Shuttles and Swords*, Oxford, 1997, p. 85. The counterpart to custom as the legitimating language of rights for the plebs, moreover, was the patrician anchoring of political legitimation in a notion of citizen virtue; a notion that in its eighteenth-century sense, as Charles Taylor has already pointed out (*Sources of the Self*, p. 196), "can't be combined with an atomist understanding of society. It assumes that the political way of life" – the exclusive vocation of the propertied virtuous citizen – "is in an important sense prior to the individuals. It establishes their identity, provides the matrix within which they can be the kinds of human beings they are." Citizen virtue too was socially turned.

70. D. Zaret, "Tradition, Human Rights, and the English Revolution", in J. Wasserstrom et al. (eds.), *Human Rights and Revolutions*, Lanham (Md.), 2000, pp. 43–58 (quoted, pp. 43, 53). Tuck, *Natural Rights Theories*, chap. 7 (and see chap. 8 for the subsequent movement in the late seventeenth century, along the path charted by Pufendorf, *away* from the understanding of rights as individual).

71. Taylor, *Sources of the Self*, pp. 11–12. J. W. Scott, "Some More Reflections on Gender and Politics", added to her *Gender and the Politics of History*, revised edn., New York, 1999, p. 217. L. Hunt, "The Paradoxical Origins of Human Rights", in Wasserstrom et al. (eds.), *Human Rights and Revolutions*, pp. 3–17 (quoted, pp. 9, 12). And cf. J. Goldstein, "Mutations of the Self in Old Regime and Postrevolutionary France", in Daston (ed.), *Biographies of Scientific Objects*, p. 107. An interesting parallel may be seen in another late-eighteenth-century development that combined notions of rights and of self, namely the history of plagiarism: as Tilar Mazzeo shows in her forthcoming *Plagiarism and Literary Property in the Romantic Period*, the 1770s and 1780s witnessed a sharp shift from earlier views of plagiarism as inevitable, given the common stock of human thoughts, to new anxieties about individualized authorship and its relationship to the self that possesses it. (I am grateful to Tilar for sharing her forthcoming work with me.)

72. Andrew, *Conscience and its Critics*, pp. 139, 146 (for Byron) and *passim* (and see above, p. 369 n. 40). See also Haakonssen, *Natural Law and Moral Philosophy*, pp. 283–4, for the route taken by James Mackintosh in pushing moral conscience from a Hartleyian socially turned understanding in the manner of David Hartley to "a genetic theory of the moral faculty" that operates independently of social reinforcement.

73. M. Zuckert, "Natural Rights in the American Revolution: The American Amalgam", in Wasserstrom et al. (eds.), *Human Rights and Revolutions*, pp. 59–76 (esp. p. 61). R. Zagarri, "The Rights of Man and Woman in Post-Revolutionary America", *William and Mary Quarterly* 3rd ser., 55 (1998), esp. pp. 211–14. O. Patterson, "Freedom, Slavery, and the Modern Construction of Rights", in O. Hufton (ed.), *Historical Change and Human Rights*, New York, 1995, pp. 156–63. D. T. Rodgers, *Contested Truths: Keywords in American Politics since Independence*, New York, 1987, p. 46 (and see to p. 66). J. P. Reid, *Constitutional History of the American Revolution*, Madison (Wis.), 1986, p. 90 (and cf. to p. 95). Haakonssen, *Natural Law and Moral Philosophy*, p. 330. A. F. Young, "*Common Sense* and the *Rights of Man* in America", in K. Gavroglu et al. (eds.), *Science, Mind and Art*, Dordrecht, 1995, p. 426. And note Paul Langford's observation (*Public Life and Propertied Englishmen 1689–1798*, pp. 523–4) that natural-rights language entered into circulation in England in the political organizations and societies of the 1780s.

74. William Godwin, *Enquiry Concerning Political Justice* (1793), ed. I. Kramnick, Harmondsworth, 1985, pp. 104–5, 107; and cf. p. 109 for Godwin's direct attack on the Romantic notion of development as that of hidden potential: "How long has the jargon [been] imposed upon the world which would persuade us that in instructing a man you do not add to, but unfold his stores?" See also William Godwin, *The Enquirer: Reflections on Education, Manners, and Literature*, London, 1797, pt. I, essays III, IV. Cf. M. Philp, *Godwin's Political Justice*, London, 1986, pp. 42–4; and Andrew, *Conscience and its Critics*, pp. 141–3.

75. Mary Hays, *Memoirs of Emma Courtney* (1796), ed. E. Ty, Oxford, 1996, p. 8; and see p. 199 for the quotation from William Godwin, *Things as They Are; or, The Adventures of Caleb Williams* (1794). The persistence of such environmental Lockean perspectives in 1790s Jacobin novels is noted in Henderson, *Romantic Identities*, chap. 3; and Richardson, *British Romanticism and the Science of the Mind*, p. 96. Richardson further discusses (pp. 94–5) the striking shift in Godwin's position in subsequent decades, as he renounced (most explicitly in his *Thoughts on Man, his Nature, Productions, and Discoveries*, London, 1831) the belief in the shaping powers of education in favor of a belief in innate "temper" rooted in the brain. Moreover, recall that we have encountered both Godwin and Hays reproducing the altered sensibilities of the new regime of identity in ways that seem to contradict their proclaimed political commitments: the one rewriting the life story of his wife, Mary Wollstonecraft, to explain away her discomfiting Amazonian side, the other rewriting the life story of Queen Elizabeth to play down her manly (perhaps even unnatural) side. The new regime of identity did not present itself as a deliberate either/or choice: a self-conscious political commitment to some tenets of the *ancien régime* did not make one immune to the pervasive, diffuse, mostly unselfconscious cultural effects of the transformation that spelled its demise.

The Panoramic View

1. Maximilien Robespierre, *Rapport fait au nom du comité de Salut Public sur les rapports des idées religieuses et morales avec les principes républicains*, Paris, 1794, p. 4. Robespierre's endorsement and editing of Le Pelletier de Saint-Fargeau's plan for primary education, in B. Baczko (ed.), *Une éducation pour la démocratie*, Paris, 1982. (I am grateful to David Bell for these citations.) J. Goldstein, "Saying 'I': Victor

Cousin, Caroline Angebert, and the Politics of Selfhood in Nineteenth-Century France", in M. S. Roth (ed.), *Rediscovering History: Culture, Politics, and the Psyche*, Stanford, 1994, p. 322. M. Ozouf, *Festivals and the French Revolution*, trans. A. Sheridan, Cambridge (Mass.), 1988, p. 203. Idem, "Regeneration", in F. Furet and M. Ozouf (eds.), *A Critical Dictionary of the French Revolution*, Cambridge (Mass.), 1989, pp. 781–90.

2. J. Goldstein, "The Advent of Psychological Modernism in France: An Alternative Narrative", in D. Ross (ed.), *Modernist Impulses in the Human Sciences 1870–1930*, Baltimore, 1994, pp. 191–2 (and see sources of quotations there); and her "Saying 'I' ", pp. 321–2.

3. J. W. Scott, "French Feminists and the Rights of 'Man': Olympe de Gouges's Declarations", *History Workshop Journal* 28 (1989), pp. 1–21 (quoted, including Chaumette, pp. 13, 17); and idem, *Only Paradoxes to Offer: French Feminists and the Rights of Man*, Cambridge (Mass.), 1996, pp. 22–3, 48, 52.

4. L. Hunt, *Politics, Culture, and Class in the French Revolution*, Berkeley, 1984, chap. 3. The many studies of this contraction in the possibilities that the revolution had opened for women (to which there has also been a revisionist reaction, on which more in a moment) include: D. Godineau, *The Women of Paris and their French Revolution*, trans. K. Streip, Berkeley, 1998 (orig. 1988); J. B. Landes, *Women and the Public Sphere in the Age of the French Revolution*, Ithaca (N.Y.), 1988; G. Fraisse, *Reason's Muse: Sexual Difference and the Birth of Democracy*, trans. J. M. Todd, Chicago, 1994 (orig. 1989); S. E. Melzer and L. W. Rabine (eds.), *Rebel Daughters: Women and the French Revolution*, Oxford, 1992, esp. the contributions by N. Schor and M.-C. Vallois; and L. Hunt, *The Family Romance of the French Revolution*, Berkeley, 1992, esp. chaps. 4, 6.

5. W. M. Reddy, *The Navigation of Feeling: A Framework for the History of Emotions*, Cambridge, 2001 (quoted, pp. 208, 226). S. M. Quinlan, "Medicine and the Social Body in France: From the Individual Self to Social Therapy in Learned Medical Practice, 1750–1850", PhD thesis, Indiana University, 2000, chap. 5. For "the Cousinian philosophical revolution" that rejected eighteenth-century notions of self see J. Goldstein, "Mutations of the Self in Old Regime and Postrevolutionary France", in L. Daston (ed.), *Biographies of Scientific Objects*, Chicago, 2000, pp. 86–116 (quoted, p. 101).

6. Cabanis's essentialism stood in conspicuous tension with his efforts to hold on to Lockean sensationalist doctrines. This "mini-genre" (noted by Quinlan, "Medicine and the Social Body") also included J.-F. Saint-Lambert's *Analyse de l'homme et de la femme* (1798–1801); A.-L. Thomas's *Essai sur le caractère, les moeurs et l'esprit naturel de femme* and Jacques-Louis Moreau de la Sarthe's *Histoire naturelle de la femme* (both 1803); and Gabriel Jouard's *Nouvel essai sur la femme considérée comparativement à l'homme* (1804). Cf. also E. Colwill, "Women's Empire and the Sovereignty of Man in *La Décade philosophique*, 1794–1807", *Eighteenth-Century Studies* 29 (1996), pp. 265–89.

7. J. Goldstein, *Console and Classify: The French Psychiatric Profession in the Nineteenth Century*, Cambridge, 1987, chap. 3 (quoted, pp. 99, 117). Like Cabanis, Pinel also had one eye looking back at mid-eighteenth-century associationist psychology while the other was looking forward to the nineteenth century. And see p. 95 for an important source for Pinel's ideas from across the Channel, the Scotsman Alexander Crichton's *Inquiry into the Nature and Origins of Mental Derangement* (1798), which similarly claimed associationist credentials while also boasting the discovery that

the passions, rather than being induced by external sensations, were an aspect of inner nature, "part of our constitution".

8. A. Benzaquén, "Childhood and Identity in Enlightenment Human Science", paper presented at the Bloomington Eighteenth-Century Workshop "Signs of the Self in the Eighteenth Century", May 2002.

9. J. V. Douthwaite, "*Homo ferus*: Between Monster and Model", in A. Curran et al. (eds.), *Faces of Monstrosity in Eighteenth-Century Thought*, special issue of *Eighteenth-Century Life* 21:2 (1997), p. 177; and idem, *The Wild Girl, Natural Man and the Monster: Dangerous Experiments in the Age of Enlightenment*, Chicago, 2002, pp. 53–69 (and cf. p. 28 for an English counterpart, in William Lawrence's early-nineteenth-century dismissal of feral children as "pathological specimens").

10. J. Caplan, "'This or That Particular Person': Protocols of Identification in Nineteenth-Century Europe", in J. Caplan and J. Torpey (eds.), *Documenting Individual Identity: The Development of State Practices in the Modern World*, Princeton, 2001, pp. 56–7. D. G. Levy et al., *Women in Revolutionary Paris 1789–1795*, Urbana (Ill.), 1980, pp. 12, 271. S. Desan, "The Politics of Intimacy in Revolutionary France: Marriage, Citizenship, and the Political Power of Love", paper presented at the Sixth Feminism and Enlightenment Colloquium, London, May 2001; idem, "Reconstituting the Social after the Terror: Family, Property and the Law in Popular Politics", *Past and Present* 164 (1999), p. 95; and idem, *The Family on Trial in the French Revolution*, Berkeley, 2004, which traces the gender-differentiating reaction to the potential new openings of the revolutionary decade to its final triumph in the Civil Code of 1804. (I am grateful to Suzanne Desan for the opportunity to read her work before publication.) J. Heuer, "Adopted Daughter of the French People: Suzanne Lepeletier and her Father, the National Assembly", *French Politics, Culture, and Society* 17:3–4 (1999), pp. 31–51 (quoted, p. 38).

11. C. Hesse, "The Cultural Contradictions of Feminism in the French Revolution", in C. Jones and D. Wahrman (eds.), *The Age of Cultural Revolutions: Britain and France 1750–1820*, Berkeley, 2002, pp. 192, 194, 199, 201; and idem, *The Other Enlightenment: How French Women Became Modern*, Princeton, 2001, esp. chap. 6. For another partly revisionist account querying the complete success of the gender differentiation during the same years, but one that nonetheless again does so within a framework of an emerging new notion of individual and self, see Colwill, "Women's Empire and the Sovereignty of Man".

12. E. Lajer-Burcharth, *Necklines: The Art of Jacques-Louis David after the Terror*, New Haven, 1999, pp. 1–2.

13. Ibid., pp. 41, 100, 102, 106, 143, 174, 240–1. Note also D. G. Grigsby's interesting analysis of Anne-Louis Girodet's ground-breaking injection of individuality – while acknowledging the unreachable depths of interiority – into the heavily physiognomic portrait of the black deputy Jean-Baptiste Belley (1797), problematized by an increasing investment in incommensurable racial difference: *Extremities: Painting Empire in Post-Revolutionary France*, New Haven, 2002, esp. pp. 23, 35–8, 48–51.

14. J. H. Johnson, "Versailles, Meet Les Halles: Masks, Carnival, and the French Revolution", *Representations* 73 (2001), pp. 89–116 (quoted, p. 91). Lajer-Burcharth, *Necklines*, pp. 112, 116, 160. And cf. Reddy, *The Navigation of Feeling*, p. 195; and A. de Baecque, *The Body Politic: Corporeal Metaphor in Revolutionary France, 1770–1800*, trans. C. Mandell, Stanford, 1997, Chap. 6.

15. Hunt, *Politics, Culture, and Class*, pp. 66–7. Johnson, "Versailles, Meet Les Halles",

p. 110 (emphasis added). Lajer-Burcharth, *Necklines*, pp. 181, 286, and *passim*. Cf. R. Wrigley, *The Politics of Appearances: Representations of Dress in Revolutionary France*, Oxford, 2002, p. 235 and chap. 6.

16. "P. Friedland, 'Parallel Stages: Theatrical and Political Representation in Early Modern and Revolutionary France", in Jones and Wahrman (eds.), *The Age of Cultural Revolutions*, pp. 218–50; and idem, *Political Actors: Representative Bodies and Theatricality in the Age of the French Revolution*, Ithaca (N.Y.), 2002. Douthwaite, *The Wild Girl, Natural Man and the Monster*. K. Nicholson, "The Ideology of Feminine 'Virtue': The Vestal Virgin in French Eighteenth-Century Allegorical Portraiture", in J. Woodall (ed.), *Portraiture: Facing the Subject*, Manchester, 1997, pp. 52–72. D. Roche, *The Culture of Clothing: Dress and Fashion in the Ancien Regime*, trans. J. Birrell, Cambridge, 1994 (quoted, p. 410). Goldstein, "Mutations of the Self in Old Regime and Postrevolutionary France". J. Dejean, *Ancients against Moderns: Culture Wars and the Making of a Fin de Siècle*, Chicago, 1997 (quoted, pp. 92–3; and for an excellent example of the *ancien régime* of gender see pp. 119ff.). Reading Dejean from the perspective of the present book, one should keep in mind that she uses "interiority" to mean "affect", which makes her story seem further apart from the one told here than it really is.

17. There were also of course many instances of direct crossovers from one side of the Channel to the other. Thus, when Lord Chesterfield expressed his bemusement in 1748 at a recent Parisian publication "titled L'Année Merveilleuse, [which] predicts . . . nothing less than the total and reciprocal metamorphosis of the two sexes", he was in fact commenting unknowingly on a twenty-five-year-old *English jeu d'esprit*, John Arbuthnot's *Annus Mirabilis*, which had in the meantime been transported across the Channel, translated without attribution into French by Abbé Gabriel-François Coyer, and now brought to Chesterfield's attention back in England. It would not be difficult to replicate this example many times over. (Philip Dormer Stanhope, 4th Earl of Chesterfield, letter of 30 July 1748, in *The French Correspondence of Philip Dormer Stanhope, Fourth Earl of Chesterfield*, 2 vols., ed. R. A. Barrell, Ottawa, 1980, i, p. 52.) For Arbuthnot's publication see above, pp. 195–6.

18. For a discussion of the constrictive backlash against imagining unstable identities in America in the 1790s, and its link to the effects of the events in France, see J. Fliegelman, *Prodigals and Pilgrims: The American Revolution against Patriarchal Authority, 1750–1800*, Cambridge, 1982, chap. 8, and esp. pp. 240–1. For examples of American "gender panic" beginning in the mid-1790s, often closely echoing those we have seen in England from the early 1780s, see R. Zagarri, "The Rights of Man and Woman in Post-Revolutionary America", *William and Mary Quarterly* 3rd ser., 55 (1998), esp. pp. 216–30. Herman Mann's biography of Deborah Sampson, *The Female Review; or, Memoirs of an American Young Lady* (1797), is cited in L. Friedli, "'Passing Women' – A Study of Gender Boundaries in the Eighteenth Century", in G. S. Rousseau and R. Porter (eds.), *Sexual Underworlds of the Enlightenment*, Manchester, 1987, p. 243; and cf. S. M. Gustafson, "The Genders of Nationalism: Patriotic Violence, Patriotic Sentiment in the Performances of Deborah Sampson Gannett", in R. Blair St. George (ed.), *Possible Pasts: Becoming Colonial in Early America*, Ithaca (N.Y.), 2000, esp. pp. 380–1.

Index